American Payroll Asso

MW00744561

PAYROLL
PRACTICE
FUNDAMENTALS

2016 Edition

In the preparation of this text, every effort has been made to offer the most current, correct, and clearly understandable information possible. Nonetheless, inadvertent errors can occur, and tax rules and regulations are constantly changing.

This text is intended to provide authoritative information in regard to the subject matter covered and can be used as a training tool. As such, it is not an evaluation device upon which to base performance reviews and/or promotions.

This material is distributed with the understanding that the publisher and author are not engaged in rendering legal, accounting, or other professional services. If legal advice or other professional assistance is required, the service of your attorney or certified public accountant should be sought. Readers are encouraged to consult with appropriate professional advisors for advice concerning specific matters before making decisions affecting their individual operations. The publisher disclaims any responsibility for positions taken by practitioners in their individual cases or for any misunderstanding on the part of readers. The information in this text is current as of January 1, 2016.

Please visit our Web site at www.americanpayroll.org

ISBN: 978-1-934951-90-3

Printed in the United States

Prove yourself.
Improve yourself.

Use Payroll Knowledge Assessments to:

- Determine the right courses for you
- Set a course of study for the CPP and FPC exams
- Evaluate employees or an entire department

Assessments are only $29.95 each!
Volume discounts available.

Pick the assessment that's right for you.

There are 5 levels of assessment:

- **Concepts and Terms**
- **Fundamental Payroll Practices**
- **Compliance, Operations, and Administration**
- **Preparing for the Fundamental Payroll Certification Exam**
- **Preparing for the Certified Payroll Professional Exam**

Each assessment provides you with confidential results and training recommendations specifically targeted to your knowledge gaps.

Group Assessments

Use group assessments to screen multiple job candidates, evaluate departmental performance, and plan sessions for a certification study group.

KNOWLEDGE ASSESSMENT CALCULATOR

Go to www.PayrollKAC.com
to measure your payroll knowledge in minutes.

APA's web-based Payroll Knowledge Assessment is supported by all popular web browsers.
One hour is allotted for each 50-question assessment. Patent Pending.

Table of Contents

Table of Contents

Table of Contents

Table of Contents

Table of Contents

Payroll Fundamentals

Payroll is the process used by an organization to pay its employees accurately and on time. Thus, the most obvious job of payroll is to issue payments to employees. Undoubtedly, few employees or others in the business community understand how complicated this task can be. Employees correctly assume that every payday their paycheck should be on time and accurate. This chapter describes some of the legal and operational factors that make issuing timely, accurate paychecks a job for professionals.

Payroll is the process used to pay employees accurately and on time.

The functions within a payroll department vary from company to company. Some common examples of payroll tasks are:

- Paying employees
- Verifying the integrity of pay data
- Collecting/inputting/auditing data
- Inputting new hire information
- Record keeping
- Reporting payroll data
- Distributing paychecks and pay stubs
- Creating Automated Clearinghouse files
- Withholding, depositing, and reporting taxes
- Communicating with employees
- Balancing payroll input
- Modifying existing employee files
- Reconciling payroll data
- Processing deductions
- Researching federal and state regulations

This list includes only a few of the responsibilities a payroll department may have. What are some of the tasks in your payroll department?

1.1 Challenges

Those who work in payroll face the following challenges:

Complexity: Many federal, state, and local laws and regulations affect the way companies can pay their workers. These laws and regulations change frequently. Thus, it is necessary to evaluate these laws and regulations in order to determine which prevail. Then, those laws and regu-lations must be incorporated into the company policies and practices.

Communication: Paychecks or pay statements are the most scrutinized products of a company. Clear, concise explanations of payroll informa-tion benefit employees as well as those who work in payroll.

Technology: New software, equipment, and web-based applications can enhance the payroll process as well as human resource functions. Such products can automate time keeping, record storage, and record retrieval.

Accuracy: Ensuring accuracy of employees' pay is only part of the accuracy required of a payroll professional. Without accuracy in tax fil-ing, management reports, and other processes, the payroll process will not be a success.

The Payroll Process

The payroll process includes the following:

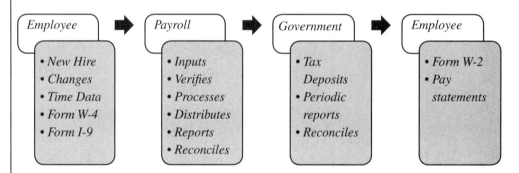

1.2 Concepts

Worker Status

Employers must make two distinctions when classifying workers.

Employers must make two distinctions when classifying workers. A worker can be an employee or an independent contractor. Employees can be exempt or nonexempt. Both of these distinctions are discussed in this chapter.

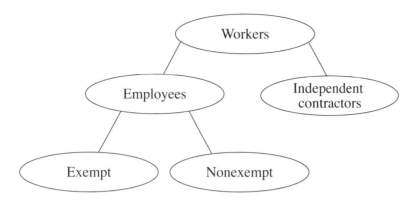

First, you need to determine who is an employee and who is not. Every worker at your company is not necessarily an employee. Is the part-time secretary in marketing an employee? How would you classify the free-lance artist who has handled all your firm's graphics for the last five years (and regularly attends the holiday party)? What is the status of a 16-year-old summer worker in shipping or a commission-only salesperson? These questions aren't academic. The answers determine whether the company must withhold taxes and pay overtime.

1.2.1 Employees vs. Independent Contractors

Employers must withhold federal income tax, social security tax, Medicare tax, state income tax, and local income tax from employees' pay. In addition, the company must pay the employer's share of social security tax and Medicare taxes and make federal and state unemployment insurance contributions based on the employee's wages. However, tax withholding is not required for independent contractors, who provide the company with a Taxpayer Identification Number (TIN). Additionally, the company does not pay social security tax or Medicare tax or federal and state unemployment insurance contributions on the payments for services provided by an independent contractor.

Withholding is generally not required for independent contractors.

Designating a worker's status as employee or independent contractor is the responsibility of the employer, not the worker. The primary way that a company determines if a worker qualifies as an employee or independent contractor is the common law test. However, exceptions do allow an employer to classify a worker qualifying as an employee under the common law test as an independent contractor when meeting the requirements of the reasonable basis test.

1.2.2 Common Law and Reasonable Basis Tests

The common law test asks these critical questions: How independent is the employee? How much control can be exercised over the worker? The table on page 1-4 compares and contrasts employees and independent contractors under the common law test. The crucial distinction is the employer's right to control the worker.

A worker cannot sign a contract stating they will be an independent contractor when the worker meets the common law test that the IRS will use in an employee/independent contractor audit.

A worker or an employer may request the IRS' determination of the worker's status by filing Form SS-8, *Determination of Worker Status for Purposes of Federal Employment Taxes and Income Tax Withholding,* (see page A-119) with the IRS.

Common Law Test for Determining Whether a Worker Is an Employee

Employee	Independent Contractor
Required to comply with employer's instructions about when, where, and how to work	Sets own hours; determines own sequence of work
Works exclusively for the employer	Can work for multiple employers; services available to the public
Hired by the employer	Is self-employed
Subject to dismissal; can quit without liability	A contract governs how the relationship can be severed
Has a continuing relationship with the employer	Works by the job
Work done personally	Permitted to employ assistants

Employee	Independent Contractor
Performs services under the company's name	Performs services under the worker's business name
Paid a salary; reimbursed for expenses; participates in company's fringe benefits programs	Payment by the job; opportunity for profit and loss
Furnished tools, equipment, materials, and training	Furnishes own tools, equipment, and training; substantial investment by the worker
If an outside salesperson: company provides leads, sets terms and conditions of the sale, assigns a territory, and controls the sales process	Controls the sales process and terms

Reasonable Basis Test

There are exceptions to the common law test. Employers can classify certain workers as independent contractors for employment tax purposes even though the workers meet the requirement of a common law employee, if they have a reasonable basis for doing so. To meet the IRS' requirements for the reasonable basis test an employer must

The reasonable basis test provides an exception to the common law test.

- Have consistently treated the worker or similar workers as an independent contractor and have filed tax returns (Form 1099-MISC) consistent with their treatment as independent contractors.

- Have a longstanding, recognized practice in a significant segment of the employer's industry of treating similar workers as independent contractors.

- Have a judicial precedent (i.e., court decisions) for treating workers in similar circumstances as independent contractors.

- Be able to demonstrate that the IRS has ruled in a "published ruling" that the workers are independent contractors and the facts relating to the workers are the same as the examples in the "published ruling".

- Have received a specific ruling from the IRS (e.g., a Private Letter Ruling) that the workers are independent contractors.

- Have had a past IRS employment tax audit of the employer that did not disallow the worker's treatment as an independent contractor.

- Have received guidance from an attorney or CPA that the worker is an independent contractor.

Exceptions to the Rule

1.2.3 Temporary Service/Leased Employees

Organizations may have individuals who are not classified as either employees or independent contractors performing services. These individuals generally are employed by organizations described as temporary service agencies, leasing companies, or Professional Employer Organizations. These organizations bear the burdens of an employer:

- Paying
- Withholding
- Reporting
- Providing benefits

The company receiving the services contracts with the temporary service agency or leasing company, not with the individual workers.

1.2.4 Misclassifying Workers

Alert

If you misclassify an employee as an independent contractor, your company can have significant problems. Misclassifications represent a potential loss of revenue for all levels of government. Therefore, the IRS, the Department of Labor, state unemployment agencies, and other state and local government agencies have entered into agreements with each other under which they look closely at employee classifications and assess severe penalties for misclassification.

1.2.5 Employment Eligibility

The Immigration Reform and Control Act of 1986 (IRCA) requires employers to verify employees' eligibility for employment in the U.S. Employers face stiff penalties for knowingly hiring individuals not eligible for employment. The key provisions of the law that affect employers are employer sanctions, antidiscrimination, and verification of eligibility.

Employer Sanctions

It is illegal to knowingly hire or recruit for a fee aliens who lack authorization to work in the U.S. The law also applies to leasing or temporary help agencies who are recruiting workers for your company. Penalties for hiring illegal aliens range from $375 for a first offense to $16,000 for a third. In addition, employers could face criminal penalties if U.S. Citizenship and Immigration Services (USCIS) determines that your company has a pattern of such violations.

Antidiscrimination

At the same time, the law prohibits discrimination in hiring or recruiting workers on the basis of national origin or citizenship.

Verification of Eligibility

The burden of verifying that any employee (regardless of nationality) is eligible to work in the United States falls on employers. Your company must check the employment eligibility of all new employees hired after the law was enacted (November 6, 1986). Employees continuously employed by the same employer since before November 6, 1986 are not required to have completed a Form I-9.

By the first day of work, the new hire must fill out Section 1 of Form I-9, *Employment Eligibility Verification* (see page A-126). Within three days of the employee's first day of work, the employer must review the employee's documents and complete Section 2 of Form I-9. Form I-9 must be retained for the longer of three years from the date of hire or one year from termination.

Form I-9 requires that the new hires document their identity and eligibility to work in the U.S. The Instructions for Form I-9 list documents that employees can use to document their identity and eligibility to work.

An authorized employee of the organization or your agent must examine and attest on Form I-9 that the new hire's documents appear genuine.

Employers can verify a newly hired employee's eligibility to work in the U.S. using DHS' E-Verify system.

1.2.6 Social Security Numbers

IRS Regulations require that employees provide employers with their social security card when requested, if it is available.

IRS Regulations require that employees provide employers with their social security card when requested, if it is available. The Social Security Administration (SSA) encourages:

1. Employers to verify an employee's name and social security number (SSN) on the employee's W-4 form as part of the hiring process for tax withholding and reporting purposes.
2. Workers NOT to carry their SSN or social security card on them because of the possibility of identity theft.

SSA processes over 240 million W-2 forms a year, with 10% of these W-2 forms having names and social security numbers that do not match. SSA places the unposted wage amounts on these W-2 forms into the Earnings Suspense File.

If an individual finds a discrepancy in their earnings, submits the discrepancy to the SSA, and it finds the record, the SSA will take the earnings out of the Earnings Suspense File and apply them to the individual's record.

An employer must be able to show that it made an initial solicitation for the employee's SSN at the time the employee began work. Generally this is accomplished by asking the employee to complete Form W-4, *Employee's Withholding Allowance Certificate*. No additional solicitations of Form W-4, the employee's name or SSN are required unless the IRS notifies the employer that the employee's name and SSN are incorrect.

Following receipt of an IRS notice that the employee's name and SSN reported on Form W-2 do not match the IRS' records, the employer is required to make up to two annual solicitations for the correct SSN.

The solicitations for the SSN must be made by December 31 of the year in which the IRS notice was received, and may be made by mail, telephone, electronically, or in person. Solicitations are not required if the individual has not received a wage reportable payment for that year.

The Role of the Social Security Number Verification Service (SSNVS) and E-Verify

Employers may use the Social Security Administration's Social Security Number Verification Service (SSNVS) or the Department of Homeland Security's (DHS) E-Verify system to verify employees' names and SSNs, but they are not required to do so in most situations. SSNVS is an optional way for employers to identify potential discrepancies and correct SSNs before receiving penalty notices. Employers are not allowed to verify names and SSNs reported on W-2 forms using the IRS TIN Matching System.

When verifying that the employee's name and SSN match through SSNVS, the employer must always provide their Federal Employer Identification Number (FEIN) plus three items for each employee to the SSA:

When verifying the employee's name and SSN, using SSNVS the employer must provide three items for each employee.

1. Employee's last name; first name; middle initial (if applicable)
2. Employee's SSN
3. Employee's date of birth

The DHS' E-Verify system verifies not only the employee's name and SSN but also their eligibility to work in the United States. Federal government contractors and employers in certain states are required to use E-Verify. Employers not required to use E-Verify may use it voluntarily.

E-Verify verifies an employee's eligibility to work in the U.S.

IRS Advice to Employers for SSN Compliance

The IRS has made the following suggestions to assist employers in maintaining compliance with the requirement to have correct social security numbers:

1. Ask each new worker for proof of his or her SSN by showing you a social security card.
2. Maintain a copy of the W-4 form the employee provides.
3. Document any subsequent solicitations for a new W-4 form you make in the event that you receive a notification from the IRS that there is a problem with the employee's name and SSN.
4. Maintain accurate records of the SSN and the name provided by the employee in the payroll records.
5. Remind workers to report any name changes due to marriage, divorce, etc. first to SSA and then provide a copy of the new social security card to the employer.
6. Validate the SSN on the W-4 form using SSA's SSNVS or DHS' E-Verify.
7. Remind employees to verify the accuracy of their name and social security number when they receive their W-2 form, checking to be sure there isn't a typo or another error.
8. Note that an Individual Taxpayer Identification Number (ITIN) can never be used to report an employee's earnings. When an employer receives a W-4 form with a social security number that begins with a 9, the employer should recognize that this is not an SSN but an ITIN. You should be aware that an ITIN cannot be used when filing W-2 forms. However, if this is the only number you have from the employee, SSA advises employers to use it.

If you take these proactive steps, they should help eliminate the possibility that any penalties will be assessed for putting incorrect information on an employee's Form W-2.

Form SS-5

Form SS-5, *Application for a Social Security Card* (see page A-114), can be used to request a replacement social security card. Form SS-5 can be mailed or taken with evidentiary documents to any Social Security office.

In early 2015, the SSA proposed regulations that would ease the transition to an electronic SSN card application process. SSA is developing a new online application that would allow certain members of the public to apply for replacement SSN cards electronically without having to visit an SSA office or mail in Form SS-5 and supporting documentary evidence. Other than the use of Form SS-5, the only other method for obtaining an SSN currently is to have an SSA representative file an application electronically through the Social Security Number Application Process (SSNAP) during an in-office interview.

Replacement Card: To apply for a replacement card, the individual must prove their identity. Individuals born outside of the U.S., will need to prove U.S. citizenship or current lawful, work-authorized immigration status.

Change of Information: To correct information on a social security card, or information shown in SSA's records (e.g., a name change, or corrected date of birth), the individual will need to prove identity and provide documents that support the change and establish the reason for the change (e.g., a birth certificate to show the corrected date or place of birth). A name change document (e.g., marriage certificate) must provide both the old and new names.

1.2.7 New Hire Reporting

Employers are required to comply with the federal and state new hire reporting requirements. For each newly hired employee, the employer must provide the following information to the state new hire directory:

- The employee's name, address, social security number, and date employment began
- The employer's name, address, and Federal Employer Identification Number (FEIN)

However, you should be aware that each state may request more information.

Employers with employees in only one state must report newly hired employees to that state, either on paper, magnetically or electronically.

Employers with employees in two or more states that report new hires magnetically or electronically may designate one state where they have employees as the state to which they will report all their new hires. Multistate employers that wish to file all their new hire reports with one state must notify the Secretary of Health and Human Services (HHS) of the state where new hires will be reported. Employers can notify HHS in one of several ways:

- By filling out an HHS form
- By writing a letter that can be mailed or faxed
- On the Internet at https://ocsp.acf.hhs.gov/OCSE/

Regardless of the method used, the following information must be provided:

1. Employer's name, address, phone number, and Federal Employer Identification Number (FEIN)
2. The state to which the employer will report new hires and the date on which multistate reporting will begin
3. Other states in which the employer hires employees
4. Employer contact information (name, title, phone number, e-mail address, fax number)
5. FEIN, name, state and zip code of any subsidiary of the employer with a different FEIN for which the employer will be reporting new hires

In general, employers must report newly hired employees within 20 calendar days of the date of hire. If an employer reports new hires magnetically or electronically, it must send at least two transmissions each calendar month which are 12–16 days apart. States can establish their own time frames for reporting new hires, but they can be no longer than the federal requirements. Multistate employers that submit reports twice monthly must submit information for a newly hired employee as soon as possible after the date of hire, but no later than the next semimonthly reporting period.

Some states may require employers to report more information or report more frequently than required by federal law. However, the federal Office of Child Support Enforcement has stated that multistate employers do not have to report the elements required by every state in which they have employees—only those required by the state the employer has selected for new hire reporting purposes.

An employee's date of hire is considered to be the first day services are performed for wages by the employee, and employees who work for as little as one day, with the exception of election workers, must be reported. If an employee has a break in employment of 60 days or more, the rehired employee is reported as a new hire.

The federal reporting requirement does not apply to independent contractors, but some states do require such reporting.

Employers can report new hires using the employee's Form W-4, or an equivalent form containing the required information, and can transmit the report by first class mail, fax, magnetically, or electronically. Using the employee's Form W-4 to meet the new hire reporting requirement entails a burden not previously faced by employers, since the employer identifying information does not otherwise need to be placed on a Form W-4 unless the form is being submitted to the IRS.

Check Your Understanding

Quiz 1.1. Answer the following questions to test your understanding of worker status.

Check Your Understanding

1. Payroll's chief product – the paycheck or pay statement – must be:
    ❑ a. Accurate
    ❑ b. Timely
    ❑ c. Both accurate and timely
    ❑ d. None of the above

2. What taxes, if any, must be withheld from an employee's pay?
    ❑ a. Federal income, social security and Medicare
    ❑ b. Federal income only
    ❑ c. Social security and Medicare only
    ❑ d. No taxes are withheld

3. What taxes, if any, must be withheld from an independent contractor's pay who provides a TIN?
    ❑ a. Federal income, social security and Medicare
    ❑ b. Federal income only
    ❑ c. Social security and Medicare only
    ❑ d. No taxes are withheld

4. Who has the responsibility to determine if the worker is an employee or independent contractor?
   - ❏ a. Employer
   - ❏ b. Social Security Administration
   - ❏ c. Worker
   - ❏ d. Internal Revenue Service

5. Prior to beginning work for a company, a chemical engineer signed a contract stating that she agreed to work as an independent contractor. She performs all her duties in the company's laboratories, where she has full access to the company's testing equipment. She works under their direction and maintains regular office hours. What is her status?
   - ❏ a. Independent contractor under common law.
   - ❏ b. Independent contractor under the reasonable basis test
   - ❏ c. Employee.

6. A retired safety inspector for the company was rehired as a consultant when the company expanded its plant operations. The retired employee was a natural choice. The tasks he undertook as a consultant were the same as the ones he performed before retirement. Paid monthly, he has agreed to work under the direction of his old boss until the new plant facilities are fully operational. What is his status?
   - ❏ a. Independent contractor under common law.
   - ❏ b. Independent contractor under the reasonable basis test.
   - ❏ c. Employee.

7. A receptionist has agreed to work afternoons at the company until they can find a full-time replacement. What is the receptionist's status?
   - ❏ a. Independent contractor under common law.
   - ❏ b. Independent contractor under the reasonable basis test.
   - ❏ c. Employee.

8. Which of the following workers is an independent contractor?
    ❑ a. A temporary receptionist from an agency
    ❑ b. A lawyer hired on a project-by-project basis, with the company providing secretarial service and office space for the lawyer
    ❑ c. A lecturer who is paid a percentage of the money collected at fund raisers when he speaks on behalf of a nonprofit clinic
    ❑ d. An outside salesperson who is paid by commission but guaranteed a minimum salary

1.3 The Fair Labor Standards Act

As we have learned, producing employees' pay is the main job of the payroll department. The payment includes more than an individual's regular wage or salary. Payments include pay for overtime work, paid time off, bonuses, and other types of compensation. Calculating the correct amount of earnings for each employee is essential.

The Fair Labor Standards Act of 1938 (FLSA), as well as state wage and hour laws, govern the payment of wages to employees.

The FLSA:

- Guarantees employees a minimum wage.
- Requires employers to pay an overtime premium.
- Limits when minors can work.
- Provides equal pay protection.

The FLSA is administered by the Wage and Hour Division of the U.S. Department of Labor (DOL). In addition, most states have enacted laws governing:

- Minimum wage
- Overtime
- Other aspects of paying employees
- Child labor

1.3.1 Exempt vs. Nonexempt Employees

Not all employees are subject to the minimum wage and overtime requirements of the Fair Labor Standards Act. Employees who meet certain criteria are exempt from minimum wage, overtime and some record keeping regulations. Employees who are covered by the FLSA's minimum wage and overtime requirements are called nonexempt employees. Those who are not covered by the FLSA's minimum wage and overtime requirements are called exempt employees.

1.3.2 Exempt Employees

Executives, administrative employees, professionals and outside salespeople are four types of white collar exempt employees.

The white collar exemptions to the FLSA overtime and minimum wage requirements are not based on job title but on the employee's:

- Actual duties
- Responsibilities
- Level of discretionary authority

In addition, for most exempt employees a minimum weekly salary must be paid.

FLSA regulations include the following four types of white collar exempt employees.

Executives

The primary duty of an executive is to manage an enterprise, a department, or a departmental subdivision. To be classified as an executive, a person must direct the work of at least two full-time workers, have hiring/firing authority, and exercise discretionary powers. The executive must be paid a minimum weekly salary of $455 ($23,660/year). Executives include department managers and supervisors who are directly associated with management decisions and the direction of the staff.

Administrative Employees

The primary duty of exempt administrative employees is either:

1. The performance of office work related to management or general business operations.
2. The administration of a school system.

Employees who perform special assignments (like purchasing agents or auditors) are exempt administrative employees. Exempt administrative employees must exercise independent judgement and discretion in matters of significance. An exempt administrative employee must also be paid a weekly salary of at least $455. Examples of administrative exempt employees might include executive secretaries or confidential or administrative assistants who are not closely supervised.

Professionals

The primary work of exempt professional employees is classified in one of two ways:

1. Learned Professionals—whose primary duty involves the use of advanced knowledge customarily acquired by specialized study
2. Creative Professionals—whose primary duty involves the use of originality and creativity

The work of either group must be intellectual and varied, not standardized. The minimum weekly salary an exempt professional employee must be paid is $455. Teachers, engineers, and attorneys are examples of professional employees.

Those working in highly skilled computer software occupations fall into a separate category of exempt professional employees. The primary duties of exempt computer professionals must include systems analysis, system, program design, or computer programming. To qualify, employees must be proficient in their field. The same minimum salary threshold of $455 per week is applicable, but computer professionals paid by the hour may also be exempt if their hourly rate exceeds $27.63.

Outside Salespeople

Outside salespeople are exempt if they meet two requirements

1. They are customarily engaged in selling or getting orders for the company's product/service.
2. They work away from the employer's premises.

Alert

There is no salary requirement for outside salespeople.

State laws. The minimum salaries and duties required of exempt employees listed above may be superseded by applicable state laws.

Special Exemptions Exist

Special Tips

In addition to the four categories of white collar exempt workers, certain classifications of employees are covered by overtime provisions different from the normal FLSA provisions. Special provisions are made in the law for the following categories of workers:

- Various transportation workers—motor and rail carrier workers, taxicab drivers, seamen, airline employees
- Agricultural workers
- Hospital and nursing home workers
- Home companion care workers
- Public sector employees, firefighters, police officers, and others

All exempt employees are exempt from FLSA regulations concerning overtime or the minimum wage. Nonexempt employees must be paid the minimum wage and overtime pay.

1.4 Federal Minimum Wage

Update

The federal government and many states have set a minimum wage for nonexempt workers. The minimum wage applies to workers' hourly compensation, not to their net pay. Thus, after deductions, a worker's take-home pay may legally fall below the required minimum wage.

The federal minimum wage, effective since July 24, 2009, is $7.25 per hour. Employees under age 20 can be paid $4.25 per hour in their first 90 calendar days on the job. Federal government contractors must pay a minimum wage of $10.15 for hours worked in 2016.

1.4.1 State Minimum Wage

Many states have set their own minimum wage higher than $7.25 per hour. If the employer is covered by both state and federal law and the two are not the same, then the employer is required to pay the higher minimum wage based on the state in which the employee works. For example, an employee who works in a state with a $7.50 per hour minimum wage must be paid $7.50 per hour, not the $7.25 per hour federal minimum wage.

Alert

1.4.2 Tip Credit

The FLSA defines a tip as an amount presented by a customer as a gift or gratuity in recognition of a service performed. The tip is to be distinguished from the payment of a charge for services performed.

A restaurant's wait staff may be paid a rate that is less than the federal minimum wage. This subminimum wage applies to wait staff, bartenders, and some other workers who typically earn tips in addition to their wages. In such cases, the employer may be able to reduce these employees' hourly rate to $2.13 per hour. The tip credit can be used to reduce these employees' hourly rate only if the employee regularly receives more than $30.00 per month in tips. Various states also regulate tip credits. Make sure you are aware of any applicable state laws, which limit the use of or reduce the federal tip credit.

However, the actual tips received plus the cash wage must equal the required minimum wage, as shown below.

Exceptions to the Rule

Effective	Federal Minimum Wage	Tip Credit	Minimum Cash Wage
July 24, 2009	$7.25 per hour	$5.12 per hour	$2.13 per hour

1.5 Additional Earnings

In addition to a wage or salary, employees may receive additional compensation, such as tips, shift premiums, paid time off, and bonuses.

In addition to a wage or salary, employees may receive additional compensation, such as tips, shift premiums, paid time off, and bonuses. The discussion below looks at some of the issues faced in handling these earnings. Your company may have other policies, which you need to follow as well.

1.5.1 Shift Premiums

Although there is no federal or state requirement, many companies pay shift premiums (also called shift differentials) to employees who work certain shifts. For example, a company might pay assembly workers $10.00 per hour for the 8:00 a.m. to 4:00 p.m. shift, $11.00 per hour for the 4:00 p.m. to midnight shift, and $12.00 per hour for the shift from midnight to 8:00 a.m.

Shift premiums must be included when determining a regular rate of pay for overtime (discussed later).

1.5.2 Paid Time Off

The FLSA does not require employers to pay employees for days or hours not worked such as holidays (e.g. Christmas or Independence Day) or vacation. The FLSA also does not require employers to pay employees for unworked sick days, holidays, or vacation days or pay a premium to employees who work on holidays (although many companies have such policies). Under the FLSA, holiday, vacation, and sick pay hours are not counted in determining the regular rate of pay for overtime.

Some states and localities require employers to provide sick leave to employees.

1.5.3 Bonuses

Employees may receive many different types of supplemental payments from their employers such as bonuses, commissions, production pay, etc., as an incentive for increased productivity. Under the FLSA, these payments may be a factor in determining an employee's regular rate of pay for overtime purposes.

Check Your Understanding

Quiz 1.2. Answer the following questions to test your understanding of calculating earnings.

1. What are exempt employees exempt from?
   - ❑ a. Minimum wage only
   - ❑ b. Overtime pay only
   - ❑ c. Minimum wage and overtime
   - ❑ d. Pay for time off

2. All of the following types of employees are classified as exempt from the FLSA's minimum wage and overtime requirements except:
   - ❑ a. Professional
   - ❑ b. Outside salesperson
   - ❑ c. Administrative
   - ❑ d. Computer repairman

3. A waitress is paid $2.25 per hour, and she receives $225.00 in tips during the week. She works 40 hours per week. Which of the following is true?
   - ❑ a. Her employer is allowed to reduce her cash wage to no less than $2.13 per hour.
   - ❑ b. Her base pay must be increased to $4.25 per hour after a 90-day training period.
   - ❑ c. She must be paid $5.12 per hour by her employer.
   - ❑ d. Her base salary must be raised to $3.00 per hour to comply with federal minimum wage requirements.

Check Your Understanding

4. What is the federal minimum wage?
   - ❑ a. $6.00
   - ❑ b. $6.50
   - ❑ c. $7.25
   - ❑ d. $8.00

5. If a state sets the minimum wage at a rate greater than the federal minimum wage the state minimum wage must be paid to workers in that state.
   - ❑ True
   - ❑ False

6. A nonexempt employee works in a state with a minimum wage of $7.35 per hour, while living in a state with a minimum wage of $8.05. What is the minimum rate he must be paid?
   - ❑ a. $7.25 per hour
   - ❑ b. $7.35 per hour
   - ❑ c. $8.05 per hour
   - ❑ d. There is no minimum because the employee is exempt.

7. Tips can be counted toward the employee's minimum wage.
   - ❑ True
   - ❑ False

8. An employee works 40 hours per week as a fry cook. During the week, she substitutes for one of the waitresses and reports $5.00 per week in tips. Can her employer pay her $2.13 per hour?
   - ❑ Yes
   - ❑ No

9. Employers who provide paid vacation leave must count the hours of paid time off when determining if the employee must receive an overtime premium when the total hours worked in a week exceed 40.
   - ❑ True
   - ❑ False

10. A nonexempt employee works the night shift (midnight to 8:00 a.m.) and works 45 hours during the week. Under the FLSA, what must his employer pay him?
    ❑ a.   Time and one-half for working Christmas.
    ❑ b.   The federal minimum wage.
    ❑ c.   Shift differential pay.

1.6 Defining Overtime

The Fair Labor Standards Act (FLSA) requires that all nonexempt employees be paid 1½ times their regular rate of pay for all hours worked over 40 in one week. Complying with these federal overtime regulations can be complex, particularly when employees earn multiple rates of pay in a workweek. Be sure to note that a state may require overtime payments based on the hours worked in a day.

Under the FLSA, the term "hours worked" includes all time an employee is required to be on duty, whether on the employer's premises or at a prescribed workplace. In addition, "hours worked" includes all time an employee is suffered or permitted to work whether or not required to do so. Hours worked is not limited to active productive labor but also may include waiting for work, remaining "on call", or traveling on the employer's business, etc. (For more information on the FLSA definition of time worked see Chapter 1.8).

Ensuring that the employee's hours worked are reported correctly is the employer's responsibility. Payroll frequently reviews the time recorded on an employee's time sheet, time card or in the electronic time and attendance system, ensuring compliance with company policy, state laws, and the FLSA. The FLSA does not require employees to approve the time reported. It is the employer's responsibilities to accurately pay the employee.

The Fair Labor Standards Act requires that all nonexempt employees be paid 1½ times their regular rate of pay when they work more than 40 hours in one week.

1.6.1 When Must Overtime Be Paid?

FLSA regulations require that all nonexempt employees be paid an overtime premium of 50% for any hours physically worked over 40 hours each workweek. Note that under the FLSA, overtime is paid only for time worked, not all time compensated. Therefore, overtime need not be paid when time worked is less than 40 hours in the week but the employee receives sick pay, holiday pay, vacation pay, jury duty pay, or similar pay for unworked hours and the paid time exceeds 40 hours.

The FLSA does not require overtime premiums to be paid for working on Saturdays, Sundays, or holidays unless actual overtime (more than 40 hours) is worked in the workweek (although many companies do pay overtime premiums for such hours). Under the FLSA, employers are not required to pay overtime premiums when employees work more than eight hours in one day (although some companies do pay overtime when an employee works more than 8 hours in a day). In addition, three states' wage and hour laws require paying overtime when an employee has worked more then 8 hours a day or for working a seventh consecutive day. With the exception of fire protection, law enforcement, and hospital employees, overtime is based on having physically worked more than 40 hours during a workweek. These exceptions are discussed later in this section.

1.6.2 Other Overtime Regulations Exist

Alert

State wage and hour rules on overtime may differ from the federal regulations. For example, a state may require that overtime be paid when employees work more than 8 hours in a day. Company policies on overtime and union contracts may also differ from the federal regulations. Generally, a company must follow the rule that most benefits the employee—federal regulations, state laws, company policies, or union contracts.

1.6.3 Defining the Workweek

A workweek is defined by the FLSA as a fixed, recurring period of 168 consecutive hours (7 days x 24 hours). An employer's workweek need not coincide with the calendar week or payroll period. It may begin on any day of the week and at any hour of the day. For example, all of the following could be considered a workweek:

- Sunday through Saturday
- Monday through Sunday

- Saturday through Friday

Employers may establish a single workweek for the entire organization or different workweeks for various groups of employees.

Each workweek stands on its own. An employee who works 35 hours in week one and 60 hours in week two is paid overtime on the 20 extra hours worked in week two. (There are exceptions for hospital, law enforcement, and fire protection workers, as explained below.)

1.6.4 Time of payment

The FLSA does not require that overtime pay be paid weekly. The general rule is to pay overtime on the next regular payday after the end of the workweek. If this doesn't permit the payroll department enough time to collect the time and complete the necessary calculations, then the overtime pay must be paid as soon as practically possible, generally the next payday. State regulations regulating when wages must be paid may differ from the federal rules.

1.6.5 Workweek Exceptions

Most employees are paid an overtime premium after working 40 hours in a workweek, but there are several exceptions.

Fluctuating Workweek

There are many variations of the standard workweek and many different regulations for each variation. For example, fluctuating workweek plans require that the employee's work schedule vary so that neither the employer nor the employee can anticipate the schedule from week to week. The employee's salary must be set at a fixed amount but must not fall below the current minimum wage when considering the number of hours the employee works each week.

Chapter 1 | Hospital/Nursing Home Special Rules

Hospitals and nursing homes have an exemption from the requirement that overtime be computed on a workweek basis.

The Fair Labor Standards Act provides hospitals and nursing homes an exemption from the requirement that overtime be computed on a work-week basis, known as the 8/80 rule. Hospitals and nursing homes can use a 14-day period to compute overtime. However, certain conditions must be met.

First, the hospital/nursing home and the employee must agree to use the 14-day period instead of the 7-day workweek for computing overtime before the work is actually performed. The agreement may be reached directly with the employee or with his or her representative. The 14-day period may begin at any hour of any day of the week, not necessarily at the beginning of a calendar day or week. The work period includes 14 consecutive 24-hour periods. The 14-day period must be used permanently or for a substantial period of time. The employer cannot change back and forth between the 7-day workweek and 14-day period in order to reduce its overtime payments.

Second, an employer is not required to compute overtime pay unless the employee works more than eight hours in any workday in the 14-day period or works more than 80 hours in the 14-day period. The employer must calculate the overtime pay under whichever scenario provides the most benefit to the employee.

Firefighters' and Police Officers' Exception

Public safety employees are also covered by another exception to the FLSA's overtime requirements.

Public safety employees (firefighters and police officers) are also covered by another exception to the FLSA's overtime requirements. Where firefighters and police officers have a work period lasting from 7 to 28 consecutive days, no overtime pay or compensatory time off is due until the ratio of the number of hours worked to the number of days in the work period exceeds the ratio of 212 hours to 28 days (171 hours to 28 days for law enforcement officers); see the following table. The firefighter exemption also includes paramedics, emergency medical technicians, rescue workers, ambulance personnel and hazardous materials workers who are trained and engage in fire prevention and suppression or respond to emergency situations. This exception allows public employers to spread hours worked for public safety employees over the entire work period, thus saving on overtime costs.

Work Periods (days)	Fire Protection Maximum Hours	Law Enforcement Maximum Hours
7	53	43
8	61	49
9	68	55
10	76	61
11	83	67
12	91	73
13	98	79
14	106	86
15	114	92
16	121	98
17	129	104
18	136	110
19	144	116
20	151	122
21	159	128
22	167	134
23	174	141
24	182	147
25	189	153
26	197	159
27	204	165
28	212	171

1.6.6 Changing Workweeks

Although the FLSA encourages employers to establish permanent workweeks, changes to the workweek may be necessary to meet changing business needs. To ensure that employees receive all overtime pay to which they are entitled when workweeks change, several steps must be taken:

Employers may change employees' workweek with specific conditions.

1. Add overlapping days to the old workweek, then calculate overtime hours and pay for both the old and new workweeks.

2. Add overlapping days to the new workweek, then calculate overtime hours and pay for both the old and new workweeks.
3. Pay the employee the greater amount from Step 1 or Step 2.

Assume that an employer changes its workweek from Monday through Sunday to Sunday through Saturday. A nonexempt employee works the following hours during a two-week period.

Old Workweek						
Mon	Tues	Wed	Thur	Fri	Sat	Sun
0	8	8	8	8	8	8

Sun	Mon	Tues	Wed	Thur	Fri	Sat
8	8	8	8	8	0	0
New Workweek						

The employee's overtime is calculated as follows:

1. Add overlapping day (Sunday) to the time worked during the old workweek (40 hours + 8 hours = 48 hours).
2. Add overlapping day (Sunday) to the time worked during the new workweek (8 hours + 32 hours = 40 hours).
3. Pay overtime based on the greater of the two amounts (48 hours)

Check Your Understanding

Check Your Understanding

Quiz 1.3. Answer the following questions to test your understanding of issues related to defining and calculating overtime.

1. The FLSA requires that time worked on Saturday be paid at overtime rates and time worked on Sunday be paid at double time rates.

   ❏ True
   ❏ False

2. If a state wage and hour law requires that a nonexempt employee be paid an overtime premium when the employee works more than 8 hours in a day and the employee works the following schedule, how many overtime hours must the employee be paid?

Sun	Mon	Tue	Wed	Thur	Fri	Sat
5	7	6	8	10	8	6

❑ a. 0
❑ b. 2
❑ c. 10
❑ d. 14

3. Last week a high school teacher spent 40 hours in the classroom, worked 10 hours grading papers and was required to put in another 8 hours on Saturday at the school-sponsored science fair. Under the FLSA, what overtime hours, if any, must the teacher be paid?

❑ a. Time and one-half for 0 hours.
❑ b. Time and one-half for 8 hours.
❑ c. Time and one-half for 10 hours.
❑ d. Time and one-half for 18 hours..

4. An employer pays semimonthly on the 15th and last day of each month. Their workweek is Sunday through Saturday. Memorial Day is May 31. A nonexempt employee worked the following hours.

MAY						
Sun	**Mon**	**Tue**	**Wed**	**Thu**	**Fri**	**Sat**
16 Hours Worked 8	**17** Hours Worked 8	**18** Hours Worked 0	**19** Hours Worked 0	**20** Hours Worked 8	**21** Hours Worked 8	**22** Hours Worked 8
23 Hours Worked 8	**24** Hours Worked 10	**25** Hours Worked 4	**26** Hours Worked 0	**27** Hours Worked 8	**28** Hours Worked 8	**29** Hours Worked 0
30 Hours Worked 8	**31** Hours Worked 12					

How many hours of overtime, if any, did the employee work during this pay period?

❑ a. 0 hours
❑ b. 4 hours
❑ c. 10 hours
❑ d. 16 hours

5. During Thanksgiving week, a nonexempt employee was paid for the following hours.

Sun	Mon	Tue	Wed	Thur	Fri	Sat
none	10 hrs. work	10 hrs. work	8 hrs. sick day	8 hrs. holiday	8 hrs. vacation day	8 hrs. work

How many hours, if any, of overtime did the employee work?
❑ a. 0 hours
❑ b. 4 hours
❑ c. 12 hours

6. When must overtime be paid?
❑ a. Each week
❑ b. With the next payroll
❑ c. As soon as practically possible

7. A nonexempt employee working at a hospital can work more than 40 hours in a week and not be paid overtime.
❑ True
❑ False

1.7 Calculating Overtime Payments

There are different ways to calculate overtime pay.

There are different ways to calculate overtime pay. In all instances, the first step is to calculate the employee's regular rate of pay.

Remember the employee is first paid for all time worked. Then the FLSA requires an overtime premium be paid in addition to the employee's pay for time worked when the employee has worked more than

40 hours in a week. In many cases, the term overtime pay will include both the pay for time worked and the overtime premium.

1.7.1 Establishing a Regular Rate of Pay

Overtime is based on an employee's regular rate of pay, which must be at or above the minimum wage. The regular rate of pay is calculated by dividing all of the employee's pay for time worked during the workweek (less exceptions, discussed later) by the number of hours worked in the workweek.

$$\frac{\text{Pay for all hours worked less exceptions}}{\text{All hours worked}}$$

The following table lists some of the types of compensation that are included and all of the compensation that is not included when determining an employee's regular rate of pay.

What to Include in the Regular Rate of Pay

Regular Rate Includes	Regular Rate Excludes
Base pay for all hours worked	Reimbursed business expenses
Nondiscretionary bonuses	Discretionary bonuses
Fair market value of noncash compensation	Employer benefit plan contributions
Shift premiums	Vacation/holiday/sick pay for unworked hours
Production bonuses	Gifts on special occasions
Cost-of-living adjustments	Overtime in excess of FLSA requirement
Retroactive pay	Stock options
All payments not specifically excluded by law	

The regular rate of pay requires dividing all pay for the week by all hours worked during the week.

1.7.2 Issues When Calculating Regular Rate of Pay

The regular rate of pay calculation requires the exclusion of some types of pay and may require averaging some types of pay over the number of hours worked during the workweek. For example, a nonexempt employee earning a commission that is earned over several workweeks will have the commission averaged over the workweeks, except when the employer can determine the amount of the commission earned each week.

Nondiscretionary Bonuses

If the bonus is not determined each week but at a later date, the bonus must be allocated to each workweek it was earned for the regular rate of pay calculation.

Any contractual or agreed-upon bonus related to production, efficiency, attendance, quality, or another measure of performance must be included in the calculation of the employee's regular rate of pay during the workweeks the bonus is earned.

If the bonus is not determined each week but at a later date (such as at the end of the month, quarter, year, or when a specific goal has been reached), the bonus must be allocated to each workweek in which it was earned for the regular rate of pay calculation. If not specifically tied to the work done during each workweek, it may be allocated equally to each workweek or each hour worked during the period for which the bonus is earned.

If, before the work is performed, the contract or bonus plan says that the bonus will be paid as a "percentage of total earnings," then the bonus satisfies the overtime requirements and no recomputation is necessary.

If, before the work is performed, the contract or bonus plan says that the bonus will be paid as a "percentage of total earnings" (which includes both pay for time worked and the overtime premium), then the bonus satisfies the overtime requirements and no recomputation is necessary.

Discretionary Bonuses

Bonuses paid for services performed are not included in the employees' regular rate of pay if the employer has the discretion whether to pay the bonus and to determine the amount of the bonus. To be a discretionary bonus, the bonus must not be promised in advance by a contract or other agreement. The employer's discretion as to when to pay the bonus and the amount of the bonus must be made at or near the end of the period during which the services were performed.

Overtime in Excess of Requirements

If your company pays double time or triple time for working more than eight hours a day, or other overtime compensation in excess of the FLSA overtime requirements, the extra compensation can be excluded from the employee's regular rate of pay calculations. The extra pay may also be credited toward the FLSA's required overtime premium payments.

Extra compensation at a premium rate of at least time and one-half for working Saturdays, Sundays, or holidays may be treated as overtime pay. However, if the premium rate is less than 50% of the regular rate of pay, it must be included in determining the regular rate of pay.

Noncash Goods and Services

The fair market value of goods and services provided to the employee by the employer must be included in calculating the regular rate of pay. An example is the lodging that an employer furnishes as part of a compensation package in addition to cash payments.

Benefit Plans

Contributions irrevocably made by an employer to a trustee or third person or to profit-sharing plans, qualified retirement plans, insurance plans, supplemental unemployment benefits, or similar plans are excluded from the regular rate of pay.

Retroactive Pay

Retroactive pay increases an employee's regular rate of pay. It must be prorated over the period covered and overtime calculated on the new regular rate.

1.7.3 Doing the Math - Calculating Overtime Pay

The formula for calculating overtime pay for hourly nonexempt employees is outlined below.

Doing the Math

	Calculating Overtime Pay	
Step 1	Total pay for workweek – Exclusions	**= Regular pay**
Step 2	Regular pay ÷ Hours worked	**= Regular Rate of Pay**
Step 3	Regular rate of pay x 0.5	**= Overtime premium rate**
Step 4	Overtime premium rate x Hours of overtime	**= Premium pay for over-time**
Step 5	Total pay for workweek + Premium pay for overtime	**= Total weekly compensation**

Note that in step 3, you multiply the regular rate of pay by 0.5 rather than 1.5 because the overtime hours have already been paid at the employee's pay rate in step 1. Therefore, you need to account for only the overtime hours worked that are paid at the overtime premium rate.

For example, calculate the total compensation for an employee who worked 44 hours last week. In addition to his regular wage of $10.00 per hour, the employee was paid $50.00 for supervising a trainee. What is the employee's total weekly compensation?

	Example Calculating Overtime Pay	
Step 1	(44 hours x $10.00/hour) + $50.00	**= $490.00 Regular pay**
Step 2	$490.00 ÷ 44 hours	**= $11.14 Regular rate of pay** (Rounded from $11.1364)
Step 3	$11.14 x .5	**= $5.57 Overtime premium rate**
Step 4	$5.57 x 4 hours	**= $22.28 Premium pay for overtime**
Step 5	$490.00 + $22.28	**= $512.28 Total weekly compensation**

Calculating Overtime Using a Weighted Average

When an employee is compensated at more than one rate of pay in the workweek, the regular rate of pay must be at least the weighted average of all rates used in the week.

For example, calculate the overtime for the following employee who was paid a shift differential for working different shifts.

Using Weighted Average to Calculate Overtime Pay				
Monday	$8.00/hour x	8 hours	=	$64.00
Tuesday	$8.00/hour x	9 hours	=	72.00
Wednesday	$9.50/hour x	8 hours	=	76.00
Thursday	$10.50/hour x	10 hours	=	105.00
Saturday	$8.00/hour x	8 hours	=	64.00
TOTAL		43 hours	=	$381.00

Doing the Math

Calculating Overtime Using a Weighted Average	
Step 1	$381.00 = **Regular Pay**
Step 2	$381.00 ÷ 43 hours = $8.86 (rounded from $8.8605) **Regular Rate of Pay**
Step 3	$8.86 x .5 = $4.43 **Overtime Premium Rate**
Step 4	$4.43 x 3 hours = $13.29 **Premium Pay for Overtime**
Step 5	$381.00 + $13.29 = $394.29 **Total Weekly Compensation**

Calculating Overtime for Pieceworkers

When an employee works on a piece rate, the regular rate of pay is calculated by adding the total earnings for the workweek from the piece rate to all other earnings (such as a bonus), and either of the following two methods may be used.

Method 1: Once the regular rate of pay is determined, the pieceworker must be paid, in addition to the piecework earnings for the workweek, an amount equal to one-half the regular rate times the number of hours worked over 40 in the workweek.

For example, assume that a lathe operator earns $1.00 for each sheet of metal cut on the machine. Last week, the employee finished 1,100 sheets and worked 45 hours. Overtime pay would be calculated as follows.

Calculating Overtime for Piecework
(Method 1)

Step 1	$1.00 x 1,100 sheets	= $1,100.00 **Regular Pay**
Step 2	$1,100.00 ÷ 45 hours	= $24.44 (rounded from $24.4444) **Regular Rate of Pay**
Step 3	$24.44 x .5	= $12.22 **Overtime Premium Rate**
Step 4	$12.22 x 5 hours	= $61.10 **Premium Pay for Overtime**
Step 5	$1,100.00 + $61.10	= $1,161.10 **Total Weekly Compensation**

Method 2: If employees agree before the work is performed, they may be paid at a rate not less than 1½ times the regular piece rate for each piece made during the overtime hours. (Other conditions must also be met that help guarantee that pieceworkers are not taken advantage of by their employers.)

For example, Sally receives $2.50 for each figurine she paints. In one 45-hour workweek, she painted 140 figurines in the first 40 hours and 18 in the next 5 hours.

Calculating Overtime for Piecework
(Method 2)

Step 1	$2.50 x 140 figurines	= $350.00 **Regular Piecework Earnings**
Step 2	$2.50 x 1.5	= $3.75 **Overtime Piecework Rate**
Step 3	$3.75 x 18 figurines	= $67.50 **Overtime Piecework Earnings**
Step 4	$350.00 + $67.50	= $417.50 **Total Earnings for Workweek**

Calculating Overtime for Commissioned Employees

When a nonexempt employee is paid a commission, the regular rate of pay is calculated by adding the total earnings for the workweek (hourly rate times hours worked, if applicable) to the commission earned during the workweek.

For example, Rachel earns $8.00 an hour and is paid a commission of 1% of her weekly sales. In a week that Rachel works 46 hours and makes sales of $2,000; her total weekly compensation is calculated as follows:

Calculating Overtime for Commissioned Employees

Step 1	$8.00 x 46 hours	= $368.00 **Pay for Hours Worked**
Step 2	1% x $2,000 sales	= $20.00 **Commission**
Step 3	$368.00 + $20	= $388.00 **Regular Pay**
Step 4	$388.00 ÷ 46 hours	= $8.43 **Regular Rate of Pay** (rounded from $8.4348)
Step 5	$8.43 x 0.5	= $4.22 **Overtime Premium Rate** (rounded from $4.215)
Step 6	$4.22 x 6	= $25.32 **Overtime Premium Pay**
Step 7	$388.00 + $25.32	= $413.32 **Total Weekly Compensation**

Doing the Math

Calculating Overtime for Salaried Employees

Under this plan, the employer pays a nonexempt employee a salary that is intended to compensate the employee for a specified number of hours per week. If the stipulated salary covers a period longer than a workweek, such as a month, it must be converted to its workweek equivalent.

For example, a nonexempt secretary is paid $1,800.00 per month for working a 40-hour week. Calculate the secretary's total weekly compensation for a week in which he or she works 48 hours.

Calculating Overtime for Salaried Employees		
Step 1	$1,800/month x 12 months = $21,600 ÷ 52 Weeks	$415.38 **Regular Pay** (rounded from $415.3846)
Step 2	$415.38 ÷ 40 hours	$10.38 **Regular Rate of Pay** (rounded from $10.3845)
Step 3	$10.38 x 1.5	$15.57 **Overtime rate** (Use 1.5 not 0.5 as the calculation in Step 1 is only for 40 hours in the workweek.)
Step 4	$15.57 x 8 hours	$124.56 **Overtime Pay**
Step 5	$415.38 + $124.56	$539.94 **Total Weekly Compensation**

In this case 1.5 was used instead of .5 as the employee has only been paid for working 40 hours not 48.

A salaried nonexempt employee who works more than 40 hours in a workweek must be paid their regular rate of pay plus the 50% overtime premium for the hours worked beyond 40 hours. Employers will calculate the overtime pay at 150% of the employee's regular rate of pay.

In many situations you will need to convert a salary to a weekly or hourly rate. Use the formulas on the following page.

Monthly to weekly

$$\text{Monthly salary} \times 12 \quad = \quad \frac{\text{Annual Salary}}{52} \quad = \quad \text{Weekly rate of pay}$$

Semimonthly to weekly*

$$\text{Semimonthly salary} \times 24 \quad = \quad \frac{\text{Annual Salary}}{52} \quad = \quad \text{Weekly rate of pay}$$

Biweekly to weekly*

$$\text{Biweekly salary} \times 26 \quad = \quad \frac{\text{Annual Salary}}{52} \quad = \quad \text{Weekly rate of pay}$$

Monthly to hourly rate

$$\text{Monthly salary} \times 12 \quad = \quad \frac{\text{Annual Salary}}{2{,}080 \text{ Hours**}} \quad = \quad \text{Hourly rate of pay}$$

*Semimonthly is defined as two pay periods per month (24 pay periods per year); biweekly means being paid every other week (26 times per year).

**Note: 2,080 hours/year is an acceptable standard for determining an hourly rate whenever the employee normally works 40 hours/week.

1.7.4 Acceptable Rounding

The Wage and Hour Division has accepted the practice of rounding an employee's worktime, especially where time cards and time and attendance systems are used, to the nearest tenth (6 minutes) or quarter (15 minutes) of an hour. The practice must be used consistently, however, so that employees are compensated, over a period of time, for all time actually worked.

Check Your Understanding

Check Your Understanding

Quiz 1.4. Answer the following questions to test your understanding of calculating overtime.

1. All of the following types of compensation are included in calculating an employee's regular rate of pay for overtime purposes except:
   - ❑ a. Shift premium of $50 for working the night shift
   - ❑ b. Production bonus of $15
   - ❑ c. 4 hours paid but not worked
   - ❑ d. 4% cost-of-living adjustment

2. What type of pay is included in the regular rate of pay calculation?
   - ❑ a. Discretionary bonuses
   - ❑ b. Paid sick leave
   - ❑ c. Paid vacation leave
   - ❑ d. Production bonuses

3. All of the following types of payments are included in the regular rate of pay calculation except:
   - ❑ a. A production bonus to be paid in June which the employer announced in January
   - ❑ b. An agreement with the union to pay one-half of one week's salary to workers with over five years of service
   - ❑ c. A traditional $50 gift certificate which the firm has paid for the past five years during the holiday season
   - ❑ d. Shift differential for working the 4 p.m. to midnight shift

4. An employee worked for 30 hours on his regular shift at $10.00 per hour and 16 hours on the late-night shift at $12.00 per hour. In addition, he earned a production bonus of $50.00. What is his total weekly compensation?
   $_____

1.8 Defining Time Worked

If an employee took only seven hours to complete an eight-hour job, must you pay for the extra hour and include it in overtime calculations? How do you treat the time spent waiting for a shift to begin or cleaning up afterwards? Issues like these make complying with the overtime regulations difficult. Here are some of the general rules on determining what hours must be included in overtime pay, but many situations must be judged on a case-by-case basis.

Determing what hours must be included in overtime pay must be judged on a case-by-case basis.

1.8.1 Portal-to-Portal Act of 1947

The Portal-to-Portal Act of 1947 defines the beginning of a workday as the time on any particular workday when an employee commences their principal activities, and it defines the end of a workday as the time on any particular workday when an employee ceases to perform their principal activities.

The beginning of a work day is when an employee commences their principal activities.

Workday
- A workday may be longer than the employee's scheduled shift, hours, tours of duty, or time on the production line.
- Workdays may vary from day to day, depending on when the employee commences or ceases principal activities.

Preliminary or Postliminary Activities
- Preliminary or postliminary activities (e.g., changing clothes or washing up) that must be completed during a portion of the workday are compensable if defined as such by a contract, custom, or practice.

Principal Activities
- Principal activities include all activities that are an integral part of the principal activity, such as those that are so closely related as to be indispensable to its performance. The following activities are examples of integral parts of an employee's principal activities:
  — At the commencement of the workday, the employee oils, greases, cleans, or installs a new part on a machine.
  — An employee is required to report 30 minutes prior to other employees in order to distribute clothing or materials to the workbenches of other employees.

The end of a work day is when the employee ceases their principal activities.

— An employee at a chemical plant cannot perform his tasks without changing clothes on the employer's premises at the beginning and at the end of the workday.
- The following activities are not integral parts of principal activities:
  — The employer allows the employee to change clothes on the employer's premises as a convenience to the employee.
  — Punching in and out and waiting in line to do so would not ordinarily be regarded as integral parts of the employee's principal activities.
  — Passing through security devices and traveling to the job site.

1.8.2 Call-back and Show-up Pay

Some companies pay call-back (or call-out) pay whenever an employee is called back to work after the shift is complete. Also, some employers pay show-up (or reporting) pay if an employee reports to work and then is sent home without working. In both situations, the hours that were paid but not physically worked by the employee do not have to be counted as hours worked when calculating overtime. However, first consult the state requirements and your legal advisors to make certain that this rule fits your specific situation.

1.8.3 Waiting to Work

Employees at times may be required to wait to begin or continue work. Depending on the circumstances, the waiting time may be considered work time.

Is the employee engaged to be waiting or waiting to be engaged?

According to the FLSA, employees do not have to be engaged in productive work to be considered working. If the employer restricts an employee's behavior and does not permit any personal business or activities to be conducted while waiting to begin work, the employee is considered to be *engaged to be waiting*. These hours would be included in the employee's time worked when figuring overtime hours.

However, the law does not require you to include the time spent on call if the employee is not physically at the employer's premises, but is merely asked to stay by the phone and is allowed to conduct personal business. In this situation, the employee is *waiting to be engaged* (in contrast to *engaged to be waiting*). Time spent *waiting to be engaged* would not be included in calculating overtime pay.

1.8.4 Preparing to Work

Employers do not have to compensate workers for insignificant periods of time spent cleaning up at the beginning or end of the day. Nor do they have to compensate for time waiting for the workday to begin. However, if an employee arrives on time and must wait for work to begin, the employee is engaged to wait. You must pay for this time.

1.8.5 Travel Time

The principles which apply in determining whether time spent traveling is compensable time depend on the kind of travel involved.

A nonexempt employee's travel time may be time worked depending on the circumstances.

Home to Work Travel
An employee who travels to work from home before the regular workday and returns to his/her home at the end of the workday is engaged in ordinary home to work travel, (commuting), which is not work time.

Home to Work on a Special One Day Assignment in Another City
An employee who regularly works at a fixed location in one city is given a special one day assignment in another city and returns home the same day. The time spent in traveling to and returning from the other city is work time, except that the employer may deduct that time the employee would normally spend commuting to the regular work site.

Travel That Is All in the Day's Work
Time spent by an employee in travel as part of his principal activity, such as travel from one job site to another job site during the workday, is work time and must be counted as hours worked. However, the Department of Labor has ruled that travel time and work time may be paid at different rates.

Travel Away from Home Community
Travel that keeps an employee away from home overnight is travel away from home. Travel away from home is work time when it cuts across the employee's scheduled workday. The time is not only hours

worked on regular working days during normal working hours but also during corresponding hours on nonworking days. Time spent in travel away from home outside of regular working hours as a passenger on an airplane, train, boat, bus, or automobile is not counted as time worked.

1.8.6 Seminars/Meetings

Employers are required to compensate employees for the time spent at seminars, meetings, or other required events.

Employers are required to compensate employees for the time spent at seminars, meetings, or other required events. This may include travel time getting to the meeting.

However, employers do not have to compensate employees for attending meetings when all of the following four conditions apply:

1. Attendance is outside the employee's normal working hours.
2. Attendance is voluntary.
3. The event is not directly job-related.
4. The employee performs no productive work during this period.

Be aware that the rules about compensating for travel time to meetings, seminars, etc., are complex. For example, you must compensate if the employee travels during normal working hours, but you do not have to compensate for travel time outside of normal business hours.

1.8.7 Remedial Education

An employer may employ a worker for a period of 10 hours in any workweek in excess of 40 hours during the workweek without having to pay the overtime premium if, during that time, the worker is involved in an employer-supported remedial education program. This program cannot include job-specific training. Rather, its purpose must be to provide individuals who lack a high-school diploma or an eighth grade education with reading and other basic skills.

1.9 Record Keeping and Systems

Payroll could easily get buried in its own records. Employment records, numerous IRS forms, state and local tax records, social security and Medicare data, paid checks, time cards, policies and procedures manuals, state unemployment records—countless records require your careful attention and retention.

It is difficult to imagine how any payroll department could function without computerized payroll systems and other technology designed to generate, store, and retrieve data. This section looks at payroll from a systems point of view. It suggests some ways you can streamline or eliminate the paperwork associated with payroll.

1.9.1 Handling Payroll Documents

The volume of documents and information flowing into and out of the payroll process is enormous. Each major responsibility is accompanied by a trail of records that could easily become an avalanche without careful planning.

How the data is obtained from the employee is determined by the employer in most instances, either on paper or electronically. The employer in most instances defines the actual elements of the data which must be obtained. However in some circumstances either the law or regulations will define the data to be obtained, e.g., marital status and allowances are obtained from Form W-4 as the IRS requires them to be obtained under penalties of perjury.

Each major payroll responsibility is accompanied by a trail of paper that could easily become an avalanche without careful processing.

Major Payroll Tasks
- Compliance with federal, state, and local regulations
- Timely and accurate issuance of paychecks
- Periodic reporting
- Record retention
- Control and security

1.9.2 Maintaining a Master File

Both federal and state regulations require employers to keep many records on employees. The following table summarizes the federal requirements for a master file. However, your company may choose to keep more information for its business needs.

What Must Be Kept in a Master File?

Employee Data

_____ Name

_____ Address

_____ Gender

_____ Birth date

_____ Social security number

_____ Occupation

_____ State where services are rendered

Employment Data

_____ Hire date

_____ Termination date

_____ Payment date

_____ Basic or hourly rate of pay

_____ Additions/deductions from pay

_____ Frequency of payment

_____ Hours worked/day

_____ Hours worked/week

_____ Workweek

_____ Straight time hours/pay

_____ Overtime hours/pay

_____ Shift premium

Tax and Payroll Data

_____ Allowances claimed

_____ Marital status

For Both Payroll Period and Calendar Year

_____ Total wages subject to federal, state, and local income taxes

_____ Total wages subject to social security tax and Medicare tax

_____ Total remuneration

_____ Total federal income tax withheld

_____ Total social security tax withheld

_____ Total Medicare tax withheld

_____ Tax paid by employer but not deducted from wages

1.9.3 Why a Master File?

Master file records are required for federal income tax withholding, social security and Medicare withholding, calculating unemployment tax, and overtime. Furthermore, without complete and accurate records, an employer has no way to verify whether an employee's claim for back pay is justified.

Without complete and accurate records, an employer has no way to verify whether an employee's claim for back pay is justified.

Media

Records may be maintained in any legible, retrievable form (electronic storage, microfilm, microfiche, hard copy, etc.). There is no federal requirement to maintain a paper copy of these records.

Updating the File

The master file should be kept up-to-date. There are no federal requirements for how often the file must be updated. The more up-to-date the records, the more reliable they are if the Department of Labor or court needs to investigate contested wages. Thus, you may want to consider updating the files more often than once per month.

The more up-to-date the record, the more reliable it is.

As the master file is updated, the information must remain in balance – the values from the prior pay period added to the changes and new entries must equal the updated master file. The most reliable balancing requires maintaining the prior period values and the changes to the value independently to ensure that the correct entries have been made to the correct data base.

Combining Files

Many organizations benefit by combining their human resources and payroll data into a single integrated database. Such a database may include, for example, tax deferral agreements, affirmative action policies, etc.

Without the information in the master file, it would be impossible to pay employees accurately or timely.

1.9.4 Record Retention

Gathering and reporting data efficiently and cost-effectively is one problem. Another problem is how long to retain that information without turning the payroll department into a warehouse of old files.

Retention Requirements

Federal retention requirements are shown in the following table.

How Long Must Documents be Kept?

5 Year Record Retention – OSHA (Occupation Safety and Health Administration)

- Log of all occupational illnesses and accidents
- Other OSHA records

4 Year Record Retention – Internal Revenue Service (IRS)/Social Security Administration (SSA)
- Duplicate copies of tax returns/tax deposits
- Returned copies of Form W-2
- Canceled/voided checks
- Employee's name/address/occupation/social security number
- Amount and date of payments for wages, annuities, pensions, tips; fair market value of wages-in-kind
- Record of allocated tips
- Amount of wages subject to withholding
- Taxes withheld (and date if different from pay date)
- Copies of Form W-4 (for at least four years after the date the last return was filed using the information on the Form W-4)
- Agreements to withhold additional amounts
- Dates when employee was absent due to injury and received payments; amount/rate of such payments (by employer or third party)
- Dates when employee was absent from work and payments were made under a contingency plan; amount/rate of such payments
- Copies of Forms 941, 941-X, 940, Schedule A (Form 940), 944, 945, 945-A, W-2, W-3, Schedule B (Form 941), 1042-S, 1042, 1099-MISC, 1099-R, and other returns filed electronically

3 Year Record Retention – Fair Labor Standards Act (FLSA)/Immigration Reform and Control Act (IRCA)

- Name of employee/address/occupation/birth date/sex
- Hours worked each day/week
- Amount and date of payment
- Amounts earned for straight time and overtime/additions to and deductions from wages
- Collective bargaining agreements
- Sales and purchase records
- Form I-9—three years after date of hire or one year after date of termination (whichever is later)

3 Year Record Retention – Family and Medical Leave Act (FMLA)

The following records must be kept for at least three years, in any format, and made available no more frequently than once every 12 months for Department of Labor inspection:

- Name, address, occupation, rate of pay, daily and weekly hours worked per pay period
- Additions to and deductions from wages, total compensation
- Dates of FMLA leave (or hours if taken in increments of less than one day)
- Copies of written FMLA notices
- Copies of general and specific notices provided to employees
- Plan descriptions/policies and procedures dealing with unpaid and paid leaves
- Premium payments for employee benefits
- Records of any disputes

2 Year Record Retention – Fair Labor Standards Act – Supplemental

- Time cards
- Wage rate tables
- Work time schedules
- Order, shipping, and billing records
- Records of additions to or deductions from wages

Some States Require You to Keep Records Longer Than the Federal Government Does

Real-world Application

In addition to the federal requirements, each state has its own requirements for state income tax, unemployment insurance tax, wage and hour, and other state-mandated requirements. Some states have longer retention requirements than the federal government. You should be aware of the applicable laws in the states where your company operates.

Should you retain documents beyond these dates? Many employers do. Clearly, the main reason for keeping records is to protect the company from audits and lawsuits. Government contracts require companies to keep records longer. For tax audits, many companies keep payroll tax returns for the life of the company, or at least seven years. The statute of limitations for back wage suits under the FLSA is two years (three years for willful violations). Your company should establish policies as to which files will be kept beyond the legal requirements.

Check Your Understanding

Check Your Understanding

Quiz 1.5. Answer the following questions to test your understanding of handling paperwork.

1. All of the following are reasons payroll keeps records except:
   - ❑ a. Compliance with laws
   - ❑ b. Demonstrate accuracy of paychecks
   - ❑ c. Demonstrate security of payroll
   - ❑ d. Periodic reporting

2. An employer maintains the following information in their employee master file:
   - Hire date
   - Termination date
   - Payment date
   - Regular rate of pay
   - Additions/deductions from pay
   - Frequency of payment

Name two other records that must be kept in order to calculate overtime pay.

3. An employer maintains their employee master file in computer files. Which of the following statements is true?
   - ❑ a. Under federal law, they are required to keep a backup copy of these records.
   - ❑ b. Employment records must be kept for seven years.
   - ❑ c. There is no federal requirement to update the data monthly.

4. All of the following types of records can be combined with payroll data in an integrated system except:
   - ❑ a. Personnel
   - ❑ b. Benefits
   - ❑ c. Purchasing
   - ❑ d. Human Resources

5. How long must you retain each of the following records in your files?
   - Proof of tax deposits
   - Form I-9
   - Copies of your quarterly tax returns
   - Wage and hour records
   - Employee time cards
   - Canceled checks
   - Name/address/occupation of each employee
   - Work time schedules
   - Form W-4
   - Total wages and tips
   - Overtime information
   - Log of injuries on the job

6. How long should employers keep payroll records beyond legal requirements?
   - ❑ a. 2 years
   - ❑ b. 3 years
   - ❑ c. 4 years
   - ❑ d. As long as the company needs the records

1.10 Withholding Allowances (Form W-4)

The amount of federal income tax withheld from an employee's paycheck is determined by prescribed formulas. These formulas take into account:

- Employee's wages
- Pay period frequency
- Marital status
- Withholding allowances

Employees provide their marital status and withholding allowances when they fill out the *Employee's Withholding Allowance Certificate*, or Form W-4.

The IRS allows employees to provide and change their marital status and withholding allowances on the Form W-4 through electronic systems. However, the IRS has placed requirements on the systems to make sure the person making the change is actually the employee.

1.10.1 Forms W-4 and W-4P

The *Employee's Withholding Allowance Certificate* (Form W-4) (see page A-37) and its counterpart for retired employees, *Withholding Certificate for Pension or Annuity Payments* (Form W-4P) (see page A-39), tell employers four crucial types of information:

1. Whether to withhold taxes at the single or married rate
2. How many withholding allowances are claimed
3. Whether the employee wants any additional amount withheld
4. Whether the employee is claiming to be exempt from withholding

The worksheet portion of Form W-4 helps employees find out how many allowances they can claim.

1.10.2 Filing Requirements

All employees should complete a Form W-4 or provide the information electronically, when they are first hired. In most cases, the form stays in effect until the employee provides a new one. Employees should provide a new Form W-4 if their marital status or allowances change or if too much or too little is being withheld from their wages.

Employees are not required to fill out Form W-4 each year.

All employees should complete a Form W-4 when they are first hired.

If an Employee Fails to Furnish a Form W-4

If a new employee does not complete a Form W-4 for the first paycheck, you must withhold as if he or she were single with no allowances. This procedure maximizes the amount of federal income tax withheld. It may also motivate the employee to complete the Form W-4.

If Allowances Increase

Current employees can file an amended Form W-4 any time their number of allowances increases, for example, at the birth or adoption of a child.

If Allowances Decrease

If allowances decrease (thus increasing the amount required to be withheld each pay period), employees must file an amended Form W-4 within 10 days of the change. This could happen when:

- An employee is divorced or legally separated.
- An employee is no longer supporting a dependent.
- A nonworking spouse takes a job.

Employers are not required to monitor employees for changes that decrease allowances.

Death of Spouse

The death of a spouse does not affect withholding marital status until the next year.

Notify Employees by December 1

The employer should notify employees by December 1 that they need to file an amended Form W-4 if their filing status or number of allowances has changed.

Changes Cannot Be Made in Advance

Employees cannot submit a revised Form W-4 before a change actually occurs. For example, if an employee expects to be married, she cannot change her marital status or number of allowances until after the wedding.

When You Must Change Withholding

Alert

After an employee files an amended Form W-4, you must reflect the change in withholding no later than the first payroll period ending on or after the 30th day after you received the amended Form W-4. Many employers choose to implement new W-4 forms with the next payroll.

1.10.3 Invalid Form W-4

Alert

An employee's Form W-4 is invalid when there is any alteration, addition, or deletion to the language or format of the form, especially to the perjury statement, which certifies the accuracy of the data. Form W-4 is also invalid if the employee indicates in any way that it is false.

If the employee gives you an invalid W-4 form, do not use it to calculate withholding. Ask the employee for a valid form. If a valid form is not provided, withhold as if the employee were single and claiming zero withholding allowances. However, if you have another form from this employee that is valid, you can withhold based on that form. A Form W-4 on which an employee requests a flat dollar amount of withholding or a percentage amount to calculate withholding is also invalid.

1.10.4 Exempt Form W-4

Employees may be exempt from withholding if they had no taxes due last year and none are expected to be due this year.

Who Is Exempt?

Unless employees are claimed as a dependent, those who earn less than the standard deduction can ordinarily claim to be exempt from withholding. See the table below. However, as discussed next, earning less than these amounts does not guarantee that an employee qualifies for an exemption.

Unless employees are claimed as a dependent, those who earn less than the standard deduction can ordinarily claim to be exempt from withholding.

Who Can Claim Exempt?	
Standard Deduction	**Applies To**
$12,600	Married persons filing jointly or qualified widows (widowers)
$9,300	Unmarried heads of household
$6,300	Single taxpayers
$6,300	Married persons filing separately
Personal Deduction	**Applies To**
$4,050	Taxpayers, their spouses, and dependents

Dependents

Being a full-time student and a dependent does not automatically exempt a part-time employee from withholding requirements. When total income (both wage and nonwage income) exceeds $1,050 and includes more than $350 of unearned income per year, an employee who is being claimed as a dependent by their parents (or someone else) cannot claim exemption from withholding. Unearned income includes interest earned on a savings account, dividends, capital gains, or other investment income.

Exempt Employees Must Refile Each Year

Employees who want to continue their exempt status each year must file a new Form W-4 with their employer by February 15 of each year. Remind employees that if no valid Form W-4 is filed by the deadline, you must withhold based on the last valid W-4 in your file for the employee. If there is none then, you must withhold as if they were single with no allowances.

Special Tips

1.10.5 Employer's Responsibilities

Employers are not required to verify whether an employee's marital status or withholding allowances are accurate. Your responsibilities center on the following activities.

Ensuring That Form W-4 Is Complete

Check to make certain that each employee has completed the form, signed and dated it, and that the social security number is accurate. Reject any Forms W-4 that are invalid.

Electronic systems should not accept W-4 information that is not complete.

Withholding as Claimed

Withhold based on the number of allowances claimed by the employee on Form W-4. Also deduct any additional amount requested on the form.

Requesting That Employees Change Forms W-4 When Appropriate

IRS regulations say that employers should remind their employees by December 1 to submit revised Forms W-4 if their marital status or number of allowances has changed.

Employees may submit an amended Form W-4 if they want their employer to withhold additional amounts to cover nonwage income. For example, if an employee sells stock during the year and incurs capital gains taxes, he may want to cover that tax obligation through payroll deductions with additional withholding rather than making quarterly estimated tax payments.

Record Keeping

Keep all Forms W-4 on file for at least four years from the last tax return filed using information from the Form W-4. Note the last tax return filed using information from the W-4 is the employee's personal income tax return (Form 1040 that is filed on April 15).

Keep all Forms W-4 on file for at least four years.

Submitting Forms W-4 to the IRS

You are not required to send Forms W-4 to the IRS unless the IRS specifically requests the form.

Lock-in Letters

If the IRS sends the employer a "lock-in letter" specifying an employee's marital status and/or withholding allowances, the employer must change the employee's W-4 form status for the first payroll period beginning after 60 days have passed from the date on the IRS' letter. This gives the employee time to try to convince the IRS that the employee is entitled to the marital status and/or allowances on the Form W-4.

Checking Forms Claiming Exempt Status

Be sure the employee understands the rules for being exempt from withholding. An employee who submits a false Form W-4 may be subject to a $500 penalty.

Chapter 1 | Be Cautious About Helping Employees Complete Form W-4

Alert

You certainly want to help employees understand Form W-4. But do not put yourself in the role of their tax adviser. If you consult with employees as to the number of allowances to claim or the amount of withholding, you may be liable for penalties for underwithholding.

Here is how you can help employees with their Forms W-4:

- Provide only published or recognized sources of information (IRS Publication 505), *Tax Withholding and Estimated Tax*.
- Before December 1, remind all employees to submit a revised Form W-4 if their allowances increase or decrease or their marital status changes.

1.10.6 Deducting Income Tax From Pension Income (Form W-4P)

Periodic taxable distributions from qualified pension plans, profit-sharing plans, and other qualified deferred compensation plans and annuities are subject to federal income tax withholding. However, recipients of such distributions can decline to have taxes withheld by filing Form W-4P, *Withholding Certificate for Pension or Annuity Payments* (see page A-39). Recipients also file Form W-4P to specify the number of withholding allowances and any additional amount they want withheld. If they do not file Form W-4P, you must figure withholding as if the recipients were claiming married with three allowances.

1.10.7 Deducting Income Tax From Sick Pay (Form W-4S)

When an employee who is disabled by a non-job-related illness or injury is being paid sick pay by a third-party insurer, no federal income tax will be withheld unless the employee requests it by submitting Form W-4S, *Request for Federal Income Tax Withholding From Sick Pay*, (see page A-43) to the third party. The employee uses this form to tell the third party to withhold a flat dollar amount. The minimum amount that can be withheld is $20 per week, and after withholding, the employee must receive at least $10. If a payment is smaller or larger than a regular payment, the amount withheld must be changed in the same proportion as the payment.

1.10.8 Obtaining Taxpayer Identification Numbers

Form W-9, *Request for Taxpayer Identification Number and Certification* is used to obtain a taxpayer identification number from a nonemployee. The form is not required to be signed when it is obtained for payments reported on Form 1099-MISC.

The payee may provide one of the following with the Form W-9:

1. Employer Identification Number (xx-xxxxxxx)
2. Social security number (xxx-xx-xxxx)

1.10.9 State Withholding Allowance Certificates

More than 40 states have a state income tax and require withholding from wages to collect it. Many of those states allow employers to use the employee's federal Form W-4 to calculate state income tax withholding. However, others require that a state withholding allowance certificate be completed and submitted to the employer.

Special Tips

1.11 Child Labor

Employers must meet specific requirements when employing minors under the age of 18. The law's purpose is to protect the health and well being of the child and ability of the child to receive an education.

Minors under 14 years of age generally are forbidden from working, other than on family farms. Minors 14 and 15 years of age are not allowed to work more than 3 hours per day or 18 hours per week while school is in session. During school sessions, the minor can only work between the hours of 7 a.m. and 7 p.m. When school is not in session, the minor may not work more than 8 hours per day, or 40 hours per week, and only between the hours of 7 a.m. and 9 p.m.

14- and 15-year-olds may not work in hazardous jobs. Minors under 16 years of age can perform certain work in retail, food service, and gasoline service establishments, but may not work in a job defined by the U. S. Department of Labor's Wage and Hour Division as hazardous, manufacturing, or mining. Actors or performers (in radio, television, movies, or theater) and newspaper carriers under the age of 14 are exempt from child labor restrictions.

Minors 16 and 17 years of age are only limited to not working in hazardous jobs. Employers may be fined up to $11,000 for each violation of the child labor laws and up to $50,000 for violations that lead to the death or serious injury of a minor.

Many states have also enacted child labor laws. In some cases, these laws are more restrictive regarding when a minor can work than the FLSA's limitations.

1.12 Family and Medical Leave Act (FMLA)

The Family and Medical Leave Act (FMLA) guarantees employees unpaid leave for the birth or adoption of children and for serious medical conditions of family members or themselves. Closely related to this act and the benefit it provides to employees are the sick and disability policies most mid-size and large employers provide. In addition, several states also provide a paid version of Family and Medical Leave.

In general, the FMLA guarantees employees 12 weeks of unpaid leave within a 12-month period to care for:

- A newborn or newly adopted or foster child.
- A child, spouse, or parent with a "serious health condition".
- Themselves if they have a serious health condition that makes it impossible for them to continue working.
- The employee's spouse, son, daughter, or parent who is a covered military member on active duty (or has been notified of an impending call or order to active duty) because of any qualifying situation in support of a contingency operation.
- "Eligible" employees of a covered employer may take unpaid leave, or substitute appropriate paid leave if the em-

ployee has earned or accrued it, for up to a total of 26 work-weeks in a "single 12-month period" to care for a covered servicemember with a serious injury or illness. The covered servicemembers were members of the armed forces during the five-year period before undergoing treatment.

The FMLA applies to all private and public (government) employers with 50 or more employees, including part-timers and employees on leave or suspension, but not laid-off employees. The definition of employee is the same as that under the Fair Labor Standards Act. An employee at a facility with less than 50 employees may still be eligible for the leave benefits, if the employer has at least 50 employees working within a 75-mile radius of the facility.

To be eligible for leave benefits, employees must:

1. Have been employed by the employer for at least 12 months (not necessarily consecutively)
2. Have worked at least 1,250 hours within the previous 12-month period

Exempt employees who have worked for the employer for at least a year are deemed to have met the 1,250-hours requirement unless the employer can prove otherwise.

The law also guarantees continuation of employee health benefits while on leave.

Check Your Understanding

Quiz 1.6. Answer the following questions to test your understanding of Form W-4.

1. The amount of federal income tax that is withheld from an employee's regular wages is determined by a formula that uses all of the following items Except:
   - ❑ a. Employee's taxable wages
   - ❑ b. Pay period
   - ❑ c. A flat rate
   - ❑ d. Marital status

Check Your Understanding

2. When does an employee first complete Form W-4?
   - ❏ a. When first hired
   - ❏ b. When they need to have federal income tax withheld
   - ❏ c. When the employee is married
   - ❏ d. When the employee is divorced

3. When must an employee amend their W-4?
   - ❏ a. After receiving a pay increase
   - ❏ b. After receiving overtime pay
   - ❏ c. After becoming divorced
   - ❏ d. After their spouse quits working

4. Which of the following events would require an employee to fill out an amended Form W-4 within 10 days of its occurrence?
   - ❏ a. Employee becomes legally separated from his or her spouse who was claimed as an allowance
   - ❏ b. Employee's spouse quits job to stay home with a new baby
   - ❏ c. Death of spouse
   - ❏ d. Adoption of a child

5. An employee was recently married. The employer pays on the 15th and last day of every month. On June 10, the employee submitted a revised Form W-4, changing his marital status and number of allowances from one to four. When must you change the amount of his withholding?
   - ❏ a. On his June 15th paycheck
   - ❏ b. On his June 30th paycheck
   - ❏ c. On his July 15th paycheck
   - ❏ d. On his July 31 paycheck

6. An employee is married with one child. His beginning salary is $1,000 semimonthly. Because of an unexpected business trip, the employee fails to submit Form W-4 by his first payday. What withholding status must the employer use for his first paycheck?
   - ❏ a. Single, no allowances
   - ❏ b. Single, 3 allowances
   - ❏ c. Married, no allowances
   - ❏ d. Married, 3 allowances

7. Under what conditions can an employee claim exemption from withholding on Form W-4?
   - ❏ a. Receiving overtime pay
   - ❏ b. Had no tax liability last year and expects no tax liability this year
   - ❏ c. Anticipates receiving a bonus
   - ❏ d. An employee takes her first job

8. A full-time student works a few hours each week as a receptionist. She is claimed as a dependent on her parents' tax return. Last year, she paid no income tax. This year, her anticipated total income is less than $500 and she expects to receive no unearned income. Which of the following statements is true?
   - ❏ a. She can claim to be exempt from withholding.
   - ❏ b. Once she files an exempt Form W-4, it stays in effect until a new Form W-4 is submitted.
   - ❏ c. She is not exempt because she is a dependent.
   - ❏ d. She is not exempt because she had no unearned income.

9. All employees must complete a new Form W-4 each year.
   - ❏ True
   - ❏ False

10. The personnel of the payroll department must assist employees in determining their marital status and number of allowances for Form W-4.
    - ❏ True
    - ❏ False

11. An employee claims exempt from withholding on his Form W-4. To continue the exempt status for the next year, a new Form W-4:
    - ❏ a. must be filed by December 31.
    - ❏ b. must be filed by February 15 of the following year.
    - ❏ c. is not necessary.
    - ❏ d. is illegal unless the employee has more than 10 allowances.

| # Answers to Quiz 1.1

1. c. An employer can face severe consequences when paychecks are not issued timely or correctly.

2. a. In addition to federal income, social security and Medicare taxes, employers may have to withhold state and local income taxes.

3. d. Independent contractors who have provided a TIN do not have taxes withheld and must pay their own taxes.

4. a. Even though the IRS and SSA have a stake in determining who is an employee, the employer is responsible for the determination.

5. c. Do not assume that the employer has fulfilled its responsibilities and is free from penalty simply by having someone sign a contract stating they are an independent contractor. Individuals do not have a right to waive their employee status in a contract.

   She is behaving like an employee (use of employer's tools, working on site, maintaining regular working hours, working under the company's direction). The IRS may rule that she is an employee. If so, the company could be subject to penalties for failure to withhold federal income tax, social security tax, and Medicare tax from her wages.

6. c. Consultants are generally treated as independent contractors. However, when an ex-employee is performing the same or a similar job as before retirement or termination, it is unlikely that he or she qualifies as an independent contractor after termination.

7. c. Whether or not an employee is full-time or part-time or works a few weeks or a lifetime for the company is not relevant here. She is an employee.

8. c. Being paid by the job rather than a guaranteed salary is a sign of an independent contractor. Workers from an agency (a) are employees of the temporary help agency. A lawyer (b) who is furnished all the equipment necessary to do a particular job is an employee. Payment of a guaranteed salary (d) usually indicates an employee.

Answers to Quiz 1.2

1. c. Most exempt employees must be paid a fixed salary for each workweek.

2. d. A computer repairman does not perform the duties required to qualify as an exempt computer professional.

3. a. Her employer can claim the full federal tip credit because she receives tips and with her tips is paid more than the current federal minimum wage. For federal minimum wage purposes, her employer must pay her at least $2.13 per hour and her hourly rate plus tips must equal at least the current federal minimum wage.

4. c. The federal minimum wage was increased to $7.25 per hour on July 24, 2009.

5. True

6. b. When the federal and state minimum wages differ, the higher must be paid. The minimum wage in the state where he works takes precedence over the federal minimum wage. The minimum wage where he lives is irrelevant.

7. True

8. No. The tip credit can be used to reduce the minimum wage only if the employee regularly receives tips and documents receiving more than $30.00 per month in tips.

9. False. Only hours worked count toward determining whether overtime premiums must be paid under the FLSA.

10. b. His employer is obliged to pay him at or above the federal minimum wage. No federal law requires either a shift premium or special holiday pay.

Answers to Quiz 1.3

1. False. Under the FLSA, overtime premiums must be paid only when the employee works more than 40 hours in a workweek.

2. c. The employee has worked 50 hours in the week and must be paid the overtime premium on the greater of the hours over 40 or more than 8 per day. In this case the employee will be paid 10 overtime hours.

3. a. Teachers are exempt under the professional exemption. Only nonexempt employees must be paid overtime.

4. a. Overtime is based on time worked in excess of 40 hours each workweek. There is no federal requirement to pay an overtime premium for long hours on one day, such as May 24 or May 31. Also, employers are not required to pay overtime for working on holidays, such as May 31, although many firms have such a policy. (Also remember to check your state's laws.)

   Further, each workweek stands alone. The employee worked 40 hours during the workweek of May 16-22 and 38 hours in the workweek of May 23-29. The hours worked on May 30-31 must be considered when determining overtime for the workweek of May 30-June 5, however, even though these hours are included in the May 31 paycheck.

5. a. None. Overtime is based on time worked, not time compensated. The employee physically worked only 28 hours that workweek. (Remember to check your state's laws.)

6. c. Overtime is to be paid with the next regular payday. However, if overtime can not be paid with the next regular payday due to administrative reasons it can be delayed until the next payday.

7. True. Employees of hospitals can have their overtime calculated on a 14-day-work period instead of a workweek. However, if the employee has worked more than 8 hours in any day during the work period, the hours over 8 in a day must be paid at the overtime premium rate.

Answers to Quiz 1.4

1. c. Only hours physically worked are included in the regular rate of pay overtime calculation under the FLSA.

2. d. The FLSA excludes paid time off and discretionary bonuses from the regular rate of pay calculation.

3. c. If a bonus paid during the holiday season or on other occasions is a gift, it may be excluded from the regular rate of pay even if it is paid with regularity and employees come to expect it. To be excluded, the employer must retain discretion over whether the bonus is paid and the amount. Preannouncements or union agreements make the bonus nondiscretionary.

4. The employee earned $577.34, calculated as follows:

Step 1	30 x $10.00 = $300.00 16 x $12.00 = $192.00 Bonus $50.00 $542.00 Regular pay
Step 2	$542.00 ÷ 46 hours = $11.78 per hour (rounded from $11.7826) Regular rate of pay
Step 3	$11.78 x .5 = $5.89 Overtime premium rate
Step 4	$5.89 x 6 hours = $35.34 Premium pay for overtime
Step 5	$542.00 + $35.34 = $577.34 Total weekly compensation

Answers to Quiz 1.5

1. c. Records are used to determine compliance, calculate pay, and produce reports.

2. To comply with Fair Labor Standards Act requirements for wage and hour reporting, you must also keep data on the following:
    *   Hours worked/day
    *   Hours worked/week
    *   Workweek
    *   Overtime hours/pay
    *   Shift bonus

3. c. While records should be current, no federal regulations mandate monthly updating. It is in the company's interest, however, to update at least that frequently. Records may be maintained in any legible media; no backup copies are required. Most employment data (wages, occupation, hours worked, etc.) must be kept for only three years.

4. c. Integrated databases include payroll, benefits, and other human resources data.

5. Remember to keep tax files for four years, most FLSA information for three years, and supplemental employment information for two years. The answers are as follows:
    - Proof of tax deposits: 4 years.
    - Form I-9: 3 years after date of hire or 1 year after date of termination, whichever is later.
    - Copies of your quarterly tax returns: 4 years.
    - Wage and hour records: 3 years.
    - Employee time cards: 2 years.
    - Canceled checks: 4 years.
    - Name/address/occupation of each employee: 3 years—FLSA/IRCA, 4 years—IRS/SSA/FUTA.
    - Work time schedules: 2 years.
    - Form W-4: for at least 4 years after the date the last return was filed using the information on the Form W-4.
    - Total wages and tips: 4 years.
    - Overtime information: 3 years.
    - Log of injuries on the job (OSHA): 5 years.

6. d. The employer's business needs determine the retention of records beyond the legal requirements.

Answers to Quiz 1.6

1. c. Only when paying a supplemental wage (covered in Chapter 3) can an employer use the optional flat rate method to calculate federal income tax.

2. a. If the new employee fails to complete a Form W-4, the IRS requires the employer to treat the employee as if they filed single with 0 allowances.

3. c. An employee must file a new Form W-4 when a change in status occurs that requires additional withholding.

4. a. When allowances increase (such as when a child is adopted or a spouse stops working), less tax is withheld; an employee can fill out a new Form W-4 any time. However, when allowances decrease (as in answer a), the employee must fill out a new Form W-4 within 10 days. In case of the death of a spouse, marital status and allowances are not affected until the next year. However, it is not the employer's responsibility to track or require these changes.

5. c. You must reflect the change in withholding no later than the first payroll period ending on or after the 30th day from the date you received the amended Form W-4.

6. a. If a new employee fails to submit a Form W-4, withhold the maximum amount for single, 0 allowances.

7. b Employees claiming exempt must owe no federal income tax both for the prior year and the current year as no tax will be withheld.

8. a. She apparently meets the requirements for exempt status. To maintain this status, however, she must file a new Form W-4 by February 15 of the following year.

9. False. Only employees wishing to continue an exempt status must file a Form W-4 each year.

10. False. Assisting employees with their Form W-4 may imply that you are providing them with tax advice.

11. b. The exempt status expires on February 15 of the following year. Employees must refile their Forms W-4 by that date to continue to be exempt from withholding.

Fundamentals of Payroll Operations

2.1 The Payroll System

A computerized payroll system has many components that must fit together. These components include the hardware (the physical components of the computer), the software (the programs), a network (providing communication), and the people who operate the system. When all its components work well together, a computerized system will improve the efficiency of the payroll department. A computerized payroll system can help the department accomplish the following tasks:

2.1.1 Complying With Federal/State/Local Regulations and Company Policies

For employers, payroll compliance means the ability to deal with federal, state, and local taxation, withholding, depositing, and reporting requirements on a timely basis. In addition, compliance requires ensuring employees are paid as the FLSA and state wage and hour rules require.

2.1.2 Timely and Accurate Issuance of Paychecks/Direct Deposit

Above all, you need a system that can reduce the human labor (and, therefore, human error) in preparing for payday. Your system must be sophisticated enough to calculate wages and tax withholding and to deal with the tax complexities of various fringe benefits.

2.1.3 Periodic Reporting

Your computer system must enable you to report not only to federal and state taxing agencies but also produce internal reports, providing management with essential information to evaluate expenses and trends.

Your system should facilitate the maintenance of records, both storage and retrieval.

2.1.4 Record Retention

Your system should facilitate the maintenance of records, both storage and retrieval.

2.1.5 Maintaining Control and Security

A payroll system must be as secure as possible.

2.2 Batch and Real-time Processing Methods

An important decision that affects your computer system is how the data are to be processed. There are two possibilities — batch processing and real-time processing.

2.2.1 Batch Processing

Real-world Application

Batch processing is a method of coding and collecting items to be processed into similar groups. In many systems the user prepares the batch, inputs the data, and ensures the batch is in balance. Batch processing is not always interactive. That is, you typically may not have computer access to the data as it is being run, unless the batch process is run in a background mode.

2.2.2 Real-time Processing

Instead of accumulating and processing information in batches, you can have a system that uses real-time processing. In an online real-time system, as the data are entered into the computer, the system does calculations, updates records, and returns the results to the user so they are available immediately. The operator has direct online computer communication with the data as the program is being run.

Batch processing is less expensive than real-time processing. However, batch processing may not provide the timely real-time communication you want from your payroll system. Many systems use both batch and online real-time processing.

2.2.3 Employee and Manager Self-Service

Many payroll systems now provide employees and managers the ability to update data. These systems provide employee and manager self-service. Other features of these systems may include the ability to view and print pay statements and W-2 forms.

2.3 Interfaces

In computer language, the term interface refers to the point where two distinct data-processing elements meet. It can be a connector between two pieces of hardware, between two software systems, or between hardware and software. When two systems are interfaced, the systems are organized so they can talk to each other.

Your system should be capable of being directly linked or interfaced with many other systems within your company that require payroll data.

Your payroll system should be capable of being directly linked (or interfaced) with many other systems within your company that require payroll data. The following are the most common systems that the payroll system should be interfaced with.

2.3.1 Human Resources/Personnel

Unless you have an integrated database for your master file, both payroll and human resources/personnel may be responsible for keeping employee information current. Therefore, you may need interfaces to cross-check data and update both files.

2.3.2 Benefits

You may need to pass information on employee pensions, insurance, and other benefits between the payroll department and other departments that are responsible for benefits administration.

2.3.3 Data Collection

There are far fewer manual errors when time clocks and other systems for tracking labor costs communicate directly with the payroll system. So you may need interfaces with systems that analyze job costs, work in progress, labor, employee time sheets, vacation, personal time accounts, etc.

2.3.4 Bank Checking Accounts

To facilitate check reconciliation, you may need communication between your system and the file generated containing issued checks.

2.3.5 Electronic Funds Transfer

To deposit money directly into employees' bank accounts or on payroll cards, you need a file in the format required by the automated clearinghouse (ACH).

2.3.6 Time and Attendance

Systems that allow employees to record time electronically and send time and attendance data directly to payroll save considerable time and eliminate many errors.

2.3.7 General Ledger/Cost Accounting

Your system should interface with the general ledger and accounting for recording payroll transactions, deductions, employer taxes, accruals and reversals, etc.

Real-world Application

With an automated interface, data is entered only once. Because the computers talk directly to each other with no need for human intervention, there is far less chance of error than in manual systems. Automated interfacing allows information to be shared on an as-needed basis By eliminating the human factor, the data exchange is not only more timely but also more accurate.

Be aware of timing issues when interfacing.

2.3.8 Integration

The ideal processing environment today has all data elements integrated in a single database and available to all users at any time. An integrated database has the following advantages:

- Helps reduce data integrity issues, since information is entered and maintained in one location only
- Eliminates timing issues, since information is always accessible
- Eliminates the need for interfacing

One of the latest trends in integration is the "enterprise-wide solution," in which all the company manufacturing, sales, financial, and payroll/human resources software is provided in one set of computer applications by one vendor.

2.3.9 Reconciliations

Interfaced and integrated systems require extensive reconciliations to ensure the data shared between the systems is accurate.

General Ledger Account Reconciliation
At regular intervals, you need to review the payroll general ledger accounts (see Chapter 6 for information on accounting entries) to make certain they are accurate and in balance. Pay particular attention to payroll liability accounts (such as tax payable accounts), other withholding accounts, and payroll cash (check, payroll card, and direct deposit) accounts.

Reconciling to Third-party Payments
In addition to making payments to employees, the payroll process begins the payment process to many third parties. These payments may be made to

- Outsource providers who manage a company's 401(k) plan or flexible spending account
- Agencies or courts administering withholding orders
- Unions.

• Other organizations providing assistance to employees

Whether these payments are generated by the payroll system or are made through accounts payable, the reconciliation of these payments is a critical part of ensuring compliance.

Check Your Understanding

Check Your Understanding

Quiz 2.1. Answer the following questions to test your understanding of computerized payroll systems.

1. A computerized payroll system can help a payroll department accomplish all the following tasks EXCEPT:
    ❑ a. compliance with laws and regulations
    ❑ b. producing timely, accurate paychecks
    ❑ c. record retention
    ❑ d. recognize changes in laws and regulations

2. If you need very rapid response time with minimal lag between input and output into your computer system, look for:
    ❑ a. batch processing.
    ❑ b. remote entry processing.
    ❑ c. real-time processing.
    ❑ d. network processing.

3. Name three systems that commonly need to be interfaced with the payroll computer system.

    _____

    _____

    _____

4. Name two key advantages of automated interfacing.

    _____

    _____

5. Name two key advantages of integrated databases.

    _____

    _____

6. Name two features found in systems providing employee self-service.

_____

_____

2.4 Control Procedures

Imagine the devastating effect on your company if the payroll department ceased to function. No direct deposit. No tax deposits. No quarterly reports. The resulting employee problems and government penalties could undermine the firm. Clearly, the payroll computer system and processes must remain functional, free from errors, and secure against misappropriations. Here are some of the control procedures you need to have in place.

The payroll computer system must remain functional, free from errors, and secure against misappropriations.

2.4.1 Edits

No system is foolproof, no matter how automated it is. Mistakes happen. Incorrect data are entered into the system. The wrong procedure is followed. That's why your system should have edit functions. Edit functions can be installed in the payroll system to check for errors and (sometimes) correct them. Such validity edits verify that the system is operating normally by alerting you when inputs or outputs are outside accepted ranges. For example, you can have the following types of edit functions:

- A special code to alert the operator when a payment is being generated for a terminated or soon-to-be terminated employee (this allows you to take the necessary steps in preparing the final payment)
- A special code to alert you of new hires so that you can verify their salary and hours
- An error message if no paycheck is generated for an active employee in the master file
- A special edit to identify compensation over a specified amount or a payment generated for an inactive employee
- An error message when the pay is negative
- A special alert for overtime hours or hours under standard time
- An alert when the rate of pay is changed

2.4.2 Balancing and Reconciliation

Another way to verify the integrity of the information in the payroll system is through balancing and account reconciliation procedures. These procedures (see Chapter 6 for reconciliation and balancing procedures) include the following:

- The master record of employee payments must be maintained and edited to substantiate federal and state tax returns.
- All payroll liability tax accounts should be reconciled monthly to verify the company's liability for unpaid taxes.
- Payroll liability accounts for deductions must be balanced to the pay registers to ensure that the amount in liability accounts is accurate.
- Bank accounts for payroll should be reconciled monthly, with all outstanding checks researched and all stale-dated checks cleared. (Also, you'll want to clear any unclaimed checks from the general account to an unclaimed wages account.)

2.4.3 Documentation

Make sure that all policies, procedures, system software, job descriptions, and file descriptions are documented.

Make sure that all policies, procedures, system software, job descriptions, and file descriptions are documented. Writing and maintaining documentation is not easy, but it is an important control mechanism. Documentation does the following.

Ensures Uniformity

By standardizing procedures, everyone in the department performs the same task the same way. Without this kind of control, it would be impossible to rotate assignments or fill in for staff members when they are sick or on vacation.

Simplifies Training

The training of new hires and retraining of veterans is far less time-consuming when the standard procedures are written down.

Staff members as well as outside auditors know what is expected and how processes should be done. Documentation can be used to verify or research a process.

The Sarbanes-Oxley Act has reemphasized the need for documentation as part of control procedures.

2.4.4 Apply Department Procedures

Based on documentation, procedures will be applied to all payroll processes. The procedures must be followed to ensure accuracy of the payroll processes.

2.4.5 Data Auditing and Validating

Data entered into the payroll system must be valid and appropriate. The computer system can check to determine if the data fall within acceptable parameters. However, reviewing a sample of the data for appropriateness can identify data problems that fall within the parameters of the system edits but are not actually valid. Your organization will have to decide how to set the parameters for the sampling to ensure validity.

Reviewing a sample of the data for appropriateness can identify data problems that fall within the parameters of the system edits but are not actually valid.

2.4.6 Batch Controls

Data entered into the payroll system must be controlled to ensure that the data that are intended to be entered have actually been entered. Batching the data into groups of similar data, developing totals of the data to be entered, and then comparing the totals of the data entered into the system to the previously developed totals is one method of batch controls. This method ensures that the amounts that are anticipated to be entered have been entered. However, it does not ensure that the data have been correctly entered into the system.

2.4.7 Correction Procedures

If system-generated totals from the data entered do not agree with either batch control totals or other controls, procedures must be in place to determine the error, its cause, and how it should be corrected. Ideally, control totals will have interim totals that correspond to interim totals that the system generates. The interim totals may be divided into divisions, plants, or any other logical sequence. Once erroneous data has been identified, it must be corrected. This will require developing batch controls for the data correction entries.

2.4.8 Accumulator Totals

Within each payroll system totals are accumulated for various periods of time – year-to-date, quarter-to-date, month-to-date, etc. Balancing these totals from pay period to pay period is critical to ensure the data has been processed correctly each pay period.

2.4.9 Upgrading/Updating the Payroll System

Payroll systems must be updated/upgraded periodically during the system's life cycle. Updates consist of end of quarter or end of year patches to ensure compliance with quarterly or annual reporting and new year processing. Specific procedures must be followed beginning with the backup of the system prior to beginning the update.

Upgrades may be more complex as they may include the addition of new features and processing requirements. In many cases the upgrade to a new version of the software is a project that closely rivals the implementation of a new system.

2.4.10 Apply Departmental Procedures

Each organization may have a different procedure but each procedure must be implemented appropriately. Ensuring that the defined procedures are implemented and used is one critical step in the success of a payroll operation.

Check Your Understanding

Quiz 2.2. Answer the following questions to test your understanding of control procedures.

1. The integrity of the data can be verified by:
   - ❏ a. balancing and reconciliations.
   - ❏ b. system edits.
   - ❏ c. validity checks.

2. Checking inputs or outputs against predetermined constraints is called:
   - ❏ a. internal control.
   - ❏ b. validity edit.
   - ❏ c. system safeguard.
   - ❏ d. parallel test.

3. Payroll tax liability accounts should be reconciled at least weekly.
   - ❏ True
   - ❏ False

4. Every month, all of the following records are reconciled EXCEPT:
   - ❏ a. payroll liability accounts.
   - ❏ b. master record of payments.
   - ❏ c. payroll bank checking account.
   - ❏ d. validity edits.

5. Payroll documentation accomplishes all of the following EXCEPT:
   - ❏ a. provide uniformity.
   - ❏ b. simplify training.
   - ❏ c. ensure procedures are followed.
   - ❏ d. provide a reference tool.

6. When system-generated totals do not agree to batch control totals, what must occur?
   - ❏ a. continue processing.
   - ❏ b. finding the cause and correcting the error.
   - ❏ c. delay finding the error until more time is available.
   - ❏ d. document the difference and continue processing.

2.4.11 Security

Payroll departments handle a sizable percentage of your company's cash. Security against embezzlement, protection against payroll check fraud, and data security must always be a top concern of payroll management. Here are some ways to protect your company.

Control Your Own Staff

There are several procedural steps payroll managers can take to guard against misappropriations by payroll staff members.

Segregate job duties - No task should be handled exclusively by one person. Make certain, particularly in cash transactions, that more than one person is involved.

Rotate personnel - Periodically switch tasks and reassign duties among the staff. This practice makes sense not only from a security point of view; it can also relieve tedium on the job and help in case of a staff emergency.

Restrict access to the system - Severely limit the number of employees who have access to your payroll system.

Special Tips

Controls for a Small Payroll Department

If your department is small (one or two people), you need to set up controls outside the payroll department, especially with human resources and accounting. You need to separate the elements of payroll. Do not keep any one function under the control of one person or small department. For instance, you might do the following:

- Store payroll checks in a locked area of the security department but keep the key in the payroll department.
- Have an independent review of the check register before releasing any payroll checks.
- Have accounting perform bank reconciliations.
- Periodically send a list of employees who were paid to department heads so they can verify that no unauthorized names are receiving paychecks.

Reconcile Bank Accounts Monthly

Reconciling your payroll checking account is more than just a necessary accounting procedure. It may also be the most effective way to guard against breaches of security. However, reconciliation of the payroll bank account should not be accomplished by those responsible for issuing paychecks.

Build Security into the System

Build security into your automated payroll environment. Your data security system should offer the following three things:

1. File security against unauthorized access
2. Password protection so only authorized personnel can gain access to protected information
3. Regular backup of data and offsite storage of data

Guard Against "Phantom Employees"

Some companies deliver payroll checks or direct deposit notifications either by mail or by having supervisors distribute them. Neither method ensures that you are not paying "phantom employees" who exist only on payday. Segregating job duties and rotating assignments will provide some safeguard against creating "phantom employees."

For even better protection against having phantom employees, conduct a surprise physical payoff (or payout) at least once a year; preferably more often. Upper management selects a team of auditors (not payroll personnel) who will pick up the paychecks and direct deposit notifications and hand-deliver them to each employee. Ideally, employees are required to show photo IDs and sign for their paychecks before they are paid.

Real-world Application

In addition, employers should check for multiple direct deposits being made to the same bank account, which may help identify phantom employees.

Define Procedures for Handling Undelivered Checks

Your company should have a written procedure for how employees' paychecks will be distributed. These procedures must define what occurs if an employee is not available to receive the check. For internal control purposes, the undelivered check should not be returned to someone who has the capability to issue the check or who reconciles the payroll bank account. Undelivered checks should be returned to someone in the organization who does not have the ability to control paycheck issue or redemption.

Define Procedures for Handling Voided Payments

Once a payment (check, direct deposit or payroll card) has been determined to not be valid, it must be voided. Your company must have specific procedures in place to ensure that the entries made are complete. In many cases, voiding the payment in the payroll system is not sufficient to meet all organizational requirements and may cause reporting issues when a payment is voided in a subsequent quarter. A voided payment may require:

- A W-2c to be issued
- A claim for refund from the IRS or other tax authorities
- Correction to state unemployment insurance reporting and taxation
- Correcting entries to the accounting records

Use Audit Trails

Audit trails are the tracks that data leave when entered into the payroll system. Each time data are entered, it must have the proper authorization. Authorization may be found in a paper document or an electronic document. Audit trails tie the authorization document into the data in the payroll system. Payroll system audit trails will also identify which operator entered the data and when the data were entered into the system. However, due to the system resources required for a complete audit trail, most system-generated audit trails are limited to critical entries, such as the entry of a new employee, pay rate changes, etc. Internal or external auditors use audit trails to trace what has happened in the processing of data.

2.5 External audits

In addition to frequent internal audits of your firm's financial accounts, publicly held firms must also undergo an annual external independent audit of their books. This information is required so that the board of directors and shareholders can assess the financial well-being of the company and protect their interests. Furthermore, the IRS may require an audited financial statement when reviewing corporate tax returns.

The primary focus of external audits is to determine the following:

- Whether the financial statements are appropriate
- Whether the firm's financial assets are being properly safe-guarded
- Whether there are risks to the company's financial well-being that will materially affect its future balance sheets or income statements

Obviously, payroll will be included in an external audit, since its actions affect a large percentage of the firm's assets. Some of the key questions you might be asked are summarized in the following table.

Questions Frequently Asked by External Auditors

- Where are the blank checks stored?
- Who signs checks?
- Who approves payroll?
- Where are files retained?
- How is the accuracy of payroll verified?
- Who reconciles the payroll checking account?
- How do you ensure that taxes are withheld accurately?
- Are timely deposits made?
- Are managers complying with new tax rules?
- Are all payroll transactions properly recorded in the general ledger?
- Are accrual accounts handled properly?

You can benefit from an audit. Don't be afraid of an audit. Rather, welcome it as a time to take a new look at your processes, control mechanisms, and procedures to safeguard company assets.

Special Tips

Auditors, both external and internal, are bound by professional requirements to maintain the confidentiality of the data they review. Data requested by auditors should be provided.

Audits can even work to your advantage. For example, if you have been requesting a certain procedure that will assist you in establishing better controls, speak to the auditors about it. If they agree, they may include this request in their letter to management.

Check Your Understanding

Check Your Understanding

Quiz 2.3. Answer the following questions to test your understanding of security.

1. Name one way payroll managers can increase security through stricter internal control of the payroll staff.

    _____

2. Which of the following is the best method of guarding against phantom employees?

    ❑ a. Monthly bank reconciliation
    ❑ b. Validity edits
    ❑ c. Physical payout
    ❑ d. Audit trails

3. Name two items that should be documented in the payroll department.

    _____

    _____

4. All of the following issues are concerns of external auditors EXCEPT:
    ❑ a. Safeguarding of the firm's financial assets
    ❑ b. Risks to the company's financial well-being
    ❑ c. Efficiency of payroll procedures
    ❑ d. Material misstatements of financial statements

5. How can one or two-person payroll departments guard against breaches of security?

    _____

2.6 Paying Employees

It is the employer's choice — by cash, check, direct deposit, or payroll card — how employees will be paid within the bounds of state law in the state where the employee works. For example, most states allow an employer to pay the employee through direct deposit but give the employee the choice of the financial institution which will receive the deposit. Other states require that when paying an employee by check, the check must be paid by a bank in the state where the employee works. Restrictions similar to those on the use of direct deposit apply when paying employees with payroll cards.

Individual states control how and when paychecks are issued. You need to be in compliance with applicable state regulations. In addition to regulating how an employee is paid, most states require employees be provided an accounting of their gross pay and deductions. Some employers now provide these statements electronically.

Individual states control how and when paychecks are issued.

2.6.1 Paying by Check

Here are some important considerations when developing policies for paying employees by check.

Advantages of a Special Payroll Checking Account

Many firms pay employees from a special payroll checking account. This facilitates reconciliation between the payroll register, the payroll checking account, and the general ledger account.

Never having more funds in the account than needed to meet a particular payroll simplifies reconciling the payroll checking account. When all payroll checks have cleared the account, the account balance should be zero, thus the name of these type of account — Zero Balance Account.

Note, however, that some firms deliberately keep a balance in excess of their payroll needs in their payroll checking account. One reason is that the excess funds help affirm and maintain their banking relationship, especially in satellite offices.

Real-world Application

Canceling and Voiding Checks

Each company will set its own procedures for the handling of canceling or voiding payroll checks. Generally, those responsible for entering payroll data are not responsible for canceling or voiding checks.

If at all possible, the canceled or voided check should be returned to the Payroll Department to ensure proper processing through the payroll system and proper notification to other parts of the organization as is appropriate—Finance, Treasury, Tax Reporting, etc.

Keeping Track of Checks

Alert

You need a procedure for keeping track of used check numbers. An account reconciliation system should automatically report any check numbers that have not been accounted for. Open check numbers must be reconciled. An open number may signify that a manual check has not been recorded or an employee has not cashed the check (for a variety of reasons).

Take Extra Security Precautions

Take extra precautions when storing blank checks that are pre-printed with company and banking information and the check-signing machine. In the wrong hands, these items could cost your company a great deal. Payroll checks should be stored under lock and key. Proper segregation of duties for the handling of checks should be in place and approved by your internal auditing department. Such steps can help guard against theft, fraud, or other misappropriations.

2.6.2 Direct Deposit

With EFT, there are no paper checks to safeguard and there are no checks to get lost.

Direct deposit or electronic funds transfer (EFT) eliminates some of the problems associated with checks. EFT allows employers to deposit employees' pay electronically in their bank account. There is no paper or check signing equipment to safeguard and no checks to get lost.

The following table summarizes the advantages and disadvantages of direct deposit for employees and employers.

Advantages and Disadvantages of Direct Deposit
For Employees

Advantages	Disadvantages
Funds available on payday; no waiting for checks to clear	Some employees are not comfortable without a physical check to cash.
Funds deposited even if employee is sick, out of town, or on vacation	Some employees do not have a bank account.
No standing in line to cash a paycheck	

For Employers

Advantages	Disadvantages
No lost checks	Not paperless; authorization must be given, notifications must be provided
Reduces paper flow	May be forced to handle two methods of pay: check for some employees and EFT for others
Eliminates early release or manual preparation of vacation checks	Difficult to stop payment on direct deposit
Reduces potential loss by theft/fraud	Costs of processing direct deposit may be passed on to employer by the originating bank
Reduces costs—checks cost more than EFT notices	Loss of "float" on payroll funds
Fewer employees taking time off work to cash checks	

For Employers

Advantages	Disadvantages
Minimizes check signing	
Fewer canceled checks to store	
Reduces unclaimed checks	
Fewer checks to balance	
Reduces check reconciliations	

Real-world Application

In general, direct deposit is more advantageous to employers than employees. One of the chief drawbacks for the employer is the loss of the "float" time on payroll funds. Float is the interest earned on the funds during the time between the writing of the paychecks and the actual withdrawal of funds to cover the paychecks. For large employers, the amount of the float can be sizable.

Because of the complexity of the direct deposit process, it may not be practical for employers with high turnover. Nevertheless, most employers offer direct deposit of payroll because it is a relatively inexpensive benefit to employees that offers advantages to the employer as well.

2.6.3 The Direct Deposit Process

The direct deposit process is regulated by the Consumer Financial Protection Bureau's Regulation E, NACHA's ACH Operating Rules, and state laws.

Educating Employees

The greater the participation in the direct deposit system, the less expensive it is to maintain. So before setting up the system, be sure to educate employees about it and encourage their participation. Employers should have frequent campaigns that actively promote direct deposit. In fact, participation levels can rise as much as 10% with each campaign.

Ways to Promote Direct Deposit

The best place to start is with new hires—include direct deposit information in employee orientation programs. Provide the employees with names of banks who are willing to provide free services to employees who elect direct deposit. Another way of promoting direct deposit is to hold "Banking Days," inviting local banks to come to your employees at their work site to explain their services and also encourage direct deposit. Paycheck attachments, e-mail messages, posters, and newsletter articles are easy ways to inform employees of the multiple benefits of direct deposit.

Setting up New Enrollees

Direct deposit is an agreement between the employer and the employee to allow the electronic transfer of funds to the employee's bank account. You need three pieces of information to set up a direct deposit of payroll for an employee:

1. The employee's bank routing number
2. The type of account into which the payroll will be deposited (checking or savings)
3. The account number

Determine which methods you will use to obtain employee information:

- E-mail
- Voice mail
- Employee self-service
- Written requests

The NACHA Operating Rules allow that "in case of credit entries, the authorization may be provided orally or by other written means." This means that you can get the information required to establish a direct deposit relationship by a phone call into the payroll department, through the company e-mail network, or other electronic means your company uses for employee communications. If a form is used, keep it simple, but be sure it asks for adequate information about the financial institution name, routing number, and type of account.

In this example, the MICR line shows the check number to the right of the account number. When the check number on the MICR line is identical to the check serial number (located in the upper right hand corner of the check), it should be included with the account number.

```
TXYZ CORPORATION                                                    1044
1100 Jack Benny Drive                          _____ 19 _____
Rochester, New York 14643

Pay to the
order of _____ $[          ]

_____Dollars

Anywhere Bank
Memo _____        _____

MICR →   012640456   123 4567        1044           0000039158
Line
            ↓           ↓              ↓                 ↓
        Routing      Account      Check Serial      Dollar Amount
        Number       Number         Number
```

When an employee authorizes a direct deposit, they are authorizing a credit to their bank account. Most companies direct deposit authorization forms also include authorization to debit the account when an overpayment has been made.

Check the Routing Number

Determine if the financial institution is in the right federal reserve district, based on the first two digits of the routing number.

Routing Numbers of Federal Reserve Districts			
Federal Reserve District Number	Location	Federal Reserve District Number	Location
01	Boston	07	Chicago
02	New York	08	St. Louis
03	Philadelphia	09	Minneapolis
04	Cleveland	10	Kansas City
05	Richmond	11	Dallas
06	Atlanta	12	San Francisco

Verify that there are nine digits in the routing number. Any exceptions should be considered potential problems, and a phone call to the ACH department of the employee's financial institution could eliminate a returned transaction. The entire routing number can be verified against a listing of financial institutions, which can be obtained from the originating depository financial institution (ODFI).

Determining Transmission Methods

The ODFI should be able to provide information about the types of electronic links that are available. Usually all that is needed is a personal computer (PC) with a high-speed communications line or Internet connection to your ODFI. This type of program can be used to transmit debits, credits, or prenotes that otherwise cannot be made until the next payroll cycle.

Sending a Prenotification

The initial entry of a direct deposit transaction can be a "prenotification." That is, the first cycle of the direct deposit can be processed with a zero amount to verify that the bank code and financial institution account are accurate and that the bank is a member of the ACH. This process alerts the receiving bank that this transaction will occur electronically and notifies the payroll department if the transaction is acceptable. The receiving depository financial institution (RDFI) should notify the ODFI, which will notify the employer of any discrepancies before the direct deposit is "live." Prenotifications are optional.

The first cycle of the direct deposit can be processed with a zero amount to verify that the bank code and financial institution account are accurate.

ACH FLOW

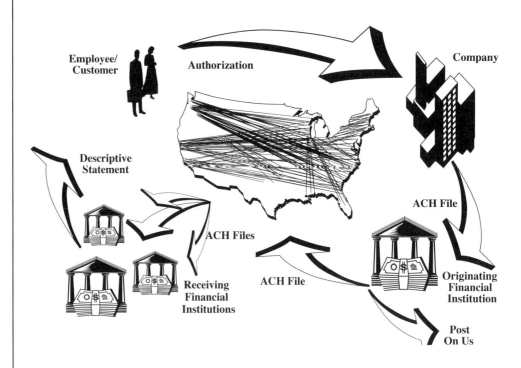

Direct Deposit Flow

Correcting Mistakes

Mistakes can happen with direct deposit as with any payroll entry. The ACH Operating Rules make it easier to correct errors such as:

- Duplicate payments
- Payments not intended to be credited to designated receivers (e.g., payments made to employees or to terminated employees)
- Payments issued in the wrong amounts

If a mistake is made, companies can simply generate a "single-entry reversal" through the ACH network within five banking days from the settlement date of the original erroneous entry.

You do not need employee authorization to correct a mistake. No debit authorizations from employees are necessary for "single-entry reversals" made in the exact amount of the original payment that are executed within the five banking days time frame for corrections.

2.6.4 Resolving Late Deposit Issues

The worst feeling an employee on direct deposit can have is going to their bank to make a withdrawal and being told that their account has no funds. In this situation, the employee will immediately contact the payroll department. The first and most important step is to reassure the employee that their money is safe. Then, the payroll department should take the following steps:

1. Verify the routing and account numbers on the employee's authorization against the numbers in the payroll system.
2. If the employee has used an automated teller machine (ATM), ask them to speak to a representative at their bank to see if the funds have been posted. ATM withdrawals may be using information that has later posting at the bank.
3. Payroll funds should be available to employees at the opening of business on payday (the settlement date with the ODFI). If the financial institution is having internal problems, they should be asked to honor an employee's pay statement as proof of the direct deposit.
4. If a solution still has not been found, contact your ODFI and speak to your account representative. Your ODFI should research the problem and respond to your request promptly.

Direct deposits should be available on the day they are settled. Financial institutions are required to make direct deposits available for cash withdrawal on the day they are settled (the date determined by your company). In most cases, the problem will be at the employee's financial institution, and that institution should be willing to take corrective action to ensure availability of funds to the employee.

2.6.5 Stopping Direct Deposit

From time to time, an employee may wish to stop direct deposit and revert to payment by check. Use these requests as opportunities to understand the employee's reasons by soliciting his or her input. In most cases, you will find that the reason for stopping direct deposit will have nothing to do with the direct deposit program.

An employee may wish to stop direct deposit and revert to payment by check.

One common reason to stop direct deposit is the termination of the employee. Company policy may prohibit the employee from receiving any further direct deposit payments once the employee has given notice or the payroll department has been notified of the employee's termination. This will reduce the employer's risk of loss of funds due to an error in the direct deposit.

A second frequent reason for an employee to request that their direct deposit be stopped is a change in the employee's bank account. The employee may move their account to a new financial institution or another account at the same financial institution. If the employee is changing banks, it may not be necessary to stop the direct deposit if the employee can have both accounts open to receive the final deposit at the old account while the new account is receiving a prenote. However, prenotes are not currently required. If the employee is changing accounts at the same financial institution, the bank may be able to provide the new account number, which can be entered without prenoting the account. Frequently, banks will provide the new account number if they change their numbering system.

2.6.6 Reversing Direct Deposit

While most payroll ACH transactions will be in the form of credits, the use of debits should not be ignored. Debiting an employee's account represents a much more efficient method for recovering an erroneous payment than requesting a check refund from the employee. An employee may be paid in error, which means a "reversal" may need to be made which will simply retrieve the funds from the account where the deposit was initially made and return such funds to your corporate account. A single item reversal is always for the exact amount of the initial deposit and must be executed within five business days from the original payment date (settlement date).

2.6.7 Federal Bank Holidays

If a direct deposit due date falls on a banking holiday, the employer dictates when employees will be paid.

If a direct deposit due date falls on a banking holiday, the employer's policy will dictate when employees will be paid. If the policy requires payment prior to the normal payday, ACH processing will occur one day earlier. The following is the ACH holiday schedule:

New Year's Day—January 1

Martin Luther King, Jr.'s Birthday—Third Monday in January

President's Day—Third Monday in February

Memorial Day—Last Monday in May

Independence Day—July 4

Labor Day—First Monday in September

Columbus Day—Second Monday in October

Veterans Day—November 11

Thanksgiving Day—Fourth Thursday in November

Christmas Day—December 25

If either January 1, July 4, November 11, or December 25 falls on a Sunday, the following Monday is a holiday. There is no provision for a Friday holiday should any of these holidays fall on a Saturday, or for state holidays that differ from these holidays, even though financial institutions may be closed on those days.

2.6.8 Payment by Payroll Card

An easy-to-use direct deposit solution for the unbanked is available. Payroll cards are prepaid, host-based, stored-value cards that can act as a tool to facilitate direct deposit of payroll for employees, whether or not they have a current banking relationship.

Payroll cards allow employers to reduce costs traditionally associated with paper-based payroll processes, including producing and handling physical paper media, fraud costs related to losses and theft, and bank processing service costs. The payroll card provides employees (especially unbanked employees) with a convenient, secure way to obtain cash, make purchases, and pay bills. In short, it's better than a paper check.

Benefits of Payroll Cards for Employers
The employee's use of a payroll card provides employers with many of the benefits associated with direct deposit—reduced costs, enhanced efficiency, and increased employee productivity and satisfaction—and it does not require that the employee using the payroll card have a bank account.

Advantages for Employees

- **Cost savings:** *Unbanked?* Having a payroll card eliminates the need for costly check-cashing services.
- **Independence:** Employees don't need to ask relatives or friends to cash paychecks or pay bills on their behalf.
- **Prestige:** With the payroll card, employees may have the prestige of carrying a branded payroll card without being subject to traditional credit or debit card underwriting requirements.
- **Safety:** Employees can obtain cash in the increments they need to meet their immediate needs, rather than cashing their checks for the full amount of their pay. With most payroll card products, a loss policy protects the employee—if their card is lost or stolen, their balance will be transferred to a replacement card.
- **Freedom:** Cash access at ATMs and purchasing power online and at millions of stores worldwide allow employees to control their funds while encouraging increased personal financial management.
- **Convenience:** Employees can receive and access their pay even when they're not on the job on payday.
- **Time:** Employees save time by avoiding check-cashing lines on payday.

Advantages for Employers

Reduce costs by eliminating:

- Exception and special payments (termination, awards, expense reimbursements, advanced adjustments, disaster recovery).
- Check loss and theft, including stop-payment fees.
- Fraudulent cashing of duplicate checks.
- Check printing, storing, retention, and reconciliation charges.

Enhance efficiency and productivity by:

- Elimination of paper payroll checks.
- Instituting electronic pay statements.
- Funding via ACH.
- Administering payroll cards through a user-friendly Web application.
- Eliminating the need for employees to be at the worksite to receive their pay.

- Eliminating the need for employees to leave work to cash checks on paydays.

Legal Compliance Requirements

Payroll cards are subject to laws and regulations that traditionally apply to electronic funds transfers, payment of employees, and credit card issuance, including recent developments related to privacy and electronic delivery of disclosures and other documentation. Additionally, state and federal labor laws impose various requirements on employers regarding the payment of wages. Many state laws require employers to provide employees with access to their net pay in full, without discount or fees. While there is no officially prescribed or approved means for meeting the requirement, employees have many means among which they may choose to obtain their pay.

Starting a Payroll Card Program

First, you need to enter into an agreement with a participating bank or payroll card provider. Next, institute a marketing campaign for your employees (make sure you ask your payroll card provider for support!) and enroll employees in the program.

Next, you need to establish a central funds pool with the payroll card provider (the funding account). Typically, enrolling employees means that you will use the payroll card provider's website to establish an "account" for each enrolled employee. The payroll card provider will then generate the cards for each enrolled employee (for payroll cards, this usually occurs within about three days) and deliver the cards to you or directly to your employees, whichever you designate. On payday, you fund the central funds pool, and the amount of each employee's net pay is credited to his/her individual account. Funding is initiated via the ACH or intra-bank transfer. When necessary, you can typically use a Web-based process to change your employee's account profile and make payroll adjustments.

Payroll Card Reversal Timing

Each employer will have policies and procedures that provide the ability to stop payment on a payroll card that has been issued to an employee and that spell out what must occur before the payment can be reissued. These procedures may include the following steps:

1. Notify the bank to reverse the payroll card payment.
2. Reissue the payroll card payment to the employee.

2.6.9 Regulation of Payment Timing

Employers have a wide variety of methods to use in paying the employee. In the past, employees were paid in cash, a method that is seldom used now. Employees are familiar with receiving checks, which are negotiable instruments. Direct deposit of employees' pay into their personal bank account has become widely accepted in recent years.

State laws govern the method of payment.

State laws govern the method of payment. Each state's requirements must be reviewed if a change in payment method is being considered.

Typically, each state requires employers to pay employees within a certain time frame. For example, the state may require the employer to pay no less frequently than monthly. In such a state, the employer may pay employees weekly, biweekly, semimonthly, or monthly.

Generally, states also limit the time period between the end of the pay period and payday. Most states do not allow employers more than 10 days between the end of the pay period and payday.

2.6.10 Unclaimed Wages

Escheat Laws

Most states dictate how long the employer must hold unclaimed wages if an employee does not cash a paycheck. Usually this occurs when an employee moves and fails to pick up a final paycheck. Typically, the unclaimed amounts must be submitted to a state agency for further retention. Check the individual laws for your state.

Escheat Processing

State law and company procedures will dictate how and when unclaimed wages are recorded and then transferred to the appropriate state agency.

Check Your Understanding

Check Your Understanding

Quiz 2.4. Answer the following questions to test your understanding of direct deposit.

1. In order to set up direct deposit of payroll, you need which three pieces of information?
   1. _____
   2. _____
   3. _____

2. What is the correct chronological sequence for the following events associated with direct deposit?
   1. Company creates ACH file
   2. Employee receives deposit in his or her bank account
   3. Company collects employee information
   4. Originating financial institution transmits data
   5. Settlement through ACH
   ❑ a. 1 3 4 2 5
   ❑ b. 3 1 5 4 2
   ❑ c. 3 1 4 5 2
   ❑ d. 1 4 5 3 2

3. All of the following regulate payments made by direct deposit EXCEPT:
   a. Consumer Financial Protection Bureau
   b. NACHA
   c. State laws
   d. Local laws

Answers to Quiz 2.1

1. d. Payroll professionals must research the constantly changing laws and regulations to ensure the payroll system remains in compliance.

2. c. In real-time systems, timeliness is critical. These are interactive systems in which the response time is measured in milliseconds. This contrasts with batch systems, which have response times measured in hours or even days.

3. Interfaces may be required between payroll and computer systems for many other functions within your organization, including the following:
   - Human Resources
   - Benefits
   - Bank checking accounts
   - Direct deposit
   - Data collection systems
   - Time and attendance
   - General ledger
   - Cost accounting

4. Some of the advantages of automated interfacing include the following:
   - Data is entered once, reducing labor time
   - Less chance of error than with manual systems
   - Allows information to be shared on an as-needed basis
   - More timely exchange of data between systems
   - More accurate data exchange

5. Some of the advantages of integrated databases are
   - Help reduce data integrity issues
   - Eliminate timing issues
   - Eliminate the need for sending data from one system to another

6. Features found in systems providing employee self-service include:
   - The ability to update personal data
   - The ability to view and print pay statements
   - The ability to view and print W-2 forms

Answers to Quiz 2.2

1. a. Balancing and reconciliations ensure that amounts in the system are correct.

2. b. One way to check for errors is to build validity edits into the system. The system automatically checks to make certain all inputs and outputs are within normally accepted ranges. If not, the operator is alerted.

3. False. Reconciliations of liability accounts should occur at least monthly.

4. d. Monthly account reconciliation helps validate the integrity of the information in your payroll system.

5. c. Payroll management is entrusted with ensuring procedures are followed.

6. b. When the system is not in balance, it must be corrected before proceeding.

Answers to Quiz 2.3

1. From a security point of view, three good ways to control the payroll staff are
    *   Segregation of job duties
    *   Rotation of personnel
    *   Restricted access to the system.

2. c. Perhaps the only way to protect your company against phantom employees is to have auditors physically hand out checks to each employee and require identification.

3. Good documentation is needed for
    *   Payroll policies
    *   Procedures
    *   System and software user manuals
    *   Employee job descriptions
    *   File descriptions.

4. c. External auditors are more concerned with truth, security, and risks to the company's well-being than they are with the efficiency of your procedures.

5. If you are in a small department, establish checkpoints with other departments (for instance, human resources and accounting), so that no one department handles a function in its entirety.

Answers to Quiz 2.4

1. The three pieces of information that are needed for direct deposit are as follows:
   - The employee's bank's routing number
   - The type of account (checking or savings)
   - The account number

2. c. The sequence is as follows:
   3. Company collects employee information
   1. Company creates ACH file
   4. Originating financial institution transmits data
   5. Settlement through ACH
   2. Employee receives deposit in his or her bank account

3. d. The Consumer Financial Protection Bureau's Regulation E allows the use of Electronic Funds Transfer. NACHA provides the operational rules for EFT. State laws facilitate the payment process.

Paycheck Fundamentals | Chapter 3

Look at any paycheck, and you will notice that the gross amount of pay is not equal to the paycheck amount. That's because certain amounts are deducted from an employee's gross pay. These deductions include amounts for benefit plans and taxes. The paycheck amount is called net pay, or take-home pay. This chapter discusses how to handle some of the deductions and additions that are made to gross pay in order to calculate net pay.

3.1 Withholding Federal Taxes

As you learned in Chapter 1, gross earnings include regular wages plus additional earnings, such as tips, shift premiums, paid time off, bonuses, and overtime pay. After calculating an employee's gross earnings, you then determine the amount to withhold for federal, state, and local taxes. Let us first concentrate on the basics of withholding federal taxes—federal income tax (FIT), social security tax, and Medicare tax.

3.1.1 Taxable Wages

The IRS defines taxable wages as all remuneration for services (including noncash benefits). As shown in the following table, determining what is taxable and what is not can be complex. Some benefits are fully taxable, some are partially taxable, and some are tax-free to the employee.

Taxable Versus Nontaxable Compensation
(federal law only)

Taxable Compensation	Nontaxable Compensation
Back pay awards	Dependent child care assistance (up to $5,000) under a Section 129 plan
Bonuses	Company vehicle (business use only)
Commissions	De minimis fringes

Taxable Compensation	Nontaxable Compensation
Company vehicle (personal use)	Disability benefits (employee contributions)
Dismissal and severance pay or final vacation pay	Educational assistance for job-related courses (no limit)
Employer-paid transit passes and transportation in commuter highway vehicle in excess of $255/month	Group-term life insurance premiums ($50,000 or less of coverage)
Employer-paid parking greater than $255/month	Medical/dental/health plans (employer contributions)
Fringe benefits (unless specifically excluded)	No-additional-cost fringe benefits
Gifts, gift cards, prizes, and awards	Qualified employee discounts on employer goods/services
Group legal services	Qualified moving expenses
Group-term life insurance over $50,000	Qualified transportation fringe benefits
Nonaccountable reimbursed business expenses	Reimbursed business expenses (if accounted for in a timely manner)
Noncash fringe benefits, unless excluded by Internal Revenue Code	Working condition fringe benefits which would be deductible if paid by employee
Sick pay and disability benefits (portion attributable to employer contributions)	Non-job-related education assistance up to $5,250
Nonqualified moving expenses	Long-term care insurance

Taxable Compensation	Nontaxable Compensation	
Overtime pay	Workers' compensation benefits	Chapter 3
Regular wages	Health Savings Accounts	
Tips		

3.1.2 Wages are Taxable When Paid

Wages become taxable when they are paid, not when they are earned. Thus, salary for hours worked during the last week of December 2015 but paid in January 2016 is taxable in 2016.

Constructive Receipt

Wages are considered paid when the employee actually receives the paycheck or when it is constructively received. A paycheck that has been set aside for an employee is considered constructively received at that time.

For example, assume that December 30 is payday at your firm. An employee takes December 30, 2016, as a vacation day and does not pick up her paycheck until January 3, 2017. Since the wages were available on December 30, they are considered constructively received on that date and would be taxable in 2016.

Overpayments/Repayments

When an employee is overpaid and the repayment occurs in the same calendar year, the repayment requested is the employee's net overpayment. The employer can claim a refund from the IRS for the federal income, social security, and Medicare taxes withheld from the employee's pay and employer's social security and Medicare taxes. The overpayment and repayment can be netted together for reporting on Form W-2.

When an employee is overpaid and the repayment occurs in a calendar year subsequent to when the payment was made in error, the repayment requested is the employee's gross overpayment less social security and

Medicare taxes. The employer can claim a refund from the IRS for the employee's withheld social security and Medicare taxes and the employer's social security and Medicare taxes. The overpayment and repayment cannot be netted together for reporting on Form W-2. The employee will deduct the repayment on the subsequent year's federal income tax return to obtain a refund of their federal income tax.

Tips

If an employee receives and reports to their employer $20.00 or more in tips in a calendar month, federal income, social security, and Medicare taxes must be withheld from the tips as well as cash wages. Employers must also pay the employer's portion of the social security and Medicare taxes and pay federal unemployment tax on the tip amount.

Tips are considered supplemental wages by the IRS. Federal income tax withholding from tips can be done at the optional flat rate of 25% or the tips can be added to the employee's wages when calculating federal income tax withholding. Even though tips are defined by the IRS as supplemental wages, for income tax purposes an employer may chose to treat tips as regular wages.

3.1.3 Factors Affecting Withholding

The amount of federal income tax withholding from an employee's taxable wages depends on a number of factors:

- The employee's marital status claimed on the employee's Form W-4 (single or married)
- The number of withholding allowances claimed on the employee's Form W-4 (discussed in Chapter 1)
- Pay frequency (weekly, biweekly, semimonthly, etc.)
- Whether the wages are regular or supplemental
- Any pretax deductions

The two most common procedures for calculating withholding on regular wages are the wage-bracket method and the percentage method.

3.1.4 Withholding Methods

Withholding on regular wages is calculated by using one of several different methods that are acceptable to the IRS. The two most common procedures are the wage-bracket method and the percentage method.

For supplemental wages, an optional flat tax rate of 25% can be used, and under some circumstances a mandatory 39.6% rate must be used.

We will briefly describe these three methods and work through some examples.

Wage-bracket Method

When calculating withholding manually, the quickest and easiest method is to use the wage-bracket tables from IRS Circular E (found in the Appendix, pages A-185–A-204).

For example, an employee who claims single and two allowances, earns a weekly salary of $700. Find the wage-bracket table for weekly – single in the Circular E to calculate her federal income tax. Simply go down the wages column to $700 but less than $710 and then across to two allowances. The amount of federal income tax to be withheld is $67 per week. (*See the following wage-bracket table*)

Wage Bracket Method Tables for Income Tax Withholding
SINGLE Persons—**WEEKLY** Payroll Period
(For Wages Paid through December 31, 2016)

And the wages are–		And the number of withholding allowances claimed is—										
At least	But less than	0	1	2	3	4	5	6	7	8	9	10
		The amount of income tax to be withheld is—										
$600	$610	$75	$64	$52	$40	$29	$17	$9	$2	$0	$0	$0
610	620	77	65	53	42	30	18	10	3	0	0	0
620	630	78	67	55	43	32	20	11	4	0	0	0
630	640	80	68	56	45	33	21	12	5	0	0	0
640	650	81	70	58	46	35	23	13	6	0	0	0
650	660	83	71	59	48	36	24	14	7	0	0	0
660	670	84	73	61	49	38	26	15	8	0	0	0
670	680	86	74	62	51	39	27	16	9	1	0	0
680	690	87	76	64	52	41	29	17	10	2	0	0
690	700	89	77	65	54	42	30	19	11	3	0	0
700	710	90	79	67	55	44	32	20	12	4	0	0
710	720	92	80	68	57	45	33	22	13	5	0	0
720	730	93	82	70	58	47	35	23	14	6	0	0
730	740	95	83	71	60	48	36	25	15	7	0	0
740	750	96	85	73	61	50	38	26	16	8	0	0
750	760	98	86	74	63	51	39	28	17	9	1	0
760	770	99	88	76	64	53	41	29	18	10	2	0
770	780	102	89	77	66	54	42	31	19	11	3	0
780	790	104	91	79	67	56	44	32	21	12	4	0
790	800	107	92	80	69	57	45	34	22	13	5	0
800	810	109	94	82	70	59	47	35	24	14	6	0
810	820	112	95	83	72	60	48	37	25	15	7	0
820	830	114	97	85	73	62	50	38	27	16	8	0
830	840	117	98	86	75	63	51	40	28	17	9	1
840	850	119	100	88	76	65	53	41	30	18	10	2
850	860	122	102	89	78	66	54	43	31	19	11	3
860	870	124	105	91	79	68	56	44	33	21	12	4
870	880	127	107	92	81	69	57	46	34	22	13	5
880	890	129	110	94	82	71	59	47	36	24	14	6
890	900	132	112	95	84	72	60	49	37	25	15	7
900	910	134	115	97	85	74	62	50	39	27	16	8
910	920	137	117	98	87	75	63	52	40	28	17	9
920	930	139	120	100	88	77	65	53	42	30	18	10
930	940	142	122	103	90	78	66	55	43	31	20	11

Generally when employees have wages in excess of the last wage bracket shown in the table, use the percentage method to figure withholding.

Special Tips

Percentage Method

The method most commonly used in computerized payroll systems is the percentage method. It applies to either single or married taxpayers for any pay frequency (daily, weekly, biweekly, semimonthly, monthly, quarterly, semiannually, and annually). Unlike the wage-bracket method, there are no limits on the amount of wages to which the percentage method can be applied. The percentage method tables are found in Circular E in the Appendix, pages A-183–A-184.

The amounts shown in the percentage method tables are net wages after the deduction for total withholding allowances (from the employee's Form W-4). The withholding allowance amounts per payroll period for 2016 are shown in the following table. To use the percentage method, you first must reduce the employee's taxable wages by the number of allowances.

2016 One Withholding Allowance Value by Payroll Period

Weekly	$77.90	Biweekly	$155.80
Semimonthly	$168.80	Monthly	$337.50
Quarterly	$1,012.50	Semiannually	$2,025.00
Annually	$4,050.00	Daily or miscellaneous	$15.60

Steps to Calculate Federal Income Tax with the Percentage Method

Step 1	Refer to the table of withholding allowances for the percentage method. Multiply the biweekly amount given in the table by the number of allowances the employee claims on Form W-4.
Step 2	Gross wages - Amount of allowances = Adjusted wages
Step 3	Refer to the appropriate percentage table
Step 4	Adjusted wages - Threshold amount = Excess amount
Step 5	Amount of tax + (Excess amount x Percentage) = Total withholding

Example 1: An employee, who claims married with four allowances, earns a biweekly salary of $1,500. Use the tables to calculate his federal income tax.

For the employee, this means:	
Step 1	If the number of withholding allowances is four and wages are paid biweekly, tthe allowance amount is $623.20 ($155.80 x 4 = $623.20).
Step 2	$1,500.00 – $623.20 = $876.80
Step 3	Look at the biweekly table for married taxpayers. The employee's net wages are over $329.00 but not over $1,042.00.
Step 4	$876.80 – $329.00 = $547.80
Step 5	$0 + ($547.80 x 10%) = $54.78

Example 2: An employee, who claims single with three allowances, earns a biweekly salary of $2,350. Use the percentage method tables to calculate her federal income tax.

For the employee, this means:	
Step 1	With three allowances and wages paid biweekly, the value of the allowances is $467.40 ($155.80 x 3 = $467.40)
Step 2	$2,350.00 – $467.40 = $1,882.60
Step 3	Look at the biweekly table for single taxpayers. The employee's net wages are over $1,535.00 but not over $3,592.00.
Step 4	1,882.60 – $1,535.00 = $347.60
Step 5	$199.40 + ($347.60 x 25%) = $199.40 + $86.90 = $286.30

Doing the Math

Doing the Math

Percentage Method Tables for Income Tax Withholding

(For Wages Paid in 2016)

TABLE 1—WEEKLY Payroll Period

(a) SINGLE person (including head of household)—

If the amount of wages (after subtracting withholding allowances) is:		The amount of income tax to withhold is:	
Not over $43		$0	
Over—	But not over—		of excess over—
$43	—$222 . .	$0.00 plus 10%	—$43
$222	—$767 . .	$17.90 plus 15%	—$222
$767	—$1,796 . .	$99.65 plus 25%	—$767
$1,796	—$3,700 . .	$356.90 plus 28%	—$1,796
$3,700	—$7,992 . .	$890.02 plus 33%	—$3,700
$7,992	—$8,025 . .	$2,306.38 plus 35%	—$7,992
$8,025		$2,317.93 plus 39.6%	—$8,025

(b) MARRIED person—

If the amount of wages (after subtracting withholding allowances) is:		The amount of income tax to withhold is:	
Not over $164		$0	
Over—	But not over—		of excess over—
$164	—$521 . .	$0.00 plus 10%	—$164
$521	—$1,613 . .	$35.70 plus 15%	—$521
$1,613	—$3,086 . .	$199.50 plus 25%	—$1,613
$3,086	—$4,615 . .	$567.75 plus 28%	—$3,086
$4,615	—$8,113 . .	$995.87 plus 33%	—$4,615
$8,113	—$9,144 . .	$2,150.21 plus 35%	—$8,113
$9,144		$2,511.06 plus 39.6%	—$9,144

TABLE 2—BIWEEKLY Payroll Period

(a) SINGLE person (including head of household)—

If the amount of wages (after subtracting withholding allowances) is:		The amount of income tax to withhold is:	
Not over $87		$0	
Over—	But not over—		of excess over—
$87	—$443 . .	$0.00 plus 10%	—$87
$443	—$1,535 . .	$35.60 plus 15%	—$443
$1,535	—$3,592 . .	$199.40 plus 25%	—$1,535
$3,592	—$7,400 . .	$713.65 plus 28%	—$3,592
$7,400	—$15,985 . .	$1,779.89 plus 33%	—$7,400
$15,985	—$16,050 . .	$4,612.94 plus 35%	—$15,985
$16,050		$4,635.69 plus 39.6%	—$16,050

(b) MARRIED person—

If the amount of wages (after subtracting withholding allowances) is:		The amount of income tax to withhold is:	
Not over $329		$0	
Over—	But not over—		of excess over—
$329	—$1,042 . .	$0.00 plus 10%	—$329
$1,042	—$3,225 . .	$71.30 plus 15%	—$1,042
$3,225	—$6,171 . .	$398.75 plus 25%	—$3,225
$6,171	—$9,231 . .	$1,135.25 plus 28%	—$6,171
$9,231	—$16,227 . .	$1,992.05 plus 33%	—$9,231
$16,227	—$18,288 . .	$4,300.73 plus 35%	—$16,227
$18,288		$5,022.08 plus 39.6%	—$18,288

TABLE 3—SEMIMONTHLY Payroll Period

(a) SINGLE person (including head of household)—

If the amount of wages (after subtracting withholding allowances) is:		The amount of income tax to withhold is:	
Not over $94		$0	
Over—	But not over—		of excess over—
$94	—$480 . .	$0.00 plus 10%	—$94
$480	—$1,663 . .	$38.60 plus 15%	—$480
$1,663	—$3,892 . .	$216.05 plus 25%	—$1,663
$3,892	—$8,017 . .	$773.30 plus 28%	—$3,892
$8,017	—$17,317 . .	$1,928.30 plus 33%	—$8,017
$17,317	—$17,388 . .	$4,997.30 plus 35%	—$17,317
$17,388		$5,022.15 plus 39.6%	—$17,388

(b) MARRIED person—

If the amount of wages (after subtracting withholding allowances) is:		The amount of income tax to withhold is:	
Not over $356		$0	
Over—	But not over—		of excess over—
$356	—$1,129 . .	$0.00 plus 10%	—$356
$1,129	—$3,494 . .	$77.30 plus 15%	—$1,129
$3,494	—$6,685 . .	$432.05 plus 25%	—$3,494
$6,685	—$10,000 . .	$1,229.80 plus 28%	—$6,685
$10,000	—$17,579 . .	$2,158.00 plus 33%	—$10,000
$17,579	—$19,813 . .	$4,659.07 plus 35%	—$17,579
$19,813		$5,440.97 plus 39.6%	—$19,813

TABLE 4—MONTHLY Payroll Period

(a) SINGLE person (including head of household)—

If the amount of wages (after subtracting withholding allowances) is:		The amount of income tax to withhold is:	
Not over $188		$0	
Over—	But not over—		of excess over—
$188	—$960 . .	$0.00 plus 10%	—$188
$960	—$3,325 . .	$77.20 plus 15%	—$960
$3,325	—$7,783 . .	$431.95 plus 28%	—$3,325
$7,783	—$16,033 . .	$1,546.45 plus 28%	—$7,783
$16,033	—$34,633 . .	$3,856.45 plus 33%	—$16,033
$34,633	—$34,775 . .	$9,994.45 plus 35%	—$34,633
$34,775		$10,044.15 plus 39.6%	—$34,775

(b) MARRIED person—

If the amount of wages (after subtracting withholding allowances) is:		The amount of income tax to withhold is:	
Not over $713		$0	
Over—	But not over—		of excess over—
$713	—$2,258 . .	$0.00 plus 10%	—$713
$2,258	—$6,988 . .	$154.50 plus 15%	—$2,258
$6,988	—$13,371 . .	$864.00 plus 25%	—$6,988
$13,371	—$20,000 . .	$2,459.75 plus 28%	—$13,371
$20,000	—$35,158 . .	$4,315.87 plus 33%	—$20,000
$35,158	—$39,625 . .	$9,318.01 plus 35%	—$35,158
$39,625		$10,881.46 plus 39.6%	—$39,625

Optional/Mandatory Flat Rate Method

Supplemental wages include any payment of wages by an employer that is not regular wages.

- Regular wages are defined as amounts paid by an employer for a payroll period either at a regular hourly rate or in a predetermined fixed amount.
- Wages that vary from payroll period to payroll period based on factors other than the amount of time worked, such as commissions and bonuses, are supplemental wages if they are paid in addition to regular wages.

The IRS regulations allow employers to determine whether or not tips and overtime payments will be considered supplemental wages.

If you pay supplemental wages (bonuses, commissions, overtime pay, back pay, etc.) along with regular wages but do not specify the amount of each, withhold income tax as if the total were a single payment for the payroll period.

However, if you pay supplemental wages separately (or combine them with regular wages but specify the amount for each in your payroll records, e.g. the employee's pay stub), you have two choices.

Optional Flat Rate Method (25%). Simply multiply the amount of the supplemental compensation by 25% and withhold that sum.

Use the Aggregate Method. Add the supplemental wages to the regular wages for the most recent payroll period or the current payroll period. Then figure the income tax as if the total were a single sum. Subtract the tax already withheld from the regular wages. Withhold the remaining tax from the supplemental wages.

Mandatory Flat Rate Method (39.6%). When year-to-date supplemental wage payments to an employee reach $1,000,000.00, the supplemental tax rate required for supplemental wage payments in excess of $1,000,000 is 39.6%. In addition, the aggregate method cannot be used when supplemental wage payments are in excess of $1,000,000.00. In this situation, withholding is based on the 39.6% rate.

Real-world Application

The IRS regulations allow employers to apply the 39.6% rate against the entire supplemental payment when a portion is below $1,000,000.00 and a portion is above $1,000,000.00. For example, an employee with year-to-date supplemental wages of $900,000.00 receives a $200,000.00 bonus. The federal income tax withholding on the bonus can be $79,200.00 (39.6% x $200,000) or $64,600.00 ((25% x $100,000.00) + (39.6% x $100,000.00)).

When to use the Aggregate Method

The optional flat rate and mandatory flat rate methods do not consider marital status or allowances from the employee's W-4. The flat rate methods can have the effect of either over- or underwithholding taxes. Therefore, if the supplemental wages are sizable (for example, in the case of commissions or bonuses), you may want to use the aggregate method.

If there is no income tax withheld from the employee's regular wages during the current or preceding years, you must use the aggregate method, except when the employee's year-to-date supplemental wages exceed $1,000,000.00. In that case, the mandatory flat 39.6% rate must be used. An employee may have no income tax withheld from regular wages, for example, when the value of the employee's allowances (from Form W-4) is greater than the wages.

Examples

Doing the Math

Optional Flat Tax Rate

An employee receives the Employee of the Month award—two tickets to a local dinner theater, valued at $50—when she has year-to-date wages of $25,000. Using the supplemental flat rate of 25%, federal income tax withholding on this award is $12.50 ($50 x 25% = $12.50).

Aggregate Method

Start by using the wage-bracket tables to calculate the tax on the employee's regular wages. In the wage-bracket method example on page 3-5, the employee's weekly withholding on her regular wages of $700 with her Form W-4 claiming single with two allowances is $67.

Now calculate her withholding on her regular wages of $700 plus the $50 award. As the tables show, withholding on $750 for single taxpayers with two allowances is $74. There is a $7 difference between the amount you already withheld ($67) and the amount you would withhold by combining her regular and supplemental wages. Using the aggregate method, you would deduct $7 from the value of the award.

Here's another example. An employee receives a $500 bonus in a separate check. Her regular wages are $645 paid weekly. She claims single and five allowances on her W-4. Using the wage-bracket table, she has $23 withheld from her regular wages for federal income tax. Using the aggregate method, she will have her regular wages added to the bonus ($645.00 + $500.00 = $1,145.00) and applied to the weekly wage-bracket table to calculate federal income tax withholding of $98. However, since $23 has already been withheld, it is subtracted from the $98, leaving $75 to be withheld from the bonus payment using the aggregate method. Her employer could also use the flat rate method and withhold $125 ($500 x 25%) from her bonus

3.1.5 A Note on Rounding

The IRS allows you to round federal income tax withholding to the nearest whole dollar as long as you do it consistently. Round up amounts ending in $0.50 to $0.99; round down amounts ending in $0.01 to $0.49. Thus, $53.04 becomes $53; $353.60 becomes $354.

3.1.6 Withholding Income Tax From Pensions

In most instances, federal income tax must be withheld from pension and annuity payments made to retired employees. Unless directed otherwise, payers and plan administrators must withhold certain amounts, depending on whether the payments are periodic, nonperiodic, or eligible rollover distributions. Retirees can have input into the amount withheld if they file a Form W-4P, *Withholding Certificate for Pension or Annuity Payments.*

3.2 Withholding Social Security and Medicare Taxes

Social security tax and Medicare tax continue to rise from their initial maximum of $30 per year in 1937 under the Federal Insurance Contributions Act. Social security covers more than retirement benefits. It also provides benefits to disabled workers and survivors of deceased workers. Medicare provides medical services to the elderly and disabled. You must withhold social security tax and Medicare tax from taxable wages (including many employer-provided benefits).

3.2.1 Tax Rate and Wage Base

The rates and wage limits for social security and Medicare taxes are shown in the following table.

Special Tips

Alert

2016 Social Security Tax and Medicare Tax					
Coverage	Employee Rate	Employer Rate	Maximum Salary	Maximum Employee Tax	Maximum Employer Tax
Social Security	6.2%	6.2%	$118,500.00	$7,347.00	$7,347.00
Medicare	1.45%	1.45%	No Max	No Max	No Max

When an employee's Medicare wages reach $200,000 the employee is subject to an additional Medicare tax of 0.9% for a total tax rate of 2.35%. Despite the increase in the employee's Medicare tax rate, the employer's Medicare tax rate remains 1.45% for all wages paid.

For example, an employee's year-to-date Medicare wages are $275,000 and the employee is paid $12,500 in the current pay period. The Medicare tax that will be withheld from the employee's pay is $293.75 (($12,500 x 1.45%) + ($12,500 x 0.9%)). The employer's portion of the Medicare tax on the $12,500 payment is $181.25 ($12,500 x 1.45%).

When an employee's wages for the current pay period cause the employee's year-to-date Medicare wages to exceed $200,000, the wages up to $200,000 are subject to the 1.45% rate while the wages in excess of $200,000 are subject to the 2.35% rate.

For example, an employee's year-to-date Medicare wages are $195,000 and the employee is paid $12,500 in the current pay period. The Medicare tax that will be withheld from the employee's pay is $248.75 (($12,500 x 1.45%) + ($7,500 x 0.9%)). The employer's portion of the Medicare tax on the $12,500 payment is $181.25 ($12,500 x 1.45%).

The following are some key facts to remember about social security tax and Medicare tax.

3.2.2 Employers Must Pay Their Portion

During 2016, the social security tax and the regular Medicare tax are the same for both employers and employees. For example, if an employee earns an annual salary of $125,000.00, the employer and employee would each pay a total tax of $9,159.50. This represents the following:

- Employers and employees each pay $7,347.00 in social security tax on the first $118,500.00 in social security wages.
- Employers and employees both pay $1,812.50 in Medicare tax on the entire $125,000.00, since there is no Medicare wage limit (1.45% x $125,000.00 = $1,812.50).

3.2.3 There Is No Age Limit

As an employer, you are required to withhold social security tax and Medicare tax and to pay the employer's portion the amount for all employees, even those who are receiving social security and Medicare benefits.

3.2.4 Employers Must Withhold up to the Maximum

When a taxpayer works for more than one employer during the calendar year, it is possible that the employee's social security wages paid by all employers will be more than the limit. Employees receive credit for any social security tax withheld in a year due to excess withholding when they file their annual tax returns. All employers are required to withhold and to pay the employer's portion the amount up to the maximum each year, regardless of an employee's previous earnings with another employer.

Check Your Understanding

Quiz 3.1. Answer the following questions to test your understanding of federal tax withholding from paychecks.

Check Your Understanding

1. Which of the following employee benefits is nontaxable compensation?
   - ❑ a. Company vehicle (personal use)
   - ❑ b. Gifts, prizes and awards
   - ❑ c. Company vehicle (business use)
   - ❑ d. Nonqualified moving expenses

2. Which of the following employee benefits is taxable compensation?
   - ❑ a. Workers' Compensation benefits
   - ❑ b. Qualified moving expenses
   - ❑ c. Sick pay
   - ❑ d. Qualified transportation fringes

3. Which of the following employee benefits is nontaxable compensation?
   - ❑ a. Group legal services
   - ❑ b. Noncash prizes and awards
   - ❑ c. Reimbursed business expenses accounted for timely
   - ❑ d. A back pay award

4. An employee's most recent pay period began on December 15, 2016, and ended on December 31, 2016. The employee was paid on January 7, 2017. In what year are his wages earned between December 15, 2016, and December 31, 2016, included in his taxable wages?

5. An employee was sick the last week in December. His paycheck, dated December 31, 2016, was held for him until he returned to work on January 6, 2017. These wages are taxable:
   - ❑ a. In 2016
   - ❑ b. In 2017

6. Use the wage-bracket method to calculate FIT withholding on an employee's weekly paycheck of $605. The employee is single with one allowance. What is the amount of his FIT withholding?

   $_____

7. Which of the following is true if the employee in Question 6 also receives a $100 bonus?
   - ❑ a. You must add the $100 to his regular wages before you calculate FIT withholding.
   - ❑ b. Using the flat rate, you would withhold $39.60 in federal income tax from his bonus.
   - ❑ c. If you use the aggregate method, you will withhold the same from his bonus as you would if you use the supplemental method.
   - ❑ d. The aggregate and flat rate methods will produce a different amount to withhold.

8. All of the following factors are used in figuring an employee's federal income tax withholding EXCEPT:
   - ❑ a. marital status.
   - ❑ b. number of allowances.
   - ❑ c. regular rate of pay.
   - ❑ d. pay frequency.

9. What is the easiest method to calculate federal income tax withholding on regular wages?
   - ❑ a. Wage-bracket
   - ❑ b. Percentage
   - ❑ c. Supplemental
   - ❑ d. Optional flat rate

10. Which method to calculate federal income tax withholding is the most common for a computerized payroll system?
   - ❑ a. Wage-bracket
   - ❑ b. Percentage
   - ❑ c. Optional flat rate
   - ❑ d. Mandatory flat rate

11. The value of one withholding allowance for a weekly pay period is?
   - ❑ a. $77.90
   - ❑ b. $155.80
   - ❑ c. $168.80
   - ❑ d. $4,050.00

12. An employee, claiming single with one allowance on her W-4, earns $18,000 annually. Your firm pays biweekly. Use the percentage method to calculate withholding for federal income tax.
   $_____

13. All of the following wages are supplemental wages EXCEPT:
   - ❑ a. salary.
   - ❑ b. bonus.
   - ❑ c. commission.
   - ❑ d. fringe benefits.

14. When using the optional flat rate method, which of the following items is considered when making the calculation?
    ☐ a. Taxable wages
    ☐ b. Pay frequency
    ☐ c. Marital status
    ☐ d. Withholding allowances

15. When paying supplemental wages, when must the aggregate with-holding method be used?
    ☐ a. When no income tax is withheld from regular wages for the current or preceding calendar year
    ☐ b. When the employee claims more than 10 withholding al-lowances
    ☐ c. When the employee is married
    ☐ d. When the employee is single

16. A firm's chief executive officer is paid $250,000 annually. He claims married with three allowances on his W-4. Using the per-centage method, what is his biweekly withholding for federal income tax?
    $_____

17. When an employee is overpaid and the repayment occurs in the same year, the repayment requested is the employee's:
    ☐ a. net overpayment.
    ☐ b. gross overpayment.
    ☐ c. gross overpayment minus social security and Medicare tax.
    ☐ d. gross overpayment minus federal income tax.

18. When calculating federal income tax, which is correct when rounding.
    ☐ a. $0.51 is rounded to $0.00
    ☐ b. $0.49 is rounded to $1.00
    ☐ c. $0.495 is rounded to $0.00
    ☐ d. $0.50 is rounded to $0.00

19. What form must a pensioner file to have input into the amount of federal income tax withheld?
    ☐ a. W-4
    ☐ b. W-4P
    ☐ c. W-4S
    ☐ d. W-9

20. When an employee begins to receive social security benefits, the employer no longer needs to withhold social security and Medicare taxes.
   ❑ True
   ❑ False

21. In 2016, an employer must pay social security tax on an employee's wages up to:
   ❑ a. $110,100.00
   ❑ b. $113,700.00
   ❑ c. $117,000.00
   ❑ d. $118,500.00

22. What is the employer's social security tax rate in 2016?
   ❑ a. 1.45%
   ❑ b. 6.2%
   ❑ c. 7.65%
   ❑ d. 12.4%

23. What is the maximum amount of social security tax that an employer must report and deposit for an employee in 2016?
   ❑ a. $7,347.00
   ❑ b. $8,950.05
   ❑ c. $14,694.00
   ❑ d. $17,901.00

3.3 Additional Deductions From Pay

So far, we have been focusing on one type of deduction from an employee's gross pay—withholding for federal taxes. In addition, other deductions are allowed or, in some cases, required. Let's review these deductions—both voluntary and involuntary ones.

3.3.1 Voluntary Deductions

In some cases, employees elect to have amounts taken directly from their paycheck. Some examples of voluntary deductions are listed below.

Besides withholding for federal taxes, other deductions from an employee's paycheck are allowed or may even be required.

Examples of Voluntary Deductions

- Contributions to United Way or other charities
- Contributions to retirement programs
- myRA contributions (direct deposit to account with U.S. Treasury)
- Purchases from employer-provided store or cafeteria
- Health insurance premiums (outside of Section 125 plans)
- Purchase of stock in the employer's company
- Repayment of loans/advances from the employer
- Union dues/fees

The following are key points to remember about voluntary deductions.

Require Authorization

All voluntary deductions require employee authorization. Authorization can be written or electronic.

Last Priority

All required deductions take precedence over voluntary ones.

All required deductions (wage attachments) take precedence over voluntary ones. As we'll see when dealing with involuntary deductions, this can be significant when there are prior claims on an employee's wages. However, the employer can choose the priority of voluntary deductions, for example, health insurance before charitable contributions.

Employer Loan Repayments

When an employee is provided a loan, it will be repaid by the employee. The agreed repayment is a voluntary deduction and must be prioritized with other voluntary deductions by the employer.

Substantiation of Charitable Contributions

IRS rules prohibit taxpayers from deducting on their Form 1040 individual charitable contributions without proper substantiation of the contribution. Regulations provide special rules for contributions made through payroll deduction. Taxpayers can substantiate these contributions with a combination of two documents:

- A document furnished by the employer showing the amount withheld from the taxpayer's wages; this document could be Form W-2 or the pay statement.
- A document prepared by the charity, such as a pledge card. This documentation need not be in any particular form or prepared at any particular time as long as the taxpayer has the document in his or her possession before filing his or her personal income tax return.

3.3.2 Involuntary Deductions

Priorities

Involuntary deductions are called wage attachments. Generally, attachments are honored in the following priorities. However, specific exceptions do exist.

1. Child support orders
2. Chapter XIII bankruptcy orders
3. Other federal agency garnishments
4. Federal tax levies
5. State tax levies
6. Local tax levies
7. Creditor garnishments
8. Student loan garnishments

Tax Levies

One type of involuntary deduction is a levy for unpaid federal or state taxes. If an employee neglects or refuses to pay federal tax liabilities, the IRS can collect the amount due through a levy on the employee's compensation. Most states have similar laws.

Take-home Pay for Federal Levies

The IRS gives these instructions on Form 668-W, *Notice of Levy on Wages, Salary, and Other Income:*

"Send us the taxpayer's take-home pay minus the exempt amount which is described below. Unless we tell you that a deduction should not be allowed, allow the taxpayer's payroll deductions which were in effect when you received this levy in determining the take-home pay. Do not allow the taxpayer to take new payroll deductions while this levy is in effect."

"Payroll deductions which were in effect" include any child support order, creditor garnishment or other involuntary deduction received prior to the date of the levy. If these orders are received after the levy, the tax levy has priority.

Deductions Beyond the Employee's Control
Payroll deduction changes that are beyond the employee's control are allowed when figuring take home pay. For example, if the employee's place of employment becomes unionized and union dues become a condition of employment, the deduction would be allowed.

Special Tips

Amount Exempt From Federal Levy

The amount exempt from a federal levy is based on the employee's filing status and the number of personal exemptions claimed on Part 3 of Form 668-W divided by the number of payroll periods in the year. Publication 1494 provided with each Form 668-W gives the exempt amounts. Publication 1494 is found in the Appendix (p. A-137).

The following example demonstrates how the deduction required by an IRS levy is calculated.

The employer receives a levy of $15,000 against the employee's wages. The employee completes Form 668-W telling his employer that he files his income tax return as married filing jointly with three personal exemptions.

The employee's pay and deductions for a biweekly pay period prior to the receipt of the levy were:

Gross Wages	$1,500.00
401(k) salary reduction	*75.00*
Federal income tax	*110.00*
State income tax	*35.00*
Social security tax	*93.00*
Medicare tax	*21.75*
Charitable contribution	*50.00*
Total Deductions	*384.75*
Take-Home Pay	$1,115.25

Based on the information provided by the employee on Form 668-W, the employee has $951.92 exempt from the levy. This amount is calculated using IRS Publication 1494, *Table for Figuring Amount Exempt from Levy on Wages, Salary, and Other Income*, see page A-139. After determining the amount exempt from levy, the exempt amount is subtracted from the take-home pay to determine the amount of the IRS levy deduction. The employee's exempt amount becomes the employee's net pay.

Take-Home Pay	$1,115.25
Amount exempt from levy	$951.92
IRS Levy deduction	$163.33

Levy Continues Until Paid

Federal levies continue until you receive a Form 668-D, *Release of Levy/Release of Property from Levy* from the IRS.

Child Support

As a payroll professional, you will face a growing number of Income Withholding Orders requiring child support withholding from employees' paychecks. Child support payments are increasingly becoming payroll's responsibility. Here are some key points to remember.

Chapter 3 | Withholding

The custodial parent can request the court to order immediate automatic withholding, even if the support payments are not past due. So child support withholding does not only come from "deadbeat dads."

All support orders require immediate withholding unless specifically waived by court order or by the written consent of both parents. All orders that are in arrears will cause immediate withholding.

Limits

The order will state the amount to be deducted for child support. However, the maximum amount of an employee's compensation that is subject to child support withholding is governed by the Consumer Credit Protection Act (CCPA). The maximum percentage that can be withheld is based on an employee's disposable earnings (gross earnings less federal/state/local taxes). The maximum withholding is limited to the following:

Special Tips

- If the employee supports a second family, the amount withheld cannot exceed 50% of the employee's disposable earnings (55% if support is in arrears).
- If the employee does not support a second family, the amount withheld cannot exceed 60% of the employee's disposable earnings (65% if support is in arrears).

The maximum withholding allowed under a state's law may be lower, but cannot be higher, than the federal limits.

Disposable Earnings

Disposable earnings equal all of an employee's earnings (generally including bonuses, and other lump salary sum payments but not including tips) after deducting taxes. Required deductions include federal, state and local taxes.

For example, assume that an employee earns $500.00 per week. From that, payroll withholds $65.00 for federal income tax, $31.00 for social security tax, $7.25 for Medicare tax, $75.00 for child support, and

$10.00 for a credit union payment. What is the disposable pay for child support and creditor garnishments?

$500.00	Gross earnings (not including tips)
- 103.25	Federal/state taxes ($65.00 + $31.00 + $7.25)
$396.75	Disposable pay

Check Applicable State Laws Governing Child Support Payments.
In many states, the state regulations are more stringent than the federal ones. Even though each state sets their own child support laws, they are limited by the federal laws in the following areas

- A state can allow the employer to deduct an administrative fee, in addition to the child support withholding, to offset the costs of maintaining the child support program.
- Federal law requires the payment to be made within seven days of withholding the child support from the employee's wages. State laws may require the payment to be made sooner.
- Federal law requires the first withholding to be made with the first pay period 14 business days after the child support order is mailed. State laws may require the first withholding to occur sooner.

All of the states, except South Carolina, have centralized collection agencies (State Disbursement Units) for the payment of withheld child support.

Uniform Interstate Family Support Act (UIFSA)
UIFSA clarifies many of the rules used in processing wage withholding orders received from out-of-state agencies. The child support order will tell us:

- The duration and specific amount of periodic payments
- The person or agency to receive payments
- Medical support, stated as a specific amount or an order to provide coverage
- The amount of periodic payments of arrears and interest on arrears, stated as sum certain

When administering the child support order, the rules from the employee's work state are used when:

- Withholding the employer's fee for processing an income withholding order.
- Determining the maximum amount permitted to be withheld from the obligor's income.
- Determining the time periods within which the employer must implement the withholding order and forward the child support.
- There are orders for more than one obligee.

Rejecting Income Withholding Orders

Employers receive IWO forms from state child support agencies, courts, attorneys, and private entities. Sometimes IWOs have been changed by the sender, which can confuse employers about an IWO's legitimacy. "Since the IWO is a standard, OMB-approved federal form sent to employers to withhold child support, there are very few changes that are acceptable," says OCSE. One of the reasons an employer can reject an IWO and return it to the sender is if the form is altered or contains invalid information.

Acceptable Changes to IWO

The following may be changed on the IWO form:

- Font.
- Pagination.
- Supplemental and/or state-specific information, such as state codes, may be added.

No Discharge Because of Withholding

The employer is prohibited from discharging, disciplining, or otherwise discriminating against an employee because the employee's wages are subject to withholding for child support. Violators can be fined an amount set by state law.

Complying With More Than One Withholding Order

If an employer receives more than one child support withholding order for an employee, state law governs how they must be handled. If the orders are from different states, the law in the state where the employee works generally applies (see UIFSA). These considerations generally come into play when the total withholding amount required by all of the orders exceeds the maximum allowed under the applicable state law. State laws handle this problem in one of three ways:

1. They require allocating the available wages to each order

depending on its percentage in relation to the total amount required to be withheld.

2. They allocate the available wages equally toward each order until each order is individually complied with or the maximum amount of allowable withholding is reached.

3. They give the orders priority depending on when the orders were received by the employer. This means the order received first must be satisfied in full (if possible) before the next oldest order is satisfied, until the maximum amount has been withheld.

Current support must be calculated prior to amounts past due (arrearages). When medical support has also been ordered, the state may require its satisfaction after current child support obligations.

Standardized Child Support Withholding Order (Income Withholding Orders)

With the assistance of the American Payroll Association, a standardized Income Withholding Order (IWO) was developed by the federal Office of Child Support Enforcement that is used when notifying employers how to handle any child support withholding order. The order must be used by all states for all court-ordered cases and welfare and nonwelfare cases. In addition to listing current child support obligations, the form lists amounts in arrears and amounts due for medical support. It allows employers to make payments using a schedule that is consistent with their existing pay cycles. The form also indicates to whom checks are payable and the payee's address. See page A-135.

A standardized form notifies employers how to handle any child support withholding order.

The IWO also states that if a child support withholding order is received that is not on the current form or directs the payment to be made to someone other than the State Disbursement Unit, the order should be returned.

Many organizations have enrolled in the Office of Child Support Enforcement's electronic Income Withholding Order (eIWO) process. eIWO provides organizations the ability to receive and respond to withholding orders in an electronic format. Some organizations receive a flat file that can be input directly into the payroll process facilitating the implementation of a withholding order. Other organizations receive orders in a PDF format. The PDF format reduces the time between when the order is issued and when the employer receives it.

Centralized Support Collections

All states except South Carolina have implemented procedures allowing employers to send the child support payments they withhold from workers' pay to a State Disbursement Unit within their state. Payroll professionals may still be sending child support withholding to local courts administering child support withholding orders issued before 1994.

Creditor Garnishments

A garnishment is a court order to attach an employee's earnings.

A creditor garnishment involves a court order to attach the employee's earnings in order to pay off a debt which the employee incurred.

Federal Limits

The Consumer Credit Protection Act limits the amount of disposable earnings (using the same definition used for child support withholding) that can be garnished by creditors in a week.

The withholding required by a garnishment cannot exceed the lesser of:

- 25% of the employee's disposable pay
- The amount by which the employee's disposable pay for the week exceeds 30 times the federal minimum wage

Alert

Be aware that the following table is subject to change when the federal minimum wage changes.

The following table simplifies this calculation so that you can find where the employee's disposable pay falls and figure the amount of the garnishment.

Garnishment Limits

(based on minimum wage of $7.25/hour effective July 24, 2009)

Weekly	Biweekly
Disposable pay no more than $217.50 – No garnishment	Disposable pay no more than $435.00 – No garnishment
Disposable pay more than $217.50 but less than $290.00 – Garnishment amount above $217.50	Disposable pay more than $435.00 but less than $580.00 – Garnishment amount above $435.00
Disposable pay at least $290.00 – Garnishment amount 25% of disposable earnings	Disposable pay at least $580.00 – Garnishment amount 25% of disposable earnings
Semimonthly	**Monthly**
Disposable pay no more than $471.25 – No garnishment	Disposable pay no more than $942.50 – No garnishment
Disposable pay more than $471.25 but less than $628.33 – Garnishment amount above $471.25	Disposable pay more than $942.50 but less than $1,256.67 – Garnishment amount above $942.50
Disposable pay at least $628.33 – Garnishment amount 25% of disposable earnings	Disposable pay at least $1,256.67 – Garnishment amount 25% of disposable earnings

If the employee has disposable pay of more than $290.00 weekly (see table above), the maximum garnishment allowed under federal law is 25% of the employee's disposable pay. An employee with weekly disposable earnings of $396.75 would have a creditor garnishment maximum of $99.19 (25% x $396.75).

The following example demonstrates how the deduction required by a creditor garnishment is calculated.

The employer receives a creditor garnishment of $5,500 against the employee's wages. The employee's pay, deductions, and disposable earnings for a biweekly pay period prior are:

Doing the Math

	Net Pay	Disposable Earnings
Gross Wages	$1,500.00	$1,500.00
401(k) salary reduction	*75.00*	
Federal income tax	*110.00*	*110.00*
State income tax	*35.00*	*35.00*
Social security tax	*93.00*	*93.00*
Medicare tax	*21.75*	*21.75*
Charitable contribution	*50.00*	
Total Deductions	384.75	$259.75
Net Pay/Disposable Earnings	$1,115.25	$1,240.25

As the employee's disposable biweekly earnings are greater than $580.00, the amount of the garnishment will be 25% of the disposable pay (25% x $1,240.25), $310.06.

Gross wages	$1,500.00
Total Deductions	384.75
Creditor Garnishment Deduction	310.06
Net Pay	$805.19

Be Aware of Your State's Laws

Alert

States may have wage garnishment laws that may be more beneficial to the employee than the federal law. Payroll is required to adhere to these laws as well as to the federal laws.

Student Loans

The Higher Education Act allows garnishment of employees' wages to repay delinquent student loans. Student loan garnishments are subject to the following restrictions:

1. If the garnishment is issued by a state guarantee agency, no more than 15% of an employee's disposable earnings may be garnished to satisfy a delinquent student loan unless the employee consents in writing to a higher percentage.
2. Employees may not be discharged or otherwise discriminated against because of a garnishment order to repay a student loan.

3. Employees must receive at least 30 days' notice before withholding begins and must be given a chance to work out a repayment schedule with the agency guaranteeing the loan to avoid garnishment.

Employer's Responsibilities. Under the regulations, the Department of Education will send the employer of a delinquent debtor a wage garnishment order directing the employer to remit a portion of the debtor's wages. The employer will also be required to certify certain payment information about the debtor.

Federal Limits on Student Loan Withholding. The garnishment limits imposed by the Consumer Credit Protection Act (CCPA) apply to garnishments under the DCIA. Accordingly, the maximum amount that should be withheld under a DCIA garnishment order is the lesser of:

- The amount indicated in the order (up to 15% of the debtor's "disposable pay")
- The amount by which the debtor's disposable pay exceeds 30 times the minimum wage

Disposable earnings for student loans is calculated the same way it is for child support withholding orders and creditor garnishments under the Consumer Credit Protection Act, gross earnings less taxes.

For example, an employer receives a student loan withholding order on May 15 requiring the withholding of the lesser of 15% of disposable earnings or the excess of the employee's weekly disposable earnings over 30 times the federal minimum wage. The following calculation shows the employee's disposable earnings for the next payday.

	Net Pay	Disposable Earnings
Gross Wages	$1,500.00	$1,500.00
Federal income tax	180.00	180.00
Social security tax	93.00	93.00
Medicare tax	21.75	21.75
State income tax	45.00	45.00
Charitable contribution	30.00	
Total deductions	369.75	339.75
Net Pay/Disposable Pay	$1,130.25	$1,160.25

The maximum that can be withheld for the student loan withholding order is:

The lesser of 15% × $1,160.25 = $174.04, or

$1,160.25 – (30 × $7.25) = $942.75

The amount deducted will be $174.04.

Bankruptcy Orders

Bankruptcy is governed by the federal Bankruptcy Code. Once an employee voluntarily declares bankruptcy or is found to be bankrupt by a court, the satisfaction of the employee's creditors is handled by the "bankruptcy trustee" appointed by the court. Until the employer is notified by the bankruptcy court or the trustee to do otherwise, the employer should continue to withhold. Once the employee's employer receives a bankruptcy order from the trustee under a court-approved plan requiring a certain amount of the employee's wages to be paid to the trustee to satisfy the employee's creditors, the employer must stop withholding on any other garnishments against the employee except for child support withholding orders.

Multiple Withholding Orders

When an amount is deducted for attachments with priority, the amount deducted will reduce the deduction available for attachments with a lower priority. For example, an employee with disposable earnings of $1,000 and a child support order of $200 can only have a deduction for a creditor garnishment of $50 (($1,000 x 25%) - $200).

Check Your Understanding

Check Your Understanding

Quiz 3.2. Answer the following questions to test your understanding of deductions from paychecks.

1. A voluntary deduction must be:
    - ❑ a. authorized by the employee.
    - ❑ b. deducted without the employee's permission.
    - ❑ c. changed to what the employer needs to deduct.

2. Required deductions must take precedence over voluntary deductions.
   ❑ True
   ❑ False

3. All of the following deductions are involuntary deductions EXCEPT:
   ❑ a.   charitable contribution.
   ❑ b.   tax levy.
   ❑ c.   child support.
   ❑ d.   creditor garnishment.

4. What does an employer use to calculate the amount to withhold for an IRS tax levy?
   ❑ a.   Disposable pay
   ❑ b.   Net pay
   ❑ c.   Take-home pay
   ❑ d.   Taxable wages

5. When does an employer stop deducting a federal tax levy from an employee's wages?
   ❑ a.   The amount on the levy is reached
   ❑ b.   The IRS issues a Form 668-D
   ❑ c.   The employee asks that the levy deduction be stopped

6. When an employer receives a child support withholding order against an employee, that means the employee is delinquent in making their child support payments.
   ❑ True
   ❑ False

7. What does an employer use to calculate the amount to withhold for a child support withholding order?
   ❑ a.   Disposable pay
   ❑ b.   Net pay
   ❑ c.   Take-home pay
   ❑ d.   Taxable wages

8. An employee earns $1,000.00 weekly. His deductions are $174.00 for federal income tax, $62.00 for social security tax, and $14.50 for Medicare tax. He is not supporting another family and has never been in arrears in his child support payments. What is the maximum child support payment that can be withheld from his wages?
   - ❑ a. $600.00
   - ❑ b. $500.00
   - ❑ c. $449.70
   - ❑ d. $500.18

9. What does an employer use to calculate the amount to withhold for a creditor garnishment?
   - ❑ a. Disposable pay
   - ❑ b. Net pay
   - ❑ c. Take-home pay
   - ❑ d. Taxable wages

10. The federal minimum wage is used when figuring the amount to withhold for a creditor garnishment.
    - ❑ True
    - ❑ False

11. Which of the following deductions requires an employee's authorization before it can be deducted from the employee's paycheck?
    - ❑ a. Garnishments
    - ❑ b. Levies
    - ❑ c. Child support payments
    - ❑ d. Repayment of employer loans

Use the following information to answer questions 12 and 13.
An employee earns $8.50 per hour and is paid biweekly. He worked two 40-hour shifts of straight time. His deductions include $40.00 for federal income tax, $10.00 for state income tax, $42.16 for social security tax, $9.86 for Medicare tax, and $10 for union dues.

12. What is the employee's disposable pay?
    - ❑ a. $567.98
    - ❑ b. $577.98
    - ❑ c. $580.00
    - ❑ d. $680.00

13. What is the maximum that can be attached from the employee's paycheck for a creditor garnishment?
$_____

3.4 State Taxes

3.4.1 State Income Taxes

Generally, the state income taxes are calculated by applying the wage-bracket or percentage method to the employee's taxable wages, using tables similar to the federal tables. Some states calculate taxes as a flat percentage of the employee's wages. Still others use a percentage of the employee's withheld federal income tax.

The following nine states currently do not have a state income tax on wages:

Alaska	New Hampshire	Texas
Florida	South Dakota	Washington
Nevada	Tennessee	Wyoming

Know Your State's Laws. Each state has different requirements that must be followed, and each state in which the employer operates should be contacted to determine that state's requirements.

Alert

3.4.2 Local Income Taxes

Local taxes are even more varied than state income taxes. Cities, counties, school districts, and other governmental authorities may have the authority to enact a tax on income that employers are required to withhold, pay, and report. Many local government units use the same methods favored by the states in determining the amount to withhold for local income taxes.

Know Your Local Tax Requirements. Each local taxing authority has different requirements that must be followed. In view of all the different requirements, each locality in which the employer operates should be contacted to determine its requirements.

3.4.3 State Disability Taxes

Six jurisdictions have laws establishing disability and family temporary leave plans to which employees and/or employers contribute. These plans provide wage replacement benefits to employees who become ill or injured off the job. The six jurisdictions are:

California	New Jersey	Puerto Rico
Hawaii	New York	Rhode Island

Generally, state disability taxes are calculated at a fixed percentage of the employees' wages up to a maximum wage. Employers in these states are required to retain records, file reports, and deduct the appropriate taxes. If the employer fails to withhold the disability tax, the employer becomes responsible for paying the tax.

3.4.4 State Unemployment Insurance Tax Withholding

Currently three states (Alaska, New Jersey, and Pennsylvania) have provisions for withholding state unemployment tax from employees in addition to the employer tax. The amount withheld is a flat percentage of wages up to the state unemployment wage base in Alaska and New Jersey. All Pennsylvania wages are subject to withholding of state unemployment tax.

3.5 Deceased Employees

If an employee dies, accrued wages, vacation pay, and other compensation paid after the date of death are taxable. However, for federal income tax it is not the employee who is subject to the tax but whomever received the payment is taxed. Because of this requirement, wages paid after death are not subject to federal income tax withholding.

If the amounts due the deceased employee are paid during the same year the employee dies, social security tax and Medicare tax must be withheld and the amounts paid must be reported as wages in Boxes 3 (social security wages) and 5 (Medicare wages) on the employee's Form W-2. The social security and Medicare tax withholding is reported in Boxes

4 (social security tax) and 6 (Medicare tax). The amount is not reported as federal income taxable wages in Box 1 but must be reported on Form 1099-MISC in Box 3 (Other Income), using the name and Taxpayer Identification Number of the deceased employee's estate or beneficiary.

If the amounts are paid after the year of death, no social security or Medicare tax is withheld or paid, and no reporting is done on Form W-2. The amount is reported on Form 1099-MISC in Box 3, using the name and Taxpayer Identification Number of the deceased employee's estate or beneficiary.

Check Your Understanding

Quiz 3.3. Answer the following questions to test your understanding of state and local tax deductions.

Check Your Understanding

1. If an employee dies and a final payment is made, the employer continues to withhold taxes as if the employee was still alive.
    ❑ True
    ❑ False

2. For a payment after the employee's death in the year of the death, what taxes, if any, will be withheld?
    ❑ a. Federal income tax only
    ❑ b. Social security and Medicare taxes only
    ❑ c. Both federal income and social security and Medicare taxes
    ❑ d. No taxes will be withheld

3. For a payment after the employee's death in the year after the death, what taxes, if any, will be withheld?
    ❑ a. Federal income tax only
    ❑ b. Social security and Medicare taxes only
    ❑ c. Federal income and social security and Medicare taxes
    ❑ d. No taxes will be withheld

3.6 Gross to Net Calculation

Once the employee's total wages have been calculated and tax withholding and other deductions have been determined, the employer can pay the employee the difference—the employee's net pay.

All of the organization's employees' net pay, gross pay, and deductions are reported on the payroll register. Individual employee earnings and deductions are posted to an Earnings Record, which accumulates all payments made during the year.

Doing the Math

Example:

Gross Wages	$1,100.00
Pre-Tax Deductions	
401(k)	*110.00*
Cafeteria (Medical)	*150.00*
Deductions	
Federal Income Tax	*175.00*
State Income Tax	*50.00*
Social Security Tax	*58.90*
Medicare Tax	*13.78*
Charitable Contributions	*35.00*
Net Pay	**$507.32**

There are several ways to pay an employee. In the past, employees were paid in cash, a method that is seldom used now. Employees are familiar with receiving checks, which are negotiable instruments. Direct deposit of employees' pay into their personal bank account has become widely accepted in recent years. Additionally, payroll cards have emerged as an easy-to-use electronic payment option, especially for unbanked employees. For more information on paying employees see Chapter 2.

Alert

Know Your State's Laws. State laws govern the method of payment. Each state's requirements must be reviewed if a change in payment method is being considered.

3.7 Employer-Paid Taxes

The calculations of employee taxes and net pay earlier in this chapter were from gross to net earnings. You began those calculations with gross taxable income and withheld taxes from that amount to arrive at a net figure. Under some circumstances, when the employer wants to pay the employee's taxes you start with the net you want the employee to receive and then calculate a gross amount that includes the tax withholding amounts. This is known as a gross-up.

3.7.1 Why Gross-up?

Some typical circumstances for grossing up include the following situations:

Real-world Application

- A salesperson receives a $100.00 bonus. The sales manager wants the salesperson to receive $100.00 in cash (after withholding taxes), so the gross bonus will be more than $100.00.
- The employer decides to pay the employee's taxes on taxable relocation expenses.
- The value of excess group-term life insurance for a terminated employee is calculated but social security tax or Medicare tax was not withheld; gross-up is required.
- The employer fails to withhold taxes from the employee's wages at the time of payment; gross-up is required.

When grossing up, the taxes paid by the employer are included in the employee's taxable income.

3.7.2 Calculating Gross-up

To calculate the gross-up, take the following steps.

Doing the Math

Calculating Gross-Up Steps	
Step 1	100% - Tax % (Federal/State/Local Taxes) = Net %
Step 2	Payment ÷ Net % = Gross Amount of Earnings
Step 3	Check by Calculating Gross to Net Pay

For example, calculate the gross-up on the salesperson's $100.00 bonus. He has year-to-date wages of $40,000.00. Bonuses are taxed at the supplemental tax rate of 25%; in addition, social security tax of 6.2% and Medicare tax of 1.45% are due. Assume that there is no state or local income tax. Thus, the tax percentage (step 1) is 32.65% (25% + 6.2% + 1.45% = 32.65%).

	Calculating Gross-Up Example
Step 1	100% – 32.65% = 67.35%
Step 2	$100 ÷ 67.35% = $148.48 Gross Amount of Earnings
Step 3	Check by calculating Gross to Net Pay $148.48 x 32.65% = $48.48 (Tax withheld) $148.48 - $48.48 = $100.00 (bonus)

3.7.3 Grossing up with Special Circumstances

In most circumstances, the gross-up formula works when paying the employee's taxes. However, if the payment of the taxes causes the employee's year-to-date social security wages to cross the social security wage base, the formula must be revised.

The following revised formula accounts for the maximum social security tax that can be withheld during one year.

	Grossing Up With Special Circumstances Steps	
Step 1	100% - Tax % (Federal/ State/Local Taxes, except Social Security) =	Net %
Step 2	Payment + [(SS Wage Base – Prior Year-to-date payments) x 6.2%] ÷ Net% =	Gross Amount of Earnings
Step 3	Check by calculating Gross to Net Pay	

Doing the Math

For example, calculate the gross-up on the salesperson's $100.00 bonus if the salesperson's year-to-date social security wages are $118,450.00. Bonuses are taxed at the supplemental tax rate of 25%. In addition, only $50 of the bonus is subject to social security tax while the entire bonus is subject to the Medicare tax. Assume that there is no state or local income tax.

	Grossing Up with Special Circumstances Example	
Step 1	100% - (25% + 1.45%)	= 73.55%
Step 2	$100 + [($118,500.00 - $118,450.00) x 6.2%] ÷ 73.55% (100.00 + $3.10) ÷ 73.55%	= $140.18
Step 3	Check by calculating Gross to Net Pay $140.18 x 26.45% = $37.08 $37.08 + $3.10 (Social Security Tax) = $40.18 $140.18 - $40.18 = $100.00	

Answers to Quiz 3.1

1. c. Of these, only the business use of a company vehicle is nontaxable. The tax treatment of certain fringe benefits (like company vehicles, educational assistance, third-party sick pay, or group-term life insurance) can get complicated. Unless otherwise specified, fringe benefits are taxable.

2. c. Of these, sick pay is taxable. The other benefits are excluded from income by law.

3. c. Only the reimbursed business expenses accounted for timely are excluded by law.

4. 2017. Wages are included in taxable income when paid on January 7, 2017.

5. a. The employee's paycheck was available in 2016. According to the concept of constructive receipt, these wages are taxable in 2016.

    However, these situations can get very tricky. Therefore, the payroll department should pay close attention to wages paid near the December 31 deadline, particularly when shipping checks to branch offices. If they arrive for distribution after December 31, they are not technically paid until the next year and should not be reported on Form W-2 for the first year.

6. Withholding on a weekly salary of $605 with one allowance is $64 for single taxpayers.

7. d. Using the aggregate method, the employee's withholding on $705 ($605 in regular wages plus $100 bonus) is $79. That is a $15 difference over his regular withholding of $64 (see question 6). Using the flat rate, the withholding is 25%, or $25 on a $100 bonus. So the withholding will be different depending on which method is used.

8. c. The regular rate of pay is part of the FLSA's overtime premium calculation.

9. a. Using the wage-bracket method does not require making any calculations.

10. b. All payroll systems use the percentage method to calculate income tax.

11. a.

12. The employee's biweekly withholding for federal income tax is $49.63. To calculate her withholding, you must first determine her biweekly salary.

$$\frac{\$18,000 \text{ annually}}{26 \text{ pay periods}} = \$692.31 \text{ (rounded from \$692.3077)}$$

Remember: biweekly (every other week) = 26 pay periods; semi-monthly (twice a month) = 24 pay periods.

Now, follow the steps for using the percentage method tables.

Step 1	If the number of withholding allowances is one and wages are paid biweekly, the allowance amount is $155.80.
Step 2	$692.31 - $155.80 = $536.51
Step 3	Look at the biweekly table for single taxpayers. The employee's net wages are over $443.00 but not over $1,535.00
Step 4	$536.51 – $443.00 = $93.51
Step 5	$35.60 + ($93.51 x 15%) = $35.60 + $14.03 = $49.63

13. a. The IRS considers a salary regular wages not supplemental wages.

14. a. When using the optional flat rate, only the taxable wages is used in the calculation.

15. a. The IRS rules require the use of the aggregate method where no income tax has been withheld in the current or preceding year.

16. The employee's biweekly withholding for federal income tax is $1,968.80.

    His biweekly gross salary is $9,615.38 ($250,000 divided by 26 pay periods). The wage-bracket tables do not go this high, so you must use the percentage method.

Step 1	If the number of withholding allowances is three and wages are paid biweekly, the allowance amount is $467.40 ($155.80 x 3 = $467.40).
Step 2	$9,615.38 – $467.40 = $9,147.98
Step 3	Look at the biweekly percentage method table for married taxpayers. The employee's net wages are over $6,171.00 but not over $9,231.00.
Step 4	$9,147.98 – $6,171.00 = $2,976.98
Step 5	$1,135.25 + ($2,976.98 x 28%) = $1,135.25 + $833.55 = $1,968.80

17. a. When an employee is overpaid and the repayment occurs in the same year, the repayment requested is the employee's net overpayment.

18. c. When rounding the nearest dollar, round down for amounts less than $0.50 and round up for $0.50 and more.

19. b.

20. False

21. d.

22. b.

23. c. Employers pay and report both the employee and employer portion of the social security tax.

Answers to Quiz 3.2

1. a. Employees must authorize voluntary deductions.

2. True. Involuntary deductions have priority over other deductions.

3. a. Charitable contributions are voluntary deductions from the employee's pay.

4. c. The IRS requires the employee's take-home-pay be used when calculating the levy deduction.

5. b. IRS interest and penalties continue to accrue on the outstanding taxes until Form 668-D is issued.

6. False. Almost all divorce decrees require child support withholding.

7. a. The employee's disposable pay (all earnings less deductions required by law) is used to determine the maximum child support withholding.

8. c. If the employee has no second family and is not in arrears, the maximum deduction is 60% of disposable pay. The employee's disposable pay is $749.50 ($1,000 – $174 – $62 – $14.50). Therefore, the maximum child support payment is $449.70 ($749.50 x .60).

9. a. As with child support withholding orders, creditor garnishments use disposable pay to determine the amount withheld.

10. True. However, in some states the state's minimum wage (when higher) is used.

11. d. You need the employee's permission for voluntary deductions.

12. b. Disposable pay does not include voluntary deductions.

$8.50/hour x 80 =

$680.00	biweekly pay
— 40.00	federal income tax
— 10.00	state income tax
— 42.16	social security tax
— 9.86	Medicare tax
$577.98	

13. $142.98 The employee's disposable biweekly pay is less than $580.00. The maximum garnishment under federal law is the difference between the disposable pay ($577.98) and $435.00 or $142.98.

Answers to Quiz 3.3

1. False. Federal income tax is not withheld from wages paid after an employee's death as the wages subject to federal income tax are paid to the employee's estate or beneficiary and reported on Form 1099-MISC.

2. b. The Social Security Act requires withholding social security and Medicare taxes from wages paid in the year of an employee's death. These wages are paid to the employee's estate or beneficiary and are reported on Form W-2.

3. d. The Social Security Act requires that social security and Medicare taxes not be withheld from wages paid in the year after an employee's death. These wages are paid to the employee's estate or beneficiary and are not reported on Form W-2.

Payroll Benefit Basics

4.1 Fringe Benefits

In general, most fringe benefits and other compensation (cash or non-cash) are included in an employee's taxable compensation. Federal income tax, social security tax, and Medicare tax are withheld from the value of the benefit. There are some exceptions, however, as seen in Table 4.1. This chapter focuses on some of those exceptions and complications — compensation that is nontaxable or partially taxable.

In general, most fringe benefits and other compensation (cash or noncash) are included in an employee's taxable compensation.

Taxable Compensation	Nontaxable Compensation
Back pay	Dependent child care assistance (up to $5,000) under a Section 129 plan
Bonuses	Company vehicle (business use only)
Commissions	De minimis fringes
Company vehicle (personal use)	Disability benefits (employee contributions)
Dismissal and severance pay or final vacation pay	Educational assistance for job-related courses (no limit)
Employer-paid transit passes and transportation in a commuter highway vehicle in excess of $255/month	Group-term life insurance premiums ($50,000 or less of coverage)
Employer-paid parking greater than $255/month	Medical/dental/health plans (employer contributions)
Fringe benefits (unless specifically excluded)	No-additional-cost fringes
Gifts, gift certificates, prizes, and awards	Qualified employee discounts on employer goods/ services

Taxable Compensation	Nontaxable Compensation
Group legal services	Qualified moving expenses
Group-term life insurance over $50,000	Qualified transportation fringes
Nonaccountable reimbursed business expenses	Reimbursed business expenses (if accounted for in a timely manner)
Noncash fringes, unless excluded by Internal Revenue Code	Working condition fringes which would be deductible if paid by employee
Nonqualified moving expenses	Non-job-related education assistance up to $5,250 under a qualified plan
Overtime pay	Long-term care insurance
Regular wages	Health Savings Accounts
Sick pay and disability benefits (portion attributable to employer contributions)	
Tips	

Table 4.1. Taxable versus nontaxable compensation (federal law only)

4.1.1 Tax Treatment of Employee Compensation

The employee's gross income for tax purposes includes everything received from the employer in payment for services for the employer.

Generally, the employee's gross income for tax purposes includes everything received from the employer in payment for services for the employer. Amounts included in gross income are not limited to wages, salaries, commissions, fees, and tips. *All* forms of compensation are included in gross income, including fringe benefits.

4.1.2 IRS Definition

The Internal Revenue Service defines wages subject to taxation as all compensation an employee receives for services performed by that employee for the employer. This includes both payments made in cash and payments in any other form, such as salaries, vacation, bonuses, commissions, and fringe benefits. Compensation paid by noncash methods is valued at the fair market value to the employee.

Neither the Internal Revenue Code (IRC) nor the Internal Revenue Service regulations have specifically defined fringe benefits, because employers may be able to identify a new fringe benefit that would not meet the definition. With this in mind, the IRS has stated that any "accession to wealth" provided by the employer to the employee for services performed is considered wages subject to taxation.

4.1.3 Fair Market Value of Noncash Compensation

The fair market value of any noncash item received as compensation for services performed less any employee after-tax contribution must be included in the employee's income unless specifically excluded by law.

In general, the fair market value of a fringe benefit is determined on the basis of all the facts and circumstances. Specifically, the fair market value of a fringe benefit is the amount the employee would have paid a third party to buy or lease the fringe benefit. When determining the value of the benefit, keep the following two statements in mind:

The fair market value of a fringe benefit is the amount the employee would have paid a third party to buy or lease the fringe benefit.

1. The employee's perceived value of the benefit is not relevant.
2. The amount the employer paid for the benefit is not a determining factor.

4.1.4 Imputed Income

Imputed income represents the value of the taxable benefits employees receive from the employer and must be included in the employees' income. In most cases, employees do not receive cash as the benefit.

Employers are required to impute income to employees for each taxable noncash benefit received by the employee. Imputing income reduces employees' net pay by increasing taxes. The employee does not receive additional pay in the form of cash. An example of imputed income is taxable group-term life insurance.

Example: An employee has $50.00 included in income for a noncash taxable fringe benefit. The employee's salary is $1,500.00 for the monthly pay period, and the employee claims single and 2 allowances on her Form W-4. Using the wage-bracket method, a calculation of the employee's taxes follows:

	Pay Without Imputed Income	Pay With Imputed Income
Salary	$1,500.00	$1,500.00
Noncash Taxable Fringe Benefit		+$50.00
Taxable Pay	$1,500.00	$1,550.00
Federal Income Tax	64.00	68.00
Social Security Tax	93.00	96.10
Medicare Tax	21.75	22.48
Noncash Fringe Benefit		50.00
Net Pay	$1,321.25	$1,313.42

Imputing should occur as frequently as possible.

Imputing should occur as frequently as possible. If the employer delays imputing income until the end of the year, increased taxes from the calculation can leave the employee's net pay greatly reduced. For example, imputing group-term life insurance could occur monthly since the employee's imputed income is based on a calculation that uses a monthly rate.

4.1.5 Recognition of Noncash Fringe Benefits

The IRS has established special rules applying to the treatment of noncash fringe benefits. These benefits must be recognized as income at least once a year, by December 31, but may be recognized more frequently, such as monthly or quarterly.

The employer may recognize fringe benefits at different frequencies for different benefits and groups of employees. Employers have the option of analyzing the benefit amounts and allocating them to each period in equal amounts. The employer has the right to set the number and frequency of periods when allocating each benefit.

4.1.6 When to Withhold and Deposit Taxes on Noncash Fringe Benefits

The recognition of fringe benefits as taxable income requires that all applicable income and employment taxes be withheld and deposited. The federal tax deposits for fringe benefits follow the deposit rules for regular income. Federal tax deposit rules are discussed in Chapter 5.

4.1.7 Withholding Tax on Fringe Benefits

Withholding and employment tax regulations apply regardless of the frequency used for reporting the taxable fringe benefit. Employers must either collect the tax from the employee or pay the tax on behalf of the employee. If the employer pays the taxes due on fringe benefits on behalf of the employee, those taxes paid become additional income.

Employers must either collect the tax from the employee or pay the tax on behalf of the employee.

Employers electing not to withhold taxes from the employee's regular wages on the benefit provided to the employee still must pay the taxes due. When the employer pays taxes on behalf of the employee, the taxes may be treated as an account receivable. Repayment must be made no later than April 1 of the following year.

4.1.8 Nonreportable Fringe Benefits

IRC Section 132 defines benefits that are excluded from taxable earnings. In most cases, these benefits are not reported on the employee's Form W-2. Section 132 benefits include the following.

IRC Section 132 defines benefits that are excluded from taxable earnings.

De Minimis (Minimal) Fringe Benefits
De minimis fringe benefits are so small in value that it is unreasonable or administratively impractical for the employer to account for them. They are not included in an employee's taxable compensation.

Examples include the following:

- Occasional typing of a personal letter by a company administrative assistant
- Occasional personal use of the employer's photocopy machine (as long as it is less than 15% of the total use of the machine)
- Occasional parties for employees
- Occasional tickets to the theater or sporting events
- Occasional supper money for working overtime
- Traditional holiday gifts like a turkey or a ham (but not cash gifts, gift cards, or gift certificates that are treated like cash)
- Coffee or donuts furnished by the employer
- Use of company telephone for personal calls

Caution: If you keep track of any of these items, no matter how small, they could become taxable. In addition, cash, gift cards, gift certificates, or cash equivalents are always taxable.

No-Additional-Cost Services

Employees can take advantage of employer services with no tax consequences when the services are sold to customers as part of the employer's regular line of business in which the employee works. As long as the employer does not incur any substantial cost in providing this service to employees, it need not be included in the employee's taxable compensation. The benefit must be offered on substantially equal terms to all employees in the same group and must not discriminate in favor of highly compensated employees.

Examples include the following:

- Free or reduced-price standby travel to employees of an airline
- Free telephone service to employees of a telephone company

Qualified Employee Discounts

The property and services must be offered for sale to customers in the ordinary course of an employer's line of business.

Employers do not include in their employees' taxable income the value of qualified employer property and services purchased at a discount from the employer if:

- The discount on property is not greater than the gross profit earned on the property at the price normally sold to customers

- The discount on services is not greater than 20% of the retail price

To be qualified, the property and services must be offered for sale to customers in the ordinary course of an employer's line of business. As with most other nontaxable fringes, if the discounts are generally available to only highly compensated employees, they must be included in the recipient's taxable compensation.

Working Condition Fringes

Work-related items, when paid for by the employee, may be deducted from the employee's individual tax return as a business expense. These items, when provided by the employer, represent nontaxable compensation.

Examples include the following:

- Business use of a company car or plane
- Subscriptions to business periodicals
- Fees to join professional organizations
- Attendance at a job-related seminar
- Goods used by employees for product testing
- Cell phone provided primarily for business purposes

Use of Athletic Facilities

The value of the use of employer-provided athletic facilities intended primarily for employees and their families may be excluded from income. The facility must be located on the employer's premises although not necessarily at the place of business. The facility must also be operated by the employer. If the facility is made available to the public, the exclusion does not apply.

Qualified Transportation Fringe Benefits

Employer-provided qualified transportation fringe benefits may be excluded from the income of an employee up to certain limits. Employers may offer a choice of transportation, a transit pass, qualified parking, or cash. If cash, it is taxable.

Qualified transportation fringes include the following:

Transportation in a Commuter Highway Vehicle (Van-Pooling)
Up to $255 per month (indexed annually) may be excluded from the employee's income for transportation in a commuter highway vehicle provided by the employer for travel between the employee's residence

Under the Protecting Americans from Tax Hikes Act of 2015 (PATH Act), the excludable amounts for the transportation fringe benefit for van-pooling and mass transit passes were made equal to the amount of the of the qualified transportation fringe benefit for qualified parking for 2015 and beyond. For 2016 all three benefits have the same monthly excludable amount ($255).

and place of work. A commuter highway vehicle is defined as a high-way vehicle that:

- Seats at least six adults (not including the driver)
- Has at least 80% of its mileage used in transporting employ-ees between their residences and their place of work and at least 50% of the adult seating capacity is occupied (not including the driver)

Transit Passes
Up to $255 per month (indexed annually) may be excluded from the employee's income when the employer provides the employee with a transit pass.

A transit pass is any pass, token, fare card, voucher, or similar item.

A transit pass is any pass, token, fare card, voucher, or similar item provid-ing the employee transportation to and/or from work (or transportation at a reduced price) when the transportation is on mass transit facilities or pro-vided by a business transporting persons in a commuter highway vehicle.

Qualified Parking
Parking provided by an employer to an employee on or near the prem-ises of the employer or at or near a location from which the employee commutes to work on mass transit or in a commuter highway vehicle may be excluded from the employee's gross income up to $255 per month (indexed annually). The amount to apply against the exclusion is what the employee would pay in a fair market value, "arms-length" transaction to obtain the parking. Employers may discriminate in favor of highly compensated employees when providing qualified parking.

Bicycle Commuters
A "qualified bicycle commuting reimbursement" can be made to em-ployees for reasonable expenses incurred by an employee who regularly uses a bicycle to commute to and from work. The maximum qualified bicycle commuting reimbursement is $20 a month. A qualified month is a month in which the employee does not receive any other qualified

Qualified retirement planning services may be provided to an employee by an employer maintaining a qualified plan.

transportation fringe benefit and *regularly* uses a bicycle for a *substan-tial portion* of travel between his/her residence and place of work.

Employer-Provided Retirement Advice
Qualified retirement planning services (i.e., retirement advice and infor-mation but not tax preparation, accounting, legal, or brokerage services) may be provided to an employee and his or her spouse by an employer maintaining a qualified plan (i.e., 401(k) plan, 403(b) annuity, SEP, or

SIMPLE plan but not a 457 plan). The amount of the services received is not included in the employee's income and wages. This exclusion does not apply to highly compensated individuals unless the services are available on substantially the same terms to other employees.

Qualified moving expense reimbursements

An employer's reimbursement or payment of an employee's moving expenses is an excludable fringe benefit when the expenses meet the qualified moving expense requirements. The expenses are qualified moving expenses when:

- The expenses would be deductible by the employee if he or she had directly paid or incurred the expenses
- The employee did not deduct the expenses in a prior year

The following rules must be met for moving expenses to be qualified:

- The distance from the employee's new workplace to his/her old residence must be at least 50 miles farther than the distance from the employee's old workplace to his/her old residence.
- The employee must work full-time in the general location of their new principal place of work for at least 39 weeks during the 12 months immediately following the move. (Note: The time test is waived if the employee dies, loses his or her job due to a disability, transfers for the employer's benefit, or is laid off or discharged for a reason other than willful misconduct.)
- The reimbursements should be made under rules similar to those relating to an accountable business expense reimbursement plan.

Deductible moving expenses that are defined in IRC Section 217 and are excluded from income when reimbursed with no dollar limitation are:

- Expenses incurred moving household goods and personal effects from the employee's old residence to the new residence.
- Expenses incurred by the employee and his/her family for traveling from the old residence to the new residence. If reimbursing mileage during a move, the rate cannot exceed $0.19 (for 2016) per mile without incurring taxation. These expenses include lodging but not meals.

Deductible expenses that are defined in Section 217 are excluded from income when reimbursed under Section 132 with no dollar limitation.

Any reimbursed or employer-paid moving expenses not meeting the qualified moving expense reimbursement requirements are included in the employee's income and are subject to employment taxes and income tax withholding. They must be reported in Boxes 1, 3, and 5 of the employee's Form W-2 but not in Box 12. Qualified moving expenses paid directly to a third party are not reportable on Form W-2. However, qualified moving expenses paid directly to the employee must be reported on Form W-2 in Box 12, Code P.

Check Your Understanding

Check Your Understanding

Quiz 4.1. Answer the following questions to test your understanding of fringe benefits.

1. Last month, an employee e-mailed her mother on the company's e-mail, photocopied fliers for her church picnic at work, and used her work computer to update her resume. These services represent:
    - ❑ a. taxable compensation.
    - ❑ b. de minimis fringes.
    - ❑ c. working condition fringes.
    - ❑ d. no-additional-cost services.

2. A retail sales clerk took advantage of the company's employee discount program to purchase clothes at 10% off the normal retail price. This service represents:
    - ❑ a. taxable compensation.
    - ❑ b. a qualified employee discount.
    - ❑ c. a working condition fringe.
    - ❑ d. a no-additional-cost service.

3. An employee belongs to a professional organization. When his company pays his dues, the payment is:
    - ❑ a. taxable compensation.
    - ❑ b. a de minimis fringe.
    - ❑ c. a working condition fringe.
    - ❑ d. a no-additional cost service.

Use the following information to answer questions 4 and 5.
In February 2016, an accountant moved from Chicago to Boston to join another firm and was still employed in Boston on December 31, 2016. Her new employer paid for her moving expenses as follows:

$3,500	Moving household items
$500	Airfare to new job site
$1,500	House-hunting trips and temporary living expenses until she closes on her new house
$2,500	Expenses of purchasing a new house

4. Which if any, of the qualified moving expense test(s) does this move meet?
   ❏ a. Distance test only
   ❏ b. Time test only
   ❏ c. Distance and time tests
   ❏ d. Neither the distance nor the time test

5. Her employer must withhold federal income tax, social security tax, and Medicare tax from how much of her reimbursement check for her moving expenses?
   ❏ a. $500.00
   ❏ b. $3,400.00
   ❏ c. $4,000.00
   ❏ d. $8,000.00

Use the following information to answer question 6.
When your company transferred an employee, whose annual salary is $45,000.00, from its Miami plant to its Dallas plant in March, it agreed to pay 100% of his moving expenses. He claimed the following expenses, which your company paid in full.

$5,000.00	Moving household goods to new residence
$243.00	Mileage/lodging for traveling to new job site at $0.19/mile
$50.00	Meals en route to the new location
$2,200.00	Pre-move house-hunting expenses and temporary living expenses after relocating in Dallas
$3,000.00	Expenses related to purchase, sale, or lease of a primary residence
$1,000.00	Real estate taxes

6. How much of these expenses is excluded from income?
   - ❏ a. $5,243.00
   - ❏ b. $7,550.00
   - ❏ c. $9,850.00
   - ❏ d. $11,500.00

7. An employee's parking garage is two blocks away from his downtown office. It costs $270.00 per month to rent a stall there, but the employee doesn't mind because it's convenient and his employer reimburses him for 100% of the costs. How much of his monthly parking is taxable?
   - ❏ a. $15.00
   - ❏ b. $130.00
   - ❏ c. $245.00
   - ❏ d. $250.00

8. An employer provides an employee $300.00 each month in bus tokens so she can commute to work. How much of this expense is nontaxable?
   - ❏ a. $130.00
   - ❏ b. $255.00
   - ❏ c. $300.00
   - ❏ d. $355.00

4.2 Prizes and Awards

Prizes and awards are included in the employee's taxable compensation.

Prizes and awards given to employees are generally included in the employee's taxable compensation and require withholding. However, length-of-service and safety awards may be excluded from income if the awards follow certain guidelines:

- For nonqualified plans, employees can receive an award costing the employer $400.00 in a calendar year.
- For qualified plans, all awards made to a single employee cannot cost the employer more than $1,600.00 in a calendar year, with the average cost of all individual awards to all employees not exceeding $400.00.
- A qualified plan is a written plan that does not favor highly compensated employees. If awards exceed the limitations above, the excess amount is considered taxable income.
- Awards must be tangible property and must be presented in a meaningful ceremony.

Other qualifications for length-of-service awards include the following:

- Awards must not be given during the first five years of employment with the employer.
- Awards can be made only at five-year intervals.

Other qualifications for safety awards include the following:

- No more than 10% of all employees may receive safety awards.
- No management, professional, administrative, or clerical employees may receive safety awards.
- The employee must work full time with at least one year of service.

4.3 Company Vehicles

Business use of a company-owned vehicle is a working condition fringe benefit and is not taxable. However, personal use of the vehicle is taxable compensation.

Accounting for Company Vehicle Use

Here are some of the factors involved in accounting for company vehicle use.

Need for Documentation

Only mileage with a documented business purpose can be excluded from taxable compensation as a working condition fringe benefit. Therefore, employees must keep detailed records of all business use of the vehicle. There is no requirement to substantiate personal use — employers determine it by subtracting business use from total use.

Employee records should include the following:

- Business miles driven
- Date of trip
- Purpose of trip
- Expenses

Business use of a company-owned vehicle is a working condition fringe benefit and is not taxable.

Personal use of the vehicle is taxable compensation.

Income tax Withholding Optional

The employer can elect not to withhold federal income tax on personal use of a company vehicle. When choosing not to withhold, employers must notify the affected employees by January 31 of each year, or 30 days after the employee is assigned a vehicle.

If federal income tax is not withheld on the personal use of a company car, the employee may be underwithheld for personal income tax and could face penalties and interest charges.

Social Security Tax and Medicare Tax Withholding and Reporting Required

Social security tax and Medicare tax must be withheld on the personal use of a company vehicle. If the employee terminates before withholding requirements are met, the employer must pay the social security tax and Medicare tax for the employee, unless the taxes can be collected from the terminated employee.

Report the Value

Even though choosing not to withhold federal income tax, the employer must add the value of personal use to the compensation reported on the employee's Form W-2. Employees may pay federal income tax on the amount when filing their personal income tax returns.

Reporting Required

The value of personal use of a company vehicle is required to be reported only once a year. However, more frequent reporting is recommended, with quarterly reporting suggested. Employers may treat the personal use of the company vehicle provided during November and December of one year (or any shorter period during those two months) as being paid during the next year.

4.3.1 Valuation Methods

Either the general valuation method or one of three safe-harbor valuation methods may be used to determine the cash value of the personal use of a company vehicle. Once an employer begins to use a safe-harbor valuation method for a vehicle, they must continue using that method as long as the employee uses that vehicle.

Under the general valuation method, the personal use of a company car is determined by the fair market value an individual would have to pay to lease the same vehicle under the same terms in the same geographic area. One of the safe-harbor methods is usually more advantageous administratively. The three safe-harbor methods are the following.

Annual Lease Value Method

This method, also called the fair market valuation method, involves determining how much it would cost to lease a comparable car on the same terms. The annual lease value table is used to determine the lease value. The first step is to determine the fair market value of the vehicle on the first day the employee uses the vehicle. The annual lease value amount is then multiplied by the percentage of personal use. For example, assume that an employee uses a company car 50% for business and 50% for personal matters. The car has a fair market value of $20,000. Using the table below, taxable compensation for personal use of the car is $2,800 ($5,600 x 50%).

Doing the Math

Annual Lease Value Table			
Fair market value	**Annual lease value**	**Fair market value**	**Annual lease value**
$0-999	$600	$22,000-22,999	$6,100
$1,000-1,999	$850	$23,000-23,999	$6,350
$2,000-2,999	$1,100	$24,000-24,999	$6,600
$3,000-3,999	$1,350	$25,000-25,999	$6,850
$4,000-4,999	$1,600	$26,000-27,999	$7,250
$5,000-5,999	$1,850	$28,000-29,999	$7,750
$6,000-6,999	$2,100	$30,000-31,999	$8,250
$7,000-7,999	$2,350	$32,000-33,999	$8,750
$8,000-8,999	$2,600	$34,000-35,999	$9,250
$9,000-9,999	$2,850	$36,000-37,999	$9,750
$10,000-10,999	$3,100	$38,000-39,999	$10,250
$11,000-11,999	$3,350	$40,000-41,999	$10,750
$12,000-12,999	$3,600	$42,000-43,999	$11,250
$13,000-13,999	$3,850	$44,000-45,999	$11,750
$14,000-14,999	$4,100	$46,000-47,999	$12,250
$15,000-15,999	$4,350	$48,000-49,999	$12,750
$16,000-16,999	$4,600	$50,000-51,999	$13,250
$17,000-17,999	$4,850	$52,000-53,999	$13,750
$18,000-18,999	$5,100	$54,000-55,999	$14,250
$19,000-19,999	$5,350	$56,000-57,999	$14,750
$20,000-20,999	$5,600	$58,000-59,999	$15,250
$21,000-21,999	$5,850		

Note: If the fair market value is greater than $59,999, the annual lease value is equal to 25% of the fair market value plus $500.

When the company provides fuel for personal use, add the cost of fuel based on the personal mileage (at a rate of $0.055 per mile or actual expenses).

The annual lease value remains the same for four calendar years. However, if the driver of the vehicle changes, the fair market value may be recalculated at that time. After four calendar years with the same driver, the fair market value must be recalculated.

Cents-per-mile method

In 2016, the mileage rate is $0.54 (54 cents) per mile.

If a vehicle is valued under $15,900, SUV valued under $17,700, vehicle in a fleet valued under $21,200 or SUV in a fleet valued under $23,100 and is first put in service in 2016, the value of personal use can be determined by multiplying the personal miles by the business standard mileage rate. In 2016, the mileage rate is $0.54 (54 cents) per mile. To qualify for this method, one of two requirements must be met:

1. The employer must reasonably expect the vehicle to be used by employees throughout the year for business.
2. The vehicle must be driven at least 10,000 miles annually (including personal use) and be used primarily by employees.

Note: Consult the "blue book" or other recognized source to determine the vehicle's fair market value.

Commuting Value Method

Include in the employee's income $1.50 per one-way commute ($3.00 for a round trip) if the personal use of the company vehicle is:

- Not undertaken by a "control employee"
- Restricted (by written company policy) to driving between work and home
- Undertaken by an employee who commutes in the company vehicle for noncompensatory business reasons

This method also applies to more than one employee commuting in the same vehicle or for company-sponsored car-pools. The amount included in income is $3 per round trip for each employee in the car-pool.

Business Use of Personal Vehicles

Employees who use their personal vehicle for business use may be reimbursed for that use at the business standard mileage rate ($0.54 per mile in 2016). The business use must be documented — date, purpose, place and number of miles driven. Employers may have different rates. However, if the rate is greater than $0.54 per mile, the excess over $0.54 per mile is subject to federal income, social security and Medicare taxes.

Check Your Understanding

Quiz 4.2. Answer the following questions to test your understanding of handling prizes and awards and company vehicles.

Use the following information to answer questions 1-3.

A salesperson drives a company-owned vehicle valued at $12,000. In the year, he logs 10,000 miles for business travel and 5,000 miles for personal use.

1. Use the annual lease value method (see table below) to calculate the value of his personal use of the vehicle.

    $ _____

Fair market value	Annual lease value
$11,000-11,999	$3,350
$12,000-12,999	$3,600
$13,000-13,999	$3,850
$14,000-14,999	$4,100

2. Determine the value of the salesperson's personal use of this vehicle using the cents-per-mile method based on 10,000 business miles and 5,200 personal miles.

    $ _____

Check Your Understanding

3. What federal taxes, if any must the salesperson's employer withhold for his personal use of the company vehicle?
    - ❑ a. Social security tax and Medicare tax only
    - ❑ b. Federal income tax only
    - ❑ c. Federal income tax, social security tax, and Medicare tax
    - ❑ d. No taxes are required to be withheld

4. For her 10 years of service, an employee was given a gold necklace valued at $100. Which of the following is true?
    - ❑ a. The gift must be included in her taxable compensation.
    - ❑ b. The gift is tax-free.
    - ❑ c. Only social security tax and Medicare tax should be withheld on the fair market value of the award.
    - ❑ d. Only federal income tax should be withheld on the fair market value of the award.

4.4 Group-Term Life Insurance

Group-term life insurance provided to an employee in excess of $50,000 is taxable compensation.

Normally, the value of group-term life insurance provided to an employee in excess of $50,000 is taxable compensation. Dependent group-term life insurance coverage of $2,000 or less is excludable from income as a de minimis benefit. If dependent group-term life insurance coverage is more than $2,000, the entire amount is taxable and subject to all withholding, unless the cost paid for the insurance is de minimis.

Tax Considerations

Here are some key points to keep in mind when dealing with excess group-term life insurance.

Exempt From Federal Income Tax Withholding

The value of excess group-term life coverage is exempt from federal income tax withholding.

The value of excess group-term life coverage is exempt from federal income tax withholding. However, the amount is taxable on the employee's individual tax return and must be reported on Form W-2.

However, the value of dependent group-term life insurance that is taxable is subject to federal income tax withholding.

Must Withhold Social Security Tax and Medicare Tax

Employers must withhold social security tax and Medicare tax from the value of the employee's excess group-term life insurance coverage and the dependent's group-term life coverage provided by the employer. This is true even if the employee pays for this benefit using pretax dollars through a cafeteria plan. Employers are required to withhold and report social security tax and Medicare tax only once a year. More frequent withholding and reporting, such as every pay period, is recommended.

Exempt From Federal Unemployment Tax

The value of excess group-term life insurance is exempt from FUTA (federal unemployment tax — discussed in Chapter 5) but must be reported on Form 940.

Calculating the Value of Excess Group-Term Life Insurance

Doing the Math

The value of excess group-term life insurance is an example of imputed income. Imputed income is the amount that a company pays on behalf of an employee but the individual does not actually receive in real dollars.

The cost of group-term life insurance increases as people age, so employers must know the age of each participant. Calculate the employee's age as of December 31 of the year in which the benefit is taxable.

Uniform Premiums — Table I	
Age	*Monthly Cost per $1,000*
Under 25	$ 0.05
25 to 29	0.06
30 to 34	0.08
35 to 39	0.09
40 to 44	0.10
45 to 49	0.15
50 to 54	0.23
55 to 59	0.43
60 to 64	0.66
65 to 69	1.27
70 and above	2.06

Table 4.3. IRS Table I, Section 79, for group-term life over $50,000 (cost per $1,000 per month of coverage)

Using the age of the participant, the taxable value can be determined by taking the following steps.

Doing the Math

Calculating the Value of Excess Group-Term Life Insurance Steps	
Step 1	Determine the amount of coverage.
Step 2	Amount of coverage - $50,000.00 = Excess Coverage
Step 3	(Excess Coverage ÷ $1,000) x Value from IRS Table I = Table Value (per month)
Step 4	Taxable Value – Employee's contributions (after–tax only) = Taxable Value of Group-Term Life (per month)

Note: Employee pretax contributions do not reduce taxable value. Only after-tax contributions reduce the taxable value. The after-tax contribution cannot reduce the taxable value below $0.00.

Sample Calculation

For example, a company offers group-term life at twice the employee's annual salary. This benefit is part of the firm's flexible benefit plan; since contributions are pretax, they do not count in step 4. Calculate the taxable value of group-term life for a 32-year-old employee who earns $30,000 as follows.

Sample Calculation		
Step 1	($30,000 x 2)	= $60,000 Amount of Coverage
Step 2	$60,000 - $50,000	= $10,000 Excess Coverage
Step 3	($10,000 ÷ $1,000) x $0.08	= $0.80 (Benefit Value (per month)
Step 4	$0.80 - $0.00 (Employee's Contributions)	= $0.80 Taxable Value of Group-Term Life (per month)

On May 1, the employee's salary increased to $35,000 per year. For the months of May through December, recalculate the taxable value of group-term life as follows.

Sample Calculation		
Step 1	($35,000 x 2)	= $70,000 Amount of Coverage
Step 2	$70,000 - $50,000	= $20,000 Excess Coverage
Step 3	($20,000 ÷ $1,000) x $0.08	= $1.60 (Benefit Value (per month)
Step 4	$1.60 - $0.00 (Employee's Contributions)	= $1.60 Taxable Value of Group-Term Life (per month)

4.5 Deferred Compensation

Your company's benefit programs may be of great value to you personally and also complex for you as a payroll practitioner. One of the key benefits many companies offer their employees is the opportunity to have some of their current income deferred and accumulated until retirement.

4.5.1 Qualified Versus Nonqualified Plans

Deferred compensation plans can be classified into two key groups.

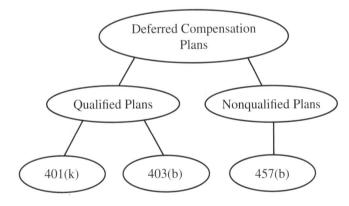

Qualified Plans

A plan is qualified if it complies with the provisions of Section 401 of the Internal Revenue Code. Qualified plans include profit-sharing plans, defined contribution plans, defined benefit plans, and the popular 401(k) plan, named after its section of the tax code.

A plan is qualified if it complies with the provisions of Section 401 of the Internal Revenue Code.

Similar plans, which fall under other sections of the tax code, have been established for certain types of employees. Section 403(b) applies to employees of public schools and nonprofit organizations. Essentially, qualified plans must:

1. Be in writing and be communicated to employees.
2. Be established for the exclusive benefit of employees or their beneficiaries.
3. Be nontransferable and nonforfeitable (that is, be vested).
4. Satisfy the rules related to eligibility and minimum vesting of employees' interest in the plan.
5. Not discriminate in favor of officers, shareholders, or highly compensated employees. However, benefits can vary with length of service.

Nonqualified Plans

Section 457(b) plans are for public sector employees.

Unlike qualified plans, nonqualified plans can be discriminatory. Section 457(b) plans for public sector employees are like nonqualified plans in that they can be discriminatory.

The table on this page compares some of the key deferred compensation plans available.

Deferred Compensation Plans				
	401(k)	**403(b)**	**457(b)**	**Nonqualified Plans**
2016 Max Contribution ($ amt)	$18,000	$18,000	$18,000	No Limit
Catch-Up Contribution	$6,000	$6,000	$6,000	No Limit
Federal Income Tax Wages?	No	No	No	No
Social Security and Medicare Tax Wages	Yes	Usually	Usually	Usually

Note that maximum contributions may be subject to additional testing and limitations.

4.5.2 401(k) Plans

Also known as cash or deferred arrangements or salary reduction plans, 401(k) plans allow employees to have their employers defer a portion of their salary until they retire or start withdrawing the funds. Here are some key facts to remember about 401(k) plans.

Maximum Contribution Under Section 402(g)

Employees cannot defer more than the statutory limit of $18,000 in 2016. (This amount is adjusted periodically for inflation.) The annual maximum on all contributions (employee before-tax, employee after-tax and employer contributions) to all qualified plans (401(k), profit-sharing, etc.) is 100% of eligible compensation or $53,000 (whichever is less).

Employees cannot defer more than the statutory limit of $18,000 in 2016.

The maximum annual limit of an employee's compensation that can be considered by qualified retirement plans and simplified employee pensions is $265,000 under Code Section 401(a)(17) in 2016. Any compensation over $265,000 is disregarded when applying certain nondiscrimination rules but may be used for elective deferrals if the employer's 401(k) plan allows it. The amount is indexed for inflation periodically.

Catch-up Contributions

The dollar limit on pre-tax employee contributions to a 401(k), 403(b) annuity, or 457(b) plan is increased by $6,000 in 2016 for employees who reach age 50 before the end of the plan year. The additional "catch-up" contribution is available for employees who otherwise would have their deferrals limited by the plan, discrimination testing or the statutory limit.

The dollar limit on pre-tax contributions is increased by $6,000 for employees age 50 or older.

Withhold no Federal Income Tax

The contributions are not subject to federal income tax at the time they are made. Income tax should not be withheld from the contribution. Also, the contribution should not be reported as income on Form W-2. However, participants will pay federal income tax as they receive distributions from their 401(k) plan, generally during retirement.

Roth 401(k) Plans

Employers may offer a 401(k) plan that contains a Roth 401(k) option. For employees participating in the Roth 401(k), their contributions will be subject to federal income tax. When the Roth 401(k) contribution is distributed to the employee it is not subject to income tax.

Withhold Social Security Tax and Medicare Tax

Contributions are taxable for social security and Medicare.

Contributions are taxable for social security and Medicare and thus must be reported as social security and Medicare wages on Form W-2.

Generally Not Subject To State Income Tax

Pennsylvania is the only state that taxes 401(k) employee contributions.

Employer Options

Contributions go into a special trust account established by the employer. The company chooses the investment options, which typically include a range of choices such as a stock mutual fund, a bond fund, and fixed income investments. Your firm's 401(k) plan may include the following:

- Employer matching funds (for example, 50 cents for every dollar contributed from employee deferrals).
- Ceilings on the amount of the contribution that are lower than the maximum set up by law. For example, your organization might limit contributions to 6% of salary.
- Automatic enrollment into the 401(k) plan with mandatory contributions.

Transfering employee 401(k) contributions to a trust fund. Contributions to a 401(k) plan must be transferred to the trust as soon as they can be reasonably segregated from the company's general assets but no later than 15 business days after the end of the month in which the contribution is made.

4.5.3 403(b) Plans

Section 403(b) of the Internal Revenue Code creates a retirement savings program for employees of tax-exempt organizations such as public schools, colleges and universities, religious groups, and public charities. Two savings options are available:

Tax-Sheltered Annuities (TSAs)

TSA contributions are invested in tax-deferred annuities issued by life insurance companies.

Tax-Sheltered Custodial Accounts (TSCAs)

TSCA contributions are invested in mutual funds held by a qualifying custodian.

The amount that may be contributed for each employee annually is limited in the same manner as 401(k) contributions are; $18,000 in elective deferrals, or 100% of compensation or $53,000 in total contributions, whichever is less.

Consult IRS Publication 571 for more details.

TSA and TSCA Contributions May Be Excluded From Gross Income. Contributions to a TSA or TSCA within the allowance are excluded from an employee's gross income for federal (and most states') income tax. However, participants may pay social security tax and Medicare tax on the contributions if the employee is subject to social security tax or Medicare tax.

Roth 403(b) Plans. Employers with 403(b) plans can allow contributions to Roth 403(b) plans that are similar to Roth 401(k) plans (page 4-24).

4.5.4 457(b) Plans

Section 457(b) of the Internal Revenue Code allows employees of states, counties, cities, towns, and special governmental districts, as well as certain tax-exempt organizations, to defer receipt of wages that otherwise would be considered current income. This type of deferred compensation is a contractual agreement between the organization and an employee wherein the organization makes a promise to defer up to a limit of $18,000 of compensation in 2016 to the participant to a future date for services currently rendered. The Internal Revenue Code requires that Section 457(b) plan assets be held in trust.

Contributions to 457(b) plans are not subject to federal income tax.

How to Treat Contributions to 457(b) Plans. Generally speaking, contributions to 457(b) plans are not subject to federal income tax. Both the employer and employee contributions may be subject to social security tax and Medicare tax (or just the Medicare portion for some public employees) if the employee is subject to social security tax or Medicare tax. A 457(b) plan is treated in some ways as a nonqualified deferred compensation plan.

Roth 457(b) Plans. Employers with 457(b) plans can allow contributions to Roth 457(b) plans that are similar to Roth 401(k) plans (page 4-24).

4.5.5 Nonqualified Deferred Compensation Plans

Companies provide additional benefits to executive in nonqualified deferred compensation plans.

One way for companies to provide additional benefits to selected key executives is to offer nonqualified deferred compensation plans. Because there are no nondiscrimination requirements for these plans, the company can pick and choose which employees may benefit from them. The plans are a written promise by the employer to pay a given amount at a later date. For example, the employer contractually promises to pay a lump sum or make periodic payments. Generally, these funds are not set aside in a special account or trust.

Usually Not Federal Income Taxable

If the employee's interest is nontransferable and is subject to a substantial risk of forfeiture or the plan meets IRC Section 409A's requirements that restrict distributions and require deferral elections before the tax year, the employee pays no federal income tax on the deferred compensation until the amount contributed to the plan is distributed to the employee. The distribution is reported on Form W-2.

Usually Social Security and Medicare Taxable

The amount deferred is subject to social security tax and Medicare tax when the services are performed or when the employee has no substantial risk of loss of the amount, whichever is later. However, the employee is usually over the maximum limit on social security withholding. To avoid double taxation (at deferral and payment), the increased value (employee and employer contribution and earnings) during the year must be subject to social security and Medicare taxation. The plan's increase in value can be included in the employee's social security and Medicare wages once a year.

The amount deferred is subject to social security tax and Medicare tax.

Get legal advice about how to treat nonqualified deferred compensation plans. The wages are taxable if they are set aside for and accessible to the employee without significant restriction.

Check Your Understanding

Quiz 4.3. Answer the following questions to test your understanding of deferred compensation programs.

Check Your Understanding

1. All of the following deferred compensation plans limit the employee to making a deferral contribution of $18,000 in 2016 except:
    - ❑ a.   401(k)
    - ❑ b.   403(b)
    - ❑ c.   457(b)
    - ❑ d.   Nonqualified

2. Under which type of plan are employee contributions subject to social security and Medicare taxes?
    - ❑ a.   401(k) only
    - ❑ b.   403(b) only
    - ❑ c.   457(b) only
    - ❑ d.   401(k), 403(b) and 457(b)

3. All of the following features are present in a qualified plan except:
   - ☐ a. discrimination in favor of highly compensated employees.
   - ☐ b. written document.
   - ☐ c. benefits for employees.
   - ☐ d. the right to benefits is nontransferable.

4. Under which type of plan are employee contributions subject to federal income tax?
   - ☐ a. 401(k)
   - ☐ b. 403(b)
   - ☐ c. 457(b)
   - ☐ d. Roth 401(k)

5. An employer may provide all of the following features in a 401(k) plan except:
   - ☐ a. matching contributions.
   - ☐ b. lower ceilings on contributions.
   - ☐ c. higher benefits for highly compensated employees.
   - ☐ d. catch-up contributions.

6. All of the following features are generally found in a nonqualified deferred compensation plan except:
   - ☐ a. equal benefits for all employees.
   - ☐ b. provided only to key executives.
   - ☐ c. discriminatory toward highly compensated.
   - ☐ d. contributions are not subject to federal income tax.

7. A superintendent of schools who will be 49 years of age on December 31, 2016, earns $100,000. His school district has a 403(b) plan. What is the maximum that he can contribute to this before taxes plan in 2016?
   - ☐ a. $17,500
   - ☐ b. $18,000
   - ☐ c. $23,500
   - ☐ d. $24,000

8. An employee earns $40,000 annually. Married with three allowances, she contributes $6,000 annually to her 401(k). How much must be withheld for federal income tax, social security, and/or Medicare tax on the contribution?
   - ❑ a. $0.00
   - ❑ b. $459.00
   - ❑ c. $918.00
   - ❑ d. $1,959.00

9. The owners of a company want to set up a retirement program for themselves, but do not want to make contributions on behalf of their employees. All of their employees are under age 30. What can they do?
   - ❑ a. Establish only a 401(k) plan that restricts eligibility to employees over age 30.
   - ❑ b. Set up a nonqualified deferred compensation plan only.
   - ❑ c. Establish only a 401(k) plan that restricts eligibility to employees over age 30, and set up a nonqualified deferred compensation plan.
   - ❑ d. Establish a 403(b) plan for all employees.

10. Which of the following plans applies only to employees of public schools, colleges and universities, and public charities?
    - ❑ a. 401(k) plans
    - ❑ b. 403(b) plans
    - ❑ c. 457(b) plans
    - ❑ d. Both b and c

11. Payroll must withhold federal income tax from:
    - ❑ a. Contributions to 401(k) plans.
    - ❑ b. Contributions to 457(b) plans.
    - ❑ c. Contributions to nonqualified deferred compensation plans.
    - ❑ d. Contributions to Roth 401(k) plans.

12. Are companies required to match employee contributions to 401(k) plans?
    - ❑ Yes
    - ❑ No

13. Which plan is specifically set up for government employees?
   - ❑ a. 401(k) plan
   - ❑ b. 457(b) plan
   - ❑ c. 403(b) plan
   - ❑ d. Nonqualified deferred compensation plan

4.6 Section 125 Flexible Benefit Plans

To accommodate the diverse needs of employees and their many types of families, employers are turning to flexible benefit plans, often called "cafeteria" plans.

Families include single parents, two-earner couples, stepparents, and a wide assortment of other arrangements. To accommodate the diverse needs of employees and their many types of families, employers are turning to flexible benefit plans, often called "cafeteria" plans.

4.6.1 Cafeteria Plans

Qualified "cafeteria" benefit plans fall under Section 125 of the Internal Revenue Code.

Qualified "cafeteria" benefit plans must meet the requirements of Section 125 of the Internal Revenue Code. They allow employees to select the types of tax-free benefits they need. Prior to the start of each plan year, employees select a benefit package from a "menu."

Once selected, benefits may be changed during the plan year only when there is a change in status, when the coverage or premiums change significantly, or when the employee leaves the company. A change in status could include marriage, divorce, death of spouse or dependent, birth or adoption, or a change in employment.

4.6.2 Possible Menu Choices

The benefit menu must include at least two benefits allowing the employee to receive cash or one or more qualified (nontaxable) benefits. Choices might include the following:

- Medical/dental coverage for the employee and/or the employee's spouse/children)
- Long-term care insurance
- Group-term life insurance
- Disability/accident coverage

- Dependent care (limited to $5,000; $2,500 if married and filing separately)
- Adoption assistance
- Vacation choices (e.g., regular vacation, "buying" additional days, or converting vacation days to cash)
- Cash or deferred arrangement (CODA)—only 401(k) plans; 403(b) and 457(b) plans cannot be included
- Two separate reimbursement or flexible spending accounts, one to pay for qualified medical expenses, such as eligible unreimbursed medical costs (limited to $2,550 in 2016), and another for dependent care
- Health Savings Accounts

Benefits that cannot be included are deferred compensation (except 401(k) plans), employee discounts, scholarship and fellowship grants, rides in commuter vans, employer-provided dependent group-term life insurance (cannot be included if benefit would also be eligible for exclusion under Section 132), and other nontaxable benefits (see the next section).

The IRS also allows after-tax employee contributions to cafeteria plans as well as pre-tax contributions. The after-tax contributions may only be made for qualified benefits.

4.6.3 Tax Implications

Most cafeteria plans allow employees to pay for their benefits with pretax dollars.

No Tax Withholding

The employer may contribute a fixed amount per employee to cover the cost of the benefits. Or the employer may deduct the cost of the chosen benefits from the employee's salary. Either way, the contributions are with pretax dollars; no amount is withheld for federal income tax. With the exception of 401(k) plans, cafeteria plan contributions are not subject to social security tax or Medicare tax. The amount set aside by the employee reduces the employee's taxable earnings.

The contributions are with pretax dollars; no amount is withheld for federal income tax.

Cafeteria plan contributions are not subject to social security tax or Medicare tax, with the exception of 401(k) plan contributions.

Cash Benefits Taxable

Any benefits converted to cash (for example, "selling" vacation days) become taxable income to the employee at the time the cash is received.

4.6.4 Flexible Spending Accounts

One type of reimbursement fund allows employees to use pretax dollars to pay for medical expenses.

Many cafeteria plans include separate reimbursement funds (also called flexible spending accounts). One type of reimbursement fund allows employees to use pretax dollars to pay for medical expenses, such as eyeglasses or eligible unreimbursed medical/dental expenses. Another type of fund allows employees to pay dependent care expenses with pretax dollars.

Use it or Lose it

During the year, employees elect to defer a portion of their wages to the fund and file claims against the fund based on their expenses incurred. Any amount not spent on benefits at the end of the plan year or its 2½-month grace period is lost to the employee. The plan may allow employees to carry over up to $500 from one plan year to the next without losing it, but a plan cannot have both a grace period and a carryover for the same year. Employees should carefully calculate how much to allocate to the reimbursement fund, because if they do not use it, they lose it.

Uniform Coverage Requirement

Employers must reimburse health-care-related flexible spending account claims up to the employee's total annual election even if the claim exceeds the employee's account balance.

Employer Options

A number of options are available to the employer for any funds remaining in the flexible spending account at the end of the plan year and any grace period, or in excess of any allowable carryover amount heath care FSA. For example, employers may use the funds to defray administrative costs of the plan.

Check Your Understanding

Quiz 4.4. Answer the following questions to test your understanding of flexible benefit plans.

1. What benefits can be provided in a Section 125 Cafeteria Plan?
    - ❑ a. Scholarships
    - ❑ b. Discounts
    - ❑ c. Medical insurance
    - ❑ d. Commuter vans

2. Cafeteria plans are authorized by what Internal Revenue Code Section?
    - ❑ a. 125
    - ❑ b. 401(k)
    - ❑ c. 403(b)
    - ❑ d. 457(b)

3. All of the following are tax implications of a Cafeteria Plan except:
    - ❑ a. no income tax withholding.
    - ❑ b. no social security and Medicare tax withholding.
    - ❑ c. must withhold income, social security and Medicare taxes.
    - ❑ d. no Form W-2 reporting.

4. One of the options in an employee's cafeteria benefit plan is a dependent care flexible spending account. He earmarked $100 per month to the account to pay for child care but spent only $1,000 by the end of the plan's grace period. At the end of the grace period, what happens to the $200 left in the account?
    - ❑ a. The amount is forfeited.
    - ❑ b. It will be added to his taxable income.
    - ❑ c. He can use it to "buy" an additional benefit.
    - ❑ d. It will carry over to the next year.

5. An employer contributes $200 per month to an employee cafeteria benefit plan. The pretax medical/dental package that she has chosen costs $250 per month. She contributes the extra $50 for this benefit plan. Payroll must withhold:
   □ a. Social security tax and Medicare tax from only the employee contribution.
   □ b. Social security tax, Medicare tax, and federal income tax from only the employee contribution.
   □ c. No tax from either the employee or employer contribution.
   □ d. Social security tax and Medicare tax from only the employer contribution.

6. An employer contributes $175 per month to an employee's cafeteria benefit plan. Since her husband has medical/dental coverage through his employer, she wants to take the $175 per month in cash. Which of the following statements is true?
   □ a. This option is not available; if the amount is not spent, it is lost.
   □ b. The $175 becomes taxable income.
   □ c. Only social security tax and Medicare tax are withheld from the $175 per month.
   □ d. The $175 is a tax-free benefit to her.

7. At the beginning of the year, an employee elected to buy group-term life insurance as part of his benefit package through his company's cafeteria benefit plan. In May, he took out an individual life insurance policy. Since he no longer needs group coverage, he wants to replace the insurance option with increased contributions to his 401(k) plan. Is this possible?
   □ a. Yes. If both group-term life and the 401(k) plan are part of the same cafeteria benefit program, he can switch.
   □ b. Yes, but he will have to pay taxes on the amount.
   □ c. No

8. All of the following features are characteristics of a Flexible Spending Account Cafeteria Plan except:
   □ a. Benefits are taxable
   □ b. Use it or lose it
   □ c. Uniform coverage
   □ d. Employer options for forfeited amounts

Answers to Quiz 4.1

1. b. These are de minimis fringes and are not taxable.

2. b. This represents a qualified employee discount. The discount is 10% less than the cost to customers (the limit is the company's gross profit percentage). Since it is available to sales clerks (and not just to highly compensated employees), it does not have to be included in her taxable compensation.

3. c. Dues to professional organizations are tax-free as working condition fringe benefits.

4. c. Both tests are met. Certainly, Chicago to Boston is over 50 miles. If the new employer also has reason to believe that the employee will meet the time test by staying in the area for 39 weeks, then the amounts are not subject to tax withholding.

5. c. The first two items (moving household items and travel to new job site) are qualified moving expense reimbursements. Meals, househunting trips, temporary living expenses ($1,500.00) and the expenses of purchasing a new home ($2,500.00) are taxable compensation under IRS regulations.

6. a. Let us review which expenses are not taxable and are excluded from income and which ones are taxable.

$5,000.00	Moving household goods (not taxable — excluded)
243.00	Traveling to new job site (not taxable — excluded)
50.00	Meals en route to the new location (taxable)
2,200.00	House-hunting and temporary living expenses (taxable)
3,000.00	Expenses related to purchase, sale, or lease of primary residence (taxable)
1,000.00	Real estate taxes (taxable)
$11,493.00	

    To summarize, $5,243.00 ($5,000.00 for moving household goods plus 243.00 (at $0.19 per mile) and lodging for travel are excluded from income.

7. a. Employer-provided parking is nontaxable up to $255.00 per month.

8. b. Employer-provided tokens for public transportation commuting expenses are nontaxable up to $255.00 per month.

Answers to Quiz 4.2

1. $1,200.00. The salesperson uses the car two-thirds for business and one-third (5,000 ÷ 15,000) for personal use. The lease value of a $12,000 automobile is $3,600, and $3,600 x 1/3 = $1,200.00.

2. $2,808.00 (5,200 miles x $0.54 per mile = $2,808.00)

3. a. If the employee is notified by January 31, the employer is not required to withhold federal income tax. Social security tax and Medicare tax must be withheld for the employee's personal use of the vehicle.

4. b. Most prizes and awards are taxable wages. One exception is qualified awards for length of service or safety.

Answers to Quiz 4.3

1. d

2. d

3. a

4. d

5. c

6. a

7. b. The maximum that employees who are not yet 50 years old can contribute to a 403(b) plan is $18,000. Such plans are available only to employees of tax-exempt organizations and public schools.

8. b. You must withhold social security tax and Medicare tax but not federal income tax from 401(k) contributions. Employee social security tax on $6,000 is $372.00 ($6,000 x 6.2%); Medicare tax is $87.00 ($6,000 x 1.45%); $372.00 + $87.00 = $459.00

9. b. Nonqualified deferred compensation plans can discriminate on behalf of key executives.

10. b. Section 403(b) of the Internal Revenue Code creates a tax-sheltered retirement plan for employees of tax-exempt nonprofit organizations like schools, colleges, universities, hospitals, or charities.

11. d. Contributions to Roth 401(k) plans are subject to withholding for federal income tax, social security tax, and Medicare tax.

12. No, although many employers do match 401(k) contributions. Employer matching can serve as an incentive to get higher participation in the plan.

13. b. 457(b) plans cover employees of state, county, and local governments.

Answers to Quiz 4.4

1. c

2. a

3. c

4. a. All money allocated to a flexible spending account (also called a reimbursement account) must be spent by the end of the year or any grace period or it is forfeited. The rule is use it or lose it.

5. c. Both the employer's contribution ($200 per month) and the employee's contribution ($50 per month) to the cafeteria benefit plan are in pretax dollars. Do not withhold any taxes.

6. b. Benefits converted to cash are added to an employee's taxable income. Federal income tax, social security tax, and Medicare tax must be withheld from the sum. The use it or lose it rule applies only to a flexible spending account.

7. c. Once selected, benefits cannot be changed or added to during the plan year (except for a change in family status).

8. a

Tax Reporting

If nothing else, just handling the various IRS forms makes your job complicated.

The payroll practitioner must be familiar with more than 40 tax forms (summarized in the following table), differentiate between various versions of the same form, know when each is to be used, and complete and file the appropriate form by the due date.

Federal Forms Used by the Payroll Department	
Form	**Title**
SS-4	*Application for Employer Identification Number*
SS-5	*Application for a Social Security Card*
SS-8	*Determination of Worker Status for Purposes of Federal Employment Taxes and Income Tax Withholding*
W-2	*Wage and Tax Statement*
W-2c	*Corrected Wage and Tax Statement*
W-3	*Transmittal of Wage and Tax Statements*
W-3c	*Transmittal of Corrected Wage and Tax Statements*
W-4	*Employee's Withholding Allowance Certificate*
W-4P	*Withholding Certificate for Pension or Annuity Payments*
W-4S	*Request for Federal Income Tax Withholding From Sick Pay*
940	*Employer's Annual Federal Unemployment (FUTA) Tax Return*
Form 940 (Schd. A)	*Multi-State Employer and Credit Reduction Information*
Form 940 (Schd. R)	*Allocation Schedule for Aggregate Form 940 Filers*
941	*Employer's Quarterly Federal Tax Return*
Form 941 (Schd. B)	*Report of Tax Liability for Semiweekly Schedule Depositors*
Form 941 (Schd. D)	*Report of Discrepancies Caused by Acquisitions, Statutory Mergers or Consolidations*

Federal Forms Used by the Payroll Department	
Form	**Title**
Form 941 (Schd. R)	*Allocation Schedule for Aggregate Form 941 Filers*
941-X	*Adjusted Employer's Quarterly Federal Tax Return or Claim for Refund*
943	*Employer's Annual Federal Return for Agricultural Employees*
943-A	*Agricultural Employer's Record of Federal Tax Liability*
944	*Employer's Annual Federal Return*
945	*Annual Return of Withheld Federal Income Tax*
945-A	*Annual Record of Federal Tax Liability*
945-X	*Adjusted Annual Return of Withheld Federal Income Tax or Claim for Refund*
1042	*Annual Withholding Tax Return for U.S. Source Income of Foreign Persons*
1042-S	*Foreign Person's U.S. Source Income Subject to Withholding*
1042-T	*Annual Summary and Transmittal of Forms 1042-S*
1094-C	*Transmittal of Employer-Provided Health Insurance Offer and Coverage Information Returns*
1095-C	*Employer-Provided Health Insurance Offer and Coverage*
1094-B	*Transmittal of Health Coverage Information Returns*
1095-B	*Employer-Provided Health Insurance Offer and Coverage*
1096	*Annual Summary and Transmittal of U.S. Information Returns*
1099-MISC	*Miscellaneous Income*
2848	*Power of Attorney and Declaration of Representative*
4419	*Application for Filing Information Returns Electronically (FIRE)*

Federal Forms Used by the Payroll Department	
Form	**Title**
4852	*Substitute for Form W-2, Wage and Tax Statement or Form 1099-R, Distribution from Pensions, Annuities, Retirement or Profit Sharing Plans, IRAs, Insurance Contracts, etc.*
Nontax forms	
I-9	Employment Eligibility Verification
SSA-131	Employer Report of Special Wage Payments

5.1 Depositing Federal Taxes

The federal government requires employers to deposit withheld federal income tax, social security tax, and Medicare tax as well as the employer's social security tax and Medicare tax according to strict schedules. Depending on the size and frequency of your payrolls, you could be required to make daily deposits. An employer may be assessed penalties for any noncompliance.

Employer Identification Numbers (EIN)

The IRS issues Employer Identification Numbers (EIN) to companies to facilitate the tracking of tax deposits and tax returns. Each company applies for an EIN using IRS Form SS-4, *Application for an Employer Identification Number.* The EIN is shown on all transactions with the IRS:

- Making tax deposits
- Filing tax returns
- Responding to IRS notices

5.1.1 Tax Deposit Requirements

Your tax deposit schedule for a calendar year is determined from the total taxes on your Form 941, *Employer's Quarterly Tax Return*, in a four-quarter lookback period. The lookback period begins July 1 of the second preceding year and ends June 30 of the prior year. The lookback period for calendar year 2016 is:

2014   2015

[Jul–Sep] [Oct–Dec]   [Jan–Mar] [Apr–June]

If you reported $50,000.00 or less in employment taxes for the look-back period, you are a monthly depositor. If you reported more than $50,000.00, you are a semiweekly depositor. Three special exceptions are the $1,000.00 (annual), $2,500.00 (quarterly), and $100,000.00 (one-day) rules. It is your responsibility to deposit using the correct timing. The deposit rules and schedule are summarized in the table below.

Deposit Schedule

Deposit Schedule	
Accumulated Payroll Taxes	**Deposit Due**
Annual If employment tax history shows a liability less than $1,000.00 during the year and aggregate annual tax liability is less than $2,500.00	January 31 or pay with Form 944
Quarterly If total liability is less than $2,500.00 for the current or previous quarter.	By end of month after end of quarter or pay quarterly with Form 941
If a Form 944 filer's aggregate tax liability is more than $2,500.00 for the year but less than $2,500.00 for the quarter.	By end of month after end of quarter; for 4th quarter, by following January 31 or pay with Form 944
Monthly If aggregate amount of employment taxes reported for the look back period is $50,000.00 or less. If a Form 944 filer's aggregate employment tax liability equals or exceeds $2,500.00 but less than $100,000.00 on any day during the month.	On or before the 15th day of the following month

Deposit Schedule	
Accumulated Payroll Taxes	**Deposit Due**
Semiweekly If aggregate amount of employment taxes reported for the look back period exceeds $50,000 and the specific liability is less than $100,000.00	• If liability occurs on Wednesday, Thursday, and/or Friday, deposit on or before following Wednesday • If liability occurs on Saturday, Sunday, Monday, and/Tuesday, deposit on or before following Friday • Or deposit on third business day after payday
One-day deposit If any accumulation of employment taxes is $100,000.00 or more during any monthly or semiweekly period	By the end of the next business day

5.1.2 Clarification of the Rules

When Does the $1,000 Annual Rule Apply?

Employers with a history of annual employment taxes of less than $1,000.00 are designated by the IRS to file Form 944, *Employer's Annual Tax Return* and will pay the taxes annually. If during a year an employer designated to file Form 944 has annual employment taxes of less than $1,000.00, the employer may pay the taxes due with Form 944 or deposit the taxes no later than January 31. If a Form 944 filer's aggregate employment tax liability exceeds $1,000.00, they can file Form 944 for the year but must file Form 941 for subsequent years and must make deposits under the monthly or semiweekly rule. If a Form 944 filer's aggregate tax liability exceeds $100,000 on any day in a deposit period, the Form 944 filer must deposit the tax liability the next day (see below) and deposit all future liabilities on a semiweekly schedule.

When Does the $2,500 Quarterly Rule Apply?

Special Tips

If an employer accumulates less than $2,500.00 of total tax liability during a quarter, or the preceding quarter no payments are required until you file the quarterly tax return. However, if you are unsure that the liability will be less than $2,500, it would be prudent to deposit in accordance with the monthly depositor rules. This avoids any penalties in case you do go over the $2,500 limit.

When Does the $100,000 One-Day Rule Apply?

If the total accumulated tax reaches $100,000.00 or more on any day during a deposit period (monthly or semiweekly), you must deposit it by the next business day. This applies whether an employer is an annual, monthly or semiweekly depositor.

For purposes of the $100,000.00 rule, do not continue accumulating employment tax liability after the end of a deposit period. A deposit period is:

- A calendar month for monthly depositors.
- Wednesday through Friday or Saturday through Tuesday for semiweekly depositors.
- The year-to-date for annual depositors.

When do Monthly Depositors Change Status?

Employers cease to be monthly depositors when they first become subject to the one-day deposit rule. At that time they become semiweekly depositors for the balance of the current year and the following year.

An employer also ceases being a monthly depositor when during the lookback period the tax liability exceeds $50,000. At the beginning of the next calendar year, the employer should deposit under the semiweekly rules.

How Is the Deposit Liability Fixed?

Deposit liability is fixed at the end of the deposit period (semiweekly - Tuesday and Friday; monthly - last day of the month), regardless of any additional liability incurred before depositing the liability.

What Are the Holiday Deposit Rules?

When a deposit is required to be made on a day that is a legal holiday in the District of Columbia, use the following rules:

- For monthly and one-day depositors, a deposit is considered to have been made in a timely manner if it is made by the close of the next business day after a holiday.
- A semiweekly depositor will have at least three business days in which to deposit the amount. Thus, a semiweekly depositor with a Friday payroll will have until the following Thursday to deposit taxes if the Monday, Tuesday, or Wednesday following payday is a federal legal holiday.

What Happens at the end of the Quarter?

Semiweekly deposit periods may not end on the last day of the quarter. Liabilities incurred covering two quarters in one semiweekly period require multiple deposits to identify the correct quarters.

What Happens When an Off-cycle Check is Issued?

Due to the constructive receipt rules (page 3-3), off-cycle checks are the same as checks issued by the payroll system in the eyes of the IRS. The IRS requires that for a semiweekly depositor the federal tax liability from the off-cycle check be deposited for the semiweekly period when the payment was made. Thus, if a off-cycle check is issued on Tuesday the taxes must be deposited by the next Friday.

Deposit liability is fixed at the end of the deposit period, regardless of any additional liability incurred before depositing the liability.

Liabilities incurred covering two quarters in one semiweekly period require multiple deposits to identify the correct quarters.

5.1.3 Safe-Harbor Rule (98% rule)

You will be considered to have satisfied the deposit requirements if you deposit in a timely manner at least 98% of your tax liability, or if any deposit shortfall does not exceed $100.00, whichever is larger. However, the IRS requires the 2% shortfall to be deposited at a later date.

When Must I Make up a Deposit Shortfall?

If you deposit 98% of your tax liability, you must make up the remaining 2%. The make-up deposit is due:

- For monthly depositors, the shortfall must be paid by the due date of quarterly Form 941. The make-up amount may be paid with Form 941-V, or deposited using the Electronic Federal Tax Payment System (EFTPS).
- For semiweekly and one-day depositors, the shortfall must be deposited, using EFTPS, on or before the first Wednesday or Friday, whichever is earlier, that falls on or after the 15th of the month after the deposit was due, or no later than the due date of quarterly Form 941.

Can I Avoid Penalties If I Deposit Less Than 98%?

Employers may request that penalties be abated when they can show that the failure to deposit the full amount of employment taxes was due to reasonable cause. For example, a reasonable cause might be when information is not available on a timely basis and you cannot reasonably estimate the missing items.

5.1.4 Making Deposits

Here are some key facts about depositing federal taxes.

The Electronic Federal Tax Payment System (EFTPS)

All employers are required to use the Electronic Federal Tax Payment System (EFTPS) to make their federal tax deposits. Annual, quarterly, and monthly depositors making a shortfall payment are able to pay the taxes due when filing Form 940 or 941.

Payments made through EFTPS use the automated clearinghouse (ACH) financial network. This network transfers funds and passes tax payment information to the IRS. The IRS has provided two primary methods to make tax deposits using EFTPS: EFTPS-Direct (ACH debit) and EFTPS-Through a Financial Institution (ACH credit). If you choose to make your payments via EFTPS-Direct you must contact the IRS to make an electronic payment. If you choose to use EFTPS-Through a Financial Institution to make your payments, you will instruct your financial institution to begin the transaction.

EFTPS-Through a Financial Institution (ACH Credit)

You need to check with your banking institution to find out its processing policy for beginning the transaction and issuing confirmation or acknowledgment notifications. EFTPS will provide your company with a PIN number that will allow access to EFTPS to verify that the IRS received the payment. Payment deadlines are set by the bank that initiates the payment. If a due date falls on a holiday, payments must be initiated on the business day before the holiday and will be effective on the next business day following the holiday.

EFTPS-Direct (ACH Debit)

After enrolling in EFTPS, the IRS will issue an electronic federal tax personal identification number which you may use to begin your transaction and to receive acknowledgment that your transaction was initiated. You use this number to initiate a deposit when using your personal

Real-world Application

Alert

If a due date falls on a holiday, payments must be initiated on the business day before the holiday.

computer or telephone. Deposits may be initiated through the IRS 24 hours a day, seven days a week. However, deposits must be initiated before 8:00 pm eastern time to be deposited the next day.

Electronic Tax Application (ETA)

Using the Federal Reserve System Fedwire transfer system through your bank allows you to make deposits on the date they are due. These deposits must reach the local Federal Reserve Bank by 5:00 pm Eastern Time.

Payment with a Tax Return

If you are not required to deposit through EFTPS, you may do so voluntarily or you can mail the payment with Form 941 or 944.

Check Your Understanding

Check Your Understanding

Quiz 5.1. Answer the following questions to test your understanding of federal tax deposits.

1. To determine if an employer is a monthly or semiweekly depositor for 2016, the lookback period is?
    - ❑ a. January 1 - December 31, 2015
    - ❑ b. October 1, 2014 - September 30, 2015
    - ❑ c. July 1, 2014 - June 30, 2015
    - ❑ d. January 1 - December 31, 2014

2. If the employer's total tax liability for the quarter is less than $2,500, when must the taxes be paid?
    - ❑ a. By the due date of Form 941
    - ❑ b. By the 15th of the month after the withholding
    - ❑ c. By Wednesday or Friday under the semiweekly rules
    - ❑ d. By the next business day

3. If the employer's total tax liability for the lookback period is $48,000, when must a tax liability of less than $100,000.00 be deposited?
   - ❑ a. By the due date of Form 941
   - ❑ b. By the 15th of the month after the withholding
   - ❑ c. By Wednesday or Friday under the semiweekly rules
   - ❑ d. By the next banking day

4. If the employer's total tax liability for the lookback period is $75,000, when must tax liability of less than $100,000.00 be deposited?
   - ❑ a. By the due date of Form 941
   - ❑ b. By the 15th of the month after the withholding
   - ❑ c. By Wednesday or Friday under the semiweekly rules
   - ❑ d. By the next business day

5. If the employer's total tax liability for a payday is $150,000, when must the taxes be deposited?
   - ❑ a. By the due date of Form 941
   - ❑ b. By the 15th of the month after the withholding
   - ❑ c. By Wednesday or Friday under the semiweekly rules
   - ❑ d. By the next business day

6. A company pays semimonthly on the 15th and the last day of the month. The company reported $40,000 for federal income tax, social security tax, and Medicare tax withheld from employees' wages and the employer's social security tax and Medicare tax during the lookback period. This month, one payday occurs on Wednesday, January 15th. When is the company required to make a tax deposit?
   - ❑ a. Within three business days of the 15th
   - ❑ b. On or before the following Wednesday
   - ❑ c. With its quarterly Form 941
   - ❑ d. On or before the 15th of the following month

7. The company (see Question 6) paid only 98% of its tax liability on the due date (February 15). Which of the following is true?
   - ❑ a. It faces a stiff penalty for failure to pay its obligation.
   - ❑ b. The remaining 2% must be paid by March 15.
   - ❑ c. The remaining 2% must be paid by the due date of its first quarter Form 941.
   - ❑ d. The remaining 2% must be paid by December 31.

8. A company filing Form 941 can pay employment taxes quarterly if its accumulated tax liability for the quarter is less than $2,500:
   - ❏ a. for the entire quarter.
   - ❏ b. at the end of the month.
   - ❏ c. at the end of the semiweekly period.
   - ❏ d. during the lookback period.

9. A company is a semiweekly depositor. On its weekly Friday payday, it has a deposit liability of $50,000.00. When must the company deposit its payroll taxes?
   - ❏ a. By the following Wednesday.
   - ❏ b. By the following Friday.
   - ❏ c. By the following Monday.
   - ❏ d. By the 15th of the following month.

10. An employer's tax deposit status always remains the same for the entire year.
    - ❏ True
    - ❏ False

11. A semiweekly depositor has a Friday payroll with a tax liability of $85,000. The next Monday is a holiday. When must the employer deposit the taxes to avoid penalties?
    - ❏ a. The next Monday
    - ❏ b. The next Wednesday
    - ❏ c. The next Thursday
    - ❏ d. The next Friday

12. A company is a semiweekly depositor. Its next deposit is due on Wednesday, which falls on a federal holiday. To be considered timely, the company's deposit of federal payroll taxes must be made on or before the close of business on:
    - ❏ a. Tuesday.
    - ❏ b. Thursday.
    - ❏ c. Monday.
    - ❏ d. Friday.

13. A semiweekly depositor has accumulated a liability of $95,000 on Friday. On Saturday, it accumulates a $10,000 liability. Does the one-day rule apply?
    - ❏ a. Yes
    - ❏ b. No

14. Under what circumstances could an employer be required to make daily deposits?
   - ❑ a. If their accumulated tax liability is $100,000 or more
   - ❑ b. If their accumulated tax deposits are $100,000 or more
   - ❑ c. This is not required by the law.

15. Between paydays, an employer must issue a off-cycle check to a terminating employee. The employer can hold the tax liability until the next regular payday to make the tax deposit.
   - ❑ True
   - ❑ False

16. If you are not using EFTPS to make a tax payment, where must it be made?
   - ❑ a. The IRS
   - ❑ b. Any local bank
   - ❑ c. The Federal Reserve Bank
   - ❑ d. The U.S. Treasury

17. What is EFTPS?
   - ❑ a. Electronic Federal Tax Payment System
   - ❑ b. Electric Federal Tax Purchase System
   - ❑ c. Everyone's Federal Tax Payment System
   - ❑ d. Electronic Federal Tax Payment Services

18. All of the following are methods to use when making EFTPS deposits EXCEPT:
   - ❑ a. ACH Credit.
   - ❑ b. Checks and Form 941.
   - ❑ c. ACH Debit.
   - ❑ d. Electronic Tax Application.

5.2 Quarterly Tax Returns

Regardless of how often tax deposits are made, most employers who withhold federal income tax, social security tax, and Medicare tax must file quarterly tax returns. Employers filing quarterly fill out Form 941, *Employer's Quarterly Federal Tax Return.* Very small employers may be designated by the IRS to file Form 944 annually to report wages and taxes, while agricultural employers file Form 943 annually.

At the time this book went to press, the IRS had released a draft of the 2016 Form 941. The Supplement to this book will include the 2016 Form 941. For 2016, Form 941 is essentially unchanged from 2015.

5.2.1 Form 941, *Employer's Quarterly Federal Tax Return*

Form 941 is used to report the following:

- Wages, tips, and other compensation
- Amount of federal income tax withheld from wages and tips
- Total wages and tips subject to social security tax and Medicare tax
- Total deposits for the quarter and the balance due or any overpayment

Form 941 is due on or before the last day of the month following the end of the quarter. (Quarters end on March 31, June 30, September 30, and December 31.) Employers can take a 10-day filing extension if they have made timely tax deposits for the full amount due. If the due date for the return falls on a Saturday, Sunday, or legal holiday, the return must be filed on the next business day.

Some Employers Do Not Have to File Form 941 Quarterly.

Exceptions to the Rule

Quarterly filing is not required for seasonal employers with no tax liabilities and no wages paid during the quarter. If you use this option, be sure that the seasonal box on Line 16 is checked when Form 941 is filed.

Employers who only employ household employees use Form 1040, Schedule H, *U.S. Individual Income Tax Return.*

Employers of farm workers use Form 943, *Employer's Annual Tax Return for Agricultural Employees.*

Business reorganizations and terminations require special review to ensure that wages and taxes are reported correctly.

Employers with a history of an annual tax liability that is less than $1,000 and that are designated by the IRS to file Form 944, *Employer's Annual Tax Return.*

Filing Form 941

File Form 941 with the IRS at the address designated on the form's instructions based on the location of your business.

When mailing Form 941, in order for the IRS to consider the form to be filed timely it must be postmarked by the form's due date. Mail the return certified, with a return receipt requested, to be able to document delivery to the IRS.

You can also send your form via a private delivery service. The IRS also allows several private delivery services (PDS) to deliver tax forms. However, to be filed timely using a PDS, the PDS must meet strict requirements and the form must be given to the PDS by the form's due date. The PDS can document the delivery of Form 941 to the IRS. The IRS has announced the following delivery companies and their specific types of service qualify as a PDS.

Federal Express (FedEx): FedEx First Overnight, FedEx Priority Overnight, FedEx Standard Overnight, FedEx 2 Day, FedEx International Next Flight Out, FedEx International Priority, FedEx International First, and FedEx International Economy

United Parcel Service (UPS): UPS Next Day Air Early AM, UPS Next Day Air, UPS Next Day Air Saver, UPS 2nd Day Air, UPS 2nd Day Air A.M., UPS Worldwide Express Plus, and UPS Worldwide Express

When you do not mail Form 941 with the U.S. Postal Service, you must use one of the delivery services listed above. Thus, the "timely mailing as timely filing" rule does not apply to any other type of delivery service offered by the designated PDSs.

5.2.2 Form 941 Preparation

Real-world Application

Form 941 is no longer processed by machine scanning. Complying with the following suggestions will assist the IRS in processing the form efficiently:

- Make dollar entries without the dollar sign and comma (0000.00).
- Enter negative amounts with a minus (-) sign preceding the amount.

A copy of the Form 941 instructions are found in the Appendix, page A-65.

When preparing Form 941, make dollar entries without the dollar sign and comma (0000.00.), and enter negative amounts with a minus (-) sign preceeding the amount.

Form **941 for 2016:** Employer's QUARTERLY Federal Tax Return
(Rev. January 2016)   Department of the Treasury — Internal Revenue Service

950114
OMB No. 1545-0029

Employer identification number (EIN) [ ][ ] — [ ][ ][ ][ ][ ][ ]

Name *(not your trade name)*

Trade name *(if any)*

Address
Number   Street   Suite or room number
City   State   ZIP code
Foreign country name   Foreign province/county   Foreign postal code

Report for this Quarter of 2016
(Check one.)

☐ **1:** January, February, March
☐ **2:** April, May, June
☐ **3:** July, August, September
☐ **4:** October, November, December

Instructions and prior year forms are available at *www.irs.gov/form941*.

Read the separate instructions before you complete Form 941. Type or print within the boxes.

Part 1: Answer these questions for this quarter.

1   Number of employees who received wages, tips, or other compensation for the pay period including: *Mar. 12* (Quarter 1), *June 12* (Quarter 2), *Sept. 12* (Quarter 3), or *Dec. 12* (Quarter 4)   **1** [   ]

2   Wages, tips, and other compensation   **2** [.]

3   Federal income tax withheld from wages, tips, and other compensation   **3** [.]

4   If no wages, tips, and other compensation are subject to social security or Medicare tax   ☐ Check and go to line 6.

		Column 1		Column 2
5a	Taxable social security wages . .	[.]	× .124 =	[.]
5b	Taxable social security tips . . .	[.]	× .124 =	[.]
5c	Taxable Medicare wages & tips. .	[.]	× .029 =	[.]
5d	Taxable wages & tips subject to Additional Medicare Tax withholding	[.]	× .009 =	[.]

5e   Add Column 2 from lines 5a, 5b, 5c, and 5d   **5e** [.]

5f   Section 3121(q) Notice and Demand—Tax due on unreported tips (see instructions)   **5f** [.]

6   Total taxes before adjustments. Add lines 3, 5e, and 5f   **6** [.]

7   Current quarter's adjustment for fractions of cents   **7** [.]

8   Current quarter's adjustment for sick pay   **8** [.]

9   Current quarter's adjustments for tips and group-term life insurance   **9** [.]

10   Total taxes after adjustments. Combine lines 6 through 9   **10** [.]

11   Total deposits for this quarter, including overpayment applied from a prior quarter and overpayments applied from Form 941-X, 941-X (PR), 944-X, or 944-X (SP) filed in the current quarter   **11** [.]

12   Balance due. If line 10 is more than line 11, enter the difference and see instructions   **12** [.]

13   Overpayment. If line 11 is more than line 10, enter the difference [.]   Check one: ☐ Apply to next return. ☐ Send a refund.

▶ You MUST complete both pages of Form 941 and SIGN it.   Next ▶

For Privacy Act and Paperwork Reduction Act Notice, see the back of the Payment Voucher.   Cat. No. 17001Z   Form **941** (Rev. 1-2016)

95021

Name *(not your trade name)*	Employer identification number (EIN)

Part 2: Tell us about your deposit schedule and tax liability for this quarter.

If you are unsure about whether you are a monthly schedule depositor or a semiweekly schedule depositor, see section 11 of Pub. 15.

14 Check one: ☐ Line 10 on this return is less than $2,500 or line 10 on the return for the prior quarter was less than $2,500, and you did not incu $100,000 next-day deposit obligation during the current quarter. If line 10 for the prior quarter was less than $2,500 but line 10 on this ret is $100,000 or more, you must provide a record of your federal tax liability. If you are a monthly schedule depositor, complete the dep schedule below; if you are a semiweekly schedule depositor, attach Schedule B (Form 941). Go to Part 3.

☐ **You were a monthly schedule depositor for the entire quarter.** Enter your tax liability for each month and to liability for the quarter, then go to Part 3.

Tax liability: Month 1 [.]

Month 2 [.]

Month 3 [.]

Total liability for quarter [.]   **Total must equal line 10.**

☐ **You were a semiweekly schedule depositor for any part of this quarter.** Complete Schedule B (Form 941), Report of Tax Liability for Semiweekly Schedule Depositors, and attach it to Form 941.

Part 3: Tell us about your business. If a question does NOT apply to your business, leave it blank.

15 If your business has closed or you stopped paying wages . . . . ☐ Check here, and

enter the final date you paid wages [/ /] .

16 If you are a seasonal employer and you do not have to file a return for every quarter of the year . . ☐ Check here.

Part 4: May we speak with your third-party designee?

Do you want to allow an employee, a paid tax preparer, or another person to discuss this return with the IRS? See the instructions for details.

☐ Yes. Designee's name and phone number [ ] [ ]

Select a 5-digit Personal Identification Number (PIN) to use when talking to the IRS. [ ][ ][ ][ ][ ]

☐ No.

Part 5: Sign here. You MUST complete both pages of Form 941 and SIGN it.

Under penalties of perjury, I declare that I have examined this return, including accompanying schedules and statements, and to the best of my knowledge and belief, it is true, correct, and complete. Declaration of preparer (other than taxpayer) is based on all information of which preparer has any knowledge.

X **Sign your name here** [ ]   Print your name here [ ]

Print your title here [ ]

Date [/ /]   Best daytime phone [ ]

Paid Preparer Use Only   Check if you are self-employed . . . ☐

Preparer's name		PTIN	
Preparer's signature		Date	/ /
Firm's name (or yours if self-employed)		EIN	
Address		Phone	
City		State	ZIP code

Form **941** (Rev. 1-20

Chapter 5 | Form 941 Line-by-Line Instructions

Following are line-by-line instructions for the Form 941 based on the draft 2016 Form 941. The supplement will contain the 2016 Form 941 and instructions.

Line 1—Number of employees

Complete this line for each quarter. Only include the number of employees who were paid during the pay period that contains March 12, June 12, September 12, or December 12, respectively. Do not include household employees, those employees not receiving pay, pensioners, or members of the armed forces.

Line 2—Total wages and tips subject to withholding, plus other compensation

Taxable amounts are reported even if income tax withholding is not required.

Enter the total wages paid, tips reported to the employer, taxable fringe benefits provided, and other compensation paid to employees that is subject to federal income tax. Taxable amounts are reported even if income tax withholding is not required, for example, group-term life insurance. Elective deferrals, such as contributions to qualified deferred compensation plans or Section 125 plans, are not included, since they are not taxable wages paid. Pension payments from qualified plans, annuities, supplemental unemployment benefits, and gambling winnings are not included even if withholding is required from the payments.

When the employer receives timely notice that employees are receiving taxable sick pay from a third party, the payments subject to income tax are reported on Form 941, Line 2.

Line 3—Total income tax withheld from wages, tips, and sick pay

Enter the income tax withheld from wages, tips, taxable fringe benefits, and supplemental unemployment compensation benefits.

The amount withheld by a third-party insurance company from sick pay provided to the employer's employees is not included in the employer's total reported as it is reported on the third-party insurance company's Form 941.

Line 4

If no wages are subject to social security or Medicare tax, check the box.

Line 5a, Column 1—Taxable social security wages

Enter the total wages subject to social security tax that were paid to employees during the quarter. Include any sick payments made to the employer's employees by third parties that were reported in a timely manner and any fringe benefits subject to social security tax. Do not include tips on this line.

When an employee's wages (including tips) exceed $118,500.00 in 2016, stop reporting the wages. However, continue to withhold Medicare and income tax when the wages exceed the social security wage base of $118,500.00.

Line 5a, Column 2—Social security tax

Multiply the wages on Line 5a, column 1 by 12.4% and place this amount in the box. The calculation determines the employees' and employer's social security tax. Do not use the amount of tax withheld to calculate social security wages. When the employer is not able to withhold the tax based on group-term life insurance provided to terminated employees, an adjustment for the tax not withheld is required on Line 9.

Line 5b, Column 1—Taxable social security tips

Enter all tips employees have reported during the quarter, until the total of the tips and wages (reported on Line 5a, column 1) reaches $118,500.00 for any single employee in 2016. Report amounts subject to social security even if the tax was not withheld.

When the employer is not able to withhold the tax on tips, an adjustment for the tax not withheld is required on Line 9.

Do not include allocated tips on this line. Allocated tips are reported on Form 8027, *Employer's Annual Information Return of Tip Income and Allocated Tips*, and Form W-2. Allocated tips are not subject to income, social security, or Medicare tax withholding.

Line 5b, Column 2—Social security tax on tips

Multiply the tips in Line 5b, column 1 by 12.4% and place this amount in the box. The calculation determines the employees' and employer's social security tax liability on tips. If the social security tax could not be withheld from the employees' tips, report the taxes not withheld on Line 9 as an adjustment.

Do not include tips on Line 5a, column 1.

Line 5c, Column 1—Taxable medicare wages and tips

Enter the total wages subject to Medicare taxes that were paid to the employees during the quarter. Include any sick pay provided to the employer's employees by third parties that were reported in a timely manner and taxable fringe benefits subject to Medicare tax.

Include tips on this line. Report tips subject to Medicare even if the tax was not withheld.

Line 5c, Column 2—Medicare tax

The calculation on line 5c, column 2 determines the employees' and employer's Medicare tax.

Multiply the wages and tips in Line 5c, column 1 by 2.9% and place this amount in the box. The calculation determines the employees' and employer's Medicare tax. If the Medicare tax could not be withheld from the employees' tips or group-term life insurance provided to terminated employees, an adjustment must be entered on Line 9. Do not use the amount of Medicare tax withheld to calculate wages.

Line 5d, Column 1—Taxable Medicare wages and tips subject to additional Medicare tax withholding

Report the Medicare wages paid an employee in excess of $200,000 during the quarter. Include any sick pay provided to the employer's employees by third parties that were reported in a timely manner and taxable fringe benefits subject to Medicare tax. Include tips and group-term life insurance even when the employer is not able to withhold Medicare tax on the tips or group-term life insurance provided to terminated employees.

Line 5d, Column 2—Additional Medicare tax

Multiply the wages and tips on Line 5d, Column 1, by 0.9% and place this amount in the box. If the additional Medicare tax on tips and group-term life insurance could not be withheld report the amount by the Medicare tax that could not be withheld. Report the additional Medicare tax on tips of group-term life insurance that could not be withheld as an adjustment in Line 9.

Line 5e—Total social security and Medicare taxes

Enter the total social security and Medicare taxes (Column 2 Line 5a + Line 5b + Line 5c + Line 5d).

Line 5f—Section 3121(q) Notice and Demand — Tax due on unreported tips

Enter here the social security and Medicare taxes you are required to pay on tips that were not reported by your employees after receiving a Notice and Demand from the IRS.

Line 6—Total taxes before adjustments

Add the total federal income tax withheld from wages, tips, and other compensation (Line 3), the total social security and Medicare taxes before adjustments (Line 5e), and the tax assessed on unreported tips (Line 5f). Enter the result on Line 6.

Lines 7-9—Tax adjustments

Adjustments included on this series of lines (7-9) must be included on Line 14 of Form 941 or on Schedule B to accurately report total tax liability. The adjustment will be deposited using the appropriate deposit methodology.

If an employee's wages or withheld taxes are being adjusted, Forms W-2c and W-3c or a "corrected" Form W-2 may be required.

Current Quarter Adjustments

Line 7—Fractions of cents

Enter fractions of cents due to rounding of the employee's social security and Medicare tax calculations in the current quarter.

Line 8—Sick pay

Enter social security and Medicare taxes withheld from employees' sick pay paid by third parties.

Line 9—Tips and group-term life insurance

Enter adjustments due to uncollected social security and Medicare taxes on tips or group-term life insurance from terminated employees with continuing coverage.

Employment tax adjustment process. If you discover an error on a previously filed Form 941, make the correction using Form 941-X, *Adjusted Employer's Quarterly Federal Tax Return or Claim for Refund*. Form 941-X is a stand-alone form, meaning you can file Form 941-X when an error is discovered, rather than waiting until the end of the quarter.

Form 941-X is used to report adjustments to amounts reported on Form 941.

Line 10—Total taxes after adjustments

Add Lines 6 through 9.

Line 11—Total deposits for the quarter

The deposits made for the quarter are entered on this line. The amounts will be accumulated from records of EFTPS deposits made for the quarter. If an overpayment was indicated on the previous quarter's Form 941 or a Form 941-X to be applied to the next return, add that amount to the current quarter's deposits.

Line 12—Balance due

Subtract Line 10 from Line 11.

For semiweekly depositors, this amount should be less than $1.00. Semiweekly depositors cannot make a payment with Form 941 and not be penalized. For a semiweekly depositor, if the amount on Line 12 is greater than $1.00, the amount must be deposited by the due date for the last shortfall deposit to avoid penalties.

For monthly depositors, if the amount on Line 10 is less than $2,500.00, they may pay the tax when filing Form 941 or deposit by the due date for Form 941.

Line 13—Overpayment

An overpayment indicates that the deposits have exceeded the amount due for the quarter.

If Line 11 is greater than Line 10, enter the difference. An overpayment indicates that the deposits have exceeded the amount due for the quarter. The overpayment may be applied to the next quarter, or a refund may be requested. The choice must be indicated by marking the appropriate check box.

Amounts should not appear on both Lines 12 and 13.

If the amounts in Lines 10 and 11 are equal, leave Lines 12 and 13 blank.

Line 14

Monthly depositors will complete Line 14 and check the monthly check box. If the employer is a semiweekly depositor, Schedule B must be completed and the semiweekly check box must be checked. If Line 10 is less than $2,500.00, neither Line 14 nor Schedule B is completed and the appropriate box is checked.

The monthly liabilities incurred are summarized:

- Month 1 is used for January, April, July, or October, respectively.

- Month 2 is used for February, May, August, or November, respectively.
- Month 3 is used for March, June, September, or December, respectively.
- Total is the total liability for the quarter (the sum of month 1, month 2, and month 3).

The amounts reported on Line 14 constitute the liability, not the amount deposited and should agree to the amount reported on Line 10.

Third-Party Designee

Employers may allow any employee, a paid tax preparer, or another person to discuss the Form 941 with the IRS. This can be done by checking the "Yes" box in Part 4 of Form 941. The designee's name, phone number and personal identification number (any five numbers chosen by the designee) are entered in the appropriate places.

When the third party is designated the IRS is authorized to call the designee to answer any question relating to the information reported on the tax return. The designee is also authorized to:

- Exchange with the IRS any information that is missing from the return.
- Request and receive written tax return information relating to this return.
- The designation does not authorize the designee to receive any refund checks, or otherwise represent your organization before the IRS.

The designation can be revoked in writing to the IRS and only applies to the issues arising from the processing of this return. The designation expires 1 year after the due date of the return.

Signing Form 941

Before filing the completed Form 941, the form must be signed by

- The individual owning the business, if the employer is a sole proprietorship.
- The president, vice president, or other principal corporate officer if the employer is a corporation.

Employers may allow any employee, individual, corporation, firm, organization, or partnership to discuss the Form 941 with the IRS.

- An authorized member or partner of an unincorporated association or partnership having knowledge of the organization's affairs.
- A fiduciary if the employer is a trust or estate.

Employers wishing to have an attorney, accountant, other representative, or employee not listed above sign their employment tax returns must obtain a proper power of attorney by completing and filing Form 2848, *Power of Attorney and Declaration of Representative*. The employer must make certain to clearly explain the extent of the authority given the representative by the power of attorney.

Paid preparers. A paid preparer must sign Form 941 and provide the information in the Paid Preparer's Use Only section of Part 5 if the preparer was paid to prepare Form 941 and is not an employee of the employer filing Form 941. Paid preparers must sign Form 941 with a manual signature. Paid preparers (not employees) must enter their SSN or Preparer Tax Identification Number and include the preparer's full address. If a firm prepares Form 941, enter the firm's EIN.

5.2.3 Alternative Forms

Some employers use forms other than Form 941 for reporting taxes withheld.

Some employers use other forms for reporting taxes withheld.

Form 941-X, *Adjusted Employer's Quarterly Federal Tax Return or Claim for Refund*

Use Form 941-X (page A-83) to correct errors on a Form 941 that you previously filed. The IRS has released a draft of Form 941-X. Further information will be in the supplement to the book. Use Form 941-X to correct:

- Wages, tips, and other compensation
- Income tax withheld from wages, tips, and other compensation
- Taxable social security wages
- Taxable social security tips
- Taxable Medicare wages and tips

Use a separate Form 941-X for each quarter that you are correcting. If you did not file a Form 941 for one or more quarters, **do not** use Form 941-X. Instead, file Form 941 for each of those quarters.

Form 943, *Employer's Annual Federal Tax Return for Agricultural Employees*

Use Form 943 to report taxes on agricultural employees. Form 943 is an annual return, and is due on January 31. If the organization has both agricultural employees and other employees, the organization will file both Forms 943 and 941.

Form 944, *Employer's Annual Federal Tax Return*

Form 944 is used by employers with a history of employment tax liabilities that are less than $1,000 annually. The IRS will only notify employers when they are eligible to file Form 944 for the first time. If a Form 944 filer's monthly employment tax liability equals or exceeds $2,500 they can file Form 944 for the year their liability equals or exceeds $2,500 but for subsequent years they must file Form 941. Form 944 must be filed by January 31.

Employers eligible to file Form 944 may file Form 941 when they anticipate their tax liability will exceed $1,000 for the year or they will file Form 941 electronically. Employers choosing to file Form 941 must notify the IRS in writing by March 15 or by phone by April 1.

Form 945, *Annual Return of Withheld Federal Income Tax*

Form 945 (page A-100) is used to report nonpayroll items and income tax withholding on pensions, annuities, IRAs, gambling winnings, and backup withholding shown on Forms 1099 and W-2G. Form 945 is an annual return that must be filed by January 31.

5.2.4 State Unemployment Insurance Reporting

All states are required by federal law to have a state unemployment compensation law. State laws work in conjunction with federal law. Federal unemployment taxes provide funds needed to administer both the federal and state programs, while state unemployment taxes fund

All states are required under federal law to have a state unemployment compensation law.

benefits that unemployed workers receive. In addition, the federal program provides loans to state programs that do not have enough funds available to finance the benefits paid to workers who lose their jobs.

The following states allow withholding from employees' wages of state unemployment taxes:

Alaska   New Jersey   Pennsylvania

While the specific procedures for calculating state unemployment tax vary from state to state, there are common threads tying them together.

Each state requires employers to submit quarterly contribution and wage reports containing some or all of the following information:

- Total wages paid
- Taxable wages paid
- Nontaxable wages paid
- Number of employees each month
- Gross wages for each employee
- Taxable/nontaxable wages breakdown for each employee
- Number of weeks worked by each employee

Employers should check the states where they operate for the reporting requirements applicable in each.

Electronic/magnetic media reporting. Many states require employers to file their quarterly wage information electronically or on some type of magnetic media, either tape, cartridge, CD, or diskette. In those states that require or permit magnetic media filing, some will accept only tape reporting, while others will accept either a tape, CD, or diskette. Some states also accept electronic reporting. There is no consensus among the states regarding electronic and magnetic media reporting requirements, so employers must carefully research the requirements in the states where they operate. Most of the states that require electronic or magnetic media reporting, however, do use a threshold for triggering the requirement that is similar to the federal threshold for filing Forms W-2 electronically.

5.2.5 FUTA (Federal Unemployment Tax Act)

The Federal Unemployment Tax Act (FUTA) was enacted to help the various states fund their federally mandated unemployment compensation programs. Since the programs themselves are regulated and administered by the states, the benefits and regulations differ from state to state. However, employers from all states must pay and report FUTA tax.

Employers from all states must pay and report FUTA.

FUTA is an employer tax. No FUTA tax is withheld from employees' wages.

FUTA does not apply to independent contractors or other nonemployees.

Rate of 6.0%

The FUTA tax rate is 6.0% of the first $7,000 of each employee's annual wages.

Credit of 5.4%

Employers in most states can take a 5.4% credit against the gross taxes paid for state unemployment tax. You can get this credit even if your state's rate is lower than 5.4%. To get full credit

- You must make timely payments to your state fund by the due date for Form 940 (discussed below).
- Your state must not be in arrears in repaying loans borrowed from FUTA funds.

For 2015, employers in 4 states and territories paid a higher FUTA tax rate due to unpaid loans needed to pay unemployment benefits.

Effective Rate of 0.6%

With the full credit, your effective FUTA tax rate is 0.6% (6.0% less 5.4% credit). Any credit loss is not computed until the end of the year and affects only your fourth-quarter payment. For the first three quarters, you pay 0.6% FUTA tax for each employee on the first $7,000 in taxable wages.

Some States may not Qualify for the Full Credit

While employers in most states have been receiving the full 5.4% credit reduction, it is not automatic.

$500 Threshold

A FUTA tax deposit is required only if the amount due for the quarter plus any previous balance for a prior quarter during the year is more than $500.

Calculating FUTA Tax

The following is an example of calculating a FUTA tax deposit.

Assume that there are 20 employees, each paid $1,400 per month. At that rate, each employee will have earned $7,000 in five months. At the beginning of the second quarter (April 1), one of the employees who was on the payroll since January leaves the firm, and a replacement is hired at $2,000 per month. For the first three quarters, FUTA tax would be as shown below. The fourth quarter has no wages subject to FUTA tax.

First Quarter Taxable Wages	FUTA TAX
$1,400 x 3 = $4,200 x 20 = $84,000 x 0.6% =	$504.00
Second Quarter Taxable Wages	**FUTA TAX**
19 x $1,400 x 2 months = $53,200 1 x $2,000 x 3 months = $6,000 $59,200 x 0.6% =	$355.20
Third Quarter Taxable Wages	**FUTA TAX**
1 x $1,000 x 1 = $1,000 x 0.6% =	$6.00

Since the first-quarter's FUTA tax liability is over $500 ($504.00), the first quarter's liability must be deposited by April 30. As the second quarter's liability ($355.20) is less than $500.00, it can be carried forward to the third quarter. The FUTA tax liability at the end of the third quarter is $361.20 ($355.20 + $6.00), which is less than the $500.00 FUTA liability deposit threshold. Therefore, the total liability at the end of the third quarter is carried forward to the fourth quarter.

Now assume that in December you learn that the federal tax credit of 5.4% is reduced by 1.2% for employers in your state. The effective FUTA tax rate is now 1.8% (6.0% – 4.2% = 1.8%). To calculate the fourth quarter liability, multiply the FUTA wages for the year by the new rate and subtract for desposits already made.

Total Taxable Wages				FUTA TAX
1Q $84,000	**2Q** $59,200	**3Q** $1,000	**4Q** $0	
Total = $144,200 x 1.8% =				$2,595.60
Less year-to-date deposits				- $504.00
Final Deposit				$2,091.60 due by January 31

Note: The $361.20 ($355.20 + $6.00) liability from the second and third quarters was not deposited as the $500 threshold had not been reached. The $361.20 liability at the end of the third quarter is deposited with the fourth quarter's liability.

5.2.6 Depositing and Reporting FUTA Tax

FUTA tax must be deposited using EFTPS each quarter. The deadline is the last day of the month after the quarter ends (see the following table). The deposit must be received no later than the due date.

FUTA tax must be deposited using EFTPS.

Deadlines for FUTA Tax Deposits	Deposit Due on or Before
First quarter	April 30
Second quarter	July 31
Third quarter	October 31
Fourth quarter	January 31

Note: If the deadline falls on a Saturday, Sunday, or legal holiday, the due date is the next business day.

Form 940

FUTA tax is reported annually using Form 940, *Employer's Annual Federal Unemployment (FUTA) Tax Return.* The report is due on January 31. If you make all FUTA tax deposits on or before the due date, you can extend this deadline by 10 days (to February 10). For good cause, an employer may be granted an additional filing extension of not more than 90 days. This request must be made before January 31; it must be in writing and signed by an officer of the firm.

Penalties

The penalties for failing to deposit or report FUTA tax are the same as those for other federal taxes.

For more information on Form 940 see Section 5.5.1

Check Your Understanding

Check Your Understanding

Quiz 5.2. Answer the following questions to test your understanding of quarterly tax returns.

1. Which form is used by an employer to report federal income tax, social security tax and Medicare tax withheld?
   - ❑ a. Form 941
   - ❑ b. Form 943
   - ❑ c. Form 944
   - ❑ d. Form 945

2. All of the following items are reported on Form 941 EXCEPT:
   - ❑ a. wages, tips and other compensation.
   - ❑ b. federal income tax withheld.
   - ❑ c. social security tax.
   - ❑ d. social security numbers.

3. Which form is used to report taxes on agricultural employees' wages?
   - ❑ a. Form 941
   - ❑ b. Form 943
   - ❑ c. Form 944
   - ❑ d. Form 945

4. A company with an employment tax liability of $150,000 for the quarter files quarterly returns. Which form should the company use to report federal income tax withholding?
   - ❑ a. Form 941
   - ❑ b. Form 943
   - ❑ c. Form 944
   - ❑ d. Form 945

5. Which form is used to quarterly report taxable social security and Medicare wages?
   - ❑ a. Form 940
   - ❑ b. Form 941
   - ❑ c. Form 944
   - ❑ d. Form 945

6. Where is Form 941 filed?
   - ❑ a. With the local IRS office
   - ❑ b. With EFTPS
   - ❑ c. At the IRS designated address
   - ❑ d. With the IRS National Office

7. If filed on its due date, Form 941 must be sent to the IRS through the U.S. Postal Service.
   - ❑ True
   - ❑ False

8. Form 941 is filed monthly.
   - ❑ True
   - ❑ False

9. A company has consistently deposited 100% of its tax liability on time. What is the last date it can file its first quarter Form 941?
   - ❑ a. April 15
   - ❑ b. April 30
   - ❑ c. May 10
   - ❑ d. May 15

5.3 Form W-2, Wage and Tax Statement

The employee's Form W-2, *Wage and Tax Statement,* (see page A-1) is a crucial report. The W-2 enables employees to file their tax returns, the Internal Revenue Service to track tax obligations, and the Social Security Administration (SSA) to provide social security benefits.

5.3.1 The W-2 Series

You need to be familiar with two forms in this series.

Form W-2

Employers must prepare Form W-2 for each employee if they did one of the following:

- Withheld federal income tax, social security tax, or Medicare tax
- Would have withheld federal income tax except that the number of allowances claimed resulted in zero withholding or the employee claimed exempt on Form W-4
- Paid at least $600 for services (including noncash compensation not subject to federal income tax withholding services) if they are in a trade or business (See page A-112) for a copy of Form 1099-MISC

Payments for services rendered by an independent contractor are reported on Form 1099-MISC.

Form W-2c

Use Form W-2c, *Corrected Wage and Tax Statement*, to correct errors in previously filed Forms W-2. Use Form W-3c, *Transmittal of Corrected Wage and Tax Statements*, to send corrected information to the Social Security Administration after Forms W-2 are filed. (See page A-35).

The Protecting Americans from Tax Hikes Act of 2015 (PATH Act) established a safe harbor for de minimis errors on information returns and payee statements. The PATH Act provides a safe harbor from the penalties for failure to file a correct information return or payee statement (e.g., W-2 or 1099) if it includes one or more de minimis errors.

For withholding, the safe harbor for any single amount is $25. For other errors the de minimis threshold for any single amount is $100. An information return or payee statement containing such errors will be treated as having all the correct information.

However, the recipient of the payee statement may elect to have a corrected form furnished to the recipient and filed with the SSA or IRS under procedures that will be established by the IRS. The safe harbor will be effective for 2016 returns and statements required to be furnished or filed in 2017.

5.3.2 Deadlines

The W-2 is a multipart form. Paper filers retain one part in their files and send the other parts to employees, state tax agencies, local tax agencies, and the Social Security Administration (SSA) (see the following table). Companies required to file Forms W-2 electronically do not send Copy A to the SSA, but upload a computer file to SSA.

Deadlines for W-2

Copy	Recipient	Deadline
Copy A	Social Security Administration	January 31 whether filing on paper or electronically
Copy 1	State/Local Tax Agencies	Varies according to state and local requirements
Copy B	Employees (filed with their federal tax return)	January 31
Copy C	Employees (for their personal files)	January 31
Copy 2	Employees (filed with their state tax return)	January 31
Copy D	Employers (for your files)	None

Note: If the deadline falls on Saturday, Sunday, or a federal holiday, Form W-2 is due on the next business day.

Deadline for Former Employees

If an employee's employment ends with your company, the deadline remains January 31 unless the former employee requests, in writing, that you prepare the Form W-2 sooner. If requested in writing, you have 30 days from the request to send former employees the employee copies of Form W-2.

Deadline When Ceasing Operations

Employers ceasing operations are required to provide Forms W-2 to their employees by the date the employer files the final Form 941. In addition, the Forms W-2 must be filed with the SSA by the end of the month following the due date of the final Form 941.

Extensions

An employer had been entitled to an automatic 30-day extension for filing Forms W-2 with the SSA by filing Form 8809 with the IRS before the due date for the Forms W-2. A second 30-day extension could be granted after filing a signed Form 8809.

In 2015 the IRS issued temporary regulations applicable to the 2017 filing season that eliminate the automatic 30-day extension of time to file forms in the W-2 series (except Form W-2G) and update the list of information returns subject to the rules on extensions of time to file. The IRS also issued related proposed regulations that would apply no sooner than the 2018 filing season and would eliminate the automatic 30-day extension of time to file the other information returns on the updated list.

The temporary regulations provide that forms in the W-2 series, except for Form W-2G, are no longer eligible for an automatic extension to file. Instead, the temporary regulations provide for a single non-automatic extension for those returns that the IRS may grant, in its discretion, if it determines that an extension is warranted based on the filer's or transmitter's explanation included on Form 8809. The IRS anticipates that it will grant extensions only in limited cases where the explanation demonstrates that there are extraordinary circumstances or a catastrophe such as a natural disaster or a fire that destroys a filer's books and records. If the IRS does not grant the extension, returns filed after their due dates are not timely filed, regardless of whether Form 8809 was filed timely.

You Must Give Written Notice of the Earned Income Tax Credit to Each Eligible Employee

If you do not include an IRS-approved Earned Income Tax Credit (EITC) notice on the employee's copy of Form W-2, you must give written notice to the employee within one week of the date you deliver Forms W-2. Posting this information on your company bulletin board will not suffice.

Your Own EITC Statement

You can use your own written statement as long as it has the exact wording of IRS Notice 797.

Report Only Wages Paid, Not Earned, During the Year

Form W-2 reports all wages paid (not earned) during the year. Do not include additional compensation earned but not paid until the next year. For example, if an employee's earnings for December 26 to 31 are paid on January 3, the earnings paid on January 3 are reported on Form W-2 for the year in which January 3 occurs.

Alert

5.3.3 Instructions for completing Forms W-2

Forms should be filed either alphabetically or in social security number sequence. This allows the SSA to locate forms once they are filed.

Follow these tips when filling out Forms W-2. Forms W-2 filed on paper with the SSA are processed by optical scanning machines. To ensure that forms are processed correctly, type the entries using black ink if possible. Do not make any erasures, whiteouts, or strikeovers, as this will cause processing errors at the SSA. Make all dollar entries without

Real-world Application

the dollar sign and/or commas but with the decimal point (0000.00). A copy of the Form W-2 and W-3 instructions is found in the Appendix (page A-3).

Form W-2 Box-by-Box Instructions

Following are box-by-box instructions for the Form W-2.

Box a—Employee's social security number

Enter the number shown on the employee's social security card. If the employee does not have a social security number but is applying for one, enter "Applied For." If filing electronically, put all zeroes in the SSN field when an SSN is not available. Do not rely on employment applications or Form W-4 to obtain the social security number. Insist on seeing the social security card to ensure you have the correct number.

Enter the number shown on the employee's social security card.

Void

When filing paper forms with SSA, if an error is made completing the form or a "corrected" W-2 has been issued, this box is checked. Be sure not to include amounts from a void W-2 on Form W-3. When filing electronically with SSA this box does not apply.

Box b—Employer's identification number (EIN)

Enter the number assigned by the IRS. If an EIN has not been assigned, write "Applied For" in the box. EINs can be obtained quickly through the IRS's and Internet TIN assignment program.

Box c—Employer's name, address, and zip code

Enter the employer's name, address, and zip code as they appear on Form 941.

Box d—Control number

This box is for the employer's use and is not required to be completed.

Box e—Employee's name (first, middle initial, last, suffix)

Enter the employee's name as shown on the employee's social security card in the appropriate box. On Form W-2, use the employee's middle initial even if the full middle name appears on the social security card. If the employee's name changes, have the employee obtain a new card from the SSA before using the new name on Form W-2. Continue to use the name on the original social security card until a new social security card is shown.

Check the employee's social security card to verify the name. Use only the first name, middle initial, and last name. Do not use titles such as Mr., Mrs., Dr., Capt., etc. and do not add academic degrees or professional certifications such as M.D. or Ph.D. Titles added as prefixes or suffixes make it difficult for the SSA's computer software to determine the employee's actual name. You can add suffixes such as Jr. or Sr. only if the suffix appears on the employee's social security card, but the SSA prefers that they not be entered on Copy A. However, suffixes may be entered on the paper W-2s provided to the employee when filing W-2s electronically.

Check the employee's social security card to verify the social security number.

Box f—Employee's address and zip code

Boxes e and f are combined on the employee's copies to allow the employer to use window envelopes or mailer forms.

Include in the address the number, street, apartment or suite number. For a foreign address, give the information in the following order: city, province or state, and country. Do not abbreviate the country's name. The U.S. Postal Service recommends that no periods or commas be used in the address.

Box 1—Wages, tips, other compensation

Generally, report taxable wages including the following:

Total wages, prizes, and awards paid during the calendar year, excluding elective deferrals into deferred compensation plans and Section 125 plans. The amount paid, not earned, is reported (e.g., wages earned

Report taxable wages, including wages, prizes, and awards paid during the calendar year.

from December 21, 2015, to January 3, 2016, but paid on January 5, 2016, are reported on the 2016 Form W-2).

- Noncash payments, including taxable fringe benefits
- All tips reported by the employee, but do not include the allocated tips reported in Box 8
- Certain employee business expense reimbursements
- Contributions to Roth 401(k), 403(b) and 457(b) plans.

Include all other compensation, such as group-term life insurance over $50,000, from which no income tax was withheld. The amounts reported in Box 1 meet the IRS's definition of gross income from employment. These amounts may or may not be subject to federal income tax withholding.

Box 2—Federal income tax withheld
Enter the total amount of federal income tax withheld or paid by the employer for the employee and, if applicable, the 20% excise tax withheld on excess golden parachute payments. Include income tax withheld by third-party sick pay providers not filing Form W-2 for the employee.

The employer may complete a separate Form W-2 for employees receiving sick pay from third parties.

Box 3—Social security wages
Report the total social security wages paid by the employer to the employee. Do not include reported tips (Box 7) or allocated tips (Box 8). Noncash amounts considered wages are included in this box. For 2016, the amount reported in Boxes 3 and 7 cannot exceed $118,500.00.

Box 4—Social security tax withheld

For 2016, the social security tax withheld cannot exceed $7,347.00

Report the total social security taxes withheld from the employee or paid by the employer for the employee. This box should contain an amount equal to 6.2% times the amount in Box 3. If amounts are reported in Box 7 (Social security tips), Box 12 Code A (uncollected social security tax on tips) or Box 12 Code M (uncollected social security tax on group-term life insurance) the reconciliation of Box 3 to Box 4 requires using the following formula:

Box 4 = [(Box 3 + Box 7) x 6.2%] – Box 12 Code A – Box 12 Code M

For 2016, the amount cannot exceed $7,347.00.

Box 5—Medicare wages and tips

Report the total Medicare wages paid by the employer and tips reported by the employee. Do not include allocated tips reported in Box 8. Non-cash fringe benefits are considered wages and are included in this box.

Report all wages subject to the Medicare tax, including those wages in excess of $200,000 that are subject to the additional Medicare tax (see page 3-12), in Box 5.

Box 6—Medicare tax withheld

Report the total Medicare tax withheld or paid by the employer for the employee.

Report all Medicare tax, including the additional Medicare tax wages on excess of $200,000 (see page 3-12), in Box 6.

If amounts are reported in Box 12 Code B (uncollected Medicare tax on tips) or Box 12 Code N (uncollected Medicare tax on group-term life insurance) the reconciliation of Box 5 to Box 6 when the Medicare wages are less than $200,000 requires using the following formula:

Box 6 = (Box 5 x 1.45%) – Box 12 Code B – Box 12 Code N

If the amount in Box 6 is in excess of $200,000 the following formula is used to reconcile Box 5 to Box 6.

Box 6 = (Box 5 x 1.45%) + ((Box 5 - $200,000) x 0.9%)

Box 7—Social security tips

The amount of tips the employee reports to the employer during the calendar year is reported. Even if the employer cannot deduct taxes, the amount of tips reported by the employee is included. The total of Boxes 3 and 7 cannot exceed $118,500.00 for 2016.

Box 8—Allocated tips

A large food or beverage establishment will place the tips allocated to the employee, calculated using Form 8027, *Employer's Annual Information Return of Tip Income and Allocated Tips*, in this box. Any amount in this box is not placed in Boxes 1 (wages, tips, other compensation), 7 (social security tips), or 5 (Medicare wages).

Even if the employer cannot deduct taxes, the amount of tips reported by the employee is included in Box 7.

Box 9—Not used for 2016

Prior to 2011, Advanced Earned Income Credit payments were reported in Box 9. The AEIC was repealed effective January 1, 2011.

Box 10—Dependent care benefits

The total value of dependent care benefits provided to an employee is reported in this box. If the amount exceeds $5,000.00, the amount greater than $5,000.00 must be reported in Boxes 1, 3, and 5 as well as Box 10. For example, if $7,000.00 of benefits are provided, $7,000 is reported in Box 10 and $2,000.00 is reported in Boxes 1, 3, and 5.

Dependent care benefits provided under a Section 125 plan (flexible spending account) may be reported as either the amount deferred from the employee's salary or the benefits provided. Benefits provided directly by the employer must include the fair market value of the benefit received, not the employer's cost of providing the benefit.

Box 11—Nonqualified plans

The purpose of Box 11 is for SSA to determine if any amounts reported in Box 1 or Boxes 3 and/or 5 were earned in a prior year. Amounts earned in a prior year will not be used by SSA in the social security earnings test.

Report distributions to employees from nonqualified deferred compensation plans or nongovernmental Section 457 plans in Box 11.

Report distributions to employees from nonqualified deferred compensation plans or nongovernmental Section 457(b) plans. Generally, this amount is included in Box 1 but not Boxes 3 or 5. If no distribution was made, report the deferrals (plus earnings) under a nonqualified plan that became taxable in the current year for social security (Box 3) and Medicare (Box 5) but do not include deferrals from current-year services.

For further information on reporting amounts in Box 11, the IRS Instructions for Forms W-2 and W-2c contain examples for Box 11 reporting (see page A-31).

Box—12

Box 12 includes a variety of codes and amounts. The code must be entered as a capital letter. If an entry is required, the code is entered in front of the amount. Employers filing paper Forms W-2 with the SSA can place only four items in Box 12. When required to place more than four items in the box, complete a second Form W-2 that contains only the employee's name, address, and SSN, the employer's name, address, and EIN, and the additional items required in Box 12. When filing Forms W-2 electronically, more than four items can be placed in Box 12. Do not report any item in Box 12 without an applicable code.

Code A—Uncollected social security tax on tips
Report the amount of social security tax on tips that the employer was not able to collect because the employee did not have enough cash wages from which to deduct the tax. Do not include this amount in Box 4, "Social Security Tax Withheld." If an amount is entered with Code A, add this amount to Box 4 when reconciling the withheld taxes to wages.

Code B—Uncollected Medicare tax on tips
Report the amount of Medicare tax on tips that the employer was not able to collect because the employee did not have enough cash wages from which to deduct the tax. Do not include this amount in Box 6, "Medicare Tax Withheld." If an amount is entered with Code B, add this amount to Box 6 when reconciling the withheld taxes to wages.

If an employee's wages and tips are in excess of $200,000 and the employee's cash wages are not sufficient to deduct the additional Medicare tax (0.9% on wages in excess of $200,000) from the tips received in excess of $200,000, the uncollected Medicare taxes are NOT reported in Box 12 with Code B.

Code C—Cost of group-term life insurance coverage in excess of $50,000
Report the value of group-term life insurance coverage in excess of $50,000 as determined from Table 1, Section 79, that is included as wages. This amount is also included in Boxes 1, 3, and 5.

Code D—Section 401(k) contributions
Report the employee's elective deferrals made into a Section 401(k) plan (including catch-up contributions). If an amount is included with this code, the retirement plan box in Box 13 must be checked. Amounts reported with Code D are not included in Box 1 but are reported in Boxes 3 and 5.

Code E—Section 403(b) contributions
Report the employee's elective deferrals made into a Section 403(b) plan (including catch-up contributions). If an amount is included with this code, the retirement plan box in Box 13 must be checked. Amounts reported with Code E are not included in Box 1 but are reported in Boxes 3 and 5.

Code F—Section 408(k)(6) contributions
Report the employee's elective deferrals made into a Section 408(k)(6) simplified employee pension (SEP) plan (including catch-up contributions). If an amount is included with this code, the retirement plan box

in Box 13 must be checked. Amounts reported with Code F are not included in Box 1 but are reported in Boxes 3 and 5.

Code G—Section 457(b) contributions
Report the employee's elective deferrals and nonelective contributions which were made by either the employee or employer into a Section 457(b) plan (including catch-up contributions). The retirement plan box is not checked for Section 457(b) contributions. Amounts reported are not included in Box 1 but are reported in Boxes 3 and 5, if applicable.

Code H—Section 501(c)(18)(D) contributions
Report the employee's elective deferrals made into a Section 501(c)(18)(D) plan. If an amount is included with this code, the retirement plan in Box 13 must be checked. Amounts reported are included in Boxes 1, 3, and 5. Employees will deduct the deferral on their federal income tax return.

Code J—Sick pay not included in income
Report the amount of sick pay not included in income (Boxes 1, 3 and 5) subject to federal income tax because the employee contributed to the sick pay plan. Amounts reported are not included in any other box.

Code K—Tax on excess golden parachute payments
Report the excise tax of 20% on any excess "golden parachute" payments made to key corporate employees. If the excess payments are considered wages, also report the excise tax as income tax withholding in Box 2.

Code L—Nontaxable part of employee business expense reimbursements
Report the amount of employee business expense treated as substantiated (nontaxable) only if employees are reimbursed for expenses using a per diem or mileage allowance and the amount reimbursed exceeds the amount treated as substantiated under IRS rules. Any amounts reimbursed at more than the allowed per diem or mileage allowance rates must be included in Boxes 1, 3, and 5, with the allowed per diem or mileage being reported with Code L.

Code M—Uncollected social security tax on the cost of group-term life insurance coverage over $50,000
Report the amount of social security tax that could not be collected on the value of group-term life insurance coverage over $50,000 for former employees who have a continuing relationship with the employer (e.g., retirees). Do not include this amount in Box 4, "Social Security

Tax Withheld." When reconciling social security tax to wages, add this amount to Box 4.

Code N—Uncollected Medicare tax on the cost of group-term life insurance coverage over $50,000

Report the amount of Medicare tax that could not be collected on the value of group-term life insurance coverage over $50,000 for former employees who have a continuing relationship with the employer (e.g., retirees). Do not include this amount in Box 6, "Medicare Tax Withheld." When reconciling Medicare tax to wages, add this amount to Box 6.

If an employee's wages and group-term life insurance are in excess of $200,000 and the employee's cash wages are not sufficient to deduct the additional Medicare tax (0.9% on wages in excess of $200,000) from the group-term life insurance received in excess of $200,000, the uncollected Medicare taxes are NOT reported in Box 12 with Code B.

Code P—Excludable moving expense reimbursements

Report qualified moving expense payments made directly to an employee. Do not report any qualified moving expenses paid to third parties with Code P. Do not report amounts reported with Code P in Boxes 1, 3, or 5.

Code Q—Nontaxable combat pay

Military employers will report nontaxable combat pay with Code Q.

Code R—Archer medical savings account contributions

Report employer contributions to an Archer medical savings account using Code R. If contributions to an Archer medical savings account are for your employee, show all the employer contributions in Box 12 using Code R. Any employer contribution that cannot be excludable from the employee's gross income also must be reported in Box 1. To the extent that it was not reasonable to believe at the time of payment that the employer contributions would be excludable from the gross income of the employee, the employer contributions also must be shown in Boxes 3 and 5.

Code S—SIMPLE retirement account contributions

Report employee elective deferrals into a SIMPLE retirement account under a Section 408(p) salary reduction agreement (including catch-up contributions) using Code S. However, if the SIMPLE account is part of a Section 401(k) arrangement, the amount is reported using Code D. If an amount is included with this code, the retirement plan box in Box

Use Code T to report employer-provided adoption benefits.

13 must be checked. Amounts reported are not included in Box 1 but are reported in Boxes 3 and 5.

Code T—Adoption benefits
Use Code T to report employer-provided adoption benefits. Show the total amount paid or expenses incurred by an employer for qualified adoption expenses furnished to an employee under an adoption assistance program. Also include benefits provided from the pretax contributions made by the employee to a Section 125 adoption plan account. Amounts reported are not included in Box 1 but are reported in Boxes 3 and 5, even if included in a Section 125 plan.

Code V—Income from the exercise of nonstatutory stock option(s)
When an employee (or former employee) exercises nonstatutory stock option(s), employers are required to report the excess of the fair market value of the stock received upon exercise of the option over the amount paid for that stock on Form W-2 in Boxes 1, 3 (up to the social security wage base), and 5. Code V reporting requires that any compensation related to the exercise of the nonstatutory stock option(s) currently included in boxes 1, 3 (if applicable), and 5 must also be shown in Box 12, using Code V.

Code W—Health Savings Accounts
Report employer contributions, including amounts the employee elected to contribute using a Section 125 (cafeteria) plan, to a Health Savings Account using code W.

Code Y—Nonqualified Deferred Compensation Deferrals
Report deferrals and earnings from current or prior year deferrals to a Section 409A nonqualified deferred compensation plan. The IRS has temporarily suspended the reporting requirement for Code Y.

Code Z—Income from 409A Nonqualified Deferred Compensation Plans
Report income that is included in Box 1 due to failure to meet the nonqualified deferred compensation plan requirements in Section 409A. This income is subject to an additional tax that is reported on the employee's Form 1040.

Code AA – Roth 401(k) deferrals
Report the employee's elective deferrals made into a Roth 401(k) plan (including catch-up contributions). If an amount is included with this code, the retirement plan box in Box 13 must be checked. Amounts reported with Code AA are included in Boxes 1, 3 and 5.

Code BB – Roth 403(b) deferrals
Report the employee's elective deferrals made into a Roth 403(b) plan (including catch-up contributions). If an amount is included with this code, the retirement plan box in Box 13 must be checked. Amounts reported with Code BB are included in Boxes 1, 3 and 5.

Code CC—Code CC is not currently used.

Code DD—Cost of employer-sponsored health coverage
Report the cost of employer-sponsored heath coverage. This amount is not reported in Boxes 1, 3 or 5.

Code EE—Roth 457(b) deferrals
Report the employee's elective deferrals made into a Roth 457(b) plan (including catch-up contributions). Amounts reported with Code EE are included in Boxes 1, 3 and 5.

Box 13—Check boxes
Mark as many boxes as are applicable. If a box is not applicable to any of an employer's employees, the box does not have to be included on the form when the employer files its Forms W-2 with the SSA electronically.

Statutory employee
This box is checked for statutory employees whose earnings are subject to social security and Medicare taxes but are not subject to federal income tax withholding.

Retirement plan
If the employee is an active participant for any part of the year in a qualified retirement plan, this box is checked. For further information defining "active participant," refer to IRS Notice 87-16. Do not check this box for participation in a nonqualified pension plan or a Section 457(b) plan.

For further information on when the Retirement Plan box is checked the IRS Instructions for Forms W-2 and W-2c contain examples (see page A-30).

Third-party sick pay
Check this box as a third-party insurance company providing W-2 information or as an employer reporting sick payments made by a third-party.

*When entering
an amount in
Box 14, the item
must have a
descriptive label.*

Box 14—Other

The employer may choose to place any item of information for the employee in this box; no items are required. When entering an amount in this box, the item must have a descriptive label.

When using the annual lease value method to calculate the personal use of a company vehicle, the amount reported in boxes 1, 3 and 5 may be reported in Box 14 or a separate statement.

Box 15—Employer's state and state I.D. number

For federal tax processing, an entry in this box is not required. If the state wages are reported using Form W-2, the employer's state identification number is entered.

*Boxes 16-20
are not required
for reporting
to the SSA, but
individual states
may require their
use.*

Boxes 16-20—State and local tax information

These boxes may be used to report state and local tax information. They are not required for reporting to the SSA, but individual states may require their use. Some states require reporting of state wages and taxes on separate forms.

The boxes can be used to report wages and taxes to two different states and localities. Ensure that each state's and locality's information is separated by the broken lines.

5.3.4 Transmitting Your Forms W-2 (Form W-3 or Electronically)

Total all the information reported on the employees' Forms W-2 and report that data either on Form W-3 (for paper filers) or on the electronic W-2 file. Form W-3 is used to transmit paper W-2 forms to the SSA. Forms W-2, whether transmitted on paper with Form W-3 or transmitted electronically, are due by January 31.

The totals on Form W-2 must be reconciled with the totals reported on the four quarterly Forms 941 for the year. The items that are reconciled by the SSA and the IRS are:

- Federal income tax withheld
- Social security wages and withholding
- Medicare wages and withholding.

Forms W-3 and W-2 filed on paper are machine-read by optical scanning equipment. Staple holes and tears cause the forms to jam the machines. Typing the entries increases the ability of the equipment to read the data accurately. Make all dollar entries without the dollar sign and comma but with the decimal point (0000.00).

Real-world Application

The SSA will reject Form W-2 electronic and paper wage reports in which any of the following conditions are present:

- Medicare wages and tips are less than the sum of social security wages and social security tips
- Social security tax is greater than zero; social security wages and social security tips are equal to zero
- Medicare tax is greater than zero; Medicare wages and tips are equal to zero

If the conditions for rejection occur in a paper wage report, the SSA will notify the employer by email or postal mail to correct the report and resubmit it to the SSA.

Electronic Filing

Filers of 250 or more Forms W-2 and W-2c are required to file the information returns electronically. When filed electronically, Forms W-2 are due January 31.

The IRS and the SSA encourage employers not required to file electronically to voluntarily use electronic filing for transmitting the information contained in Forms W-2, W-2c, and W-3.

The 250-form electronic filing threshold applies separately to each type of information return filed (Form W-2, Forms 1098 and Forms 1099).

Hardship waiver. If filing electronically poses a particular hardship, you can get a waiver from this requirement by filing Form 8508, *Request for Waiver From Filing Information Returns Electronically*, with the IRS. You must apply for this waiver at least 45 days before the due date of the return.

Do not send paper returns to the SSA or IRS if you file electronically.

To file your W-2s electronically through the Internet, access SSA's employer web site at www.socialsecurity.gov/employer/.

Submitting Forms by Mail or Private Delivery Service

Real-world Application

Forms W-2 and W-3 should be mailed certified or registered or sent using an approved IRS private delivery service (PDS) (see page 5-15) to the Social Security Administration no later than the last day of February, for the employer to avoid incurring penalties. The IRS-designated PDSs that can be used are the same as those listed earlier in the discussion of Form 941. The date on which an item is given to the PDS (for DHL and UPS) or the date marked on the label attached to the cover of the item (for FedEx) is considered the postmark date of the item.

If filing paper *Forms* W-2, they should be sent, along with Form W-3, to the following address if the U.S. Postal Service is used:

> Social Security Administration
> Data Operations Center
> Wilkes-Barre, PA 18769-0001

If filing Copy A by certified mail, use zip code 18769-0002.

For a carrier other than the U.S. Postal Service, if filing paper Forms W-2, they should be sent, along with Form W-3, to the following address:

> Social Security Administration
> Attn: W-2 Process
> 1150 E. Mountain Drive
> Wilkes-Barre, PA 18702-7997

5.4 Penalties

The IRS and other agencies impose stiff penalties on employers for a variety of errors, failures, and omissions related to withholding, depositing, and reporting taxes. Summarized in the table below are key penalty provisions for 2016.

Errors, failures, and omissions related to withholding, depositing, and reporting taxes can result in stiff penalties.

Failure to File Correct Information Returns	
• Failure to file an information return with SSA or IRS by due date • Failure to include all the information required on a return • Including incorrect information on a return such as names or social security numbers Note: 2016 Forms W-2 are due January 31, 2017, whether filed on paper or electronically.	A three-tier penalty 1. $50 per Form W-2 if corrected within 30 days of the due date with a maximum penalty of $532,000 per year ($186,000 for small businesses) 2. $100 per Form W-2 if corrected more than 30 days after the due date but by August 1 with a maximum penalty of $1,596,500 per year ($532,000 for small businesses) 3. $260 per Form W-2 if corrected after August 1, do not file corrections, or do not file required Forms W-2 with a maximum penalty of $3,193,000 per year ($1,064,000 for small businesses) Note: If the information returns are filed timely and corrected by August 1, a de minimis number of corrections (the greater of 10 or 0.5% of the returns filed) will not be penalized. For intentional disregard of these obligations, the penalty is $530 per return in 2016, and there is no calendar year limit.

• Failure to furnish payee statement • Failure to include all required information on payee statement	A three-tier penalty 1. $50 per Form W-2 if corrected within 30 days of the due date with a maximum penalty of $532,000 per year ($186,000 for small businesses) 2. $100 per Form W-2 if corrected more than 30 days after the due date but by August 1 with a maximum penalty of $1,596,500 per year ($532,000 for small businesses) 3. $260 per Form W-2 if corrected after August 1, do not file corrections, or do not file required Forms W-2 with a maximum penalty of $3,193,000 per year ($1,064,000 for small businesses) For intentional disregard of these obligations, the penalty is $530 per return in 2016, and there is no calendar year limit.
Accuracy-Related Failures	
• Understatement of taxes	• 20% of the underpayment • 75% of the underpayment if due to fraud

Failure to Make Timely Deposits	
• Failure to deposit taxes on the due date	A four-tier penalty structure 1. 2% of underpayment if failure is for not more than 5 days 2. 5% if failure is for more than 5 days but not more than 15 days 3. 10% if failure is for more than 15 days 4. 15% if tax is not deposited within 10 days of first delinquency notice
Withholding Failures	
• Failure to withhold income tax, social security tax, and Medicare tax • Failure to pay withholding to the IRS	100% of the withholding. In addition, officers, or employees could be personally liable for an equal amount

Check Your Understanding

Quiz 5.3. Answer the following questions to test your understanding of Form W-2.

Check Your Understanding

1. An employer is required to file a Form W-2 in all of the following situations EXCEPT:
   - ❑ a. A part-time employee in shipping who claimed exempt from withholding on his Form W-4
   - ❑ b. A free-lance writer who was paid $5,200.00 to prepare ad copy for the employer
   - ❑ c. A salesperson who retired in May
   - ❑ d. A student who is exempt from social security tax

2. An employee quit his position on April 10. Generally, when must the company send the former employee copies of his W-2?
   - ❑ a. By May 10
   - ❑ b. By May 30
   - ❑ c. By December 31
   - ❑ d. By January 31

3. Generally, the filing deadline for Form W-3 is:
    - ❑ a. January 31.
    - ❑ b. the last day in February.
    - ❑ c. April 15.
    - ❑ d. the last day of the month following the end of each quarter.

4. Your firm made a mistake in reporting an employee's taxable wages on his Form W-2. Which form is used to correct this error?
    - ❑ a. W-2
    - ❑ b. W-2c
    - ❑ c. W-3
    - ❑ d. W-3c

5. The payroll department made a series of errors on 100 of the 350 Forms W-2 sent to the Social Security Administration electronically before January 31, 2017. Shortly after filing, they realized their errors and corrected the returns by February 15, 2017. What is the penalty for these mistakes?
    - ❑ a. $3,000.00
    - ❑ b. $4,500.00
    - ❑ c. $6,000.00
    - ❑ d. $10,000.00

6. An employer's accumulated employment taxes were $53,000.00 in federal income tax, $27,868.41 in social security tax, and $7,771.00 in Medicare tax. On the due date, they deposited $80,000.00 through EFTPS. Five days later, they deposited an additional $8,639.41. What is the penalty, if any, for this action?
    - ❑ a. $137.33
    - ❑ b. $172.79
    - ❑ c. $186.00
    - ❑ d. No penalty

7. Under what circumstances could certain officers or employees of a corporation become personally liable for payment of taxes under federal law?
    - ❑ a. For failure to withhold and/or pay federal income tax, social security tax, and Medicare tax
    - ❑ b. For filing fraudulent information returns
    - ❑ c. For depositing taxes late
    - ❑ d. For filing incorrect information returns

8. Which of the following is true of electronic reporting?
   - ❏ a. Form W-3 is used to transmit Forms W-2 to the SSA.
   - ❏ b. It is recommended if you file more than 250 Forms W-2.
   - ❏ c. Do not send paper copies of Forms W-2 if you file electronically
   - ❏ d. Filers of Forms 1099-MISC must file electronically.

9. All employees must receive notice of the Earned Income Credit required by the IRS.
   - ❏ True
   - ❏ False

10. An employee claims married with five allowances on Form W-4 and earns $1,000 per month. Although he hasn't claimed exempt status on his Form W-4, no federal income tax is withheld from his wages. Which of the following is true?
    - ❏ a. The employee will not be eligible for the earned income tax credit.
    - ❏ b. If he filed Form 1040 last year, he will continue to receive EIC payments this year.
    - ❏ c. You must provide the employee detailed information about the EIC.
    - ❏ d. The employee can get the EIC even if he doesn't file a tax return.

5.5 Unemployment Tax Returns

The Federal Unemployment Tax Act (FUTA) was enacted to help the states fund their federally mandated unemployment compensation programs. Since the programs themselves are regulated and administered by the states, the benefits and regulations differ from state to state. However, employers from all states must pay and report FUTA tax.

5.5.1 Form 940

FUTA tax is reported annually using Form 940, *Employer's Annual Federal Unemployment (FUTA) Tax Return* (page A-47). The report is due on January 31. If you make all FUTA tax deposits on or before the due date, you can extend this deadline by 10 days (to February 10). For good cause, an employer may be granted an additional filing extension of not more than 90 days. This request must be made before January 31; it must be in writing and signed by an officer of the firm.

Forms 940 are filled annually.

Penalties

The penalties for failing to deposit or report FUTA tax are the same as those for other federal taxes.

Form 940, Employer's Annual Federal Unemployment (FUTA) Tax Return

Employers are required to complete Form 940 for 2016 when:

- Wages of $1,500 or more were paid in any quarter during 2015 or 2016, or
- At least one employee was employed for some part of a day in any of 20 different weeks in 2015 or 2016. Count all regular, temporary, and part-time employees. A partnership does not count the partners.

Changes in business ownership If the business changes hands during the year, each employer meeting either test must file. Do not report the wages paid by the other.

Organizations that are exempt from income tax do not owe FUTA. Religious, educational, charitable, etc., organizations described in Section 501(c)(3) of the Internal Revenue Code and exempt from income tax under Section 501(a) are not subject to FUTA tax and are not required to complete Form 940.

Generally, a credit for state unemployment taxes paid is allowed against the federal tax. The credit for state taxes cannot be more than 5.4% of the taxable wages. Employers in some states will have the 5.4% credit reduced if the state has borrowed amounts from the federal unemployment program and failed to repay them within a prescribed time period. In 2015, 4 states and territories had not timely repaid loans and were credit reduction states. These states' 5.4% credit for paying state unemployment taxes was reduced anywhere from 1.5% to 2.1%, depending on how long the state had been a credit reduction state. The credit may also be reduced if the employer does not deposit the state unemployment taxes in a timely manner.

Federal unemployment taxes are imposed on the employer and may not be withheld from the employees' wages.

Federal unemployment taxes are imposed on the employer and may not be withheld from the employees' wages.

The 2016 Form 940 is expected to be released by the IRS in November 2016. The material in this publication is based on the 2015 Form 940 and is subject to revision by the IRS.

A copy of Form 940 is found below. The instructions are in the Appendix (page A-53).

Form **940 for 2015:** **Employer's Annual Federal Unemployment (FUTA) Tax Return**
Department of the Treasury — Internal Revenue Service

850113

OMB No. 1545-0028

Employer identification number (EIN) ☐☐ – ☐☐☐☐☐☐☐

Name *(not your trade name)*

Trade name *(if any)*

Address

Number   Street   Suite or room number

City   State   ZIP code

Foreign country name   Foreign province/county   Foreign postal code

Type of Return
(Check all that apply.)

☐ **a.** Amended

☐ **b.** Successor employer

☐ **c.** No payments to employees in 2015

☐ **d.** Final: Business closed or stopped paying wages

Instructions and prior-year forms are available at *www.irs.gov/form940*.

Read the separate instructions before you complete this form. Please type or print within the boxes.

Part 1: **Tell us about your return. If any line does NOT apply, leave it blank. See instructions before completing Part 1.**

1a If you had to pay state unemployment tax in one state only, enter the state abbreviation . **1a** ☐☐

1b If you had to pay state unemployment tax in more than one state, you are a multi-state employer . . . . **1b** ☐ Check here. Complete Schedule A (Form 940).

2 If you paid wages in a state that is subject to CREDIT REDUCTION . . . . **2** ☐ Check here. Complete Schedule A (Form 940).

Part 2: **Determine your FUTA tax before adjustments. If any line does NOT apply, leave it blank.**

3 Total payments to all employees . . . . **3** ☐

4 Payments exempt from FUTA tax . . . . **4** ☐

Check all that apply: **4a** ☐ Fringe benefits   **4c** ☐ Retirement/Pension   **4e** ☐ Other
4b ☐ Group-term life insurance   **4d** ☐ Dependent care

5 Total of payments made to each employee in excess of $7,000 . . . . **5** ☐

6 Subtotal (line 4 + line 5 = line 6) . . . . **6** ☐

7 Total taxable FUTA wages (line 3 – line 6 = line 7) (see instructions) . . . . **7** ☐

8 FUTA tax before adjustments (line 7 x .006 = line 8) . . . . **8** ☐

Part 3: **Determine your adjustments. If any line does NOT apply, leave it blank.**

9 If ALL of the taxable FUTA wages you paid were excluded from state unemployment tax, multiply line 7 by .054 (line 7 x .054 = line 9). Go to line 12 . . . . **9** ☐

10 If SOME of the taxable FUTA wages you paid were excluded from state unemployment tax, OR you paid ANY state unemployment tax late (after the due date for filing Form 940), complete the worksheet in the instructions. Enter the amount from line 7 of the worksheet . . **10** ☐

11 If credit reduction applies, enter the total from Schedule A (Form 940) . . . . . . **11** ☐

Part 4: **Determine your FUTA tax and balance due or overpayment. If any line does NOT apply, leave it blank.**

12 Total FUTA tax after adjustments (lines 8 + 9 + 10 + 11 = line 12) . . . . **12** ☐

13 FUTA tax deposited for the year, including any overpayment applied from a prior year . **13** ☐

14 Balance due (If line 12 is more than line 13, enter the excess on line 14.)
• If line 14 is more than $500, you must deposit your tax.
• If line 14 is $500 or less, you may pay with this return. (see instructions) . . . . **14** ☐

15 Overpayment (If line 13 is more than line 12, enter the excess on line 15 and check a box below.) . . . . **15** ☐

▶ You **MUST** complete both pages of this form and **SIGN** it.   Check one: ☐ Apply to next return.   ☐ Send a refund.

Next ▶

For Privacy Act and Paperwork Reduction Act Notice, see the back of Form 940-V, Payment Voucher.   Cat. No. 11234O   Form **940** (2015)

850212

Name (not your trade name)	Employer identification number (EIN)

Part 5: Report your FUTA tax liability by quarter only if line 12 is more than $500. If not, go to Part 6.

16 Report the amount of your FUTA tax liability for each quarter; do NOT enter the amount you deposited. If you had no liability for a quarter, leave the line blank.

16a **1st quarter** (January 1 – March 31) . . . . 16a [.   ]

16b **2nd quarter** (April 1 – June 30) . . . . 16b [.   ]

16c **3rd quarter** (July 1 – September 30) . . . . 16c [.   ]

16d **4th quarter** (October 1 – December 31) . . . . . . 16d [.   ]

17 **Total tax liability for the year** (lines 16a + 16b + 16c + 16d = line 17) 17 [.   ] **Total must equal line 12.**

Part 6: May we speak with your third-party designee?

Do you want to allow an employee, a paid tax preparer, or another person to discuss this return with the IRS? See the instructions for details.

☐ **Yes.** Designee's name and phone number [   ] [   ]

Select a 5-digit Personal Identification Number (PIN) to use when talking to IRS [ ] [ ] [ ] [ ] [ ]

☐ **No.**

Part 7: Sign here. You MUST complete both pages of this form and SIGN it.

Under penalties of perjury, I declare that I have examined this return, including accompanying schedules and statements, and to the best of my knowledge and belief, it is true, correct, and complete, and that no part of any payment made to a state unemployment fund claimed as a credit was, or is to be, deducted from the payments made to employees. Declaration of preparer (other than taxpayer) is based on all information of which preparer has any knowledge.

✗ **Sign your name here** [   ]

Print your name here [   ]

Print your title here [   ]

Date [/   /   ]

Best daytime phone [   ]

Paid Preparer Use Only   Check if you are self-employed . ☐

Preparer's name	[ ]	PTIN [ ]
Preparer's signature	[ ]	Date [/ /]
Firm's name (or yours if self-employed)	[ ]	EIN [ ]
Address	[ ]	Phone [ ]
City	[ ] State [ ]	ZIP code [ ]

Form 940 Line-by-Line Instructions

The following instructions are based on the 2015 Form 940. Generally, the IRS releases the form in November each year.

Type of Return
a. Amended If this return corrects a previously filed return, check box a.

b. Successor employer If you are a successor employer due to a merger or acquisition, and you are reporting wages or claiming state unemployment tax that was deposited by a previous employer before acquiring the business, check box b.

c. No payments to employees in 2016. If no payments subject to FUTA tax were made to employees, check box c.

d. Final If this a final return because the business stopped paying wages or is no longer in business, check box d.

Part 1: Tell us About Your Return.
Line 1a. If you pay state unemployment taxes in only one state, enter that state's U.S. Postal Service abbreviation.

Line 1b. If you pay state unemployment taxes in more than one state, check box 1b and complete (Schedule A) Form 940, *Multi-State Employer and Credit Reduction Information.*

Line 2. Line 2 is completed when there are one or more credit reduction states. In 2015, 4 states and territories were credit reduction states.

In 2015, 4 states and territories were credit reduction states.

Part 2: Determine FUTA tax Before Adjustment.
If any line in Part 2 does not apply, it should be left blank.

Line 3 Total payments to all employees
The total payments made to employees are reported. Included are amounts electively deferred from wages by the employee. The amount includes all payments, even if the payment is not taxable — salaries; wages; commissions; Section 125 deferrals; deferred compensation deferrals; bonuses; fees; vacation allowances; amounts paid to temporary or part-time employees; the value of goods, lodging, food, clothing, and noncash fringe benefits; and tips reported by employees.

How the payments are made is not important in determining if the payments are wages. For items paid in forms other than cash, use the fair market value of the item.

Line 4 Payments Exempt from FUTA tax

"Wages" and "employment" for FUTA tax purposes do not include every payment and every kind of service an employee may perform. In general, payments that are not wages and payments for services that are not employment are not subject to tax. These payments may be deducted from "total payments" only if they are reported on Line 4. Enter the total amount of exempt payments on Line 4 and check all of the appropriate boxes: 4a (Fringe benefits), 4b (Group-term life insurance), 4c (Retirement/pension), 4d (Dependent care), and 4e (Other amounts paid to employees that are exempt from FUTA tax).

Circular E provides further detail (see page A-175) on payments that are excluded and would require box 4e to be checked. For example:

- Value of certain meals and lodging
- Payments attributable to the employee's contributions to a sick pay plan
- Payments under a workers' compensation law

Line 5 Payments made to each employee in excess of $7,000

Calculate the total payments made to the employee and subtract the items listed on Line 4. If this amount exceeds $7,000, enter the amount in excess of $7,000 on this line. If you checked box b above because you are a successor employer, include in Line 5 amounts paid by the other employer for employees who continued to work for you after the merger/acquisition if the following:

- The other employer was required to file Form 940.
- You have agreed to report the wages for the other employer.

Line 6 Subtotal

Add Lines 4 and 5.

Line 7 Total taxable FUTA wages

Subtract Line 6 from Line 3 and enter the amount in Line 7.

Line 8 FUTA tax before adjustments

Multiply Line 7 by 0.6% and enter the amount on Line 8

Part 3: Determine Your Adjustments.
If any line in Part 3 does not apply, it should be left blank.

Line 9 If all the FUTA wages paid were exempt from state unemployment tax.
Multiply Line 7 by .054 (5.4%) and enter the amount in Line 9. Then skip to Line 12, do not complete Lines 10 or 11.

Line 10 If some of the FUTA wages paid were exempt from state unemployment tax or you paid any state unemployment tax late.
Complete the following worksheet and enter the total in Line 10.
For employers that paid state contributions after January 31, the credit for such payments is limited to 90% of the amount paid, and the total Line 6 credit is determined as follows:

1 Maximum Allowed Credit—Enter the maximum allowable credit
(Multiply line 7 by .054 (5.4%))   1._____

2 Credit for timely state unemployment tax payments?—How much did you pay on time?—Enter the state unemployment tax payments that were made timely; if this line is equal to or greater than line 1, you are not required to complete the remainder of the worksheet.
                                                     2._____

3 Additional credit—Were all of your assigned experience rates 5.4% or more?—If all state unemployment tax rates were 5.4% or more, enter 0 and go to line 4. If any state unemployment tax rate was less than 5.4% calculate the additional credit as follows:

State	Computation Rate— difference between 5.4% and the assigned rate	Taxable state unemployment wages	Additional Credit
1.____	_____	x_____	= _____
2.____	_____	x_____	= _____
3.____	_____	x_____	= _____
		Total	_____

Enter this amount in line 3.   3._____
4 Subtotal Add lines 2 and 3.   4._____
    If Line 4 is equal to or more than Line 1, do not continue completing the work sheet and enter 0.00 on Line 10 of Form 940.

5 Credit for paying state unemployment taxes late—

5a. What is the remaining allowable credit
(Line 1 – 4)   _____

5b. How much state unemployment tax was
paid late   _____

5c. Enter the smaller of Lines 5a or 5b on 5c.   _____

5d. Enter the allowable credit for state
unemployment taxes paid late (Line 5c x .90 (90%))
                                            5d _____

6 FUTA tax credit (Add Line 4 and 5d), if Line 6
is equal to or greater than Line 1, enter 0 on
Line 10 of Form 940. If Line 6 is greater than
Line 1, continue this worksheet.   6._____

7 Adjustment (Line 1 – Line 6 = Line 7). Enter
Line 7 on Line 10 of Form 940.   7._____

Line 11 When credit reduction applies, copy Line 3 from Schedule A (Form 940).

Part 4: Determine Your FUTA Tax.
If any line in Part 4 does not apply, it should be left blank.

Line 12 Total FUTA tax after adjustments
Add Lines 8, 9, 10 and 11.

Line 13 FUTA tax deposited for the year, including any payments applied from a prior year.
Enter the total amount of deposits made for the year. If the previous year's overpayment was applied to the current year, include that amount.

Line 14 Balance due
Subtract Line 12 from Line 13. If this amount is greater than $500.00, an additional deposit must be made by January 31. If the amount due is between $1.00 and $500.00, the amount can be paid with Form 940. Amounts less than $1.00 do not have to be paid.

Line 15 Overpayment
Subtract Line 13 from Line 12 and enter the amount. Check the appropriate box to indicate if a refund is desired or if the amount due will be applied to the next year. *Do not enter amounts on both Line 14 and Line 15.*

Part 5: Report FUTA Tax Liability by Quarter

If Line 12 is less than $500.00, do not complete Part 5 and go to Part 6.

Line 16 Report the FUTA tax liability for each quarter. Do NOT enter the deposits made for each quarter.

Line 16a Enter the FUTA tax liability for the first quarter (January 1 – March 31)

Line 16b Enter the FUTA tax liability for the second quarter (April 1 –June 30)

Line 16c Enter the FUTA tax liability for the third quarter (July 1 – September 30)

Line 16d Enter the FUTA tax liability for the fourth quarter (October 1 – December 31)

Line 17 Total tax liability for the year.
Add Lines 16a, 16b, 16c, and 16d. This total must equal Line 12.

Part 6: Third Party Designee

To allow an employee or an individual paid preparer the ability to discuss your Form 940 with the IRS, check the "Yes" box in Part 6. Also, enter the designee's name, and any five numbers the designee chooses as his or her personal identification number (PIN). The designation must specify an individual and may not refer to a tax preparation firm. The designee authorization cannot be revoked. However, the authorization applies only to issues that arise during the processing of this return and will automatically expire one year after the due date of the return.

By checking the "Yes" box, you are authorizing the IRS to call the designated individual and provide answers to questions arising during the returns process. You are also authorizing the designee to:
- Give the IRS any information missing from your return,
- Call the IRS for information about the processing of your return,
- Respond to certain IRS notices concerning math errors and return preparation, when you have provided the notice to the designee (Note: The IRS will not send notices to the designee).

You are not authorizing the designee to receive any refund check, bind you to anything (including additional tax liability), or otherwise represent you before the IRS.

Part 7: Sign Here
Before filing the completed Form 940, the form must be signed by:

- The individual owning the business, if the employer is a sole proprietorship.
- The president, vice president, or other principal corporate officer if the employer is a corporation.
- An authorized member or partner of an unincorporated association or partnership having knowledge of the organization's affairs.
- The owner of the limited liability company (LLC) if it is a single member limited liability company treated as a disregarded entity.
- A fiduciary if the employer is a trust or estate.

Employers wishing to have an attorney, accountant, other representative, or employee not listed above sign their employment tax returns must obtain a proper power of attorney by completing and filing Form 2848, *Power of Attorney and Declaration of Representative.* The employer must make certain to clearly explain the extent of the authority given the representative by the power of attorney.

If you were paid to prepare this return and are not an employee of the filing entity, you must sign the form. Do not complete this section if you are filing the return as a reporting agent and have a valid Form 8655, *Reporting Agent Authorization*, on file with the IRS. You are not required to complete this section.

Schedule A (Form 940)

Schedule A, (Form 940) *Multi-State Employer and Credit Reduction Information* (page A-51) line-by-line instructions provide instructions for employers paying state unemployment tax in more than one state or paying wages in a state that is subject to credit reduction.

Check the box for each state in which wages were paid that were subject to state unemployment taxes. If any state does not apply, do not check the box.

Fill out this part to tell the IRS about wages paid in any state that is subject to credit reduction.

If any state is subject to credit reduction, as 4 states and territories were in 2015, the FUTA taxable wages from that state are entered. If wages are paid in a state that is not subject to credit reduction, do not enter an amount.

Multiply each credit reduction state wages by the designated percentage (the credit reduction amount) and enter the amount in the credit reduction column.

Total Credit Reduction
Add the amounts entered in the credit reduction column and enter on Line 11 of Form 940.

5.5.2 Form 1099-MISC

A Form 1099-MISC, *Miscellaneous Income* (page A-112), is filed for each person or non-corporate entity who has been paid:

- At least $10 in royalties or broker payments in lieu of dividends or tax-exempt interest,
- At least $600 in rents, services (including parts and materials), prizes and awards, other income payments, medical and health care payments; and
- At least $600 in gross proceeds paid to attorneys, or
- Any fishing boat proceeds.

Form 1099-MISC is due to the recipient of the payment no later than January 31.

Form 1099-MISC must be filed (whether on paper or electronically) on or before January 31, 2017, when reporting nonemployee compensation payments in Box 7. Otherwise, Form 1099-MICS must be filed by February 28, 2017, if filing on paper, or by March 31, 2017, if filing electronically.

| # Trade or Business

Report payments only when they are made in the course of a trade or business. Personal payments are not reportable. However, nonprofit organizations and governmental entities are considered to be engaged in a trade or business and are subject to the reporting requirements. Payments made by federal, state, or local government agencies are also reportable.

Some payments are not required to be reported on Form 1099-MISC, although they may be taxable to the recipient. Payments for which a Form 1099-MISC is not required include the following.

(1) Payments to a corporation, except those required to be reported in Box:

- 6 (medical and health care payments)
- 7 (services provided by an attorney)
- 7 (payments by a federal executive agency for services)
- 8 (substitute payments in lieu of dividends or interest)
- 14 (gross proceeds paid to an attorney in connection with legal services)

(2) Payments for merchandise
(3) Payments of rent to real estate agents
(4) Wages paid to employees (report on Form W-2)
(5) Business travel allowances paid to employees (may be reported on Form W-2)

In addition, use Form 1099-MISC to report direct sales of at least $5,000 of consumer products to a buyer for resale. File Form 1099-MISC for each person from whom any federal income tax was withheld under the backup withholding rules regardless of the amount of the payment. Report only payments made in the course of the payor's trade or business, including those payments made by federal, state, or local government agencies and nonprofit organizations.

CAUTION: Be sure to report payments in the proper box because the IRS uses this information to determine whether the recipient has properly reported the payment.

Backup Withholding

When a company makes a payment reportable on Form 1099-MISC and does not have a taxpayer identification number from the recipient of the payment, the company, under IRS regulations, is required to withhold backup withholding. Backup withholding is withheld at the rate of 28% of the payment. Backup withholding is reported on Form 945, *Annual Return of Federal Income Tax* (page A-100).

Companies may request the independent contractor's TIN with Form W-9.

For example, a company makes a $1,000.00 payment that is to be reported on Form 1099-MISC to an independent contractor that has not provided his taxpayer identification number. The company is to withhold $280.00 from the payment, making a net payment of $720.00. The $280.00 backup withholding will be reported on Form 1099-MISC in box 4, federal income tax withholding.

The backup withholding will be deposited using the same rules as previously discussed in this chapter. The only difference is that the lookback period for Form 945 is the second preceding calendar year. For 2016, the Form 945 lookback period is 2014.

Form 4070

The purpose of Form 4070, *Employee's Report of Tips to Employer*, is for employees to provide the total of all tips the employee receives in a period of time that is no longer than one month. Employees receiving less than $20 in tips a month are not required to report the tips to their employer. Employers are not required to provide Form 4070 for employees to report tips. Employers can use a variety of methods including electronic reporting. In addition, employers can require that tips be reported more frequently than once a month.

Check Your Understanding

Quiz 5.4. Answer the following questions to test your understanding of reporting requirements and federal penalties.

1. What is the FUTA tax rate?
    - ❑ a.   0.6%
    - ❑ b.   5.4%
    - ❑ c.   6.0%
    - ❑ d.   7.65%

2. What is the FUTA tax rate that most employers pay?
    - ❑ a.   0.6%
    - ❑ b.   5.4%
    - ❑ c.   6.0%
    - ❑ d.   7.65%

3. What is the FUTA wage base in 2016?
    - ❑ a. $5,000.00
    - ❑ b. $7,000.00
    - ❑ c. $113,700.00
    - ❑ d. $117,000.00

4. Employers in a state with a credit reduction will pay FUTA taxes at a rate different from 0.6%.
    - ❑ True
    - ❑ False

5. Generally, how frequently are FUTA taxes deposited?
    - ❑ a.   Daily
    - ❑ b.   Semiweekly
    - ❑ c.   Monthly
    - ❑ d.   Quarterly

6. An employer has 20 employees in a state that does not have a FUTA credit reduction. The three top managers of the firm earn $10,000, $7,500, and $5,000 per month. Its ten engineers are paid $3,000 per month. The remaining employees, all support staff, are paid $1,400 per month. Calculate its FUTA deposit for the first quarter.
    $_____

7. By when is the company in Question 6 required to make its first quarter FUTA deposit?
   - ❑ a. April 15
   - ❑ b. April 30
   - ❑ c. May 30
   - ❑ d. It may be carried forward and deposited with the second quarter payment.

8. At the beginning of the second quarter, the employer in Question 6 hires an additional engineer at a monthly salary of $3,300. What is its second-quarter FUTA liability?
   $_____

9. No new staff are added until the fourth quarter, when the employer in Question 6 hires an office manager on December 1 at a monthly salary of $2,000. One of its engineers, with the firm for over 10 years, retires on November 30. On December 31, the employer learns that its FUTA credit is reduced by .3%. What is its fourth-quarter deposit?
   $_____

Answers to Quiz 5.1

1. c. The lookback period for 2016 is July 1, 2014, through June 30, 2015.

2. a. A quarterly depositor has a total tax liability for the quarter that is less than or equal to $2,500.

3. b. A monthly depositor had a tax liability of $50,000 or less during the lookback period and deposits employer taxes by the 15th of the next month.

4. c. A semiweekly depositor has a tax liability greater than $50,000 during the lookback period and makes tax deposits by the Wednesday or Friday after the end of the deposit period.

5. d. A tax liability of $100,000 or more must be deposited on the next business day.

6. d. The company is a monthly depositor because the aggregate amount of employment taxes for the lookback period was $50,000 or less and must deposit the taxes by the 15th of the following month.

7. c. The safe-harbor rule allows depositors to avoid penalties as long as they deposit 98% of their tax liability by the due date. All monthly depositors must deposit the full amount by the due date of their first quarter Form 941 (April 30).

8. a. If an employer accumulates less than $2,500 tax liability during one quarter, taxes may be deposited or paid with the tax return for the quarter.

9. a. Under the semiweekly rule, tax liabilities on payments made on Wednesday, Thursday, and/or Friday must be deposited by the following Wednesday. Tax liabilities on payments made on Saturday, Sunday, Monday, and/or Tuesday must be deposited by the following Friday.

10. False. A monthly depositor with a liability in excess of $100,000 in a deposit period becomes a semiweekly depositor.

11. c. Semiweekly depositors always have three business days to make their deposits after the deposit period ends.

12. b. Because Wednesday is a holiday, the company has until Thursday to deposit its payroll taxes.

13. No. For purposes of the $100,000 rule, do not continue to accumulate employment tax liability after the end of the semiweekly deposit period. The company's deposit period ended on Friday.

14. a. Deposits are due on the first banking day after accumulating $100,000 of more in federal income tax, social security tax, and Medicare tax withheld from employees' wages and the employer's portion of social security tax and Medicare tax.

15. False. The IRS requires semiweekly depositors to deposit the tax liability at the end of each deposit period.

16. d. Annual and quarterly depositors can pay the taxes due when filing Form 941 or 944. The payment must be made to the U.S. Treasury.

17. a

18. b

Answers to Quiz 5.2

1. a. The employer must withhold federal income tax, social security tax and Medicare tax from employees wages and report it on Form 941.

2 d. The employee's social security number is not reported on Form 941.

3. b. Report total taxes on agricultural employees on Form 943.

4. a. Report total taxes withheld from wages, tips, and other compensation on Form 941.

5. b. Report taxable social security and Medicare wages on Form 941.

6. c. Tax returns are sent to the IRS address found in each form's instructions.

7. False. Tax returns can also be sent using a "private delivery service."

8. False. Form 941 is filed quarterly.

9. c. Employers who make timely deposits of the full amount of employment taxes can get a 10-day filing extension. The filing deadline for the first quarter (January 1 to March 31) is normally April 30. The deadline can be extended to May 10.

Answers to Quiz 5.3

1. b. Send W-2s to all employees, current or not, who received wages (even if you didn't withhold taxes). Report earnings of independent contractors, such as the freelance writer, on Form 1099-MISC.

2. d. Unless the former employee has asked in writing to get his W-2 earlier, you can send it along with all employees' wage and tax statements. If he does ask in writing to get the W-2 earlier, you have 30 days to send it to him.

3. a. Form W-3 is used to transmit Copy A of Form W-2 to the Social Security Administration. Its deadline is the same as the deadline for Form W-2 Copy A.

4. b. Correct the error on Form W-2c; transmit the corrected form to the SSA with Form W-3c.

5. b. Each time an employer fails to put correct information on a 2016 Form W-2 or 1099 filed electronically, the employer may be assessed a $50 penalty per form (if corrected within 30 days of the due date), a $100 penalty per form (if corrected more than 30 days after the due date but by August 1), or a $260 penalty per form (if not corrected by August 1).

   Employers are not penalized for timely filed returns with incorrect or incomplete information that are corrected before August 1, up to 10 returns or 0.50% of the total number of information returns the employer must file during the year, whichever is greater.

   0.50% of total number of returns employer must file: 1.75. Therefore the de minimis of 10 will not be penalized so only 90 returns will be penalized at $50 (90 x $50 = $4,500).

6. a. The employer was required to deposit 98% of their accumulated tax liability of $88,639.41, or $86,866.62 . They underdeposited by $6,866.62. The penalty is 2% of the underpayment since they deposited the correct amount within five days. So, the penalty would be $137.33 (2% x $6,866.62).

7. a. The 100% penalty can apply when federal income tax, social security tax, and Medicare tax are not withheld and/or paid. Under this penalty, certain officers of the firm could be found personally responsible for payment of the taxes and penalized an equal amount.

8. c. Do not send paper returns if you file electronically; one of the reasons why the federal government requires large employers to file electronically is to reduce paper.

9. False. Only employees meeting the IRS eligibility requirement must receive notice of the EIC. However, some states require all employees to be notified of the EIC.

10. c. Employers are required to provide EIC information to all employees who do not claim exempt status yet have no federal income tax withheld. Eligible employees can receive EIC when they file their tax return.

Answers to Quiz 5.4

1. c. The FUTA tax rate is 6.0%.

2. a. Most employers are able to take a 5.4% credit for the state unemployment taxes paid for an effective rate of 0.6% (6.0% - 5.4%).

3. b

4. True. Employers in credit reduction states will have their FUTA credit reduced by 0.3% for each year they are in credit reduction status.

5. d. Employers with a quarterly FUTA tax liability of $500 or more must deposit the tax quarterly.

6. The employer's first-quarter FUTA deposit is $722.40.

Note that 13 of its 20 employees will earn over $7,000 in the first three months. Calculate the firm's first-quarter FUTA deposit as follows:

FUTA
Taxable Wages

13 x $7,000.00　　　　= $91,000.00
7 x $1,400.00 x 3 months　= $29,400.00
　　　　　　　　　$120,400.00　x 0.6% = $722.40

7. b. The first quarter deadline is April 30. If the amount (plus any amount not yet deposited for any earlier quarter of the year) is more than $500, deposit it no later than the last day of the first month after the quarter.

8. Its second-quarter FUTA liability is $159.60, calculated as follows.

FUTA
Taxable Wages

1 x $7,000.00   = $7,000.00
7 x $1,400.00 x 2 months   = $19,600.00
          $26,600.00   x 0.6% = $159.60

Note: Thirteen employees had wages in excess of $7,000 in the first quarter. Seven employees had wages of $4,200 each in the first quarter.

Since the liability is less than $500 no deposit is required.

9. Its fourth-quarter FUTA deposit is $618.60.

The FUTA credit is now 5.1% (reduced by .3%). So the employer's effective rate is now 0.9% (6.0% – 5.1% = 0.9%). To calculate their January deposit, recalculate their tax liability at the new rate, subtract for deposits they have already made, and add amounts due for unpaid balances or the fourth quarter. Note: The retirement has no effect on their final deposit since they already covered this employee's wages in the first quarter.

FUTA
Taxable Wages

1Q	$120,400.00	
2Q	$26,600.00	
3Q	0.00	
4Q	$2,000.00	

     $149,000.00   x. 0.9% = $1,341.00

Less year-to-date deposits –   722.40 ($722.40 from the first quarter)

Final deposit $618.60 (due January 31)

Payroll Accounting

6.1 Accounting Basics

Accounting is the basic language of business. It is the art of measuring, communicating, and interpreting financial activity. Accounting enables your organization to do the following:

- Keep track of all its monetary transactions
- Report its financial transactions to shareholders and various federal, state, and local taxing authorities
- Control expenses
- Monitor and safeguard company assets
- Make decisions and plan for the future

Since salaries and employee benefits are typically the largest expenses for most companies, payroll is under close financial scrutiny from top management. And while you may never be required to do double-entry accounting or prepare a balance sheet, your activities have a profound effect on your company's books. This chapter provides a look at some of the ways payroll affects your firm's financial statements.

6.1.1 Recording Transactions

The first phase in the accounting process involves recording each financial transaction as it occurs. The second phase of the accounting process is the posting of the transaction, first to the journal and then to the general ledger. In the final phase, this data is used to prepare financial statements that describe the company's financial position, its cash flow, profits, losses, assets, liabilities, and net worth. These statements, in turn, enable managers, shareholders, bankers, union officials, and others to make decisions about the company's future.

The first phase in the accounting process involves recording each financial transaction as it occurs.

Let us look at how payroll transactions appear on the books. Even though most companies' "books" are stored in the memory of their computers, some terms referencing "physical books" are used to describe the various documents that record transactions.

Accounting data begins with a transaction. Information about each transaction is first posted in the journal. Information from the journal is periodically transferred to the ledger. The updated ledger accounts are eventually used by the organization's accountants to prepare financial statements, such as the balance sheet and income statement. Thus, the accounting flow is as follows:

Transaction ➔ Journal ➔ Ledger ➔ Financial statements

Accounting Principles

Accounting standards are not set by law but by private organizations. The **Financial Accounting Standards Board** (FASB) sets the standards for recording financial transactions. Before FASB, a variety of organizations issued the following set of concepts and principles that have come to be known as **Generally Accepted Accounting Principles** (GAAP).

1. **Business entity concept.** Every organization that operates independently (an entity) is treated as a business under the business entity concept. The purpose of accounting is to report each entity's financial position on a balance sheet and its profitability on an income statement. The employees, owners, and managers of a business entity must keep their personal transactions separate from those of the business entity.

2. **Continuing concern concept.** This concept assumes that a business entity will continue to operate indefinitely as a business. In most cases, "continuing concerns" value their assets at the cost of the assets. If a business is for sale, a business would not be a "continuing concern," and its assets would be valued at their fair market value, not at their cost.

3. **Time period concept.** Each organization must determine its own accounting period based on the type of business in which it is engaged. For its annual accounting period, an organization can choose either the calendar year or another 12-month period.

4. **Cost principle.** Because organizations are assumed to continue as going concerns, all goods and services purchased are recorded at the cost of acquiring them. The cost is measured by the cash spent or the cash equivalent of goods or services provided in return for those purchased. Once valued, an asset remains at that value for its life minus any depreciation in accordance with the continuing concern concept and the "objectivity principle."

5. **Objectivity principle.** Transactions must be recorded objectively to ensure that personal opinions and emotions are not part of the recorded transaction. This principle ensures that accounting information will be useful for lenders and investors. Generally, valuing an asset at cost meets this principle since it requires a deal between a buyer and a seller with different goals in completing the transaction.

6. **Matching principle.** Expenses, revenue, and liabilities must be matched to the accounting period in which they were earned or incurred to satisfy the matching principle. Under the matching principle, transactions may be recorded before any money actually changes hands, but after the essence of the transaction has been completed. The matching principle allows a comparison between different organizations' financial statements.

7. **Realization principle.** The realization principle governs the recording of revenue. Revenue is the income received for goods and services provided by an organization. Revenue is recognized (or realized) and reported when earned, which is during the accounting period when the goods have been transferred or the services provided. The amount recognized is the cash received or the fair market value of goods and services received.

8. **Consistency principle.** Transactions must be recorded in a consistent manner based on the particular accounting method, principle, or period. Users of accounting information require that transactions be recorded consistently so they can make sound financial decisions regarding the organization, especially when comparing previous accounting periods to the current period.

Chart of Accounts

In today's computerized systems, account numbers are far more important than their names. The chart of accounts lists all accounts by name and number. Below is an example of a standard numbering system.

- Asset accounts: 100 series
- Liability accounts: 200 series
- Equity accounts: 300 series
- Revenue accounts: 400 series
- Expense accounts: 500 series
- General overhead: 800 series

Journal

A journal is a chronological record of the daily transactions of a business. For each transaction, the journal shows the debits and credits to be entered in specific ledger accounts and a description of the account. For example, the journal might contain the following entries.

Date		Debit	Credit
June 30	Deposit in payroll checking account	$100,000.00	
	Withdrawal from corporate account		$100,000.00
	Description: transfer cash to cover payroll expense		
July 2	Purchase of computers	$5,000.00	
	Cash		$5,000.00
	Description: Cash purchase of capital equipment		

General ledger

All the subsidiary ledgers together are summarized into the general ledger for the enterprise.

The general ledger is a record of business transactions by account. For example, you might have a subsidiary ledger for payroll expenses, another for federal income tax liabilities, a third for payroll checking, and so on. All the subsidiary ledgers together are summarized into the general ledger for the enterprise.

6.1.2 Types of Accounts

Payroll usually generates entries to three types of accounts.

Asset Accounts

Assets are anything of value that is owned by the company.

Assets are anything of value that is owned by the company, and normally have debit balances.

Examples of assets in the payroll department include the following:

- Computers
- Payroll software
- Calculating machines

- Word processors
- Furniture
- Money in a payroll checking account

Over a period of time, many assets lose value as they age and need to be replaced; therefore, they are sometimes referred to as depreciating assets.

However, the asset most significantly impacted by the payroll process is cash. The cash account represents the cash available to pay the amounts due to the employees.

Liability Accounts

Liabilities are debts. They represent a claim against the company's assets and normally have credit balances. Many payroll transactions represent liabilities, including the following:

- Taxes withheld but not yet deposited
- Contributions to a company benefit plan not yet paid, for example, Section 125 or 401(k)
- A leasing contract for a payroll hardware/software system
- Wages payable to the employees not yet paid

Expense Accounts

Expenses are the cost of goods or services used in the process of obtaining revenue for the company and normally have debit balances. Examples of expenses include the following:

- Salaries of employees
- Cost of employer-paid benefit programs
- Lease payments for hardware/software systems
- Purchasing stationery and computer supplies
- Employer portion of payroll taxes

Your organization's accounting system includes two other types of accounts that payroll typically does not affect directly.

Revenue Accounts

Revenue is income received for goods sold and services rendered and normally has a credit balance.

Equity Accounts

Equity is the net worth of the company and normally have a credit balance. The company's assets minus its liabilities equal its net worth, or shareholders' equity. These accounts are sometimes referred to as retained earnings accounts or capital accounts.

6.1.3 Balance Sheet and Income Statement

A company's financial statements include the balance sheet, retained earnings statement, income statement, cash flow statement, the footnotes to the statements, and a report for the independent auditors.

The balance sheet provides a look at the company's financial condition at a specific point in time by listing its assets, liabilities, and equity.

The income (or profit and loss) statement shows the company's net income or loss for an accounting period. Net income or loss is the difference between revenue and expenses for the accounting period. In most cases, the income statement provides both the current year and prior year's information.

Most organizations publish annual financial statements after they have been audited by independent certified public accountants (not employees of the company's finance department). Other than the auditor's report, all the financial statements are significantly impacted by information and records gathered and recorded by the payroll department. Poor payroll processing and reporting practices can lead to financial statements that materially misrepresent a company's financial condition.

The following is an example of a company's balance sheet.

Assets	
Current Assets	
Cash	121,000
Marketable securities	218,000
Accounts receivables	483,500
Inventory	750,700
Prepaid expenses	62,500
Investments	387,400
Total current assets	2,023,100
Property, plant, and equipment	
Land and Improvements	96,400
Buildings	570,350
Machinery and equipment	1,577,000
(Less accumulated depreciation)	(834,650)
Total Fixed assets	1,409,100
Deferred Assets	
Trademark, goodwill, and contract rights	131,600
Other	
Total Other Assets	131,600
Total Assets	**3,563,800**

Liabilities and Owner's Equity	
Current Liabilities	
Notes/loan payable	95,100
Accounts payable and accrued expenses	672,000
Accrued Taxes	239,100
Total current liabilities	1,006,200
Long-Term Liabilities	
Long-term debt	287,500
Total long-term liabilities	287,500
Stockholders' Equity	
Common stock (no par value)	62,300
Retained earnings	2,093,600
Paid-in capital	114,200
Total Equity	2,270,100
Total Liabilities and Owner's Equity	**3,563,800**

The following is a sample of a company's income statement.

Revenue	20xx
Net Sales	5,900,00
Cost of Goods Sold	(3,307,000)
Gross Profit on Sales	**2,593,000**

Expenses	
Selling, General and Administrative, and equipment depreciation	1,760,000
Operating Income	**833,000**
Non-operating revenues, expenses, gains, losses	70,000
(Less: interest expense)	(37,000)
Income Before Taxes	866,000
(Less: income tax expense)	(270,000)
Net Income	**596,000**

Balance Sheet

On a typical balance sheet, assets are listed first, followed by liabilities and net worth (shareholders' equity). Each major portion of the balance sheet is further divided into smaller segments—the types of assets and liabilities.

Structure of a Typical Balance Sheet

Assets are listed first, followed by liabilities and stockholders' equity (or net worth). Assets and liabilities are listed in order of how quickly they can be converted to cash; first the current assets/liabilities are listed and then longer term assets/liabilities.

Current Assets

The first assets listed on the balance sheet are current assets—those that can be converted into cash within one year. They are listed in order of liquidity, or how long it will take to turn them into cash. Cash is listed first, followed by other assets based on the length of time before they can be converted into cash. Payroll's impact on current assets is the payment of employees' wages, the remittance of deductions from those wages, and the payment of employment taxes, all of which generate entries crediting, or reducing, the cash account. In organizations that produce inventory for sale, the account for that inventory may have entries for salary expenses because the cost of goods sold often includes a portion of employees' wages.

Plant, Property, and Equipment

These assets are expected to be held for more than one year. Payroll will have input into this balance sheet item if the organization builds its own plant, property, and equipment. The labor that goes into constructing the plant facilities will be capitalized, with the amount being the portion of the employees' wages, benefits, and taxes identified as a cost of producing the asset. Until the construction is completed, the capitalized wages, benefits, and taxes are part of the construction in progress account.

Deferred Assets

These assets generally include intangible assets such as goodwill or the value of a patent. While the payroll impact on deferred assets may be minimal, if the organization has a funded or funds designated for a nonqualified deferred compensation plan, the funds will be recognized as a corporate asset.

Current Liabilities

These liabilities must be paid within the next year. Most payroll journal entries affect accounts classified as current liabilities, since most payroll liabilities must be paid within a few days or weeks (for example, withheld taxes, child support and garnishment deductions, union dues, employment taxes, and so forth). Accrued vacation or personal leave that must be taken by employees during the current year is also recorded as a current liability under generally accepted accounting principles (GAAP).

Long-Term Liabilities

If a company's accrued leave policy allows leave time to be carried over from one year to the next, the liability for leave not taken may be split between current and long-term liability. The allocation of the split depends on the carryover history of the company. The continuation of health benefits for a company's retirees requires another allocation between current and long-term liability.

Shareholders' Equity (Net Worth)

The shareholders' equity represents the owners' share of the business after all debts have been accounted for. Balance sheet items typically include the following:

- Common stock—listed at a nominal (par) value that has no relationship to its actual market value
- Retained earnings—income reinvested in the business rather than distributed to the owners
- Contributed (paid-in) capital—additions to equity that do not come from revenue, but are receipts on stock issues or donations

Income Statement

The income statement summarizes the organization's revenues and expenses, reporting the organization's earnings for the current and preceding fiscal years. All companies whose shares are traded on a stock exchange (publicly held companies) and that sell bonds must prepare annual income statements that are audited by independent auditors, and most prepare the income statement more often, usually at least quarterly.

Gross Margin on Sales

Gross margin on sales is measured as the net sales (gross sales less returns and discounts) minus the cost of goods sold (supplies, raw materials, labor), but prior to deductions for the cost of overhead and taxes, and prior to additions for revenue generated other than by sales (for example, interest income, and extraordinary items).

Operating Income (Operating Profit)

The company's operating income takes into consideration overhead costs, such as depreciation and selling and administrative expenses, but not the organization's income tax expense or nonoperating revenue/expenses (for example, interest income/expenses). Operating income provides a good look at how profitable a firm's business operations are in terms of goods and services produced and sold.

Nonoperating Revenue

Nonoperating revenue includes income earned other than from the sale of goods or services produced by the company, such as interest on a checking/savings account or bonds or capital gains from investments.

Nonoperating Expenses

Nonoperating expenses include interest expenses, such as interest paid on loans or bonds and income taxes.

Net Earnings (Net Income/Loss)

Net earnings is the "bottom line" of the income statement. It shows how much profit or loss the company has after paying its taxes.

6.1.4 Double-Entry Accounting

There are single-entry accounting systems and double-entry accounting systems. Your checkbook is an example of a single-entry accounting system. Almost all enterprises keep track of changes in their assets, liabilities, expenses, revenues, and net worth with a double-entry accounting system.

As the name implies, double-entry accounting systems require entering a dollar amount twice for each transaction. Let's look at an example.

Suppose you wrote a check for $1,000.00 to pay for the services of an independent contractor, John Doe. If this were a single-entry system (like the one you keep for your personal checking account), you would enter the check once.

Doing the Math

Number	*Date*	*Check Issued To*	*Amount*
1001	9/1	John Doe	$1,000.00

With a double-entry system, that check is recorded twice, in two different accounts. Paying the independent contractor simultaneously decreases your assets and increases your expenses as shown below.

	Debit	*Credit*
Expenses	$1,000.00	
Asscts (checking account)		$1,000.00

Debits and Credits

In accounting terms, a debit is the left-hand side of an account while a credit is the right-hand side. An account like this is often described as a T account because it forms the letter T.

Debit	*Credit*

Real-world Application

The basic advantage of having a left (debit) side and a right (credit) side is that it provides a built-in check of the system. At the end of the accounting period, perhaps after thousands of entries, the debits and credits from the various accounts must balance. In many computerized accounting systems the debit entry is a plus and the credit entry is a minus.

Posting Entries Into Various Accounts

Whether you record a transaction on the debit or credit side depends on the type of account. In an asset account (for example, the payroll checking account), anything increasing assets appears as a debit, while anything decreasing assets is recorded as a credit. So depositing money in a checking account (increasing assets) is a debit. Writing a check on that account (decreasing your assets) is a credit.

Liability accounts are the opposite. Taking out a loan (increasing your liabilities) is a credit. Paying back the loan (decreasing liabilities) is a debit.

Expense accounts operate like asset accounts. Revenue accounts operate like liability accounts.

Initially, you may find it easier to learn double-entry accounting by memorizing the information in the table below.

Debit or credit?

Any Asset or Expense Account

Debit	Credit
increases	decreases

Any Liability, Revenue, or Capital Account

Debit	Credit
decreases	increases

The following two examples show how to record an off-cycle check and company payroll in the company's journal.

Example #1: Recording an Off-Cycle Check

Let's see how the accounting process works by recording an off-cycle paycheck for an employee. On payday, the newly hired employee did not receive a paycheck in the regular processing. Payroll was required to issue an off-cycle check to the employee so he could be paid at the same time as other employees.

The employee's gross biweekly pay is $1,000.00. In addition to federal income tax ($120.00), state income tax ($50.00), social security tax ($58.28), and Medicare tax ($13.63), he has $60.00 deducted for health insurance (pre-tax). His net pay is $698.09. The company owes the employer's share of social security tax and Medicare tax, as well as federal unemployment tax of $6.00 and state unemployment tax of $24.00.

Doing the Math

Here is how you would record the employee's salary expenses in the journal.

Item	Debit	Credit	Type of Account
Salary expense	$1,000.00		Expense
Wages payable		$1,000.00	Liability

The employee's payroll deductions would be recorded in the journal as follows.

Item	Debit	Credit	Type of Account
Wages payable	$301.91		Liability
Employee's FIT payable		$120.00	Liability
Employee's SIT payable		50.00	Liability
Social security tax payable		58.28	Liability
Medicare tax payable		13.63	Liability
Employee's health insurance payable		60.00	Liability

The actual check paid to the employee would also be entered in the journal. Note how the entries to wages payable for the deductions and the actual paycheck equal the amount posted to the accrued account ($301.91 + $698.09 = $1,000.00).

Item	Debit	Credit	Type of Account
Wages payable	$698.09		Liability
Payroll checking account (cash)		$698.09	Asset

The company must also record the employer's payroll tax expenses on the employee's paycheck.

Item	Debit	Credit	Type of Account
Payroll tax expense	$101.91		Expense
Social security tax payable		$58.28	Liability
Medicare tax payable		13.63	Liability
Federal unemployment tax payable		6.00	Liability
State unemployment tax payable		24.00	Liability

The employee's deductions and the company's tax expense will be combined with the amounts from the regular payroll to make the payments. Remember, tax deposits for manual checks may be required before the next payday. All of the amounts related to Joe's manual check should be recorded in the payroll system for accumulation totals and Form W-2 reporting.

Example #2: Recording Payroll

Assume that your organization's gross pay for the next payroll period is $100,000.00. From that sum, you withhold $20,000.00 for federal tax payable, $6,200.00 for social security tax payable, $1,450.00 for Medicare tax payable, and $6,000.00 for state tax payable. The employer also incurs an expense of $1,500.00 for the employer's share of the medical insurance. And you owe $6,200.00 for the employer's share of social security tax and $1,450.00 for the employer's share of Medicare tax.

Until paid, the amounts payable all increase the firm's liabilities. Here is how they would be posted in your firm's accounts before payday.

Item	Debit	Credit	Type of Account
Salary expense	$100,000.00		Expense
Employer's social security tax expense	6,200.00		Expense
Employer's Medicare tax expense	1,450.00		Expense
Employer's insurance expense	1,500.00		Expense
Federal income tax payable		$20,000.00	Liability
Social security tax payable		12,400.00	Liability
Medicare tax payable		2,900.00	Liability
State income tax payable		6,000.00	Liability
Medical insurance payable		1,500.00	Liability
Net payroll payable		66,350.00	Liability

When payments are made, the liability accounts are debited and the cash account is credited.

6.1.5 Accrual

Accounting Period

An accounting period is a period of time covered by information on an income statement. It may be a month, a quarter, a half-year, or a year. A firm's fiscal accounting year may not be the same as the calendar year.

Not all transactions occur within one accounting period. For example, a pay period may be within two accounting periods and/or fiscal years. When a transaction overlaps two or more accounting periods, accountants must make an approximation (an accrual entry) of its value for each period. Without such an approximation, it is impossible to accurately measure your company's financial position.

Accruals and Reversals

A basic rule of accounting is the "matching principle"— expenses should always be posted against the revenues they produced.

A basic rule of accounting is the "matching principle"—expenses (such as salaries, taxes, or fringe benefits) should always be recorded against the revenues they produced. Thus, you should recognize expenses in the month they occur, not necessarily when they are paid. To do this, you may be required to accrue the expense and, later, reverse it when it is actually paid. Following is an example.

Salaries. The accounting month ends on the last day of each month, but you pay biweekly. Salaries earned during the last part of the month and paid during the next month must be accrued.

- The biweekly pay period beginning Sunday, October 10, and ending Saturday, October 23 is paid on Friday, October 29.
- The next biweekly pay period begins Sunday, October 24, and ends Saturday, November 6 is paid on Friday, November 12.
- The workweek is Monday through Friday.
- There is a five-day accrual for the wages earned in October but paid in November.
- If our previous biweekly gross wages were $50,000.00, our accrual would be five-tenths of that figure or $25,000.00.

The accounting entry for October would be:

Item	Debit	Credit
Salary Expense	$25,000.00	
Accrued Salaries		$25,000.00

In November, when the wages were paid, our October accrual would be reversed and the actual gross wages would be expensed. The reversing entry for November would be:

Item	Debit	Credit
Salary Expense		$25,000.00
Accrued Salaries	$25,000.00	

Check Your Understanding

Quiz 6.1. Answer the following questions to test your understanding of accounting basics and double-entry accounting.

1. A record of the daily transactions of a business is a:
    - ❏ a. balance sheet.
    - ❏ b. journal.
    - ❏ c. ledger.
    - ❏ d. chart of accounts.

2. A record of the business transactions by account is found in the:
    - ❏ a. balance sheet.
    - ❏ b. journal.
    - ❏ c. ledger.
    - ❏ d. chart of accounts.

3. What is normal accounting flow?
    - ❏ a. Ledger ➔ Journal ➔ Transaction ➔ Financial statements
    - ❏ b. Transaction ➔ Ledger ➔ Journal ➔ Financial statements
    - ❏ c. Transaction ➔ Journal ➔ Ledger ➔ Financial statements
    - ❏ d. Journal ➔ Transaction ➔ Ledger ➔ Financial statements

Check Your Understanding

4. A financial transaction is first posted in your organization's:
   - ❏ a. chart of accounts.
   - ❏ b. ledger.
   - ❏ c. journal.
   - ❏ d. balance sheet.

5. In which type of account (asset, liability, expense or revenue) would each of the following entries appear on the books?
   - ❏ a. A new payroll computer
   - ❏ b. Purchase of computer paper
   - ❏ c. Money in a payroll checking account
   - ❏ d. Wages paid to employees
   - ❏ e. Social security tax and Medicare tax withheld but not deposited
   - ❏ f. Employer cost of group-term life insurance
   - ❏ g. Office furniture
   - ❏ h. Deposit of employer portion of social security tax and Medicare tax
   - ❏ i. Mortgage on the addition to your building

6. How would each of the following be posted?
   - ❏ a. Increase an asset account.
   - ❏ b. Decrease a liability account.
   - ❏ c. Increase an expense account.
   - ❏ d. Decrease an asset account.
   - ❏ e. Increase a revenue account.

7. Would each of the following entries be posted in the account as a debit (DR) or a credit (CR)?
   - ❏ a. Purchase of a desk in an asset account
   - ❏ b. Purchase of stationery in an expense account
   - ❏ c. Withdrawal from a payroll checking account
   - ❏ d. Employer contributions to a 401(k) plan in an expense account
   - ❏ e. State income tax withheld but not deposited in a liability account
   - ❏ f. Federal income tax withheld but not paid in a liability account
   - ❏ g. Mortgage payment in a liability account

Answers to Quiz 6.1

1. b. The journal is a chronological record of transactions, in order of their occurrence.

2. c. The ledger is a record of business transactions by account.

3. c. The accounting flow is: Transaction →Journal →Ledger →Financial statements.

4. c. The journal is the first place a transaction is recorded.

5. a. Asset
    b. Expense (It is used to produce a service.)
    c. Asset
    d. Expense

    e. Liability
    f. Expense
    g. Asset
    h. Expense
    i. Liability

6. It may be helpful to visualize the accounts.

Asset/ *Expense*			*Liability/* *Revenue*	
Debit (DR)	Credit (CR)		Debit (DR)	Credit (CR)
incr	decr		decr	incr

    a. Debit (DR)
    b. Debit (DR)
    c. Debit (DR)
    d. Credit (CR)
    e. Credit (CR)

7. Remember how increases (and decreases) are posted in each type of account.

    a. Debit (DR)
    b. Debit (DR)
    c. Credit (CR)
    d. Debit (DR)
    e. Credit (CR)
    f. Credit (CR)
    g. Debit (DR)

Professional Payroll Skills and Responsibilities

7.1 Customer Service

When we think about customer service, it is usually in relation to the support we will receive after we purchase a product or the help given when deciding which product to buy. This is important for the consumer who is willing to pay extra for good service. Examples include tipping for prompt service or purchasing a service contract. The payroll department's product, in addition to being timely and accurate, should also include customer service.

This section includes information that will help you:

- Define customer service
- Identify customer service principles
- Relate customer service to the payroll department
- Look at providing the art of customer service

The payroll department's product, in addition to being timely and accurate, should also include good customer service.

Definition

Customer service is problem solving, soothing the irate, reassuring the timid, and even sometimes "pulling a rabbit out of a hat."

7.1.1 Principles of customer service

There are five principles associated with optimum customer service in payroll.

Reliability

Reliability is the ability to provide what was promised, dependably and accurately. In payroll, this is part of the standard process.

Employees need to receive their paycheck on the scheduled payday. Penalties can be assessed if paychecks are not produced in a timely manner.

The paycheck is only one of the deliverables a payroll department produces. Payroll should be reliable in all its products. When a commitment to a process is made, it should be realistic and attainable.

Responsiveness

Responsiveness is the willingness to help customers promptly. The payroll department is faced with many deadlines. Each may have a significant priority, making it difficult to respond quickly to each inquiry. The ability to meet critical deadlines by responding to employee needs in a timely manner is an important skill to develop.

Assurance

Assurance is the knowledge and the courtesy you show to your customers and your ability to convey trust, competence, and confidence. When an employee contacts the payroll department, he or she needs to know that the information they receive is accurate. You must project confidence in your responses. When uncertain, it is better to ask the employee for time to research the answer rather than give incorrect information. However, the promise to answer cannot be open-ended. The employee must be told when to expect the response.

Empathy

Empathy is the degree of caring and individual attention shown to your customers.

Employees are not experts on how their pay is calculated. The information they seek is important to them, regardless of how basic it may seem to those working in the payroll department. Employees need to receive individual attention when contacting the payroll department.

Tangibles

Tangibles are the physical facilities and equipment and your own (and others') appearance.

The organization of the payroll department may be visible to employees. If there are mounds of paper and things appear to be in disarray, how effective will the department be in explaining a valid reason why a new hire form was not processed promptly rather than being lost in the paper shuffle?

Staff Evolution

Simply stating that tomorrow the payroll department will provide optimum customer service will not work. Like management skills, customer service skills are different for each member of the payroll team.

Educating the payroll staff on the desired results rather than on a specific procedure is more effective. Let's briefly review a couple of instructional strategies for showing the payroll staff customer service expectations.

Role-Play

Role-play are perhaps the most interactive way of looking at customer service situations. During a training session, employees can supply their own examples of customer service experiences.

Use a structured role-play format. Volunteers can act out the scenario and the group will provide feedback on how they would handle the same situation.

Customer service role-play, if handled properly, can be engaging and educational. However, do not force people to participate.

Case Studies

If the payroll department training environment is not conducive to role playing, written case study examples can be used. As a group, the payroll staff can evaluate written customer service scenarios and make recommendations for improvement. Case studies can be included as part of training or regular meeting processes.

7.2 Professional Responsibilities

Payroll Professionals face many issues beyond the production of paychecks. The way you respond to these issues demonstrates your professional manners.

7.2.1 Compliance (Penalties, Notices, Inquiries)

It is not uncommon to receive penalty notices or other inquires from governmental agencies concerning an employee or the company. These notices must be responded to as quickly as possible.

Penalty notices will continue to accrue interest and other fees if the notice is not handled promptly. Even a short letter to the agency stating that the issue is being reviewed can reduce the penalties that may be assessed.

Requests for employee information must be handled within company policy. Failure to provide information that an employee has requested may prevent the employee from purchasing a new home.

7.2.2 Confidentiality

Everyone is entitled to maintain a certain degree of privacy. This section will review the extent to which an employee's privacy rights are protected in the work environment.

Employees' privacy rights are governed by federal and state law and company policy.

Compliance in this area requires the same coordination of regulations as several of the other sections covered in this book. Employee's privacy rights are governed by federal, state and company policy.

In payroll, you are privileged to varying degrees to the personal information about other employees. For example, you may have access to the following types of data:

Employment application	Resume	Telephone number
Form W-4	Home address	Hours of work
Pay level	Pay Increases	Involuntary
Voluntary deductions	Termination reason	deductions
Form I-9	Age	Pay schedule
Social Security number	Salary history	Bank account

In addition to this basic information you may have access to performance appraisals, disciplinary warnings, and medical information.

Whether this information is stored on a computer or in a file cabinet, the employer has a responsibility to protect its confidentially and avoid releasing information to unauthorized persons. When information is inappropriately released, an employee may have a privacy claim.

Review your company policies concerning releasing information about an employee. If guidance is not available, request the employee authorize the release by signing a document that lists the specific data and to whom it may be released.

Unintentional Release of Private Information
Not all information is deliberately released, but its unintentional release can have the same impact on the company if privacy is not maintained. Some tips for protecting data include the following:

Real-world Application

- Secure system access
- Lock files containing employee information
- Limit conversation concerning employee data to secure areas
- Protect internal communications such as e-mail and intra-company mail voice messages

Whistleblower Policies
Employers should have a whistleblower policy that encourages their employees when acting in good faith, to report suspected or actual wrongful conduct. Employers must be committed to protecting employees from interference with making a protected disclosure and from retaliation for having made a protected disclosure or for having refused an illegal order as defined in the employer's whistleblower policy. Management should be prevented from retaliating against an employee

who has made a protected disclosure or who has refused to obey an illegal order. Management and employees may not directly or indirectly use or attempt to use their authority or the influence of their position for the purpose of interfering with the right of another employee to make a protected disclosure to the individual's immediate supervisor or other appropriate administrator or supervisor within the scope of the employer's policy.

7.2.3 Problem Solving

If a problem is identified or perceived, the payroll professional must strive to resolve the issue. If an employee perceives a problem, the payroll professional's starting point is to assemble the documentation that supports the payment to the employee. Some of the data that must be obtained includes time reports, pay authorization, direct deposit authorization, Form W-4, and many more documents. For example, if an employee feels they have been incorrectly paid, the information may be manually assembled and the employee's pay may be calculated and compared to the system-generated calculations. Then the detail information can be presented to the employee documenting their pay and, if an error has occurred, informing the employee how it will be corrected.

In many cases, problems will be identified by the payroll professional in their review of the system controls and edits. If system-generated totals from the data entered do not agree with either batch control totals or other controls, procedures must be in place to determine the error, its cause, and how it should be corrected. Ideally, control totals will have interim totals that correspond to interim totals that the system generates. The interim totals may be divided into divisions, plants, or any other logical sequence. Once the data entered in error has been identified, it must be corrected. This will require developing batch controls for the data correction entries.

7.3 Resources

To ensure compliance in payroll processing, payroll professionals must be aware of legislative and regulatory changes. Analyzing these changes and how they impact payroll processing will ensure continued compliance.

Resources Available to Stay Abreast of Legislative and Regulatory Changes

The United States Congress passes bills, and, with the president's signature, these bills are enacted as laws. In many cases, these laws are very general, and, to allow the provisions of the laws to be applied effectively, agencies of the executive branch of the United States government issue guidance. Regulations—proposed, temporary, interim, and final—provide direction on how the provisions of the laws are to be implemented.

The Internal Revenue Service provides additional guidance:

- Revenue Procedures are procedural directions on the implementation of sections of the Internal Revenue Code.
- Revenue Rulings are directions on how the law will be enforced by the Internal Revenue Service.
- Private Letter Rulings are directions to taxpayers requesting guidance on how the law will be enforced given specific actions that the taxpayer may have taken or wishes to take. These rulings can be used as precedents only by the taxpayer asking for the ruling.

The Wage and Hour Division of the Department of Labor issues guidance in the form of Administrator's Interpretations. These letters are issued when the Administrator feels that further clarity is needed regarding a statutory or regulatory issue under the FLSA or FMLA. Opinion letters based on an employer's specific actions are no longer issued by the Wage and Hour Division.

One of the most important aspects of the payroll department's responsibilities is keeping on top of current developments in the payroll field. As such, payroll is expected not only to stay abreast of the latest tax law amendments and regulatory changes, but also to understand what the new laws and regulations will mean to the employee, the payroll process, and the company as a whole. Payroll professionals must be:

- Aware of other employment-related laws that might affect compliance
- Well-versed in the company's union contracts
- Well-versed in the company's policies and procedures

The American Payroll Association's membership compliance newsletter *Payroll Currently* provides payroll professionals insight into the constantly changing aspects of payroll. In addition, APA members periodically receive compliance update emails with the latest changes that affect payroll professionals.

APA also offers members special subscription rates on *PayState Update*, APA's newsletter covering the latest state and local payroll compliance news. Get information about the newsletter and subscribing on APA's Publications web page (click the link for *PayState Update*),

APA members can also attend timely and topical webinars (live or on demand) at special member rates. Check APA's Course & Conferences web page (www.americanpayroll.org/course-conf/) for the latest information on APA's webinars and other payroll education.

Check Your Understanding

Check Your Understanding

Quiz 7.1. Answer the following questions to test your understanding of professional payroll skills and responsibilities.

1. Which of the following is not a principle of customer service?
   - ❑ a. Reliability
   - ❑ b. Responsiveness
   - ❑ c. Role plays
   - ❑ d. Assurance

2. Which of the following methods are NOT to be used in practicing customer service skills?
   - ❑ a. Role plays
   - ❑ b. Arguing with customers
   - ❑ c. Case studies

3. An employee goes to the payroll department to ask a question about his paycheck. When he arrives, no one is at their desk, files are open, desk tops are covered with paper, and the floor has stacks of reports askew. Which customer service principle could be improved in this payroll department?
   - ❑ a. Reliability
   - ❑ b. Responsiveness
   - ❑ c. Assurance
   - ❑ d. Empathy
   - ❑ e. Tangibles

4. An employee changed her United Way deduction. For two pay periods, the amount deducted was correct. Then, for the following period the amount doubled. When she called the payroll department, the payroll coordinator told her that the situation would be corrected and gave her the option of having the amount added to her next paycheck or receiving a special check for the amount. Which customer service principle is being displayed here?
   - ❑ a. Reliability
   - ❑ b. Responsiveness
   - ❑ c. Assurance
   - ❑ d. Empathy
   - ❑ e. Tangibles

5. A plant supervisor met with the payroll department to schedule a special pay run that would accommodate the shutdown for the holidays. After payroll committed to the date, they realized that to meet this deadline would require working a weekend. Which customer service principle will be compromised if the deadline is not met?
   - ❑ a. Reliability
   - ❑ b. Responsiveness
   - ❑ c. Assurance
   - ❑ d. Empathy
   - ❑ e. Tangibles

6. On Thursday, an employee receives news of a family emergency that requires him to take a flight home that evening. Payday is not until Friday at 3:00 pm, but he needs his paycheck to pay for the flight. When he contacts the payroll department and explains his situation, he is told that a check will be ready for him when he stops by. Which principle of customer service has the payroll department exhibited?
   - ❑ a. Reliability
   - ❑ b. Responsiveness
   - ❑ c. Assurance
   - ❑ d. Empathy
   - ❑ e. Tangibles

7. You receive a penalty notice from a governmental agency. The information is not readily available. What should you do first?
   - ❑ a. Conduct a thorough investigation and send the report to the agency.
   - ❑ b. Ignore the letter because it will take time to locate the information.
   - ❑ c. Send a short letter to the agency stating that the issue is being reviewed.
   - ❑ d. Call the agency and tell them you plan to locate the information and send it in a few months.

8. What should happen with a notice the payroll department receives from the IRS?
   - ❑ a. It should be ignored
   - ❑ b. It should be handled quickly
   - ❑ c. It should be handled after all other duties
   - ❑ d. It should be take to the CEO

9. You receive a letter of inquiry concerning an employee. What should you do?
   - ❑ a. Follow your company's policy on the release of employee information.
   - ❑ b. Ignore the letter because it's the employee's issue.
   - ❑ c. Send a short letter to the agency stating that the issue is being reviewed.
   - ❑ d. Call the requestor and tell them you plan to locate the information and send it in a few months.

10. Payroll personnel should tell their neighbors about the following payroll information.
    - ❑ a. Salary history
    - ❑ b. Termination reasons
    - ❑ c. Pay level
    - ❑ d. None of the above

Answers to Quiz 7.1

1. c. Role plays are the technique used in practicing customer service situations.

2. b. Role plays and case studies are used when practicing customer service skills.

3. e. Tangibles are the physical appearance of the department. Tangibles can have an effect on employees' perception of how effective the department is.

4. b. Correcting the situation promptly and giving the employee options as to how the problem will be corrected are examples of responsiveness.

5. a. Reliability is providing what is promised.

6. d. Understanding the employee's individual situation is an example of empathy.

7. c. These notices must be responded to as quickly as possible. Penalty notices will continue to accrue interest and other fees if the notice is not handled promptly. Even a short letter to the agency stating that the issue is being reviewed can reduce the penalties that may be assessed.

8. b

9. a. Requests for employee information must be handled within company policy. Failure to provide information that an employee has requested may prevent the employee from purchasing a new home.

10. d. Confidentiality is a key tenet for all payroll professionals.

Preparing for the FPC Exam

In recent years, the pressures of economic and legislative developments on the payroll function have broadened the scope of payroll beyond its basic purpose — paying employees. Today's payroll utilizes the latest electronic processing technologies for executing the payroll and, in most cases, interfacing or integrating data with other systems in the organization. During the same time, payroll has come under a wide array of mandates, from the federal income tax withholding that affects nearly all employees to salary deferrals into retirement plans and child support withholding. Among all the internal operations of contemporary U.S. business, none are subject to as many governmental regulations and requirements as payroll.

Among all the internal operations of contemporary U.S. business, none is subject to as many governmental regulations and requirements as payroll.

METHODS OF TESTING AND RECERTIFICATION

As part of its ongoing effort to increase the professionalism and recognition of payroll practitioners, the American Payroll Association has made some significant changes in the methods and processes it uses to certify and recertify payroll professionals. Candidates for the Fundamental Payroll Certification (FPC) Examination now take the test electronically and can choose the day on which they take the test, within a given testing period or on the final day of participating in APA's Payroll Learning Center course—*Payroll 101: Foundations of Payroll Certificate Program.*

Also, for individuals holding the Fundamental Payroll Certification who wish to recertify through continuing education, the process for doing so has been streamlined to make recertification less of an administrative burden. Be sure to read the following sections closely, and the detailed information in the FPC Candidate Handbook and in recertification information sent by email to each FPC by the APA.

8.1 History and Purpose of Certification

Originally a technical skill, payroll has developed into today's professional discipline. Payroll professionals are knowledgeable in all aspects of payroll, stay abreast of changes in processing technologies

Chapter 8

A payroll professional must be proficient in all aspects of taxation and tax reporting, information technology, human resources (including benefits), and accounting.

and, through independent research, remain current with the legislative and regulatory environment applicable to their business. A payroll professional must be proficient in all aspects of taxation and tax reporting, information technology, human resources (including benefits), and accounting as each of these relate to the payroll environment. Today's payroll professional functions as an integral member of the management team, involved in many issues which affect today's corporate operations. Since 1985, the American Payroll Association (APA) has offered certification to recognize those who have achieved a professional skill level.

Certification criteria. Certification is the recognition of one's professional skills by one's peers. APA awards the Fundamental Payroll Certification designation to those who successfully complete the examination and subscribe to the APA Code of Ethics.

Fundamental Payroll Certification is granted for a three-year period, at which time recertification is required.

APA's Fundamental Payroll Certification Committee. The Fundamental Payroll Certification Committee oversees the program and is one of two committees that make up APA's Certification Board. The Committee consists of seven Payroll Professionals serving staggered two-year terms. APA has contracted with Pearson VUE, to administer the exam in accordance with accepted testing standards.

Goals of APA's Fundamental Payroll Certification Committee

1. Promote the standard for payroll practitioners that is accepted by the business community and the public at large.
2. Encourage professional growth and individual study by the payroll practitioner.
3. Provide the standard of requisite knowledge for the payroll practitioner.
4. Measure by means of the certification examination the attainment and application of that standard.
5. Recognize formally those colleagues who continue to meet the requirements of the APA's Fundamental Payroll Certification Committee.

Members of the APA's Certification Advisory Group assist the Certification Board's Fundamental Payroll Certification Committee by writing questions for possible inclusion in APA's bank of FPC exam questions. The questions are reviewed by editors to ensure compliance with accepted question-writing techniques. The edited questions are then reviewed and revised, if necessary, by the FPC Committee for accuracy and relevancy to the activities of payroll professionals entering payroll practice. Approved questions are then included in the bank of questions from which exam items are selected to create new examination forms for each testing window.

8.2 Examination Eligibility Requirements

The Fundamental Payroll Certification exam is open to all those who wish to demonstrate a baseline of payroll competency.

The Fundamental Payroll Certification exam is open to all those who wish to demonstrate a baseline of payroll competency.

Testing dates and registration. For the Fall 2016 exam, testing will occur from September 17 through October 15 at locations in the U.S. and Canada. Registration to reserve a seat at the testing center begins July 12, 2016. You should register as early as possible, because testing centers have a finite number of seats. For the Spring 2017 exam, testing will occur from March 25 through April 22, 2017, at sites across the country and in Canada, with registration beginning on January 17, 2017.

The FPC exam is administered year-round at APA Learning Centers after the Payroll 101 course, Military locations, South America, Europe, Middle East, Africa and Asia/Pacific.

8.3 Examination Fees

The current fee for examinations taken in North America at the APA Learning Centers and for the Militay (which is subject to change) is $305.00. The exam fee for those taking the exam in South America, Europe, Middle East, Africa and Asia/Pacific is $360.00 (subject to change). The examination fee is due at the time the reservation is made.

Candidates are individually liable for the full amount of the examination fee. Once an appointment for an examination has been initiated, the candidate is responsible for paying the full fee. If the candidate cannot test for any reason, or decides not to test, the appointment must either be changed or cancelled according to policy. To change or cancel a reservation and receive a full refund, you must cancel at least 24 hours before your scheduled examination date. If you cancel less than 24 hours before your scheduled examination, you will forfeit the full examination fee.

Candidates are responsible for knowing all regulations regarding fees and examination scheduling as presented in the FPC Candidate Handbook.

Candidates are responsible for knowing all regulations regarding fees and examination scheduling as presented in the Fundamental Payroll Certification Candidate Handbook. There are no exceptions. Examination fees are non-refundable and non-transferable other than under the conditions explained above. For more details, see the FPC Candidate Handbook.

8.4 What to Take With You to the Examination

Take the following items with you to the test center on examination day:

- Two forms of identification. One form of government-issued identification containing a photograph and name exactly as the name under which the candidate registered (e.g., drivers licence, state ID, military ID, passport) and one form showing the name exactly as the name under which the candidate registered (e.g., credit card, social security card). Candidates will not be admitted without proper identification.
- The confirmation number you were given by Pearson VUE when you made your examination reservation.

If you do not present the above items on examination day, you will be denied admission to the test and will be considered absent and the examination fee will be forfeited.

8.5 Testing Center Rules

Each exam center will be staffed by APA's testing vendor. After all candidates have been admitted, the proctor will discuss the rules for the testing site. Pay careful attention to the instructions and ask questions to insure no misunderstandings exist concerning the rules of the testing site. Before your examination begins, you will have the opportunity to review an online tutorial that highlights all of the features and functions of the computerized testing system that you will use. You will also be able to request assistance regarding computer features and functions during the examination.

The following are general guidelines which are followed for all testing centers.

Pay careful attention to the instructions and ask questions to ensure no misunderstandings exist concerning the rules of the site.

- Be on time. You should report to the testing center no later than one-half hour before the scheduled time for the examination. The exact reporting time, date, and location of the examination will be provided when you make your reservation. Allow sufficient time to find parking and the testing room. For security purposes, Pearson VUE will capture each candidate's digital signature, photograph, and palm vein recognition upon check-in. Your photo will be displayed on your score report. You must be on time. You will have three hours to complete the examination.

- Dress appropriately. While every attempt is made to provide a comfortable testing temperature, heating or cooling may sometimes not function properly. You may want to take a coat or sweater to your center. Except in extreme cases, test administrations are not cancelled because of heating or cooling problems at a center.

- You must take your confirmation number to your testing center. You will be admitted only at the testing center and on the date and time you made a reservation to take the exam.

- You must have two forms of identification. One form of government-issued identification containing a photograph and name exactly as the name under which the candidate registered, candidates will not be admitted without proper identification. Government-issued photo ID's include a driver's license with photo, state-issued non-driver ID with photo, military photo ID, or a passport. The second form of identification includes a credit card, social security card, work ID, etc.

- An electronic supplement that is required to take the exam is provided to you within the testing software. The supplement contains all payroll tables required to complete the exam's questions.

- Personal writing tools will not be allowed into the testing area.
  Pearson VUE will provide a whiteboard and erasable pen for you to use when making calculations for test questions.
- Ear plugs are available at each test site for candidate use. Request them if needed.
- You are encouraged to use a calculator during the examination. Only silent, non-printing, battery or solar-powered calculators will be allowed. PROGRAMMABLE CALCU-LATORS WITH ALPHABETIC KEY PADS FROM A - Z ARE NOT ACCEPTABLE AND WILL BE CONFISCATED PRIOR TO TAKING THE EXAM. Sharing of calculators by examinees will not be allowed. Please note that a malfunction of your calculator during the examination will not entitle you to either additional testing time or reason to challenge your examination results. Battery-operated calculators are preferable, since lighting at the test centers may not be bright enough to activate solar calculators.
- You may not take books, papers, or other reference materials into the testing room.
- You may not take personal belongings such as wallets, purses, firearms or other weapons, hats, bags, coats, books, notes, pens or pencils, other reference materials, cell phones, iPods, tablets, hand-held computers/personal digital assistants (PDAs) or other electronic devices, or watches into the examination room.
- No smoking will be allowed in the testing room.
- You may not ask questions about the test after the examination begins.
- Visitors are not allowed in the testing room.
- No group breaks are scheduled during the examination. You are permitted to take individual breaks at the proctor's discretion, but no additional time will be allotted for you to complete the examination. If you are permitted by the proctor to leave the examination room for a break, you will be escorted while outside of the examination room. You may not take any examination materials with you, and you must not speak with anyone while on your break. If you fail to follow this policy, you will be denied re-admittance, will forfeit all fees paid, and your examination will not be scored.

- Any candidate who gives or receives assistance during the examination will be required to turn in all test materials immediately and to leave the room. The candidate's exam will not be scored, no fees will be refunded, and to retest the candidate will have to re-apply to take the examination, including payment of all applicable fees. APA's testing vendor reserves the right to cancel any test score if there is a non-standard test administration.
- It is of utmost importance that all candidates listen carefully to all instructions given by the proctor and follow the directions completely.
- If you experience any problems during the testing, please make a report to the test center manager before leaving.

8.6 Format of the Examination

The examination will be administered on a computer testing station. You will have three hours to complete the examination. The certification examination consists of 150 multiple-choice questions, including 25 pre-test questions placed randomly throughout the exam.

The questions are designed to test your payroll knowledge. An electronic exam supplement containing tables required to correctly answer some questions is included in the testing computer software. Each question has four answer choices listed, only one of which is correct. The answer to each question can be derived independently of the answer to any other question.

All questions are based on federal rules and procedures in effect on January 1, 2016. For example, the $7.25 minimum wage, 6.2% employee social security tax rate and $118,500.00 social security wage base may be tested.

The pre-test items are not counted in the scoring of the examination. They are distributed among the other scorable items and will be used for statistical purposes. The items are similar to the scorable items on the exam and candidates will not know which items are scorable and which are not. Candidates should answer all examination questions.

Each question has the same weight when the passing score is determined. Failing to answer a question is the same as answering the question incorrectly. If you have difficultly answering a question, mark the question for review and if time permits, return to it later.

| Electronic Testing

Your examination will be administered on a computer testing station. The test station will enable you to easily select an answer, change the answer, skip questions, mark questions for review, check your exam status, keep track of your remaining time, and access the online supplement containing all the tables required to complete the exam. In addition, the test station has a "Request Assistance" button that electronically connects you to the Test Center Manager's station. If you click on the "Request Assistance" button, the Test Center Manager will immediately be alerted to your need for help. The Test Center Administration Station monitors all individual Test Stations electronically. The Test Center Manager can oversee the administration of all examinations, respond to requests for help, and ensure the security and privacy of each testing situation.

Before your examination begins, you will have 15 minutes to go through a tutorial that consists of a series of screens that will teach you how to use all of the features and functions of the test station and the exam supplement. The time you spend in the initial tutorial section will not reduce the amount of time you have to work on your examination.

Once you have answered all the questions on the exam, the computer will display a screen stating "review" and "continue". **By selecting "continue" you will end your test and will not be able to go back to any questions you may have skipped or marked for review.** So be certain that when you select "continue" you are ready to end your test and submit your exam to be scored.

8.7 Possible Study Aids

A successful study plan will be one that allows sufficient time for all materials to be covered.

A number of study aids are available. None should be considered the only method available for study. When you study, you should use a number of texts to insure a wide diversity of information. The following list is not to be considered a complete list of all materials available for your use in studying.

APA Courses

> APA's ePayroll Learning Center's Fundamentals of Payroll
> APA's Payroll 101: Foundations of Payroll Certificate Program
> APA's Foundation of Payroll Certificate Program
> FPC Boot Camp Virtual Classroom
> Calculating Paychecks Webinar on Demand

Payroll Practice Essentials
APA's PayTrain®

APA Publications

APA's Payroll Practice Fundamentals
APA's The Payroll Source®
APA's Basic Guide to Payroll
APA's The Guide to Successful Electronic Payments

Internal Revenue Service Publications

Circular E, Employer's Tax Guide (#15)
Employer's Supplemental Tax Guide (#15-A)
Employer's Tax Guide to Fringe Benefits (#15-B)
Taxable and Nontaxable Income (#525)
Note: IRS forms and publications are available online at https://apps.irs.gov/app/picklist/list/formsPublications.html

Wage and Hour Division Publications

Bulletin on Overtime Compensation (#1262)
Exemption for Executive, Administrative, Professional, Computer & Outside Sales Employees Under the Fair Labor Standards Act (Fact Sheet #17A)
Hours Worked Under FLSA (#1312)
Records to Be Kept by Employers (#1261)
Note: Wage and Hour publications are available online at www.dol.gov/whd/publications/

Other Publications

Payroll Accounting by Bieg
BNA's Payroll Administration Guide
CCH's Payroll Management Guide
Thomson Reuters RIA's Payroll Guide
Thomson Reuters RIA's Principles of Payroll Administration
IDG's Accounting Workbook for Dummies
IDG's Customer Service for Dummies

Study plans. A successful study plan will be one that allows sufficient time for all materials to be covered. Using APA's Payroll Knowledge Assessment Calculator (www.payrollkac.com) can assist you in developing your study plan. Waiting until the last minute to study is a sure course for failure. The successful candidate will have begun their course of study at least two months before the exam date, using a variety of sources and techniques.

CHAPTER STUDY GROUPS AVAILABLE A number of the chapters of the American Payroll Association have study programs. Group study has been shown to be a successful method of preparation for the FPC exam. In addition, having familiar faces from the study group at the exam can reduce your nervousness. To find out more about a chapter study group in your area, call APA at 210-226-4600 and ask for the Chapter Relations department.

When preparing for the exam, what your company does may not be applicable. The exam is based on federal laws and regulations in effect January 1, 2016. Some contents of the exam are based on common payroll knowledge, where the practice must be widely known and observed. Be careful to study a variety of widely respected sources, since limiting the sources studied limits your exposure to the common body of knowledge.

Successful completion of the Fall 2016 or Spring 2017 exam requires demonstration of the knowledge of payroll practice and applicable regulations which were in effect as of January 1, 2016. For the Fall 2016 or Spring 2017 examinations, tables and forms required to answer questions will be those that were in effect as of January 1, 2016, and will be provided to you as the electronic exam supplement. The 2016 Form W-2 will be applicable for the Fall 2016 and Spring 2017 exams.

8.8 Content of the Certification Examination

Each certification examination is weighted in approximately the following manner (these statistics include the pre-test questions):

Core Payroll Concepts	40%	approximately 60 questions
Compliance /Research and Resources	20%	approximately 30 questions
Calculation of the Paycheck	22%	approximately 32 questions
Payroll Process and Supporting Systems and Administration	2%	approximately 4 questions
Payroll Administration and Management	7%,	approximately 11 questions
Audits	5%	approximately 7 questions
Accounting	4%	approximately 6 questions

To successfully complete the exam, you do not need to pass all five parts.

Exam content outline. Each question on the exam falls within a specific portion of the exam's content outline. You should begin your study with a review of the content outline to identify areas of weakness. In developing your study plan, concentrate on those areas of weakness. However, do not neglect the areas with which you are familiar in your study plan. You should be aware of areas in which the methods used by your organization differ from federal law. Always using an employee's highest pay rate for overtime calculations rather than using the employee's weighted average pay rate. The complete content outline of the examination is as follows:

I.   Core Payroll Concepts
    A.   Worker Status
    B.   Fair Labor Standards Act
    C.   Employment Taxes
    D.   Employee Benefits
    E.   Employee/Employer Forms
    F.   Professional Responsibility
    G.   Methods and Timing of Pay

II.   Compliance/Research and Resources
    A.   Escheatment
    B.   Regulatory – Maintain compliance and accuracy of payroll processing
    C.   Reporting
    D.   Record Retention
    E.   Penalties

III. Calculation of the Paycheck
    A.   Compensation/Benefits
    B.   Involuntary Deductions / Taxes
    C.   Voluntary Deductions (pre- and post-tax)
    D.   Employer Taxes and Contributions
    E.   Net Pay

IV.   Payroll Process and Supporting Systems and Administration
    A.   Maintain Master File Components
    B.   Concepts and Functionalities
    C.   Disaster Recovery Plan

V. Payroll Administration and Management
    A. Policies and Procedures (e.g., overtime, benefits, leave)
    B. Management Skills and Practices
    C. Communication / Customer Service

VI. Audits
    A. Internal Controls
    B. Payroll System Controls
    C. Accounting System Controls
    D. Audit Policies and Procedures

VII. Accounting
    A. Accounting Principles
    B. General Ledger Account Classification
    C. Payroll Journal Entry
    D. Account Reconciliation

For more details on the topics to be tested, download the FPC Exam's knowledge, skills, and abilities statement from the certification page of APA's web site: www.americanpayroll.org/certification/certification-fpcinfo/. Click on the link for "FPC Knowledge, Skills, and Abilities" found on the page.

8.9 Test Taking Hints

The most difficult aspect of the Fundamental Payroll Certification exam is that it will probably be an unknown — something new — a testing experience that you have not experienced before. Many individuals taking the exam for the first time have not taken an exam for many years. Because the exam is an unknown, the key to success is being relaxed. Reducing anxiety will allow you to be relaxed.

The following are tips on reducing anxiety and being relaxed during the exam.

- Know the location of the testing center. If possible locate it before the day of the exam.
- Allow sufficient time to arrive at the testing center 30 minutes before your appointment. Plan for unexpected delays on the way to the testing center. You may encounter bad weather, road construction, or road closures.

- Know where you will be able to park near the testing center.
- Get a good night's sleep the night before the exam. Last minute cramming will only increase your anxiety. Generally, last minute study only introduces confusion and is not productive.
- Plan your study schedule to leave the night before the exam free from study requirements.
- Wear comfortable clothing to the exam. Business attire is not required when taking the exam. Tight clothing is not comfortable and will restrict your ability to be relaxed.
- Practice with your calculator before the exam. Use it at work and during your study. The calculator should be battery-powered so be sure that fresh batteries have been placed in the calculator.
- Be aware of the time remaining on the exam. Use the clock in the testing program. You will be surprised how quickly it goes by.
- Do not spend excess time on any one question. Easy questions are worth the same number of points as difficult questions. So, if a question stumps you, mark it for review and go to the next question. After completing the remaining questions, come back to the question which stumped you. But remember that selecting "continue" will end your test and your exam will be scored.
- Each question requiring calculation will have incorrect answers that can be derived by using an incorrect method. If time is available, you may want to double check your calculations. Write the steps you have taken in deriving the calculations on the white board provided by the testing center for your review.
- Read each exam question carefully. Be careful of questions which use the words NOT, EXCEPT, MOST, BEST.
- Before beginning the first question of the exam, be sure you are comfortable with using the test station and have completed the online tutorial. Ask questions of the testing personnel at the testing center before you look at the first test question.
- Verify all answers to gross-up questions.

Because the exam is an unknown, the key to success is being relaxed.

There are no penalties for answering questions incorrectly. Passing or failing the exam is based on the number of questions correctly answered. Questions not answered cannot be counted as correct answers and give no credit toward passing. If you have difficulty with a question, mark it for review to ensure that you have time to answer all questions.

There are no penalties for answering questions incorrectly.

8.10 How Your Examination Is Scored

Your answers to the exam and the correct answers are stored on computer files from which your score and statistical reports are generated. Pearson VUE understands the importance of your test results, so it uses many quality control procedures ensuring the accuracy and confidentiality of your answers, the correct answers and your score. As you answer questions, your answer will be compared to the correct answer and the result will be stored. If you change an answer, it will revise the previously stored result. Pearson VUE's test station will produce your raw and scaled score when you complete the exam. A minimum scaled score of 300 is required to pass the exam.

Your Score Report

Your individual score report will be given to you when you complete the exam. It will provide your total test scaled score and indicate whether you passed or failed the examination. Passing or failing is based on your total test scaled score. A scaled score of at least 300 is required to pass.

How the Passing Score Was Set

The passing score for this examination was recommended by a panel of payroll professionals.

The passing score for the FPC examination was recommended by a panel of payroll professionals who used a method called item mapping. The item mapping process incorporates actual performance of the test questions by graphically presenting the difficulty of questions in the test bank. This graphic presentation, or item map, displays questions along a scale based on their difficulty. The panel then judges the performance of a minimally qualified candidate with regard to the test questions displayed on the item map. The cut score study concludes when the panel reaches agreement on which questions have a high likelihood of being answered correctly and which have a low probability of being answered correctly by a minimally qualified candidate. Using this process, the panel recommended the passing score to the Fundamental Payroll Certification Committee, which set the passing score. The passing score of 300 represents the minimum level of knowledge that must be demonstrated to pass the examination.

Raw Scores and Scaled Scores

A raw score on this examination is the number of questions answered correctly. When all examinees take exactly the same examination, their raw scores can be used to compare their performances. However, when there are different forms of an examination (different forms of an examination measure the same knowledge, but use different questions), some exams will be easier or more difficult than other exams. Because of this variation in difficulty, raw scores do not reliably relate the performances of examinees who take different exams.

To make it possible to compare the performances of examinees taking different forms of an examination, a statistical procedure called equating is used to compensate for any variations in difficulty between exams. After equating, the passing raw score for each exam is converted to 300 on a common scale for all exams. Since all exams are equated and all scores are converted to the same scale, all examinees who receive the same scaled score have demonstrated equivalent ability, regardless of which exam they took.

Since different versions of the Fundamental Payroll Certification Examination are administered with each examination period, there are a number of different versions of the examination. Equating and scaled scores are therefore used to ensure that each examinee who achieves the passing scaled score of 300 on his or her examination has demonstrated equivalent minimal competency regardless of the examination form taken.

Different versions of the Fundamental Payroll Certification Examination are administered during each examination period.

Examination Results

Your scores are strictly confidential. Unless you request an official transcript, they will be reported only to you, and the APA.

If you have questions concerning your test results, you should direct them in writing to APA's Certification Department via email, fax, or by mail. However, because of the need to maintain test security, test questions and answers cannot be made available for review. Neither the APA nor Pearson VUE will provide a list of questions you answered incorrectly or correctly. The only information available regarding your performance on the test is provided on your score report.

8.11 Attainment of Certification

Payroll professionals who pass the certification examination and accept the APA Code of Ethics (see following), will receive a certificate and will be entitled to use the letters "FPC" (Fundamental Payroll Certification) after their names for 3 years. To retain the right to use the FPC designation after the initial 3-year period, an individual with the Fundamental Payroll Certification must recertify either by retaking the exam or through continuing education.

8.12 Recertification

The FPC designation is valid for three full calendar years following the year in which certification is originally or previously obtained. FPCs awarded in 2013, for example, will expire on December 31, 2016. The designation of individuals certified or recertified during 2016 will expire on December 31, 2019.

Current FPCs may recertify for an additional three years by retaking and passing the certification examination during the third year or by meeting the continuing education requirements.

The APA will email all FPCs advance notice with their applicable recertification deadline during March and November of the year in which they are scheduled to recertify. FPCs who do not receive this notice should contact APA's Certification Department at recert@americanpayroll.org. It is the responsibility of each FPC to contact APA Membership Services to report name or contact information changes before the recertification deadline. Whether a FPC receives notice of the recertification deadline from APA or not, the FPC is responsible for recertifying by the deadline. FPCs are responsible for maintaining a record of qualifying educational programs attended during their recertification period.

Recertification by Exam

FPCs choosing to recertify by examination must pass the FPC exam in the third year of their certification period. For example, an FPC who passed the FPC exam in 2013 recertifying by exam, must pass the FPC exam by December 31, 2016.

If you allow your certification to expire, however, the recertification policies do not apply, and you must retake the examination. The certification status of all applicants seeking to take the examination for recertification will be verified by APA.

Recertification by Continuing Education

The second option for recertification is to accumulate at least 60 hours of qualifying and approved payroll-related continuing education during the three-year period before certification expires. FPC continuing education is tracked as Recertification Credit Hours (RCHs).

Recertification Credit Hours can be earned by participating in any approved seminars or program designed and administered by the American Payroll Association, APA chapter or APA approved provider. The APA awards Continuing Education Units (CEUs) and RCHs for all its programs and seminars, and 1 CEU is defined as 10 Recertification Credit Hours. To recertify, you may also attend approved APA local chapter educational activities, various payroll-related seminars or educational events sponsored by organizations other than the APA or its affiliates, or College/University courses, if they are offered by APA approved providers.

Recertification Credit Hours must qualify as payroll-related in one of two ways. The educational subject must be covered on the Content Outline for the FPC exam, or the subject must fit in any one of five categories:

1. Payroll management
2. Payroll accounting
3. Payroll systems/human resource systems
4. Payroll taxation (training or update programs)
5. Human resources/personnel training

Whether the FPC elects to accumulate Recertification Credit Hours or to re-take the examination every three years, the APA is confident that the FPC designation will continue to mirror the high standards of the payroll professional.

Recertification Credits for APA Professional Membership

All national-level APA members are granted three (3) Recertification Credit Hours (RCHs) per year for being a member in good standing. RCHs are awarded at the end of the APA member's membership year based on anniversary date and will be applied in-full to the year awarded. Partial credit(s) will not be awarded for a membership term of less than one full year.

8.13 American Payroll Association Code of Ethics

1. To be mindful of the personal aspect of the payroll relationship between employer and employee, and to ensure that harmony is maintained through constant concern for the Payroll Professional's fellow employees
2. To strive for perfect accuracy and timeliness of all payroll activities
3. To keep abreast of the state of the payroll art with regard to developments in payroll technologies
4. To be current with legislative developments and actions on the part of regulatory bodies, insofar as they affect payroll
5. To maintain the absolute confidentiality of the payroll, within the procedures of the employer
6. To refrain from using Association activities for one's personal self-interest or financial gain
7. To take as one's commitment the enhancement of one's professional abilities through the resources of the American Payroll Association
8. To support one's fellow Payroll Professionals, both within and outside one's organization

8.14 Fundamental Payroll Certification Exam Practice Test Number 1

1. When a payroll department does not respond promptly to a penalty notice from a governmental agency against an employee, this is an example of:
    A. poor problem solving.
    B. breach of confidentiality.
    C. lack of compliance.
    D. responding to higher priorities.

2. What is the formula for calculating an employee's net pay?
    A. Gross pay - Deductions for taxes + Other deductions
    B. Other deductions + Gross pay - Deductions for taxes
    C. Gross pay + Deductions for taxes + Other deductions
    D. Gross pay - Deductions for taxes - Other deductions

3. Under the FLSA how old must a minor be to be employed?
    A. 12
    B. 13
    C. 14
    D. 16

4. What is the FUTA tax rate?
    A. 0.6%
    B. 1.45%
    C. 5.4%
    D. 6.0%

5. On Form 941, the employer reports:
    A. unemployment wages.
    B. disability deferred compensation excise tax.
    C. social security wages.
    D. unemployment taxes.

6. All of the following are payroll control procedures EXCEPT:
    A. external audits.
    B. edits.
    C. system selection.
    D. security.

7. If the human resources and payroll systems are not integrated, what individual employee data should be retained in both systems?
   A. Garnishment deductions
   B. Taxable earnings
   C. Gross earnings
   D. Pay rate

8. An employee's monthly income is insufficient to pay for all his deductions. The deductions were issued and received by the employer in the following order:

   • $60.00 in creditor garnishments
   • $125.00 direct payment for his mortgage
   • $300.00 for child support
   • $105.00 federal tax levy.

   Generally, which deduction has SECOND priority?
   A. Direct mortgage payment
   B. Child support
   C. Federal tax levy
   D. Creditor garnishment

9. Which of the following plans can discriminate in favor of highly compensated employees?
   A. 403(b) plans
   B. Section 125 benefit plans
   C. Defined contribution plans
   D. Nonqualified deferred compensation plans

10. What is the federal minimum wage per hour on January 1, 2016?
   A. $5.15
   B. $5.85
   C. $6.55
   D. $7.25

11. A company is located in a state with no state or local income taxes. When grossing up holiday bonuses for employees who have already earned more than $118,500.00 but less than $500,000.00, the payroll department should divide the amount of the bonus by what percentage?
    A.   75.00%
    B.   73.55%
    C.   71.55%
    D.   67.35%

12. An employee died on Saturday. His payday was the previous Friday, and he had not yet cashed his check. What, if anything, should the payroll department do?
    A.   Reissue the check to the employee's estate/beneficiary
    B.   Reissue the check without the federal income tax withholding
    C.   Reissue the check with no tax withholding
    D.   Nothing

13. What law determines the time limits with which employees must be paid after wages are earned?
    A.   Fair Labor Standards Act
    B.   Internal Revenue Code
    C.   Social Security Act
    D.   State laws

14. To convey assurance to a customer, a payroll practitioner should:
    A.   display confidence and competence.
    B.   have organizational skills.
    C.   provide a benefit employees can purchase with after-tax dollars.
    D.   get things done promptly.

15. Cafeteria plans are authorized by what Internal Revenue Code Section?
    A.   125
    B.   401(k)
    C.   403(b)
    D.   457(b)

16. The direct deposit data sent to the bank after payroll processing is an example of a(n):
    A. reasonability test.
    B. hash total.
    C. interface.
    D. validity edit.

17. What taxes, if any, must be withheld from payments to an independent contractor who provided a TIN?
    A. Federal income tax only
    B. Social security and Medicare taxes only
    C. Federal income, social security, and Medicare taxes
    D. No taxes are withheld

18. Which of the following employees is an exempt employee?
    A. A production supervisor paid a weekly salary of $1,000.00 who is responsible for hiring, reviewing, and scheduling employees and handling employee complaints
    B. A laboratory assistant paid a weekly salary of $600.00 who is responsible for cleaning and maintaining the facilities and performing some quality control testing, which is reviewed by her supervisor
    C. An assistant office manager earning over $455.00 per week but not managing the department or supervising other employees on a regular basis
    D. A purchasing agent paid a weekly salary of $400.00 a week

19. An external audit:
    A. provides assurance that fraud has not occurred.
    B. allows investment in the company.
    C. provides assurance that the finances have been handled correctly.
    D. allows an objective assessment of the financial statements.

20. If a payroll practitioner is empathetic, she should:
    A. arrive at work on time.
    B. have good time management skills.
    C. show sensitivity and treat all employees as individuals.
    D. share confidential information with the employees when they request it

21. Which of the following statements is true regarding payroll tax deposits?
    A. Employers are penalized for failing to deposit 100% of their tax liability by the due date.
    B. Employers with accumulated payroll taxes under $2,500 for a month can deposit the amount due with their quarterly tax return.
    C. Employers accumulating a tax liability of more than $50,000 in the lookback period file Schedule B with Form 941.
    D. Employers must withhold taxes on noncash fringe benefits at least quarterly.

22. Employees' privacy rights are governed by all the following EXCEPT:
    A. federal regulation.
    B. state regulation.
    C. company policy.
    D. local legislation.

23. Under the FLSA, what basis is used to determine whether a nonexempt employee is to be paid overtime?
    A. Hours worked in a day
    B. Hours worked in a workweek
    C. Hours worked in a pay period
    D. Hours worked in a month

24. Overtime payments are included in the calculation of what tax, if any?
    A. Federal income tax
    B. Social security tax
    C. Medicare tax
    D. They are included in all tax calculations

25. What is the 2016 wage base for social security tax?
    A. $113,700.00
    B. $117,000.00
    C. $118,500.00
    D. $200,000.00

26. Which of the following types of compensation is taxable?
    A.   Bonuses
    B.   Qualified moving expenses reimbursements
    C.   De minimis fringe benefits
    D.   Job-related educational assistance

27. If an employee does not have federal income tax withheld and has not claimed exempt, what must the employer do?
    A.   Provide the employee with the EITC notice
    B.   Withhold federal income tax in the subsequent year
    C.   Request that the employee submit a new Form W-4.
    D.   Not report the amount of the payments in Box 1 of Form W-2

28. What advantages does a payroll checking account provide?
    A.   Prevents fraud
    B.   Facilitates reconciliations
    C.   Ensures that reconciliations are completed in a timely manner
    D.   Ensures that checks are issued correctly

29. A computerized payroll system can help a payroll department accomplish all of the following tasks EXCEPT:
    A.   recognize changes in laws and regulations.
    B.   maintain compliance with laws and regulations.
    C.   produce timely, accurate paychecks.
    D.   retain records.

30. An employee's profit sharing bonus is payable in the year following his death. How should the bonus be taxed and reported?
    A.   Withhold no taxes and report the bonus on Form 1099-MISC
    B.   Withhold social security and Medicare taxes only and report on both Form W-2 and 1099-MISC
    C.   Withhold social security and Medicare taxes only and report the bonus on Form W-2
    D.   Withhold FIT at the optional flat rate and social security and Medicare taxes; report the bonus on Form W-2

31. In what ways can a computerized payroll system increase the accuracy of employee paychecks?
    A.   By reducing human error
    B.   By providing reports detailing the calculations
    C.   By making multiple calculations very quickly
    D.   By making multiple calculations in the same way

32. What federal taxes must an employer withhold from an employee's reported tips?
    A.   Federal income tax only
    B.   Social security tax only
    C.   Medicare tax only
    D.   Federal income, social security and Medicare tax

33. All of the following are voluntary deductions EXCEPT:
    A.   credit union payments.
    B.   united Way deduction.
    C.   creditor garnishment.
    D.   charitable contribution.

34. The main purpose of batch controls is to:
    A.   facilitate tax reporting.
    B.   make filing easier.
    C.   validate data entry accuracy.
    D.   meet unemployment requirements.

35. Which of the following types of compensation is taxable?
    A.   Backpay awards
    B.   Business use of a company vehicle
    C.   No-additional-cost fringe benefits
    D.   Qualified transportation fringe benefits

36. Payroll faces challenges from all of the following items EXCEPT:
    A.   technology.
    B.   communication.
    C.   complexity.
    D.   tax rates.

37. Which of the following amounts is used when calculating an employee's gross-up?
    A.   Disposable income
    B.   Take-Home pay
    C.   Gross income
    D.   Net pay

38. An employee is receiving a $500.00 net bonus. The employee is married with 3 allowances. The employee's YTD gross pay is $98,000.00 and the employee is paid biweekly. The employee lives and works in a state where there is no income tax. Calculate the gross amount of the bonus pay.
    A. $500.00
    B. $679.81
    C. $742.39
    D. $777.00

39. Under the FLSA, when determining whether a nonexempt employee is to be paid overtime, the employer uses the hours worked in a:
    A.   day.
    B.   workweek.
    C.   pay period.
    D.   month.

40. Employees can provide their employer with their marital status and allowances for income tax withholding purposes by:
    A.   telling their supervisor.
    B.   completing Form W-4.
    C.   completing their employment application.
    D.   a telephone call.

41. Generally, what is the largest expense for most companies?
    A.   Salaries and benefits
    B.   Cost of goods
    C.   Depreciation
    D.   Nonoperating expenses

42. What is a major payroll task that requires processing?
    A.   Completing forms for employees
    B.   Retaining records
    C.   Calculating taxes
    D.   Filing tax forms

43. Which of the following statements is correct regarding Section 125 plans?
    A. Employees working 10 hours a week or more must be included in the company's Section 125 plan.
    B. Any benefits received in cash are not taxed.
    C. At the end of the plan year, employees receive cash payments for amounts remaining.
    D. Benefits can be changed during the plan year if there is a qualified change in status.

44. The amount of federal income tax that is withheld from an employee's regular wages is determined by a formula that uses all of the following information items EXCEPT:
    A. pay period.
    B. marital status.
    C. a flat rate.
    D. employee's taxable wages.

45. What authority controls the frequency with which employees must be paid?
    A. State laws
    B. FLSA rules
    C. Local laws
    D. IRS rules

46. All of the following statements about FLSA overtime regulations are true EXCEPT:
    A. a bonus paid under a union contract is included in the regular rate of pay.
    B. a holiday bonus, paid at the discretion of the employer, is excluded from the regular rate of pay.
    C. the week's regular rate of pay must include shift premiums.
    D. employers must pay overtime when employees work more than eight hours in a workday.

47. Payroll documentation accomplishes all of the following goals EXCEPT:
    A. ensuring uniformity.
    B. providing a reference tool.
    C. ensuring that procedures are followed.
    D. simplifying training.

48. All of the following statements are correct regarding online processing EXCEPT:
    A.   the data is changed immediately.
    B.   the system is interactive.
    C.   the operator can communicate with the system as the data is being processed.
    D.   the data to be processed may be batched.

49. What is the general ledger?
    A.   A summary of transactions by date
    B.   The first place transactions are recorded
    C.   A chronological record of daily transactions
    D.   A record of transactions by account

50. What, if any, is the 2016 wage base for Medicare tax?
    A. $117,000.00
    B. $118,500.00
    C. $200,000.00
    D.   There is no limit

Fundamental Payroll Certification Exam Practice Test Number 2

1. An employee works from midnight to 8:00 a.m. on a company paid holiday but does not work more than 40 hours during the workweek. Under the FLSA, the employee must be paid:
    a.   double time for working the holiday.
    b.   time and one-half for working the holiday.
    c.   a shift differential for working the late-night shift.
    d.   at least the federal minimum wage.

2. Which of the following statements about the FLSA overtime requirements is correct?
    a.   An employer may establish one workweek for clerical employees and another for assembly workers.
    b.   An employer's workweek must coincide with the calendar week.
    c.   Employers must pay overtime when employees work more than eight hours in a workday.
    d.   Employers must pay overtime for hours worked on federal holidays.

3. Which of the following employees is entitled to file a Form W-4 claiming exempt?
    a.   A part-time student earning an average of $300.00 per week and claimed as a dependent
    b.   A full-time student earning $500.00 per week and claimed as a dependent
    c.   An employee exempt in 2015 who hasn't filed a new Form W-4 by February 15, 2016, earning $500.00 per week
    d.   An employee who paid no taxes last year and expects to pay none this year

4. An employer should remind employees to complete an amended Form W-4 if they have any changes in status:
    a.   is not the employer's responsibility.
    b.   by December 31 of each year.
    c.   whenever notified of a change in marital status.
    d.   by December 1 of each year.

5. If an employee provides an invalid Form W-4, the employer must:
   a. accept the form until the employee completes a new form.
   b. implement the form and notify the IRS.
   c. refuse to accept the form.
   d. implement the form as is.

6. Under the FLSA, an employee's workday is defined as the:
   a. entire time spent on the job site.
   b. time recorded on the employee's time sheet.
   c. time the employee is performing principal activities.
   d. scheduled shift.

7. What taxes, if any, must be withheld from an independent contractor providing a TIN?
   a. Federal income tax only
   b. Social security and Medicare taxes only
   c. Federal income, social security, and Medicare taxes only
   d. No federal employment taxes are required to be withheld

8. An exempt employee under the FLSA is exempt from:
   a. minimum wage only.
   b. federal income tax withholding.
   c. both minimum wage and overtime.
   d. overtime payments only.

9. Under the FLSA, rounding must:
   a. be consistent.
   b. be at the employer's discretion.
   c. be at the employee's discretion.
   d. done in 30 minute increments.

10. Who verifies eligibility to work in the U.S.?
    a. U.S. Citizenship and Immigration Services
    b. Department of Labor
    c. Employee
    d. Employer

11. Under the FLSA, what type of pay is included in a nonexempt employee's regular rate of pay calculation?
    a. Paid vacation leave
    b. Paid sick leave
    c. Discretionary bonuses
    d. Production bonuses

12. An employee who files an exempt Form W-4 is exempt from the withholding of:
    a.   federal income tax only.
    b.   social security tax only.
    c.   medicare tax only.
    d.   all taxes.

13. An employer's responsibilities with Form W-4 include:
    a.   requesting a new Form W-4 from each employee each year.
    b.   filing all new Forms W-4 with the IRS every year.
    c.   advising employees about the number of allowances they can claim..
    d.   implementing the Form W-4 within the time allowed.

14. When does an exempt Form W-4 expire?
    a.   At the end of each quarter
    b.   February 15 of the next year
    c.   It continues as long as the employee is subject to social security tax
    d.   December 31 of each year

15. An employee's monthly income is insufficient to pay for all his deductions. The deductions were issued and received by the employer in the following order:

    • $60.00 in creditor garnishments
    • $125.00 direct payment for his mortgage
    • $300.00 for child support
    • $105.00 federal tax levy.

    Generally, which deduction has SECOND priority?
    a.   Child support
    b.   Direct mortgage payment
    c.   Creditor garnishment
    d.   Federal tax levy

16. A commission is included in the calculation of which tax, if any?
    a.   Federal income tax only
    b.   Social security and Medicare taxes only
    c.   Federal income, social security and Medicare taxes only
    d.   All federal taxes

17. A waitperson earns $175.00 in tips this week. As a full-time employee, she often works overtime. Can her employer take the tip credit on the overtime hours?
    a. Yes, if the state minimum wage is greater than the federal minimum wage.
    b. No, the FLSA does not provide for time and one-half on tips.
    c. Yes, the tip credit applies to all hours worked.
    d. Yes, if the federal minimum wage is greater than the state minimum wage.

18. The definition of disposable earnings for a creditor garnishment is:
    a. gross wages less all deductions required by law.
    b. all compensation for services, including wages, salary, commissions, and bonuses.
    c. gross wages less federal, state, and local taxes, court-ordered child support, and levies.
    d. gross wages less federal, state, and local taxes and court-ordered child support.

19. For tipped employees to be paid $2.13 per hour, what is the minimum amount of tips they must receive each month?
    a. $20.00
    b. $30.00
    c. $40.00
    d. $50.00

20. The formula for calculating an employee's net pay is:
    a. other deductions plus gross pay less tax deductions.
    b. gross pay less taxes withheld plus other deductions.
    c. gross pay plus tax deductions plus other deductions.
    d. gross pay less taxes withheld less other deductions.

21. What action must an employer take when receiving a child support order?
    a. Tell the employee to resolve the issue with the courts.
    b. Discipline the employee because of the deduction.
    c. Make the deduction as required.
    d. Terminate the employee because of the deduction.

22. IRS regulations define all of the following payment as supplemental payments EXCEPT:
    a.   tips.
    b.   severance.
    c.   salary.
    d.   bonus.

23. What is the minimum amount of tips an employee reports each month that requires an employer withhold federal taxes from the employee's tips?
    a. $20.00
    b. $30.00
    c. $40.00
    d. $50.00

24. Which of the following information is required to correctly calculate federal income tax withholding?
    a.   Regular rate of pay
    b.   After-tax deductions
    c.   Tax levies in effect
    d.   Marital status

25. The payroll department received a court order to begin withholding $125.00 from an employee's weekly paycheck for child support. This means that:
    a.   payroll must get the employee's written permission to withhold child support.
    b.   the employee has been in arrears in making child support payments.
    c.   the employee's ex-spouse is on welfare.
    d.   the payroll department must withhold no more than $125.00 from the employee's paycheck.

26. When calculating an employee's net pay, all of the following amounts are subtracted from gross earnings EXCEPT:
    a.   cafeteria plan contributions.
    b.   401(k) contributions.
    c.   federal income tax.
    d.   regular rate of pay.

27. When making a supplemental wage payment to an employee whose supplemental YTD wages exceed $1,000,000.00, what tax rate is used to calculate federal income tax withholding?
    a. 7.65%
    b. 25%
    c. 28%
    d. 39.6%

28. Under the FLSA, calculate the overtime premium pay for a nonexempt employee who is paid $10.00 per hour and works 45 hours in the workweek.
    a. $25.00
    b. $75.00
    c. $450.00
    d. $475.00

29. All of the following factors are used in calculating an employee's federal income tax withholding EXCEPT:
    a. pay frequency.
    b. number of allowances.
    c. marital status.
    d. regular rate of pay.

30. Which of the following amounts is used when calculating an employee's gross-up?
    a. Disposable income
    b. Gross income
    c. Taxable income
    d. Net pay

31. Under the FLSA, calculate the weekly compensation due to a nonexempt employee who is paid $10.00 per hour and works 45 hours in the workweek.
    a. $25.00
    b. $75.00
    c. $450.00
    d. $475.00

32. For an employee in a state with no state income tax and YTD wages in the amount of $50,000.00, when calculating a gross-up, the employee's desired net payment of $5,000.00 is divided by 100% less the:
    a. federal income tax percentage only
    b. Medicare tax percentage only
    c. social security, and Medicare tax percentages only
    d. federal income, social security and Medicare tax percentages only

33. Last month, an employee had an administrative assistant type a personal letter and photocopy 50 fliers for a club's garage sale. The employee also purchased gifts using the company's Internet connection. How does the IRC define these services?
    a. No-additional-cost services
    b. Working condition fringes
    c. Taxable compensation
    d. De minimis fringes

34. Qualified transportation fringe benefits are subject to what taxes, if any?
    a. No federal taxes
    b. Federal income tax only
    c. Social security and Medicare taxes only
    d. Federal income, social security, and Medicare taxes

35. Which of the following statements is true regarding 401(k) plans?
    a. Employers must match employee 401(k) deferrals.
    b. In 2016, the maximum 401(k) deferral for employees under 50 years of age to a 401(k) plan is $18,000.
    c. Employee deferrals to a 401(k) plan are not subject to social security and Medicare taxes.
    d. 401(k) plans must allow eligible employees to defer up to 15% of their wages.

36. All of the following benefits are taxable wages EXCEPT:
    a. bonuses.
    b. commissions.
    c. overtime compensation.
    d. de minimis fringe benefits.

37. Which of the following plans can discriminate in favor of highly compensated employees?
    a. Section 125 benefit plans
    b. Defined contribution plans
    c. 401(k) plans
    d. Nonqualified deferred compensation plans

38. All of the following benefits are taxable EXCEPT:
    a. a trip for two to Las Vegas given to an outside salesperson for exceeding sales goals by 150%.
    b. a $5,000.00 check to a marketing representative for sales efforts.
    c. a $1,000.00 savings bond awarded to a payroll supervisor for cost-cutting suggestions.
    d. a gold watch (costing $300.00) awarded to an employee for 30 years of service with the company.

39. How frequently must an employer include noncash fringe benefits in an employee's income?
    a. Each pay period
    b. Quarterly
    c. Semiannually
    d. Annually

40. A semiweekly depositor has a liability of $79,000.00 from Wednesday's payday and a liability of $50,000.00 from Friday's payday. The deposit is due by the:
    a. next Monday.
    b. next Wednesday.
    c. next Friday.
    d. 15th of the month.

41. Employers reduce their total taxes on Form 941 by what amount, if any?
    a. Social security tax
    b. Medicare tax
    c. Additional Medicare tax
    d. The taxes cannot be reduced

42. If the cumulative FUTA tax liability is more than $500.00, when must it be deposited?
    a. Semiweekly
    b. Monthly
    c. Quarterly
    d. Along with the regular tax deposit

43. FUTA taxes of more than $500.00 on wages paid in the first quarter must be deposited no later than:
    a. March 31.
    b. April 15.
    c. April 30.
    d. May 1.

44. A semiweekly depositor that has a payroll tax liability of $50,000 from a Monday payroll must deposit the liability by:
    a. Tuesday.
    b. Wednesday.
    c. Thursday.
    d. Friday.

45. All of the following items are reported on Form W-2 EXCEPT:
    a. wages subject to Medicare tax.
    b. cost of group-term life insurance.
    c. payment for services to an independent contractor.
    d. withheld federal income tax.

46. When an employee has a legal name change, what does the IRS require the employer to see before reporting the new name on Form W-2?
    a. An amended Form I-9
    b. A court document
    c. An amended Form W-4
    d. A corrected social security card

47. An accounting document containing records of all business transactions by account is the:
    a. journal.
    b. income statement.
    c. chart of accounts.
    d. general ledger.

48. Accounting data begins with a transaction. This information is first posted:
    a.   on the income statement.
    b.   in the general ledger.
    c.   in the chart of accounts.
    d.   in the journal.

49. Salaries earned but not yet paid in the current month must be recorded as a:
    a.   debit to salary payable.
    b.   credit to salary expense.
    c.   debit to cash.
    d.   debit to salary expense.

50. Generally, the largest expense for most companies is:
    a.   nonoperating expenses.
    b.   depreciation.
    c.   cost of goods.
    d.   salaries and benefits.

Fundamental Payroll Certification Exam Practice Test Number 1 Answer Key

1.	A	18.	A	35.	A
2.	D	19.	D	36.	D
3.	C	20.	C	37.	D
4.	D	21.	C	38.	C
5.	C	22.	D	39.	B
6.	C	23.	B	40.	B
7.	D	24.	D	41.	A
8.	C	25.	C	42.	C
9.	D	26.	A	43.	D
10.	D	27.	A	44.	C
11.	B	28.	B	45.	A
12.	A	29.	A	46.	D
13.	D	30.	A	47.	C
14.	A	31.	A	48.	C
15.	A	32.	D	49.	D
16.	C	33.	C	50.	D
17.	D	34.	C		

**Fundamental Payroll Certification Exam Practice Test
Number 2 Answer Key**

1.	D	18.	A	35.	B
2.	A	19.	B	36.	D
3.	D	20.	D	37.	D
4.	D	21.	C	38.	D
5.	C	22.	C	39.	D
6.	C	23.	A	40.	A
7.	D	24.	D	41.	D
8.	C	25.	D	42.	C
9.	A	26.	D	43.	C
10.	D	27.	D	44.	D
11.	D	28.	A	45.	C
12.	A	29.	D	46.	D
13.	D	30.	D	47.	D
14.	B	31.	D	48.	D
15.	D	32.	D	49.	D
16.	D	33.	D	50.	D
17.	C	34.	A		

Glossary of Common Payroll Terms

accounting period: the period of time covered by an income statement (e.g., month, year); also known as the business cycle (6.1.2)

accrual: the recognition of expenses, and revenues after the cash value has been determined but before it has been transferred (6.1.4)

ACH: Automated Clearing House (2.6.2)

ACH credit entry: a transaction in which a tax-payer instructs its financial institution to originate a federal tax deposit through the ACH system to the appropriate Treasury account, also known as EFTPS - through a financial institution (5.1.4)

ACH debit entry: a transaction in which the IRS, after receiving instructions from the employer, instructs the employer's financial institution to withdraw funds from the employer's account for a federal tax deposit and to route the deposit to the appropriate Treasury account through the ACH system, also known as EFTPS-Direct (5.1.4)

adoption assistance: benefit provided by an employer to an employee to help with the child adoption process. It is excluded from federal income tax withholding, though not from social security and Medicare taxes

aggregate method: method of withholding federal income tax from supplemental wages in which the supplemental wage payment is combined with the regular wages paid during the most recent payroll period; after calculating withholding on the total amount using the wage-bracket or percentage method, the amount already withheld from the last wage payment is subtracted to reach the amount that must be withheld from the supplemental wage payment (3.1.4)

asset: resource acquired by a business that is consumed by the business (6.1.2)

ATM: automated teller machine

Automated Clearing House (ACH): A Federal Reserve Bank or private financial institution acting on behalf of an association operating a facility that serves as a clearinghouse for direct deposit or other payment transactions; entries are received and transmitted by the ACH under the rules of the association (2.6.2)

balance sheet: a financial statement that presents a business's financial position in terms of its assets, liabilities, and owner's equity as of a certain date (generally the end of the company's fiscal year, but may be issued quarterly as well) (6.1.2)

batch: sample or limited amount of all of the data being processed (2.2.1)

batch control: control that is designed to ensure that a batch of data has been entered successfully (2.4.5)

biweekly: once every two weeks; type of payroll period that can be used in the percentage method or the wage-bracket method of withholding (1.7.3)

cafeteria plan: a plan that offers flexible benefits under IRC §125. Employees choose their benefits from a "menu" of cash and benefits, some of which can be paid for with pretax deductions from wages (4.6.1)

cash or deferred arrangement (CODA): an arrangement under a retirement plan that allows employees to either receive cash or have the employer contribute an equivalent amount to the plan (4.5.1)

chart of accounts: lists each account by a name and an identification number; the numbering scheme is designed to identify the type of account (6.1.1)

CODA: Cash or deferred arrangement (4.5.1)

commission: percentage of sales, collections, etc., paid to an employee

common law test: a test that measures the control and direction that an employer has the authority to exercise over a worker; where the employer has the right to direct the worker as to how, where, and when the work will be completed, in addition to controlling the result of the

work, the worker is a common law employee (1.3.2)

compensation: all cash and noncash remuneration given to an employee for services performed for the employer (1.3)

constructive receipt: occurs when wages are made available to an employee, not when the wages were earned (3.1.2)

customer service: in a payroll environment, customer service consists of reliability, responsiveness, assurance, empathy, and tangibles (7.1)

deduction: an amount subtracted from an employee's gross pay to reach net pay, or an amount allowed to taxpayers as an offset against income (3.3)

deferred compensation: in general, the deferral of a wage payment to a future date. Usually describes a portion of wages set aside by an employer for an employee and put into a retirement plan on a pretax basis (4.5)

defined benefit plan: a retirement plan that uses a formula (generally based on an employee's salary and length of service) to calculate an employee's retirement benefits and is not funded by employee contributions to the plan (4.5.1)

defined contribution plan: a retirement plan with benefits determined by the amount in an employee's account at the time of retirement. The account may be funded by contributions from both the employer and the employee (4.5.1)

dependent care assistance program: an employer plan providing dependent care services or reimbursement for such services

direct deposit: the electronic transfer of an employee's net pay directly into financial institution accounts designated by the employee, thus avoiding the need for a paycheck (2.6.2)

discretionary bonus: bonus paid for services performed; in order to be considered discretionary, the bonus cannot be paid because of a promise made in advance, a contract, or another agreement (1.7.2)

disposable earnings: that part of an employee's earnings remaining after deductions required by law (e.g., taxes); it is used to determine the amount of an employee's pay that is subject to a garnishment, attachment, student loan, or child support withholding order (3.3.2)

Earned Income Credit (EIC): tax credit that is available to low-income employees; it is taken when the employee files his or her individual tax return

EFT: electronic funds transfer (2.6.2)

EFTPS: Electronic Federal Tax Payment System (4.1.4)

Electronic Federal Tax Payment System (EFTPS): allows employers to make federal tax deposits electronically through the ACH network (5.1.4)

electronic funds transfer (EFT): the transfer of money electronically from an account in one financial institution to an account in another financial institution (see direct deposit) (2.6.2)

electronic tax application (ETA): a "same-day settlement" EFTPS procedure under which tax deposits are initiated and settled on the same day (5.1.4)

employee: an individual who performs services for another individual or an organization in return for compensation (1.2.1)

employer identification number (EIN): the employer's account number with the Internal Revenue Service, it consists of nine digits (00-0000000) (4.1)

equity: represents the owner's investment in a company, i.e., the company's net worth (6.1.2)

ETA: electronic tax application (4.1.4)

excise tax: tax imposed on a specific transaction

exempt (Form W-4): if an employee claims exempt on his or her Form W-4, the employer does not withhold federal income tax from the employee's wages (1.9.4)

exempt employees: an employee not covered under the Fair Labor Standards Act, it generally means those employees who are exempt from the minimum wage, overtime pay, and certain recordkeeping requirements of the Federal Wage-Hour Law (1.3.2)

expense account: shows costs for goods and services consumed by the company during the accounting period (6.1.2)

Fair Labor Standards Act: law which regulates such areas as minimum wage, overtime pay, and child labor for employers and employees covered by the law (1.3)

fair market value (FMV): used to determine the value of noncash, employer-provided benefits for payroll tax purposes, or the value of facilities provided to employees in lieu of wages (1.7.1)

Family and Medical Leave Act (FMLA): law guaranteeing 12 weeks' unpaid leave to most employees to care for newborn or newly adopted children, or to deal with a serious illness or injury suffered by the employee or an ailing child, spouse, or parent of the employee, because of any qualifying exigency arising out of the fact that the employee's spouse, son, daughter, or parent is a covered military member on active duty (or has been notified of an impending call or order to active duty) in support of a contingency operation, or, "eligible" employees of a covered employer may take unpaid leave, or substitute appropriate paid leave if the employee has earned or accrued it, for up to a total of 26 workweeks in a "single 12-month period" to care for a covered servicemember with a serious injury or illness. (1.12)

federal income tax withholding (FITW): FIT withheld from employees' wages when they are paid (3.1.4)

Federal Insurance Contributions Act (FICA): describes the combined taxes levied for social security and Medicare (3.2)

Federal Unemployment Tax Act (FUTA): requires employers to pay a certain percentage of their employees' wages (up to a maximum wage limit) as a payroll tax to help fund unemployment compensation benefits for separated employees (5.2.5 and 5.5.1)

filing status: marital status of an employee for withholding purposes

FIT: federal income tax (3.1.4)

FITW: federal income tax withholding (3.1.4)

flat rate method: method of withholding federal income tax on supplemental wages in which the supplemental payment and regular wages are treated separately; the employer withholds 25% or 39.6% of the supplemental wages (3.1.4)

FLSA: Fair Labor Standards Act of 1938 (1.3)

FMLA: Family and Medical Leave Act of 1993 (1.12)

Form 940, Employer's Annual Federal Unemployment Tax Return: reports payments and calculates the FUTA tax (5.5.1)

Form 941, Employer's Quarterly Federal Tax Return: provides the IRS with a report of each employer's total taxable wages paid and payroll tax liability (5.2.1)

Form 941-X, Adjusted Employer's Quarterly Federal Tax Return or Claim for Refund: use Form 941-X to correct errors on a Form 941 that you previously filed. Use Form 941-X to correct wages, tips, and other compensation; income tax withheld from wages, tips, and other compensation; taxable social security wages; taxable social security tips and taxable Medicare wages and tips

Form 1099-MISC, Miscellaneous Income: reports how much an independent contractor was paid for services rendered during the past calendar year (5.5.2)

Form W-2, Wage and Tax Statement: a form employers must file to report the total amount of wages paid and taxes withheld for each employee in a calendar year (5.3)

Form W-2c, Corrected Wage and Tax Statement: a form that must be completed by an employer if incorrect information has been entered on Form W-2 that has been sent to the SSA

Form W-3, Transmittal of Wage and Tax Statements: a form which an employer must also file when filing paper Forms W-2 (Copy A) with the SSA; contains totals of the amounts reported on the employer's W-2 forms, acting as a "reconciliation" of these forms (5.3.4)

Form W-3c, Transmittal of Corrected Wage and Tax Statements: a form that accompanies Form W-2c when it is sent to the SSA that totals the information from all the W-2c forms being submitted

Form W-4, Employee's Withholding Allowance Certificate: the W-4 form tells the employer how many withholding allowances the employee is claiming along with the employee's marital status; it also tells the employer if the employee claims exemption from withholding (1.10)

Form W-4P, Withholding Certificate for Pension or Annuity Payments: a form that allows retired employees to have input into the amount of federal income tax withheld from a pension or annuity (1.10.6)

Form W-4S, Request for Federal Income Tax Withholding From Sick Pay: a form filed when an employee receives sick pay from a third-party insurer due to a disabling non-job-related illness or injury; the employee uses the form to tell the third party how much to withhold from his or her pay (1.10.7)

FTD: Federal Tax Deposit (5.1)

FUTA: Federal Unemployment Tax Act, requires employers to pay a certain percentage of their employees' wages (up to a maximum wage limit) as a payroll tax to help fund unemployment programs (5.2.5 and 5.5.1)

garnishment: a legal proceeding authorizing an involuntary transfer of an employee's wages to a creditor to satisfy a debt (3.3.2)

general ledger: ledger containing all of the transactions in the debit and credit accounts of a business (6.1.1)

golden parachute payment: a payment made to business executives in excess or their usual compensation (e.g., stock options, bonuses) in the event the business is sold and the executives are terminated from employment

gross income: the compensation for services, including fees, commissions, fringe benefits, and similar items (3.6)

gross pay: the total amount received from the employer before any deductions are made (3.6)

group-term life insurance (GTLI): term life insurance that is provided by employers for employees, with the cost being borne by the employer, the employee, or both (4.4)

highly compensated employee (HCE): in the context of certain fringe benefit plans, an employee who is an owner or officer of a business or whose salary exceeds a certain amount (indexed each year for inflation). Many benefits offered by employers do not qualify for favorable tax treatment if they discriminate in favor of highly compensated employees. And employers may also be restricted in their use of safe-harbor valuations of benefits provided to such employees

Immigration Reform and Control Act of 1986 (IRCA): The law that prohibits employers from hiring persons who are not authorized to work in the U.S. and from discriminating against those who are authorized to work in the U.S. based on their national origin or citizenship (1.2.5)

income statement: financial statement showing a company's results of operations for an accounting period or fiscal year

independent contractor: a nonemployee contracted by a business to perform services; although the business specifies the result of the work to be performed, it has no right to control the details of when, how, or who will ultimately perform the work (1.2.1)

information return: a return sent to the IRS (for example, 1099 series) or the SSA (for example, Form W-2) that indicates information relevant to tax liability

interface: the place where two systems meet (2.3)

Internal Revenue Code (IRC): federal tax laws; generally referred to as the Internal Revenue Code of 1986, which was the year of the latest major overhaul of the Code; the IRC also comprises Title 26 of the United States Code

involuntary deductions: deductions over which employers and employees have no control (3.3.2)

IRA: Individual Retirement Arrangement

IRCA: Immigration Reform and Control Act

leased employees: Employees of a leasing agency who are hired and trained for the client firm through the agency. Withholding, depositing, and reporting responsibilities remain with the leasing agency (1.2.3)

liability: debt of a business that has yet to be paid (6.1.2)

long-term care insurance: An insurance contract providing for coverage of qualified long-term care services, including diagnostic, preventive, treating, mitigating and rehabilitative services, which is treated as an accident and health insurance contract for payroll tax purposes

lookback period: the 12-month period running from July 1 of the second preceding calendar year through June-30 of the preceding calendar year; the employer's payroll tax liability during this period determines its depositor status for the current year (5.1.1)

Medicare: federal hospital insurance program for individuals age 65 or older and some disabled persons; it is funded through the hospital insurance (HI) component of the FICA tax commonly called the Medicare Tax (3.2)

minimum wage: lowest amount that an employer can pay its employees per hour under federal or state law; the federal minimum wage on January 1, 2016, is $7.25 per hour (1.4)

monthly: once per month; type of payroll period

net pay: that part of an employee's wages that remains after all deductions have been subtracted (e.g., taxes, health insurance premiums, union dues, etc.) (3.6)

net worth: amount by which a company's assets exceed liabilities

noncash fringe benefits: benefits provided to employees in some form other than cash (e.g., company car, health and life insurance, parking facility, etc.), which may be taxable or nontaxable (4.1)

nondiscretionary bonus: contractual or agreed-upon bonus or incentive related to production, efficiency, attendance, quality, or some other measure of performance (1.7.2)

nonexempt employees: employees who are covered by the minimum wage and overtime provisions of the Fair Labor Standards Act; they may be paid on an hourly or salary basis (1.3.1)

nonqualified plan: in the context of employee benefits, an employer plan that does not meet IRS qualification requirements (4.5.1)

ODFI: Originating Depository Financial Institution (2.6.3)

one-day deposit rule: if an employer's accumulated employment tax liability reaches $100,000 on any day during a monthly or semiweekly deposit period, the taxes must be deposited by the close of the next banking day (5.1.2)

originating depository financial institution (ODFI): a financial institution that is qualified to initiate deposit entries submitted by an employer as part of the direct deposit process (2.6.3)

overtime: hours worked by nonexempt employees in excess of maximums set by federal or state law that must be compensated at a premium rate of pay (e.g., under the FLSA, all hours worked over 40 in a workweek must be paid at not less than 1.5 times the employee's regular rate of pay) (1.6)

overtime premium: amount equal to one-half of an employee's regular rate of pay times all overtime hours worked (1.6.1)

paid time off: payment received for time not worked due to holiday, illness, vacation, jury duty, bereavement, or the failure of the employer to provide sufficient work (1.5.3)

payroll expense: expense that may be recorded in the payroll expense journal by function or by type of pay (6.1.2)

payroll register: report listing and summarizing the compensation paid and deductions taken from each employee's wages for the payroll period (3.6)

PDS: private delivery services (5.2.1)

percentage method: one method for calculating federal income tax withholding from an employee's wages, most often used when the calculation is automated (3.1.4)

pieceworker: worker who is paid per unit, or piece, produced (1.7.3)

posting: recording a transaction in a journal entry, or recording a journal entry in the general ledger (6.1.3)

private delivery services (PDS): delivery service which may meet IRS criteria for submitting tax forms (5.2.1)

profit: occurs when income exceeds expenses

qualified plan: a benefit plan that meets IRS qualification requirements for tax-favored treatment (for example, nondiscrimination) (4.5.1)

quarterly: once every three months or four times per year

reasonable basis: a standard used to determine whether a worker can be treated as an independent contractor whether or not the common law test is met, based on prior court and administrative rulings, IRS audits, or long-standing practice in the industry (1.2.2)

reconcile: to ensure that amounts withheld, deposited, paid, and reported by employers agree with each other and, if they do not, to determine the reasons and make the necessary corrections (2.4.2)

reconciliation: process of ensuring that amounts withheld, deposited, paid, and reported by employers agree with each other and that if they do not, determining the reasons and making the necessary corrections (2.4.2)

regular rate of pay: hourly pay rate determined by dividing the total regular pay actually earned for the workweek by the total number of hours worked (1.7.1)

reimbursed expense: payment for business-related expenses incurred by an employee on behalf of, or for the convenience of, the employer

remuneration: payment for services, including benefits

retained earnings: amount that a company's revenue exceeds its expenses, reduced by any amount returned to the owners

retroactive pay: pay for time worked in a previous workweek; retroactive pay must be applied to both regular and overtime hours (1.7.2)

revenue: income received for goods and services provided by an organization (6.1.2)

revenue account: identifies amounts received for goods sold and services rendered during the accounting period (6.1.2)

safe-harbor: an IRS-approved alternative method for complying with IRS rules, regulations, and procedures (for example, per diem allowances and high-low substantiation)

semiannual: twice per year or once every six months

semimonthly: twice per month; type of payroll period

SEP: simplified employee pension

severance pay: a payment made by an employer to terminated employees (usually those who are terminated through no fault of their own) that is designed to tide them over until new employment is secured

shift differential: extra pay received by employees for working a less-than-desirable shift (e.g., evenings or late nights) (1.5.2)

sick pay: replacement wages paid to an employee who cannot work because of an illness or injury that is not work-related

simplified employee pension (SEP): an Individual Retirement Arrangement (IRA) with special participation requirements that is available to certain small employers

SIT: state income tax

social security: Old Age, Survivors, and Disability Insurance (OASDI) component of the FICA tax (3.2)

Social Security Administration (SSA): the federal government agency that administers social security

social security number (SSN): an individual's taxpayer identification number, it consists of nine digits (000-00-0000) (5.3.3)

SSA: Social Security Administration

SSN: social security number (5.3.3)

statement of cash flow: financial statement that shows the sources and uses of cash during the accounting period

statutory employees: special groups of employees identified by law (for example, full-time life insurance sales-people, certain homeworkers) whose wages are not subject to FITW, but are subject to FICA and FUTA

subsidiary ledger: replaces a journal; summarized entries are posted from subsidiary ledgers directly to the general ledger; arose with the computerization of most companies' accounting systems

supplemental wages: compensation received by employees other than their regular pay, such as bonuses, commissions, and severance pay; income tax may be withheld from such payments at a flat rate under certain circumstances (3.1.4)

system edit: warning or alert built into computer software; a system edit checks for errors and either corrects them or notifies the operator that something may be wrong; system edits generally check for values outside accepted ranges (e.g., negative net pay) (2.4.1)

T account: diagram used for recording entries into an account (6.1.3)

take-home pay: in the context of a federal tax levy, the amount of an employee's wages that remains after all normal deductions in effect at the time the levy was received (3.3.2)

tangible: type of asset which includes land and improvements; buildings; computers and software; furniture; and automobiles

tax levy: requires employers to deduct an amount of money that the employee owes, plus any penalties and interest payments, from the employee's wages and remit it to the proper government agency (3.3.2)

taxpayer identification number (TIN): a social security number (SSN), employer identification number (EIN), or individual taxpayer identification number (ITIN) which serves as the taxpayer's account number with the IRS and many state and local tax agencies

temporary help agency employees: Workers hired through temporary help agencies who are screened and trained by the agency to provide services for client firms. They are employees of the agency, rather than the client firm (1.2.3)

TIN: taxpayer identification number

tip credit: reduction in the minimum wage allowed for tipped employees (1.4.2)

validity edit: shows whether or not data entered meet the requirements set forth by a company (2.4.1)

wage base: wage limit beyond which an employee's wages are not taxed (3.2.1 and 5.2.5)

wage-bracket method: method for calculating the amount of federal income tax to be withheld from an employee's wages based on wage-bracket tables classified by the employee's marital status and payroll period (3.1.4)

weekly: once per week; type of payroll period

white collar employees: in the context of the Federal Wage-Hour Law, these are executive, administrative, professional (including computer-related professionals), or outside sales employees who are exempt from the law's minimum wage, overtime pay, and certain recordkeeping requirements (1.3.2)

withholding: subtracting amounts from an employee's wages for taxes, garnishments, or levies, and other deductions (e.g., medical insurance premiums, union dues); these amounts are then paid over to the government agency or other party to whom they are owed (3.1)

withholding allowance: reduces the amount of wages subject to federal income tax withholding based on exemptions and deductions claimed on federal income tax Form 1040 (3.1.4)

workweek: basis for determining an employee's regular rate of pay and overtime pay due under the Fair Labor Standards Act; it can be any consecutive 7-day (168-hour) period chosen by the employer (e.g., Saturday through Friday, Wednesday through Tuesday) (1.6.3)

APPENDIX A

22222	Void ☐	**a** Employee's social security number	For Official Use Only ▶ OMB No. 1545-0008	

b Employer identification number (EIN)	**1** Wages, tips, other compensation	**2** Federal income tax withheld
c Employer's name, address, and ZIP code	**3** Social security wages	**4** Social security tax withheld
	5 Medicare wages and tips	**6** Medicare tax withheld
	7 Social security tips	**8** Allocated tips
d Control number	**9**	**10** Dependent care benefits
e Employee's first name and initial Last name Suff.	**11** Nonqualified plans	**12a** See instructions for box 12
	13 Statutory employee ☐ Retirement plan ☐ Third-party sick pay ☐	**12b**
	14 Other	**12c**
f Employee's address and ZIP code		**12d**

15 State	Employer's state ID number	**16** State wages, tips, etc.	**17** State income tax	**18** Local wages, tips, etc.	**19** Local income tax	**20** Locality name

Form **W-2** Wage and Tax Statement   **2016**   Department of the Treasury—Internal Revenue Service

Copy A For Social Security Administration — Send this entire page with Form W-3 to the Social Security Administration; photocopies are **not** acceptable.

For Privacy Act and Paperwork Reduction Act Notice, see the separate instructions.

Cat. No. 10134D

Do Not Cut, Fold, or Staple Forms on This Page

DO NOT STAPLE

33333	a Control number	For Official Use Only ▶ OMB No. 1545-0008		

b Kind of Payer (Check one)
- 941
- CT-1
- Military
- Hshld. emp.
- 943
- Medicare govt. emp.
- 944

Kind of Employer (Check one)
- None apply
- State/local non-501c
- 501c non-govt.
- State/local 501c
- Federal govt.

Third-party sick pay (Check if applicable)

c Total number of Forms W-2	d Establishment number	1 Wages, tips, other compensation	2 Federal income tax withheld
e Employer identification number (EIN)		3 Social security wages	4 Social security tax withheld
f Employer's name		5 Medicare wages and tips	6 Medicare tax withheld
		7 Social security tips	8 Allocated tips
		9	10 Dependent care benefits
		11 Nonqualified plans	12a Deferred compensation
g Employer's address and ZIP code			
h Other EIN used this year		13 For third-party sick pay use only	12b
15 State Employer's state ID number		14 Income tax withheld by payer of third-party sick pay	
16 State wages, tips, etc.	17 State income tax	18 Local wages, tips, etc.	19 Local income tax
Employer's contact person		Employer's telephone number	For Official Use Only
Employer's fax number		Employer's email address	

Under penalties of perjury, I declare that I have examined this return and accompanying documents and, to the best of my knowledge and belief, they are true, correct, and complete.

Signature ▶   Title ▶   Date ▶

Form **W-3** Transmittal of Wage and Tax Statements   **2016**   Department of the Treasury
Internal Revenue Service

Send this entire page with the entire Copy A page of Form(s) W-2 to the Social Security Administration (SSA). Photocopies are not acceptable. Do not send Form W-3 if you filed electronically with the SSA.
Do not send any payment (cash, checks, money orders, etc.) with Forms W-2 and W-3.

Reminder

Separate instructions. See the 2016 General Instructions for Forms W-2 and W-3 for information on completing this form. Do not file Form W-3 for Form(s) W-2 that were submitted electronically to the SSA.

Purpose of Form

A Form W-3 Transmittal is completed only when paper Copy A of Form(s) W-2, Wage and Tax Statement, is being filed. Do not file Form W-3 alone. All paper forms **must** comply with IRS standards and be machine readable. Photocopies are **not** acceptable. Use a Form W-3 even if only one paper Form W-2 is being filed. Make sure both the Form W-3 and Form(s) W-2 show the correct tax year and Employer Identification Number (EIN). Make a copy of this form and keep it with Copy D (For Employer) of Form(s) W-2 for your records. The IRS recommends retaining copies of these forms for four years.

E-Filing

The SSA strongly suggests employers report Form W-3 and Forms W-2 Copy A electronically instead of on paper. The SSA provides two free e-filing options on its Business Services Online (BSO) website:

• **W-2 Online.** Use fill-in forms to create, save, print, and submit up to 50 Forms W-2 at a time to the SSA.

• **File Upload.** Upload wage files to the SSA you have created using payroll or tax software that formats the files according to the SSA's *Specifications for Filing Forms W-2 Electronically (EFW2)*.

W-2 Online fill-in forms or file uploads will be on time if submitted by March 31, 2017. For more information, go to *www.socialsecurity.gov/employer*. First time filers, select *"Go to Register"*; returning filers select *"Go To Log In."*

When To File

Mail Form W-3 with Copy A of Form(s) W-2 by February 28, 2017.

Where To File Paper Forms

Send this entire page with the entire Copy A page of Form(s) W-2 to:

**Social Security Administration
Data Operations Center
Wilkes-Barre, PA 18769-0001**

Note: If you use "Certified Mail" to file, change the ZIP code to "18769-0002." If you use an IRS-approved private delivery service, add "ATTN: W-2 Process, 1150 E. Mountain Dr." to the address and change the ZIP code to "18702-7997." See Publication 15 (Circular E), Employer's Tax Guide, for a list of IRS-approved private delivery services.

For Privacy Act and Paperwork Reduction Act Notice, see the separate instructions.

Cat. No. 10159Y

20**16**

Department of the Treasury
Internal Revenue Service

General Instructions for Forms W-2 and W-3

(Including Forms W-2AS, W-2CM, W-2GU, W-2VI, W-3SS, W-2c, and W-3c)

Section references are to the Internal Revenue Code unless otherwise noted.

Future Developments

For the latest information about developments related to Forms W-2 and W-3 and their instructions, such as legislation enacted after they were published, go to *www.irs.gov/w2*.

What's New

New due date for filing with SSA. The due date for filing 2016 Forms W-2, W-2AS, W-2CM, W-2GU, W-2VI, W-3 and W-3SS with the SSA is now January 31, 2017, whether you file using paper forms or electronically.

Extensions of time to file. Extensions of time to file Form W-2 with the SSA are no longer automatic. For filings due on or after January 1, 2017, you may request one 30-day extension to file Form W-2 by submitting a complete application on Form 8809, Application for Extension of Time to File Information Returns, including a detailed explanation of why you need additional time and signed under penalties of perjury. The IRS will only grant the extension in extraordinary circumstances or catastrophe. See *Extension to file* for more information. This does not affect extensions of time to furnish Forms W-2 to employees. See *Extension of time to furnish Forms W-2 to employees* for more information.

Penalties increased. Higher penalties apply for:
- Failure to file correct Forms W-2 by the due date,
- Intentional disregard of filing requirements,
- Failure to furnish Forms W-2, and
- Intentional disregard of payee statement requirements.

The higher penalty amounts apply to returns required to be filed after December 31, 2015 and are indexed for inflation. See *Penalties* for more information.

New penalty safe harbor. Forms W-2 with incorrect dollar amounts may fall under a new safe harbor for certain de minimis errors. See *Penalties* for more information.

Same-sex marriage. For federal tax purposes, marriages of couples of the same sex are treated the same as marriages of couples of the opposite sex. The term "spouse" includes an individual married to a person of the same sex. However, individuals who have entered into a registered domestic partnership, civil union, or other similar relationship that is not considered a marriage under state law are not considered married for federal tax purposes. For more information, see Revenue Ruling 2013-17, 2013-38 I.R.B. 201, available at *https://www.irs.gov/irb/2013-38_IRB/ar07.html*. Notice 2013-61 provides special administrative procedures for employers to make claims for refunds or adjustments of overpayments of social security and Medicare taxes with respect to certain same-sex spouse benefits before expiration of the period of limitations. Notice 2013-61, 2013-44 I.R.B. 432 is available at *https://www.irs.gov/irb/2013-44_IRB/ar10.html*.

Third-party sick pay recap reporting. See Form 8922, Third-Party Sick Pay Recap.

Reminders

Get it done faster...
***E-file your Forms W-2 and W-2c with the SSA. See** E-filing.*

Rejected wage reports from the Social Security Administration (SSA). The SSA will reject Form W-2 electronic and paper wage reports under the following conditions:
- Medicare wages and tips are less than the sum of social security wages and social security tips,
- Social security tax is greater than zero; social security wages and social security tips are equal to zero, and
- Medicare tax is greater than zero; Medicare wages and tips are equal to zero.

Additionally, Forms W-2 and W-2c electronic and paper wage reports for household employers will be rejected under the following conditions:

Jan 05, 2016

Cat. No. 25979S

- The sum of social security wages and social security tips is less than the minimum yearly earnings subject to social security and Medicare tax withholding for a household employee, and
- The Medicare wages and tips are less than the minimum yearly earnings subject to social security and Medicare tax withholding for a household employee.

If the above conditions occur in an electronic wage report, the SSA will notify the submitter by email or postal mail to correct the report and resubmit it to the SSA. If the above conditions occur in a paper wage report, the SSA will notify the employer by email or postal mail to correct the report and resubmit it to the SSA.

Note: Do not write "corrected" or "amended" on any resubmitted reports.

Household employers, see Pub. 926, Household Employer's Tax Guide.

Social security numbers. Do not truncate social security numbers shown on Forms W-2, W-2AS, W-2GU, and W-2VI. Social security numbers are required on Forms W-2. See *Taxpayer identification numbers*, later. See also Regulations section 301.6109-(4)(b)(2).

Filers of other forms, such as certain Forms 1099/1098, may truncate the social security number (XXX-XX-4567) to combat identity theft.

Limit on health flexible spending arrangement (FSA). For 2016, a cafeteria plan may not allow an employee to request salary reduction contributions for a health FSA in excess of $2,550. The salary reduction contribution limitation of $2,550 does not include any amount (up to $500) carried over from a previous year. For more information, see *Health flexible spending arrangement (FSA)*.

Additional Medicare Tax. In addition to withholding Medicare tax at 1.45%, an employer is required to withhold a 0.9% Additional Medicare Tax on any Federal Insurance Contributions Act (FICA) wages or Railroad Retirement Tax Act (RRTA) compensation it pays to an employee in excess of $200,000 in a calendar year. An employer is required to begin withholding Additional Medicare Tax in the pay period in which it pays wages or compensation in excess of $200,000 to an employee and continue to withhold it until the end of the calendar year. Additional Medicare Tax is only imposed on the employee. There is no employer share of Additional Medicare Tax. All wages and compensation that are subject to Medicare tax are subject to Additional Medicare Tax withholding if paid in excess of the $200,000 withholding threshold.

For more information on Additional Medicare Tax, go to IRS.gov and enter "Additional Medicare Tax" in the search box.

Unless otherwise noted, references to Medicare tax include Additional Medicare Tax.

Medicaid waiver payments. Notice 2014-7 provides that certain Medicaid waiver payments are excludable from income for federal income tax purposes. See Notice 2014-7, 2014-4 I.R.B. 445 available at *www.irs.gov/irb/ 2014-4_IRB/ar06.html*. Also, see *www.irs.gov/Individuals/*

Certain-Medicaid-Waiver-Payments-May-Be-Excludable-From-Income for questions and answers on the notice.

Business Services Online (BSO). The SSA has enhanced its secure BSO website to make it easier to register and navigate. Use BSO's online fill-in forms to create, save, and submit Forms W-2 and W-2c to the SSA electronically. BSO lets you print copies of these forms to file with state or local governments, distribute to your employees, and keep for your records. BSO generates Form W-3 automatically based on your Forms W-2. You also can use BSO to upload wage files to the SSA, check on the status of previously submitted wage reports, and take advantage of other convenient services for employers and businesses. Visit the SSA's Employer W-2 Filing Instructions & Information website at *www.socialsecurity.gov/employer* for more information about using BSO to save time for your organization. Here you also will find forms and publications used for wage reporting, information about verifying employee social security numbers online, how to reach an SSA employer services representative for your region, and more.

 Preview BSO by viewing a brief online tutorial. Go to www.socialsecurity.gov/employer and select "Business Services Online Tutorial" under "Handbooks, Tutorials & Videos."

Correcting wage reports. You can use BSO to create, save, print, and submit Forms W-2c, Corrected Wage and Tax Statement, online for the current year as well as for prior years. After logging into BSO, navigate to the Electronic Wage Reporting home page and click on the "Forms W-2c/W-3c Online" tab. Also, see *E-filing* and *E-filing Forms W-2c and W-3c*.

Tax relief for victims of terrorist attacks. Disability payments for injuries incurred as a direct result of a terrorist attack directed against the United States (or its allies) are not included in income. Because federal income tax withholding is only required when a payment is includable in income, no federal income tax should be withheld from these payments.

Distributions from governmental section 457(b) plans of state and local agencies. Generally, report distributions from section 457(b) plans of state and local agencies on Form 1099-R, Distributions From Pensions, Annuities, Retirement or Profit-Sharing Plans, IRAs, Insurance Contracts, etc. See Notice 2003-20 on page 894 of Internal Revenue Bulletin 2003-19 at *www.irs.gov/pub/irs-irbs/irb03-19.pdf*.

Earned income credit (EIC) notice (not applicable to Forms W-2AS, W-2CM, W-2GU, and W-2VI). You must notify employees who have no income tax withheld that they may be able to claim an income tax refund because of the EIC. You can do this by using the official Internal Revenue Service (IRS) Form W-2 with the EIC notice on the back of Copy B or a substitute Form W-2 with the same statement. You must give your employee Notice 797, Possible Federal Tax Refund Due to the Earned Income Credit (EIC), or your own statement that contains the same wording if (a) you use a substitute Form W-2 that does not contain the EIC notice, (b) you are not required to furnish Form W-2, or (c) you do not furnish a timely Form W-2 to your employee. For more information, see section 10 in Pub. 15 (Circular E), Employer's Tax Guide.

Electronic statements for employees. Furnishing Copies B, C, and 2 of Forms W-2 to your employees electronically may save you time and effort. See Pub. 15-A, Employer's Supplemental Tax Guide, *Furnishing Form W-2 to employees electronically,* for additional information.

E-filing. The SSA encourages all employers to *e-file.* E-filing can save you time and effort and helps ensure accuracy. You must *e-file* if you are required to file 250 or more Forms W-2 or W-2c. If you are required to *e-file* but fail to do so, you may incur a penalty.

January 31 due date for e-filers. The due date for e-filing 2016 Form W-2 with the SSA is January 31, 2017.

Waiver from e-filing. You can request a waiver from this requirement by filing Form 8508, Request for Waiver From Filing Information Returns Electronically. Submit Form 8508 to the IRS at least 45 days before the due date of Form W-2, or 45 days before you file your first Form W-2c. See Form 8508 for information about filing this form.

The SSA's BSO website makes e-filing easy by providing two ways to submit your Forms W-2 or W-2c Copy A and Forms W-3 or W-3c information.
- If you need to file 50 or fewer Forms W-2 or 25 or fewer Forms W-2c at a time, you can use BSO to create them online. BSO guides you through the process of creating Forms W-2 or W-2c, saving and printing them, and submitting them to the SSA when you are ready. You do not have to wait until you have submitted Forms W-2 or W-2c to the SSA before printing copies for your employees. BSO generates Form W-3 or W-3c automatically based on your Forms W-2 or W-2c.
- If you need to file more than 50 Forms W-2 or more than 25 Forms W-2c, BSO's "file upload" feature might be the best e-filing method for your business or organization. To obtain file format specifications, visit the SSA's Employer W-2 Filing Instructions & Information website at *www.socialsecurity.gov/employer*, select "Publications & Forms", click on "Specifications for Filing Forms W-2 and W-2c Electronically (EFW2/EFW2C)", and select the appropriate document. This information is also available by calling the SSA's Employer Reporting Service Center at 1-800-772-6270 (toll free).

 If you e-file, *do not file the same returns using paper forms.*

For more information about e-filing Forms W-2 or W-2c and a link to the BSO website, visit the SSA's Employer W-2 Filing Instructions & Information website at *www.socialsecurity.gov/employer*.

In a few situations, reporting instructions vary depending on the filing method you choose. For example, you can include every type of box 12 amount in one employee wage record if you upload an electronic file. If you file on paper or create Forms W-2 online, you can include only four box 12 amounts per Form W-2. See the *TIP* for *Box 12—Codes* under *Specific Instructions for Form W-2.*

Form 944. Use the "944" checkbox in box b of Form W-3 or Form W-3SS if you filed Form 944, Employer's ANNUAL Federal Tax Return. Also use the "944" checkbox if you filed Formulario 944(SP), the Spanish-language version of Form 944.

Forms W-2 for U.S. possessions. In these instructions, reference to Forms W-2 and W-3 includes Forms W-2AS, W-2CM, W-2GU, W-2VI, and W-3SS, unless otherwise noted. These instructions are not applicable to wage and tax statements for Puerto Rico. Form W-2AS is used to report American Samoa wages paid by American Samoa employers, Form W-2CM is used to report the Commonwealth of the Northern Mariana Islands (CNMI) wages paid by CNMI employers, Form W-2GU is used to report Guam wages paid by Guam employers, and Form W-2VI is used to report U.S. Virgin Islands (USVI) wages paid by USVI employers. Do not use these forms to report wages subject to U.S. income tax withholding. Instead, use Form W-2 to show U.S. income tax withheld.

Treatment of military differential pay. Employers paying their employees while they are on active duty in the United States uniformed services should treat these payments as wages subject to income tax withholding. See *Military differential pay* under *Specific Instructions for Form W-2.*

Military Spouses Residency Relief Act (MSRRA). You may be required to report wages and taxes on a form different from the form you generally use if an employee claims residence or domicile under MSRRA in a different jurisdiction in one of the 50 states, the District of Columbia, American Samoa, the Commonwealth of the Northern Mariana Islands, Guam, Puerto Rico, or the U.S. Virgin Islands.

Under MSRRA, the spouse of an active duty servicemember (civilian spouse) may keep his or her prior residence or domicile for tax purposes (tax residence) when accompanying the servicemember spouse, who is relocating under military orders, to a new military duty station in one of the 50 states, the District of Columbia, or a U.S. possession. Before relocating, both spouses must have had the same tax residence.

For example, if a civilian spouse is working in Guam but properly claims tax residence in one of the 50 states under MSRRA, his or her income from services would not be taxable income for Guam tax purposes. Federal income taxes should be withheld and remitted to the IRS. State and local income taxes may need to be withheld and remitted to state and local tax authorities. You should consult with state, local, or U.S. possession tax authorities regarding your withholding obligations under MSRRA.

Nonqualified deferred compensation plans. You are not required to complete box 12 with code Y (Deferrals under a section 409A nonqualified deferred compensation plan). Section 409A provides that all amounts deferred under a nonqualified deferred compensation (NQDC) plan for all tax years are includible in gross income unless certain requirements are satisfied. See *Nonqualified deferred compensation plans* under *Special Reporting Situations for Form W-2* and the *Nonqualified Deferred Compensation Reporting Example Chart.*

Reporting aid charts. To aid in reporting, a *Form W-2 Box 13 Retirement Plan Checkbox Decision Chart* and a *Nonqualified Deferred Compensation Reporting Example Chart* have been added to these instructions. See pages 28 and 29.

Reporting the cost of group health insurance coverage. You must report the cost of employer-sponsored health coverage in box 12 using code DD. However, transitional relief applies to certain employers and certain types of plans. For more information, see *Box 12—Codes* for *Code DD—Cost of employer-sponsored health coverage*

Severance payments. Severance payments are wages subject to social security and Medicare taxes. As noted in section 15 of Pub. 15 (Circular E), severance payments are also subject to income tax withholding and FUTA tax.

Substitute forms. You may use an acceptable substitute form instead of an official IRS form.

Form W-2. If you are not using the official IRS form to furnish Form W-2 to employees or to file with the SSA, you may use an acceptable substitute form that complies with the rules in Pub. 1141, General Rules and Specifications for Substitute Forms W-2 and W-3. Pub. 1141 is a revenue procedure that explains the requirements for format and content of substitute Forms W-2 and W-3. Your substitute forms must comply with the requirements in Pub. 1141.

Pub. 1141 prohibits advertising on Form W-2. You must not include advertising on any copy of Form W-2, including coupons providing discounts on tax preparation services attached to the employee copies. See Pub. 1141 for further information.

Form W-2c. If you are not using the official IRS form to furnish Form W-2c to employees or to file with the SSA, you may use an acceptable substitute form that complies with the rules in Pub. 1223, General Rules and Specifications for Substitute Forms W-2c and W-3c. Pub. 1223 is a revenue procedure that explains the requirements for format and content of substitute Forms W-2c and W-3c. Your substitute forms must comply with the requirements in Pub. 1223.

Pub. 1223 prohibits advertising on Form W-2c. You must not include advertising on any copy of Form W-2c, including coupons providing discounts on tax preparation services attached to the employee copies. See Pub. 1223 for further information.

Need Help?

Help with e-filing. If you have questions about how to register or use BSO, call 1-800-772-6270 (toll free) to speak with an employer reporting technician at the SSA. The hours of operation are Monday through Friday from 7:00 a.m. to 7:00 p.m. Eastern time. If you experience problems using any of the services within BSO, call 1-888-772-2970 (toll free) to speak with a systems operator in technical support at the SSA. To speak with the SSA's Employer Services Liaison Officer (ESLO) for the U.S. Virgin Islands, call 1-212-264-1462 (not a toll-free number). For Guam, the Commonwealth of the Northern Mariana Islands, or American Samoa, call 1-510-970-8247 (not a toll-free number). For all other employers, contact the ESLO that services your region. For a complete telephone listing, visit the SSA's Employer W-2 Filing Instructions & Information website at *www.socialsecurity.gov/employer.*

Information reporting customer service site. The IRS operates a centralized customer service site to answer questions about reporting on Forms W-2, W-3, 1099, and other information returns. If you have questions about reporting on these forms, call 1-866-455-7438 (toll free).

TTY/TDD equipment. Telephone help is available using TTY/TDD equipment for persons who are deaf, hard of hearing, or have a speech disability. If you have questions about reporting on information returns (Forms 1096, 1097, 1098, 1099, 3921, 3922, 5498, W-2, W-2G, and W-3), call 1-304-579-4827.

Employment tax information. Detailed employment tax information is given in:
* Pub. 15 (Circular E), Employer's Tax Guide,
* Pub. 15-A, Employer's Supplemental Tax Guide,
* Pub. 15-B, Employer's Tax Guide to Fringe Benefits,
* Pub. 51 (Circular A), Agricultural Employer's Tax Guide, and
* Pub. 80 (Circular SS), Federal Tax Guide for Employers in the U.S. Virgin Islands, Guam, American Samoa, and the Commonwealth of the Northern Mariana Islands.

You also can call the IRS with your employment tax questions at 1-800-829-4933 or visit IRS.gov and type "employment taxes" in the search box.

How To Get Forms and Publications

Internet. You can access IRS.gov 24 hours a day, 7 days a week to:
* Download, view, and order tax forms, instructions, and publications.
* Access commercial tax preparation and *e-file* services.
* Research your tax questions online.
* See answers to frequently asked tax questions.
* Search publications online by topic or keyword.
* View Internal Revenue Bulletins published in the last few years.
* Sign up to receive local and national tax news by email.

You can order forms, instructions, and publications at *www.irs.gov/orderforms.* For any other tax information, go to *www.irs.gov/uac/Tax-Law-Questions.*

 Do not print Copy A of Forms W-2, W-3, W-2c, or W-3c from IRS.gov and then file them with the SSA. The SSA accepts only e-filed reports and the official red-ink versions (or approved substitute versions) of these forms. For more information about acceptable substitute versions, see Substitute forms. *For information about e-filing, see* E-filing.

Mail. You can send your order for forms, instructions, and publications to the following address. You should receive a response within 10 days after your request is received.

Internal Revenue Service
1201 N. Mitsubishi Motorway
Bloomington, IL 61705-6613

Free tax services. To find out what services are available, get Pub. 910, IRS Guide to Free Tax Services. It contains lists of free tax information sources, including publications, services, and free tax education and assistance programs. Accessible versions of IRS published products are available on request in a variety of alternative formats.

Common Errors on Forms W-2

Forms W-2 provide information to your employees, the SSA, the IRS, and state and local governments. Avoid making the following errors, which cause processing delays.

Do not:
* Omit the decimal point and cents from entries.
* Make entries using ink that is too light. Use only black ink.
* Make entries that are too small or too large. Use 12-point Courier font, if possible.
* Add dollar signs to the money-amount boxes. They have been removed from Copy A and are not required.
* Inappropriately check the "Retirement plan" checkbox in box 13. See *Retirement plan.*
* Misformat the employee's name in box e. Enter the employee's first name and middle initial in the first box, his or her surname in the second box, and his or her suffix (such as "Jr.") in the third box (optional).
* Cut, fold, or staple Copy A paper forms mailed to SSA.
* Download Copy A of Forms W-2, W-2AS, W-2GU, W-2VI, W-3SS, or Form W-3 from IRS.gov and file with SSA.

General Instructions for Forms W-2 and W-3

Who must file Form W-2. Every employer engaged in a trade or business who pays remuneration, including noncash payments, of $600 or more for the year (all amounts if any income, social security, or Medicare tax was withheld) for services performed by an employee must file a Form W-2 for each employee (even if the employee is related to the employer) from whom:
* Income, social security, or Medicare tax was withheld.
* Income tax would have been withheld if the employee had claimed no more than one withholding allowance or had not claimed exemption from withholding on Form W-4, Employee's Withholding Allowance Certificate.

Unless otherwise noted, references to Medicare tax include Additional Medicare Tax.

If you are required to file 250 or more Forms W-2 or want to take advantage of the benefits of e-filing, see *E-filing.*

Who must file Form W-3. Anyone required to file Form W-2 must file Form W-3 to transmit Copy A of Forms W-2. Make a copy of Form W-3, keep it and Copy D (For Employer) of Forms W-2 with your records for 4 years. Be sure to use Form W-3 for the correct year. If you are filing Forms W-2 electronically, also see *E-filing.*

Household employers. Even employers with only one household employee must file Form W-3 to transmit Copy

A of Form W-2. On Form W-3 check the "Hshld. emp." checkbox in box b. For more information, see Schedule H (Form 1040), Household Employment Taxes, and its separate instructions. You must have an employer identification number (EIN). See *Box b—Employer identification number (EIN).*

Who may sign Form W-3. A transmitter or sender (including a service bureau, reporting agent, paying agent, or disbursing agent) may sign Form W-3 (or use its PIN to e-file) for the employer or payer only if the sender satisfies both of the following.
* It is authorized to sign by an agency agreement (whether oral, written, or implied) that is valid under state law; and
* It writes "For (name of payer)" next to the signature (paper Form W-3 only).

 Use of a reporting agent or other third-party payroll service provider does not relieve an employer of the responsibility to ensure that Forms W-2 are furnished to employees and that Forms W-2 and W-3 are filed with the SSA, correctly and on time. See Penalties *for more information.*

Be sure that the payer's name and EIN on Forms W-2 and W-3 are the same as those used on the Form 941, Employer's QUARTERLY Federal Tax Return; Form 943, Employer's Annual Federal Tax Return for Agricultural Employees; Form 944; Form CT-1, Employer's Annual Railroad Retirement Tax Return; or Schedule H (Form 1040) filed by or for the payer.

When to file. If you file using paper forms, you must file Copy A of Form W-2 with Form W-3 by January 31, 2017. If you e-file, the due date is also January 31, 2017. You may owe a penalty for each Form W-2 that you file late. See *Penalties.* If you terminate your business, see *Terminating a business.*

Extension to file. You may request only one extension of time to file Form W-2 with the SSA by submitting a complete application on Form 8809, Application for Extension of Time To File Information Returns. Include a detailed explanation of why you need additional time. You must sign the application under penalties of perjury. Send the application to the address shown on Form 8809. You must request the extension before the due date of Forms W-2. If the IRS grants your request for extension, you will have an additional 30 days to file. The IRS will grant extensions to file Forms W-2 only in limited cases for extraordinary circumstances or catastrophe, such as a natural disaster or fire destroying the books and records needed for filing the forms. No additional extension of time to file will be allowed. See Form 8809 for details.

 Even if you request and are granted an extension of time to file Form W-2, you still must furnish Form W-2 to your employees by January 31, 2017. But see Extension of time to furnish Forms W-2 to employees.

Where to file paper Forms W-2 and W-3. File Copy A of Form W-2 with Form W-3 at the following address.

Social Security Administration
Data Operations Center
Wilkes-Barre, PA 18769-0001

 If you use "Certified Mail" to file, change the ZIP code to "18769-0002." If you use an IRS-approved private delivery service, add "Attn: W-2 Process, 1150 E. Mountain Dr." to the address and change the ZIP code to "18702-7997." See Pub. 15 (Circular E) for a list of IRS-approved private delivery services.

 Do not send cash, checks, money orders, or other forms of payment with the Forms W-2 and W-3 that you submit to the SSA. *Employment tax forms (for example, Form 941 or Form 943), remittances, and Forms 1099 must be sent to the IRS.*

Copy 1. Send Copy 1 of Form W-2, if required, to your state, city, or local tax department. For more information concerning Copy 1 (including how to complete boxes 15 through 20), contact your state, city, or local tax department.

American Samoa. File Copy 1 of Form W-3SS and Forms W-2AS at the following address.

American Samoa Tax Office
Executive Office Building
First Floor
Pago Pago, AS 96799

Guam. File Copy 1 of Form W-3SS and Forms W-2GU at the following address.

Guam Department of Revenue and Taxation
P.O. Box 23607
GMF, GU 96921

For additional information about Form W-2GU, see *www.guamtax.com*.

United States Virgin Islands. File Copy 1 of Form W-3SS and Forms W-2VI at the following address.

Virgin Islands Bureau of Internal Revenue
6115 Estate Smith Bay
Suite 225
St. Thomas, VI 00802

For additional information about Form W-2VI, see *www.viirb.com*.

Commonwealth of the Northern Mariana Islands. File Form OS-3710 and Copy 1 of Forms W-2CM at the following address.

Division of Revenue and Taxation
Commonwealth of the Northern Mariana Islands
P.O. Box 5234 CHRB
Saipan, MP 96950

Forms OS-3710 and W-2CM are not IRS forms. For additional information about Form W-2CM, see *www.cnmidof.net*.

Shipping and mailing. If you file more than one type of employment tax form, group Forms W-2 of the same type with a separate Form W-3 for each type, and send them in separate groups. See the specific instructions for *Box b—Kind of Payer* and *Box b—Kind of Employer* in *Specific Instructions for Form W-3.*

Prepare and file Forms W-2 either alphabetically by employees' last names or numerically by employees' social security numbers. Do not staple or tape Form W-3 to the related Forms W-2 or Forms W-2 to each other. These forms are machine read. Staple holes or tears interfere with machine reading. Also, do not fold Forms W-2 and W-3. Send the forms to the SSA in a flat mailing.

Furnishing Copies B, C, and 2 to employees.
Generally, you must furnish Copies B, C, and 2 of Form W-2 to your employees by January 31, 2017. You will meet the "furnish" requirement if the form is properly addressed and mailed on or before the due date.

If employment ends before December 31, 2016, you may furnish copies to the employee at any time after employment ends, but no later than January 31, 2017. If an employee asks for Form W-2, give him or her the completed copies within 30 days of the request or within 30 days of the final wage payment, whichever is later. However, if you terminate your business, see *Terminating a business.*

You may furnish Forms W-2 to employees on IRS official forms or on acceptable substitute forms. See *Substitute forms.* Be sure the Forms W-2 you provide to employees are clear and legible and comply with the requirements in Pub. 1141.

Forms W-2 that include logos, slogans, and advertisements (including advertisements for tax preparation software) may be confused with questionable Forms W-2. An employee may not recognize the importance of the employee copy for tax reporting purposes due to the use of logos, slogans, and advertisements. Therefore, the IRS has determined that logos, slogans, and advertising will not be allowed on Forms W-3, Copy A of Forms W-2, or any employee copies reporting wages paid. See Pub. 1141 for more information.

Extension of time to furnish Forms W-2 to employees. You may request an extension of time to furnish Forms W-2 to employees by sending a letter to:

Internal Revenue Service
Attn: Extension of Time Coordinator
240 Murall Drive, Mail Stop 4360
Kearneysville, WV 25430

Mail your letter on or before the due date for furnishing Forms W-2 to employees. It must include:
- Your name and address,
- Your EIN,
- A statement that you are requesting an extension to furnish "Forms W-2" to employees,
- The reason for delay, and
- Your signature or that of your authorized agent.

Requests for an extension of time to furnish Forms W-2 to employees are not automatically granted. If approved, an extension will generally be for no more than 15 days from the due date, unless the need for up to a total of 30 days is clearly shown. See Pub. 1220. Requests for an extension of time to furnish recipient statements for more than 10 payers must be submitted electronically.

Undeliverable Forms W-2. Keep for 4 years any employee copies of Forms W-2 that you tried to but could not deliver. However, if the undelivered Form W-2 can be produced electronically through April 15th of the fourth year after the year at issue, you do not need to keep undeliverable employee copies. Do not send undeliverable employee copies of Forms W-2 to the Social Security Administration (SSA).

Taxpayer identification numbers (TINs). Employers use an employer identification number (EIN) (00-0000000). Employees use a social security number (SSN) (000-00-0000). When you list a number, separate the nine digits properly to show the kind of number. Do not accept an IRS individual taxpayer identification number (ITIN) in place of an SSN for employee identification or for Form W-2 reporting. An ITIN is only available to resident and nonresident aliens who are not eligible for U.S. employment and need identification for other tax purposes. An ITIN will expire for any taxpayer who fails to file a federal income tax return for five consecutive tax years. You can identify an ITIN because it is a 9-digit number formatted like an SSN beginning with the number "9" and with a number in one of the following ranges in the fourth and fifth digit: 70-88, 90-92, or 94-99 (for example, 9NN-70-NNNN). Do not auto populate an ITIN into *box a—Employee's social security number* on Form W-2. See section 4 of Pub. 15 (Circular E).

 An individual with an ITIN who later becomes eligible to work in the United States must obtain an SSN from the Social Security Administration.

The IRS uses SSNs to check the payments that you report against the amounts shown on employees' tax returns. The SSA uses SSNs to record employees' earnings for future social security and Medicare benefits. When you prepare Form W-2, be sure to show the correct SSN for each employee. Do not truncate the employees' SSNs on Form W-2. For information about verifying SSNs, see section 4 of Pub. 15 (Circular E) or visit the SSA's Employer W-2 Filing Instructions & Information website at *www.socialsecurity.gov/employer*.

 Form W-2 e-filed with the SSA must contain the same TINs as shown on all copies of Form W-2 furnished to employees.

Special Reporting Situations for Form W-2

Adoption benefits. Amounts paid or expenses incurred by an employer for qualified adoption expenses under an adoption assistance program are not subject to federal income tax withholding and are not reportable in box 1. However, these amounts (including adoption benefits paid from a section 125 (cafeteria) plan, but not including adoption benefits forfeited from a cafeteria plan) are subject to social security, Medicare, and railroad retirement taxes and must be reported in boxes 3 and 5. (Use box 14 if railroad retirement taxes apply.) Also, the total amount must be reported in box 12 with code T.

For more information on adoption benefits, see Notice 97-9, 1997-1 C.B. 365, which is on page 35 of Internal Revenue Bulletin 1997-2 at *www.irs.gov/pub/irs-irbs/ irb97-02.pdf*. Advise your employees to see the Instructions for Form 8839, Qualified Adoption Expenses.

Agent reporting. An agent who has an approved Form 2678, Employer/Payer Appointment of Agent, should enter the following in box c of Form W-2:

> **(Name of agent)**
> **Agent for (name of employer)**
> **Address of agent**

Each Form W-2 should reflect the EIN of the agent in box b. An agent files one Form W-3 for all of the Forms W-2 and enters its own information in boxes e, f, and g of Form W-3 as it appears on the agent's related employment tax returns (for example, Form 941). Enter the client-employer's EIN in box h of Form W-3 if the Forms W-2 relate to only one employer (other than the agent); if not, leave box h blank.

If the agent (a) is acting as an agent for two or more employers or is an employer and is acting as an agent for another employer, and (b) pays social security wages to an individual on behalf of more than one employer, the agent should file separate Forms W-2 for the affected employee reflecting the wages paid by each employer.

See Rev. Proc. 2013-39, 2013-52 I.R.B. 830 available at *www.irs.gov/irb/2013-52_IRB/ar15.html*; and Form 2678 instructions for procedures to be followed in applying to be an agent.

 Generally, an agent is not responsible for refunding excess social security or railroad retirement (RRTA) tax withheld from employees. If an employee worked for more than one employer during 2016 and had more than $7,347 in social security and Tier 1 RRTA tax withheld, he or she should claim the excess on the appropriate line of Form 1040, Form 1040A, or Form 1040NR. If an employee had more than $4321.80 in Tier 2 RRTA tax withheld from more than one employer, the employee should claim a refund on Form 843, Claim for Refund and Request for Abatement.

Archer MSA. An employer's contribution to an employee's Archer MSA is not subject to federal income tax withholding or social security, Medicare, or railroad retirement taxes if it is reasonable to believe at the time of the payment that the contribution will be excludable from the employee's income. However, if it is not reasonable to believe at the time of payment that the contribution will be excludable from the employee's income, employer contributions are subject to income tax withholding and social security and Medicare taxes (or railroad retirement taxes, if applicable) and must be reported in boxes 1, 3, and 5. (Use box 14 if railroad retirement taxes apply.)

You must report all employer contributions to an Archer MSA in box 12 of Form W-2 with code R. Employer contributions to an Archer MSA that are not excludable from the income of the employee also must be reported in boxes 1, 3, and 5 (box 14 if railroad retirement taxes apply).

An employee's contributions to an Archer MSA are includible in income as wages and are subject to federal income tax withholding and social security and Medicare taxes (or railroad retirement taxes, if applicable). Employee contributions are deductible, within limits, on the employee's Form 1040.

For more information, see Pub. 969, Health Savings Accounts and Other Tax-Favored Health Plans, and Notice 96-53, which is found on page 5 of Internal Revenue Bulletin 1996-51 at *www.irs.gov/pub/irs-irbs/ irb96-51.pdf*.

Clergy and religious workers. For certain members of the clergy and religious workers who are not subject to social security and Medicare taxes as employees, boxes 3 and 5 of Form W-2 should be left blank. You may include a minister's parsonage and/or utilities allowance in box 14. For information on the rules that apply to ministers and certain other religious workers, see Pub. 517, Social Security and Other Information for Members of the Clergy and Religious Workers, and section 4 in Pub. 15-A.

Deceased employee's wages. If an employee dies during the year, you must report the accrued wages, vacation pay, and other compensation paid after the date of death. Also report wages that were available to the employee while he or she was alive, regardless of whether they actually were in the possession of the employee, as well as any other regular wage payment, even if you may have to reissue the payment in the name of the estate or beneficiary.

If you made the payment after the employee's death but in the same year the employee died, you must withhold social security and Medicare taxes on the payment and report the payment on the employee's Form W-2 only as social security and Medicare wages to ensure proper social security and Medicare credit is received. On the employee's Form W-2, show the payment as social security wages (box 3) and Medicare wages and tips (box 5) and the social security and Medicare taxes withheld in boxes 4 and 6. Do not show the payment in box 1.

If you made the payment after the year of death, do not report it on Form W-2, and do not withhold social security and Medicare taxes.

Whether the payment is made in the year of death or after the year of death, you also must report it in box 3 of Form 1099-MISC, Miscellaneous Income, for the payment to the estate or beneficiary. Use the name and taxpayer identification number (TIN) of the payment recipient on Form 1099-MISC. However, if the payment is a reissuance of wages that were constructively received by the deceased individual while he or she was still alive, do not report it on Form 1099-MISC.

Example. Before Employee A's death on June 15, 2016, A was employed by Employer X and received $10,000 in wages on which federal income tax of $1,500 was withheld. When A died, X owed A $2,000 in wages and $1,000 in accrued vacation pay. The total of $3,000

(less the social security and Medicare taxes withheld) was paid to A's estate on July 6, 2016. Because X made the payment during the year of death, X must withhold social security and Medicare taxes on the $3,000 payment and must complete Form W-2 as follows.

- Box a – Employee A's SSN
- Box e – Employee A's name
- Box f – Employee A's address
- Box 1 – 10000.00 (does not include the $3,000 accrued wages and vacation pay)
- Box 2 – 1500.00
- Box 3 – 13000.00 (includes the $3,000 accrued wages and vacation pay)
- Box 4 – 806.00 (6.2% of the amount in box 3)
- Box 5 – 13000.00 (includes the $3,000 accrued wages and vacation pay)
- Box 6 – 188.50 (1.45% of the amount in box 5)

 Employer X also must complete Form 1099-MISC as follows.

- *Boxes for recipient's name, address, and TIN—the estate's name, address, and TIN.*
- *Box 3: 3000.00 (Even though amounts were withheld for social security and Medicare taxes, the gross amount is reported here.)*

If Employer X made the payment after the year of death, the $3,000 would not be subject to social security and Medicare taxes and would not be shown on Form W-2. However, the employer would still file Form 1099-MISC.

Designated Roth contributions. Under section 402A, a participant in a section 401(k) plan, under a 403(b) salary reduction agreement, or in a governmental 457(b) plan that includes a qualified Roth contribution program, may elect to make designated Roth contributions to the plan or program in lieu of elective deferrals. Designated Roth contributions are subject to federal income tax withholding and social security and Medicare taxes (and railroad retirement taxes, if applicable) and must be reported in boxes 1, 3, and 5. (Use box 14 if railroad retirement taxes apply.)

Section 402A requires separate reporting of the yearly designated Roth contributions. Designated Roth contributions to 401(k) plans will be reported using code AA in box 12; designated Roth contributions under 403(b) salary reduction agreements will be reported using code BB in box 12; and designated Roth contributions under a governmental section 457(b) plan will be reported using code EE in box 12. For reporting instructions, see *Box 12—Codes* for Code AA, Code BB, and Code EE.

Educational assistance programs. Employer-provided educational assistance that qualifies as a working condition benefit is excludable from an employee's wages. For employer-provided educational assistance that does not qualify as a working condition benefit, a $5,250 exclusion may apply if the assistance is provided under an educational assistance program under section 127. See Pub. 970, Tax Benefits for Education, and section 2 of Pub. 15-B for more information. Also see *Box 1—Wages, tips, other compensation.*

Election workers. Report on Form W-2 payments of $600 or more to election workers for services performed in state, county, and municipal elections. File Form W-2 for payments of less than $600 paid to election workers if social security and Medicare taxes were withheld under a section 218 (Social Security Act) agreement. Do not report election worker payments on Form 1099-MISC.

If the election worker is employed in another capacity with the same government entity, see Rev. Rul. 2000-6, which is on page 512 of Internal Revenue Bulletin 2000-6 at *www.irs.gov/pub/irs-irbs/irb00-06.pdf*.

Employee business expense reimbursements. Reimbursements to employees for business expenses must be reported as follows.
• Generally, payments made under an accountable plan are excluded from the employee's gross income and are not reported on Form W-2. However, if you pay a per diem or mileage allowance and the amount paid for substantiated miles or days traveled exceeds the amount treated as substantiated under IRS rules, you must report as wages on Form W-2 the amount in excess of the amount treated as substantiated. The excess amount is subject to income tax withholding and social security and Medicare taxes (or railroad retirement taxes, if applicable). Report the amount treated as substantiated (that is, the nontaxable portion) in box 12 using code L. See *Box 12—Codes* for *Code L— Substantiated employee business expense reimbursements.* (Use box 14 if railroad retirement taxes apply.)
• Payments made under a nonaccountable plan are reported as wages on Form W-2 and are subject to federal income tax withholding and social security and Medicare taxes (or railroad retirement taxes, if applicable). (Use box 14 if railroad retirement taxes apply.)

For more information on accountable plans, nonaccountable plans, amounts treated as substantiated under a per diem or mileage allowance, the standard mileage rate, the per diem substantiation method, and the high-low substantiation method, see Pub. 463, Travel, Entertainment, Gift, and Car Expenses; and section 5 of Pub. 15 (Circular E).

Employee's social security and Medicare taxes (or railroad retirement taxes, if applicable) paid by employer. If you paid your employee's share of social security and Medicare taxes rather than deducting them from the employee's wages, you must include these payments as wages subject to federal (or American Samoa, CNMI, Guam, or U.S. Virgin Islands) income tax withholding and social security, Medicare, and federal unemployment (FUTA) taxes. If you paid your employee's share of railroad retirement taxes, you must include these amounts as compensation subject to railroad retirement taxes. The amount to include as wages and/or compensation is determined by using the formula contained in the discussion of *Employee's Portion of Taxes Paid by Employer* in section 7 of Pub. 15-A and in Rev. Proc. 83-43, 1983-24 I.R.B. 60.

 This does not apply to household and agricultural employers. If you pay a household or agricultural employee's social security and Medicare taxes, you must include these payments in the employee's wages for income tax withholding purposes. However, the wage increase due to the tax payments is not subject to social security, Medicare, or FUTA taxes. For information on completing Forms W-2 and W-3 in this situation, see the Instructions for Schedule H (Form 1040) and section 4 of Pub. 51 (Circular A).

Foreign agricultural workers. You must report compensation of $600 or more paid in a calendar year to an H-2A visa agricultural worker for agricultural labor. If the H-2A visa agricultural worker furnishes a valid taxpayer identification number, report these payments in box 1 of Form W-2. If the worker does not furnish a valid taxpayer identification number, report the payments on Form 1099-MISC. See *Form 1099-MISC* below.

On Form W-2, no amount should be reported in boxes 3 or 5. In most cases, you do not need to withhold federal income tax from compensation paid to H-2A visa agricultural workers. Employers should withhold federal income tax only if the H-2A visa agricultural worker and the employer agree to withhold. The H-2A visa agricultural worker must provide a completed Form W-4. If the employer withholds income tax, the employer must report the tax withheld in box 2 of Form W-2 and on line 8 of Form 943. See Pub. 51 (Circular A).

Form 1099-MISC. If the H-2A visa agricultural worker fails to furnish a taxpayer identification number to the employer, and the total annual payments made to the H-2A visa agricultural worker are $600 or more, the employer must begin backup withholding on the payments made until the H-2A visa agricultural worker furnishes a valid taxpayer identification number. Employers must report the compensation paid and any backup withholding on Forms 1099-MISC and Form 945, Annual Return of Withheld Federal Income Tax. See the 2016 Instructions for Form 1099-MISC and the 2016 Instructions for Form 945.

For more information, enter "foreign agricultural workers" in the search box on IRS.gov.

Fringe benefits. Include all taxable fringe benefits in box 1 of Form W-2 as wages, tips, and other compensation and, if applicable, in boxes 3 and 5 as social security and Medicare wages. Although not required, you may include the total value of fringe benefits in box 14 (or on a separate statement). However, if you provided your employee a vehicle and included 100% of its annual lease value in the employee's income, you must separately report this value to the employee in box 14 (or on a separate statement). The employee can then figure the value of any business use of the vehicle and report it on Form 2106, Employee Business Expenses. Also see Pub. 15-B for more information.

 If you used the commuting rule or the vehicle cents-per-mile rule to value the personal use of the vehicle, you cannot include 100% of the value of the use of the vehicle in the employee's income. See Pub. 15-B.

Golden parachute payments (not applicable to Forms W-2AS, W-2CM, W-2GU, or W-2VI). Include any golden parachute payments in boxes 1, 3, and 5 of Form W-2. Withhold federal income, social security, and Medicare taxes (or railroad retirement taxes, if applicable) as usual and report them in boxes 2, 4, and 6, respectively. (Use box 14 if railroad retirement taxes apply.) Excess parachute payments are also subject to a 20% excise tax. If the excess payments are considered wages, withhold the 20% excise tax and include it in box 2 as income tax withheld. Also report the excise tax in box 12 with code K. For definitions and additional information, see Regulations section 1.280G-1 and Rev. Proc. 2003-68, 2003-34 I.R.B. 398, available at *www.irs.gov/irb/2003-34_IRB/ar16.html*.

Government employers. Federal, state, and local governmental agencies have two options for reporting their employees' wages that are subject to only Medicare tax for part of the year and both social security and Medicare taxes for part of the year.

The first option (which the SSA prefers) is to file a single set of Forms W-2 per employee for the entire year, even if only part of the year's wages are subject to both social security and Medicare taxes. Check "941" (or "944") in box b of Form W-3 or check "941-SS" in box b of Form W-3SS. The wages in box 5 of Form W-2 must be equal to or greater than the wages in box 3 of Form W-2.

The second option is to file one set of Forms W-2 for wages subject only to Medicare tax and another set for wages subject to both social security and Medicare taxes. Use a separate Form W-3 to transmit each set of Forms W-2. For the Medicare-only Forms W-2, check "Medicare govt. emp." in box b of Form W-3. For the Forms W-2 showing wages subject to both social security and Medicare taxes, check "941" (or "944") in box b of Form W-3 or check "941-SS" in box b of Form W-3SS. The wages in box 5 of Form W-2 must be equal to or greater than the wages in box 3 of Form W-2.

Group-term life insurance. You must include in boxes 1, 3, and 5 (or 14, if railroad retirement taxes apply) the cost of group-term life insurance that is more than the cost of $50,000 of coverage, reduced by the amount the employee paid toward the insurance. Use Table 2-2 in Pub. 15-B to determine the cost of the insurance. Also, show the amount in box 12 with code C. For employees, you must withhold social security and Medicare taxes, but not federal income tax. For coverage provided to former employees, the former employees must pay the employee part of social security and Medicare taxes (or railroad retirement taxes, if applicable) on the taxable cost of group-term life insurance over $50,000 on Form 1040. You are not required to collect those taxes. However, you must report the uncollected social security tax (or railroad retirement taxes, if applicable) with code M and the uncollected Medicare tax (or RRTA Medicare tax, if applicable) with code N in box 12 of Form W-2. However, any uncollected Additional Medicare Tax (on the cost of group-term life insurance, which, in combination with other wages, is in excess of $200,000) is not reported with code N in box 12.

Health flexible spending arrangement (FSA). For plan year 2016, a cafeteria plan may not allow an employee to request salary reduction contributions for a health FSA in excess of $2,550 (as indexed for inflation).

If a cafeteria plan timely complies with the written plan requirement limiting health FSA salary reduction contributions, but one or more employees are erroneously allowed to elect a salary reduction of more than $2,550 for a plan year, the cafeteria plan will continue to be a section 125 cafeteria plan for that plan year if:
- The terms of the plan apply uniformly to all participants,
- The error results from a reasonable mistake by the employer (or the employer's agent) and is not due to willful neglect by the employer (or the employer's agent), and
- Salary reduction contributions in excess of $2,550 are paid to the employee and reported as wages for income tax withholding and employment tax purposes on the employee's Form W-2 (or Form W-2c) for the employee's taxable year in which, or with which, ends the cafeteria plan year in which the correction is made.

 The salary reduction contribution limit of $2,550 does not include any amount (up to $500) carried over from a previous year.

For more information, see Notice 2012-40, 2012-26 I.R.B. 1046, available at *www.irs.gov/irb/2012-26_IRB/ar09.html* and Notice 2013-71, 2013-47 I.R.B. 532 available at *www.irs.gov/irb/2013-47_IRB/ar10.html*.

Health savings account (HSA). An employer's contribution (including an employee's contributions through a cafeteria plan) to an employee's HSA is not subject to federal income tax withholding or social security, Medicare, or railroad retirement taxes (or FUTA tax) if it is reasonable to believe at the time of the payment that the contribution will be excludable from the employee's income. However, if it is not reasonable to believe at the time of payment that the contribution will be excludable from the employee's income, employer contributions are subject to federal income tax withholding, social security and Medicare taxes (or railroad retirement taxes, if applicable), and FUTA tax, and must be reported in boxes 1, 3, and 5 (use box 14 if railroad retirement taxes apply), and on Form 940, Employer's Annual Federal Unemployment (FUTA) Tax Return.

You must report all employer contributions (including an employee's contributions through a cafeteria plan) to an HSA in box 12 of Form W-2 with code W. Employer contributions to an HSA that are not excludable from the income of the employee also must be reported in boxes 1, 3, and 5. (Use box 14 if railroad retirement taxes apply.)

An employee's contributions to an HSA (unless made through a cafeteria plan) are includible in income as wages and are subject to federal income tax withholding and social security and Medicare taxes (or railroad retirement taxes, if applicable). Employee contributions are deductible, within limits, on the employee's Form 1040. For more information about HSAs, see Notice 2004-2, Notice 2004-50, and Notice 2008-52. Notice 2004-2, 2004-2 I.R.B. 269, is available at *www.irs.gov/irb/2004-02_IRB/ar09.html*. Notice 2004-50, 2004-33 I.R.B.

196, is available at *www.irs.gov/irb/2004-33_IRB/ar08.html*. Notice 2008-52, 2008-25 I.R.B. 1166, is available at *www.irs.gov/irb/2008-25_IRB/ar10.html*. Also see Form 8889, Health Savings Accounts (HSAs), and Pub. 969.

Lost Form W-2—reissued statement. If an employee loses a Form W-2, write "REISSUED STATEMENT" on the new copy and furnish it to the employee. You do not have to add "REISSUED STATEMENT" on Forms W-2 provided to employees electronically. Do not send Copy A of the reissued Form W-2 to the SSA. Employers are not prohibited (by the Internal Revenue Code) from charging a fee for the issuance of a duplicate Form W-2.

Military differential pay. Employers paying their employees while they are on active duty in the United States uniformed services should treat these payments as wages. Differential wage payments made to an individual while on active duty for periods scheduled to exceed 30 days are subject to income tax withholding, but are not subject to social security, Medicare, and unemployment taxes. Report differential wage payments in box 1 and any federal income tax withholding in box 2. Differential wage payments made to an individual while on active duty for 30 days or less are subject to income tax withholding, social security, Medicare, and unemployment taxes, and are reported in boxes 1, 3, and 5. See Rev. Rul. 2009-11, 2009-18 I.R.B. 896, available at *www.irs.gov/irb/2009-18_IRB/ar07.html*.

Moving expenses. Report moving expenses as follows.
• Qualified moving expenses that an employer paid to a third party on behalf of the employee (for example, to a moving company) and services that an employer furnished in kind to an employee are not reported on Form W-2.
• Qualified moving expense reimbursements paid directly to an employee by an employer are reported only in box 12 of Form W-2 with code P.
• Nonqualified moving expense reimbursements are reported in boxes 1, 3, and 5 (use box 14 if railroad retirement taxes apply) of Form W-2. These amounts are subject to federal income tax withholding and social security and Medicare taxes (or railroad retirement taxes, if applicable).

For more information on qualified and nonqualified moving expenses, see Pub. 521, Moving Expenses.

Nonqualified deferred compensation plans. Section 409A provides that all amounts deferred under a nonqualified deferred compensation (NQDC) plan for all tax years are currently includible in gross income to the extent not subject to a substantial risk of forfeiture and not previously included in gross income, unless certain requirements are met. Generally, section 409A is effective with respect to amounts deferred in tax years beginning after December 31, 2004, but deferrals made before that year may be subject to section 409A under some circumstances.

It is not necessary to show amounts deferred during the year under an NQDC plan subject to section 409A. If you report section 409A deferrals, show the amount in box 12 using code Y. For more information, see Notice 2008-115,

2008-52 I.R.B. 1367, available at *www.irs.gov/irb/2008-52_IRB/ar10.html*.

Income included under section 409A from an NQDC plan will be reported in box 1 and in box 12 using code Z. This income is also subject to an additional tax of 20% that is reported on Form 1040. For more information on amounts includible in gross income and reporting requirements, see Notice 2008-115 avaiable at *www.irs.gov/irb/2008-52_IRB/ar10.html*. For information on correcting failures to comply with section 409A and related reporting, see Notice 2008-113, 2008-51 I.R.B. 1305, available at *www.irs.gov/irb/2008-51_IRB/ar12.html*; Notice 2010-6, 2010-3 I.R.B. 275, available at *www.irs.gov/irb/2010-3_IRB/ar08.html*; and Notice 2010-80, 2010-51 I.R.B. 853, available at *www.irs.gov/irb/2010-51_IRB/ar08.html*.

See the *Nonqualified Deferred Compensation Reporting Example Chart*.

Railroad employers (not applicable to Forms W-2AS, W-2CM, W-2GU, or W-2VI). Railroad employers must file Form W-2 to report their employees' wages and income tax withholding in boxes 1 and 2. You must file a separate Form W-3 to transmit the Forms W-2 if you have employees covered under the Federal Insurance Contributions Act (FICA) (social security and Medicare) **and** the Railroad Retirement Tax Act (RRTA).

• On the Form W-3, check the "CT-1" checkbox in box b "Kind of Payer" used to transmit Forms W-2 for employees with box 1 wages and box 2 tax withholding. On the Form W-2, use box 14 for employees covered by RRTA tax, report the RRTA compensation, Tier 1, Tier 2, Medicare, and any Additional Medicare Tax withheld. Label them "RRTA compensation," "Tier 1 tax," "Tier 2 tax," "Medicare tax," and "Additional Medicare Tax." Include tips reported by the employee to the employer in "RRTA compensation."
• On the Form W-3, check the "941" checkbox in box b "Kind of Payer" used to transmit Forms W-2 for employees covered by social security and Medicare. On the Form W-2, complete boxes 3, 4, 5, 6, and 7 to show the social security and Medicare wages and taxes. These boxes apply only to covered social security and Medicare wages and taxes. They are **not** to be used to report railroad retirement compensation and taxes.

Repayments. If an employee repays you for wages received in error, do not offset the repayments against current year wages unless the repayments are for amounts received in error in the current year. Repayments made in the current year, but related to a prior year or years, must be repaid in gross, not net, and require special tax treatment by employees in some cases. You may advise the employee of the total repayments made during the current year and the amount (if any) related to prior years. This information will help the employee account for such repayments on his or her federal income tax return.

If the repayment was for a prior year, you must file Form W-2c with the SSA to correct only social security and Medicare wages and taxes, and furnish a copy to the employee. Do not correct "Wages, tips, other compensation" in box 1, or "Federal income tax withheld" in box 2, on Form W-2c. Also, do not correct any Additional Medicare Tax withheld on the repaid wages (reported with Medicare tax withheld in box 6) on Form W-2c. File the "X" return that is appropriate for the return on which the wages or compensation was originally reported (Forms 941-X, 943-X, 944-X, or CT-1X). Correct the social security and Medicare wages and taxes for the period during which the wages or compensation was originally paid. For information on reporting adjustments to Forms 941, 941-SS, 943, 944, or Form CT-1, see section 13 of Pub. 15 (Circular E), the Instructions for Form CT-1X, or section 9 of Pub. 51 (Circular A).

 Tell your employee that the wages paid in error in a prior year remain taxable to him or her for that year. This is because the employee received and had use of those funds during that year. The employee is not entitled to file an amended return (Form 1040X) to recover the income tax on these wages. Instead, the employee is entitled to a deduction (or a credit, in some cases) for the repaid wages on his or her Form 1040 for the year of repayment. However, the employee is entitled to file an amended return (Form 1040X) to recover Additional Medicare Tax on these wages, if any. Refer your employee to Repayments in Pub. 525.

Scholarship and fellowship grants. Give a Form W-2 to each recipient of a scholarship or fellowship grant only if you are reporting amounts includible in income under section 117(c) (relating to payments for teaching, research, or other services required as a condition for receiving the qualified scholarship). Also see Pub. 15-A and Pub. 970. These payments are subject to federal income tax withholding. However, their taxability for social security and Medicare taxes (or railroad retirement taxes, if applicable) depends on the nature of the employment and the status of the organization. See *Students, scholars, trainees, teachers, etc.*, in section 15 of Pub. 15 (Circular E).

Sick pay. If you had employees who received sick pay in 2016 from an insurance company or other third-party payer and the third party notified you of the amount of sick pay involved, you may be required to report the information on the employees' Forms W-2. If the insurance company or other third-party payer did not notify you in a timely manner about the sick pay payments, it must prepare Forms W-2 and W-3 for your employees showing the sick pay. For specific reporting instructions, see section 6 of Pub. 15-A.

SIMPLE retirement account. An employee's salary reduction contributions to a SIMPLE (savings incentive match plan for employees) retirement account are not subject to federal income tax withholding but are subject to social security, Medicare, and railroad retirement taxes. Do not include an employee's contribution in box 1, but do include it in boxes 3 and 5. (Use box 14 if railroad retirement taxes apply.) An employee's total contribution also must be included in box 12 with code D or S.

An employer's matching or nonelective contribution to an employee's SIMPLE retirement account is not subject to federal income tax withholding or social security, Medicare, or railroad retirement taxes, and is not to be shown on Form W-2.

For more information on SIMPLE retirement accounts, see Notice 98-4, 1998-1 C.B. 269. You can find Notice 98-4 on page 25 of Internal Revenue Bulletin 1998-2 at *www.irs.gov/pub/irs-irbs/irb98-02.pdf*.

Successor/predecessor employers. If you buy or sell a business during the year, see Rev. Proc. 2004-53 for information on who must file Forms W-2 and employment tax returns. Rev. Proc. 2004-53, 2004-34 I.R.B. 320, is available at *www.irs.gov/irb/2004-34_IRB/ar13.html*.

Terminating a business. If you terminate your business, you must provide Forms W-2 to your employees for the calendar year of termination by the due date of your final Forms 941, 944, or 941-SS. You also must file Forms W-2 with the SSA by the last day of the month that follows the due date of your final Forms 941, 944, or 941-SS. If filing on paper, make sure you obtain Forms W-2 and W-3 preprinted with the correct year. If e-filing, make sure your software has been updated for the current tax year.

However, if any of your employees are immediately employed by a successor employer, see *Successor/ predecessor employers* above. Also, for information on automatic extensions for furnishing Forms W-2 to employees and filing Forms W-2, see Rev. Proc. 96-57, which is on page 14 of Internal Revenue Bulletin 1996-53 at *www.irs.gov/pub/irs-irbs/irb96-53.pdf*.

 Get Schedule D (Form 941), Report of Discrepancies Caused by Acquisitions, Statutory Mergers, or Consolidations, for information on reconciling wages and taxes reported on Forms W-2 with amounts reported on Forms 941, 941-SS, 943, or 944.

Uniformed Services Employment and Reemployment Rights Act of 1994 (USERRA) makeup amounts to a pension plan. If an employee returned to your employment after military service and certain makeup amounts were contributed to a pension plan for a prior year(s) under the USERRA, report the prior year contributions separately in box 12. See the *TIP* above Code D in *Box 12—Codes*. You also may report certain makeup amounts in box 14. See *Box 14—Other* in *Specific Instructions for Form W-2*.

Instead of reporting in box 12 (or box 14), you may choose to provide a separate statement to your employee showing USERRA makeup contributions. The statement must identify the type of plan, the year(s) to which the contributions relate, and the amount contributed for each year.

Virtual currency. For federal tax purposes, virtual currency is treated as property. Bitcoin is an example of virtual currency. Transactions using virtual currency (such as Bitcoin) must be reported in U.S. dollars.

The fair market value of virtual currency (such as Bitcoin) paid as wages is subject to federal income tax withholding, FICA tax, and FUTA tax and must be reported on Form W-2. Notice 2014-21, 2014-16 I.R.B. 938 describes how virtual currency is treated for federal tax purposes and is available at *www.irs.gov/irb/2014-16_IRB/ar12.html*.

Penalties

The following penalties apply to the person or employer required to file Form W-2. The penalties apply to both paper filers and e-filers.

 Employers are responsible for ensuring that Forms W-2 are furnished to employees and that Forms W-2 and W-3 are filed with the SSA correctly and on time, even if the employer contracts with a third party to perform these acts. The IRS strongly suggests that the employer's address, not the third party's address, be the address on record with the IRS. This will ensure that you remain informed of tax matters involving your business because the IRS will correspond to the employer's address of record if there are any issues with an account. If you choose to outsource any of your payroll and related tax duties (that is, withholding, reporting, and paying over social security, Medicare, FUTA, and income taxes) to a third party payer, visit IRS.gov and enter "outsourcing payroll duties" in the search box for helpful information on this topic.

Failure to file correct information returns by the due date. If you fail to file a correct Form W-2 by the due date and cannot show reasonable cause, you may be subject to a penalty as provided under section 6721. The penalty applies if you:

- Fail to file timely,
- Fail to include all information required to be shown on Form W-2,
- Include incorrect information on Form W-2,
- File on paper forms when you are required to *e-file*,
- Report an incorrect TIN,
- Fail to report a TIN, or
- Fail to file paper Forms W-2 that are machine readable.

The amount of the penalty is based on when you file the correct Form W-2. Penalties are indexed for inflation. The penalty amounts shown below apply for tax years beginning in 2016. The penalty is:

- $50 per Form W-2 if you correctly file within 30 days of the due date (for example, by February 28 if the due date is January 31); the maximum penalty is $532,000 per year ($186,000 for small businesses, defined in *Small businesses*).
- $100 per Form W-2 if you correctly file more than 30 days after the due date but by August 1; the maximum penalty is $1,596,500 per year ($532,000 for small businesses).
- $260 per Form W-2 if you file after August 1, do not file corrections, or do not file required Forms W-2; the maximum penalty is $3,193,000 per year ($1,064,000 for small businesses).

 If you do not file corrections and you do not meet any of the exceptions to the penalty, the penalty is $260 per information return. The maximum penalty is $3,193,000 per year ($1,064,000 for small businesses).

Exceptions to the penalty. The following are exceptions to the failure to file correct information returns penalty.

1. The penalty will not apply to any failure that you can show was due to reasonable cause and not to willful neglect. In general, you must be able to show that your failure was due to an event beyond your control or due to significant mitigating factors. You also must be able to show that you acted in a responsible manner and took steps to avoid the failure.

2. An inconsequential error or omission is not considered a failure to include correct information. An inconsequential error or omission does not prevent or hinder the SSA/IRS from processing the Form W-2, from correlating the information required to be shown on the form with the information shown on the payee's tax return, or from otherwise putting the form to its intended use. Errors and omissions that are never inconsequential are those relating to:

- A TIN,
- A payee's surname, and
- Any money amounts.

3. De minimis rule for corrections. Even though you cannot show reasonable cause, the penalty for failure to file correct Forms W-2 will not apply to a certain number of returns if you:

- Filed those Forms W-2 on or before the required filing date,
- Either failed to include all of the information required on the form or included incorrect information, and
- Filed corrections of these forms by August 1.

If you meet all of the de minimis rule conditions, the penalty for filing incorrect information returns (including Form W-2) will not apply to the greater of 10 information returns (including Form W-2) or one-half of 1% of the total number of information returns (including Form W-2) that you are required to file for the calendar year.

4. Forms W-2 with incorrect dollar amounts may fall under a safe harbor for certain de minimis errors. The safe harbor applies if no single amount in error differs from the correct amount by more than $100 and no single amount reported for tax withheld differs from the correct amount by more than $25.

If the safe harbor applies, you will not have to correct the Form W-2 and it will be treated as having been filed with all of the correct required information. However, the safe harbor does not apply if the payee elects to have you issue a corrected return.

Small businesses. For purposes of the lower maximum penalties shown in *Failure to file correct information returns by the due date,* you are a small business if your average annual gross receipts for the 3 most recent tax years (or for the period that you were in existence, if shorter) ending before the calendar year in which the Forms W-2 were due are $5 million or less.

Intentional disregard of filing requirements. If any failure to timely file a correct Form W-2 is due to intentional disregard of the filing or correct information requirements, the penalty is at least $530 per Form W-2 with no maximum penalty.

Failure to furnish correct payee statements. If you fail to provide correct payee statements (Forms W-2) to your employees and cannot show reasonable cause, you may be subject to a penalty as provided under section 6722.

The penalty applies if you fail to provide the statement by January 31, 2017, if you fail to include all information required to be shown on the statement, or if you include incorrect information on the statement.

The amount of the penalty is based on when you furnish the correct payee statement. This penalty is an additional penalty and is applied in the same manner, and with the same amounts, as in *Failure to file correct information returns by the due date.*

Exceptions to the penalty. An inconsequential error or omission is not considered a failure to include correct information. An inconsequential error or omission cannot reasonably be expected to prevent or hinder the payee from timely receiving correct information and reporting it on his or her income tax return or from otherwise putting the statement to its intended use. Errors and omissions that are never inconsequential are those relating to:

- A dollar amount,
- A significant item in a payee's address, and
- The appropriate form for the information provided, such as whether the form is an acceptable substitute for the official IRS form.

See *Exceptions to the penalty* in *Failure to file correct information returns by the due date*, for additional exceptions to the penalty for failure to file correct payee statements.

Intentional disregard of payee statement requirements. If any failure to provide a correct payee statement (Form W-2) to an employee is due to intentional disregard of the requirements to furnish a correct payee statement, the penalty is $530 per Form W-2 with no maximum penalty.

Civil damages for fraudulent filing of Forms W-2. If you willfully file a fraudulent Form W-2 for payments that you claim you made to another person, that person may be able to sue you for damages. If you are found liable, you may have to pay $5,000 or more in damages. You may also be subject to criminal sanctions.

Specific Instructions for Form W-2

How to complete Form W-2. Form W-2 is a multi-part form. Ensure all copies are legible. Send Copy A to the SSA; Copy 1, if required, to your state, city, or local tax department; and Copies B, C, and 2 to your employee. Keep Copy D, and a copy of Form W-3, with your records for 4 years.

Enter the information on Form W-2 using black ink in 12-point Courier font. Copy A is read by machine and must be typed clearly with no corrections made to the entries and with no entries exceeding the size of the boxes. Entries completed by hand, in script or italic fonts, or in colors other than black cannot be read by the machines. Make all dollar entries on Copy A without the dollar sign and comma but with the decimal point (00000.00). Show the cents portion of the money amounts. If a box does not apply, leave it blank.

Send the whole Copy A page of Form W-2 with Form W-3 to the SSA even if one of the Forms W-2 on the page is blank or void. Do not staple Forms W-2 together or to Form W-3. File Forms W-2 either alphabetically by employees' last names or numerically by employees' SSNs.

Also see the *Caution* in *How To Get Forms and Publications*.

Calendar year basis. The entries on Form W-2 must be based on wages paid during the calendar year. Use Form W-2 for the correct tax year. For example, if the employee worked from December 21, 2016, through January 8, 2017, and the wages for that period were paid on January 10, 2017, include those wages on the 2017 Form W-2.

Multiple forms. If necessary, you can issue more than one Form W-2 to an employee. For example, you may need to report more than four coded items in box 12 or you may want to report other compensation on a second form. If you issue a second Form W-2, complete boxes a, b, c, d, e, and f with the same information as on the first Form W-2. Show any items that were not included on the first Form W-2 in the appropriate boxes.

Do not report the same federal, American Samoa, CNMI, Guam, or U.S. Virgin Islands tax data to the SSA on more than one Copy A.

 For each Form W-2 showing an amount in box 3 or box 7, make certain that box 5 equals or exceeds the sum of boxes 3 and 7.

Void. Check this box when an error is made on Form W-2 and you are voiding it because you are going to complete a new Form W-2. Do not include any amounts shown on "Void" forms in the totals you enter on Form W-3. See *Corrections*.

Box a—Employee's social security number. Enter the number shown on the employee's social security card.

If the employee does not have a card, he or she should apply for one by completing Form SS-5, Application for a Social Security Card. The SSA lets you verify employee names and SSNs online. For information about these free services, visit the Employer W-2 Filing Instructions & Information website at *www.socialsecurity.gov/employer*. If you have questions about using these services, call 1-800-772-6270 (toll free) to speak with an employer reporting technician at the SSA.

If the employee has applied for a card but the number is not received in time for filing, enter "Applied For" in box a on paper Forms W-2 filed with the SSA. If e-filing, enter zeros (000-00-0000 if creating forms online or 000000000 if uploading a file).

Ask the employee to inform you of the number and name as they are shown on the social security card when it is received. Then correct your previous report by filing Form W-2c showing the employee's SSN. If the employee needs to change his or her name from that shown on the card, the employee should call the SSA at 1-800-772-1213.

If you do not provide the correct employee name and SSN on Form W-2, you may owe a penalty unless you have reasonable cause. For more information, see Pub. 1586, Reasonable Cause Regulations & Requirements for Missing and Incorrect Name/TINs.

ITINs for aliens. Do not accept an ITIN in place of an SSN for employee identification or for work. An ITIN is only available to resident and nonresident aliens who are not eligible for U.S. employment and need identification for other tax purposes. You can identify an ITIN because it is a 9-digit number formatted like an SSN beginning with the number "9" and with a number in one of the following ranges in the fourth and fifth digit: 70-88, 90-92, or 94-99 (for example, 9NN-70-NNNN). An individual with an ITIN who later becomes eligible to work in the United States must obtain an SSN.

 Do not auto-populate an ITIN into box a.

Box b—Employer identification number (EIN). Show the EIN assigned to you by the IRS (00-0000000). This should be the same number that you used on your federal employment tax returns (Forms 941, 941-SS, 943, 944, CT-1, or Schedule H (Form 1040)). Do not use a prior owner's EIN. If you do not have an EIN when filing Forms W-2, enter "Applied For" in box b; do not use your SSN. You can get an EIN by applying online at IRS.gov, or by filing Form SS-4, Application for Employer Identification Number. Also see *Agent reporting*.

Box c—Employer's name, address, and ZIP code. This entry should be the same as shown on your Forms 941, 941-SS, 943, 944, CT-1, or Schedule H (Form 1040). The U.S. Postal Service recommends that no commas or periods be used in return addresses. Also see *Agent reporting*.

Box d—Control number. You may use this box to identify individual Forms W-2. You do not have to use this box.

Boxes e and f—Employee's name and address. Enter the name as shown on your employee's social security card (first name, middle initial, last name). If the name does not fit in the space allowed on the form, you may show the first and middle name initials and the full last name. It is especially important to report the exact last name of the employee. If you are unable to determine the correct last name, use of the SSA's Social Security Number Verification System may be helpful. Separate parts of a compound name with either a hyphen or a blank. Do not join them into a single word. Include all parts of a compound name in the appropriate name field. For example, for the name "John R Smith-Jones," enter "Smith-Jones" or "Smith Jones" in the last name field. If the name has changed, the employee must get a corrected social security card from any SSA office. Use the name on the original card until you see the corrected card. Do not show titles or academic degrees, such as "Dr.," "RN," or "Esq.," at the beginning or end of the employee's name. Generally, do not enter "Jr.," "Sr.," or other suffix in the "Suff." box on Copy A unless the suffix appears on the card. However, the SSA still prefers that you do not enter the suffix on Copy A.

Include in the address the number, street, and apartment or suite number (or P.O. box number if mail is not delivered to a street address). The U.S. Postal Service recommends that no commas or periods be used in delivery addresses. For a foreign address, give the information in the following order: city, province or state, and country. Follow the country's practice for entering the postal code. Do not abbreviate the country name.

Box 1—Wages, tips, other compensation. Show the total taxable wages, tips, and other compensation that you paid to your employee during the year. However, do not include elective deferrals (such as employee contributions to a section 401(k) or 403(b) plan) except section 501(c)(18) contributions. Include the following.

1. Total wages, bonuses (including signing bonuses), prizes, and awards paid to employees during the year. See *Calendar year basis.*

2. Total noncash payments, including certain fringe benefits. See *Fringe benefits.*

3. Total tips reported by the employee to the employer (not allocated tips).

4. Certain employee business expense reimbursements. See *Employee business expense reimbursements.*

5. The cost of accident and health insurance premiums for 2%-or-more shareholder-employees paid by an S corporation.

6. Taxable benefits from a section 125 (cafeteria) plan if the employee chooses cash.

7. Employee contributions to an Archer MSA.

8. Employer contributions to an Archer MSA if includible in the income of the employee. See *Archer MSA.*

9. Employer contributions for qualified long-term care services to the extent that such coverage is provided through a flexible spending or similar arrangement.

10. Taxable cost of group-term life insurance in excess of $50,000. See *Group-term life insurance.*

11. Unless excludable under *Educational assistance programs,* payments for non-job-related education expenses or for payments under a nonaccountable plan. See Pub. 970.

12. The amount includible as wages because you paid your employee's share of social security and Medicare taxes (or railroad retirement taxes, if applicable). See *Employee's social security and Medicare taxes (or railroad retirement taxes, if applicable) paid by employer.* If you also paid your employee's income tax withholding, treat the grossed-up amount of that withholding as supplemental wages and report those wages in boxes 1, 3, 5, and 7. (Use box 14 if railroad retirement taxes apply.) No exceptions to this treatment apply to household or agricultural wages.

13. Designated Roth contributions made under a section 401(k) plan, a section 403(b) salary reduction agreement, or a governmental section 457(b) plan. See *Designated Roth contributions.*

14. Distributions to an employee or former employee from an NQDC plan (including a rabbi trust) or a nongovernmental section 457(b) plan.

15. Amounts includible in income under section 457(f) because the amounts are no longer subject to a substantial risk of forfeiture.

16. Payments to statutory employees who are subject to social security and Medicare taxes but not subject to

federal income tax withholding must be shown in box 1 as other compensation. See *Statutory employee.*

17. Cost of current insurance protection under a compensatory split-dollar life insurance arrangement.

18. Employee contributions to a health savings account (HSA).

19. Employer contributions to an HSA if includible in the income of the employee. See *Health savings account (HSA).*

20. Amounts includible in income under an NQDC plan because of section 409A. See *Nonqualified deferred compensation plans* under *Special Reporting Situations for Form W-2.*

21. Payments made to former employees while they are on active duty in the Armed Forces or other uniformed services.

22. All other compensation, including certain scholarship and fellowship grants. See *Scholarship and fellowship grants.* Other compensation includes taxable amounts that you paid to your employee from which federal income tax was not withheld. You may show other compensation on a separate Form W-2. See *Multiple forms.*

Box 2—Federal income tax withheld. Show the total federal income tax withheld from the employee's wages for the year. Include the 20% excise tax withheld on excess parachute payments. See *Golden parachute payments.*

For Forms W-2AS, W-2CM, W-2GU, or W-2VI, show the total American Samoa, CNMI, Guam, or U.S. Virgin Islands income tax withheld.

Box 3—Social security wages. Show the total wages paid (before payroll deductions) subject to employee social security tax but not including social security tips and allocated tips. If reporting these amounts in a subsequent year (due to lapse of risk of forfeiture), the amount must be adjusted by any gain or loss. See *Box 7—Social security tips* and *Box 8—Allocated tips.* Generally, noncash payments are considered to be wages. Include employee business expense reimbursements reported in box 1. If you paid the employee's share of social security and Medicare taxes rather than deducting them from wages, see *Employee's social security and Medicare taxes (or railroad retirement taxes, if applicable) paid by employer.* The total of boxes 3 and 7 cannot exceed $118,500 (2016 maximum social security wage base).

Report in box 3 elective deferrals to certain qualified cash or deferred compensation arrangements and to retirement plans described in box 12 (codes D, E, F, G, and S) even though the deferrals are not includible in box 1. Also report in box 3 designated Roth contributions made under a section 401(k) plan, under a section 403(b) salary reduction agreement, or under a governmental section 457(b) plan described in box 12 (codes AA, BB, and EE).

Amounts deferred (plus earnings or less losses) under a section 457(f) or nonqualified plan or nongovernmental section 457(b) plan must be included in boxes 3 and/or 5 as social security and/or Medicare wages as of the later of when the services giving rise to the deferral are performed or when there is no substantial forfeiture risk of the rights to the deferred amount. Include both elective and nonelective deferrals for purposes of nongovernmental section 457(b) plans.

Wages reported in box 3 also include:
• Signing bonuses an employer pays for signing or ratifying an employment contract. See Rev. Rul. 2004-109, 2004-50 I.R.B. 958 available at *www.irs.gov/irb/2004-50_IRB/ar07.html.*
• Taxable cost of group-term life insurance over $50,000 included in box 1. See *Group-term life insurance.*
• Cost of accident and health insurance premiums for 2%-or-more shareholder-employees paid by an S corporation, but only if not excludable under section 3121(a)(2)(B).
• Employee and nonexcludable employer contributions to an MSA or HSA. However, do not include employee contributions to an HSA that were made through a cafeteria plan. See *Archer MSA* and *Health savings account (HSA).*
• Employee contributions to a SIMPLE retirement account. See *SIMPLE retirement account.*
• Adoption benefits. See *Adoption benefits.*

Box 4—Social security tax withheld. Show the total employee social security tax (not your share) withheld, including social security tax on tips. For 2016, the amount should not exceed $7,347 ($118,500 × 6.2%). Include only taxes withheld (or paid by you for the employee) for 2016 wages and tips. If you paid your employee's share, see *Employee's social security and Medicare taxes (or railroad retirement taxes, if applicable) paid by employer.*

Box 5—Medicare wages and tips. The wages and tips subject to Medicare tax are the same as those subject to social security tax (boxes 3 and 7) except that there is no wage base limit for Medicare tax. Enter the total Medicare wages and tips in box 5. Be sure to enter tips that the employee reported even if you did not have enough employee funds to collect the Medicare tax for those tips. See *Box 3—Social security wages,* for payments to report in this box. If you paid your employee's share of taxes, see *Employee's social security and Medicare taxes (or railroad retirement taxes, if applicable) paid by employer.*

If you are a federal, state, or local governmental agency with employees paying only Medicare tax, enter the Medicare wages in this box. See *Government employers.*

Example of how to report social security and Medicare wages. You paid your employee $140,000 in wages. Enter in box 3 (social security wages) 118500.00 but enter in box 5 (Medicare wages and tips) 140000.00. There is no limit on the amount reported in box 5. If the amount of wages paid was $118,500 or less, the amounts entered in boxes 3 and 5 will be the same.

Box 6—Medicare tax withheld. Enter the total employee Medicare tax (including any Additional Medicare Tax) withheld. Do not include your share. Include only tax withheld for 2016 wages and tips. If you paid your employee's share of the taxes, see *Employee's social security and Medicare taxes (or railroad retirement taxes, if applicable) paid by employer.*

For more information on Additional Medicare Tax, go to IRS.gov and enter "Additional Medicare Tax" in the search box.

Box 7—Social security tips. Show the tips that the employee reported to you even if you did not have enough employee funds to collect the social security tax for the tips. The total of boxes 3 and 7 should not be more than $118,500 (the maximum social security wage base for 2016). Report all tips in box 1 along with wages and other compensation. Include any tips reported in box 7 in box 5 also.

Box 8—Allocated tips (not applicable to Forms W-2AS, W-2CM, W-2GU, or W-2VI). If you operate a large food or beverage establishment, show the tips allocated to the employee. See the Instructions for Form 8027, Employer's Annual Information Return of Tip Income and Allocated Tips. Do not include this amount in boxes 1, 3, 5, or 7.

Box 9. Do not enter an amount in box 9.

Box 10—Dependent care benefits (not applicable to Forms W-2AS, W-2CM, W-2GU, or W-2VI). Show the total dependent care benefits under a dependent care assistance program (section 129) paid or incurred by you for your employee. Include the fair market value (FMV) of care in a daycare facility provided or sponsored by you for your employee and amounts paid or incurred for dependent care assistance in a section 125 (cafeteria) plan. Report all amounts paid or incurred (regardless of any employee forfeitures), including those in excess of the $5,000 exclusion. This may include (a) the FMV of benefits provided in kind by the employer, (b) an amount paid directly to a daycare facility by the employer or reimbursed to the employee to subsidize the benefit, or (c) benefits from the pre-tax contributions made by the employee under a section 125 dependent care flexible spending account. Include any amounts over $5,000 in boxes 1, 3, and 5. For more information, see Pub. 15-B.

 An employer that amends its cafeteria plan to provide a grace period for dependent care assistance may continue to rely on Notice 89-111 by reporting in box 10 the salary reduction amount elected by the employee for the year for dependent care assistance (plus any employer matching contributions attributable to dependent care). Also see Notice 2005-42, 2005-23 I.R.B. 1204, available at www.irs.gov/irb/2005-23_IRB/ar11.html.

Box 11—Nonqualified plans. The purpose of box 11 is for the SSA to determine if any part of the amount reported in box 1 or boxes 3 and/or 5 was earned in a prior year. The SSA uses this information to verify that they have properly applied the social security earnings test and paid the correct amount of benefits.

Report distributions to an employee from a nonqualified plan or nongovernmental section 457(b) plan in box 11. Also report these distributions in box 1. Make only one entry in this box. Distributions from governmental section 457(b) plans must be reported on Form 1099-R, not in box 1 of Form W-2.

Under nonqualified plans or nongovernmental 457(b) plans, deferred amounts that are no longer subject to a

substantial risk of forfeiture are taxable even if not distributed. Report these amounts in boxes 3 (up to the social security wage base) and 5. Do not report in box 11 deferrals included in boxes 3 and/or 5 and deferrals for current year services (such as those with no risk of forfeiture).

 If you made distributions and also are reporting any deferrals in boxes 3 and/or 5, do not complete box 11. See Pub. 957, Reporting Back Pay and Special Wage Payments to the Social Security Administration, and Form SSA-131, Employer Report of Special Wage Payments, for instructions on reporting these and other kinds of compensation earned in prior years. However, **do not file Form SSA-131 if this situation applies and the employee was not 61 years old or more during the tax year for which you are filing Form W-2.**

Unlike qualified plans, NQDC plans do not meet the qualification requirements for tax-favored status for this purpose. NQDC plans include those arrangements traditionally viewed as deferring the receipt of current compensation. Accordingly, welfare benefit plans, stock option plans, and plans providing dismissal pay, termination pay, or early retirement pay are not generally NQDC plans.

Report distributions from NQDC or section 457 plans to beneficiaries of deceased employees on Form 1099-MISC, not on Form W-2.

Military employers must report military retirement payments on Form 1099-R.

 Do not report special wage payments, such as accumulated sick pay or vacation pay, in box 11. For more information on reporting special wage payments, see Pub. 957.

Box 12—Codes. Complete and code this box for all items described below. Note that the codes do not relate to where they should be entered in boxes 12a through 12d on Form W-2. For example, if you are only required to report code D in box 12, you can enter code D and the amount in box 12a of Form W-2. Report in box 12 any items that are listed as codes A through EE. Do not report in box 12 section 414(h)(2) contributions (relating to certain state or local government plans). Instead, use box 14 for these items and any other information that you wish to give to your employee. For example, union dues and uniform payments may be reported in box 14.

 On Copy A (Form W-2), do not enter more than four items in box 12. If more than four items need to be reported in box 12, use a separate Form W-2 to report the additional items (but enter no more than four items on each Copy A (Form W-2)). On all other copies of Form W-2 (Copies B, C, etc.), you may enter more than four items in box 12 when using an approved substitute Form W-2. See Multiple forms.

Use the IRS code designated below for the item you are entering, followed by the dollar amount for that item. Even if only one item is entered, you must use the IRS code designated for that item. Enter the code using a capital letter(s). Use decimal points but not dollar signs or commas. For example, if you are reporting $5,300.00 in elective deferrals under a section 401(k) plan, the entry would be D 5300.00 (not A 5300.00 even though it is the first or only entry in this box). Report the IRS code to the left of the vertical line in boxes 12a through 12d and the money amount to the right of the vertical line.

See the *Form W-2 Reference Guide for Box 12 Codes.* See also the detailed instructions next for each code.

Code A—Uncollected social security or RRTA tax on tips. Show the employee social security or Railroad Retirement Tax Act (RRTA) tax on all of the employee's tips that you could not collect because the employee did not have enough funds from which to deduct it. Do not include this amount in box 4.

Code B—Uncollected Medicare tax on tips. Show the employee Medicare tax or RRTA Medicare tax on tips that you could not collect because the employee did not have enough funds from which to deduct it. Do not show any uncollected Additional Medicare Tax. Do not include this amount in box 6.

Code C—Taxable cost of group-term life insurance over $50,000. Show the taxable cost of group-term life insurance coverage over $50,000 provided to your employee (including a former employee). See *Group-term life insurance.* Also include this amount in boxes 1, 3 (up to the social security wage base), and 5. Include the amount in box 14 if you are a railroad employer.

Codes D through H, S, Y, AA, BB, and EE. Use these codes to show elective deferrals and designated Roth contributions made to the plans listed. Do not report amounts for other types of plans. See the example for reporting elective deferrals under a section 401(k) plan, later.

The amount reported as elective deferrals and designated Roth contributions is only the part of the employee's salary (or other compensation) that he or she did not receive because of the deferrals or designated Roth contributions. Only elective deferrals and designated Roth contributions should be reported in box 12 for all coded plans; except, when using code G for section 457(b) plans, include both elective and nonelective deferrals.

For employees who were 50 years of age or older at any time during the year and made elective deferral and/or designated Roth "catch-up" contributions, report the elective deferrals and the elective deferral "catch-up" contributions as a single sum in box 12 using the appropriate code, and the designated Roth contributions and designated Roth "catch-up" contributions as a single sum in box 12 using the appropriate code.

 If any elective deferrals, salary reduction amounts, or nonelective contributions under a section 457(b) plan during the year are makeup amounts under the Uniformed Services Employment and Reemployment Rights Act of 1994 (USERRA) for a prior year, you must enter the prior year contributions separately. Beginning with the earliest year, enter the code, the year, and the amount. For example, elective deferrals of $2,250 for 2014 and $1,250 for 2015 under USERRA under a section 401(k) plan are reported in box 12 as follows:

D 14 2250.00, D 15 1250.00. A 2016 contribution of $7,000 does not require a year designation; enter it as D 7000.00. Report the code (and year for prior year USERRA contributions) to the left of the vertical line in boxes 12a through 12d.

The following are not elective deferrals and may be reported in box 14, but not in box 12.
• Nonelective employer contributions made on behalf of an employee.
• After-tax contributions that are not designated Roth contributions, such as voluntary contributions to a pension plan that are deducted from an employee's pay. See *Box 12—Codes* for Code AA, Code BB, and Code EE for reporting designated Roth contributions.
• Required employee contributions.
• Employer matching contributions.

Code D—Elective deferrals under a section 401(k) cash or deferred arrangement (plan). Also show deferrals under a SIMPLE retirement account that is part of a section 401(k) arrangement.

Example of reporting excess elective deferrals and designated Roth contributions under a section 401(k) plan. For 2016, Employee A (age 45) elected to defer $18,300 under a section 401(k) plan. The employee also made a designated Roth contribution to the plan of $1,000, and made a voluntary (non-Roth) after-tax contribution of $600. In addition, the employer, on A's behalf, made a qualified nonelective contribution of $2,000 to the plan and a nonelective profit-sharing employer contribution of $3,000.

Even though the 2016 limit for elective deferrals and designated Roth contributions is $18,000, the employee's total elective deferral amount of $18,300 is reported in box 12 with code D (D 18300.00). The designated Roth contribution is reported in box 12 with code AA (AA 1000.00). The employer must separately report the actual amounts of $18,300 and $1,000 in box 12 with the appropriate codes. The amount deferred in excess of the limit is not reported in box 1. The return of excess salary deferrals and excess designated contributions, including earnings on both, is reported on Form 1099-R.

The $600 voluntary after-tax contribution may be reported in box 14 (this is optional) but not in box 12. The $2,000 nonelective contribution and the $3,000 nonelective profit-sharing employer contribution are not required to be reported on Form W-2, but may be reported in box 14.

Check the "Retirement plan" box in box 13.

Code E—Elective deferrals under a section 403(b) salary reduction agreement.

Code F—Elective deferrals under a section 408(k) (6) salary reduction SEP.

Code G—Elective deferrals and employer contributions (including nonelective deferrals) to any governmental or nongovernmental section 457(b) deferred compensation plan. Do not report either section 457(b) or section 457(f) amounts that are subject to a substantial risk of forfeiture.

Code H—Elective deferrals under section 501(c)(18)(D) tax-exempt organization plan. Be sure to include this amount in box 1 as wages. The employee will deduct the amount on his or her Form 1040.

Code J—Nontaxable sick pay. Show any sick pay that was paid by a third-party and was not includible in income (and not shown in boxes 1, 3, and 5) because the employee contributed to the sick pay plan. Do not include nontaxable disability payments made directly by a state.

Code K—20% excise tax on excess golden parachute payments (not applicable to Forms W-2AS, W-2CM, W-2GU, or W-2VI). If you made excess golden parachute payments to certain key corporate employees, report the 20% excise tax on these payments. If the excess payments are considered to be wages, report the 20% excise tax withheld as income tax withheld in box 2.

Code L—Substantiated employee business expense reimbursements. Use this code only if you reimbursed your employee for employee business expenses using a per diem or mileage allowance and the amount that you reimbursed exceeds the amount treated as substantiated under IRS rules. See *Employee business expense reimbursements.*

Report in box 12 only the amount treated as substantiated (such as the nontaxable part). Include in boxes 1, 3 (up to the social security wage base), and 5 the part of the reimbursement that is more than the amount treated as substantiated. Report the unsubstantiated amounts in box 14 if you are a railroad employer.

Code M—Uncollected social security or RRTA tax on taxable cost of group-term life insurance over $50,000 (for former employees). If you provided your former employees (including retirees) more than $50,000 of group-term life insurance coverage for periods during which an employment relationship no longer exists, enter the amount of uncollected social security or RRTA tax on the coverage in box 12. Do not include this amount in box 4. Also see *Group-term life insurance.*

Code N—Uncollected Medicare tax on taxable cost of group-term life insurance over $50,000 (for former employees). If you provided your former employees (including retirees) more than $50,000 of group-term life insurance coverage for periods during which an employment relationship no longer exists, enter the amount of uncollected Medicare tax or RRTA Medicare tax on the coverage in box 12. Do not show any uncollected Additional Medicare Tax. Do not include this amount in box 6. Also see *Group-term life insurance.*

Code P—Excludable moving expense reimbursements paid directly to employee. Show the total moving expense reimbursements that you paid directly to your employee for qualified (deductible) moving expenses. See *Moving expenses.*

Code Q—Nontaxable combat pay. If you are a military employer, report any nontaxable combat pay in box 12.

Code R—Employer contributions to an Archer MSA. Show any employer contributions to an Archer MSA. See *Archer MSA.*

Code S—Employee salary reduction contributions under a section 408(p) SIMPLE plan. Show deferrals under a section 408(p) salary reduction SIMPLE retirement account. However, if the SIMPLE plan is part of a section 401(k) arrangement, use code D. If you are reporting prior year contributions under USERRA, see the *TIP* above Code D in *Box 12—Codes.*

Code T—Adoption benefits. Show the total that you paid or reimbursed for qualified adoption expenses furnished to your employee under an adoption assistance program. Also include adoption benefits paid or reimbursed from the pre-tax contributions made by the employee under a section 125 (cafeteria) plan. However, do not include adoption benefits forfeited from a section 125 (cafeteria) plan. Report all amounts including those in excess of the $13,460 exclusion. For more information, see *Adoption benefits.*

Code V—Income from the exercise of nonstatutory stock option(s). Show the spread (that is, the fair market value of stock over the exercise price of option(s) granted to your employee with respect to that stock) from your employee's (or former employee's) exercise of nonstatutory stock option(s). Include this amount in boxes 1, 3 (up to the social security wage base), and 5. Include this amount in box 14 if you are a railroad employer.

This reporting requirement does not apply to the exercise of a statutory stock option, or the sale or disposition of stock acquired pursuant to the exercise of a statutory stock option. For more information about the taxability of employee stock options, see Pub. 15-B.

Code W—Employer contributions to a health savings account (HSA). Show any employer contributions (including amounts the employee elected to contribute using a section 125 (cafeteria) plan) to an HSA. See *Health savings account (HSA).*

Code Y—Deferrals under a section 409A nonqualified deferred compensation plan. It is not necessary to show deferrals in box 12 with code Y. For more information, see Notice 2008-115. However, if you report these deferrals, show current year deferrals, including earnings during the year on current year and prior year deferrals. See *Nonqualified deferred compensation plans* under *Special Reporting Situations for Form W-2.*

Code Z—Income under a nonqualified deferred compensation plan that fails to satisfy section 409A. Enter all amounts deferred (including earnings on amounts deferred) that are includible in income under section 409A because the NQDC plan fails to satisfy the requirements of section 409A. Do not include amounts properly reported on a Form 1099-MISC, corrected Form 1099-MISC, Form W-2, or Form W-2c for a prior year. Also, do not include amounts that are considered to be subject to a substantial risk of forfeiture for purposes of section 409A. For more information, see Regulations sections 1.409A-1, -2,-3, and -6; and Notice 2008-115.

The amount reported in box 12 using code Z is also reported in box 1 and is subject to an additional tax reported on the employee's Form 1040. See *Nonqualified deferred compensation plans* under *Special Reporting Situations for Form W-2.*

For information regarding correcting section 409A errors and related reporting, see Notice 2008-113, Notice 2010-6, and Notice 2010-80.

Code AA—Designated Roth contributions under a section 401(k) plan. Use this code to report designated Roth contributions under a section 401(k) plan. Do not use this code to report elective deferrals under code D. See *Designated Roth contributions.*

Code BB—Designated Roth contributions under a section 403(b) plan. Use this code to report designated Roth contributions under a section 403(b) plan. Do not use this code to report elective deferrals under code E. See *Designated Roth contributions.*

Code DD—Cost of employer-sponsored health coverage. Use this code to report the cost of employer-sponsored health coverage. **The amount reported with code DD is not taxable.** Additional reporting guidance, including information about the transitional reporting rules that apply, is available on the Affordable Care Act Tax Provisions page of IRS.gov.

Code EE—Designated Roth contributions under a governmental section 457(b) plan. Use this code to report designated Roth contributions under a governmental section 457(b) plan. Do not use this code to report elective deferrals under code G. See *Designated Roth contributions.*

Box 13—Checkboxes. Check all boxes that apply.

Statutory employee. Check this box for statutory employees whose earnings are subject to social security and Medicare taxes but not subject to federal income tax withholding. Do not check this box for common-law employees. There are workers who are independent contractors under the common-law rules but are treated by statute as employees. They are called statutory employees.

1. A driver who distributes beverages (other than milk) or meat, vegetable, fruit, or bakery products; or who picks up and delivers laundry or dry cleaning, if the driver is your agent or is paid on commission.

2. A full-time life insurance sales agent whose principal business activity is selling life insurance or annuity contracts, or both, primarily for one life insurance company.

3. An individual who works at home on materials or goods that you supply and that must be returned to you or to a person you name, if you also furnish specifications for the work to be done.

4. A full-time traveling or city salesperson who works on your behalf and turns in orders to you from wholesalers, retailers, contractors, or operators of hotels, restaurants, or other similar establishments. The goods sold must be merchandise for resale or supplies for use in the buyer's business operation. The work performed for you must be the salesperson's principal business activity.

For details on statutory employees and common-law employees, see section 1 in Pub. 15-A.

Retirement plan. Check this box if the employee was an "active participant" (for any part of the year) in any of the following.

1. A qualified pension, profit-sharing, or stock-bonus plan described in section 401(a) (including a 401(k) plan).

2. An annuity plan described in section 403(a).

3. An annuity contract or custodial account described in section 403(b).

4. A simplified employee pension (SEP) plan described in section 408(k).

5. A SIMPLE retirement account described in section 408(p).

6. A trust described in section 501(c)(18).

7. A plan for federal, state, or local government employees or by an agency or instrumentality thereof (other than a section 457(b) plan).

Generally, an employee is an active participant if covered by (a) a defined benefit plan for any tax year that he or she is eligible to participate in or (b) a defined contribution plan (for example, a section 401(k) plan) for any tax year that employer or employee contributions (or forfeitures) are added to his or her account. For additional information on employees who are eligible to participate in a plan, contact your plan administrator. For details on the active participant rules, see Notice 87-16, 1987-1 C.B. 446; Notice 98-49, 1998-2 C.B. 365; section 219(g)(5); and Pub. 590-A, Contributions to Individual Retirement Arrangements (IRAs). You can find Notice 98-49 on page 5 of Internal Revenue Bulletin 1998-38 at *www.irs.gov/pub/irs-irbs/irb98-38.pdf.* Also see Notice 2000-30, which is on page 1266 of Internal Revenue Bulletin 2000-25 at *www.irs.gov/pub/irs-irbs/irb00-25.pdf.*

 Do not check this box for contributions made to a nonqualified or section 457(b) plan.

See the *Form W-2 Box 13 Retirement Plan Checkbox Decision Chart.*

Third-party sick pay. Check this box only if you are a third-party sick pay payer filing a Form W-2 for an insured's employee or are an employer reporting sick pay payments made by a third party. See section 6 of Pub. 15-A.

Box 14—Other. If you included 100% of a vehicle's annual lease value in the employee's income, it also must be reported here or on a separate statement to your employee. You also may use this box for any other information that you want to give to your employee. Label each item. Examples include state disability insurance taxes withheld, union dues, uniform payments, health insurance premiums deducted, nontaxable income, educational assistance payments, or a minister's parsonage allowance and utilities. In addition, you may enter the following contributions to a pension plan: (a) nonelective employer contributions made on behalf of an employee, (b) voluntary after-tax contributions (but not designated Roth contributions) that are deducted from an employee's pay, (c) required employee contributions, and (d) employer matching contributions.

If you are reporting prior year contributions under USERRA (see the *TIP* above Code D in *Box 12—Codes* and *Uniformed Services Employment and Reemployment Rights Act of 1994 (USERRA) makeup amounts to a pension plan*), you may report in box 14 makeup amounts for nonelective employer contributions, voluntary after-tax contributions, required employee contributions, and employer matching contributions. Report such amounts separately for each year.

Railroad employers, see *Railroad employers* for amounts reportable in box 14.

Boxes 15 through 20—State and local income tax information (not applicable to Forms W-2AS, W-2CM, W-2GU, or W-2VI). Use these boxes to report state and local income tax information. Enter the two-letter abbreviation for the name of the state. The employer's state ID numbers are assigned by the individual states. The state and local information boxes can be used to report wages and taxes for two states and two localities. Keep each state's and locality's information separated by the broken line. If you need to report information for more than two states or localities, prepare a second Form W-2. See *Multiple forms.* Contact your state or locality for specific reporting information.

Specific Instructions for Form W-3

How to complete Form W-3. The instructions under *How to complete Form W-2* generally apply to Form W-3. Use black ink for all entries. Scanners cannot read entries if the type is too light. Be sure to send the entire page of the Form W-3.

 Amounts reported on related employment tax forms (for example, Forms W-2, 941, 941-SS, 943, or 944) should agree with the amounts reported on Form W-3. If there are differences, you may be contacted by the IRS and SSA. Retain your reconciliation information for future reference. See Reconciling Forms W-2, W-3, 941, 941-SS, 943, 944, CT-1, and Schedule H (Form 1040).

Box a—Control number. This is an optional box that you may use for numbering the whole transmittal.

Box b—Kind of Payer. Check the box that applies to you. Check only one box. If you have more than one type of Form W-2, send each type with a separate Form W-3. **Note.** The "Third-party sick pay" indicator box does not designate a separate kind of payer.

941 or 941-SS. Check this box if you file Forms 941 or 941-SS and no other category applies. A church or church organization should check this box even if it is not required to file Forms 941, 941-SS, or 944. If you are a railroad employer sending Forms W-2 for employees covered under the Railroad Retirement Tax Act (RRTA), check the "CT-1" box.

Military. Check this box if you are a military employer sending Forms W-2 for members of the uniformed services.

943. Check this box if you are an agricultural employer and file Form 943 and you are sending Forms W-2 for agricultural employees. For nonagricultural employees, send their Forms W-2 with a separate Form W-3, checking the appropriate box.

944. Check this box if you file Form 944 (or Formulario 944(SP), its Spanish-language version), and no other category applies.

CT-1. Check this box if you are a railroad employer sending Forms W-2 for employees covered under the Railroad Retirement Tax Act (RRTA). Do not show employee RRTA tax in boxes 3 through 7. These boxes are only for social security and Medicare information. If you also have employees who are subject to social security and Medicare taxes, send that group's Forms W-2 with a separate Form W-3 and check the "941" checkbox on that Form W-3.

Hshld. emp. Check this box if you are a household employer sending Forms W-2 for household employees and you did not include the household employee's taxes on Forms 941, 941-SS, 943, or 944.

Medicare govt. emp. Check this box if you are a U.S., state, or local agency filing Forms W-2 for employees subject only to Medicare tax. See *Government employers.*

Box b—Kind of Employer. Check the box that applies to you. Check only one box unless the second checked box is "Third-party sick pay." See Pub. 557, Tax-Exempt Status for Your Organization, for information about 501(c)(3) tax-exempt organizations.

None apply. Check this box if none of the checkboxes discussed next apply to you.

501c non-govt. Check this box if you are a non-governmental tax-exempt section 501(c) organization. Types of 501(c) non-governmental organizations include private foundations, public charities, social and recreation clubs, and veterans organizations. For additional examples of 501(c) non-governmental organizations, see chapters 3 and 4 of Pub. 557.

State/local non-501c. Check this box if you are a state or local government or instrumentality. This includes cities, townships, counties, special-purpose districts, public schools districts, or other publicly-owned entities with governmental authority.

State/local 501c. Check this box if you are a state or local government or instrumentality, and you have received a determination letter from the IRS indicating that you are also a tax-exempt organization under section 501(c)(3).

Federal govt. Check this box if you are a Federal government entity or instrumentality.

Box b—Third-party sick pay. Check this box if you are a third-party sick pay payer (or are reporting sick pay payments made by a third party) filing Forms W-2 with the "Third-party sick pay" checkbox in box 13 checked. File a single Form W-3 for the regular and "Third-party sick pay" Forms W-2. See *941 or 941-SS.*

Box c—Total number of Forms W-2. Show the number of completed individual Forms W-2 that you are transmitting with this Form W-3. Do not count "Void" Forms W-2.

Box d—Establishment number. You may use this box to identify separate establishments in your business. You may file a separate Form W-3, with Forms W-2, for each establishment even if they all have the same EIN; or you may use a single Form W-3 for all Forms W-2 of the same type.

Box e—Employer identification number (EIN). Enter the nine-digit EIN assigned to you by the IRS. The number should be the same as shown on your Forms 941, 941-SS, 943, 944, CT-1, or Schedule H (Form 1040) and in the following format: 00-0000000. Do not use a prior owner's EIN. See *Box h—Other EIN used this year.*

If you do not have an EIN when filing your Form W-3, enter "Applied For" in box e, not your social security number (SSN), and see *Box b—Employer identification number (EIN).*

Box f—Employer's name. Enter the same name as shown on your Forms 941, 941-SS, 943, 944, CT-1, or Schedule H (Form 1040).

Box g—Employer's address and ZIP code. Enter your address.

Box h—Other EIN used this year. If you have used an EIN (including a prior owner's EIN) on Forms 941, 941-SS, 943, 944, or CT-1 submitted for 2016 that is different from the EIN reported on Form W-3 in box e, enter the other EIN used. Agents generally report the employer's EIN in box h. See *Agent reporting.*

Employer's contact person, Employer's telephone number, Employer's fax number, and Employer's email address. Include this information for use by the SSA if any questions arise during processing. SSA will notify the employer by email or postal mail to correct and resubmit reports from the information provided on Form W-3.

 Payroll service providers enter your client's information for these fields.

 The amounts to enter in boxes 1 through 19, described next, are totals from only the Forms W-2 (excluding any Forms W-2 marked "VOID") that you are sending with this Form W-3.

Boxes 1 through 8. Enter the totals reported in boxes 1 through 8 on the Forms W-2.

Box 9. Do not enter an amount in box 9.

Box 10—Dependent care benefits (not applicable to Forms W-2AS, W-2CM, W-2GU, and W-2VI). Enter the total reported in box 10 on Forms W-2.

Box 11—Nonqualified plans. Enter the total reported in box 11 on Forms W-2.

Box 12a—Deferred compensation. Enter the total of all amounts reported with codes D through H, S, Y, AA, BB, and EE in box 12 on Forms W-2. Do not enter a code.

 The total of Form W-2 box 12 amounts reported with Codes A through C, J through R, T through W, Z, and DD is not reported on Form W-3.

Box 13—For third-party sick pay use only. Leave this box blank. See Form 8922.

Box 14—Income tax withheld by payer of third-party sick pay. Complete this box only if you are the employer and have employees who had federal income tax withheld on third-party payments of sick pay. Show the total income tax withheld by third-party payers on payments to all of your employees. Although this tax is included in the box 2 total, it must be separately shown here.

Box 15—State/Employer's state ID number (territorial ID number for Forms W-2AS, W-2CM, W-2GU, and W-2VI). Enter the two-letter abbreviation for the name of the state or territory being reported on Form(s) W-2. Also enter your state- or territory-assigned ID number. If the Forms W-2 being submitted with this Form W-3 contain wage and income tax information from more than one state or territory, enter an "X" under "State" and do not enter any state or territory ID number.

Boxes 16 through 19 (not applicable to Forms W-2AS, W-2CM, W-2GU, and W-2VI). Enter the total of state/local wages and income tax shown in their corresponding boxes on the Forms W-2 included with this Form W-3. If the Forms W-2 show amounts from more than one state or locality, report them as one sum in the appropriate box on Form W-3. Verify that the amount reported in each box is an accurate total of the Forms W-2.

Reconciling Forms W-2, W-3, 941, 941-SS, 943, 944, CT-1, and Schedule H (Form 1040)

Reconcile the amounts shown in boxes 2, 3, 5, and 7 from all 2016 Forms W-3 with their respective amounts from the 2016 yearly totals from the quarterly Forms 941 or 941-SS or annual Forms 943, 944, CT-1 (box 2 only), and Schedule H (Form 1040). When there are discrepancies between amounts reported on Forms W-2 and W-3 filed with the SSA and on Forms 941, 941-SS, 943, 944, CT-1, or Schedule H (Form 1040) filed with the IRS, you will be contacted to resolve the discrepancies.

 To help reduce discrepancies on Forms W-2:

- Report bonuses as wages and as social security and Medicare wages on Form W-2, and on Forms 941, 941-SS, 943, 944, and Schedule H (Form 1040).
- Report both social security and Medicare wages and taxes separately on Forms W-2 and W-3, and on Forms 941, 941-SS, 943, 944, and Schedule H (Form 1040).
- Report social security taxes withheld on Form W-2 in box 4, not in box 3.
- Report Medicare taxes withheld on Form W-2 in box 6, not in box 5.
- Do not report a nonzero amount in box 4 if boxes 3 and 7 are both zero.
- Do not report a nonzero amount in box 6 if box 5 is zero.
- Do not report an amount in box 5 that is less than the sum of boxes 3 and 7.
- Make sure that the social security wage amount for each employee does not exceed the annual social security wage base limit ($118,500 for 2016).
- Do not report noncash wages that are not subject to social security or Medicare taxes as social security or Medicare wages.
- If you use an EIN on any quarterly Forms 941 or 941-SS for the year (or annual Forms 943, 944, CT-1, or Schedule H (Form 1040)) that is different from the EIN reported in box e on Form W-3, enter the other EIN in box h on Form W-3.

To reduce the discrepancies between amounts reported on Forms W-2 and W-3, and Forms 941, 941-SS, 943, 944, CT-1, and Schedule H (Form 1040):

- Be sure that the amounts on Form W-3 are the total amounts from Forms W-2.
- Reconcile Form W-3 with your four quarterly Forms 941 or 941-SS (or annual Forms 943, 944, CT-1, or Schedule H (Form 1040)) by comparing amounts reported for:

1. Income tax withholding (box 2).

2. Social security wages, Medicare wages and tips, and social security tips (boxes 3, 5, and 7). Form W-3 should include Forms 941 or 941-SS or Forms 943, 944, or Schedule H (Form 1040) adjustments only for the current year. If the Forms 941, 941-SS, 943, or 944 adjustments include amounts for a prior year, do not report those prior year adjustments on the current year Forms W-2 and W-3.

3. Social security and Medicare taxes (boxes 4 and 6). The amounts shown on the four quarterly Forms 941 or 941-SS (or annual Forms 943, 944, or Schedule H (Form 1040)), including current year adjustments, should be approximately twice the amounts shown on Form W-3.

Amounts reported on Forms W-2 and W-3, and Forms 941, 941-SS, 943, 944, CT-1, or Schedule H (Form 1040) may not match for valid reasons. If they do not match, you should determine that the reasons are valid. Retain your reconciliation information in case you receive inquiries from the IRS or the SSA.

General Instructions for Forms W-2c and W-3c

Applicable forms. Use with the current version of Form W-2c and the current version of Form W-3c.

Purpose of forms. Use Form W-2c to correct errors on Forms W-2, W-2AS, W-2CM, W-2GU, W-2VI, or W-2c filed with the SSA. Also use Form W-2c to provide corrected Forms W-2, W-2AS, W-2CM, W-2GU, W-2VI, or W-2c to employees.

Corrections reported on Form W-2c may require you to make corrections to your previously filed employment tax returns using the corresponding "X" form, such as Form 941-X, Adjusted Employer's QUARTERLY Federal Tax Return or Claim for Refund; Form 943-X, Adjusted Employer's Annual Federal Tax Return for Agricultural Employees or Claim for Refund; Form 944-X, Adjusted Employer's ANNUAL Federal Tax Return or Claim for Refund; or Form CT-1X, Adjusted Employer's Annual Railroad Retirement Tax Return or Claim for Refund. See section 13 of Pub. 15 (Circular E) and the Instructions for Form CT-1X for more information. If you are making corrections to a previously filed Schedule H (Form 1040), see Pub. 926, Household Employer's Tax Guide. If an employee repaid you for wages received in a prior year, also see *Repayments.*

Do not use Form W-2c to report corrections to back pay. Instead, see Pub. 957, Reporting Back Pay and Special Wage Payments to the Social Security

Administration, and Form SSA-131, Employer Report of Special Wage Payments.

Do not use Form W-2c to correct Form W-2G, Certain Gambling Winnings. Instead, see the General Instructions for Certain Information Returns for the current reporting year.

Use Form W-3c to send Copy A of Form W-2c to the SSA. Always file Form W-3c when submitting one or more Forms W-2c.

E-filing Forms W-2c and W-3c. The SSA encourages all employers to *e-file* using its secure BSO website. E-filing can save you effort and helps ensure accuracy. See *E-filing.*

Where to file paper Forms W-2c and W-3c. If you use the U.S. Postal Service, send Forms W-2c and W-3c to:

Social Security Administration
Data Operations Center
P.O. Box 3333
Wilkes-Barre, PA 18767-3333

If you use a carrier other than the U.S. Postal Service, send Forms W-2c and W-3c to:

Social Security Administration
Data Operations Center
Attn: W-2c Process
1150 E. Mountain Drive
Wilkes-Barre, PA 18702-7997

See Pub. 15 (Circular E) for a list of IRS-designated private delivery services.

 Do not send Forms W-2, W-2AS, W-2CM, W-2GU, or W-2VI to either of these addresses. Instead, see Where to file paper Forms W-2 and W-3.

When to file. File Forms W-2c and W-3c as soon as possible after you discover an error. Also provide Form W-2c to employees as soon as possible.

How to complete. If you file Forms W-2c and W-3c on paper, make all entries using dark or black ink in 12-point Courier font, if possible, and make sure all copies are legible. See *How to complete Form W-2.*

If any item shows a change in the dollar amount and one of the amounts is zero, enter "-0-." Do not leave the box blank.

Who may sign Form W-3c. Generally, employers must sign Form W-3c. See *Who may sign Form W-3.*

Special Situations for Forms W-2c and W-3c

Undeliverable Forms W-2c. See *Undeliverable Forms W-2.*

Correcting Forms W-2 and W-3

Corrections. Use the current version of Form W-2c to correct errors (such as incorrect name, SSN, or amount) on a previously filed Form W-2 or Form W-2c. File Copy A of Form W-2c with the SSA. To *e-file* your corrections, see *Correcting wage reports.*

If the SSA issues your employee a replacement card after a name change, or a new card with a different social security number after a change in alien work status, file a Form W-2c to correct the name/SSN reported on the most recently filed Form W-2. It is not necessary to correct the prior years if the previous name and number were used for the years prior to the most recently filed Form W-2.

File Form W-3c whenever you file a Form W-2c with the SSA, even if you are only filing a Form W-2c to correct an employee's name or SSN. However, see *Employee's incorrect address on Form W-2*, later, for information on correcting an employee's address. See *Correcting an incorrect tax year and/or EIN incorrectly reported on Form W-2 or Form W-3*, later, if an error was made on a previously filed Form W-3.

If you discover an error on Form W-2 after you issue it to your employee but before you send it to the SSA, check the "Void" box at the top of the incorrect Form W-2 on Copy A. Prepare a new Form W-2 with the correct information, and send Copy A to the SSA. Write "CORRECTED" on the employee's new copies (B, C, and 2), and furnish them to the employee. If the "Void" Form W-2 is on a page with a correct Form W-2, send the entire page to the SSA. The "Void" form will not be processed. Do not write "CORRECTED" on Copy A of Form W-2.

If you are making a correction for previously filed Forms 941, 941-SS, 943, 944, or CT-1, use the corresponding "X" forms, such as Forms 941-X, 943-X, 944-X, or CT-1X for the return period in which you found the error. See section 13 of Pub. 15 (Circular E) and the Instructions for Form CT-1X for more details. If you are making corrections to a previously filed Schedule H (Form 1040), see Pub. 926. Issue the employee a Form W-2c if the error discovered was for the prior year.

Correcting an employee's name and/or SSN only. If you are correcting only an employee's name and/or SSN, complete Form W-2c boxes d through i. Do not complete boxes 1 through 20. Advise your employee to correct the SSN and/or name on his or her original Form W-2.

If your employee is given a new social security card following an adjustment to his or her resident status that shows a different name or SSN, file a Form W-2c for the most current year only.

Correcting an employee's name and SSN if the SSN was reported as blanks or zeros and the employee name was reported as blanks. If you need to correct an employee's name and SSN, and the SSN was reported as blanks or zeros and the employee's name was reported as blanks, do not use Form W-2c to report the corrections. You must contact the SSA at 1-800-772-6270 for instructions.

Correcting an incorrect tax year and/or EIN incorrectly reported on Form W-2 or Form W-3. To correct an incorrect tax year and/or EIN on a previously submitted Form W-2 or Form W-3, you must prepare two sets of Forms W-2c and W-3c.
• Prepare one Form W-3c along with a Form W-2c for each affected employee. On the Form W-3c, enter the incorrect tax year in box a, and the incorrect EIN originally

reported in box h. Enter in the "Previously reported" boxes the money amounts that were on the original Form W-2. In the "Correct information" boxes, enter zeros.
• Prepare a second Form W-3c along with a second Form W-2c for each affected employee. On the Form W-3c, enter the correct tax year in box a and/or the correct EIN in box e. Enter zeros in the "Previously reported" boxes, and enter the correct money amounts in the "Correct information" boxes.

Correcting more than one Form W-2 for an employee. There are two ways to prepare a correction for an employee for whom more than one Form W-2 was filed under the same EIN for the tax year. You can (1) consider all the Forms W-2 when determining the amounts to enter on Form W-2c or (2) file a single Form W-2c to correct only the incorrect Form W-2.

However, state, local, and federal government employers who are preparing corrections for Medicare Qualified Government Employment (MQGE) employees also must follow the instructions in the *Caution* for state, local, and federal government employers in the *Specific Instructions for Form W-2c.*

Correcting more than one kind of form. You must use a separate Form W-3c for each type of Form W-2 (Forms W-2, W-2AS, W-2CM, W-2GU, W-2VI, or W-2c) being corrected. You also must use a separate Form W-3c for each kind of payer/employer combination in box c. If you are correcting more than one kind of form, please group forms of the same kind of payer/employer combination, and send them in separate groups.

Employee's incorrect address on Form W-2. If you filed a Form W-2 with the SSA that reported an incorrect address for the employee, but all other information on the Form W-2 was correct, do not file Form W-2c with the SSA merely to correct the address.

However, if the address was incorrect on the Form W-2 furnished to the employee, you must do one of the following.
• Issue a new, corrected Form W-2 to the employee that includes the new address. Indicate "REISSUED STATEMENT" on the new copies. Do not send Copy A of Form W-2 to the SSA.
• Issue a Form W-2c to the employee that shows the correct address in box i and all other correct information. Do not send Copy A of Form W-2c to the SSA.
• Reissue the Form W-2 with the incorrect address to the employee in an envelope showing the correct address or otherwise deliver it to the employee.

Two Forms W-2 were filed under the same EIN, but only one should have been filed.

Example. Two Forms W-2 were submitted for Mary Smith under the same EIN for the same tax year. One Form W-2 correctly reported social security wages of $20,000. The other Form W-2 incorrectly reported social security wages of $30,000. There are two ways to correct this situation.
• File a Form W-3c along with one Form W-2c, entering $50,000 in box 3 under "Previously reported" and $20,000 in box 3 under "Correct information," or

- File a Form W-3c along with one Form W-2c, entering $30,000 in box 3 under "Previously reported" and $0.00 in box 3 under "Correct information."

Two Forms W-2 were filed under the same EIN, but wages on one were incorrect.

Example. Two Forms W-2 were submitted for Mary Smith under the same EIN for the same tax year. One Form W-2 correctly reported social security wages of $20,000. The other Form W-2 incorrectly reported social security wages of $30,000, whereas $25,000 should have been reported. There are two ways to correct this situation.

- File a Form W-3c along with one Form W-2c, entering $50,000 in box 3 under "Previously reported" and $45,000 in box 3 under "Correct information," or
- File a Form W-3c along with one Form W-2c, entering $30,000 in box 3 under "Previously reported" and $25,000 in box 3 under "Correct information."

Specific Instructions for Form W-2c

Box a—Employer's name, address, and ZIP code. This entry should be the same as shown on your Forms 941, 941-SS, 943, 944, CT-1, or Schedule H (Form 1040).

Box b—Employer's Federal EIN. Show the correct nine digit EIN assigned to you by the IRS in the format 00-0000000.

Box c—Tax year/Form corrected. If you are correcting Form W-2, enter all four digits of the year of the form you are correcting. If you are correcting Form W-2AS, W-2CM, W-2GU, W-2VI, or W-2c, enter all four digits of the year you are correcting, and also enter "AS," "CM," "GU," "VI," or "c" to designate the form you are correcting. For example, "2014" and "GU" shows that you are correcting a 2014 Form W-2GU.

Box d—Employee's correct SSN. You must enter the employee's correct SSN even if it was correct on the original Form W-2. If you are correcting an employee's SSN, you also must complete boxes e through i.

Box e—Corrected SSN and/or name. Check this box only if you are correcting the employee's SSN, name, or both SSN and name. You also must complete boxes d and f through i.

Box f—Employee's previously reported SSN. Complete this box if you are correcting an employee's previously reported incorrect SSN and/or name. If the previous SSN was reported as blanks or not available, then box f should be all zeroes.

Box g—Employee's previously reported name. Complete this box if you are correcting an employee's previously reported incorrect SSN and/or name. You must enter the employee's previously reported full name in box g exactly as it was previously reported. If the previous reported name was reported as blanks or not available, then box g should be all blanks.

 *For boxes f and g, if both the previous SSN and the previous name were reported as blanks, **do not** use Form W-2c. Contact the SSA at 1-800-772-6270.*

Box h—Employee's first name and initial, Last name, Suff. Always enter the employee's correct name. See *Boxes e and f—Employee's name and address* for name formatting information.

Box i—Employee's address and ZIP code. Always enter the employee's correct address. See *Boxes e and f—Employee's name and address* for address formatting information.

 You must enter the employee's full name in boxes g and h.

Boxes 1 through 20. For the items you are changing, enter under "Previously reported" the amount reported on the original Form W-2 or on a prior Form W-2c. Enter under "Correct information" the correct amount.

Do not make an entry in any of these boxes on Copy A unless you are making a change. However, see the *CAUTION* for state, local, or federal government employers below.

Box 2—Federal income tax withheld. Use this box only to make corrections because of an administrative error. (An administrative error occurs only if the amount you entered in box 2 of the incorrect Form W-2 was not the amount you actually withheld.) If you are correcting Forms W-2AS, W-2CM, W-2GU, or W-2VI, box 2 is for income tax withheld for the applicable U.S. possession.

Boxes 5 and 6. Complete these boxes to correct Medicare wages and tips and Medicare tax withheld. (Exception – do not correct Additional Medicare Tax withheld unless you need to correct an administrative error. An administrative error occurs only if the amount you entered in box 6 of the incorrect Form W-2 is not the amount you actually withheld.) State, local, or federal government employers also should use these boxes to correct MQGE wages. Box 5 must equal or exceed the sum of boxes 3 and 7.

 A state, local, or federal government employer correcting only social security wages and/or social security tips (boxes 3 and/or 7) for an MQGE employee also must complete Medicare wages and tips in box 5. Enter the total Medicare wages and tips, including MQGE-only wages, even if there is no change to the total Medicare wages and tips previously reported.

Boxes 8, 10, and 11. Use these boxes to correct allocated tips, dependent care benefits, or deferrals and distributions relating to nonqualified plans.

Box 12—Codes. Complete these boxes to correct any of the coded items shown on Forms W-2. Examples include uncollected social security and/or Medicare taxes on tips, taxable cost of group-term life insurance coverage over $50,000, elective deferrals (codes D through H, S, Y, AA, BB, and EE), sick pay not includible as income, and employee business expenses. See *Box 12—Codes* in *Specific Instructions for Form W-2* for the proper format to use in reporting coded items from box 12 of Forms W-2.

Employers should enter both the code and dollar amount for both fields on Form W-2c.

If a single Form W-2c does not provide enough blank spaces for corrections, use additional Forms W-2c.

Box 13. Check the boxes in box 13, under "Previously reported," as they were checked on the original Form W-2. Under "Correct information," check them as they should have been checked. For example, if you checked the "Retirement plan" box on the original Form W-2 by mistake, check the "Retirement plan" checkbox in box 13 under "Previously reported," but do not check the "Retirement plan" checkbox in box 13 under "Correct information."

Box 14. Use this box to correct items reported in box 14 of the original Form W-2 or on a prior Form W-2c. If possible, complete box 14 on Copies B, C, 1, and 2 of Form W-2c only, not on Copy A.

Boxes 15 through 20—State/local taxes. If your only changes to the original Form W-2 are to state or local data, do not send Copy A of Form W-2c to the SSA. Instead, send Form W-2c to the appropriate state or local agency and furnish copies to your employees.

Correcting state information. Contact your state or locality for specific reporting information.

Specific Instructions for Form W-3c

Do not staple or tape the Forms W-2c to Form W-3c or to each other. File a separate Form W-3c for each tax year, for each type of form, and for each kind of payer/employer combination. (The "Third-party sick pay" indicator box does not designate a separate kind of payer or employer.) Make a copy of Form W-3c for your records.

In the money boxes of Form W-3c, total the amounts from each box and column on the Forms W-2c you are sending.

Box a—Tax year/Form corrected. Enter all four digits of the year of the form you are correcting and the type of form you are correcting. For the type of form, enter "2," "2AS," "2CM," "2GU," "2VI," "2c," "3," "3SS," or "3c." For example, entering "2014" and "2" indicates that all the forms being corrected are 2014 Forms W-2.

Box b—Employer's name, address, and ZIP code. This should be the same as shown on your Forms 941, 941-SS, 943, 944, CT-1, or Schedule H (Form 1040). Include the suite, room, or other unit number after the street address. If the post office does not deliver mail to the street address and you use a P.O. box, show the P.O. box number instead of the street address.

 The IRS will not use Form W-3c to update your address of record. If you wish to change your address, file Form 8822 or Form 8822-B.

Box c—Kind of Payer. Check the box that applies to you. Check only one box. If your previous Form W-3 or Form W-3SS was checked incorrectly, report your prior incorrect payer type in the "Explain decreases here" area below boxes 18 and 19.

941/941-SS. Check this box if you file Form 941 or Form 941-SS. If you are a railroad employer sending Forms W-2c for employees covered under the Railroad Retirement Tax Act (RRTA), check the "CT-1" checkbox.

Military. Check this box if you are a military employer correcting Forms W-2 for members of the uniformed services.

943. Check this box if you file Form 943 and you are correcting Forms W-2 for agricultural employees. For nonagricultural employees, send Forms W-2c with a separate Form W-3c, generally with the 941/941-SS box checked.

944. Check this box if you file Form 944.

CT-1. Check this box if you are a railroad employer correcting Forms W-2 for employees covered under the Railroad Retirement Tax Act (RRTA). If you also have to correct forms of employees who are subject to social security and Medicare taxes, complete a separate Form W-3c with the "941/941-SS" box or "944" box checked instead.

Hshld. emp. Check this box if you are a household employer correcting Forms W-2 for household employees and you file Schedule H (Form 1040). If you also have to correct forms of employees who are not household employees, complete a separate Form W-3c.

Medicare govt. emp. Check this box if you are a U.S., state, or local agency filing corrections for employees subject only to Medicare taxes.

Box c—Kind of Employer. Check the box that applies to you. Check only one box. If your previous Form W-3 or W-3SS was checked incorrectly, report your prior incorrect employer type in the "Explain decreases here" area below boxes 18 and 19.

None apply. Check this box if none of the checkboxes described next apply to you.

501c non-govt. Check this box if you are a non-governmental tax-exempt 501(c) organization. Types of 501(c) non-governmental organizations include private foundations, public charities, social and recreation clubs, and veterans organizations. For additional examples of 501(c) non-governmental organizations, see chapters 3 and 4 of Pub. 557, Tax-Exempt Status for Your Organization.

State/local non 501c. Check this box if you are a state or local government or instrumentality. This includes cities, townships, counties, special-purpose districts, public schools districts, or other publicly-owned entities with governmental authority.

State/local 501c. Check this box if you are a state or local government or instrumentality, and you have received a determination letter from the IRS indicating that you are also a tax-exempt organization under section 501(c)(3).

Federal govt. Check this box if you are a Federal government entity or instrumentality.

Box c—Third-party sick pay. Check this box if you are a third-party sick pay payer (or are reporting sick pay payments made by a third party) correcting Forms W-2 with the "Third-party sick pay" checkbox in box 13 of Form W-2c under "Correct information" checked. File a separate Form W-3c for each payer/employer combination reporting "Third-party sick pay" on Form W-2c.

Box d—Number of Forms W-2c. Show the number of individual Forms W-2c filed with this Form W-3c or enter

"-0-" if you are correcting only a previously filed Form W-3 or Form W-3SS.

Box e—Employer's Federal EIN. Enter the correct number assigned to you by the IRS in the following format: 00-0000000. If you are correcting your EIN, enter the originally reported Federal EIN you used in box h.

Box f—Establishment number. You may use this box to identify separate establishments in your business. You may file a separate Form W-3c, with Forms W-2c, for each establishment or you may use a single Form W-3c for all Forms W-2c. You do not have to complete this item; it is optional.

Box g—Employer's state ID number. You are not required to complete this box. This number is assigned by the individual state where your business is located. However, you may want to complete this item if you use copies of this form for your state returns.

Box h—Employer's originally reported Federal EIN. Your correct number must appear in box e. Make an entry here only if the number on the original form was incorrect.

Box i—Incorrect establishment number. You may use this box to correct an establishment number.

Box j—Employer's incorrect state ID number. Use this box to make any corrections to your previously reported state ID number.

Boxes 1 through 8, 10, and 11. Enter the total of amounts reported in boxes 1 through 8, 10, and 11 as "Previously reported" and "Correct information" from Forms W-2c.

Box 12a—Deferred compensation. Enter the total of amounts reported with codes D through H, S, Y, AA, BB, and EE as "Previously reported" and "Correct information" from Forms W-2c.

 The total of Form W-2c box 12 amounts reported with Codes A through C, J through R, T through W, Z, and DD is not reported on Form W-3c.

Box 14—Inc. tax w/h by third-party sick pay payer. Enter the amount previously reported and the corrected amount of income tax withheld on third-party payments of sick pay. Although this tax is included in the box 2 amounts, it must be shown separately here.

Boxes 16 through 19. If your only changes to the Forms W-2c and W-3c are to the state and local data, do not send either Copy A of Form W-2c or Form W-3c to the SSA. Instead, send the forms to the appropriate state or local agency and furnish copies of Form W-2c to your employees.

Explain decreases here. Explain any decrease to amounts "Previously reported." Also report here any previous incorrect entry in box c, "Kind of Payer" or "Kind of Employer." Enclose (but do not attach) additional sheets explaining your decreases, if necessary. Include your name and EIN on any additional sheets.

Signature. Sign and date the form. Also enter your title and employer's contact person, employer's telephone number, employer's fax number, and employer's email address, if available. If you are not the employer, see *Who may sign Form W-3*.

Privacy Act and Paperwork Reduction Act Notice. We ask for the information on Forms W-2 and W-3 to carry out the Internal Revenue laws of the United States. We need it to figure and collect the right amount of tax. Section 6051 and its regulations require you to furnish wage and tax statements to employees, the Social Security Administration, and the Internal Revenue Service. Section 6109 requires you to provide your employer identification number (EIN). Failure to provide this information in a timely manner or providing false or fraudulent information may subject you to penalties.

You are not required to provide the information requested on a form that is subject to the Paperwork Reduction Act unless the form displays a valid OMB control number. Books or records relating to a form or its instructions must be retained as long as their contents may become material in the administration of any Internal Revenue law.

Generally, tax returns and return information are confidential, as required by section 6103. However, section 6103 allows or requires the Internal Revenue Service to disclose or give the information shown on your return to others as described in the Code. For example, we may disclose your tax information to the Department of Justice for civil and/or criminal litigation, and to cities, states, the District of Columbia, and U.S. commonwealths and possessions for use in administering their tax laws. We may also disclose this information to other countries under a tax treaty, to federal and state agencies to enforce federal nontax criminal laws, or to federal law enforcement and intelligence agencies to combat terrorism.

The time needed to complete and file these forms will vary depending on individual circumstances. The estimated average times are: Form W-2—30 minutes; Form W-3—28 minutes; Form W-2c—40 minutes; Form W-3c—51 minutes. If you have comments concerning the accuracy of these time estimates or suggestions for making these forms simpler, we would be happy to hear from you. You can write to the Internal Revenue Service, Tax Forms and Publications Division, 1111 Constitution Ave. NW, IR-6526, Washington, DC 20224. Do not send Forms W-2 and W-3 to this address. Instead, see *Where to file paper Forms W-2 and W-3*.

Form W-2 Reference Guide for Box 12 Codes

A	Uncollected social security or RRTA tax on tips	K	20% excise tax on excess golden parachute payments	V	Income from exercise of nonstatutory stock option(s)
B	Uncollected Medicare tax on tips (but not Additional Medicare Tax)	L	Substantiated employee business expense reimbursements	W	Employer contributions (including employee contributions through a cafeteria plan) to an employee's health savings account (HSA)
C	Taxable cost of group-term life insurance over $50,000	M	Uncollected social security or RRTA tax on taxable cost of group-term life insurance over $50,000 (former employees only)	Y	Deferrals under a section 409A nonqualified deferred compensation plan
D	Elective deferrals under a section 401(k) cash or deferred arrangement plan (including a SIMPLE 401(k) arrangement)	N	Uncollected Medicare tax on taxable cost of group-term life insurance over $50,000 (but not Additional Medicare Tax)(former employees only)	Z	Income under a nonqualified deferred compensation plan that fails to satisfy section 409A
E	Elective deferrals under a section 403(b) salary reduction agreement	P	Excludable moving expense reimbursements paid directly to employee	AA	Designated Roth contributions under a section 401(k) plan
F	Elective deferrals under a section 408(k)(6) salary reduction SEP	Q	Nontaxable combat pay	BB	Designated Roth contributions under a section 403(b) plan
G	Elective deferrals and employer contributions (including nonelective deferrals) to a section 457(b) deferred compensation plan	R	Employer contributions to an Archer MSA	DD	Cost of employer-sponsored health coverage
H	Elective deferrals to a section 501(c)(18)(D) tax-exempt organization plan	S	Employee salary reduction contributions under a section 408(p) SIMPLE plan	EE	Designated Roth contributions under a governmental section 457(b) plan
J	Nontaxable sick pay	T	Adoption benefits		

See *Box 12—Codes.*

Form W-2 Box 13 Retirement Plan Checkbox Decision Chart

Type of Plan	Conditions	Check Retirement Plan Box?
Defined benefit plan (for example, a traditional pension plan)	Employee qualifies for employer funding into the plan, due to age/years of service – even though the employee may not be vested or ever collect benefits	Yes
Defined contribution plan (for example, a 401(k) or 403(b) plan, a Roth 401(k) or 403(b) account, but not a 457 plan)	Employee is eligible to contribute but does not elect to contribute any money in this tax year	No
Defined contribution plan (for example, a 401(k) or 403(b) plan; a Roth 401(k) or 403(b) account; but not a 457 plan)	Employee is eligible to contribute and elects to contribute money in this tax year	Yes
Defined contribution plan (for example, a 401(k) or 403(b) plan; a Roth 401(k) or 403(b) account; but not a 457 plan)	Employee is eligible to contribute but does not elect to contribute any money in this tax year, but the employer does contribute funds	Yes
Defined contribution plan (for example, a 401(k) or 403(b) plan; a Roth 401(k) or 403(b) account; but not a 457 plan)	Employee contributed in past years but not during the current tax year under report	No (even if the account value grows due to gains in the investments)
Profit sharing plan	Plan includes a grace period after the close of the plan year when profit sharing can be added to the participant's account	Yes

See *Box 13—Checkboxes.*

Nonqualified Deferred Compensation Reporting Example Chart

Example	How to report on Form W-2
Example 1—Deferral, immediately vested (no risk of forfeiture). Regular wages: $200 Defer, vested: $20 Employer match, vested: $10	Box 1 = $180 ($200 – $20) Boxes 3 and 5 = $210 ($200 + $10) Box 11 = $0
Example 2—Deferral, delayed vesting (risk of forfeiture) of employee and employer portions. Regular wages: $200 Defer, not vested: $20 Employer match, not vested: $10	Box 1 = $180 ($200 – $20) Boxes 3 and 5 = $180 ($200 – $20) Box 11 = $0
Example 3—Deferral, immediately vested. Prior year deferrals and employer matches are now vesting. Regular wages: $200 Defer, vested: $20 Vesting of prior-year deferrals and employer matches: $100 + $15 (earnings on $100)	Box 1 = $180 ($200 – $20) Boxes 3 and 5 = $315 ($200 + $100 + $15) Box 11 = $115 ($100 + $15)
Example 4—No deferrals, but there are distributions. No vesting of prior year deferrals. Regular wages: $100 Distribution: $50	Box 1 = $150 ($100 + $50) Boxes 3 and 5 = $100 Box 11 = $50
Special Rule for W-2 Box 11: Distributions and Deferrals in the Same Year – Form SSA-131	If, in the same year, there are NQDC distributions and deferrals that are reportable in boxes 3 and/or 5 (current or prior year deferrals), do not complete box 11. Instead, report on Form SSA-131 the total amount the employee earned during the year. Generally, the amount earned by the employee during the tax year for purposes of item 6 of Form SSA-131 is the amount reported in box 1 of Form W-2 plus current year deferrals that are vested (employee and employer portions) less distributions. Do not consider prior-year deferrals that are vesting in the current year. If there was a plan failure, the box 1 amount in this calculation should be as if there were no plan failure. Submit the SSA-131 to the nearest SSA office or give it to the employee.
Example 5—Deferral, immediately vested, and distributions. No vesting of prior year deferrals. Regular wages: $200 Defer, vested: $20 Employer match, vested: $10 Distribution: $50	Box 1 = $230 ($200 – $20 + $50) Boxes 3 and 5 = $210 ($200 + $10) Box 11 = $0 Form SSA-131 = $210 ($230 (box 1) – $50 (distribution) + $30 (vested employee and employer deferrals))
Example 6—Deferral, delayed vesting, and distributions. No vesting of prior year deferrals. Regular wages: $200 Defer, not vested: $20 Distribution: $50	Box 1 = $230 ($200 – $20 + $50) Boxes 3 and 5 = $180 ($200 – $20) Box 11 = $50
Example 7—Deferral, immediately vested, and distributions. Prior-year deferrals and employer matches are now vesting. Regular wages: $200 Defer, vested: $20 Distribution: $50 Vesting of prior-year deferrals and employer matches: $100 + $15 (earnings on the $100)	Box 1 = $230 ($200 – $20 + $50) Boxes 3 and 5 = $315 ($200 + $100 + $15) Box 11 = $0 Form SSA-131 = $200 ($230 (box 1) – $50 (distribution) + $20 (vested deferral))
Example 8—Deferral, delayed vesting, and distributions. Prior-year deferrals and employer matches are now vesting. Regular wages: $200 Defer, not vested: $20 Distribution: $50 Vesting of prior-year deferrals and employer matches: $100 + $15 (earnings on the $100)	Box 1 = $230 ($200 – $20 + $50) Boxes 3 and 5 = $295 ($200 – $20 + $100 + $15) Box 11 = $0 Form SSA-131 = $180 ($230 (box 1) – $50 (distribution))

See *Nonqualified deferred compensation plans.*

Nonqualified Deferred Compensation Reporting Example Chart—*(Continued)*

Example	How to report on Form W-2
Special Rule for Payment of Social Security, Medicare, and Unemployment Taxes If the amount cannot be reasonably ascertained (the employer is unable to calculate an amount for a year by December 31), the employer has two methods it can use. For example, immediately-vested employer contributions to NQDC made late in the year would have no effect on W-2 box 1, but they would affect FICA and FUTA taxes.	*Estimated Method* Under the estimated method, an employer may treat a reasonably estimated amount as wages paid on the last day of the calendar year (the "first year"). If the employer underestimates the amount deferred and, thereby, underdeposits social security, Medicare, or FUTA taxes, it can choose to treat the shortfall as wages either in the first year or the first quarter of the next year. The shortfall does not include income credited to the amount deferred after the first year. Conversely, if the amount deferred is overestimated, the employer can claim a refund or credit. If the employer chooses to treat the shortfall as wages in the first year, the employer must issue a Form W-2c. Also, the employer must correct the information on the Form 941 for the last quarter of the first year. In such a case, the shortfall will not be treated as a late deposit subject to penalty if it is deposited by the employer's first regular deposit date following the first quarter of the next year. *Lag Method* Under the lag method, an employer may calculate the end-of-the-year amount on any date in the first quarter of the next calendar year. The amount deferred will be treated as wages on that date, and the amount deferred that would otherwise have been taken into account on the last day of the first year must be increased by income earned on that amount through the date on which the amount is taken into account.
Section 409A NQDC Plan Failure Example 9—Deferral, immediately vested. No distributions. Plan failure. Plan balance on January 1, 2010: $325, vested. Regular wages: $100 Defer, vested: $50 Employer match, vested: $25 Plan failure in 2010.	Box 12, Code Z = $400 • Amount in the plan account on December 31, 2010, not subject to risk of forfeiture and not included in prior-year income: $400 ($325 + $50 + $25) • Current-year distributions: $0 • $400 ($0 + $400) Box 1 = $450 ($100 – $50 + $400) Boxes 3 and 5 = $125 ($100 + $25) Box 11 = $0 SSA-131 = not required
Section 409A NQDC Plan Failure Example 10—Deferral, some delayed vesting, and distributions. Plan failure. Plan balance on January 1, 2010: $250 vested; $75 not vested. Regular wages: $100 Defer, vested: $50 Employer match, not vested: $25 Distribution: $200 Plan failure in 2010. Vesting of prior-year deferrals and employer matches: $0	Box 12, Code Z = $300 • Amount in the plan account on December 31, 2010, not subject to risk of forfeiture and not included in prior-year income: $100 ($250 + $50 – $200) • Current-year distributions: $200 • $100 + $200 = $300 Box 1 = $350 ($100 – $50 + $300 (code Z amount, which already includes the distribution)) Boxes 3 and 5 = $100 Box 11 = $0 SSA-131 = $100 ($250 (what box 1 would have been without plan failure) – $200 (distributions) + $50 (vested deferral))

See *Nonqualified deferred compensation plans.*

Index

DO NOT CUT, FOLD, OR STAPLE THIS FORM

44444	For Official Use Only ▶ OMB No. 1545-0008		

a Employer's name, address, and ZIP code

c Tax year/Form corrected

/ **W-2**

d Employee's correct SSN

e Corrected SSN and/or name (Check this box and complete boxes f and/or g if incorrect on form previously filed.) ☐

Complete boxes f and/or g only if incorrect on form **previously filed** ▶

f Employee's **previously reported** SSN

b Employer's Federal EIN

g Employee's **previously reported** name

h Employee's first name and initial | Last name | Suff.

Note. Only complete money fields that are being corrected (exception: for corrections involving MQGE, see the General Instructions for Forms W-2 and W-3, under Specific Instructions for Form W-2c, boxes 5 and 6).

i Employee's address and ZIP code

Previously reported	Correct information	Previously reported	Correct information
1 Wages, tips, other compensation	**1** Wages, tips, other compensation	**2** Federal income tax withheld	**2** Federal income tax withheld
3 Social security wages	**3** Social security wages	**4** Social security tax withheld	**4** Social security tax withheld
5 Medicare wages and tips	**5** Medicare wages and tips	**6** Medicare tax withheld	**6** Medicare tax withheld
7 Social security tips	**7** Social security tips	**8** Allocated tips	**8** Allocated tips
9	**9**	**10** Dependent care benefits	**10** Dependent care benefits
11 Nonqualified plans	**11** Nonqualified plans	**12a** See instructions for box 12 Code	**12a** See instructions for box 12 Code
13 Statutory employee ☐ Retirement plan ☐ Third-party sick pay ☐	**13** Statutory employee ☐ Retirement plan ☐ Third-party sick pay ☐	**12b** Code	**12b** Code
14 Other (see instructions)	**14** Other (see instructions)	**12c** Code	**12c** Code
		12d Code	**12d** Code

State Correction Information

Previously reported	Correct information	Previously reported	Correct information
15 State	**15** State	**15** State	**15** State
Employer's state ID number	Employer's state ID number	Employer's state ID number	Employer's state ID number
16 State wages, tips, etc.	**16** State wages, tips, etc.	**16** State wages, tips, etc.	**16** State wages, tips, etc.
17 State income tax	**17** State income tax	**17** State income tax	**17** State income tax

Locality Correction Information

Previously reported	Correct information	Previously reported	Correct information
18 Local wages, tips, etc.	**18** Local wages, tips, etc.	**18** Local wages, tips, etc.	**18** Local wages, tips, etc.
19 Local income tax	**19** Local income tax	**19** Local income tax	**19** Local income tax
20 Locality name	**20** Locality name	**20** Locality name	**20** Locality name

For Privacy Act and Paperwork Reduction Act Notice, see separate instructions.

Copy A—For Social Security Administration

Form **W-2c** (Rev. 8-2014) **Corrected Wage and Tax Statement** Cat. No. 61437D

Department of the Treasury
Internal Revenue Service

DO NOT CUT, FOLD, OR STAPLE

55555	a Tax year/Form corrected ――――――――― / W- ―――――――――	For Official Use Only ▶ OMB No. 1545-0008

b Employer's name, address, and ZIP code	c **Kind of Payer** (Check one)		Kind of Employer (Check one)	Third-party sick pay

c Kind of Payer (Check one)

941/941-SS	Military	943	944
☐	☐	☐	☐

CT-1	Hshld. emp.	Medicare govt. emp.
☐	☐	☐

Kind of Employer (Check one)

None apply	501c non-govt.
☐	☐

State/local non-501c	State/local 501c	Federal govt.
☐	☐	☐

Third-party sick pay
☐ (Check if applicable)

d Number of Forms W-2c	e Employer's Federal EIN	f Establishment number	g Employer's state ID number

Complete boxes h, i, or j only if incorrect on last form filed.	h Employer's **originally reported** Federal EIN	i **Incorrect** establishment number	j Employer's **incorrect** state ID number

Total of amounts previously reported as shown on enclosed Forms W-2c.	**Total of corrected amounts as shown on enclosed Forms W-2c.**	**Total of amounts previously reported as shown on enclosed Forms W-2c.**	**Total of corrected amounts as shown on enclosed Forms W-2c.**
1 Wages, tips, other compensation	1 Wages, tips, other compensation	2 Federal income tax withheld	2 Federal income tax withheld
3 Social security wages	3 Social security wages	4 Social security tax withheld	4 Social security tax withheld
5 Medicare wages and tips	5 Medicare wages and tips	6 Medicare tax withheld	6 Medicare tax withheld
7 Social security tips	7 Social security tips	8 Allocated tips	8 Allocated tips
9	9	10 Dependent care benefits	10 Dependent care benefits
11 Nonqualified plans	11 Nonqualified plans	12a Deferred compensation	12a Deferred compensation
14 Inc. tax w/h by third-party sick pay payer	14 Inc. tax w/h by third-party sick pay payer	12b	12b
16 State wages, tips, etc.	16 State wages, tips, etc.	17 State income tax	17 State income tax
18 Local wages, tips, etc.	18 Local wages, tips, etc.	19 Local income tax	19 Local income tax

Explain decreases here:

Has an adjustment been made on an employment tax return filed with the Internal Revenue Service? ☐ Yes ☐ No

If "Yes," give date the return was filed ▶

Under penalties of perjury, I declare that I have examined this return, including accompanying documents, and, to the best of my knowledge and belief, it is true, correct, and complete.

Signature ▶   Title ▶   Date ▶

Employer's contact person	Employer's telephone number	For Official Use Only
Employer's fax number	Employer's email address	

Form **W-3c** (Rev. 11-2015)   **Transmittal of Corrected Wage and Tax Statements**   Department of the Treasury
Internal Revenue Service

Purpose of Form

Use this form to transmit Copy A of the most recent version of **Form(s) W-2c,** Corrected Wage and Tax Statement. Make a copy of Form W-3c and keep it with Copy D (For Employer) of Forms W-2c for your records. File Form W-3c even if only one Form W-2c is being filed or if those Forms W-2c are being filed only to correct an employee's name and social security number (SSN) or the employer identification number (EIN). See the General Instructions for Forms W-2 and W-3 for information on completing this form.

E-Filing

The SSA strongly suggests employers report Form W-3c and Forms W-2c Copy A electronically instead of on paper. The SSA provides two free e-filing options on its Business Services Online (BSO) website:

• **W-2c Online.** Use fill-in forms to create, save, print, and submit up to 25 Forms W-2c at a time to the SSA.

• **File Upload.** Upload wage files to the SSA you have created using payroll or tax software that formats the files according to the SSA's *Specifications for Filing Forms W-2c Electronically (EFW2C).*

For more information, go to *www.socialsecurity.gov/employer.* First time filers, select "Go To Register"; returning filers select "Go To Log In."

For Paperwork Reduction Act Notice, see separate instructions.

When To File

File this form and Copy A of Form(s) W-2c with the Social Security Administration as soon as possible after you discover an error on Forms W-2, W-2AS, W-2GU, W-2CM, W-2VI, or W-2c. Provide Copies B, C, and 2 of Form W-2c to your employees as soon as possible.

Where To File

If you use the U.S. Postal Service, send Forms W-2c and W-3c to the following address:

**Social Security Administration
Data Operations Center
P.O. Box 3333
Wilkes-Barre, PA 18767-3333**

If you use a carrier other than the U.S. Postal Service, send Forms W-2c and W-3c to the following address:

**Social Security Administration
Data Operations Center
Attn: W-2c Process
1150 E. Mountain Drive
Wilkes-Barre, PA 18702-7997**

Cat. No. 10164R

A-36

Form W-4 (2016)

Purpose. Complete Form W-4 so that your employer can withhold the correct federal income tax from your pay. Consider completing a new Form W-4 each year and when your personal or financial situation changes.

Exemption from withholding. If you are exempt, complete **only** lines 1, 2, 3, 4, and 7 and sign the form to validate it. Your exemption for 2016 expires February 15, 2017. See Pub. 505, Tax Withholding and Estimated Tax.

Note: If another person can claim you as a dependent on his or her tax return, you cannot claim exemption from withholding if your income exceeds $1,050 and includes more than $350 of unearned income (for example, interest and dividends).

Exceptions. An employee may be able to claim exemption from withholding even if the employee is a dependent, if the employee:

• Is age 65 or older,

• Is blind, or

• Will claim adjustments to income; tax credits; or itemized deductions, on his or her tax return.

The exceptions do not apply to supplemental wages greater than $1,000,000.

Basic instructions. If you are not exempt, complete the **Personal Allowances Worksheet** below. The worksheets on page 2 further adjust your withholding allowances based on itemized deductions, certain credits, adjustments to income, or two-earners/multiple jobs situations.

Complete all worksheets that apply. However, you may claim fewer (or zero) allowances. For regular wages, withholding must be based on allowances you claimed and may not be a flat amount or percentage of wages.

Head of household. Generally, you can claim head of household filing status on your tax return only if you are unmarried and pay more than 50% of the costs of keeping up a home for yourself and your dependent(s) or other qualifying individuals. See Pub. 501, Exemptions, Standard Deduction, and Filing Information, for information.

Tax credits. You can take projected tax credits into account in figuring your allowable number of withholding allowances. Credits for child or dependent care expenses and the child tax credit may be claimed using the **Personal Allowances Worksheet** below. See Pub. 505 for information on converting your other credits into withholding allowances.

Nonwage income. If you have a large amount of nonwage income, such as interest or dividends, consider making estimated tax payments using Form 1040-ES, Estimated Tax for Individuals. Otherwise, you may owe additional tax. If you have pension or annuity income, see Pub. 505 to find out if you should adjust your withholding on Form W-4 or W-4P.

Two earners or multiple jobs. If you have a working spouse or more than one job, figure the total number of allowances you are entitled to claim on all jobs using worksheets from only one Form W-4. Your withholding usually will be most accurate when all allowances are claimed on the Form W-4 for the highest paying job and zero allowances are claimed on the others. See Pub. 505 for details.

Nonresident alien. If you are a nonresident alien, see Notice 1392, Supplemental Form W-4 Instructions for Nonresident Aliens, before completing this form.

Check your withholding. After your Form W-4 takes effect, use Pub. 505 to see how the amount you are having withheld compares to your projected total tax for 2016. See Pub. 505, especially if your earnings exceed $130,000 (Single) or $180,000 (Married).

Future developments. Information about any future developments affecting Form W-4 (such as legislation enacted after we release it) will be posted at www.irs.gov/w4.

Personal Allowances Worksheet (Keep for your records.)

A	Enter "1" for **yourself** if no one else can claim you as a dependent	A _____
B	Enter "1" if: { • You are single and have only one job; or • You are married, have only one job, and your spouse does not work; or • Your wages from a second job or your spouse's wages (or the total of both) are $1,500 or less. } . . .	B _____
C	Enter "1" for your **spouse.** But, you may choose to enter "-0-" if you are married and have either a working spouse or more than one job. (Entering "-0-" may help you avoid having too little tax withheld.)	C _____
D	Enter number of **dependents** (other than your spouse or yourself) you will claim on your tax return	D _____
E	Enter "1" if you will file as **head of household** on your tax return (see conditions under **Head of household** above) . .	E _____
F	Enter "1" if you have at least $2,000 of **child or dependent care expenses** for which you plan to claim a credit . . .	F _____
	(**Note:** Do **not** include child support payments. See Pub. 503, Child and Dependent Care Expenses, for details.)	
G	**Child Tax Credit** (including additional child tax credit). See Pub. 972, Child Tax Credit, for more information.	
	• If your total income will be less than $70,000 ($100,000 if married), enter "2" for each eligible child; then **less** "1" if you have two to four eligible children or **less** "2" if you have five or more eligible children.	
	• If your total income will be between $70,000 and $84,000 ($100,000 and $119,000 if married), enter "1" for each eligible child . .	G _____
H	Add lines A through G and enter total here. (**Note:** This may be different from the number of exemptions you claim on your tax return.) ▶ H	_____

For accuracy, complete all worksheets that apply.	{	• If you plan to **itemize** or **claim adjustments to income** and want to reduce your withholding, see the **Deductions and Adjustments Worksheet** on page 2. • If you are **single and have more than one job** or are **married and you and your spouse both work** and the combined earnings from all jobs exceed $50,000 ($20,000 if married), see the **Two-Earners/Multiple Jobs Worksheet** on page 2 to avoid having too little tax withheld. • If **neither** of the above situations applies, **stop here** and enter the number from line H on line 5 of Form W-4 below.

--------------------------- **Separate here and give Form W-4 to your employer. Keep the top part for your records.** ---------------------------

Form W-4 — Employee's Withholding Allowance Certificate

Department of the Treasury
Internal Revenue Service

OMB No. 1545-0074

2016

▶ Whether you are entitled to claim a certain number of allowances or exemption from withholding is subject to review by the IRS. Your employer may be required to send a copy of this form to the IRS.

1 Your first name and middle initial	Last name	2 Your social security number
Home address (number and street or rural route)	3 ☐ Single ☐ Married ☐ Married, but withhold at higher Single rate. **Note:** If married, but legally separated, or spouse is a nonresident alien, check the "Single" box.	
City or town, state, and ZIP code	4 If your last name differs from that shown on your social security card, check here. You must call 1-800-772-1213 for a replacement card. ▶ ☐	

5	Total number of allowances you are claiming (from line **H** above **or** from the applicable worksheet on page 2)	5	
6	Additional amount, if any, you want withheld from each paycheck	6	$
7	I claim exemption from withholding for 2016, and I certify that I meet **both** of the following conditions for exemption.		
	• Last year I had a right to a refund of **all** federal income tax withheld because I had **no** tax liability, **and**		
	• This year I expect a refund of **all** federal income tax withheld because I expect to have **no** tax liability.		
	If you meet both conditions, write "Exempt" here . . . . ▶	7	

Under penalties of perjury, I declare that I have examined this certificate and, to the best of my knowledge and belief, it is true, correct, and complete.

Employee's signature
(This form is not valid unless you sign it.) ▶

Date ▶

8 Employer's name and address (Employer: Complete lines 8 and 10 only if sending to the IRS.)	9 Office code (optional)	10 Employer identification number (EIN)

For Privacy Act and Paperwork Reduction Act Notice, see page 2.

Cat. No. 10220Q

Form **W-4** (2016)

Deductions and Adjustments Worksheet

Note: Use this worksheet *only* if you plan to itemize deductions or claim certain credits or adjustments to income.

1	Enter an estimate of your 2016 itemized deductions. These include qualifying home mortgage interest, charitable contributions, state and local taxes, medical expenses in excess of 10% (7.5% if either you or your spouse was born before January 2, 1952) of your income, and miscellaneous deductions. For 2016, you may have to reduce your itemized deductions if your income is over $311,300 and you are married filing jointly or are a qualifying widow(er); $285,350 if you are head of household; $259,400 if you are single and not head of household or a qualifying widow(er); or $155,650 if you are married filing separately. See Pub. 505 for details . . .	**1**	$ _____
2	Enter: { $12,600 if married filing jointly or qualifying widow(er) ; $9,300 if head of household ; $6,300 if single or married filing separately }	**2**	$ _____
3	**Subtract** line 2 from line 1. If zero or less, enter "-0-"	**3**	$ _____
4	Enter an estimate of your 2016 adjustments to income and any additional standard deduction (see Pub. 505)	**4**	$ _____
5	**Add** lines 3 and 4 and enter the total. (Include any amount for credits from the *Converting Credits to Withholding Allowances for 2016 Form W-4* worksheet in Pub. 505.)	**5**	$ _____
6	Enter an estimate of your 2016 nonwage income (such as dividends or interest)	**6**	$ _____
7	**Subtract** line 6 from line 5. If zero or less, enter "-0-"	**7**	$ _____
8	**Divide** the amount on line 7 by $4,050 and enter the result here. Drop any fraction	**8**	_____
9	Enter the number from the **Personal Allowances Worksheet,** line H, page 1	**9**	_____
10	**Add** lines 8 and 9 and enter the total here. If you plan to use the **Two-Earners/Multiple Jobs Worksheet,** also enter this total on line 1 below. Otherwise, **stop here** and enter this total on Form W-4, line 5, page 1	**10**	_____

Two-Earners/Multiple Jobs Worksheet (See *Two earners or multiple jobs* on page 1.)

Note: Use this worksheet *only* if the instructions under line H on page 1 direct you here.

1	Enter the number from line H, page 1 (or from line 10 above if you used the **Deductions and Adjustments Worksheet**)	**1**	_____
2	Find the number in **Table 1** below that applies to the **LOWEST** paying job and enter it here. **However,** if you are married filing jointly and wages from the highest paying job are $65,000 or less, do not enter more than "3"	**2**	_____
3	If line 1 is **more than or equal to** line 2, subtract line 2 from line 1. Enter the result here (if zero, enter "-0-") and on Form W-4, line 5, page 1. **Do not** use the rest of this worksheet	**3**	_____

Note: If line 1 is **less than** line 2, enter "-0-" on Form W-4, line 5, page 1. Complete lines 4 through 9 below to figure the additional withholding amount necessary to avoid a year-end tax bill.

4	Enter the number from line 2 of this worksheet	**4**	_____	
5	Enter the number from line 1 of this worksheet	**5**	_____	
6	**Subtract** line 5 from line 4	**6**	_____	
7	Find the amount in **Table 2** below that applies to the **HIGHEST** paying job and enter it here	**7**	$ _____	
8	**Multiply** line 7 by line 6 and enter the result here. This is the additional annual withholding needed . .	**8**	$ _____	
9	Divide line 8 by the number of pay periods remaining in 2016. For example, divide by 25 if you are paid every two weeks and you complete this form on a date in January when there are 25 pay periods remaining in 2016. Enter the result here and on Form W-4, line 6, page 1. This is the additional amount to be withheld from each paycheck	**9**	$ _____	

Table 1

Married Filing Jointly		**All Others**	
If wages from **LOWEST** paying job are—	Enter on line 2 above	If wages from **LOWEST** paying job are—	Enter on line 2 above
$0 - $6,000	0	$0 - $9,000	0
6,001 - 14,000	1	9,001 - 17,000	1
14,001 - 25,000	2	17,001 - 26,000	2
25,001 - 27,000	3	26,001 - 34,000	3
27,001 - 35,000	4	34,001 - 44,000	4
35,001 - 44,000	5	44,001 - 75,000	5
44,001 - 55,000	6	75,001 - 85,000	6
55,001 - 65,000	7	85,001 - 110,000	7
65,001 - 75,000	8	110,001 - 125,000	8
75,001 - 80,000	9	125,001 - 140,000	9
80,001 - 100,000	10	140,001 and over	10
100,001 - 115,000	11		
115,001 - 130,000	12		
130,001 - 140,000	13		
140,001 - 150,000	14		
150,001 and over	15		

Table 2

Married Filing Jointly		**All Others**	
If wages from **HIGHEST** paying job are—	Enter on line 7 above	If wages from **HIGHEST** paying job are—	Enter on line 7 above
$0 - $75,000	$610	$0 - $38,000	$610
75,001 - 135,000	1,010	38,001 - 85,000	1,010
135,001 - 205,000	1,130	85,001 - 185,000	1,130
205,001 - 360,000	1,340	185,001 - 400,000	1,340
360,001 - 405,000	1,420	400,001 and over	1,600
405,001 and over	1,600		

Form **W-4P**

Department of the Treasury
Internal Revenue Service

**Withholding Certificate for
Pension or Annuity Payments**

OMB No. 1545-0074

2016

Purpose. Form W-4P is for U.S. citizens, resident aliens, or their estates who are recipients of pensions, annuities (including commercial annuities), and certain other deferred compensation. Use Form W-4P to tell payers the correct amount of federal income tax to withhold from your payment(s). You also may use Form W-4P to choose (a) not to have any federal income tax withheld from the payment (except for eligible rollover distributions or payments to U.S. citizens delivered outside the United States or its possessions) or (b) to have an additional amount of tax withheld.

Your options depend on whether the payment is periodic, nonperiodic, or an eligible rollover distribution, as explained on pages 3 and 4. Your previously filed Form W-4P will remain in effect if you do not file a Form W-4P for 2016.

What do I need to do? Complete lines **A** through **G** of the **Personal Allowances Worksheet**. Use the additional worksheets on page 2 to further adjust your withholding allowances for itemized deductions, adjustments to income, any additional standard deduction, certain credits, or multiple pensions/more-than-one-income situations. If you do not want any federal income tax withheld (see *Purpose*, earlier), you can skip the worksheets and go directly to the Form W-4P below.

Sign this form. Form W-4P is not valid unless you sign it.

Future developments. The IRS has created a page on IRS.gov for information about Form W-4P and its instructions, at *www.irs.gov/w4p*. Information about any future developments affecting Form W-4P (such as legislation enacted after we release it) will be posted on that page.

Personal Allowances Worksheet (Keep for your records.)

A   Enter "1" for **yourself** if no one else can claim you as a dependent . . . .   **A** _____

B   Enter "1" if:
{
• You are single and have only one pension; or
• You are married, have only one pension, and your spouse has no income subject to withholding; or
• Your income from a second pension or a job or your spouse's pension or wages (or the total of all) is $1,500 or less.
}   . . . .   **B** _____

C   Enter "1" for your **spouse**. But, you may choose to enter "-0-" if you are married and have either a spouse who has income subject to withholding or more than one source of income subject to withholding. (Entering "-0-" may help you avoid having too little tax withheld.) . . . .   **C** _____

D   Enter number of **dependents** (other than your spouse or yourself) you will claim on your tax return . . . . .   **D** _____

E   Enter "1" if you will file as **head of household** on your tax return . . . .   **E** _____

F   **Child Tax Credit** (including additional child tax credit). See Pub. 972, Child Tax Credit, for more information.

    • If your total income will be less than $70,000 ($100,000 if married), enter "2" for each eligible child; then **less** "1" if you have two to four eligible children or **less** "2" if you have five or more eligible children.

    • If your total income will be between $70,000 and $84,000 ($100,000 and $119,000 if married), enter "1" for each eligible child . . . .   **F** _____

G   Add lines A through F and enter total here. (**Note:** This may be different from the number of exemptions you claim on your tax return.) ▶   **G** _____

For accuracy, complete all worksheets that apply.
{
• If you plan to **itemize** or **claim adjustments to income** and want to reduce your withholding, see the **Deductions and Adjustments Worksheet** on page 2.
• If you are **single and have more than one source of income subject to withholding** or are **married and you and your spouse both have income subject to withholding** and your combined income from all sources exceeds $50,000 ($20,000 if married), see the **Multiple Pensions/More-Than-One-Income Worksheet** on page 2 to avoid having too little tax withheld.
• If **neither** of the above situations applies, **stop here** and enter the number from line G on line 2 of Form W-4P below.
}

- - - - - - - - - -   **Separate here and give Form W-4P to the payer of your pension or annuity. Keep the top part for your records.**   - - - - - - - - - -

Form **W-4P**

Department of the Treasury
Internal Revenue Service

**Withholding Certificate for
Pension or Annuity Payments**

▶ **For Privacy Act and Paperwork Reduction Act Notice, see page 4.**

OMB No. 1545-0074

2016

Your first name and middle initial	Last name	Your social security number

Home address (number and street or rural route)	Claim or identification number (if any) of your pension or annuity contract
City or town, state, and ZIP code	

Complete the following applicable lines.

1   Check here if you **do not want any** federal income tax withheld from your pension or annuity. (Do not complete line 2 or 3.) ▶   ☐

2   Total number of allowances and marital status you are claiming for withholding from each **periodic** pension or annuity payment. (You also may designate an additional dollar amount on line 3.) . . . . ▶   _____
    Marital status: ☐ Single   ☐ Married   ☐ Married, but withhold at higher Single rate.   *(Enter number of allowances.)*

3   Additional amount, if any, you want withheld from each pension or annuity payment. (**Note:** For periodic payments, you cannot enter an amount here without entering the number (including zero) of allowances on line 2.) . . . . . ▶ $ _____

Your signature ▶   Date ▶

Cat. No. 10225T   Form **W-4P** (2016)

Deductions and Adjustments Worksheet

Note: Use this worksheet *only* if you plan to itemize deductions or claim certain credits or adjustments to income.

1 Enter an estimate of your 2016 itemized deductions. These include qualifying home mortgage interest, charitable contributions, state and local taxes, medical expenses in excess of 10% (7.5% if either you or your spouse was born before January 2, 1952) of your income, and miscellaneous deductions. For 2016, you may have to reduce your itemized deductions if your income is over $311,300 and you are married filing jointly or are a qualifying widow(er); $285,350 if you are head of household; $259,400 if you are single and not head of household or a qualifying widow(er); or $155,650 if you are married filing separately. See Pub. 505 for details . . . . **1** $ _____

2 Enter:
$12,600 if married filing jointly or qualifying widow(er)
$9,300 if head of household
$6,300 if single or married filing separately
. . . . **2** $ _____

3 **Subtract** line 2 from line 1. If zero or less, enter "-0-" . . . . **3** $ _____

4 Enter an estimate of your 2016 adjustments to income and any additional standard deduction (see Pub. 505) . . . . **4** $ _____

5 **Add** lines 3 and 4 and enter the total. (Include any credit amounts from the *Converting Credits to Withholding Allowances for 2016 Form W-4* worksheet in Pub. 505.) . . . . **5** $ _____

6 Enter an estimate of your 2016 income not subject to withholding (such as dividends or interest) . . **6** $ _____

7 **Subtract** line 6 from line 5. If zero or less, enter "-0-" . . . . **7** $ _____

8 **Divide** the amount on line 7 by $4,050 and enter the result here. Drop any fraction . . . . . . **8** _____

9 Enter the number from the **Personal Allowances Worksheet, line G, page 1** . . . . **9** _____

10 **Add** lines 8 and 9 and enter the total here. If you use the **Multiple Pensions/More-Than-One-Income Worksheet,** also enter this total on line 1 below. Otherwise, **stop here** and enter this total on Form W-4P, line 2, page 1 . . . . **10** _____

Multiple Pensions/More-Than-One-Income Worksheet

Note: Complete *only* if the instructions under line G, page 1, direct you here. This applies if you (and your spouse if married filing jointly) have more than one source of income subject to withholding (such as more than one pension, or a pension and a job, or you have a pension and your spouse works).

1 Enter the number from line G, page 1 (or from line 10 above if you used the **Deductions and Adjustments Worksheet**) . . . . **1** _____

2 Find the number in **Table 1** below that applies to the **LOWEST** paying pension or job and enter it here. **However,** if you are married filing jointly and the amount from the highest paying pension or job is $65,000 or less, do not enter more than "3" . . . . **2** _____

3 If line 1 is **more than or equal to** line 2, subtract line 2 from line 1. Enter the result here (if zero, enter "-0-") and on Form W-4P, line 2, page 1. **Do not** use the rest of this worksheet . . . . **3** _____

Note: If line 1 is **less than** line 2, enter "-0-" on Form W-4P, line 2, page 1. Complete lines 4 through 9 below to figure the additional withholding amount necessary to avoid a year-end tax bill.

4 Enter the number from line 2 of this worksheet . . . . **4** _____

5 Enter the number from line 1 of this worksheet . . . . **5** _____

6 **Subtract** line 5 from line 4 . . . . **6** _____

7 Find the amount in **Table 2** below that applies to the **HIGHEST** paying pension or job and enter it here **7** $ _____

8 **Multiply** line 7 by line 6 and enter the result here. This is the additional annual withholding needed . . **8** $ _____

9 **Divide** line 8 by the number of pay periods remaining in 2016. For example, divide by 12 if you are paid every month and you complete this form in December 2015. Enter the result here and on Form W-4P, line 3, page 1. This is the additional amount to be withheld from each payment . . . . **9** $ _____

Table 1				Table 2			
Married Filing Jointly		**All Others**		**Married Filing Jointly**		**All Others**	
If wages from **LOWEST** paying job or pension are—	Enter on line 2 above	If wages from **LOWEST** paying job or pension are—	Enter on line 2 above	If wages from **HIGHEST** paying job or pension are—	Enter on line 7 above	If wages from **HIGHEST** paying job or pension are—	Enter on line 7 above
$0 - $6,000	0	$0 - $9,000	0	$0 - $75,000	$610	$0 - $38,000	$610
6,001 - 14,000	1	9,001 - 17,000	1	75,001 - 135,000	1,010	38,001 - 85,000	1,010
14,001 - 25,000	2	17,001 - 26,000	2	135,001 - 205,000	1,130	85,001 - 185,000	1,130
25,001 - 27,000	3	26,001 - 34,000	3	205,001 - 360,000	1,340	185,001 - 400,000	1,340
27,001 - 35,000	4	34,001 - 44,000	4	360,001 - 405,000	1,420	400,001 and over	1,600
35,001 - 44,000	5	44,001 - 75,000	5	405,001 and over	1,600		
44,001 - 55,000	6	75,001 - 85,000	6				
55,001 - 65,000	7	85,001 - 110,000	7				
65,001 - 75,000	8	110,001 - 125,000	8				
75,001 - 80,000	9	125,001 - 140,000	9				
80,001 - 100,000	10	140,001 and over	10				
100,001 - 115,000	11						
115,001 - 130,000	12						
130,001 - 140,000	13						
140,001 - 150,000	14						
150,001 and over	15						

Additional Instructions

Section references are to the Internal Revenue Code.

When should I complete the form? Complete Form W-4P and give it to the payer as soon as possible. Get Pub. 505, Tax Withholding and Estimated Tax, to see how the dollar amount you are having withheld compares to your projected total federal income tax for 2016. You also may use the IRS Withholding Calculator at *www.irs.gov/individuals* for help in determining how many withholding allowances to claim on your Form W-4P.

Multiple pensions/more-than-one-income. To figure the number of allowances that you may claim, combine allowances and income subject to withholding from all sources on one worksheet. You may file a Form W-4P with each pension payer, but do not claim the same allowances more than once. Your withholding usually will be most accurate when all allowances are claimed on the Form W-4P for the highest source of income subject to withholding and zero allowances are claimed on the others.

Other income. If you have a large amount of income from other sources not subject to withholding (such as interest, dividends, or capital gains), consider making estimated tax payments using Form 1040-ES, Estimated Tax for Individuals. Get Form 1040-ES and Pub. 505 at *www.irs.gov/formspubs*.

If you have income from wages, see Pub. 505 to find out if you should adjust your withholding on Form W-4 or Form W-4P.

Note: Social security and railroad retirement payments may be includible in income. See Form W-4V, Voluntary Withholding Request, for information on voluntary withholding from these payments.

Withholding From Pensions and Annuities

Generally, federal income tax withholding applies to the taxable part of payments made from pension, profit-sharing, stock bonus, annuity, and certain deferred compensation plans; from individual retirement arrangements (IRAs); and from commercial annuities. The method and rate of withholding depend on (a) the kind of payment you receive; (b) whether the payments are delivered outside the United States or its commonwealths and possessions; and (c) whether the recipient is a nonresident alien individual, a nonresident alien beneficiary, or a foreign estate. Qualified distributions from a Roth IRA are nontaxable and, therefore, not subject to withholding. See page 4 for special withholding rules that apply to payments outside the United States and payments to foreign persons.

Because your tax situation may change from year to year, you may want to refigure your withholding each year. You can change the amount to be withheld by using lines 2 and 3 of Form W-4P.

Choosing not to have income tax withheld. You (or in the event of death, your beneficiary or estate) can choose not to have federal income tax withheld from your payments by using line 1 of Form W-4P. For an estate, the election to have no income tax withheld may be made by the executor or personal representative of the decedent. Enter the estate's employer identification number (EIN) in the area reserved for "Your social security number" on Form W-4P.

You may not make this choice for eligible rollover distributions. See *Eligible rollover distribution—20% withholding* on page 4.

Caution: There are penalties for not paying enough federal income tax during the year, either through withholding or estimated tax payments. New retirees, especially, should see Pub. 505. It explains your estimated tax requirements and describes penalties in detail. You may be able to avoid quarterly estimated tax payments by having enough tax withheld from your pension or annuity using Form W-4P.

Periodic payments. Withholding from periodic payments of a pension or annuity is figured in the same manner as withholding from wages. Periodic payments are made in installments at regular intervals over a period of more than 1 year. They may be paid annually, quarterly, monthly, etc.

If you want federal income tax to be withheld, you must designate the number of withholding allowances on line 2 of Form W-4P and indicate your marital status by checking the appropriate box. Under current law, you cannot designate a specific dollar amount to be withheld. However, you can designate an additional amount to be withheld on line 3.

If you do not want any federal income tax withheld from your periodic payments, check the box on line 1 of Form W-4P and submit the form to your payer. However, see *Payments to Foreign Persons and Payments Outside the United States* on page 4.

Caution: If you do not submit Form W-4P to your payer, the payer must withhold on periodic payments as if you are married claiming three withholding allowances. Generally, this means that tax will be withheld if your pension or annuity is at least $1,720 a month.

If you submit a Form W-4P that does not contain your correct social security number (SSN), the payer must withhold as if you are single claiming zero withholding allowances even if you checked the box on line 1 to have no federal income tax withheld.

There are some kinds of periodic payments for which you cannot use Form W-4P because they are already defined as wages subject to federal income tax withholding. These payments include retirement pay for service in the U.S. Armed Forces and payments from certain nonqualified deferred compensation plans and deferred compensation plans described in section 457 of tax-exempt organizations. Your payer should be able to tell you whether Form W-4P applies.

For periodic payments, your Form W-4P stays in effect until you change or revoke it. Your payer must notify you each year of your right to choose not to have federal income tax withheld (if permitted) or to change your choice.

Nonperiodic payments—10% withholding. Your payer must withhold at a flat 10% rate from nonperiodic payments (but see *Eligible rollover distribution—20% withholding* on page 4) **unless** you choose not to have federal income tax withheld. Distributions from an IRA that are payable on demand are treated as nonperiodic payments. You can choose not to have federal income tax withheld from a nonperiodic payment (if permitted) by submitting Form W-4P (containing your correct SSN) to your payer and checking the box on line 1. Generally, your choice not to have federal income tax withheld will apply to any later payment from the same plan. You cannot use line 2 for nonperiodic payments. But you may use line 3 to specify an additional amount that you want withheld.

Caution: If you submit a Form W-4P that does not contain your correct SSN, the payer cannot honor your request not to have income tax withheld and must withhold 10% of the payment for federal income tax.

Eligible rollover distribution—20% withholding. Distributions you receive from qualified pension or annuity plans (for example, 401(k) pension plans and section 457(b) plans maintained by a governmental employer) or tax-sheltered annuities that are eligible to be rolled over tax free to an IRA or qualified plan are subject to a flat 20% federal withholding rate. The 20% withholding rate is required, and you cannot choose not to have income tax withheld from eligible rollover distributions. Do not give Form W-4P to your payer unless you want an additional amount withheld. Then, complete line 3 of Form W-4P and submit the form to your payer.

Note: The payer will not withhold federal income tax if the entire distribution is transferred by the plan administrator in a direct rollover to a traditional IRA or another eligible retirement plan (if allowed by the plan), such as a qualified pension plan, governmental section 457(b) plan, section 403(b) contract, or tax-sheltered annuity.

Distributions that are (a) required by law, (b) one of a specified series of equal payments, or (c) qualifying "hardship" distributions are **not** "eligible rollover distributions" and are not subject to the mandatory 20% federal income tax withholding. See Pub. 505 for details. See also *Nonperiodic payments—10% withholding* on page 3.

Tax relief for victims of terrorist attacks. For tax years ending after September 10, 2001, disability payments for injuries incurred as a direct result of a terrorist attack directed against the United States (or its allies), whether outside or within the United States, are not included in income. You may check the box on line 1 of Form W-4P and submit the form to your payer to have no federal income tax withheld from these disability payments. However, you must include in your income any amounts that you received or you would have received in retirement had you not become disabled as a result of a terrorist attack. See Pub. 3920, Tax Relief for Victims of Terrorist Attacks, for more details.

Changing Your "No Withholding" Choice

Periodic payments. If you previously chose not to have federal income tax withheld and you now want withholding, complete another Form W-4P and submit it to your payer. If you want federal income tax withheld at the rate set by law (married with three allowances), write "Revoked" next to the checkbox on line 1 of the form. If you want tax withheld at any different rate, complete line 2 on the form.

Nonperiodic payments. If you previously chose not to have federal income tax withheld and you now want withholding, write "Revoked" next to the checkbox on line 1 and submit Form W-4P to your payer.

Payments to Foreign Persons and Payments Outside the United States

Unless you are a nonresident alien, withholding (in the manner described above) is required on any periodic or nonperiodic payments that are delivered to you outside the United States or its possessions. You cannot choose not to have federal income tax withheld on line 1 of Form W-4P. See Pub. 505 for details.

In the absence of a tax treaty exemption, nonresident aliens, nonresident alien beneficiaries, and foreign estates generally are subject to a 30% federal withholding tax under section 1441 on the taxable portion of a periodic or nonperiodic pension or annuity payment that is from U.S. sources. However, most tax treaties provide that private pensions and annuities are exempt from withholding and tax. Also, payments from certain pension plans are exempt from withholding even if no tax treaty applies. See Pub. 515, Withholding of Tax on Nonresident Aliens and Foreign Entities, and Pub. 519, U.S. Tax Guide for Aliens, for details. A foreign person should submit Form W-8BEN, Certificate of Foreign Status of Beneficial Owner for United States Tax Withholding, to the payer before receiving any payments. The Form W-8BEN must contain the foreign person's taxpayer identification number (TIN).

Statement of Federal Income Tax Withheld From Your Pension or Annuity

By January 31 of next year, your payer will furnish a statement to you on Form 1099-R, Distributions From Pensions, Annuities, Retirement or Profit-Sharing Plans, IRAs, Insurance Contracts, etc., showing the total amount of your pension or annuity payments and the total federal income tax withheld during the year. If you are a foreign person who has provided your payer with Form W-8BEN, your payer instead will furnish a statement to you on Form 1042-S, Foreign Person's U.S. Source Income Subject to Withholding, by March 15 of next year.

Privacy Act and Paperwork Reduction Act Notice

We ask for the information on this form to carry out the Internal Revenue laws of the United States. You are required to provide this information only if you want to (a) request federal income tax withholding from periodic pension or annuity payments based on your withholding allowances and marital status, (b) request additional federal income tax withholding from your pension or annuity, (c) choose not to have federal income tax withheld, when permitted, or (d) change or revoke a previous Form W-4P. To do any of the aforementioned, you are required by sections 3405(e) and 6109 and their regulations to provide the information requested on this form. Failure to provide this information may result in inaccurate withholding on your payment(s). Providing false or fraudulent information may subject you to penalties.

Routine uses of this information include giving it to the Department of Justice for civil and criminal litigation, and to cities, states, the District of Columbia, and U.S. commonwealths and possessions for use in administering their tax laws. We may also disclose this information to other countries under a tax treaty, to federal and state agencies to enforce federal nontax criminal laws, or to federal law enforcement and intelligence agencies to combat terrorism.

You are not required to provide the information requested on a form that is subject to the Paperwork Reduction Act unless the form displays a valid OMB control number. Books or records relating to a form or its instructions must be retained as long as their contents may become material in the administration of any Internal Revenue law. Generally, tax returns and return information are confidential, as required by section 6103.

The average time and expenses required to complete and file this form will vary depending on individual circumstances. For estimated averages, see the instructions for your income tax return.

If you have suggestions for making this form simpler, we would be happy to hear from you. See the instructions for your income tax return.

Request for Federal Income Tax Withholding From Sick Pay

▶ Give this form to the third-party payer of your sick pay.
▶ Information about Form W-4S is available at *www.irs.gov/w4s*.

OMB No. 1545-0074

2016

Type or print your first name and middle initial.	Last name	Your social security number

Home address (number and street or rural route)

City or town, state, and ZIP code

Claim or identification number (if any) . . . .

I request federal income tax withholding from my sick pay payments. I want the following amount to be withheld from each payment. (See **Worksheet** below.) . . . . $

Employee's signature ▶   Date ▶

--------------------------------- **Separate here and give the top part of this form to the payer. Keep the lower part for your records.** ---------------------------------

Worksheet (Keep for your records. Do not send to the Internal Revenue Service.)

1 Enter amount of adjusted gross income that you expect in 2016	**1**	
2 If you plan to itemize deductions on Schedule A (Form 1040), enter the estimated total of your deductions. For 2016, you may have to reduce your itemized deductions if your income is over $311,300 and you are married filing jointly or are a qualifying widow(er); $285,350 if you are head of household; $259,400 if you are single and not head of household or a qualifying widow(er); or $155,650 if you are married filing separately. See Pub. 505 for details. If you do not plan to itemize deductions, enter the standard deduction. (See the instructions on page 2 for the standard deduction amount, including additional amounts for age and blindness.)	**2**	
3 Subtract line 2 from line 1	**3**	
4 Exemptions. Multiply $4,050 by the number of personal exemptions	**4**	
5 Subtract line 4 from line 3	**5**	
6 Tax. Figure your tax on line 5 by using the 2016 Tax Rate Schedule X, Y, or Z on page 2. Do not use the Tax Table or Tax Rate Schedule X, Y, or Z in the 2015 Form 1040, 1040A, or 1040EZ instructions	**6**	
7 Credits (child tax and higher education credits, credit for child and dependent care expenses, etc.)	**7**	
8 Subtract line 7 from line 6	**8**	
9 Estimated federal income tax withheld or to be withheld from other sources (including amounts withheld due to a prior Form W-4S) during 2016 or paid or to be paid with 2016 estimated tax payments	**9**	
10 Subtract line 9 from line 8	**10**	
11 Enter the number of sick pay payments you expect to receive this year to which this Form W-4S will apply . .	**11**	
12 Divide line 10 by line 11. Round to the nearest dollar. This is the amount that should be withheld from each sick pay payment. Be sure it meets the requirements for the amount that should be withheld, as explained under *Amount to be withheld* below. If it does, enter this amount on Form W-4S above	**12**	

General Instructions

Purpose of form. Give this form to the third-party payer of your sick pay, such as an insurance company, if you want federal income tax withheld from the payments. You are not required to have federal income tax withheld from sick pay paid by a third party. However, if you choose to request such withholding, Internal Revenue Code sections 3402(o) and 6109 and their regulations require you to provide the information requested on this form. Do not use this form if your employer (or its agent) makes the payments because employers are already required to withhold federal income tax from sick pay.

Note: If you receive sick pay under a collective bargaining agreement, see your union representative or employer.

Definition. Sick pay is a payment that you receive:

• Under a plan to which your employer is a party and

• In place of wages for any period when you are temporarily absent from work because of your sickness or injury.

Amount to be withheld. Enter on this form the amount that you want withheld from each payment. The amount that you enter:

• Must be in whole dollars (for example, $35, not $34.50).

• Must be at least $4 per day, $20 per week, or $88 per month based on your payroll period.

• Must not reduce the net amount of each sick pay payment that you receive to less than $10.

For payments larger or smaller than a regular full payment of sick pay, the amount withheld will be in the same proportion as your regular withholding from sick pay. For example, if your regular full payment of $100 a week normally has $25 (25%) withheld, then $20 (25%) will be withheld from a partial payment of $80.

Caution: You may be subject to a penalty if your tax payments during the year are not at least 90% of the tax shown on your tax return. For exceptions and details, see Pub. 505, Tax Withholding and Estimated Tax. You may pay tax during the year through withholding or estimated tax payments or both. To avoid a penalty, make sure that you have enough tax withheld or make estimated tax payments using Form 1040-ES, Estimated Tax for Individuals. You may estimate your federal income tax liability by using the worksheet above.

Sign this form. Form W-4S is not valid unless you sign it.

Statement of income tax withheld. After the end of the year, you will receive a Form W-2, Wage and Tax Statement, reporting the taxable sick pay paid and federal income tax withheld during the year. These amounts are reported to the Internal Revenue Service.

(continued on back)

For Paperwork Reduction Act Notice, see page 2.   Cat. No. 10226E   Form **W-4S** (2016)

Changing your withholding. Form W-4S remains in effect until you change or revoke it. You may do this by giving a new Form W-4S or a written notice to the payer of your sick pay. To revoke your previous Form W-4S, complete a new Form W-4S and write "Revoked" in the money amount box, sign it, and give it to the payer.

Specific Instructions for Worksheet

You may use the worksheet on page 1 to estimate the amount of federal income tax that you want withheld from each sick pay payment. Use your tax return for last year and the worksheet as a basis for estimating your tax, tax credits, and withholding for this year.

You may not want to use Form W-4S if you already have your total tax covered by estimated tax payments or other withholding.

If you expect to file a joint return, be sure to include the income, deductions, credits, and payments of both yourself and your spouse in figuring the amount you want withheld.

Caution: If any of the amounts on the worksheet change after you give Form W-4S to the payer, you should use a new Form W-4S to request a change in the amount withheld.

Line 2—Deductions

Itemized deductions. For 2016, you may have to reduce your itemized deductions if your income is over $311,300 and you are married filing jointly or are a qualifying widow(er); $285,350 if you are head of household; $259,400 if you are single and not head of household or a qualifying widow(er); or $155,650 if you are married filing separately. See Pub. 505 for details.

Standard deduction. For 2016, the standard deduction amounts are:

Filing Status	Standard Deduction
Married filing jointly or qualifying widow(er)	$12,600*
Head of household	$9,300*
Single or Married filing separately	$6,300*

*If you are age 65 or older or blind, add to the standard deduction amount the additional amount that applies to you as shown in the next paragraph. If you can be claimed as a dependent on another person's return, see *Limited standard deduction for dependents,* later.

Additional amount for the elderly or blind. An additional standard deduction of $1,250 is allowed for a married individual (filing jointly or separately) or qualifying widow(er) who is 65 or older or blind, $2,500 if 65 or older **and** blind. If both spouses are 65 or older or blind, an additional $2,500 is allowed on a joint return ($2,500 on a separate return if you can claim an exemption for your spouse). If both spouses are 65 or older **and** blind, an additional $5,000 is allowed on a joint return ($5,000 on a separate return if you can claim an exemption for your spouse). An additional $1,550 is allowed for an unmarried individual (single or head of household) who is 65 or older or blind, $3,100 if 65 or older **and** blind.

Limited standard deduction for dependents. If you can be claimed as a dependent on another person's return, your standard deduction is the greater of (a) $1,050 or (b) your earned income plus $350 (up to the regular standard deduction for your filing status). If you are 65 or older or blind, see Pub. 505 for additional amounts that you may claim.

Certain individuals not eligible for standard deduction. For the following individuals, the standard deduction is zero.

• A married individual filing a separate return if either spouse itemizes deductions.

• A nonresident alien individual.

• An individual filing a return for a period of less than 12 months because of a change in his or her annual accounting period.

Line 7—Credits

Include on this line any tax credits that you are entitled to claim, such as the child tax and higher education credits, credit for child and dependent care expenses, earned income credit, or credit for the elderly or the disabled.

Line 9—Tax Withholding and Estimated Tax

Enter the federal income tax that you expect will be withheld this year on income other than sick pay and any payments made or to be made with 2016 estimated tax payments. Include any federal income tax already withheld or to be withheld from wages and pensions.

2016 Tax Rate Schedules

Schedule X—Single

If line 5 is: Over—	But not over—	The tax is:	of the amount over—
$0	$9,275	$0 + 10%	$0
9,275	37,650	927.50 + 15%	9,275
37,650	91,150	5,183.75 + 25%	37,650
91,150	190,150	18,558.75 + 28%	91,150
190,150	413,350	46,278.75 + 33%	190,150
413,350	415,050	119,934.75 + 35%	413,350
415,050	and greater	120,529.75 + 39.6%	415,050

Schedule Z—Head of household

If line 5 is: Over—	But not over—	The tax is:	of the amount over—
$0	$13,250	$0 + 10%	$0
13,250	50,400	1,325 + 15%	13,250
50,400	130,150	6,897.50 + 25%	50,400
130,150	210,800	26,835 + 28%	130,150
210,800	413,350	49,417 + 33%	210,800
413,350	441,000	116,258.50 + 35%	413,350
441,000	and greater	125,936 + 39.6%	441,000

Schedule Y-1—Married filing jointly or Qualifying widow(er)

If line 5 is: Over—	But not over—	The tax is:	of the amount over—
$0	$18,550	$0 + 10%	$0
18,550	75,300	1,855 + 15%	18,550
75,300	151,900	10,367.50 + 25%	75,300
151,900	231,450	29,517.50 + 28%	151,900
231,450	413,350	51,791.50 + 33%	231,450
413,350	466,950	111,818.50 + 35%	413,350
466,950	and greater	130,578.50 + 39.6%	466,950

Schedule Y-2—Married filing separately

If line 5 is: Over—	But not over—	The tax is:	of the amount over—
$0	$9,275	$0 + 10%	$0
9,275	37,650	927.50 + 15%	9,275
37,650	75,950	5,183.75 + 25%	37,650
75,950	115,725	14,758.75 + 28%	75,950
115,725	206,675	25,895.75 + 33%	115,725
206,675	233,475	55,909.25 + 35%	206,675
233,475	and greater	65,289.25 + 39.6%	233,475

Paperwork Reduction Act Notice. We ask for the information on this form to carry out the Internal Revenue laws of the United States.

You are not required to provide the information requested on a form that is subject to the Paperwork Reduction Act unless the form displays a valid OMB control number. Books or records relating to a form or its instructions must be retained as long as their contents may become material in the administration of any Internal Revenue law. Generally, tax returns and return information are confidential, as required by Code section 6103.

The average time and expenses required to complete and file this form will vary depending on individual circumstances. For estimated averages, see the instructions for your income tax return.

If you have suggestions for making this form simpler, we would be happy to hear from you. See the instructions for your income tax return.

Form **8508** (October 2015)	Department of the Treasury - Internal Revenue Service **Request for Waiver From Filing Information Returns Electronically** *(Forms W-2, W-2G, 1042-S, 1097-BTC, 1098 Series, 1099 Series, 3921, 3922, 5498 Series, and 8027, or ACA Forms 1095-B, 1095-C or an Authoritative Transmittal Form 1094-C (Refer to Instructions for Form 1094-C and 1095-C))* *(Please type or print in **black ink** when completing this form - Refer to instructions on the back.)*	OMB Number 1545-0957

Note: Only the person required to file electronically can sign Form 8508. A transmitter cannot sign Form 8508 for the payer, unless a power of attorney has been established. If you have a power of attorney, attach a copy to this form.

1. Type of submission   ☐ Original   ☐ Reconsideration

2. Payer name, **complete** address, and contact person. (A *separate* Form 8508 must be filed for *each payer* requesting a waiver.)

Payer name _____

Address _____

City _____ State ___ Zip code _____

Contact person _____

3. Taxpayer Identification Number *(9-digit EIN/SSN)*
_____

4. Telephone number
(___) ___ - _____

Email address _____

5. Waiver Requested for:

Waiver Requested for:	Enter the Number of Returns that:		Waiver Requested for:	Enter the Number of Returns that:	
	(a) You expect to file on paper	(b) You expect to file next tax year		(a) You expect to file on paper	(b) You expect to file next tax year
☐ 1042-S			☐ 1099-Q		
☐ 1094-C/1095-C			☐ 1099-R		
☐ 1095-B			☐ 1099-S		
☐ 1097-BTC			☐ 1099-SA		
☐ 1098			☐ 3921		
☐ 1098-C			☐ 3922		
☐ 1098-E			☐ 5498		
☐ 1098-T			☐ 5498-ESA		
☐ 1099-A			☐ 5498-SA		
☐ 1099-B			☐ 8027		
☐ 1099-C			☐ W-2		
☐ 1099-CAP			☐ W-2AS		
☐ 1099-DIV			☐ W-2G		
☐ 1099-G			☐ W-2GU		
☐ 1099-INT			☐ W-2PR		
☐ 1099-K			☐ W-2VI		
☐ 1099-LTC					
☐ 1099-MISC					
☐ 1099-OID					
☐ 1099-PATR					

6. Is this waiver requested for corrections ONLY?   ☐ Yes   ☐ No

7. Is this the first time you requested a waiver from the electronic filing requirements for any of the forms listed in Block 5?

☐ Yes *(Skip to signature line)*   ☐ No *(Complete Block 8 if your request is due to undue hardship)*

8. Enter **two current cost estimates** provided to you by third parties for software, software upgrades or programming for your current system, or costs to prepare your files for you.

Cost estimates for any reason other than the preparation of electronic files will not be acceptable.

Attach the two **current** cost estimates to Form 8508.

Note: Failure to provide current cost estimates and/or signature will result in a denial of your waiver request.

$ _____

$ _____

Under penalties of perjury, I declare that I have examined this document, including any accompanying statements, and, to the best of my knowledge and belief, it is true, correct, and complete.

9. Signature	Title	Date

Catalog Number 63499V   www.irs.gov   Form **8508** (Rev. 10-2015)

General Instructions

Purpose of Form. Use this form to request a waiver from filing Forms W-2, W-2AS, W-2G, W-2GU, W-2PR, W-2VI, 1042-S, 1097-BTC, 1098 Series, 1099 Series, 3921, 3922, 5498 Series, 8027, or Affordable Care Act (ACA) Forms 1095-B, 1095-C or an Authoritative Transmittal Form 1094-C (Refer to Instructions for Form 1094-C and 1095-C) electronically for the current tax year. Complete a Form 8508 for each Taxpayer Identification Number *(TIN)*. You may use one Form 8508 for multiple types of forms. After evaluating your request, an approval or denial letter will be issued.

Note: When completing this form, type or print clearly in **BLACK ink**.

Specific Instructions

Block 1. Indicate the type of submission by checking the appropriate box. An original submission is your first request for a waiver for the current year. A reconsideration indicates that you are submitting additional information to the IRS that you think may reverse a denial of an originally submitted request.

Block 2. Enter the name and complete address of the payer and person to contact if additional information is needed.

Block 3. Enter the nine-digit Taxpayer Identification Number *(TIN)* [Employer Identification Number *(EIN)* or the Social Security Number *(SSN)*] of the payer.

Block 4. Enter the telephone number and email address of the contact person.

Block 5. Check the box(es) beside the form(s) for which the waiver is being requested.

Block 5a. For each type of information return checked, enter the total number of forms you expect to file on paper.

Block 5b. Provide an estimate of the total number of information returns you expect to file for the following tax year.

Block 6. Indicate whether or not this waiver is requested for corrections only. If you request a waiver for original documents and it is approved, you will automatically receive a waiver for corrections. However, if you can submit your original returns electronically, but not your corrections, a waiver must be requested for corrections only.

Block 7. If this is the first time you have requested a waiver for any of the forms listed in Block 5, for any tax year, check "YES" and skip to Block 9, *Signature*. However, if you have requested a waiver in the past and check "NO," complete Block 8 to establish undue hardship. Waivers, after the first year, are granted only in the case of undue hardship or catastrophic event.

Note: Under Regulations Section 301.6011-2(c)(2),"The principal factor in determining hardship will be the amount, if any, by which the cost of filing the information returns in accordance with this section exceeds the cost of filing the returns on other media."

Block 8. Enter the cost estimates from two service bureaus or other third parties. These cost estimates must reflect the total amount that each service bureau will charge for software, software upgrades or programming for your current system, or costs to prepare your electronic file only. If you do not provide two written cost estimates from service bureaus or other third parties, we will automatically deny your request. Cost estimates from prior years will not be accepted.

Note: If your request is not due to undue hardship, as defined above, attach a detailed explanation of why you need a waiver.

Block 9. The waiver request must be signed by the payer or a person duly authorized to sign a return or other document on his behalf. Only the person required to file electronically can sign Form 8508. A transmitter cannot sign Form 8508 for the payer, unless a power of attorney has been established. If you have a power of attorney, attach a copy to this form.

Filing Instructions

When to File. You should file Form 8508 at least 45 days before the due date of the returns for which you are requesting a waiver. Refer to *General Instructions for Certain Information Returns, Publication 1239, Specifications for Electronic Filing of Form 8027, Employer's Annual Information Return of Tip Income and Allocated Tips,* and ACA Forms 1095-B, 1095-C and 1094-C Form Instructions for the due dates. Waiver requests will be processed beginning January 1st of the calendar year for which the returns are due.

Where to File By Mail:

> Internal Revenue Service
> Attn: Extension of Time Coordinator
> 240 Murall Drive Mail Stop 4360
> Kearneysville, WV 25430

By Fax: 1-877-477-0572
    304-579-4105 (International)

Please either fax or mail, do not do both.
For additional information on filing of information returns electronically, contact the IRS at:

> 866-455-7438
> 304-263-8700 (International)

Penalty. If you are required to file electronically but fail to do so and you do not have an approved waiver on record, you may be subject to a penalty of $250 per return unless you establish reasonable cause.

Paperwork Reduction Act Notice. We ask for the information on these forms to carry out the Internal Revenue Laws of the United States. You are not required to provide the information requested on a form that is subject to the Paperwork Reduction Act unless the form displays a valid OMB control number. Books or records relating to a form must be retained as long as their contents may become material in the administration of any Internal Revenue law. Generally, tax returns and return information are confidential, as required by Code section 6103. The time needed to provide this information would vary depending on individual circumstances. The estimated average time is:

Preparing Form 8508 . . . . **15 min.**

If you have comments concerning the accuracy of these time estimates or suggestions for making this form simpler, we would be happy to hear from you. You can write to the Internal Revenue Service, Tax Products Coordinating Committee, SE:W:CAR:MP:T:T:SP, 1111 Constitution Ave. NW, IR-6406, Washington, DC 20224.

Form **940 for 2015:** **Employer's Annual Federal Unemployment (FUTA) Tax Return**

850113

Department of the Treasury — Internal Revenue Service

OMB No. 1545-0028

Employer identification number (EIN) ☐☐ — ☐☐☐☐☐☐☐

Name *(not your trade name)* _____

Trade name *(if any)* _____

Address _____

Number _____ Street _____ Suite or room number _____

City _____ State _____ ZIP code _____

Foreign country name _____ Foreign province/county _____ Foreign postal code _____

Type of Return
(Check all that apply.)

☐ **a.** Amended

☐ **b.** Successor employer

☐ **c.** No payments to employees in 2015

☐ **d.** Final: Business closed or stopped paying wages

Instructions and prior-year forms are available at *www.irs.gov/form940.*

Read the separate instructions before you complete this form. Please type or print within the boxes.

Part 1: Tell us about your return. If any line does NOT apply, leave it blank. See instructions before completing Part 1.

1a If you had to pay state unemployment tax in one state only, enter the state abbreviation . **1a** ☐☐

1b If you had to pay state unemployment tax in more than one state, you are a multi-state employer . . . . **1b** ☐ Check here. Complete Schedule A (Form 940).

2 If you paid wages in a state that is subject to **CREDIT REDUCTION** . . . . **2** ☐ Check here. Complete Schedule A (Form 940).

Part 2: Determine your FUTA tax before adjustments. If any line does NOT apply, leave it blank.

3 Total payments to all employees . . . . **3** _____ .

4 Payments exempt from FUTA tax . . . . . . **4** _____ .

Check all that apply: **4a** ☐ Fringe benefits **4c** ☐ Retirement/Pension **4e** ☐ Other
4b ☐ Group-term life insurance **4d** ☐ Dependent care

5 Total of payments made to each employee in excess of $7,000 . . . . . **5** _____ .

6 Subtotal (line 4 + line 5 = line 6) . . . . **6** _____ .

7 Total taxable FUTA wages (line 3 – line 6 = line 7) (see instructions) . . . . **7** _____ .

8 FUTA tax before adjustments (line 7 x .006 = line 8) . . . . **8** _____ .

Part 3: Determine your adjustments. If any line does NOT apply, leave it blank.

9 If ALL of the taxable FUTA wages you paid were excluded from state unemployment tax, multiply line 7 by .054 (line 7 × .054 = line 9). Go to line 12 . . . . **9** _____ .

10 If SOME of the taxable FUTA wages you paid were excluded from state unemployment tax, OR you paid ANY state unemployment tax late (after the due date for filing Form 940), complete the worksheet in the instructions. Enter the amount from line 7 of the worksheet . . **10** _____ .

11 If credit reduction applies, enter the total from Schedule A (Form 940) . . . . . . **11** _____ .

Part 4: Determine your FUTA tax and balance due or overpayment. If any line does NOT apply, leave it blank.

12 Total FUTA tax after adjustments (lines 8 + 9 + 10 + 11 = line 12) . . . . **12** _____ .

13 FUTA tax deposited for the year, including any overpayment applied from a prior year . **13** _____ .

14 Balance due (If line 12 is more than line 13, enter the excess on line 14.)
• If line 14 is more than $500, you must deposit your tax.
• If line 14 is $500 or less, you may pay with this return. (see instructions) . . . . . **14** _____ .

15 Overpayment (If line 13 is more than line 12, enter the excess on line 15 and check a box below.) . . . . **15** _____ .

▶ You **MUST** complete both pages of this form and **SIGN** it. Check one: ☐ Apply to next return. ☐ Send a refund.

Next ▶

For Privacy Act and Paperwork Reduction Act Notice, see the back of Form 940-V, Payment Voucher. Cat. No. 11234O Form **940** (2015)

Name *(not your trade name)*	Employer identification number (EIN)

Part 5: Report your FUTA tax liability by quarter only if line 12 is more than $500. If not, go to Part 6.

16 Report the amount of your FUTA tax liability for each quarter; do NOT enter the amount you deposited. If you had no liability for a quarter, leave the line blank.

16a **1st quarter** (January 1 – March 31) . . . . **16a** [.]

16b **2nd quarter** (April 1 – June 30) . . . . **16b** [.]

16c **3rd quarter** (July 1 – September 30) . . . . **16c** [.]

16d **4th quarter** (October 1 – December 31) . . . . . . **16d** [.]

17 **Total tax liability for the year** (lines 16a + 16b + 16c + 16d = line 17) **17** [.] **Total must equal line 12.**

Part 6: May we speak with your third-party designee?

Do you want to allow an employee, a paid tax preparer, or another person to discuss this return with the IRS? See the instructions for details.

☐ **Yes.** Designee's name and phone number [_____] [_____]

Select a 5-digit Personal Identification Number (PIN) to use when talking to IRS [ ][ ][ ][ ][ ]

☐ **No.**

Part 7: Sign here. You MUST complete both pages of this form and SIGN it.

Under penalties of perjury, I declare that I have examined this return, including accompanying schedules and statements, and to the best of my knowledge and belief, it is true, correct, and complete, and that no part of any payment made to a state unemployment fund claimed as a credit was, or is to be, deducted from the payments made to employees. Declaration of preparer (other than taxpayer) is based on all information of which preparer has any knowledge.

✗ **Sign your name here** [_____]

Print your name here [_____]

Print your title here [_____]

Date [__ / __ / __]

Best daytime phone [_____]

Paid Preparer Use Only   Check if you are self-employed . ☐

Preparer's name	[_____]	PTIN	[_____]
Preparer's signature	[_____]	Date	[__ / __]
Firm's name (or yours if self-employed)	[_____]	EIN	[_____]
Address	[_____]	Phone	[_____]
City	[_____] State [_____]	ZIP code	[_____]

Form 940-V,
Payment Voucher

Purpose of Form

Complete Form 940-V if you are making a payment with Form 940. We will use the completed voucher to credit your payment more promptly and accurately, and to improve our service to you.

Making Payments With Form 940

To avoid a penalty, make your payment with your 2015 Form 940 **only if** your FUTA tax for the fourth quarter (plus any undeposited amounts from earlier quarters) is $500 or less. If your total FUTA tax after adjustments (Form 940, line 12) is more than $500, you must make deposits by electronic funds transfer. See *When Must You Deposit Your FUTA Tax?* in the Instructions for Form 940. Also see sections 11 and 14 of Pub. 15 for more information about deposits.

 Use Form 940-V when making any payment with Form 940. However, if you pay an amount with Form 940 that should have been deposited, you may be subject to a penalty. See Deposit Penalties *in section 11 of Pub. 15.*

Specific Instructions

Box 1—Employer Identification Number (EIN). If you don't have an EIN, you may apply for one online. Go to IRS.gov and type "EIN" in the search box. You may also apply for an EIN by faxing or mailing Form SS-4 to the IRS. If you haven't received your EIN by the due date of Form 940, write "Applied For" and the date you applied in this entry space.

Box 2—Amount paid. Enter the amount paid with Form 940.

Box 3—Name and address. Enter your name and address as shown on Form 940.

• Enclose your check or money order made payable to "United States Treasury." Be sure to enter your EIN, "Form 940," and "2015" on your check or money order. Don't send cash. Don't staple Form 940-V or your payment to Form 940 (or to each other).

• Detach Form 940-V and send it with your payment and Form 940 to the address provided in the Instructions for Form 940.

Note: You must also complete the entity information above Part 1 on Form 940.

✂ ▼ **Detach Here and Mail With Your Payment and Form 940.** ▼ ✂

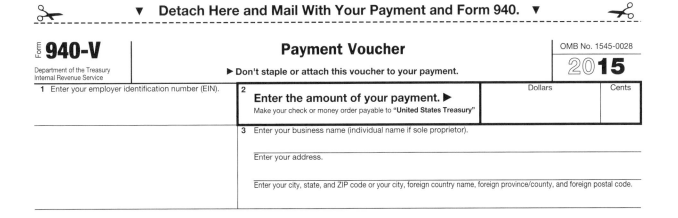

Form **940-V**

Department of the Treasury
Internal Revenue Service

Payment Voucher

► **Don't staple or attach this voucher to your payment.**

OMB No. 1545-0028

20**15**

| 1 Enter your employer identification number (EIN). | 2 **Enter the amount of your payment.** ►
 Make your check or money order payable to "**United States Treasury**" | Dollars | Cents |

3 Enter your business name (individual name if sole proprietor).

Enter your address.

Enter your city, state, and ZIP code or your city, foreign country name, foreign province/county, and foreign postal code.

A-49

Privacy Act and Paperwork Reduction Act Notice. We ask for the information on this form to carry out the Internal Revenue laws of the United States. We need it to figure and collect the right amount of tax. Chapter 23, Federal Unemployment Tax Act, of Subtitle C, Employment Taxes, of the Internal Revenue Code imposes a tax on employers with respect to employees. This form is used to determine the amount of the tax that you owe. Section 6011 requires you to provide the requested information if you are liable for FUTA tax under section 3301. Section 6109 requires you to provide your identification number. If you fail to provide this information in a timely manner or provide a false or fraudulent form, you may be subject to penalties.

You aren't required to provide the information requested on a form that is subject to the Paperwork Reduction Act unless the form displays a valid OMB control number. Books and records relating to a form or instructions must be retained as long as their contents may become material in the administration of any Internal Revenue law.

Generally, tax returns and return information are confidential, as required by section 6103. However, section 6103 allows or requires the IRS to disclose or give the information shown on your tax return to others as described in the Code. For example, we may disclose your tax information to the Department of Justice for civil and criminal litigation, and to cities, states, the District of Columbia, and U.S. commonwealths and possessions to administer their tax laws. We may also disclose this information to other countries under a tax treaty, to federal and state agencies to enforce federal non-tax criminal laws, or to federal law enforcement and intelligence agencies to combat terrorism.

The time needed to complete and file this form will vary depending on individual circumstances. The estimated average time is:

Recordkeeping . . . . 9 hr., 40 min.

Learning about the law or the form . . 1 hr., 23 min.

Preparing, copying, assembling, and sending the form to the IRS . . . . 40 min.

If you have comments concerning the accuracy of these time estimates or suggestions for making Form 940 simpler, we would be happy to hear from you. You can send us comments from *www.irs.gov/formspubs.* Click on *More Information* and then click on *Give us feedback.* Or you can send your comments to Internal Revenue Service, Tax Forms and Publications Division, 1111 Constitution Avenue, NW, IR-6526, Washington, DC 20224. **Don't** send Form 940 to this address. Instead, see *Where Do You File?* in the Instructions for Form 940.

Schedule A (Form 940) for 2015:

Multi-State Employer and Credit Reduction Information

Department of the Treasury — Internal Revenue Service

860312

OMB No. 1545-0028

See the instructions on page 2. File this schedule with Form 940.

Employer identification number (EIN) ☐☐ – ☐☐☐☐☐☐☐

Name *(not your trade name)*

Place an "X" in the box of EVERY state in which you had to pay state unemployment tax this year. For each state with a credit reduction rate greater than zero, enter the FUTA taxable wages, multiply by the reduction rate, and enter the credit reduction amount. Don't include in the *FUTA Taxable Wages* box wages that were excluded from state unemployment tax (see the instructions for Step 2). If any states don't apply to you, leave them blank.

Postal Abbreviation	FUTA Taxable Wages	Reduction Rate	Credit Reduction	Postal Abbreviation	FUTA Taxable Wages	Reduction Rate	Credit Reduction
☐ AK	.	× .000	.	☐ NC	.	× .000	.
☐ AL	.	× .000	.	☐ ND	.	× .000	.
☐ AR	.	× .000	.	☐ NE	.	× .000	.
☐ AZ	.	× .000	.	☐ NH	.	× .000	.
☐ CA	.	× .015	.	☐ NJ	.	× .000	.
☐ CO	.	× .000	.	☐ NM	.	× .000	.
☐ CT	.	× .021	.	☐ NV	.	× .000	.
☐ DC	.	× .000	.	☐ NY	.	× .000	.
☐ DE	.	× .000	.	☐ OH	.	× .015	.
☐ FL	.	× .000	.	☐ OK	.	× .000	.
☐ GA	.	× .000	.	☐ OR	.	× .000	.
☐ HI	.	× .000	.	☐ PA	.	× .000	.
☐ IA	.	× .000	.	☐ RI	.	× .000	.
☐ ID	.	× .000	.	☐ SC	.	× .000	.
☐ IL	.	× .000	.	☐ SD	.	× .000	.
☐ IN	.	× .000	.	☐ TN	.	× .000	.
☐ KS	.	× .000	.	☐ TX	.	× .000	.
☐ KY	.	× .000	.	☐ UT	.	× .000	.
☐ LA	.	× .000	.	☐ VA	.	× .000	.
☐ MA	.	× .000	.	☐ VT	.	× .000	.
☐ MD	.	× .000	.	☐ WA	.	× .000	.
☐ ME	.	× .000	.	☐ WI	.	× .000	.
☐ MI	.	× .000	.	☐ WV	.	× .000	.
☐ MN	.	× .000	.	☐ WY	.	× .000	.
☐ MO	.	× .000	.	☐ PR	.	× .000	.
☐ MS	.	× .000	.	☐ VI	.	× .015	.
☐ MT	.	× .000	.				

Total Credit Reduction. Add all amounts shown in the *Credit Reduction* boxes. Enter the total here and on Form 940, line 11 . . . .

For Privacy Act and Paperwork Reduction Act Notice, see the Instructions for Form 940.   Cat. No. 16997C   Schedule A (Form 940) 2015

Instructions for Schedule A (Form 940) for 2015:

Multi-State Employer and Credit Reduction Information

Specific Instructions: Completing Schedule A

Step 1. Place an "X" in the box of every state (including the District of Columbia, Puerto Rico, and the U.S. Virgin Islands) in which you had to pay state unemployment taxes this year, even if the state's credit reduction rate is zero.

Note: Make sure that you have applied for a state reporting number for your business. If you do not have an unemployment account in a state in which you paid wages, contact the state unemployment agency to receive one. For a list of state unemployment agencies, visit the U.S. Department of Labor's website at *www.workforcesecurity.doleta.gov/unemploy/agencies.asp.*

The table below provides the two-letter postal abbreviations used on Schedule A.

State	Postal Abbreviation	State	Postal Abbreviation
Alabama	AL	Montana	MT
Alaska	AK	Nebraska	NE
Arizona	AZ	Nevada	NV
Arkansas	AR	New Hampshire	NH
California	CA	New Jersey	NJ
Colorado	CO	New Mexico	NM
Connecticut	CT	New York	NY
Delaware	DE	North Carolina	NC
District of Columbia	DC	North Dakota	ND
Florida	FL	Ohio	OH
Georgia	GA	Oklahoma	OK
Hawaii	HI	Oregon	OR
Idaho	ID	Pennsylvania	PA
Illinois	IL	Rhode Island	RI
Indiana	IN	South Carolina	SC
Iowa	IA	South Dakota	SD
Kansas	KS	Tennessee	TN
Kentucky	KY	Texas	TX
Louisiana	LA	Utah	UT
Maine	ME	Vermont	VT
Maryland	MD	Virginia	VA
Massachusetts	MA	Washington	WA
Michigan	MI	West Virginia	WV
Minnesota	MN	Wisconsin	WI
Mississippi	MS	Wyoming	WY
Missouri	MO	Puerto Rico	PR
		U.S. Virgin Islands	VI

Step 2. You are subject to credit reduction if you paid FUTA taxable wages that were also subject to state unemployment taxes in any state listed that has a credit reduction rate greater than zero.

If you paid FUTA taxable wages that were also subject to state unemployment taxes in any state that is subject to credit reduction, find the line for each state.

In the *FUTA Taxable Wages* box, enter the total FUTA taxable wages that you paid in that state. (The FUTA wage base for all states is $7,000.) However, don't include in the *FUTA Taxable Wages* box wages that were excluded from state unemployment tax. For example, if you paid $5,000 in FUTA taxable wages in a credit reduction state but $1,000 of those wages were excluded from state unemployment tax, report $4,000 in the *FUTA Taxable Wages* box for that state.

Note: Don't enter your state unemployment wages in the *FUTA Taxable Wages* box.

Then multiply the total FUTA taxable wages by the reduction rate.

Enter your total in the *Credit Reduction* box at the end of the line.

Step 3. Total credit reduction

To calculate the total credit reduction, add up all of the *Credit Reduction* boxes and enter the amount in the *Total Credit Reduction* box.

Then enter the total credit reduction on Form 940, line 11.

Example 1

You paid $20,000 in wages to each of three employees in State A. State A is subject to credit reduction at a rate of .003 (.3%). Because you paid wages in a state that is subject to credit reduction, you must complete Schedule A and file it with Form 940.

Total payments to all employees in State A	$60,000
Payments exempt from FUTA tax (see the Instructions for Form 940)	$0
Total payments made to each employee in excess of $7,000 (3 x ($20,000 - $7,000))	$39,000
Total FUTA taxable wages you paid in State A entered in the *FUTA Taxable Wages* box ($60,000 - $0 - $39,000)	$21,000
Credit reduction rate for State A	.003
Total credit reduction for State A ($21,000 x .003)	$63

 CAUTION *Don't include in the FUTA Taxable Wages box wages in excess of the $7,000 wage base for each employee subject to state unemployment insurance in the credit reduction state. The credit reduction applies only to FUTA taxable wages that were also subject to state unemployment tax.*

In this case, you would write $63.00 in the *Total Credit Reduction* box and then enter that amount on Form 940, line 11.

Example 2

You paid $48,000 ($4,000 a month) in wages to Employee A and no payments were exempt from FUTA tax. Employee A worked in State B (not subject to credit reduction) in January and then transferred to State C (subject to credit reduction) on February 1. Because you paid wages in more than one state, you must complete Schedule A and file it with Form 940.

The total payments in State B that are not exempt from FUTA tax are $4,000. Since this payment to Employee A does not exceed the $7,000 FUTA wage base, the total FUTA taxable wages paid in State B are $4,000.

The total payments in State C that are not exempt from FUTA tax are $44,000. However, $4,000 of FUTA taxable wages was paid in State B with respect to Employee A. Therefore, the total FUTA taxable wages with respect to Employee A in State C are $3,000 ($7,000 (FUTA wage base) - $4,000 (total FUTA taxable wages paid in State B)). Enter $3,000 in the *FUTA Taxable Wages* box, multiply it by the *Reduction Rate*, and then enter the result in the *Credit Reduction* box.

Attach Schedule A to Form 940 when you file your return.

20**15**

Instructions for Form 940

Employer's Annual Federal Unemployment (FUTA) Tax Return

Section references are to the Internal Revenue Code unless otherwise noted.

Future Developments

For the latest information about developments related to Form 940 and its instructions, such as legislation enacted after they were published, go to *www.irs.gov/form940*.

What's New

Credit reduction state. A state that hasn't repaid money it borrowed from the federal government to pay unemployment benefits is a "credit reduction state." The Department of Labor determines these states. If an employer pays wages that are subject to the unemployment tax laws of a credit reduction state, that employer must pay additional federal unemployment tax when filing its Form 940.

For 2015, there are credit reduction states. If you paid any wages that are subject to the unemployment compensation laws of a credit reduction state, your credit against federal unemployment tax will be reduced based on the credit reduction rate for that credit reduction state. Use Schedule A (Form 940) to figure the credit reduction. For more information, see the Schedule A (Form 940) instructions or visit IRS.gov.

Reminders

If you change your business name, business address, or responsible party. For a definition of "responsible party" and how to notify IRS of a change in the identity of your responsible party, see the Form 8822-B Instructions. Notify the IRS immediately if you change your business name, business address, or responsible party. Write to the IRS office where you file your returns (using the *Without a payment* address under *Where Do You File*, later) to notify the IRS of any name change. See Pub. 1635 to see if you need to apply for a new employer identification number (EIN). Complete and mail Form 8822-B to notify the IRS of an address change.

Federal tax deposits must be made by electronic funds transfer (EFT). You must use EFT to make all federal tax deposits. Generally, an EFT is made using the Electronic Federal Tax Payment System (EFTPS). If you don't want to use EFTPS, you can arrange for your tax professional, financial institution, payroll service, or other trusted third party to make electronic deposits on your behalf. Also, you may arrange for your financial institution to initiate a same-day wire payment on your behalf. EFTPS is a free service provided by the Department of Treasury. Services provided by your tax professional, financial institution, payroll service, or other third party may have a fee.

For more information on making federal tax deposits, see section 11 of Pub. 15. To get more information about EFTPS or to enroll in EFTPS, visit *www.eftps.gov*, or call 1-800-555-4477, 1-800-733-4829 (TDD), or 1-800-244-4829 (Spanish). Additional information about EFTPS is also available in Pub. 966.

Aggregate Form 940 filers. Agents must complete Schedule R (Form 940), Allocation Schedule for Aggregate Form 940 Filers, when filing an aggregate Form 940. Aggregate Forms 940 are filed by agents of home care service recipients approved by the IRS under section 3504. To request approval to act as an agent for an employer, the agent files Form 2678 with the IRS unless you are a state or local government agency acting as agent under the special procedures provided in Rev. Proc. 2013-39, 2013-52 I.R.B. 830, available at *www.irs.gov/irb/ 2013-52_IRB/ar15.html*.

Disregarded entities and qualified subchapter S subsidiaries (QSubs). Business entities that are disregarded as separate from their owner, including qualified subchapter S subsidiaries, are required to withhold and pay employment taxes and file employment tax returns using the name and EIN of the disregarded entity. For more information, see *Disregarded entities*, later.

State unemployment information. When you registered as an employer with your state, the state assigned you a state reporting number. If you don't have a state unemployment account and state experience tax rate, or if you have questions about your state account, you must contact your state unemployment agency. For a list of state unemployment agencies, visit the U.S. Department of Labor's website at *www.workforcesecurity.doleta.gov/unemploy/agencies.asp*.

You can file and pay electronically. Using electronic options available from the IRS can make filing a return and paying your federal tax easier. You can use IRS *e-file* to file a return and EFTPS to make deposits or pay in full whether you rely on a tax professional or prepare your own taxes.
• For e-file, visit the IRS website at *www.irs.gov/efile* for additional information.
• For EFTPS, visit *www.eftps.gov*, or call EFTPS Customer Service at 1-800-555-4477, 1-800-733-4829 (TDD), or 1-800-244-4829 (Spanish).

Electronic funds withdrawal (EFW). If you file Form 940 electronically, you can e-file and e-pay (EFW) the balance due in a single step using tax preparation software or through a tax professional. However, don't use EFW to make federal tax deposits. For more information on paying your taxes using EFW, visit the IRS website at *www.irs.gov/payments*. A fee may be charged to file electronically.

You can pay your balance due by credit or debit card. You may pay your FUTA tax shown on line 14 using a credit card or debit card. However, don't use a credit or debit card to pay taxes that are required to be deposited (see *When Must You Deposit Your FUTA Tax*, later). For more information on paying your taxes with a credit or debit card, visit the IRS website at *www.irs.gov/payments*.

Online payment agreement. You may be eligible to apply for an installment agreement online if you have a balance due when you file your return. For more information, see *What if you can't pay in full*, later.

Outsourcing payroll duties. You are responsible to ensure that tax returns are filed and deposits and payments are made, even if you contract with a third party to perform these acts. You remain responsible if the third party fails to perform any required action. If you choose to outsource any of your payroll and related tax duties (that is, withholding, reporting, and paying over social security, Medicare, FUTA, and income taxes) to a third-party payer, such as a payroll service provider or reporting agent, visit IRS.gov and enter "outsourcing payroll duties" in the search box for helpful information on this topic.

Oct 28, 2015   Cat. No. 13660I

Photographs of missing children. The IRS is a proud partner with the National Center for Missing and Exploited Children. Photographs of missing children selected by the Center may appear in instructions on pages that would otherwise be blank. You can help bring these children home by looking at the photographs and calling 1-800-THE-LOST (1-800-843-5678) if you recognize a child.

How Can You Get More Help?

If you want more information about this form, see Pub. 15, visit our website at IRS.gov, or call the Business and Specialty Tax Line toll free at 1-800-829-4933 or 1-800-829-4059 (TDD/TTY for persons who are deaf, hard of hearing, or have a speech disability) Monday–Friday from 7:00 a.m.–7:00 p.m. local time (Alaska and Hawaii follow Pacific time).

For a list of related employment tax topics, visit IRS.gov and enter "employment taxes" in the search box. You can order forms, instructions, and publications at *www.irs.gov/orderforms*.

General Instructions:

What's the Purpose of Form 940?

These instructions give you some background information about Form 940. They tell you who must file the form, how to fill it out line by line, and when and where to file it.

Use Form 940 to report your annual Federal Unemployment Tax Act (FUTA) tax. Together with state unemployment tax systems, the FUTA tax provides funds for paying unemployment compensation to workers who have lost their jobs. Most employers pay both a federal and a state unemployment tax. Only employers pay FUTA tax. Don't collect or deduct FUTA tax from your employees' wages.

The FUTA tax applies to the first $7,000 you pay to each employee during a calendar year after subtracting any payments exempt from FUTA tax.

Who Must File Form 940?

Except as noted below, if you answer "Yes" to either one of these questions, you must file Form 940.
• Did you pay wages of $1,500 or more to employees in any calendar quarter during 2014 or 2015?
• Did you have one or more employees for at least some part of a day in any 20 or more different weeks in 2014 or 20 or more different weeks in 2015? Count all full-time, part-time, and temporary employees. However, if your business is a partnership, don't count its partners.

If your business was sold or transferred during the year, each employer who answered "Yes" to at least one question above must file Form 940. However, don't include any wages paid by the predecessor employer on your Form 940 unless you are a successor employer. For details, see *Successor employer* under *Type of Return*.

If you aren't liable for FUTA tax for 2015 because you made no payments to employees in 2015, check box *c* in the top right corner of the form. Then go to Part 7, sign the form, and file it with the IRS.

If you won't be liable for filing Form 940 in the future because your business has closed or because you stopped paying wages, check box *d* in the top right corner of the form. See *Final: Business closed or stopped paying wages* under *Type of Return* for more information.

For Employers of Household Employees . . .

If you are a household employer, you must pay FUTA tax on wages that you paid to your household employees only if you paid cash wages of $1,000 or more in any calendar quarter in 2014 or 2015.

A household employee performs household work in a:
• Private home,
• Local college club, or
• Local chapter of a college fraternity or sorority.

Generally, employers of household employees must file Schedule H (Form 1040) instead of Form 940.

However, if you have other employees in addition to household employees, you can choose to include the FUTA taxes for your household employees on Form 940 instead of filing Schedule H (Form 1040). If you choose to include household employees on your Form 940, you must also file Form 941, Employer's QUARTERLY Federal Tax Return; Form 943, Employer's Annual Federal Tax Return for Agricultural Employees; or Form 944, Employer's ANNUAL Federal Tax Return; to report social security, Medicare, and any withheld federal income taxes for your household employees. See Pub. 926 for more information.

For Agricultural Employers . . .

File Form 940 if you answer "Yes" to either of these questions.
• Did you pay cash wages of $20,000 or more to farmworkers during any calendar quarter in 2014 or 2015?
• Did you employ 10 or more farmworkers during some part of the day (whether or not at the same time) during any 20 or more different weeks in 2014 or 20 or more different weeks in 2015?

Count wages you paid to aliens who were admitted to the United States on a temporary basis to perform farmwork (workers with H-2A visas). However, wages paid to "H-2A visa workers" aren't subject to FUTA tax. See Pub. 51 for more information.

For Indian Tribal Governments . . .

Services rendered by employees of a federally recognized Indian tribal government employer (including any subdivision, subsidiary, or business enterprise wholly owned by the tribe) are exempt from FUTA tax and no Form 940 is required. However, the tribe must have participated in the state unemployment system for the full year and be in compliance with applicable state unemployment law. For more information, see section 3309(d).

For Tax-Exempt Organizations . . .

Religious, educational, scientific, charitable, and other organizations described in section 501(c)(3) and exempt from tax under section 501(a) aren't subject to FUTA tax and don't have to file Form 940.

For Employers of State or Local Governments. . .

Services rendered by employees of a state, political subdivision or instrumentality of the state are exempt from FUTA tax and no Form 940 is required.

When Must You File Form 940?

The due date for filing Form 940 for 2015 is February 1, 2016. However, if you deposited all your FUTA tax when it was due, you may file Form 940 by February 10, 2016.

If we receive your return after the due date, we will treat your return as filed on time if the envelope containing your return is properly addressed, contains sufficient postage, and is postmarked by the U.S. Postal Service on or before the due date or sent by an IRS-designated private delivery service on or before the due date. However, if you don't follow these guidelines, we will consider your return filed when it is actually received. For a list of IRS-designated private delivery services, see Pub. 15.

Where Do You File?

Where you file depends on whether you include a payment (check or money order) with your return. However, mail your amended return to the *Without a payment* address even if a payment is included.

If you are in . . .		Without a payment . . .	With a payment . . .
Connecticut	New Jersey	Department of the Treasury Internal Revenue Service Cincinnati, OH 45999-0046	Internal Revenue Service P.O. Box 804521 Cincinnati, OH 45280-4521
Delaware	New York		
District of Columbia	North Carolina		
	Ohio		
Florida	Pennsylvania		
Georgia	Rhode Island		
Illinois	South Carolina		
Indiana	Tennessee		
Kentucky	Vermont		
Maine	Virginia		
Maryland	West Virginia		
Massachusetts	Wisconsin		
Michigan			
New Hampshire			
Alabama	Missouri	Department of the Treasury Internal Revenue Service Ogden, UT 84201-0046	Internal Revenue Service P.O. Box 37940 Hartford, CT 06176-7940
Alaska	Montana		
Arizona	Nebraska		
Arkansas	Nevada		
California	New Mexico		
Colorado	North Dakota		
Hawaii	Oklahoma		
Idaho	Oregon		
Iowa	South Dakota		
Kansas	Texas		
Louisiana	Utah		
Minnesota	Washington		
Mississippi	Wyoming		
Puerto Rico		Internal Revenue Service P.O. Box 409101 Ogden, UT 84409	Internal Revenue Service P.O. Box 37940 Hartford, CT 06176-7940
U.S. Virgin Islands			
If the location of your legal residence, principal place of business, office, or agency isn't listed . . .		Internal Revenue Service P.O. Box 409101 Ogden, UT 84409	Internal Revenue Service P.O. Box 37940 Hartford, CT 06176-7940
EXCEPTION for tax-exempt organizations, Federal, State and Local Governments, and Indian Tribal Governments, regardless of your location		Department of the Treasury Internal Revenue Service Ogden, UT 84201-0046	Internal Revenue Service P.O. Box 37940 Hartford, CT 06176-7940

 Private delivery services can't deliver to P.O. boxes. You must use the U.S. Postal Service to mail an item to a P.O. box address.

Credit for State Unemployment Tax Paid to a State Unemployment Fund

You get a credit for amounts you pay to a state (including the District of Columbia, Puerto Rico, and the U.S. Virgin Islands) unemployment fund by February 1, 2016 (or February 10, 2016, if that is your Form 940 due date). Your FUTA tax will be higher if you don't pay the state unemployment tax timely. If you didn't pay all state unemployment tax by the due date of Form 940, see the line 10 instructions.

State unemployment taxes are sometimes called "contributions." These contributions are payments that a state requires an employer to make to its unemployment fund for the payment of unemployment benefits. They don't include:

* Any payments deducted or deductible from your employees' pay;
* Penalties, interest, or special administrative taxes; and
* Voluntary amounts you paid to get a lower assigned state experience rate.

Additional credit. You may receive an additional credit if you have a state experience rate lower than 5.4% (.054). This applies even if your rate varies during the year. This additional credit is the difference between your actual state unemployment tax payments and the amount you would have been required to pay at 5.4%.

Special credit for successor employers. You may be eligible for a credit based on the state unemployment taxes paid by a predecessor. You may claim this credit if you are a successor employer who acquired a business in 2015 from a predecessor who wasn't an employer for FUTA purposes and, therefore, wasn't required to file Form 940 for 2015. See section 3302(e). You can include amounts paid by the predecessor on the *Worksheet—Line 10* as if you paid them. For details on successor employers, see *Successor employer* under *Type of Return*. If the predecessor was required to file Form 940, see the line 5 instructions.

When Must You Deposit Your FUTA Tax?

Although Form 940 covers a calendar year, you may have to deposit your FUTA tax before you file your return. If your FUTA tax is more than $500 for the calendar year, you must deposit at least one quarterly payment.

You must determine when to deposit your tax based on the amount of your quarterly tax liability. If your FUTA tax is $500 or less in a quarter, carry it over to the next quarter. Continue carrying your tax liability over until your cumulative tax is more than $500. At that point, you must deposit your tax for the quarter. Deposit your FUTA tax by the last day of the month after the end of the quarter. If your tax for the next quarter is $500 or less, you aren't required to deposit your tax again until the cumulative amount is more than $500.

Fourth quarter liabilities. If your FUTA tax for the fourth quarter (plus any undeposited amounts from earlier quarters) is more than $500, deposit the entire amount by February 1, 2016. If it is $500 or less, you can either deposit the amount or pay it with your Form 940 by February 1, 2016.

In years when there are credit reduction states, you must include liabilities owed for credit reduction with your fourth quarter deposit.

When To Deposit Your FUTA Tax

If your undeposited FUTA tax is more than $500 on . . .*	Deposit your tax by . . .
March 31	April 30
June 30	July 31
September 30	October 31
December 31	January 31
*Also, see the instructions for line 16.	

 If any deposit due date falls on a Saturday, Sunday, or legal holiday, you may deposit on the next business day. See Timeliness of federal tax deposits, *later.*

How Do You Figure Your FUTA Tax Liability for Each Quarter?

You owe FUTA tax on the first $7,000 you pay to each employee during the calendar year after subtracting any payments exempt from FUTA tax. The FUTA tax is 6.0% (.060) for 2015. Most employers receive a maximum credit of up to 5.4% (.054) against this FUTA tax. Every quarter, you must figure how much of the first $7,000 of each employee's annual wages you paid during that quarter.

Figure Your Tax Liability

Before you can figure the amount to deposit, figure your FUTA tax liability for the quarter. To figure your tax liability, add the first $7,000 of each employee's annual wages you paid during the quarter for FUTA wages paid and multiply that amount by .006.

The tax rates are based on your receiving the maximum credit against FUTA taxes. You are entitled to the maximum credit if you paid all state unemployment tax by the due date of your Form 940 or if you weren't required to pay state unemployment tax during the calendar year due to your state experience rate.

Example. During the first quarter, you had three employees: Employees A, B, and C. You paid $11,000 to Employee A, $2,000 to Employee B, and $4,000 to Employee C. None of the payments made were exempt from FUTA tax.

To figure your liability for the first quarter, add the first $7,000 of each employee's wages subject to FUTA tax:

$7,000	Employee A's wages subject to FUTA tax
2,000	Employee B's wages subject to FUTA tax
+ 4,000	Employee C's wages subject to FUTA tax
$13,000	Total wages subject to FUTA tax for the first quarter

$13,000	Total wages subject to FUTA tax for the first quarter
x .006	Tax rate (based on maximum credit of 5.4%)
$78	Your liability for the first quarter

In this example, you don't have to make a deposit because your liability is $500 or less for the first quarter. However, you must carry this liability over to the second quarter.

If any wages subject to FUTA tax aren't subject to state unemployment tax, you may be liable for FUTA tax at the maximum rate of 6.0%. For instance, in certain states, wages paid to corporate officers, certain payments of sick pay by unions, and certain fringe benefits are excluded from state unemployment tax.

Example. Employee A and Employee B are corporate officers whose wages are excluded from state unemployment tax in your state. Employee C's wages aren't excluded from state unemployment tax. During the first quarter, you paid $11,000 to Employee A, $2,000 to Employee B, and $4,000 to Employee C.

$9,000	Total FUTA wages for Employees A and B in first quarter
x .060	Tax rate
$540	Your liability for the first quarter for Employees A and B

$4,000	Total FUTA wages subject to state unemployment tax
x .006	Tax rate (based on maximum credit of 5.4%)
$24	Your liability for the first quarter for Employee C

$540	Your liability for the first quarter for Employees A and B
+ 24	Your liability for first quarter for Employee C
$564	Your liability for the first quarter for Employees A, B, and C

In this example, you must deposit $564 by April 30 because your liability for the first quarter is more than $500.

How Must You Deposit Your FUTA Tax?

You Must Deposit Your FUTA Tax Using EFT

You must use EFT to make all federal tax deposits. Generally, an EFT is made using EFTPS. To get more information or to enroll in EFTPS, visit EFTPS website at *www.eftps.gov*, or call 1-800-555-4477, 1-800-733–4829 (TDD), or 1-800-244-4829 (Spanish). Additional information about EFTPS is also available in Pub. 966.

If your business is new, IRS will automatically pre-enroll you in EFTPS when you apply for an EIN. Follow the instructions on your EIN package to activate your enrollment.

 For an EFTPS deposit to be on time, you must submit the deposit by 8 p.m. Eastern time the day before the date the deposit is due.

Same-day wire payment option. If you fail to submit a deposit transaction on EFTPS by 8 p.m. Eastern time the day before the date a deposit is due, you can still make your deposit on time by using the Federal Tax Collection Service (FTCS). To use the same-day wire payment method, you will need to make arrangements with your financial institution ahead of time. Please check with your financial institution regarding availability, deadlines, and costs. Your financial institution may charge you a fee for payments made this way. To learn more about the information you will need to provide to your financial institution to make a same-day wire payment, visit the IRS website at *www.irs.gov/payments* and click on *Same-day wire*.

Timeliness of federal tax deposits. If a deposit is required to be made on a day that isn't a business day, the deposit is considered timely if it is made by the close of the next business day. A business day is any day other than a Saturday, Sunday, or legal holiday. The term "legal holiday" for deposit purposes includes only those legal holidays in the District of Columbia. For a list of legal holidays, see Pub. 15.

How Can You Avoid Penalties and Interest?

Penalties and interest are assessed at a rate set by law on taxes paid late, returns filed late or incorrectly, insufficient payments made, and failure to make deposits using EFT.

You can avoid paying penalties and interest if you:
- Deposit or pay your tax when it is due,
- File your completed Form 940 accurately and on time, and
- Ensure your tax payments are honored by your financial institution.

If you receive a notice about a penalty after you file this return, reply to the notice with an explanation and we will determine if you meet reasonable-cause criteria. Don't attach an explanation when you file your Form 940.

Can You Amend a Return?

You use the 2015 Form 940 to amend a return that you previously filed for 2015. If you are amending a return for a previous year, use that previous year's Form 940.

Follow the steps below to amend your return.
- Use a paper return to amend a Form 940 filed under an electronic filing program.
- Check the amended return box in the top right corner of Form 940, page 1, box a.
- Fill in all the amounts that should have been on the original form.
- Sign the form.
- Attach an explanation of why you are amending your return. For example, tell us if you are filing to claim credit for tax paid to your state unemployment fund after the due date of Form 940.
- File the amended return using the *Without a payment* address (even if a payment is included) under *Where Do You File*.
- If you file an amended return for an aggregate Form 940, be sure to attach Schedule R (Form 940). Complete Schedule R (Form 940) only for employers who have adjustments on the amended Form 940.

Completing Your Form 940

Follow These Guidelines to Correctly Fill Out the Form

To help us accurately scan and process your form, please follow these guidelines.
- Make sure your business name and EIN are on every page of the form and any attachments.
- If you type or use a computer to fill out your form, use a 12-point Courier font, if possible. Portable Document Format (PDF) forms on IRS.gov have fillable fields with acceptable font specifications.
- Make sure you enter dollars to the left of the preprinted decimal point and cents to the right.
- Don't enter dollar signs or decimal points. Commas are optional.
- You may choose to round your amounts to the nearest dollar, instead of reporting cents on this form. If you choose to round, you must round all entries. To round, drop the amounts under 50 cents and increase the amounts from 50 to 99 cents to the next dollar. For example, $1.49 becomes $1.00 and $2.50 becomes $3.00. If you use two or more amounts to figure an entry on the form, use cents to figure the answer and round the answer only.
- If you have a line with the value of zero, leave it blank.

Employer Identification Number (EIN), Name, Trade Name, and Address

Enter Your Business Information at the Top of the Form

Enter your EIN, name, and address in the spaces provided. You must enter your name and EIN here and on page 2. Enter the business (legal) name that you used when you applied for your EIN on Form SS-4. For example, if you are a sole proprietor, enter "Ronald Smith" on the *Name* line and "Ron's Cycles" on the *Trade Name* line. Leave the *Trade Name* line blank if it is the same as your *Name*.

If you pay a tax preparer to fill out Form 940, make sure the preparer shows your business name exactly as it appeared when you applied for your EIN.

Employer identification number (EIN). An EIN is a unique nine-digit number assigned to sole proprietors, corporations, partnerships, estates, trusts, and other entities for tax filing and reporting purposes. Businesses that need an EIN must apply for a number and use it throughout the life of the business on all tax returns, payments, and reports.

Your business should have only one EIN. If you have more than one and are unsure which one to use, call 1-800-829-4933 to verify your correct EIN.

If you don't have an EIN, apply for one by:
- Visiting IRS.gov and entering "EIN" in the search box, or
- Filling out Form SS-4 and mailing it to the address in the Instructions for Form SS-4 or faxing it to the number in the Instructions for Form SS-4.

Employers outside the United States may also apply for an EIN by calling 267-941-1099 (toll call), but domestic entities may not apply by telephone.

If you haven't received your EIN by the time a return is due, write *"Applied For"* and the date you applied in the space shown for the EIN on pages 1 and 2 of your return.

 If you are filing your tax return electronically, a valid EIN is required at the time the return is filed. If a valid EIN isn't provided, the return won't be accepted. This may result in penalties.

 Always be sure the EIN on the form you file exactly matches the EIN that the IRS assigned to your business. Don't use a social security number (SSN) or individual taxpayer identification number (ITIN) on forms that ask for an EIN. Filing a Form 940 with an incorrect EIN or using the EIN of another's business may result in penalties and delays in processing your return.

Tell Us if You Change Your Business Name or Business Address

Notify the IRS immediately if you change your business name or address.
- If your business name changes, write to the IRS using the *Without a payment* address under *Where Do You File*. Also see Pub. 1635 for general information on EINs.
- If your business address changes, complete and mail Form 8822-B. Don't attach Form 8822-B to your Form 940. Mail Form 8822-B separately to the address indicated on Form 8822-B.

Type of Return

Review the box at the top of the form. If any line applies to you, check the appropriate box to tell us which type of return you are filing. You may check more than one box.

Amended. If this is an amended return that you are filing to correct a return that you previously filed, check box *a*.

Successor employer. Check box *b* if you are a successor employer and:
- You are reporting wages paid before you acquired the business by a predecessor who was required to file a Form 940 because the predecessor was an employer for FUTA tax purposes, or
- You are claiming a special credit for state unemployment tax paid before you acquired the business by a predecessor who wasn't required to file a Form 940 because the predecessor wasn't an employer for FUTA tax purposes.

A successor employer is an employer who:

• Acquires substantially all the property used in a trade or business of another person (predecessor) or used in a separate unit of a trade or business of a predecessor, and
• Immediately after the acquisition, employs one or more people who were employed by the predecessor.

No payments to employees in 2015. If you aren't liable for FUTA tax for 2015 because you made no payments to employees in 2015, check box *c.* Then go to Part 7, sign the form, and file it with the IRS.

Final: Business closed or stopped paying wages. If this is a final return because you went out of business or stopped paying wages and you won't be liable for filing Form 940 in the future, check box *d.* Complete all applicable lines on the form, sign it in Part 7, and file it with the IRS. Include a statement showing the address at which your records will be kept and the name of the person keeping the records.

Disregarded entities. A disregarded entity is required to file Form 940 using its name and EIN, not the name and EIN of its owner. An entity that has a single owner and is disregarded as separate from its owner for federal income tax purposes is treated as a separate entity for purposes of payment and reporting federal employment taxes. If the entity doesn't currently have an EIN, it must apply for one using one of the methods under *Employer identification number (EIN)*, earlier. Disregarded entities include single-owner limited liability companies (LLCs) that haven't elected to be taxed as a corporation for federal income tax purposes, qualified subchapter S subsidiaries, and certain foreign entities treated as disregarded entities for U.S. income tax purposes. Although a disregarded entity is treated as a separate entity for employment tax purposes, it isn't subject to FUTA tax if it is owned by a tax-exempt organization under section 501(c)(3) and isn't required to file Form 940. For more information, see *Disregarded entities and qualified subchapter S subsidiaries* in the *Introduction* section of Pub. 15.

Specific Instructions

Part 1: Tell Us About Your Return

1. If You Were Required to Pay Your State Unemployment Tax In . . .

 You must complete line 1a or line 1b even if you were not required to pay any state unemployment tax because your state unemployment tax rate(s) was zero. You may leave lines 1a and 1b blank only if all of the wages you paid to all employees in all states were excluded from state unemployment tax. If you leave lines 1a and 1b blank, you must complete line 9 because all of the taxable FUTA wages you paid were excluded from state unemployment tax.

Identify the state(s) where you were required to pay state unemployment taxes.

1a. One state only. Enter the two-letter U.S. Postal Service abbreviation for the state where you were required to pay your state unemployment tax on line 1a. For a list of state abbreviations, see the Schedule A (Form 940) instructions or visit the website for the U.S. Postal Service at *www.usps.com*.

1b. More than one state (you are a multi-state employer). Check the box on line 1b. Then fill out Schedule A (Form 940) and attach it to your Form 940.

2. If You Paid Wages in a State That is Subject to Credit Reduction

If you paid wages that are subject to the unemployment tax laws of a credit reduction state, you may have to pay more FUTA tax when filing your Form 940.

A state that hasn't repaid money it borrowed from the federal government to pay unemployment benefits is called a "credit reduction state." The U.S. Department of Labor determines which states are credit reduction states.

For tax year 2015, there are credit reduction states. If you paid wages subject to the unemployment tax laws of these states, check the box on line 2 and fill out Schedule A (Form 940). See the instructions for line 9 before completing the Schedule A (Form 940).

Part 2: Determine Your FUTA Tax Before Adjustments

If any line in Part 2 doesn't apply, leave it blank.

3. Total Payments to All Employees

Report the total payments you made during the calendar year on line 3. Include payments for the services of all employees, even if the payments aren't taxable for FUTA. Your method of payment doesn't determine whether payments are wages. You may have paid wages hourly, daily, weekly, monthly, or yearly. You may have paid wages for piecework or as a percentage of profits. Include:

• **Compensation,** such as:

—Salaries, wages, commissions, fees, bonuses, vacation allowances, and amounts you paid to full-time, part-time, or temporary employees.

• **Fringe benefits,** such as:

—Sick pay (including third-party sick pay if liability is transferred to the employer). For details on sick pay, see Pub. 15-A, Employer's Supplemental Tax Guide.
—The value of goods, lodging, food, clothing, and non-cash fringe benefits.
—Section 125 (cafeteria) plan benefits.

• **Retirement/Pension,** such as:

—Employer contributions to a 401(k) plan, payments to an Archer MSA, payments under adoption assistance programs, and contributions to SIMPLE retirement accounts (including elective salary reduction contributions).
—Amounts deferred under a non-qualified deferred compensation plan.

• **Other payments,** such as:

—Tips of $20 or more in a month that your employees reported to you.
—Payments made by a predecessor employer to the employees of a business you acquired.
—Payments to nonemployees who are treated as your employees by the state unemployment tax agency.

 Wages may be subject to FUTA tax even if they are excluded from your state's unemployment tax.

For details on wages and other compensation, see section 5 of Pub. 15-A.

Example:

You had 3 employees. You paid $44,000 to Employee A, $8,000 to Employee B, and $16,000 to Employee C.

$44,000	Amount paid to Employee A
8,000	Amount paid to Employee B
+ 16,000	Amount paid to Employee C
$68,000	Total payments to employees. You would enter this amount on line 3.

4. Payments Exempt from FUTA Tax

If you enter an amount on line 4, check the appropriate box or boxes on lines 4a through 4e to show the types of payments exempt from FUTA tax. **You only report a payment as exempt from FUTA tax on line 4 if you included the payment on line 3.**

Some payments are exempt from FUTA tax because the payments aren't included in the definition of wages or the services aren't included in the definition of employment. Payments exempt from FUTA tax may include:

- **Fringe benefits**, such as:

    —The value of certain meals and lodging.
    —Contributions to accident or health plans for employees, including certain employer payments to a Health Savings Account or an Archer MSA.
    —Employer reimbursements (including payments to a third party) for qualified moving expenses, to the extent that these expenses would otherwise be deductible by the employee.
    —Payments for benefits excluded under section 125 (cafeteria) plans.

- **Group term life insurance.**

    For information about group term life insurance and other payments for fringe benefits that may be exempt from FUTA tax, see Pub. 15-B.

- **Retirement/Pension**, such as employer contributions to a qualified plan, including a SIMPLE retirement account (other than elective salary reduction contributions) and a 401(k) plan.

- **Dependent care**, such as payments (up to $5,000 per employee, $2,500 if married filing separately) for a qualifying person's care that allows your employees to work and that would be excludable by the employee under section 129.

- **Other payments**, such as:

    —All non-cash payments and certain cash payments for agricultural labor, and all payments to "H-2A" visa workers. See *For Agricultural Employers*, earlier, or see Pub. 51.
    —Payments made under a workers' compensation law because of a work-related injury or sickness. See section 6 of Pub. 15-A.
    —Payments for domestic services if you didn't pay cash wages of $1,000 or more (for all domestic employees) in any calendar quarter in 2014 or 2015, or if you file Schedule H (Form 1040). See *For Employers of Household Employees*, earlier, or Pub. 926.
    —Payments for services provided to you by your parent, spouse, or child under the age of 21. See section 3 of Pub. 15.
    —Payments for certain fishing activities. See Pub. 334, Tax Guide for Small Business.
    —Payments to certain statutory employees. See section 1 of Pub. 15-A.
    —Payments to nonemployees who are treated as your employees by the state unemployment tax agency.

See section 3306 and its related regulations for more information about FUTA taxation of retirement plan contributions, dependent care payments, and other payments.

For more information on payments exempt from FUTA tax, see section 15 in Pub. 15.

Example:

You had 3 employees. You paid $44,000 to Employee A including $2,000 in health insurance benefits. You paid $8,000 to Employee B, including $500 in retirement benefits. You paid $16,000 to Employee C, including $2,000 in health and retirement benefits.

$ 2,000	Health insurance benefits for Employee A
500	Retirement benefits for Employee B
+ 2,000	Health and retirement benefits for Employee C
$4,500	Total payments exempt from FUTA tax. You would enter this amount on line 4 and check boxes 4a and 4c.

5. Total of Payments Made to Each Employee in Excess of $7,000

Only the first $7,000 you paid to each employee in a calendar year, after subtracting any payments exempt from FUTA tax, is subject to FUTA tax. This $7,000 is called the *FUTA wage base.*

Enter on line 5 the total of the payments over the FUTA wage base you paid to each employee during 2015 **after subtracting any payments exempt from FUTA tax shown on line 4.**

Following our example:

You had three employees. You paid $44,000 to Employee A, $8,000 to Employee B, and $16,000 to Employee C, including a total of $4,500 in payments exempt from FUTA tax for all three employees. To determine the total payments made to each employee in excess of the FUTA wage base, the payments exempt from FUTA tax and the FUTA wage base must be subtracted from total payments. These amounts are shown in parentheses.

Employees	A	B	C
Total payments to employees	$44,000	$8,000	$16,000
Payments exempt from FUTA tax	(2,000)	(500)	(2,000)
FUTA wage base	(7,000)	(7,000)	(7,000)
	$35,000	$ 500	$ 7,000
Total of payments made to each employee in excess of the FUTA wage base. You would enter this amount on line 5.			$42,500

If you are a successor employer . . . When you figure the payments made to each employee in excess of the FUTA wage base, you may include the payments that the predecessor made to the employees who continue to work for you **only** if the predecessor was an employer for FUTA tax purposes resulting in the predecessor being required to file Form 940.

Example for successor employers:

During the calendar year, the predecessor employer paid $5,000 to Employee A. You acquired the predecessor's business. After the acquisition, you employed Employee A and paid Employee A an additional $3,000 in wages. None of the amounts paid to Employee A were payments exempt from FUTA tax.

$5,000	Wages paid by predecessor employer
+ 3,000	Wages paid by you
$8,000	Total payments to Employee A. You would include this amount on line 3.
$8,000	Total payments to Employee A
− 7,000	FUTA wage base
$1,000	Payments made to Employee A in excess of the FUTA wage base.
$1,000	Payments made to Employee A in excess of the FUTA wage base.
+ 5,000	Taxable FUTA wages paid by predecessor employer
$6,000	You would include this amount on line 5.

6. Subtotal

To figure your subtotal, add the amounts on lines 4 and 5 and enter the result on line 6.

$$
\begin{array}{r}
\text{line 4} \\
+ \text{ line 5} \\
\hline
\text{line 6}
\end{array}
$$

7. Total Taxable FUTA Wages

To figure your total taxable FUTA wages, subtract line 6 from line 3 and enter the result on line 7.

$$
\begin{array}{r}
\text{line 3} \\
- \text{ line 6} \\
\hline
\text{line 7}
\end{array}
$$

8. FUTA Tax Before Adjustments

To figure your total FUTA tax before adjustments, multiply line 7 by .006 and then enter the result on line 8.

$$
\begin{array}{r}
\text{line 7} \\
\times \text{ .006} \\
\hline
\text{line 8}
\end{array}
$$

Part 3: Determine Your Adjustments

If any line in Part 3 doesn't apply, leave it blank.

9. If ALL of the Taxable FUTA Wages You Paid Were Excluded from State Unemployment Tax. . .

 Line 9 doesn't apply to FUTA wages on which you paid no state unemployment tax only because the state assigned you a tax rate of zero percent.

If all of the taxable FUTA wages you paid were excluded from state unemployment tax, multiply line 7 by .054 and enter the result on line 9.

$$
\begin{array}{r}
\text{line 7} \\
\times \text{ .054} \\
\hline
\text{line 9}
\end{array}
$$

If you weren't required to pay state unemployment tax because all of the wages you paid were excluded from state unemployment tax, you must pay FUTA tax at the 6.0% (.060) rate. For example, if your state unemployment tax law excludes wages paid to corporate officers or employees in specific occupations, and the only wages you paid were to corporate officers or employees in those specific occupations, you must pay FUTA tax on those wages at the full FUTA rate of 6.0% (.060). When you figured the FUTA tax before adjustments on line 8, it was based on the maximum allowable credit (5.4%) for state unemployment tax payments. Because you didn't pay state unemployment tax, you don't have a credit and must figure this adjustment.

If line 9 applies to you, lines 10 and 11 don't apply to you. Therefore, leave lines 10 and 11 blank. Don't fill out the worksheet in these instructions. Complete Schedule A (Form 940) only if you are a multi-state employer.

10. If SOME of the Taxable FUTA Wages You Paid Were Excluded From State Unemployment Tax, or You Paid any State Unemployment Tax Late...

You must fill out the worksheet on the next page if:
• Some of the taxable FUTA wages you paid were excluded from state unemployment, or
• Any of your payments of state unemployment tax were late.
The worksheet takes you step by step through the process of figuring your credit. At the end of the worksheet you'll find an example of how to use it. Don't complete the worksheet if line 9 applied to you (see the instructions for line 9 above).

Before you can properly fill out the worksheet, you will need to gather the following information.
• Taxable FUTA wages (Form 940, line 7).
• Taxable state unemployment wages (state and federal wage bases may differ).
• The experience rates assigned to you by the states where you paid wages.
• The amount of state unemployment taxes you paid on time. (*On time* means that you paid the state unemployment taxes by the due date for filing Form 940.)
• The amount of state unemployment taxes you paid late. (*Late* means after the due date for filing Form 940.)

 Don't include any penalties, interest, or unemployment taxes deducted from your employees' pay in the amount of state unemployment taxes. Also, don't include as state unemployment taxes any special administrative taxes or voluntary contributions you paid to get a lower assigned experience rate or any surcharges, excise taxes, or employment and training taxes. (These items are generally listed as separate items on the state's quarterly wage report.)

For line 3 of the worksheet:
• If any of the experience rates assigned to you were less than 5.4% for any part of the calendar year, you must list each assigned experience rate separately on the worksheet.
• If you were assigned six or more experience rates that were less than 5.4% for any part of the calendar year, you must use another sheet to figure the additional credits and then include those additional credits in your line 3 total.

After you complete the worksheet, enter the amount from line 7 of the worksheet on Form 940, line 10. **Don't attach the worksheet to your Form 940.** Keep it with your records.

Worksheet—Line 10

Before you begin: Read the *Example* on the next page before completing this worksheet.

Use this worksheet to figure your credit if:

- ✓ Some of the wages you paid were excluded from state unemployment tax, OR
- ✓ You paid any state unemployment tax late.

For this worksheet, **don't round your figures**.

Before you can properly fill out this worksheet, you must gather this information:

- ■ Taxable FUTA wages (Form 940, line 7)
- ■ Taxable state unemployment wages
- ■ The experience rates assigned to you by the states where you paid wages
- ■ The amount of state unemployment taxes you paid on time. (*On time* means that you paid the state unemployment taxes by the due date for filing Form 940.) Include any state unemployment taxes you paid on nonemployees who were treated as employees by your state unemployment agency.
- ■ The amount of state unemployment taxes you paid late. (*Late* means after the due date for filing Form 940.)

1. **Maximum allowable credit** — Enter Form 940, line 7 _____ . x .054 on line 1   1. _____ .
(Form 940, line 7 x .054 = line 1).

2. **Credit for timely state unemployment tax payments — How much did you pay on time?**   2. _____ .

- • If line 2 is **equal to** or **more than** line 1, **STOP here**. (STOP) You have completed the worksheet. Leave Form 940, line 10 blank.
- • If line 2 is **less than** line 1, continue this worksheet.

3. **Additional credit — Were ALL of your assigned experience rates 5.4% or more?**

- • **If yes**, enter zero on line 3. Then go to line 4 of this worksheet.
- • **If no**, fill out the computations below. List ONLY THOSE STATES for which your assigned experience rate for any part of the calendar year was less than 5.4%.

State	Computation rate The difference between 5.4% (.054) and your assigned experience rate (.054 – .XXX (assigned experience rate) = computation rate)		Taxable state unemployment wages at assigned experience rate		Additional Credit
1. _____	_____ . _____	x	_____ .	=	_____ .
2. _____	_____ . _____	x	_____ .	=	_____ .
3. _____	_____ . _____	x	_____ .	=	_____ .
4. _____	_____ . _____	x	_____ .	=	_____ .
5. _____	_____ . _____	x	_____ .	=	_____ .

If you need more lines, use another sheet and include those additional credits in the total.   **Total** _____ .

Enter the total on line 3.

3. _____ .

4. **Subtotal** (line 2 + line 3 = line 4)   4. _____ .

- • If line 4 is equal to or more than line 1, **STOP here**. (STOP) You have completed the worksheet. Leave Form 940, line 10 blank.
- • If line 4 is less than line 1, continue this worksheet.

5. **Credit for paying state unemployment taxes late:**

5a. **What is your remaining allowable credit?** (line 1 – line 4 = 5a)   5a. _____ .

5b. **How much state unemployment tax did you pay late?**   5b. _____ .

5c. **Which is smaller, line 5a or line 5b?** Enter the smaller number here.   5c. _____ .

5d. **Your allowable credit for paying state unemployment taxes late** (line 5c x .90 = line 5d)   5d. _____ .

6. **Your FUTA credit** (line 4 + line 5d = line 6)   6. _____ .

- • If line 6 is equal to or more than line 1, **STOP here**. (STOP) You have completed the worksheet. Leave Form 940, line 10 blank.
- • If line 6 is less than line 1, continue this worksheet.

7. **Your adjustment** (line 1 – line 6 = line 7)   Enter line 7 from this worksheet on Form 940, line 10.   7. _____ .

Don't attach this worksheet to your Form 940. Keep it for your records.

Example for using the worksheet:

Employee A and Employee B are corporate officers whose wages are excluded from state unemployment tax in your state. Employee C's wages aren't excluded from state unemployment tax. During 2015, you paid $44,000 to Employee A, $22,000 to Employee B, and $16,000 to Employee C. Your state's wage base is $8,000. You paid some state unemployment tax on time, some late, and some remains unpaid.

Here are the records:

Total taxable FUTA wages (Form 940, line 7)	$21,000.00
Taxable state unemployment wages	$ 8,000.00
Experience rate for 2015	.041(4.1%)
State unemployment tax paid on time	$100.00
State unemployment tax paid late	$78.00
State unemployment tax not paid	$150.00

1. Maximum allowable credit

$21,000.00 (Form 940, line 7)
x .054 (maximum credit rate)
——————————
$1,134.00   **1.** $1,134.00

2. Credit for timely state unemployment tax payments   **2.** $100.00

3. Additional credit   **3.** $104.00

.054 (maximum credit rate) $8,000
− .041 (your experience rate)   x .013
——————————————————
.013 (your computation rate) $104.00

4. Subtotal (line 2 + line 3)   **4.** $204.00

$100
+ 104
————
$204

5. Credit for paying state unemployment taxes late

5a. **Remaining allowable credit: (line 1 - line 4)**   **5a.** $930.00

$1,134.00
− 204.00
—————
$930.00

5b. **State unemployment tax paid late:**   **5b.** $78.00

5c. **Which is smaller? Line 5a or line 5b?**   **5c.** $78.00

5d. **Allowable credit (for paying late)**   **5d.** $70.20

$78.00
x .90
————
$70.20

6. Your FUTA credit (line 4 + line 5d)   **6.** $274.20

$204.00
+ 70.20
—————
$274.20

7. Your adjustment (line 1 - line 6)   **7.** $859.80

$1,134.00
− 274.20
—————
$859.80 **You would enter this amount on Form 940, line 10.**

11. If Credit Reduction Applies . . .

If you paid FUTA taxable wages that were also subject to state unemployment taxes in any states that are subject to credit reduction, enter the total amount from Schedule A (Form 940) on Form 940, line 11. However, if you entered an amount on line 9 because all the FUTA taxable wages you paid were excluded from state unemployment tax, skip line 11 and go to line 12.

Part 4: Determine Your FUTA Tax and Balance Due or Overpayment

If any line in Part 4 doesn't apply, leave it blank.

12. Total FUTA Tax After Adjustments

Add the amounts shown on lines 8, 9, 10, and 11, and enter the result on line 12.

line 8
line 9
line 10
+ line 11
————————
line 12

 If line 9 is greater than zero, lines 10 and 11 must be zero because they don't apply.

13. FUTA Tax Deposited for the Year

Enter the amount of FUTA tax that you deposited for the year, including any overpayment that you applied from a prior year.

14. Balance Due

If line 13 is less than line 12, enter the difference on line 14.

line 12
− line 13
————————
line 14

If line 14 is:
- More than $500, you must deposit your tax. See *When Must You Deposit Your FUTA Tax,* earlier.
- $500 or less, you can deposit your tax, pay your tax with a credit card or debit card, pay your tax by EFW if filing electronically, or pay your tax by check or money order with your return. For more information on electronic payment options, visit the IRS website at *www.irs.gov/payments*.
- Less than $1, you don't have to pay it.

 If you don't deposit as required and pay any balance due with Form 940, you may be subject to a penalty.

If you pay by EFT, credit card, or debit card, file your return using the *Without a payment* address under *Where Do You File.* Don't file Form 940-V, Payment Voucher.

What if you can't pay in full? If you can't pay the full amount of tax you owe, you can apply for an installment agreement online. You can apply for an installment agreement online if:
- You can't pay the full amount shown on line 14,
- The total amount you owe is $25,000 or less, and
- You can pay the liability in full in 24 months.

To apply using the Online Payment Agreement Application, go to IRS.gov, click on *Tools*, then click on *Online Payment Agreement*.

Under an installment agreement, you can pay what you owe in monthly installments. There are certain conditions you must meet to enter into and maintain an installment agreement, such as paying the liability within 24 months, and making all required deposits and timely filing tax returns during the length of the agreement.

If your installment agreement is accepted, you will be charged a fee and you will be subject to penalties and interest on the amount of tax not paid by the due date of the return.

15. Overpayment

If line 13 is more than line 12, enter the difference on line 15.

$$
\begin{array}{r}
\text{line 13} \\
- \text{line 12} \\
\hline
\text{line 15}
\end{array}
$$

If you deposited more than the FUTA tax due for the year, you may choose to have us either:
- Apply the refund to your next return, or
- Send you a refund.

Check the appropriate box in line 15 to tell us which option you select. If you don't check either box, we will automatically refund your overpayment, less any amount we apply to any past due tax account shown in our records under your EIN.

If line 15 is less than $1, we will send you a refund or apply it to your next return only if you ask for it in writing.

Part 5: Report Your FUTA Tax Liability by Quarter Only if Line 12 is More Than $500

Fill out Part 5 **only** if line 12 is more than $500. If line 12 is $500 or less, leave Part 5 blank and go to Part 6.

16. Report the Amount of Your FUTA Tax Liability for Each Quarter

Enter the amount of your FUTA tax liability for each quarter on lines 16a–d. Don't enter the amount you deposited. If you had no liability for a quarter, leave the line blank.

    16a. 1st quarter (January 1 to March 31)
    16b. 2nd quarter (April 1 to June 30)
    16c. 3rd quarter (July 1 to September 30)
    16d. 4th quarter (October 1 to December 31)

To figure your FUTA tax liability for the fourth quarter, complete Form 940 through line 12. Then copy the amount from line 12 onto line 17. Lastly, subtract the sum of lines 16a through 16c from line 17 and enter the result on line 16d.

Example:
You paid wages on March 28 and your FUTA tax on those wages was $200. You weren't required to make a deposit for the 1st quarter because your accumulated FUTA tax was $500 or less. You paid additional wages on June 28 and your FUTA tax on those wages was $400. Because your accumulated FUTA tax for the 1st and 2nd quarters exceeded $500, you were required to make a deposit of $600 by July 31.

You would enter $200 in line 16a because your liability for the 1st quarter is $200. You would also enter $400 in line 16b to show your 2nd quarter liability.

 In years when there are credit reduction states, you must include liabilities owed for credit reduction with your fourth quarter deposit. You may deposit the anticipated extra liability throughout the year, but it isn't due until the due date for the deposit for the fourth quarter, and the associated liability should be recorded as being incurred in the fourth quarter.

17. Total Tax Liability for the Year

Your total tax liability for the year **must equal** line 12. Copy the amount from line 12 onto line 17.

Part 6: May We Speak With Your Third-Party Designee?

If you want to allow an employee, your paid tax preparer, or another person to discuss your Form 940 with the IRS, check the "Yes" box. Then enter the name and phone number of the person you choose as your designee. Be sure to give us the specific name of a person — not the name of the firm that prepared your tax return.

Have your designee select a five-digit Personal Identification Number (PIN) that he or she must use as identification when talking to the IRS about your form.

By checking "Yes," you authorize us to talk to your designee about any questions that we may have while we process your return. Your authorization applies only to this form, for this year; it doesn't apply to other forms or other tax years.

You are authorizing your designee to:
- Give us any information that is missing from your return,
- Ask us for information about processing your return, and
- Respond to certain IRS notices that you have shared with your designee about math errors and in preparing your return. We won't send notices to your designee.

You aren't authorizing your designee to:
- Receive any refund check,
- Bind you to anything (including additional tax liability), or
- Otherwise represent you before the IRS.

The authorization will automatically expire 1 year after the due date for filing your Form 940 (regardless of extensions). If you or your designee want to end the authorization before it expires, write to the IRS office for your location using the *Without a payment* address under *Where Do You File.*

If you want to expand your designee's authorization or if you want us to send your designee copies of your notices, see Pub. 947.

Part 7: Sign Here (Approved Roles)

You MUST Fill Out Both Pages of This Form and SIGN It

Failure to sign will delay the processing of your return.

On page 2 in Part 7, sign and print your name and title. Then enter the date and the best daytime telephone number, including area code, where we can reach you if we have any questions.

Who Must Sign Form 940?

The following persons are authorized to sign the return for each type of business entity.
- **Sole proprietorship**—The individual who owns the business.
- **Partnership (including a limited liability company (LLC) treated as a partnership) or unincorporated organization**— A responsible and duly authorized partner, member, or officer having knowledge of its affairs.

- **Corporation (including an LLC treated as a corporation)** —The president, vice president, or other principal officer duly authorized to sign.
- **Single member LLC treated as a disregarded entity for federal income tax purposes**—The owner of the LLC or a principal officer duly authorized to sign.
- **Trust or estate**—The fiduciary.

Form 940 may also be signed by a duly authorized agent of the taxpayer if a valid power of attorney or reporting agent authorization (Form 8655) has been filed.

Alternative signature method. Corporate officers or duly authorized agents may sign Form 940 by rubber stamp, mechanical device, or computer software program. For details and required documentation, see Rev. Proc. 2005-39, 2005-28 I.R.B. 82, available at *www.irs.gov/irb/2005-28_IRB/ar16.html*.

Paid preparers. A paid preparer must sign Form 940 and provide the information in the *Paid Preparer Use Only* section of Part 7 if the preparer was paid to prepare Form 940 and isn't an employee of the filing entity. Paid preparers must sign paper returns with a manual signature. The preparer must give you a copy of the return in addition to the copy to be filed with IRS.

If you are a paid preparer, enter your Preparer Tax Identification Number (PTIN) in the space provided. Include your complete address. If you work for a firm, write the firm's name and the EIN of the firm. You can apply for a PTIN online or by filing Form W-12. For more information about applying for a PTIN online, visit the IRS website at *www.irs.gov/ptin*. You can't use your PTIN in place of the EIN of the tax preparation firm.

Generally, don't complete the Paid Preparer Use Only section if you are filing the return as a reporting agent and have a valid Form 8655 on file with the IRS. However, a reporting agent must complete this section if the reporting agent offered legal advice, for example, by advising the client on determining whether its workers are employees or independent contractors for Federal tax purposes.

Privacy Act and Paperwork Reduction Act Notice We ask for the information on Form 940 to carry out the Internal Revenue laws of the United States. We need it to figure and collect the right amount of tax. Subtitle C, Employment Taxes, of the Internal Revenue Code imposes unemployment tax under the Federal Unemployment Tax Act. Form 940 is used to determine the amount of the taxes that you owe. Section 6011 requires you to provide the requested information if the tax is applicable to you. Section 6109 requires you to provide your identification number. If you fail to provide this information in a timely manner, or provide false or fraudulent information, you may be subject to penalties.

You aren't required to provide the information requested on a form that is subject to the Paperwork Reduction Act unless the form displays a valid OMB control number. Books or records relating to a form or instructions must be retained as long as their contents may become material in the administration of any Internal Revenue law.

Generally, tax returns and return information are confidential, as required by section 6103. However, section 6103 allows or requires the IRS to disclose or give the information shown on your tax return to others as described in the Code. For example, we may disclose your tax information to the Department of Justice for civil and criminal litigation, and to cities, states, the District of Columbia, and U.S. commonwealths and possessions to administer their tax laws. We may also disclose this information to other countries under a tax treaty, to federal and state agencies to enforce federal nontax criminal laws, or to federal law enforcement and intelligence agencies to combat terrorism.

If you have comments concerning the accuracy of these time estimates or suggestions for making these forms simpler, we would be happy to hear from you. You can send us comments from *www.irs.gov/formspubs*. Click on *More Information* and then click on *Give us feedback*. Or you can send your comments to Internal Revenue Service, Tax Forms and Publications Division, 1111 Constitution Avenue, NW, IR-6526, Washington, DC 20224. Don't send Form 940 to this address. Instead, see *Where Do You File*, earlier.

Estimated average times

The time needed to complete and file this form will vary depending on individual circumstances. The estimated average time is:		
Form	Recordkeeping	Preparing, copying, assembling, and sending the form to the IRS
Schedule A (Form 940)	16 hrs., 1 min.	15 min.
Worksheet (Form 940)	1 hr., 41 min.	21 min.

Form **941 for 2016:** **Employer's QUARTERLY Federal Tax Return**
(Rev. January 2016)   Department of the Treasury — Internal Revenue Service

950114

OMB No. 1545-0029

Employer identification number (EIN) ☐☐ – ☐☐☐☐☐☐☐

Name *(not your trade name)*

Trade name *(if any)*

Address
Number   Street   Suite or room number
City   State   ZIP code
Foreign country name   Foreign province/county   Foreign postal code

DRAFT AS
June 17, 2015

Report for this Quarter of 2016
(Check one.)

☐ **1:** January, February, March

☐ **2:** April, May, June

☐ **3:** July, August, September

☐ **4:** October, November, December

Instructions and prior year forms are available at *www.irs.gov/form941*.

Read the separate instructions before you complete Form 941. Type or print within the boxes.

Part 1: Answer these questions for this quarter.

1   Number of employees who received wages, tips, or other compensation for the pay period including: *Mar. 12* (Quarter 1), *June 12* (Quarter 2), *Sept. 12* (Quarter 3), or *Dec. 12* (Quarter 4)   **1** ☐

2   Wages, tips, and other compensation . . . .   **2** ☐ .

3   Federal income tax withheld from wages, tips, and other compensation . . . . . .   **3** ☐ .

4   If no wages, tips, and other compensation are subject to social security or Medicare tax   ☐ Check and go to line 6.

		Column 1		Column 2
5a	Taxable social security wages . .	☐ .	× .124 =	☐ .
5b	Taxable social security tips . . .	☐ .	× .124 =	☐ .
5c	Taxable Medicare wages & tips. .	☐ .	× .029 =	☐ .
5d	Taxable wages & tips subject to Additional Medicare Tax withholding	☐ .	× .009 =	☐ .

5e   Add Column 2 from lines 5a, 5b, 5c, and 5d . . . .   **5e** ☐ .

5f   Section 3121(q) Notice and Demand—Tax due on unreported tips (see instructions) . .   **5f** ☐ .

6   Total taxes before adjustments. Add lines 3, 5e, and 5f . . . .   **6** ☐ .

7   Current quarter's adjustment for fractions of cents . . . .   **7** ☐ .

8   Current quarter's adjustment for sick pay . . . .   **8** ☐ .

9   Current quarter's adjustments for tips and group-term life insurance . . . .   **9** ☐ .

10   Total taxes after adjustments. Combine lines 6 through 9 . . . .   **10** ☐ .

11   Total deposits for this quarter, including overpayment applied from a prior quarter and overpayments applied from Form 941-X, 941-X (PR), 944-X, or 944-X (SP) filed in the current quarter . . . .   **11** ☐ .

12   Balance due. If line 10 is more than line 11, enter the difference and see instructions . . .   **12** ☐ .

13   Overpayment. If line 11 is more than line 10, enter the difference ☐ .   Check one: ☐ Apply to next return.   ☐ Send a refund.

▶ **You MUST complete both pages of Form 941 and SIGN it.**

Next ▶

For Privacy Act and Paperwork Reduction Act Notice, see the back of the Payment Voucher.   Cat. No. 17001Z   Form **941** (Rev. 1-2016)

Name *(not your trade name)* | **Employer identification number (EIN)**

Part 2: Tell us about your deposit schedule and tax liability for this quarter.

If you are unsure about whether you are a monthly schedule depositor or a semiweekly schedule depositor, see section 11 of Pub. 15.

14 Check one: ☐ Line 10 on this return is less than $2,500 or line 10 on the return for the prior quarter was less than $2,500, and you did not incur a $100,000 next-day deposit obligation during the current quarter. If line 10 for the prior quarter was less than $2,500 but line 10 on this return is $100,000 or more, you must provide a record of your federal tax liability. If you are a monthly schedule depositor, complete the deposit schedule below; if you are a semiweekly schedule depositor, attach Schedule B (Form 941). Go to Part 3.

☐ **You were a monthly schedule depositor for the entire quarter.** Enter your tax liability for each month and total liability for the quarter, then go to Part 3.

Tax liability: Month 1 [.   ]

Month 2 [.   ]

Month 3 [.   ]

Total liability for quarter [.   ] Total must equal line 10.

☐ **You were a semiweekly schedule depositor for any part of this quarter.** Complete Schedule B (Form 941), Report of Tax Liability for Semiweekly Schedule Depositors, and attach it to Form 941.

Part 3: Tell us about your business. If a question does NOT apply to your business, leave it blank.

15 If your business has closed or you stopped paying wages . . . . ☐ Check here, and

enter the final date you paid wages [/   /   ] .

16 If you are a seasonal employer and you do not have to file a return for every quarter of the year . . ☐ Check here.

Part 4: May we speak with your third-party designee?

Do you want to allow an employee, a paid tax preparer, or another person to discuss this return with the IRS? See the instructions for details.

☐ Yes. Designee's name and phone number [   ] [   ]

Select a 5-digit Personal Identification Number (PIN) to use when talking to the IRS. ☐ ☐ ☐ ☐ ☐

☐ No.

Part 5: Sign here. You MUST complete both pages of Form 941 and SIGN it.

Under penalties of perjury, I declare that I have examined this return, including accompanying schedules and statements, and to the best of my knowledge and belief, it is true, correct, and complete. Declaration of preparer (other than taxpayer) is based on all information of which preparer has any knowledge.

✗ **Sign your name here** [   ]

Print your name here [   ]

Print your title here [   ]

Date [/   /   ]

Best daytime phone [   ]

Paid Preparer Use Only

Check if you are self-employed . . . ☐

Preparer's name	[ ]	PTIN	[ ]
Preparer's signature	[ ]	Date	[/ /]
Firm's name (or yours if self-employed)	[ ]	EIN	[ ]
Address	[ ]	Phone	[ ]
City	[ ]	State	[ ]	ZIP code	[ ]

Form 941-V,
Payment Voucher

Purpose of Form

Complete Form 941-V if you are making a payment with Form 941. We will use the completed voucher to credit your payment more promptly and accurately, and to improve our service to you.

Making Payments With Form 941

To avoid a penalty, make your payment with Form 941 **only if:**

• Your total taxes after adjustments for either the current quarter or the preceding quarter (Form 941, line 10) are less than $2,500, you didn't incur a $100,000 next-day deposit obligation during the current quarter, and you are paying in full with a timely filed return; or

• You are a monthly schedule depositor making a payment in accordance with the Accuracy of Deposits Rule. See section 11 of Pub. 15 for details. In this case, the amount of your payment may be $2,500 or more.

Otherwise, you must make deposits by electronic funds transfer. See section 11 of Pub. 15 for deposit instructions. Don't use Form 941-V to make federal tax deposits.

 Use Form 941-V when making any payment with Form 941. However, if you pay an amount with Form 941 that should have been deposited, you may be subject to a penalty. See Deposit Penalties *in section 11 of Pub. 15.*

Specific Instructions

Box 1—Employer identification number (EIN). If you don't have an EIN, you may apply for one online. Go to IRS.gov and type "EIN" in the search box. You may also apply for an EIN by faxing or mailing Form SS-4 to the IRS. If you haven't received your EIN by the due date of Form 941, write "Applied For" and the date you applied in this entry space.

Box 2—Amount paid. Enter the amount paid with Form 941.

Box 3—Tax period. Darken the circle identifying the quarter for which the payment is made. Darken only one circle.

Box 4—Name and address. Enter your name and address as shown on Form 941.

• Enclose your check or money order made payable to "United States Treasury." Be sure to enter your EIN, "Form 941," and the tax period on your check or money order. Don't send cash. Don't staple Form 941-V or your payment to Form 941 (or to each other).

• Detach Form 941-V and send it with your payment and Form 941 to the address in the Instructions for Form 941.

Note: You must also complete the entity information above Part 1 on Form 941.

✂ ▼ **Detach Here and Mail With Your Payment and Form 941.** ▼ ✂

Form **941-V** Department of the Treasury Internal Revenue Service	**Payment Voucher** ▶ **Don't staple this voucher or your payment to Form 941.**	OMB No. 1545-0029 20**16**

1 Enter your employer identification number (EIN).	2 **Enter the amount of your payment.** ▶ Make your check or money order payable to "**United States Treasury**"		Dollars	Cents

3 Tax Period		4 Enter your business name (individual name if sole proprietor).

○ 1st Quarter	○ 3rd Quarter	Enter your address.

○ 2nd Quarter	○ 4th Quarter	Enter your city, state, and ZIP code or your city, foreign country name, foreign province/county, and foreign postal code.

Privacy Act and Paperwork Reduction Act Notice.
We ask for the information on Form 941 to carry out the Internal Revenue laws of the United States. We need it to figure and collect the right amount of tax. Subtitle C, Employment Taxes, of the Internal Revenue Code imposes employment taxes on wages and provides for income tax withholding. Form 941 is used to determine the amount of taxes that you owe. Section 6011 requires you to provide the requested information if the tax is applicable to you. Section 6109 requires you to provide your identification number. If you fail to provide this information in a timely manner, or provide false or fraudulent information, you may be subject to penalties.

You aren't required to provide the information requested on a form that is subject to the Paperwork Reduction Act unless the form displays a valid OMB control number. Books and records relating to a form or its instructions must be retained as long as their contents may become material in the administration of any Internal Revenue law.

Generally, tax returns and return information are confidential, as required by section 6103. However, section 6103 allows or requires the IRS to disclose or give the information shown on your tax return to others as described in the Code. For example, we may disclose your tax information to the Department of Justice for civil and criminal litigation, and to cities, states, the District of Columbia, and U.S. commonwealths and possessions for use in administering their tax laws. We may also disclose this information to other countries under a tax treaty, to federal and state agencies to enforce federal nontax criminal laws, or to federal law enforcement and intelligence agencies to combat terrorism.

The time needed to complete and file Form 941 will vary depending on individual circumstances. The estimated average time is:

Recordkeeping	11 hr.
Learning about the law or the form	47 min.
Preparing, copying, assembling, and sending the form to the IRS	1 hr.

If you have comments concerning the accuracy of these time estimates or suggestions for making Form 941 simpler, we would be happy to hear from you. You can send us comments from *www.irs.gov/formspubs*. Click on *More Information* and then click on *Give us feedback*. Or you can send your comments to Internal Revenue Service, Tax Forms and Publications Division, 1111 Constitution Ave. NW, IR-6526, Washington, DC 20224. **Don't** send Form 941 to this address. Instead, see *Where Should You File?* in the Instructions for Form 941.

Instructions for Form 941

Department of the Treasury
Internal Revenue Service

(Rev. January 2016)

Employer's QUARTERLY Federal Tax Return

Section references are to the Internal Revenue Code unless otherwise noted.

Future Developments

For the latest information about developments related to Form 941 and its instructions, such as legislation enacted after they were published, go to *www.irs.gov/form941*.

What's New

Social security and Medicare tax for 2016. The social security tax rate is 6.2% each for the employee and employer, unchanged from 2015. The social security wage base limit is $XXX,XXX.

The Medicare tax rate is 1.45% each for the employee and employer, unchanged from 2015. There is no wage base limit for Medicare tax.

Social security and Medicare taxes apply to the wages of household workers you pay $X,XXX or more in cash or an equivalent form of compensation in 2016. Social security and Medicare taxes apply to election workers who are paid $X,XXX or more in cash or an equivalent form of compensation in 2016.

Reminders

COBRA premium assistance credit. Effective for tax periods beginning after December 31, 2013, the credit for COBRA premium assistance payments can't be claimed on Form 941. Instead, after filing your Form 941, file Form 941-X, Adjusted Employer's QUARTERLY Federal Tax Return or Claim for Refund, to claim the COBRA premium assistance credit. Filing a Form 941-X before filing a Form 941 for the quarter may result in errors or delays in processing your Form 941-X. For more information, visit IRS.gov and enter "COBRA" in the search box.

 If you are entitled to claim the COBRA premium assistance credit, but aren't otherwise required to file Form 941, file a Form 941 with -0- entered on line 12 before filing a Form 941-X to claim the credit.

Additional Medicare Tax withholding. In addition to withholding Medicare tax at 1.45%, you must withhold a 0.9% Additional Medicare Tax from wages you pay to an employee in excess of $200,000 in a calendar year. You are required to begin withholding Additional Medicare Tax in the pay period in which you pay wages in excess of $200,000 to an employee and continue to withhold it each pay period until the end of the calendar year. Additional Medicare Tax is only imposed on the employee. There is no employer share of Additional Medicare Tax. All wages that are subject to Medicare tax are subject to Additional Medicare Tax withholding if paid in excess of the $200,000 withholding threshold.

For more information on what wages are subject to Medicare tax, see the chart, *Special Rules for Various Types of Services and Payments*, in section 15 of Pub. 15, Employer's Tax Guide. For more information on Additional Medicare Tax, visit IRS.gov and enter "Additional Medicare Tax" in the search box.

Aggregate Form 941 filers. Agents must complete Schedule R (Form 941), Allocation Schedule for Aggregate Form 941 Filers, when filing an aggregate Form 941. Aggregate Forms 941 are filed by agents approved by the IRS under section 3504. To request approval to act as an agent for an employer, the agent files Form 2678 with the IRS.

Correcting a previously filed Form 941. If you discover an error on a previously filed Form 941, make the correction using Form 941-X. Form 941-X is filed separately from Form 941. For more information, see section 13 of Pub. 15 or visit IRS.gov and enter "correcting employment taxes" in the search box.

Employers can choose to file Forms 941 instead of Form 944. Employers that would otherwise be required to file Form 944, Employer's ANNUAL Federal Tax Return, can notify the IRS if they want to file quarterly Forms 941 instead of annual Form 944. To request to file quarterly Forms 941 to report your social security and Medicare taxes for the 2016 calendar year, you must either call the IRS at 1-800-829-4933 between January 1, 2016, and April 1, 2016, or send a written request postmarked between January 1, 2016, and March 15, 2016. After you contact the IRS, the IRS will send you a written notice that your filing requirement has been changed to Forms 941. You must receive written notice from the IRS to file Forms 941 instead of Form 944 before you may file these forms. If you don't receive this notice, you must file Form 944 for calendar year 2016. See Rev. Proc. 2009-51, 2009-45 I.R.B. 625, available at *www.irs.gov/irb/2009-45_IRB/ar12.html*.

Requesting to file Form 944 instead of Forms 941. If you are required to file Forms 941 but believe your employment taxes for the calendar year will be $1,000 or less, you may request to file Form 944 instead of Forms 941 by calling the IRS at 1-800-829-4933 between January 1, 2016, and April 1, 2016, or sending a written request postmarked between January 1, 2016, and March 15, 2016. After you contact the IRS, the IRS will send you a written notice that your filing requirement has been changed to Form 944. You must receive written notice from the IRS to file Form 944 instead of Forms 941 before you may file this form. If you don't receive this notice, you must file Forms 941 for calendar year 2016. See Rev. Proc. 2009-51, 2009-45 I.R.B. 625, available at *www.irs.gov/irb/2009-45_IRB/ar12.html*.

Federal tax deposits must be made by electronic funds transfer (EFT). You must use EFT to make all federal tax deposits. Generally, an EFT is made using the Electronic Federal Tax Payment System (EFTPS). If you don't want to use EFTPS, you can arrange for your tax professional, financial institution, payroll service, or other trusted third party to make electronic deposits on your behalf. Also, you may arrange for your financial institution to initiate a same-day wire payment on your behalf. EFTPS is a free service provided by the Department of Treasury. Services provided by your tax professional, financial institution, payroll service, or other third party may have a fee.

For more information on making federal tax deposits, see section 11 of Pub. 15. To get more information about EFTPS or to enroll in EFTPS, visit *www.eftps.gov*, or call 1-800-555-4477 or 1-800-733-4829 (TDD). Additional information about EFTPS is also available in Pub. 966.

 For an EFTPS deposit to be on time, you must submit the deposit by 8 p.m. Eastern time the day before the date the deposit is due.

Same-day wire payment option. If you fail to submit a deposit transaction on EFTPS by 8 p.m. Eastern time the day before the date a deposit is due, you can still make your deposit on time by using the Federal Tax Collection Service (FTCS). To use the same-day wire payment method, you will need to make arrangements with your financial institution ahead of time. Please check with your financial institution regarding availability, deadlines, and costs. Your financial institution may charge you a fee for payments made this way. To learn more about the information you will need to provide your financial institution to make a same-day wire payment, visit the IRS website at *www.irs.gov/payments* and click on *Same-day wire*.

Timeliness of federal tax deposits. If a deposit is required to be made on a day that isn't a business day, the deposit is considered timely if it is made by the close of the next business day. A business day is any day other than a Saturday, Sunday, or legal holiday. The term "legal holiday" for deposit purposes includes only those legal holidays in the District of Columbia. Legal holidays in the District of Columbia are provided in Pub. 15.

Electronic filing and payment. Now, more than ever before, businesses can enjoy the benefits of filing tax returns and paying their federal taxes electronically. Whether you rely on a tax professional or handle your own taxes, the IRS offers you convenient programs to make filing and paying easier. Spend less time and worry about taxes and more time running your business. Use e-file and EFTPS to your benefit.
• For e-file, visit the IRS website at *www.irs.gov/efile* for additional information.
• For EFTPS, visit *www.eftps.gov*, or call EFTPS Customer Service at 1-800-555-4477 or 1-800-733-4829 (TDD) for additional information.

 If you are filing your tax return or paying your federal taxes electronically, a valid employer identification number (EIN) is required at the time the return is filed or the payment is made. If a valid EIN isn't provided, the return or payment won't be processed. This may result in penalties.

Electronic funds withdrawal (EFW). If you file Form 941 electronically, you can e-file and e-pay (EFW) the balance due in a single step using tax preparation software or through a tax professional. However, don't use EFW to make federal tax deposits. For more information on paying your taxes using EFW, visit the IRS website at *www.irs.gov/payments*. A fee may be charged to file electronically.

Credit or debit card payments. Employers can pay the balance due shown on Form 941 by credit or debit card. Don't use a credit or debit card to make federal tax deposits. For more information on paying your taxes with a credit or debit card, visit the IRS website at *www.irs.gov/payments*.

Online payment agreement. You may be eligible to apply for an installment agreement online if you have a balance due when you file your return. For more information, see *What if you can't pay in full*, later.

Paid preparers must sign Form 941. Paid preparers must complete and sign the paid preparer's section of Form 941.

Outsourcing payroll duties. You are responsible to ensure that tax returns are filed and deposits and payments are made, even if you contract with a third party to perform these acts. You remain responsible if the third party fails to perform any required action. If you choose to outsource any of your payroll and related tax duties (that is, withholding, reporting, and paying over social security, Medicare, FUTA, and income taxes) to a third-party payer, such as a payroll service provider or reporting agent, visit IRS.gov and enter "outsourcing payroll duties" in the search box for helpful information on this topic.

Where can you get telephone help? For answers to your questions about completing Form 941 or tax deposit rules, you can call the IRS at 1-800-829-4933 or 1-800-829-4059 (TDD/TTY for persons who are deaf, hard of hearing, or have a speech disability), Monday–Friday from 7:00 a.m. to 7:00 p.m. local time (Alaska and Hawaii follow Pacific time).

Photographs of missing children. The IRS is a proud partner with the National Center for Missing and Exploited Children. Photographs of missing children selected by the Center may appear in instructions on pages that would otherwise be blank. You can help bring these children home by looking at the photographs and calling 1-800-THE-LOST (1-800-843-5678) if you recognize a child.

General Instructions:

Purpose of Form 941

These instructions give you some background information about Form 941. They tell you who must file Form 941, how to complete it line by line, and when and where to file it.

If you want more in-depth information about payroll tax topics relating to Form 941, see Pub. 15 or visit IRS.gov and enter "employment taxes" in the search box.

Federal law requires you, as an employer, to withhold certain taxes from your employees' pay. Each time you pay wages, you must withhold – or take out of your employees' pay – certain amounts for federal income tax, social security tax, and Medicare tax. You must also withhold Additional Medicare Tax from wages you pay to an employee in excess of $200,000 in a calendar year. Under the withholding system, taxes withheld from your employees are credited to your employees in payment of their tax liabilities.

Federal law also requires you to pay any liability for the employer's portion of social security and Medicare taxes. This portion of social security and Medicare taxes isn't withheld from employees.

Who Must File Form 941?

Use Form 941 to report the following amounts.
• Wages you have paid.
• Tips your employees have received.
• Federal income tax you withheld.
• Both the employer's and the employee's share of social security and Medicare taxes.

Instructions for Form 941 (Rev. 1-2016)

- Additional Medicare Tax withheld from employees.
- Current quarter's adjustments to social security and Medicare taxes for fractions of cents, sick pay, tips, and group-term life insurance.

Don't use Form 941 to report backup withholding or income tax withholding on nonpayroll payments such as pensions, annuities, and gambling winnings. Report these types of withholding on Form 945, Annual Return of Withheld Federal Income Tax.

After you file your first Form 941, you must file a return for each quarter, even if you have no taxes to report, unless you filed a final return or one of the exceptions listed next applies.

Exceptions

Special rules apply to some employers.
- **Seasonal employers** don't have to file a Form 941 for quarters in which they have no tax liability because they have paid no wages. To tell the IRS that you won't file a return for one or more quarters during the year, check the box on line 16 every quarter you file Form 941. See section 12 of Pub. 15 for more information.
- Employers of **household employees** don't usually file Form 941. See Pub. 926 and Schedule H (Form 1040) for more information.
- Employers of **farm employees** don't usually file Form 941. See Form 943 and Pub. 51 for more information.

 If none of the above exceptions applies and you haven't filed a final return, you must file Form 941 each quarter even if you didn't pay wages during the quarter. Use IRS e-file, if possible.

What if You Reorganize or Close Your Business?

If You Sell or Transfer Your Business . . .

If you sell or transfer your business, you and the new owner must each file a Form 941 for the quarter in which the transfer occurred. Report only the wages you paid.

When two businesses merge, the continuing firm must file a return for the quarter in which the change took place and the other firm should file a final return.

Changing from one form of business to another—such as from a sole proprietorship to a partnership or corporation—is considered a transfer. If a transfer occurs, you may need a new EIN. See section 1 of Pub. 15. Attach a statement to your return with:
- The new owner's name (or the new name of the business);
- Whether the business is now a sole proprietorship, partnership, or corporation;
- The kind of change that occurred (a sale or transfer);
- The date of the change; and
- The name of the person keeping the payroll records and the address where those records will be kept.

If Your Business Has Closed . . .

If you go out of business or stop paying wages to your employees, you must file a final return. To tell the IRS that Form 941 for a particular quarter is your final return, check the box on line 15 and enter the date you last paid wages. Also attach a statement to your return showing the name of the person keeping the payroll records and the address where those records will be kept.

Instructions for Form 941 (Rev. 1-2016)

See the General Instructions for Forms W-2 and W-3 for information about earlier dates for the expedited furnishing and filing of Forms W-2, Wage and Tax Statement, when a final Form 941 is filed.

If you participated in a statutory merger or consolidation, or qualify for predecessor-successor status due to an acquisition, you should generally file Schedule D (Form 941), Report of Discrepancies Caused by Acquisitions, Statutory Mergers, or Consolidations. See the Instructions for Schedule D (Form 941) to determine whether you should file Schedule D (Form 941) and when you should file it.

When Must You File?

File your initial Form 941 for the quarter in which you first paid wages that are subject to social security and Medicare taxes or subject to federal income tax withholding. See the table titled *When To File Form 941*, later.

Then you must file for every quarter after that—every 3 months—even if you have no taxes to report, unless you are a seasonal employer or are filing your final return. See *Seasonal employers* and *If Your Business Has Closed* above.

File Form 941 only once for each quarter. If you filed electronically, don't file a paper Form 941. For more information about filing Form 941 electronically, see *Electronic filing and payment*, earlier.

When To File Form 941

Your Form 941 is due by the last day of the month that follows the end of the quarter.		
The Quarter Includes . . .	**Quarter Ends**	**Form 941 Is Due**
1. January, February, March	March 31	April 30
2. April, May, June	June 30	July 31
3. July, August, September	September 30	October 31
4. October, November, December	December 31	January 31

For example, you generally must report wages you pay during the first quarter—which is January through March—by April 30. If you made timely deposits in full payment of your taxes for the quarter, you may file by the 10th day of the second month that follows the end of the quarter. For example, you may file Form 941 by May 10 if you made timely deposits in full payment of your taxes for the first quarter.

If we receive Form 941 after the due date, we will treat Form 941 as filed on time if the envelope containing Form 941 is properly addressed, contains sufficient postage, and is postmarked by the U.S. Postal Service on or before the due date, or sent by an IRS-designated private delivery service on or before the due date. If you don't follow these guidelines, we generally will consider Form 941 filed when it is actually received. See Pub. 15 for more information on IRS-designated private delivery services.

If any due date for filing falls on a Saturday, Sunday, or legal holiday, you may file your return on the next business day.

How Should You Complete Form 941?

Type or print your EIN, name, and address in the spaces provided. Also enter your name and EIN on the top of page 2.

-3-

Don't use your social security number (SSN) or individual taxpayer identification number (ITIN). Generally, enter the business (legal) name you used when you applied for your EIN on Form SS-4. For example, if you are a sole proprietor, enter "Haleigh Smith" on the "Name" line and "Haleigh's Cycles" on the "Trade name" line. Leave the "Trade name" line blank if it is the same as your "Name."

Employer identification number (EIN). To make sure businesses comply with federal tax laws, the IRS monitors tax filings and payments by using a numerical system to identify taxpayers. A unique nine-digit EIN is assigned to all corporations, partnerships, and some sole proprietors. Businesses needing an EIN must apply for a number and use it throughout the life of the business on all tax returns, payments, and reports.

Your business should have only one EIN. If you have more than one and aren't sure which one to use, write to the IRS office where you file your returns (using the *Without a payment* address under *Where Should You File*, later) or call the IRS at 1-800-829-4933.

If you don't have an EIN, you may apply for one online. Go to IRS.gov and enter "EIN" in the search box. You may also apply for an EIN by faxing or mailing Form SS-4 to the IRS. If you haven't received your EIN by the due date of Form 941, write "Applied For" and the date you applied in this entry space.

 If you are filing your tax return electronically, a valid EIN is required at the time the return is filed. If a valid EIN isn't provided, the return won't be accepted. This may result in penalties.

 Always be sure the EIN on the form you file exactly matches the EIN the IRS assigned to your business. Don't use your SSN or ITIN on forms that ask for an EIN. Filing a Form 941 with an incorrect EIN or using another business's EIN may result in penalties and delays in processing your return.

If you change your business name, business address, or responsible party... Notify the IRS immediately if you change your business name, business address, or responsible party.
- Write to the IRS office where you file your returns (using the *Without a payment* address under *Where Should You File*, later) to notify the IRS of any business name change. See Pub.1635 to see if you need to apply for a new EIN.
- Complete and mail Form 8822-B to notify the IRS of a business address or responsible party change. Don't mail Form 8822-B with your Form 941. For a definition of "responsible party" see the Form 8822-B instructions.

Check the Box for the Quarter

Under "Report for this Quarter of 2016" at the top of Form 941, check the appropriate box of the quarter for which you are filing. Make sure the quarter checked is the same as shown on any attached Schedule B (Form 941), Report of Tax Liability for Semiweekly Schedule Depositors.

Completing and Filing Form 941

Make entries on Form 941 as follows to enable accurate scanning and processing.
- Use 10-point Courier font (if possible) for all entries if you are typing or using a computer to complete your form. Portable Document Format (PDF) forms on IRS.gov have fillable fields with acceptable font specifications.

- Don't enter dollar signs and decimal points. Commas are optional. Enter dollars to the left of the preprinted decimal point and cents to the right of it.
- Leave blank any data field (except lines 1, 2, and 10) with a value of zero.
- Enter negative amounts using a minus sign (if possible). Otherwise, use parentheses.
- Enter your name and EIN on all pages and attachments.
- Staple multiple sheets in the upper left corner when filing.

Required Notice to Employees About the Earned Income Credit (EIC)

To notify employees about the EIC, you must give the employees one of the following items.
- Form W-2 which has the required information about the EIC on the back of Copy B.
- A substitute Form W-2 with the same EIC information on the back of the employee's copy that is on Copy B of Form W-2.
- Notice 797, Possible Federal Tax Refund Due to the Earned Income Credit (EIC).
- Your written statement with the same wording as Notice 797.

For more information, see section 10 of Pub. 15 and Pub. 596.

Reconciling Forms 941 and Form W-3

The IRS matches amounts reported on your four quarterly Forms 941 with Form W-2 amounts totaled on your yearly Form W-3, Transmittal of Wage and Tax Statements. If the amounts don't agree, you may be contacted by the IRS or the Social Security Administration (SSA). The following amounts are reconciled.
- Federal income tax withholding.
- Social security wages.
- Social security tips.
- Medicare wages and tips.

For more information, see section 12 of Pub. 15 and the Instructions for Schedule D (Form 941).

Where Should You File?

Where you file depends on whether you include a payment with Form 941.

If you are in . . .		Without a payment . . .	With a payment . . .
Connecticut	New Jersey	Department of the	Internal Revenue
Delaware	New York	Treasury	Service
District of	North Carolina	Internal Revenue	P.O. Box 804522
Columbia	Ohio	Service	Cincinnati, OH
Florida	Pennsylvania	Cincinnati, OH	45280-4522
Georgia	Rhode Island	45999-0005	
Illinois	South Carolina		
Indiana	Tennessee		
Kentucky	Vermont		
Maine	Virginia		
Maryland	West Virginia		
Massachusetts	Wisconsin		
Michigan			
New Hampshire			

Instructions for Form 941 (Rev. 1-2016)

If you are in . . .		Without a payment . . .	With a payment . . .
Alabama	Missouri	Department of the Treasury Internal Revenue Service Ogden, UT 84201-0005	Internal Revenue Service P.O. Box 37941 Hartford, CT 06176-7941
Alaska	Montana		
Arizona	Nebraska		
Arkansas	Nevada		
California	New Mexico		
Colorado	North Dakota		
Hawaii	Oklahoma		
Idaho	Oregon		
Iowa	South Dakota		
Kansas	Texas		
Louisiana	Utah		
Minnesota	Washington		
Mississippi	Wyoming		
No legal residence or principal place of business in any state		Internal Revenue Service P.O. Box 409101 Ogden, UT 84409	Internal Revenue Service P.O. Box 37941 Hartford, CT 06176-7941
Special filing addresses for exempt organizations; federal, state, and local governmental entities; and Indian tribal governmental entities; regardless of location		Department of the Treasury Internal Revenue Service Ogden, UT 84201-0005	Internal Revenue Service P.O. Box 37941 Hartford, CT 06176-7941

 Your filing address may have changed from that used to file your employment tax return in prior years. Don't send Form 941 or any payments to the SSA. Private delivery services can't deliver to P.O. boxes.

Depositing Your Taxes

 You must deposit all depository taxes electronically by EFT. For more information, see Federal tax deposits must be made by electronic funds transfer (EFT) *under* Reminders.

Must You Deposit Your Taxes?

You may have to deposit the federal income taxes you withheld and both the employer and employee social security taxes and Medicare taxes.

• **If your total taxes (line 10) are less than $2,500 for the current quarter or the preceding quarter, and you didn't incur a $100,000 next-day deposit obligation during the current quarter.** You don't have to make a deposit. To avoid a penalty, you must pay the amount in full with a timely filed return or you must deposit the amount timely. For more information on paying with a timely filed return, see the instructions for line 12, later. If you aren't sure your total tax liability for the current quarter will be less than $2,500 (and your liability for the preceding quarter wasn't less than $2,500), make deposits using the semiweekly or monthly rules so you won't be subject to failure to deposit penalties.

• **If your total taxes (line 10) are $2,500 or more for the current quarter and the preceding quarter.** You must make deposits according to your deposit schedule. See section 11 of Pub. 15 for information and rules about federal tax deposits.

You may reduce your deposits during the quarter by the amount of the COBRA premium assistance credit that will be reflected on your Form 941-X, only if you use the claim process and not the adjustment process to claim the COBRA premium assistance credit on your Form 941-X for the quarter.

The COBRA premium assistance credit is treated as a credit on the first day of the return period (that is, January 1, April 1, July 1, or October 1). However, because the credit is now claimed on Form 941-X filed after submission of the Form 941, an employer that reduces its required deposits in anticipation of the credit will receive a system-generated notice reflecting a balance due and associated penalties and interest, if applicable. The balance due, including any related penalties and interest, resulting from the reduction in deposits in anticipation of the credit will be abated when the credit is applied. Such abatement will generally occur without any further action from the employer.

Alternatively, to prevent triggering a system-generated balance due notice, the employer can make its deposits without a reduction in anticipation of the COBRA premium assistance credit and follow the ordinary procedures for filing a claim for refund or adjusted return using Form 941-X.

When Must You Deposit Your Taxes?

Determine if You Are a Monthly or Semiweekly Schedule Depositor for the Quarter

The IRS uses two different sets of deposit rules to determine when businesses must deposit their social security, Medicare, and withheld federal income taxes. These schedules tell you when a deposit is due after you have a payday.

Your deposit schedule isn't determined by how often you pay your employees. Your deposit schedule depends on the total tax liability you reported on Form 941 during the previous four-quarter lookback period (July 1 of the second preceding calendar year through June 30 of the preceding calendar year). See section 11 of Pub. 15 for details. If you filed Form 944 in either 2014 or 2015, your lookback period is the 2014 calendar year.

Before the beginning of each calendar year, determine which type of deposit schedule you must use.
• If you reported $50,000 or less in taxes during the lookback period, you are a **monthly schedule depositor**.
• If you reported more than $50,000 of taxes during the lookback period, you are a **semiweekly schedule depositor**.

 If you are a monthly schedule depositor and accumulate a $100,000 tax liability on any day during the deposit period, you become a semiweekly schedule depositor on the next day and remain so for at least the rest of the calendar year and for the following calendar year. See $100,000 Next-Day Deposit Rule *in section 11 of Pub. 15 for more information.*

What About Penalties and Interest?

Avoiding Penalties and Interest

You can avoid paying penalties and interest if you do all of the following.
• Deposit or pay your taxes when they are due.
• File your fully completed Form 941 on time.
• Report your tax liability accurately.
• Submit valid checks for tax payments.
• Furnish accurate Forms W-2 to employees.
• File Form W-3 and Copy A of Forms W-2 with the SSA on time and accurately.

Instructions for Form 941 (Rev. 1-2016) -5-

Penalties and interest are charged on taxes paid late and returns filed late at a rate set by law. See sections 11 and 12 of Pub. 15 for details.

Use Form 843 to request abatement of assessed penalties or interest. Don't request abatement of assessed penalties or interest on Form 941 or Form 941-X.

 If amounts that must be withheld aren't withheld or aren't deposited or paid to the United States Treasury, the trust fund recovery penalty may apply. The penalty is the full amount of the unpaid trust fund tax. This penalty may apply to you if these unpaid taxes can't be immediately collected from the employer or business.

The trust fund recovery penalty may be imposed on all persons who are determined by the IRS to be responsible for collecting, accounting for, or paying over these taxes, and who acted willfully in not doing so. For more information, see section 11 of Pub. 15.

Adjustment of Tax on Tips

If, by the 10th of the month after the month you received an employee's report on tips, you don't have enough employee funds available to withhold the employee's share of social security and Medicare taxes, you no longer have to collect it. Report the entire amount of these tips on line 5b (Taxable social security tips), line 5c (Taxable Medicare wages and tips), and, if the withholding threshold is met, line 5d (Taxable wages and tips subject to Additional Medicare Tax withholding). Include as an adjustment on line 9 the total uncollected employee share of the social security and Medicare taxes.

Specific Instructions:

Part 1: Answer These Questions for This Quarter

1. Number of Employees Who Received Wages, Tips, or Other Compensation This Quarter

Enter the number of employees on your payroll for the pay period including March 12, June 12, September 12, or December 12, for the quarter indicated at the top of Form 941. Don't include:

- Household employees,
- Employees in nonpay status for the pay period,
- Farm employees,
- Pensioners, or
- Active members of the Armed Forces.

 If you enter "250" or more on line 1, you must file Forms W-2 electronically. For details, call the SSA at 1-800-772-6270 or visit SSA's Employer W-2 Filing Instructions & Information website at www.socialsecurity.gov/employer.

2. Wages, Tips, and Other Compensation

Enter amounts on line 2 that would also be included in box 1 of your employees' Forms W-2. Include sick pay paid by a third party if you were given timely notice of the payments and the third party transferred liability for the employer's taxes to you. See the General Instructions for Forms W-2 and W-3 for details.

If you are a third-party payer of sick pay, don't include sick pay that you paid to policyholders' employees here if you gave the policyholders timely notice of the payments.

3. Federal Income Tax Withheld From Wages, Tips, and Other Compensation

Enter the federal income tax you withheld (or were required to withhold) from your employees on this quarter's wages, tips, taxable fringe benefits, and supplemental unemployment compensation benefits. Don't include any income tax withheld by a third-party payer of sick pay even if you reported it on Forms W-2. You will reconcile this difference on Form W-3. Also include here any excise taxes you were required to withhold on golden parachute payments (section 4999).

If you are a third-party payer of sick pay, enter the federal income tax you withheld (or were required to withhold) on third-party sick pay here.

4. If No Wages, Tips, and Other Compensation are Subject to Social Security or Medicare Tax . . .

If no wages, tips, and other compensation on line 2 are subject to social security or Medicare tax, check the box on line 4. If this question doesn't apply to you, leave the box blank. For more information about exempt wages, see section 15 of Pub. 15 and section 4 of Pub. 15-A, Employer's Supplemental Tax Guide.

 If you are a government employer, wages you pay aren't automatically exempt from social security and Medicare taxes. Your employees may be covered by law or by a voluntary Section 218 Agreement with the SSA. For more information, see Pub. 963, Federal-State Reference Guide.

5a–5e. Taxable Social Security and Medicare Wages and Tips

5a. Taxable social security wages. Enter the total wages, sick pay, and taxable fringe benefits subject to social security taxes you paid to your employees during the quarter. For this purpose, sick pay includes payments made by an insurance company to your employees for which you received timely notice from the insurance company. See section 6 in Pub. 15-A for more information about sick pay reporting.

Enter the amount before deductions. Don't include tips on this line. For information on types of wages subject to social security taxes, see section 5 of Pub. 15.

For 2016, the rate of social security tax on taxable wages is 6.2% (.062) each for the employer and employee or 12.4% (.124) for both. Stop paying social security tax on and entering an employee's wages on line 5a when the employee's taxable wages (including tips) reach $XXX,XXX for the year. However, continue to withhold income and Medicare taxes for the whole year on wages and tips even when the social security wage base of $XXX,XXX has been reached.

line 5a (column 1)
x   .124
line 5a (column 2)

Instructions for Form 941 (Rev. 1-2016)

5b. Taxable social security tips. Enter all tips your employees reported to you during the quarter until the total of the tips and wages for an employee reach $XXX,XXX for the year. Include all tips your employee reported to you even if you were unable to withhold the employee tax of 6.2%.

Your employee must report cash tips to you by the 10th day of the month after the month the tips are received. The report should include charged tips (for example, credit and debit card charges) you paid over to the employee for charge customers, tips the employee received directly from customers, and tips received from other employees under any tip-sharing arrangement. Both directly and indirectly tipped employees must report tips to you. No report is required for months when tips are less than $20. Employees may use Form 4070 (available only in Pub. 1244), or submit a written statement or electronic tip record.

Don't include allocated tips on this line. Instead, report them on Form 8027. Allocated tips aren't reportable on Form 941 and aren't subject to withholding of federal income, social security, or Medicare taxes.

$$
\begin{array}{r}
\text{line 5b \quad (column 1)} \\
\text{x} \quad \underline{\text{.124}} \\
\text{line 5b \quad (column 2)}
\end{array}
$$

5c. Taxable Medicare wages & tips. Enter all wages, tips, sick pay, and taxable fringe benefits that are subject to Medicare tax. Unlike social security wages, there is no limit on the amount of wages subject to Medicare tax.

The rate of Medicare tax is 1.45% (.0145) each for the employer and employee or 2.9% (.029) for both. Include all tips your employees reported during the quarter, even if you were unable to withhold the employee tax of 1.45%.

$$
\begin{array}{r}
\text{line 5c \quad (column 1)} \\
\text{x} \quad \underline{\text{.029}} \\
\text{line 5c \quad (column 2)}
\end{array}
$$

For more information on tips, see section 6 of Pub. 15.

5d. Taxable wages & tips subject to Additional Medicare Tax withholding. Enter all wages, tips, sick pay, and taxable fringe benefits that are subject to Additional Medicare Tax withholding. You are required to begin withholding Additional Medicare Tax in the pay period in which you pay wages in excess of $200,000 to an employee and continue to withhold it each pay period until the end of the calendar year. Additional Medicare Tax is only imposed on the employee. There is no employer share of Additional Medicare Tax. All wages that are subject to Medicare tax are subject to Additional Medicare Tax withholding if paid in excess of the $200,000 withholding threshold.

For more information on what wages are subject to Medicare tax, see the chart, *Special Rules for Various Types of Services and Payments*, in section 15 of Pub. 15. For more information on Additional Medicare Tax, visit IRS.gov and enter "Additional Medicare Tax" in the search box.

Once wages and tips exceed the $200,000 withholding threshold, include all tips your employees reported during the quarter, even if you were unable to withhold the employee tax of 0.9%.

$$
\begin{array}{r}
\text{line 5d \quad (column 1)} \\
\text{x} \quad \underline{\text{.009}} \\
\text{line 5d \quad (column 2)}
\end{array}
$$

5e. Total social security and Medicare taxes. Add the column 2 amounts on lines 5a–5d. Enter the result on line 5e.

5f. Section 3121(q) Notice and Demand—Tax Due on Unreported Tips

Enter the tax due from your Section 3121(q) Notice and Demand on line 5f. The IRS issues a Section 3121(q) Notice and Demand to advise an employer of the amount of tips received by employees who failed to report or underreported tips to the employer. An employer isn't liable for the employer share of the social security and Medicare taxes on unreported tips until notice and demand for the taxes is made to the employer by the IRS in a Section 3121(q) Notice and Demand. The tax due may have been determined from tips reported to the IRS on employees' Forms 4137, Social Security and Medicare Tax on Unreported Tip Income, or other tips that weren't reported to their employer as determined by the IRS during an examination. For additional information, see Rev. Rul. 2012-18, 2012-26 I.R.B. 1032, available at *www.irs.gov/irb/2012-26_IRB/ar07.html*.

Deposit the tax within the time period required under your deposit schedule to avoid any possible deposit penalty. The tax is treated as accumulated by the employer on the "Date of Notice and Demand" as printed on the Section 3121(q) Notice and Demand. The employer must include this amount on the appropriate line of the record of federal tax liability (Part 2 of Form 941 for a monthly schedule depositor or Schedule B (Form 941) for a semiweekly schedule depositor).

6. Total Taxes Before Adjustments

Add the total federal income tax withheld from wages, tips, and other compensation (line 3), the total social security and Medicare taxes before adjustments (line 5e), and any tax due under a Section 3121(q) Notice and Demand (line 5f). Enter the result on line 6.

7–9. Tax Adjustments

Enter tax amounts on lines 7–9 that result from current quarter adjustments. Use a minus sign (if possible) to show an adjustment that decreases the total taxes shown on line 6 instead of parentheses. Doing so enhances the accuracy of our scanning software. For example, enter "-10.59" instead of "(10.59)." However, if your software only allows for parentheses in entering negative amounts, you may use them.

Current quarter's adjustments. In certain cases, you must adjust the amounts you entered as social security and Medicare taxes in column 2 of lines 5a–5d to figure your correct tax liability for this quarter's Form 941. See section 13 of Pub. 15.

7. Current quarter's adjustment for fractions of cents. Enter adjustments for fractions of cents (due to rounding) relating to the employee share of social security and Medicare taxes withheld. The employee share of amounts shown in column 2 of lines 5a–5d may differ slightly from amounts actually withheld from employees' pay due to the rounding of social security and Medicare taxes based on statutory rates.

8. Current quarter's adjustment for sick pay. Enter the adjustment for the employee share of social security and Medicare taxes that were withheld and deposited by your third-party sick pay payer with regard to sick pay paid by the third-party. These wages should be included on line 5a, line 5c, and, if the withholding threshold is met, line 5d. If you are the third-party sick pay payer, enter the adjustment for any employer share of these taxes required to be paid by the employer.

9. Current quarter's adjustments for tips and group-term life insurance. Enter adjustments for:
• Any uncollected employee share of social security and Medicare taxes on tips, and
• The uncollected employee share of social security and Medicare taxes on group-term life insurance premiums paid for former employees.

Prior quarter's adjustments. If you need to correct any adjustment reported on a previously filed Form 941, complete and file Form 941 X. Form 941-X is an adjusted return or claim for refund and is filed separately from Form 941. See section 13 of Pub. 15.

10. Total Taxes After Adjustments

Combine the amounts shown on lines 6–9 and enter the result on line 10.

• **If line 10 is less than $2,500 or line 10 on the preceding quarterly return was less than $2,500, and you didn't incur a $100,000 next-day deposit obligation during the current quarter.** You may pay the amount with Form 941 or you may deposit the amount. To avoid a penalty, you must pay the amount in full with a timely filed return or you must deposit the amount timely. For more information on paying with a timely filed return, see the instructions for line 12 below.
• **If line 10 is $2,500 or more and line 10 on the preceding quarterly return was $2,500 or more, or if you incurred a $100,000 next-day deposit obligation during the current quarter.** You must make deposits according to your deposit schedule. The amount shown on line 10 must equal the "Total liability for quarter" shown on line 14 or the "Total liability for the quarter" shown on Schedule B (Form 941).

For more information and rules about federal tax deposits, see *Depositing Your Taxes*, earlier, and section 11 of Pub. 15.

 If you are a semiweekly depositor, you must complete Schedule B (Form 941). If you fail to complete and submit Schedule B (Form 941), the IRS may assert deposit penalties based on available information.

11. Total Deposits for This Quarter

Enter your deposits for this quarter, including any overpayment from a prior quarter. Also include in the amount shown any overpayment that you applied from filing Form 941-X, 941-X (PR), 944-X, or 944-X (SP), in the current quarter.

12. Balance Due

If line 10 is more than line 11, enter the difference on line 12. Otherwise, see *Overpayment*, later.

Never make an entry on both lines 12 and 13.

You don't have to pay if line 12 is under $1. Generally, you should have a balance due only if your total taxes (line 10) for the current quarter or preceding quarter are less than $2,500, and you didn't incur a $100,000 next-day deposit obligation during the current quarter. However, see section 11 of Pub. 15 for information about payments made under the accuracy of deposits rule.

If you were required to make federal tax deposits, pay the amount shown on line 12 by EFT. If you weren't required to make federal tax deposits, you may pay the amount shown on line 12 by EFT, credit card, debit card, check, money order, or EFW. For more information on electronic payment options, visit the IRS website at *www.irs.gov/payments*.

If you pay by EFT, credit card, or debit card, file your return using the *Without a payment* address under *Where Should You File*, earlier, and don't file Form 941-V, Payment Voucher.

If you pay by check or money order, make it payable to the "United States Treasury." Enter your EIN, Form 941, and the tax period on your check or money order. Complete Form 941-V and enclose with Form 941.

If line 10 is $2,500 or more and you have deposited all taxes when due, the balance due on line 12 should be zero, unless you have reduced your deposits in anticipation of filing a Form 941-X to claim COBRA premium assistance credits. See *Depositing Your Taxes*, earlier.

 If you are required to make deposits and instead pay the taxes with Form 941, you may be subject to a penalty. See Must You Deposit Your Taxes*, earlier.*

What if you can't pay in full? If you can't pay the full amount of tax you owe, you can apply for an installment agreement online. You can apply for an installment agreement online if:
• You can't pay the full amount shown on line 12,
• The total amount you owe is $25,000 or less, and
• You can pay the liability in full in 24 months.

To apply using the Online Payment Agreement Application, go to IRS.gov, click on *Tools*, then click on *Online Payment Agreement*.

Under an installment agreement, you can pay what you owe in monthly installments. There are certain conditions you must meet to enter into and maintain an installment agreement, such as paying the liability within 24 months, and making all required deposits and timely filing tax returns during the length of the agreement.

If your installment agreement is accepted, you will be charged a fee and you will be subject to penalties and interest on the amount of tax not paid by the due date of the return.

13. Overpayment

If line 11 is more than line 10, enter the difference on line 13. **Never make an entry on both lines 12 and 13.**

If you deposited more than the correct amount for the quarter, you can choose to have the IRS either refund the overpayment or apply it to your next return. Check only one box on line 13. If you don't check either box or if you check both boxes, generally we will apply the overpayment to your account. We may apply your overpayment to any past due tax account that is shown in our records under your EIN.

If line 13 is under $1, we will send a refund or apply it to your next return only if you ask us in writing to do so.

-8-

Instructions for Form 941 (Rev. 1-2016)

A-76

Complete Both Pages

You must complete both pages of Form 941 and sign on page 2. Failure to do so may delay processing of your return.

Part 2: Tell Us About Your Deposit Schedule and Tax Liability for This Quarter

14. Tax Liability for the Quarter

• **De minimis exception.** If line 10 is less than $2,500 or line 10 on the preceding quarterly return was less than $2,500, and you didn't incur a $100,000 next-day deposit obligation during the current quarter, check the appropriate box on line 14 and go to Part 3.

 If you meet the de minimis exception based on the prior quarter and line 10 for the current quarter is $100,000 or more, you must provide a record of your federal tax liability. If you are a monthly schedule depositor, complete the deposit schedule on line 14. If you are a semiweekly schedule depositor, attach Schedule B (Form 941).

• If you reported $50,000 or less in taxes during the lookback period, you are a monthly schedule depositor unless the *$100,000 Next-Day Deposit Rule* discussed in section 11 of Pub. 15 applies. Check the appropriate box on line 14 and enter your tax liability for each month in the quarter. Add the amounts for each month. Enter the result in the *Total liability for quarter* box.

Note that your total tax liability for the quarter must equal your total taxes shown on line 10. If it doesn't, your tax deposits and payments may not be counted as timely. Don't change your tax liability on line 14 by adjustments reported on any Forms 941-X.

You are a monthly schedule depositor for the calendar year if the amount of your Form 941 taxes reported for the lookback period is $50,000 or less. The lookback period is the four consecutive quarters ending on June 30 of the prior year. For 2016, the lookback period begins July 1, 2014, and ends June 30, 2015. For details on the deposit rules, see section 11 of Pub. 15. If you filed Form 944 in either 2014 or 2015, your lookback period is the 2014 calendar year.

 The amounts entered on line 14 are a summary of your monthly tax liability, not a summary of deposits you made. If you don't properly report your liabilities when required or if you are a semiweekly schedule depositor and enter your liabilities on line 14 instead of on Schedule B (Form 941), you may be assessed an "averaged" failure-to-deposit (FTD) penalty. See Deposit Penalties *in section 11 of Pub. 15 for more information.*

• If you reported more than $50,000 of taxes for the lookback period, you are a semiweekly schedule depositor. Check the appropriate box on line 14.

You must complete Schedule B (Form 941) and submit it with your Form 941. Don't use Schedule B (Form 941) if you are a monthly schedule depositor.

Don't change your tax liability on Schedule B (Form 941) by adjustments reported on any Forms 941-X.

Part 3: Tell Us About Your Business

In Part 3, answer only those questions that apply to your business. If the questions don't apply, leave them blank and go to Part 4.

15. If Your Business Has Closed . . .

If you go out of business or stop paying wages, you must file a final return. To tell the IRS that a particular Form 941 is your final return, check the box on line 15 and enter the date you last paid wages in the space provided. For additional filing requirements, see *If Your Business Has Closed*, earlier.

16. If You are a Seasonal Employer . . .

If you hire employees seasonally—such as for summer or winter only—check the box on line 16. Checking the box tells the IRS not to expect four Forms 941 from you throughout the year because you haven't paid wages regularly.

Generally, we won't ask about unfiled returns if you file at least one return showing tax due each year. However, you must check the box every time you file a Form 941.

Also, when you complete Form 941, be sure to check the box on the top of the form that corresponds to the quarter reported.

Part 4: May We Speak With Your Third-party Designee?

If you want to allow an employee, a paid tax preparer, or another person to discuss your Form 941 with the IRS, check the "Yes" box in Part 4. Enter the name, phone number, and the five-digit personal identification number (PIN) of the specific person to speak with—not the name of the firm that prepared your tax return. The designee may choose any five numbers as his or her PIN.

By checking "Yes," you authorize the IRS to talk to the person you named (your designee) about any questions we may have while we process your return. You also authorize your designee to do all of the following.
• Give us any information that is missing from your return.
• Call us for information about processing your return.
• Respond to certain IRS notices that you have shared with your designee about math errors and return preparation. The IRS won't send notices to your designee.

You aren't authorizing your designee to bind you to anything (including additional tax liability) or to otherwise represent you before the IRS. If you want to expand your designee's authorization, see Pub. 947.

The authorization will automatically expire 1 year from the due date (without regard to extensions) for filing your Form 941. If you or your designee want to terminate the authorization, write to the IRS office for your location using the *Without a payment* address under *Where Should You File*, earlier.

Part 5: Sign Here (Approved Roles)

Complete all information in Part 5 and sign Form 941. The following persons are authorized to sign the return for each type of business entity.

• **Sole proprietorship—** The individual who owns the business.

• **Corporation (including a limited liability company (LLC) treated as a corporation)—** The president, vice president, or other principal officer duly authorized to sign.

• **Partnership (including an LLC treated as a partnership) or unincorporated organization—** A responsible and duly authorized member, partner, or officer having knowledge of its affairs.

• **Single member LLC treated as a disregarded entity for federal income tax purposes—** The owner of the LLC or a principal officer duly authorized to sign.

• **Trust or estate—** The fiduciary.

Form 941 may be signed by a duly authorized agent of the taxpayer if a valid power of attorney has been filed.

Alternative signature method. Corporate officers or duly authorized agents may sign Form 941 by rubber stamp, mechanical device, or computer software program. For details and required documentation, see Rev. Proc. 2005-39, 2005-28 I.R.B. 82, at *www.irs.gov/irb/2005-28_IRB/ar16.html*.

Paid Preparer Use Only

A paid preparer must sign Form 941 and provide the information in the *Paid Preparer Use Only* section of Part 5 if the preparer was paid to prepare Form 941 and isn't an employee of the filing entity. Paid preparers must sign paper returns with a manual signature. The preparer must give you a copy of the return in addition to the copy to be filed with the IRS.

If you are a paid preparer, enter your Preparer Tax Identification Number (PTIN) in the space provided. Include your complete address. If you work for a firm, enter the firm's name and the EIN of the firm. You can apply for a PTIN online or by filing Form W-12. For more information about applying for a PTIN online, visit the IRS website at *www.irs.gov/ptin*. You can't use your PTIN in place of the EIN of the tax preparation firm.

Generally, don't complete this section if you are filing the return as a reporting agent and have a valid Form 8655 on file with the IRS. However, a reporting agent must complete this section if the reporting agent offered legal advice, for example, advising the client on determining whether its workers are employees or independent contractors for federal tax purposes.

How to Order Forms, Instructions, and Publications from the IRS

 Visit *www.irs.gov/orderforms*.

Other IRS Forms, Notices, and Publications You May Need

- Form SS-4, Application for Employer Identification Number
- Form W-2, Wage and Tax Statement
- Form W-2c, Corrected Wage and Tax Statement
- Form W-3, Transmittal of Wage and Tax Statements
- Form W-3c, Transmittal of Corrected Wage and Tax Statements
- Form W-4, Employee's Withholding Allowance Certificate
- Form 940, Employer's Annual Federal Unemployment (FUTA) Tax Return
- Form 941-X, Adjusted Employer's QUARTERLY Federal Tax Return or Claim for Refund
- Form 943, Employer's Annual Federal Tax Return for Agricultural Employees
- Form 944, Employer's ANNUAL Federal Tax Return
- Form 944-X, Adjusted Employer's ANNUAL Federal Tax Return or Claim for Refund
- Form 8027, Employer's Annual Information Return of Tip Income and Allocated Tips
- Form 8655, Reporting Agent Authorization
- Notice 797, Possible Federal Tax Refund Due to the Earned Income Credit (EIC)
- Pub. 15, Employer's Tax Guide
- Pub. 15-A, Employer's Supplemental Tax Guide
- Pub. 15-B, Employer's Tax Guide to Fringe Benefits
- Pub. 596, Earned Income Credit
- Pub. 1244, Employee's Daily Record of Tips and Report to Employer
- Pub. 926, Household Employer's Tax Guide
- Schedule B (Form 941), Report of Tax Liability for Semiweekly Schedule Depositors
- Schedule D (Form 941), Report of Discrepancies Caused by Acquisitions, Statutory Mergers, or Consolidations
- Schedule H (Form 1040), Household Employment Taxes
- Schedule R (Form 941), Allocation Schedule for Aggregate Form 941 Filers

Schedule B (Form 941):

Report of Tax Liability for Semiweekly Schedule Depositors

960311

OMB No. 1545-0029

(Rev. January 2014)   Department of the Treasury — Internal Revenue Service

Employer identification number (EIN) ☐☐ – ☐☐☐☐☐☐☐

Name *(not your trade name)*

Calendar year ☐☐☐☐   *(Also check quarter)*

Report for this Quarter...
(Check one.)

☐ **1:** January, February, March

☐ **2:** April, May, June

☐ **3:** July, August, September

☐ **4:** October, November, December

Use this schedule to show your TAX LIABILITY for the quarter; DO NOT use it to show your deposits. When you file this form with Form 941 or Form 941-SS, DO NOT change your tax liability by adjustments reported on any Forms 941-X or 944-X. You must fill out this form and attach it to Form 941 or Form 941-SS if you are a semiweekly schedule depositor or became one because your accumulated tax liability on any day was $100,000 or more. Write your daily tax liability on the numbered space that corresponds to the date wages were paid. See Section 11 in Pub. 15 (Circular E), Employer's Tax Guide, for details.

Month 1

1	9	17	25	**Tax liability for Month 1**
2	10	18	26	
3	11	19	27	
4	12	20	28	
5	13	21	29	
6	14	22	30	
7	15	23	31	
8	16	24		

Month 2

1	9	17	25	**Tax liability for Month 2**
2	10	18	26	
3	11	19	27	
4	12	20	28	
5	13	21	29	
6	14	22	30	
7	15	23	31	
8	16	24		

Month 3

1	9	17	25	**Tax liability for Month 3**
2	10	18	26	
3	11	19	27	
4	12	20	28	
5	13	21	29	
6	14	22	30	
7	15	23	31	
8	16	24		

Fill in your total liability for the quarter (Month 1 + Month 2 + Month 3) ▶

Total must equal line 10 on Form 941 or Form 941-SS.

Total liability for the quarter

For Paperwork Reduction Act Notice, see separate instructions.   IRS.gov/form941   Cat. No. 11967Q   Schedule B (Form 941) (Rev. 1-2014)

A-79

Instructions for Schedule B (Form 941)

Department of the Treasury
Internal Revenue Service

(Rev. January 2014)

Report of Tax Liability for Semiweekly Schedule Depositors

Section references are to the Internal Revenue Code unless otherwise noted.

Future Developments

For the latest information about developments related to Schedule B and its instructions, such as legislation enacted after they were published, go to *www.irs.gov/form941*.

Reminders

Reporting prior period adjustments. Prior period adjustments are reported on Form 941-X, Adjusted Employer's QUARTERLY Federal Tax Return or Claim for Refund, or Form 944-X, Adjusted Employer's ANNUAL Federal Tax Return or Claim for Refund, and are not taken into account when figuring the tax liability for the current quarter.

When you file Schedule B with your Form 941 (or Form 941-SS), do not change your tax liability by adjustments reported on any Form 941-X or 944-X.

Amended Schedule B. If you have been assessed a failure-to-deposit (FTD) penalty, you may be able to file an amended Schedule B. See *Correcting Previously Reported Tax Liability*, later.

General Instructions

Purpose of Schedule B

These instructions tell you about Schedule B, Report of Tax Liability for Semiweekly Schedule Depositors. To determine if you are a semiweekly depositor, visit IRS.gov and type "semiweekly depositor" in the search box. Also see Pub. 15 (Circular E), Employer's Tax Guide, or Pub. 80 (Circular SS), Federal Tax Guide for Employers in the U.S. Virgin Islands, Guam, American Samoa, and the Commonwealth of the Northern Mariana Islands.

Federal law requires you, as an employer, to withhold certain taxes from your employees' paychecks. Each time you pay wages, you must withhold – or take out of your employees' paychecks – certain amounts for federal income, social security, and Medicare taxes (payroll taxes). Under the withholding system, taxes withheld from your employees are credited to your employees in payment of their tax liabilities.

Federal law also requires employers to pay any liability for the employer's portion of social security and Medicare taxes. This portion of social security and Medicare taxes is not withheld from employees.

On Schedule B, list your **tax liability** for each day. Your liability includes:
- The federal income tax you withheld from your employees' paychecks, and
- Both employee and employer social security and Medicare taxes.

Do not use the Schedule B to show federal tax deposits. The IRS gets deposit data from electronic funds transfers.

 The IRS uses Schedule B to determine if you have deposited your federal employment tax liabilities on time. If you do not properly complete and file your Schedule B with Form 941 or Form 941-SS, the IRS may propose an "averaged" failure-to-deposit penalty. See Deposit Penalties *in section 11 of Pub. 15 (Circular E) for more information.*

Who Must File?

File Schedule B if you are a semiweekly schedule depositor. You are a semiweekly depositor if you reported more than $50,000 of employment taxes in the lookback period or accumulated a tax liability of $100,000 or more on any given day in the current or prior calendar year. See section 11 of Pub. 15 (Circular E) for more information.

Do not complete Schedule B if you have a tax liability that is less than $2,500 during the quarter.

When Must You File?

Schedule B is filed with Form 941, Employer's QUARTERLY Federal Tax Return, or Form 941-SS, Employer's QUARTERLY Federal Tax Return (American Samoa, Guam, the Commonwealth of the Northern Mariana Islands, and the U.S. Virgin Islands). Therefore, the due date of Schedule B is the same as the due date for the applicable Form 941 or Form 941-SS.

Do not file Schedule B as an attachment to Form 944, Employer's ANNUAL Federal Tax Return. Instead, if required to file a report of tax liability with Form 944, use Form 945-A, Annual Record of Federal Tax Liability.

Specific Instructions

Completing Schedule B

Enter Your Business Information

Carefully enter your employer identification number (EIN) and name at the top of the schedule. Make sure that they exactly match the name of your business and the EIN that the IRS assigned to your business and also agree with the name and EIN shown on the attached Form 941 or Form 941-SS.

Calendar Year

Enter the calendar year that applies to the quarter checked.

Check the Box for the Quarter

Under *Report for this Quarter* at the top of Schedule B, check the appropriate box of the quarter for which you are filing this schedule. Make sure the quarter checked on the top of the Schedule B matches the quarter checked on your Form 941 or Form 941-SS.

Enter Your Tax Liability by Month

Schedule B is divided into the 3 months that make up a quarter of a year. Each month has 31 numbered spaces that correspond to the dates of a typical month. Enter your tax liabilities in the spaces that correspond to the dates you **paid** wages to your employees, not the date payroll deposits were made.

For example, if your payroll period ended on December 31, 2013, and you **paid** the wages for that period on January 6, 2014, you would:

• Go to Month 1 (because January is the first month of the quarter), and

• Enter your tax liability on line 6 (because line 6 represents the sixth day of the month).

 Make sure you have checked the appropriate box in Part 2 of Form 941 or Form 941-SS to show that you are a semiweekly schedule depositor.

Total Liability for the Quarter

To find your total liability for the quarter, add your monthly tax liabilities.

Tax Liability for Month 1
+Tax Liability for Month 2
+Tax Liability for Month 3
Total Liability for the Quarter

Your total liability for the quarter must equal line 10 on Form 941 or Form 941-SS.

Example 1. Employer A is a **semiweekly** schedule depositor who pays wages for each month on the last day of the month. On December 24, 2013, Employer A also paid its employees year-end bonuses (subject to employment taxes). Employer A must report employment tax liabilities on Schedule B for the 4th quarter (October, November, December), as follows.

Month	Lines for dates wages were paid
1 (October)	line 31 (pay day, last day of the month)
2 (November)	line 30 (pay day, last day of the month)
3 (December)	line 24 (bonus paid December 24, 2013)
3 (December)	line 31 (pay day, last day of the month)

Example 2. Employer B is a **semiweekly** schedule depositor who pays employees every other Friday. Employer B accumulated a $20,000 employment tax liability on each of these pay dates: 01/04/13, 01/18/13, 02/01/13, 02/15/13, 03/01/13, 03/15/13, and 03/29/13. Employer B must report employment tax liabilities on Schedule B as follows.

Month	Lines for dates wages were paid
1 (January)	lines 4 and 18
2 (February)	lines 1 and 15
3 (March)	lines 1, 15, and 29

Example 3. Employer C is a new business and **monthly** schedule depositor for 2013. Employer C paid wages every Friday and accumulated a $2,000 employment tax liability on 01/11/13. On 01/18/13, and on every subsequent Friday during 2013, Employer C accumulated a $110,000 employment tax liability. Under the deposit rules, employers **become semiweekly schedule depositors** on the day after any day they accumulate $100,000 or more of employment tax liability in a deposit period. Employer C became a semiweekly schedule depositor on 1/19/13, because Employer C had a total

accumulated employment tax liability of $112,000 on 1/18/13. For more information, see section 11 of Pub. 15 (Circular E) or section 8 of Pub. 80 (Circular SS).

Employer C must complete Schedule B as shown below and file it with Form 941 or 941-SS.

Month	Lines for dates wages were paid	Amount to report
1 (January)	line 11	$2,000
1 (January)	lines 18, 25	$110,000
2 (February)	lines 1, 8, 15, and 22	$110,000
3 (March)	lines 1, 8, 15, 22, and 29	$110,000

Correcting Previously Reported Tax Liability

Semiweekly schedule depositors. If you have been assessed a failure-to-deposit (FTD) penalty for a quarter and you made an error on Schedule B and the correction will not change the total liability for the quarter you reported on Schedule B, you may be able to reduce your penalty by filing a corrected Schedule B.

Example. You reported a liability of $3,000 on day 1 of month 1. However, the liability was actually for month 3. Prepare an amended Schedule B showing the $3,000 liability on day 1 of month 3. Also, you must enter the liabilities previously reported for the quarter that did not change. Write "Amended" at the top of Schedule B. The IRS will refigure the penalty and notify you of any change in the penalty.

Monthly schedule depositors. You can file a Schedule B if you have been assessed an FTD penalty for a quarter and you made an error on the monthly tax liability section of Form 941. When completing Schedule B, only enter the monthly totals. The daily entries are not required.

Where to file. File your amended Schedule B at the address provided in the penalty notice you received. You do not have to submit your original Schedule B.

Form 941-X

Tax decrease. If you are filing Form 941-X for a quarter, you can file an amended Schedule B with Form 941-X if both of the following apply.

1. You have a tax decrease.

2. You were assessed an FTD penalty.

File your amended Schedule B with Form 941-X. The total liability for the quarter reported on your corrected Schedule B must equal the corrected amount of tax reported on Form 941-X. If your penalty is decreased, the IRS will include the penalty decrease with your tax decrease.

Tax increase — Form 941-X filed timely. If you are filing a timely Form 941-X, do not file an amended Schedule B, unless you were assessed an FTD penalty caused by an incorrect, incomplete, or missing Schedule B. If you are filing an amended Schedule B, do not include the tax increase reported on Form 941-X.

Tax increase — Form 941-X filed late. If you owe tax and are filing a late Form 941-X, that is, after the due date of the return for the return period in which you discovered the error, you must file an amended Schedule B with Form 941-X. Otherwise, the IRS may assess an "averaged" FTD penalty. The total tax reported on the "Total liability for the quarter" line of the amended Schedule B must match the corrected tax (Form 941, line 10, combined with any correction reported on Form 941-X, line 18, minus any advance EIC reported on Form 941-X, line 19) for the quarter, less any previous abatements and interest-free tax assessments.

Note. Form 941-X will be revised in April 2014. If you are using the April 2014 revision, the total tax reported on the "Total liability for the quarter" line of the amended Schedule B must match the corrected tax (Form 941, line 10, combined with any correction reported on Form 941-X, line 18) for the quarter, less any previous abatements and interest-free tax assessments.

Paperwork Reduction Act Notice. We ask for the information on Schedule B to carry out the Internal Revenue laws of the United States. You are required to give us the information. We need it to ensure that you are complying with these laws and to allow us to figure and collect the right amount of tax.

You are not required to provide the information requested on a form that is subject to the Paperwork Reduction Act unless the form displays a valid OMB control number. Books or records relating to a form or its instructions must be retained as long as their contents may become material in the administration of any Internal Revenue law. Generally, tax returns and return information are confidential, as required by Code section 6103.

The time needed to complete and file Schedule B will vary depending on individual circumstances. The estimated average time is 2 hours, 53 minutes.

If you have comments concerning the accuracy of this time estimate or suggestions for making Schedule B simpler, we would be happy to hear from you. You can send us comments from *www.irs.gov/formspubs*. Click on *More Information* then click on *Comment on Tax Forms and Publications*. Or you can send your comments to Internal Revenue Service, Tax Forms and Publications Division, 1111 Constitution Ave. NW, IR-6526, Washington, DC 20224. **Do not** send Schedule B to this address. Instead, see *Where Should You File?* in the Form 941 or Form 941-SS instructions.

Form **941-X:** **Adjusted Employer's QUARTERLY Federal Tax Return or Claim for Refund**
(Rev. April 2015)   Department of the Treasury — Internal Revenue Service   OMB No. 1545-0029

Employer identification number (EIN) ☐☐ – ☐☐☐☐☐☐☐

Name *(not your trade name)*

Trade name *(if any)*

Address
Number   Street   Suite or room number

City   State   ZIP code

Foreign country name   Foreign province/county   Foreign postal code

DRAFT AS December 16 DO NOT FILE

Return You Are Correcting ...

Check the type of return you are correcting:

☐ 941

☐ 941-SS

Check the ONE quarter you are correcting:

☐ **1:** January, February, March

☐ **2:** April, May, June

☐ **3:** July, August, September

☐ **4:** October, November, December

Enter the calendar year of the quarter you are correcting:

[_____] (YYYY)

Enter the date you discovered errors:

☐☐ / ☐☐ / ☐☐☐☐
(MM / DD / YYYY)

Read the separate instructions before completing this form. Use this form to correct errors you made on Form 941 or 941-SS. Use a separate Form 941-X for each quarter that needs correction. Type or print within the boxes. You MUST complete all three pages. Do not attach this form to Form 941 or 941-SS.

Part 1: Select ONLY one process. See page 4 for additional guidance.

☐ **1. Adjusted employment tax return.** Check this box if you underreported amounts. Also check this box if you overreported amounts and you would like to use the adjustment process to correct the errors. You must check this box if you are correcting both underreported and overreported amounts on this form. The amount shown on line 20, if less than zero, may only be applied as a credit to your Form 941, Form 941-SS, or Form 944 for the tax period in which you are filing this form.

☐ **2. Claim.** Check this box if you overreported amounts only and you would like to use the claim process to ask for a refund or abatement of the amount shown on line 20. Do not check this box if you are correcting ANY underreported amounts on this form.

Part 2: Complete the certifications.

☐ **3.** I certify that I have filed or will file Forms W-2, Wage and Tax Statement, or Forms W-2c, Corrected Wage and Tax Statement, as required.

Note. If you are correcting underreported amounts only, go to Part 3 on page 2 and skip lines 4 and 5. If you are correcting overreported amounts, for purposes of the certifications on lines 4 and 5, Medicare tax does not include Additional Medicare Tax. Form 941-X cannot be used to correct overreported amounts of Additional Medicare Tax unless the amounts were not withheld from employee wages or an adjustment is being made for the current year.

4. If you checked line 1 because you are adjusting overreported amounts, check all that apply. You must check at least one box.
I certify that:

☐ **a.** I repaid or reimbursed each affected employee for the overcollected federal income tax or Additional Medicare Tax for the current year and the overcollected social security tax and Medicare tax for current and prior years. For adjustments of employee social security tax and Medicare tax overcollected in prior years, I have a written statement from each affected employee stating that he or she has not claimed (or the claim was rejected) and will not claim a refund or credit for the overcollection.

☐ **b.** The adjustments of social security tax and Medicare tax are for the employer's share only. I could not find the affected employees or each affected employee did not give me a written statement that he or she has not claimed (or the claim was rejected) and will not claim a refund or credit for the overcollection.

☐ **c.** The adjustment is for federal income tax, social security tax, Medicare tax, or Additional Medicare Tax that I did not withhold from employee wages.

5. If you checked line 2 because you are claiming a refund or abatement of overreported employment taxes, check all that apply. You must check at least one box.
I certify that:

☐ **a.** I repaid or reimbursed each affected employee for the overcollected social security tax and Medicare tax. For claims of employee social security tax and Medicare tax overcollected in prior years, I have a written statement from each affected employee stating that he or she has not claimed (or the claim was rejected) and will not claim a refund or credit for the overcollection.

☐ **b.** I have a written consent from each affected employee stating that I may file this claim for the employee's share of social security tax and Medicare tax. For refunds of employee social security tax and Medicare tax overcollected in prior years, I also have a written statement from each affected employee stating that he or she has not claimed (or the claim was rejected) and will not claim a refund or credit for the overcollection.

☐ **c.** The claim for social security tax and Medicare tax is for the employer's share only. I could not find the affected employees; or each affected employee did not give me a written consent to file a claim for the employee's share of social security tax and Medicare tax; or each affected employee did not give me a written statement that he or she has not claimed (or the claim was rejected) and will not claim a refund or credit for the overcollection.

☐ **d.** The claim is for federal income tax, social security tax, Medicare tax, or Additional Medicare Tax that I did not withhold from employee wages.

Next ▶

For Paperwork Reduction Act Notice, see the instructions.   IRS.gov/form941x   Cat. No. 17025J   Form **941-X** (Rev. 4-2015)

A-83

Name *(not your trade name)*	Employer identification number *(EIN)*	Correcting quarter (1, 2, 3, 4)
		Correcting calendar year (YYYY)

Part 3: Enter the corrections for this quarter. If any line does not apply, leave it blank.

		Column 1 Total corrected amount (for ALL employees)		*Column 2* Amount originally reported or as previously corrected (for ALL employees)		*Column 3* Difference (If this amount is a negative number, use a minus sign.)		*Column 4* Tax correction
6.	**Wages, tips and other compensation** (Form 941, line 2)	.	−	.	=	.	Use the amount in Column 1 when you prepare your Forms W-2 or Forms W-2c.	
7.	**Federal income tax withheld from wages, tips, and other compensation** (Form 941, line 3)	.	−	.	=	.	Copy Column 3 here ▶	.
8.	**Taxable social security wages** (Form 941 or 941-SS, line 5a, Column 1)	.	−	.	=	.	× .124* =	.
	If you are correcting a 2011 or 2012 return, use .104. If you are correcting your employer share only, use .062. See instructions.							
9.	**Taxable social security tips** (Form 941 or 941-SS, line 5b, Column 1)	.	−	.	=	.	× .124* =	.
	If you are correcting a 2011 or 2012 return, use .104. If you are correcting your employer share only, use .062. See instructions.							
10.	**Taxable Medicare wages and tips** (Form 941 or 941-SS, line 5c, Column 1)	.	−	.	=	.	× .029* =	.
	If you are correcting your employer share only, use .0145. See instructions.							
11.	**Taxable wages & tips subject to Additional Medicare Tax withholding** (Form 941 or 941-SS, line 5d; only for quarters beginning after December 31, 2012)	.	−	.	=	.	× .009* =	.
	Certain wages and tips reported in Column 3 should not be multiplied by .009. See instructions.							
12.	**Section 3121(q) Notice and Demand — Tax due on unreported tips** (Form 941 or 941-SS, line 5f (line 5e for quarters ending before January 1, 2013))	.	−	.	=	.	Copy Column 3 here ▶	.
13.	**Tax adjustments** (Form 941 or 941-SS, lines 7–9)	.	−	.	=	.	Copy Column 3 here ▶	.
14.	**Special addition to wages for federal income tax**	.	−	.	=	.	See instructions	.
15.	**Special addition to wages for social security taxes**	.	−	.	=	.	See instructions	.
16.	**Special addition to wages for Medicare taxes**	.	−	.	=	.	See instructions	.
17.	**Special addition to wages for Additional Medicare Tax**	.	−	.	=	.	See instructions	.
18.	Combine the amounts on lines 7–17 of Column 4							.
19a.	**COBRA premium assistance payments** (see instructions)	.	−	.	=	.	See instructions	.
19b.	**Number of individuals provided COBRA premium assistance** (see instructions)	.	−	.	=	.		
20.	**Total.** Combine the amounts on lines 18 and 19a of Column 4							.

If line 20 is less than zero:

- If you checked line 1, this is the amount you want applied as a credit to your Form 941 for the tax period in which you are filing this form. (If you are currently filing a Form 944, Employer's ANNUAL Federal Tax Return, see the instructions.)
- If you checked line 2, this is the amount you want refunded or abated.

If line 20 is more than zero, this is the amount you owe. Pay this amount by the time you file this return. For information on how to pay, see *Amount You Owe* in the instructions.

Next ▶

Form **941-X** (Rev. 4-2015)

A-84

Name *(not your trade name)*	Employer identification number *(EIN)*	Correcting quarter (1, 2, 3, 4)
		Correcting calendar year (YYYY)

Part 4: Explain your corrections for this quarter.

☐ **21.** **Check here if any corrections you entered on a line include both underreported and overreported amounts.** Explain both your underreported and overreported amounts on line 23.

☐ **22.** **Check here if any corrections involve reclassified workers.** Explain on line 23.

23. **You must give us a detailed explanation of how you determined your corrections.** See the instructions.

Part 5: Sign here. You must complete all three pages of this form and sign it.

Under penalties of perjury, I declare that I have filed an original Form 941 or Form 941-SS and that I have examined this adjusted return or claim, including accompanying schedules and statements, and to the best of my knowledge and belief, they are true, correct, and complete. Declaration of preparer (other than taxpayer) is based on all information of which preparer has any knowledge.

X **Sign your name here**

Print your name here

Print your title here

Date ___/___/___

Best daytime phone

Paid Preparer Use Only

Check if you are self-employed . . ☐

Preparer's name		PTIN	
Preparer's signature		Date	___/___/___
Firm's name (or yours if self-employed)		EIN	
Address		Phone	
City		State	ZIP code	

Page **3**

Form **941-X** (Rev. 4-2015)

A-85

Type of errors you are correcting	Form 941-X: Which process should you use?		
Underreported amounts ONLY	**Use the adjustment process** to correct underreported amounts. • Check the box on line 1. • Pay the amount you owe from line 20 by the time you file Form 941-X.		
Overreported amounts ONLY	The process you use depends on **when** you file Form 941-X.	**If you are filing Form 941-X MORE THAN 90 days before the period of limitations on credit or refund for Form 941 or Form 941-SS expires...**	Choose either the adjustment process or the claim process to correct the overreported amounts. **Choose the adjustment process** if you want the amount shown on line 20 credited to your Form 941, Form 941-SS, or Form 944 for the period in which you file Form 941-X. Check the box on line 1. OR **Choose the claim process** if you want the amount shown on line 20 refunded to you or abated. Check the box on line 2.
		If you are filing Form 941-X WITHIN 90 days of the expiration of the period of limitations on credit or refund for Form 941 or Form 941-SS...	You must use the **claim process** to correct the overreported amounts. Check the box on line 2.
BOTH underreported and overreported amounts	The process you use depends on **when** you file Form 941-X.	**If you are filing Form 941-X MORE THAN 90 days before the period of limitations on credit or refund for Form 941 or Form 941-SS expires...**	Choose either the adjustment process or both the adjustment process and the claim process when you correct both underreported and overreported amounts. **Choose the adjustment process** if combining your underreported amounts and overreported amounts results in a balance due or creates a credit that you want applied to Form 941, Form 941-SS, or Form 944. • File one Form 941-X, and • Check the box on line 1 and follow the instructions on line 20. OR **Choose both the adjustment process and the claim process** if you want the overreported amount refunded to you or abated. File two separate forms. **1. For the adjustment process,** file one Form 941-X to correct the underreported amounts. Check the box on line 1. Pay the amount you owe from line 20 by the time you file Form 941-X. **2. For the claim process,** file a second Form 941-X to correct the overreported amounts. Check the box on line 2.
		If you are filing Form 941-X WITHIN 90 days of the expiration of the period of limitations on credit or refund for Form 941 or Form 941-SS...	You must **use both the adjustment process and the claim process**. File two separate forms. 1. For the adjustment process, file one Form 941-X to correct the underreported amounts. Check the box on line 1. Pay the amount you owe from line 20 by the time you file Form 941-X. 2. For the claim process, file a second Form 941-X to correct the overreported amounts. Check the box on line 2.

Form **941-X** (Rev. 4-2015)

Instructions for Form 941-X

(April 2015)

Department of the Treasury
Internal Revenue Service

Adjusted Employer's QUARTERLY Federal Tax Return or Claim for Refund

Section references are to the Internal Revenue Code unless otherwise noted.

Future Developments

For the latest information about developments related to Form 941-X and its instructions, such as legislation enacted after they were published, go to *www.irs.gov/form941x*.

Reminders

Claiming the COBRA premium assistance credit. Effective for tax periods beginning after December 31, 2013, the COBRA premium assistance credit cannot be claimed on Form 941 or 941-SS. Instead, use Form 941-X, lines 19a and 19b, to claim the credit. Form 941-X should be filed after filing your Form 941 or 941-SS. Filing a Form 941-X before filing a Form 941 or 941-SS for the quarter may result in errors or delays in processing your Form 941-X. For more information, visit IRS.gov and enter "COBRA" in the search box.

 If you are entitled to claim the COBRA premium assistance credit, but are not otherwise required to file Form 941 or 941-SS, file a Form 941 or 941-SS with -0- entered on line 12 before filing your Form 941-X to claim the credit.

Period of limitations to make certain corrections expired. Generally, you may correct overreported taxes on a previously filed Form 941 if you file Form 941-X within 3 years of the date Form 941 was filed or 2 years from the date you paid the tax reported on Form 941, whichever is later. For purposes of the period of limitations, Forms 941 for a calendar year are considered filed on April 15 of the succeeding year if filed before that date.

The period of limitations to correct the qualified employer's tax exemption on wages/tips paid to qualified employees (for quarters ending after March 31, 2010, and before January 1, 2011); the qualified employer's tax credit on wages/tips paid to qualified employees March 19–31, 2010; and advance earned income credit (EIC) payments expired on April 15, 2014, for most employers. The lines formerly used for these corrections were removed from Form 941-X. If the period of limitations for any of these corrections is still open, you will need to file the April 2013 revision of Form 941-X. The April 2013 revision of Form 941-X is available on IRS.gov.

Correcting wages and tips subject to Additional Medicare Tax withholding. Beginning with the first quarter of 2013, wages and tips subject to Additional Medicare Tax withholding are reported on Form 941, line 5d. Any errors discovered on a previously filed Form 941 are corrected on Form 941-X, line 11. For more information about Additional Medicare Tax withholding, see the Instructions for Form 941 and go to IRS.gov and enter "Additional Medicare Tax" in the search box. See the instructions for line 11 for more information on the types of errors that can be corrected and how the correction is reported on Form 941-X.

Correcting the COBRA premium assistance credit. For tax periods ending before January 1, 2014, employers who made COBRA premium assistance payments for assistance eligible individuals were allowed a credit on their Form 941 or 941-SS. Any errors discovered on a previously filed Form 941 or 941-SS for this credit are corrected on Form 941-X, lines 19a and 19b.

Effective for tax periods beginning after December 31, 2013, Form 941-X, is used to both report the total COBRA premium assistance credit an employer is entitled to claim and correct any previously reported credit. For more information, see the instructions for lines 19a and 19b, later.

Social security tax rate for 2011 and 2012. In 2011 and 2012, the employee social security tax rate was 4.2% and the employer social security tax rate was 6.2% (10.4% total). Be sure to use the correct rate when reporting corrections on lines 8 and 9.

Aggregate Form 941. Agents must complete Schedule R (Form 941), Allocation Schedule for Aggregate Form 941 Filers, when correcting an aggregate Form 941. Schedule R (Form 941) is completed only for those clients who have corrections reported on Form 941-X. Schedule R (Form 941) is filed as an attachment to Form 941-X. Aggregate Forms 941 are filed by agents approved by the IRS under section 3504. To request approval to act as an agent for an employer, the agent files Form 2678, Employer/Payer Appointment of Agent, with the IRS.

Retroactive increase in excludible transit benefits for 2012. The American Taxpayer Relief Act (ATRA) increased the monthly transit benefit exclusion from $125 per participating employee to $240 per participating employee for the period of January 1, 2012, through December 31, 2012. Employers were provided instructions on how to correct the social security and Medicare taxes on the excess transit benefits in Notice 2013-8, 2013-7 I.R.B. 486, available at *www.irs.gov/irb/2013-07_IRB/ar08.html*.

General Instructions:

What Is the Purpose of Form 941-X?

 For tax periods beginning after December 31, 2013, Forms 941 and 941-SS will no longer be used to claim the credit for COBRA premium assistance payments. Instead use Form 941-X. For more information, see the instructions for lines 19a and 19b.

Use Form 941-X to correct errors on a Form 941 that you previously filed. Use Form 941-X to correct:
- Wages, tips, and other compensation;
- Income tax withheld from wages, tips, and other compensation;
- Taxable social security wages;
- Taxable social security tips;
- Taxable Medicare wages and tips;
- Taxable wages and tips subject to Additional Medicare Tax withholding; and
- Credits for COBRA premium assistance payments.

Use Form 843, Claim for Refund and Request for Abatement, to request a refund or abatement of assessed interest or penalties. **Do not** request abatement of assessed interest or penalties on Form 941 or Form 941-X.

 References to Form 941 on Form 941-X and in these instructions also apply to Form 941-SS, Employer's QUARTERLY Federal Tax Return—American Samoa, Guam, the Commonwealth of the Northern Mariana Islands, and the U.S. Virgin Islands, unless otherwise noted. We use the

terms "correct" and "corrections" on Form 941-X and in these instructions to include interest-free adjustments under sections 6205 and 6413 and claims for refund and abatement under sections 6402, 6414, and 6404. See Rev. Rul. 2009-39 for examples of how the interest-free adjustment and claim for refund rules apply in 10 different situations. You can find Rev. Rul. 2009-39, 2009-52, I.R.B. 951 at www.irs.gov/irb/2009-52_IRB/ar14.html.

When you discover an error on a previously filed Form 941, you must:
- Correct that error using Form 941-X,
- File a separate Form 941-X for each Form 941 that you are correcting, and
- File Form 941-X separately. Do not file Form 941-X with Form 941.

If you did not file a Form 941 for one or more quarters, **do not** use Form 941-X. Instead, file Form 941 for each of those quarters. See also *When Should You File Form 941-X?* below. However, if you did not file Forms 941 because you improperly treated workers as independent contractors or nonemployees and are now reclassifying them as employees, see the instructions for line 22, later.

Report the correction of underreported and overreported amounts for the same tax period on a single Form 941-X, unless you are requesting a refund or abatement. If you are requesting a refund or abatement and are correcting both underreported and overreported amounts, file one Form 941-X correcting the underreported amounts only and a second Form 941-X correcting the overreported amounts.

You will use the adjustment process if you underreported employment taxes and are making a payment, or if you overreported employment taxes and will be applying the credit to Form 941 for the period during which you file Form 941-X. However, see the *Caution* under *Is There a Deadline for Filing Form 941-X*, later, if you are correcting overreported amounts during the last 90 days of a period of limitations. You will use the claim process if you overreported employment taxes and are requesting a refund or abatement of the overreported amount. Follow the chart on the back of Form 941-X for help in choosing whether to use the adjustment process or the claim process. Be sure to give us a detailed explanation on line 23 for each correction that you show on Form 941-X.

Continue to report current quarter fractions of cents, third-party sick pay, tips, and group-term life insurance on Form 941, lines 7–9.

You have additional requirements to complete when filing Form 941-X, such as certifying that you filed (or will file) all applicable Forms W-2, Wage and Tax Statements, and Forms W-2c, Corrected Wage and Tax Statements, with the Social Security Administration (SSA). For corrections of overreported federal income tax, social security tax, Medicare tax, or Additional Medicare Tax, you must make any certifications that apply to your situation.

 Do not use Form 941-X to correct Form CT-1, 943, 944, 944-SS, or 945. Instead, use the "X" form that corresponds to those forms (Form CT-1 X, 943-X, 944-X, or 945-X).

Where Can You Get Help?

For help filing Form 941-X or for questions about federal employment taxes and tax corrections, you can:
- Call the IRS Business and Specialty Tax Line at 1-800-829-4933 or 1-800-829-4059 (TDD/TTY for persons who are deaf, hard of hearing, or have a speech disability) Monday–

Friday from 7:00 a.m. to 7:00 p.m. local time (Alaska and Hawaii follow Pacific time),
- Visit IRS.gov and enter "employment taxes" in the search box, or
- See Pub. 15 (Circular E), Employer's Tax Guide, for correcting Form 941, or Pub. 80 (Circular SS), Federal Tax Guide for Employers in the U.S. Virgin Islands, Guam, American Samoa, and the Commonwealth of the Northern Mariana Islands, for correcting Form 941-SS.

See also *How Can You Order Forms, Instructions, and Publications from the IRS*, later.

When Should You File Form 941-X?

File Form 941-X when you discover an error on a previously filed Form 941.

However, if your only errors on Form 941 relate to the number of employees who received wages or to federal tax liabilities reported on Form 941, Part 2, or on Schedule B (Form 941), Report of Tax Liability for Semiweekly Schedule Depositors, do not file Form 941-X. For more information about correcting federal tax liabilities reported on Form 941, Part 2, or on Schedule B (Form 941), see the Instructions for Schedule B (Form 941).

Due dates. The due date for filing Form 941-X depends on when you discover an error and if you underreported or overreported tax. If you underreported tax, see *Underreported tax* next. For overreported amounts, you may choose to either make an interest-free adjustment or file a claim for refund or abatement. If you are correcting overreported amounts, see *Overreported tax—adjustment process* or *Overreported tax—claim process*, later.

If any due date falls on a Saturday, Sunday, or legal holiday, you may file Form 941-X on the next business day. If we receive Form 941-X after the due date, we will treat Form 941-X as filed on time if the envelope containing Form 941-X is properly addressed, contains sufficient postage, and is postmarked by the U.S. Postal Service on or before the due date, or sent by an IRS-designated private delivery service on or before the due date. If you do not follow these guidelines, we will consider Form 941-X filed when it is actually received. See Pub. 15 (Circular E) or Pub. 80 (Circular SS) for more information on legal holidays and IRS-designated private delivery services.

Underreported tax. If you are correcting underreported tax, you must file Form 941-X by the due date of the return for the return period in which you discovered the error and **pay** the amount you owe by the time you file. Doing so will generally ensure that your correction is interest free and not subject to failure-to-pay or failure-to-deposit penalties. See *What About Penalties and Interest*, later. For details on how to make a payment, see the instructions for line 20, later.

If Form 941-X is filed late (after the due date of the return for the return period in which you discovered the error), you must attach an amended Schedule B (Form 941) to Form 941-X. Otherwise, the IRS may assess an "averaged" failure-to-deposit penalty. The total tax reported on the "Total liability for the quarter" line of Schedule B (Form 941) must match the corrected tax (Form 941, line 10, combined with any correction entered on Form 941-X, line 18) for the quarter, less any previous abatements and interest-free tax assessments.

Instructions for Form 941-X (Rev. 4-2015)

If you discover an error in	Form 941-X is due . . .
1. January, February, March	April 30
2. April, May, June	July 31
3. July, August, September	October 31
4. October, November, December	January 31

The dates shown in the table above apply only to corrections of underreported amounts. If any due date falls on a Saturday, Sunday, or legal holiday, you may file Form 941-X on the next business day.

Example—You owe tax. On February 11, 2015, you discovered that you underreported $10,000 of social security and Medicare wages on your 2014 fourth quarter Form 941. File Form 941-X and pay the amount you owe by April 30, 2015, because you discovered the error in the first quarter of 2015, and April 30, 2015, is the due date for that quarter. If you file Form 941-X before April 30, 2015, pay the amount you owe by the time you file.

Overreported tax—adjustment process. If you overreported tax on Form 941 and choose to apply the credit to Form 941 or Form 944, file an adjusted return on Form 941-X soon after you discovered the error but more than 90 days before the period of limitations on the credit or refund for Form 941 expires. See *Is There a Deadline for Filing Form 941-X?* below.

 If you reduced your deposits during the quarter by the amount of the COBRA premium assistance credit that will be reflected on your Form 941-X, do not use the adjustment process to claim the COBRA premium assistance credit. Use the claim process. See the instructions for lines 19a and 19b, later.

Overreported tax—claim process. If you overreported tax on Form 941, you may choose to file a claim for refund or abatement on Form 941-X any time before the period of limitations on credit or refund expires on Form 941. If you also need to correct **any** underreported amounts, you must file another Form 941-X reporting only corrections to the underreported amounts. See *Is There a Deadline for Filing Form 941-X?* next.

 You may not file a refund claim to correct federal income tax or Additional Medicare Tax actually withheld from employees.

Is There a Deadline for Filing Form 941-X?

Generally, you may correct overreported taxes on a previously filed Form 941 if you file Form 941-X within 3 years of the date Form 941 was filed or 2 years from the date you paid the tax reported on Form 941, whichever is later. You may correct underreported taxes on a previously filed Form 941 if you file Form 941-X within 3 years of the date the Form 941 was filed. We call each of these time frames a "period of limitations." For purposes of the period of limitations, Forms 941 for a calendar year are considered filed on April 15 of the succeeding year if filed before that date.

Example. You filed your 2012 fourth quarter Form 941 on January 27, 2013, and payments were timely made. The IRS treats the return as if it were filed on April 15, 2013. On January 22, 2014, you discovered that you overreported social security and Medicare wages on that form by $350. To correct the error you must file Form 941-X by April 15, 2016, which is the end of the period of limitations for Form 941, and use the claim process.

 If you file Form 941-X to correct overreported amounts in the last 90 days of a period of limitations (after January 15, 2016, in the example above), you must use the claim process. You cannot use the adjustment process. If you are also correcting underreported amounts, you must file another Form 941-X to correct the underreported amounts using the adjustment process and pay any tax due.

Where Should You File Form 941-X?

Send your completed Form 941-X to the address shown next.

IF you are in	THEN use this address . . . . .
Connecticut, Delaware, District of Columbia, Florida, Georgia, Illinois, Indiana, Kentucky, Maine, Maryland, Massachusetts, Michigan, New Hampshire, New Jersey, New York, North Carolina, Ohio, Pennsylvania, Rhode Island, South Carolina, Tennessee, Vermont, Virginia, West Virginia, Wisconsin	Department of the Treasury Internal Revenue Service Cincinnati, OH 45999-0005
Alabama, Alaska, Arizona, Arkansas, California, Colorado, Hawaii, Idaho, Iowa, Kansas, Louisiana, Minnesota, Mississippi, Missouri, Montana, Nebraska, Nevada, New Mexico, North Dakota, Oklahoma, Oregon, South Dakota, Texas, Utah, Washington, Wyoming	Department of the Treasury Internal Revenue Service Ogden, UT 84201-0005
No legal residence or principal place of business in any state	Internal Revenue Service P.O. Box 409101 Ogden, UT 84409
Special filing addresses for exempt organizations; federal, state, and local governmental entities; and Indian tribal governmental entities; regardless of location	Department of the Treasury Internal Revenue Service Ogden, UT 84201-0005

How Should You Complete Form 941-X?

Use a Separate Form 941-X for Each Quarter You Are Correcting

Use a separate Form 941-X for each Form 941 that you are correcting. For example, if you found errors on your Forms 941 for the third and fourth quarters of 2014, file one Form 941-X to correct the 2014 third quarter Form 941. File a second Form 941-X to correct the 2014 fourth quarter Form 941.

EIN, Name, and Address

Enter your EIN, name, and address in the spaces provided. Also enter your name and EIN on the top of pages 2 and 3, and on any attachments. If your address has changed since you filed your Form 941, enter the corrected information and the IRS will update your address of record. Be sure to write your name, EIN, " Form 941-X," the calendar quarter you are correcting (for example "Quarter 2"), and the calendar year of the quarter you are correcting on the top of any attachments.

Return You Are Correcting

In the box at the top of page 1, check the type of return (Form 941 or Form 941-SS) you are correcting. Check the appropriate box for the **one** quarter you are correcting. Enter the calendar year of the Form 941 you are correcting. Enter the quarter and calendar year on pages 2 and 3. Be sure to write your name,

EIN, "Form 941-X," the quarter you are correcting (for example, "Quarter 2"), and the calendar year of the quarter you are correcting on the top of any attachments.

Enter the Date You Discovered Errors

You **must** enter the date you discovered errors. You discover an error when you have enough information to be able to correct it. If you are reporting several errors that you discovered at different times, enter the earliest date you discovered them here. Report any subsequent dates and related errors on line 23.

Must You Make an Entry on Each Line?

You must provide all of the information requested at the top of page 1. You must check one box (but not both) in Part 1. In Part 2, you must check the box on line 3 and any applicable boxes on lines 4 and 5. In Part 3, if any line does not apply, leave it blank. Complete Parts 4 and 5 as instructed.

How Should You Report Negative Amounts?

Form 941-X uses negative numbers to show reductions in tax (credits) and positive numbers to show additional tax (amounts you owe).

When reporting a negative amount in columns 3 and 4, use a minus sign instead of parentheses. For example, enter "-10.59" instead of "(10.59)." However, if you are completing the return on your computer and your software only allows you to use parentheses to report negative amounts, you may use them.

How Should You Make Entries on Form 941-X?

You can help the IRS process Form 941-X timely and accurately if you follow these guidelines.
* Type or print your entries.
* Use Courier font (if possible) for all typed or computer-generated entries.
* Omit dollar signs. You may use commas and decimal points, if desired. Enter dollar amounts to the left of any preprinted decimal point and cents to the right of it.
* Always show an amount for cents. Do not round entries to whole dollars.
* Complete all three pages and sign Form 941-X on page 3.
* Staple multiple sheets in the upper-left corner.

What About Penalties and Interest?

Generally, your correction of an underreported amount will not be subject to a failure-to-pay penalty, failure-to-deposit penalty, or interest if you:
* File on time (by the due date of the quarter in which you discover the error),
* Pay the amount shown on line 20 **by the time you file** Form 941-X,
* Enter the date you discovered the error, and
* Explain in detail the grounds and facts relied on to support the correction.

No correction will be eligible for interest-free treatment if any of the following apply.
* The amounts underreported relate to an issue that was raised in an examination of a prior period.
* You knowingly underreported your employment tax liability.
* You received a notice and demand for payment.
* You received a Notice of Determination of Worker Classification.

If you receive a notice about a penalty after you file this return, reply to the notice with an explanation and we will determine if you meet the reasonable-cause criteria. Do not attach an explanation when you file your return.

Overview of the Process

The process to correct a previously filed Form 941 or file a claim is outlined below.

If you underreported the tax. If you underreported the tax on a previously filed Form 941, check the box on line 1 and **pay** any additional amount you owe by the time you file Form 941-X. For details on how to make a payment, see the instructions for line 20, later.

Example—You underreported employment taxes. On June 19, 2015, you discover an error that results in additional tax on your 2014 fourth quarter Form 941. File Form 941-X by July 31, 2015, and pay the amount you owe by the time you file. See *When Should You File Form 941-X*, earlier. **Do not** attach Form 941-X to your 2015 second quarter Form 941.

If you overreported the tax. If you overreported the tax on a previously filed Form 941, you may **choose** one of the following options.
* Use the adjustment process. Check the box on line 1 to apply any credit (negative amount) from line 20 to Form 941 for the quarter during which you file Form 941-X.
* Use the claim process. Check the box on line 2 to file a claim on Form 941-X requesting a refund or abatement of the amount shown on line 20.

 To ensure that the IRS has enough time to process a credit for an **overreporting adjustment** in the quarter during which you file Form 941-X, you are encouraged to file Form 941-X correcting the overreported amount in the first two months of a quarter. For example, if you discover an overreported amount in March, June, September, or December, you may want to file Form 941-X in the first two months of the next quarter. However, there must be 90 days remaining on the period of limitations when you file Form 941-X. See the Caution under Is There a Deadline for Filing Form 941-X, *earlier. This should ensure that the IRS will have enough time to process Form 941-X so the credit will be posted before you file Form 941, thus avoiding an erroneous balance due notice from the IRS. See the example below.*

Example—You want your overreported tax applied as a credit to Form 941. On June 19, 2015, you discover you overreported your tax on your 2014 fourth quarter Form 941 and want to choose the adjustment process. To allow the IRS enough time to process the credit, you file Form 941-X on July 1, 2015, and take the credit on your third quarter 2015 Form 941.

 If you currently file Form 944 and you are making a correction to a previously filed Form 941 that will be claimed as a credit on Form 944, file Form 941-X before December in any year before the expiration of the period of limitations for the previously filed Form 941. In the year that the period of limitations for the previously filed Form 941 expires, file Form 941-X at least 90 days before the expiration date.

Specific Instructions:

Part 1: Select ONLY One Process

Because Form 941-X may be used to file either an adjusted employment tax return or a claim for refund or abatement, you **must** check one box on either line 1 or line 2. Do not check both boxes.

1. Adjusted Employment Tax Return

Check the box on line 1 if you are correcting underreported amounts or overreported amounts and you would like to use the adjustment process to correct the errors.

If you are correcting both underreported amounts and overreported amounts on this form, you **must** check this box. If you check this box, any negative amount shown on line 20 will be applied as a credit (tax deposit) to your Form 941 or Form 944 for the period in which you are filing this form. See *Example—You want your overreported tax applied as a credit to Form 941*, earlier.

If you owe tax. Pay the amount shown on line 20 by the time you file Form 941-X. Generally, you will not be charged interest if you file on time, pay on time, enter the date you discovered the error, and explain the correction on line 23.

If you have a credit. You overreported employment taxes (you have a negative amount on line 20) and want the IRS to apply the credit to Form 941 or Form 944 for the period during which you filed Form 941-X. The IRS will apply your credit on the first day of the Form 941 or Form 944 period during which you filed Form 941-X. However, the credit you show on Form 941-X, line 20, may not be fully available on your Form 941 or Form 944 if the IRS corrects it during processing or you owe other taxes, penalties, or interest. The IRS will notify you if your claimed credit changes or if the amount available as a credit on Form 941 or Form 944 was reduced because of unpaid taxes, penalties, or interest.

 Do not check the box on line 1 if you are either: (a) correcting overreported amounts and the period of limitations on credit or refund for Form 941 will expire within 90 days of the date you file Form 941-X, or (b) claiming a credit for COBRA premium assistance payments and you reduced your deposits in anticipation of the credit. Instead, in either case, check the box on line 2 to file a Form 941-X under the claim process. See Is There a Deadline for Filing Form 941-X, *earlier. Also see the instructions for lines 19a and 19b, later.*

2. Claim

Check the box on line 2 to use the claim process if you are correcting **overreported amounts only** and you are claiming a refund or abatement for the negative amount (credit) shown on line 20. Do not check this box if you are correcting any underreported amounts on this form.

You must check the box on line 2 if you have a credit and the period of limitations on credit or refund for Form 941 will expire within 90 days of the date you file Form 941-X. See *Is There a Deadline for Filing Form 941-X*, earlier.

The IRS usually processes claims shortly after they are filed. The IRS will notify you if your claim is denied, accepted as filed, or selected to be examined. See Pub. 556, Examination of Returns, Appeal Rights, and Claims for Refund, for more information.

Unless the IRS corrects Form 941-X during processing or you owe other taxes, penalties, or interest, the IRS will refund the amount shown on line 20, plus any interest that applies.

 You may not file a refund claim to correct federal income tax or Additional Medicare Tax actually withheld from employees.

Part 2: Complete the Certifications

You must complete all certifications that apply by checking the appropriate boxes. If all of your corrections relate to underreported amounts, complete line 3 only; skip lines 4 and 5 and go to Part 3. If your corrections relate to overreported amounts, you have a duty to ensure that your employees' rights to recover overpaid employee social security and Medicare taxes that you withheld are protected. The certifications on lines 4 and 5 address the requirement to:

- Repay or reimburse your employees for the overcollection of employee social security and Medicare taxes, or
- Obtain consents from your employees to file a claim on their behalf.

3. Filing Forms W-2 or Forms W-2c

Check the box on line 3 to certify that you filed or will file Forms W-2 or Forms W-2c with the SSA, as required, showing your employees' correct wage and tax amounts. See the General Instructions for Forms W-2 and W-3 for detailed information about filing requirements. References to Form W-2 on Form 941-X and in these instructions also apply to Forms W-2AS, W-2CM, W-2GU, and W-2VI unless otherwise noted.

You must check the box on line 3 to certify that you filed Forms W-2 or Forms W-2c even if your corrections on Form 941-X do not change amounts shown on those forms. For example, if your only correction to Form 941 involves misstated tax adjustments (see the instructions for line 13, later), check the box on line 3 to certify that you already filed all required Forms W-2 and W-2c with the SSA.

4. Certifying Overreporting Adjustments

If you overreported federal income tax, social security tax, Medicare tax, or Additional Medicare Tax and checked the box on line 1, check the appropriate box on line 4. You may need to check more than one box. If you obtained written statements from some employees but you could not locate or secure the cooperation of the remaining employees, check all applicable boxes. Provide a summary on line 23 of the amount of the corrections both for the employees who provided written statements and for those who did not.

4a. Check the box on line 4a if your overreported amount includes each affected employee's share of overcollected taxes. You are certifying that you repaid or reimbursed the employee's share of current and prior year taxes and you received written statements from the employees stating that they did not and will not receive a refund or credit for the prior year taxes. You are certifying that you adjusted federal income tax or Additional Medicare Tax withheld from employees for the current calendar year only.

> **Example.** The following is an example of the written statement that is required from employees.
>
> Employee name _____
> Employer name _____
> I have received a repayment of $_____ as overcollected social security and Medicare taxes for 20____. I have not claimed a refund of or credit for the overcollected taxes from the IRS, or if I did, that claim has been rejected; and I will not claim a refund or a credit of the amount.
> Employee signature _____
> Date _____

Do not send these statements to the IRS. Keep them for your records. Generally, all employment tax records must be kept for at least 4 years.

4b. Check the box on line 4b to certify that your overreported amount is only for the employer share of taxes on those employees who you were unable to find or those who would not (or could not) give you a statement described on line 4a.

4c. Check the box on line 4c to certify that your overreported amount is only for federal income tax, social security tax, Medicare tax, or Additional Medicare Tax that you did not withhold from your employees.

5. Certifying Claims

If you are filing a claim for refund or abatement of overreported federal income tax, social security tax, Medicare tax, or

Additional Medicare Tax and checked the box on line 2, check the appropriate box on line 5. You may need to check more than one box. If you obtained written statements or consents from some employees but you could not locate or secure the cooperation of the remaining employees, check all applicable boxes. Provide a summary on line 23 of the amount of the corrections for both the employees who provided statements or consents and for those who did not.

 You cannot file a refund claim to correct federal income tax or Additional Medicare Tax actually withheld from employees in a prior year.

5a. Check the box on line 5a if your overreported tax includes each affected employee's share of social security and Medicare taxes. You are certifying that you repaid or reimbursed to the employees their share of social security and Medicare taxes. For refunds of employee social security and Medicare taxes overcollected in prior years, you are certifying that you received written statements from those employees stating that they did not and will not receive a refund or credit for the prior year taxes.

5b. Check the box on line 5b if your overreported tax includes each affected employee's share of social security and Medicare taxes and you have not yet repaid or reimbursed the employee share of taxes. You are certifying that you received consent from each affected employee to file a claim on the employee share of those taxes and you received written statements from those employees stating that they did not and will not receive a refund or credit for the prior year taxes.

Example. The following is an example of the consent and written statement that is required from employees when you are filing a claim for refund and have not yet paid or reimbursed the employee share of taxes.

Employee name _____
Employer name _____
I give my consent to have my employer (named above) file a claim on my behalf with the IRS requesting $_____ in overcollected social security and Medicare taxes for 20___. I have not claimed a refund of or credit for the overcollected taxes from the IRS, or if I did, that claim has been rejected; and I will not claim a refund or a credit of the amount.
Employee signature _____
Date _____

Do not send these statements to the IRS. Keep them for your records. Generally, all employment tax records must be kept for at least 4 years.

In certain situations, you may not have repaid or reimbursed your employees or obtained their consents prior to filing a claim, such as in cases where the period of limitations on credit or refund is about to expire. In those situations, file Form 941-X, but do not check a box on line 5. Tell us on line 23 that you have not repaid or reimbursed employees or obtained consents. However, you must certify that you have repaid or reimbursed your employees or obtained consents before the IRS can grant the claim.

5c. Check the box on line 5c to certify that your overreported tax is only for the employer share of social security and Medicare taxes. Affected employees did not give you consent to file a claim for refund for the employee share of social security and Medicare taxes, they could not be found, or would not (or could not) give you a statement described on line 5b.

5d. Check the box on line 5d to certify that your overreported amount is only for federal income tax, social security tax, Medicare tax, or Additional Medicare Tax that you did not withhold from your employees.

Part 3: Enter the Corrections for This Quarter

What Amounts Should You Report in Part 3?

On lines 6–11, columns 1 and 2, show amounts for **all** of your employees, not just for those employees whose amounts you are correcting.

If a correction that you report in column 4 includes both underreported and overreported amounts (see the instructions for line 21, later), give us details for each on line 23.

Because special circumstances apply for lines 12–17, 19a, and 19b, read the instructions for each line carefully before entering amounts in the columns.

 If you previously adjusted or amended Form 941 by using Form 941-X or because of an IRS examination change, show amounts in column 2 that include those previously reported corrections.

6. Wages, Tips, and Other Compensation

If you are correcting the wages, tips, and other compensation you reported on Form 941, line 2, enter the total corrected amount for ALL employees in column 1. In column 2, enter the amount you originally reported. In column 3, enter the difference between columns 1 and 2. This line does not apply to Form 941-SS.

If you or the IRS previously corrected the amount reported on Form 941, line 2, enter in column 2 the amount after any previous corrections.

line 6 (column 1)	
- line 6 (column 2)	
line 6 (column 3)	If the amount in column 2 is larger than the amount in column 1, use a minus sign in column 3.

Example —Wages, tips, and other compensation increased. You reported $9,000 as total wages, tips, and other compensation on line 2 of your 2015 first quarter Form 941. In May of 2015, you discovered that you had overlooked $1,000 in tips for one of your part-time employees. To correct the error, figure the difference on Form 941-X as shown.

Column 1 (corrected amount)	10,000.00
Column 2 (Form 941, line 2)	- 9,000.00
Column 3 (difference)	1,000.00

Example —Wages, tips, and other compensation decreased. You reported $9,000 as wages, tips, and other compensation on line 2 of your 2015 first quarter Form 941. In May of 2015, you discovered that you included $2,000 in wages for one of your employees twice. To correct the error, figure the difference on Form 941-X as shown.

Column 1 (corrected amount)	7,000.00
Column 2 (Form 941, line 2)	- 9,000.00
Column 3 (difference)	-2,000.00

Example—Auto allowance; wages, tips, and other compensation increased. You paid one of your employees a $500 monthly auto allowance from October through December 2014, and did not treat the payments as taxable wages. In February 2015, you realized that the payments were wages because they were not reimbursements of deductible business expenses that were substantiated and paid under an accountable plan. You correct the error by treating the auto allowance as wages subject to income, social security, and Medicare taxes. Report the additional $1,500 of wages on lines 6, 8, and 10.

 The amount on line 6, column 1, should be used on your Forms W-2 or Forms W-2c. This amount should also be used for any business expense deduction on your income tax return (or amended return) for wages paid.

7. Federal Income Tax Withheld from Wages, Tips, and Other Compensation

If you are correcting the federal income tax withheld from wages, tips, and other compensation you reported on Form 941, line 3, enter the total corrected amount in column 1. In column 2, enter the amount you originally reported or as previously corrected. In column 3, enter the difference between columns 1 and 2. This line does not apply to Form 941-SS.

line 7 (column 1)	
- line 7 (column 2)	
line 7 (column 3)	If the amount in column 2 is larger than the amount in column 1, use a minus sign in column 3.

Copy the amount in column 3 to column 4. Include any minus sign shown in column 3.

 *Generally, you may correct federal income tax withholding errors **only** if you discovered the errors in the same calendar year you paid the wages. However, you may correct federal income tax withholding errors for prior years if the amounts shown on Form 941 do not agree with the amounts you actually withheld, that is, an administrative error or if section 3509 rates apply. See section 13 of Pub. 15 (Circular E) for more information about corrections during the calendar year and about administrative errors. See section 2 of Pub. 15 (Circular E) for more information about section 3509.*

Example—Failure to withhold income tax when required. You were required to withhold $400 of federal income tax from an employee's bonus that was paid in December of 2014 but you withheld nothing. You discovered the error on March 16, 2015. You cannot file Form 941-X to correct your 2014 fourth quarter Form 941 because the error involves a previous year and the amount previously reported for the employee represents the actual amount withheld from the employee during 2014.

Example—Administrative error reporting income tax. You had three employees. In the fourth quarter of 2014, you withheld $1,000 of federal income tax from employee A, $2,000 from employee B, and $6,000 from employee C. The total amount of federal income tax you withheld was $9,000. You mistakenly reported $6,000 on line 3 of your 2014 fourth quarter Form 941. You discovered the error on March 13, 2015. This is an example of an administrative error that may be corrected in a later calendar year because the amount actually withheld from employees' wages differs from the amount reported on Form 941. Use Form 941-X to correct the error. Enter $9,000 in column 1 and $6,000 in column 2. Subtract the amount in column 2 from the amount in column 1.

Column 1 (corrected amount)	9,000.00
Column 2 (Form 941, line 3)	- 6,000.00
Column 3 (difference)	3,000.00

Report the $3,000 as a tax correction in column 4.

Be sure to explain the reasons for this correction on line 23.

8. Taxable Social Security Wages

 The 2011 and 2012 employee tax rate for social security was 4.2%.

If you are correcting the taxable social security wages you reported on Form 941, line 5a, column 1, enter the total corrected amount in column 1. In column 2, enter the amount you originally reported or as previously corrected. In column 3, enter the difference between columns 1 and 2.

line 8 (column 1)	
- line 8 (column 2)	
line 8 (column 3)	If the amount in column 2 is larger than the amount in column 1, use a minus sign in column 3.

Multiply the amount in column 3 by .124 (.104 for corrections to a 2011 or 2012 return) and enter that result in column 4.

line 8 (column 3)	
x .124	(Use .104 for corrections to a 2011 or 2012 return.)
line 8 (column 4)	If the amount in column 3 used a minus sign, also use a minus sign in column 4.

Note. If you are correcting only the employer share of tax on a decrease to social security wages, use .062 (6.2%) when multiplying the amount shown in column 3. If you are correcting both shares of tax for some employees and only the employer share for other employees, enter the properly calculated amount in column 4. Be sure to show your calculations on line 23.

Example—Social security wages decreased. Following Example—Wages, tips, and other compensation decreased in the instructions for line 6, the wages that you counted twice were also taxable social security wages. To correct the error, figure the difference on Form 941-X as shown.

Column 1 (corrected amount)	7,000.00
Column 2 (Form 941, line 5a, column 1)	- 9,000.00
Column 3 (difference)	-2,000.00

Use the difference in column 3 to determine your tax correction.

Column 3 (difference)	-2,000.00
Tax rate (12.4%)	x .124
Column 4 (tax correction)	-248.00

Be sure to explain the reasons for this correction on line 23.

Note. If the example above was for a correction to a 2011 or 2012 return, the amount in column 3 would be multiplied by .104.

9. Taxable Social Security Tips

 The 2011 and 2012 employee tax rate for social security was 4.2%.

If you are correcting the taxable social security tips you reported on Form 941, line 5b, column 1, enter the total corrected amount in column 1. In column 2, enter the amount you originally reported or as previously corrected. In column 3, enter the difference between columns 1 and 2.

line 9 (column 1)
- line 9 (column 2)
line 9 (column 3)   If the amount in column 2 is larger than the amount in column 1, use a minus sign in column 3.

Multiply the amount in column 3 by .124 (.104 for corrections to a 2011 or 2012 return) and report that result in column 4.

line 9 (column 3)
x .124   (Use .104 for corrections to a 2011 or 2012 return.)
line 9 (column 4)   If the amount in column 3 used a minus sign, also use a minus sign in column 4.

Note. If you are correcting only the employer share of tax on a decrease to social security tips, use .062 (6.2%) when multiplying the amount shown in column 3. If you are correcting both shares of tax for some employees and only the employer share for other employees, report the properly calculated amount in column 4. Be sure to show your calculations on line 23.

Example—Social security tips increased. Following the *Example—Wages, tips, and other compensation increased* in the instructions for line 6, the tips that you overlooked were also taxable social security tips. To correct the error, figure the difference on Form 941-X as shown.

Column 1 (corrected amount)	10,000.00
Column 2 (Form 941, line 5b, column 1)	- 9,000.00
Column 3 (difference)	1,000.00

Use the difference in column 3 to determine your tax correction.

Column 3 (difference)	1,000.00
Tax rate (12.4%)	x .124
Column 4 (tax correction)	124.00

Be sure to explain the reasons for this correction on line 23.

Note. If the example above was for a correction to a 2011 or 2012 return, the amount in column 3 would be multiplied by .104.

10. Taxable Medicare Wages and Tips

If you are correcting the taxable Medicare wages and tips you reported on Form 941, line 5c, column 1, enter the total corrected amount in column 1. In column 2, enter the amount you originally reported or as previously corrected. In column 3, enter the difference between columns 1 and 2.

line 10 (column 1)
- line 10 (column 2)
line 10 (column 3)   If the amount in column 2 is larger than the amount in column 1, use a minus sign in column 3.

Multiply the amount in column 3 by .029 (2.9% tax rate) and enter that result in column 4.

line 10 (column 3)
x .029
line 10 (column 4)   If the amount in column 3 used a minus sign, also use a minus sign in column 4.

Note. If you are correcting only the employer share of tax on a decrease to Medicare wages and tips, use .0145 (1.45%) when multiplying the amount in column 3. If you are correcting both shares of tax for some employees and only the employer share for other employees, enter the properly calculated amount in column 4. Be sure to explain your calculations on line 23.

Example—Medicare wages and tips decreased. Following *Example—Wages, tips, and other compensation decreased* in the instructions for line 6, the wages that you counted twice were also taxable Medicare wages and tips. To correct the error, figure the difference on Form 941-X as shown.

Column 1 (corrected amount)	7,000.00
Column 2 (Form 941, line 5c, column 1)	- 9,000.00
Column 3 (difference)	-2,000.00

Use the difference in column 3 to determine your tax correction.

Column 3 (difference)	-2,000.00
Tax rate (2.9%)	x .029
Column 4 (tax correction)	-58.00

Be sure to explain the reasons for this correction on line 23.

11. Taxable Wages and Tips Subject to Additional Medicare Tax Withholding

Generally, you may correct errors to Additional Medicare Tax withholding **only** if you discovered the errors in the same calendar year the wages and tips were paid to employees. However, you may correct errors to Additional Medicare Tax withholding for prior years if the amount reported on Form 941, line 5d, column 2, does not agree with the amount you actually withheld. This type of error is an administrative error. You may also correct errors to Additional Medicare Tax withholding for prior years if section 3509 rates apply. If section 3509 rates apply, see the instructions for line 17.

If a prior year error was a nonadministrative error, you may correct only the **wages and tips** subject to Additional Medicare Tax withholding that were originally reported on Form 941, line 5d, column 1, or previously corrected on Form 941-X. You cannot correct the tax reported on Form 941, line 5d, column 2.

Errors discovered in the same calendar year or prior year administrative errors. If you are correcting the taxable wages and tips subject to Additional Medicare Tax withholding that you reported on Form 941, line 5d, column 1, enter the total corrected amount in column 1. In column 2, enter the amount you originally reported or as previously corrected. In column 3, enter the difference between columns 1 and 2.

line 11 (column 1)
- line 11 (column 2)
line 11 (column 3)   If the amount in column 2 is larger than the amount in column 1, use a minus sign in column 3.

Multiply the amount in column 3 by .009 (0.9% tax rate) and enter that result in column 4.

line 11 (column 3)
x .009
_____
line 11 (column 4)   If the amount in column 3 used a minus sign, also use a minus sign in column 4.

Example—Prior year administrative error (incorrectly reported amount of Additional Medicare Tax actually withheld). Employee A's wages exceeded the $200,000 withholding threshold for Additional Medicare Tax in November 2014. The total wages paid to Employee A for 2014 were $230,000. You withheld $270 ($30,000 x .009) from the employee's wages. However, on your fourth quarter 2014 Form 941 you mistakenly reported $3,000 on line 5d, column 1, and Additional Medicare Tax withheld of $27 on line 5d, column 2. You discover the error on March 16, 2015. This is an example of an administrative error that may be corrected in a later calendar year because the amount actually withheld differs from the amount reported on your fourth quarter 2014 Form 941. Use Form 941-X, line 11, to correct the error as shown below.

Column 1 (corrected amount)	30,000.00
Column 2 (Form 941, line 5d, column 1)	- 3,000.00
Column 3 (difference)	27,000.00

Use the difference in column 3 to determine your tax correction.

Column 3 (difference)	27,000.00
Tax rate (0.9%)	x .009
Column 4 (tax correction)	243.00

Be sure to explain the reasons for this correction on line 23.

Prior year nonadministrative errors. You may correct **only** the taxable wages and tips subject to Additional Medicare Tax withholding that you reported on Form 941, line 5d, column 1. Enter the total corrected amount in column 1. In column 2, enter the amount you originally reported or as previously corrected. In column 3, enter the difference between columns 1 and 2.

line 11 (column 1)
- line 11 (column 2)
_____
line 11 (column 3)   If the amount in column 2 is larger than the amount in column 1, use a minus sign in column 3.

Do not multiply the amount in column 3 by .009 (0.9% tax rate). Leave column 4 blank and explain the reasons for this correction on line 23.

Example—Prior year nonadministrative error (failure to withhold Additional Medicare Tax when required). Employee B's wages exceeded the $200,000 withholding threshold for Additional Medicare Tax in December 2014. The total wages paid to Employee B for 2014 were $220,000. You were required to withhold $180 ($20,000 x .009) but you withheld nothing and did not report an amount on line 5d of your fourth quarter 2014 Form 941. You discover the error on March 16, 2015. File Form 941-X to correct wages and tips subject to Additional Medicare Tax withholding for your 2014 fourth quarter Form 941, but you may not correct the Additional Medicare Tax withheld (column 4) because the error involves a previous year

and the amount previously reported for the employee represents the actual amount withheld from the employee during 2014.

Combination of prior year administrative and nonadministrative errors. If you are reporting both administrative errors and nonadministrative errors for the same quarter of a prior year, enter the total corrected amount in column 1. In column 2, enter the amount you originally reported or as previously corrected. In column 3, enter the difference between columns 1 and 2. However, multiply only the amount of wages and tips reported in column 3 that are related to administrative errors by .009 (0.9% tax rate). **Do not** multiply any wages and tips reported in column 3 that are related to nonadministrative errors by .009 (0.9% tax rate). Use line 23 to explain in detail your corrections. The explanation must include the reasons for the corrections and a breakdown of the amount reported in column 3 into the amounts related to administrative errors and nonadministrative errors.

Example—Combination of prior year administrative and nonadministrative errors. Employee A's wages exceeded the $200,000 withholding threshold for Additional Medicare Tax in November 2014. The total wages paid to Employee A for 2014 were $230,000. You withheld $270 ($30,000 x .009) from the employee's wages. However, on your fourth quarter 2014 Form 941 you mistakenly reported $3,000 on line 5d, column 1, and Additional Medicare Tax withheld of $27 on line 5d, column 2. The difference in wages subject to Additional Medicare Tax related to this administrative error is $$27,000 ($30,000 - $3,000).

Employee B's wages exceeded the $200,000 withholding threshold for Additional Medicare Tax in December 2014. The total wages paid to Employee B for 2014 were $220,000. You were required to withhold $180 ($20,000 x .009) but you withheld nothing and did not report Employee B's $20,000 in wages subject to Additional Medicare Tax withholding on line 5d of your fourth quarter 2014 Form 941.

You discover both errors on March 16, 2015. Use Form 941-X, line 11, to correct the errors as shown below.

Column 1 (corrected amount)	50,000.00
Column 2 (Form 941, line 5d, column 1)	- 3,000.00
Column 3 (difference)	47,000.00

Determine the portion of wages and tips reported in column 3 that is related to the administrative error ($47,000 - $20,000 (nonadministrative error) = $27,000 (administrative error)). Multiply this portion of column 3 by .009 (0.9% tax rate) to determine your tax correction.

Difference related to administrative error	27,000.00
Tax rate (0.9%)	x .009
Column 4 (tax correction)	243.00

Be sure to explain the reasons for these corrections on line 23. You must also report that $20,000 of the amount shown in column 3 was related to the correction of a prior year nonadministrative error and $27,000 of the amount shown in column 3 was related to the correction of an administrative error.

12. Section 3121(q) Notice and Demand—Tax on Unreported Tips

Enter any corrections, including amounts reported on Form 941, line 5e (for quarters ending in 2011 or 2012), and amounts reported on Form 941, line 5f (for quarters ending after 2012), to the tax due from a Section 3121(q) Notice and Demand on line 12. The IRS issues a Section 3121(q) Notice and Demand to advise an employer of the amount of tips received by employees who failed to report or underreported tips to the employer. An employer is not liable for the employer share of the social security and Medicare taxes on unreported tips until a Section 3121(q) Notice and Demand for the taxes is made to the employer by the IRS.

13. Tax Adjustments

Use line 13 to correct any adjustments reported on Form 941, lines 7–9. Enter in column 1 the total **corrected** amount for Form 941, lines 7–9.

Enter in column 2 the total originally reported or previously corrected amounts from Form 941, lines 7–9. In column 3, enter the difference between columns 1 and 2.

line 13 (column 1)
-line 13 (column 2)
line 13 (column 3)

 You may need to report negative numbers in any column. Make sure that the difference you enter in column 3 accurately represents the change to adjustments originally reported or previously corrected on Form 941, lines 7–9.

Copy the amount in column 3 to column 4. Include any minus sign shown in column 3.

On line 23, describe what you misreported on Form 941. Tell us if your adjustment is for fractions of cents, third-party sick pay, tips, or group-term life insurance.

Example—Current quarter's third-party sick pay underreported. You reported $6,900 (shown as "-6,900.00") as a third-party sick pay adjustment (reduction to tax) on line 8 of your 2014 second quarter Form 941. You did not report any amounts on lines 7 and 9. Your third-party sick pay adjustment should have been $9,600 (shown as "-9,600.00") because your third-party sick pay payer withheld that amount of social security and Medicare taxes from your employees. You discovered the error in April of 2015. To correct the error, figure the difference on Form 941-X as shown.

Column 1 (corrected amount)	-9,600.00
Column 2 (Form 941, line 8)	- (6,900.00)
Column 3 (difference)	-2,700.00

Here is how you would enter the numbers on Form 941-X.

Column 1	Column 2	Column 3
(corrected amount)	(Form 941, line 8)	(difference)
-9,600.00	-6,900.00	-2,700.00

Report "-2,700.00" as your correction in column 4.

In this example, you are claiming a credit for $2,700 in overreported tax for your 2014 second quarter Form 941. Always enter the same amount in column 4 (including any minus sign) that you enter in column 3.

Be sure to explain the reasons for this correction on line 23.

14–17. Special Additions to Wages for Federal Income Tax, Social Security Taxes, Medicare Taxes, and Additional Medicare Tax

Section 3509 provides special rates for the employee share of income tax, social security tax, Medicare tax, and Additional Medicare Tax withholding when workers are reclassified as employees in certain circumstances. The applicable rate depends on whether you filed required information returns. An employer cannot recover any tax paid under this provision from the employees. The full employer share of social security tax and Medicare tax is due for all reclassifications.

Note. Section 3509 rates are not available if you intentionally disregarded the requirements to withhold taxes from the employee, or if you withheld income tax but did not withhold social security and Medicare taxes. Section 3509 rates are also not available for certain statutory employees.

On lines 14–17 enter **only** corrections to wages resulting from reclassifying certain workers as employees when section 3509 rates are used to calculate the taxes.

If the employer issued the required information returns, use the section 3509 rates as follows.
• For social security taxes, use the employer rate of 6.2% plus 20% of the employee rate of 6.2% (4.2% for 2011 and 2012), for a total rate of 7.44% (7.04% for 2011 and 2012) of wages.
• For Medicare taxes, use the employer rate of 1.45% plus 20% of the employee rate of 1.45%, for a total rate of 1.74% of wages.
• For Additional Medicare Tax; 0.18% (20% of the employee rate of 0.9%) of wages subject to Additional Medicare Tax.
• For income tax withholding, the rate is 1.5% of wages.

If the employer did not issue the required information returns, use the section 3509 rates as follows.
• For social security taxes, use the employer rate of 6.2% plus 40% of the employee rate of 6.2% (4.2% for 2011 and 2012), for a total rate of 8.68% (7.88% for 2011 and 2012) of wages.
• For Medicare taxes, use the employer rate of 1.45% plus 40% of the employee rate of 1.45%, for a total rate of 2.03% of wages.
• For Additional Medicare Tax; 0.36% (40% of the employee rate of 0.9%) of wages subject to Additional Medicare Tax.
• For income tax withholding, the rate is 3.0% of wages.

Unlike other lines on Form 941-X, enter in column 1 only the corrected wages for workers being reclassified, **not** the amount paid to ALL employees. Enter in column 2 previously reported wages (if any) to reclassified employees. To get the amount for column 4, use the applicable section 3509 rates. If you filed the required information returns for some employees but did not file them for other employees, be sure to use the applicable rates for each employee when calculating the amounts in column 4 and show your calculations on line 23. The tax correction in column 4 will be a positive number if you increased the amount of wages you previously reported. See the instructions for line 22 for more information.

18. Subtotal

Combine the amounts from column 4 on lines 7–17.

Instructions for Form 941-X (Rev. 4-2015)

Example. You entered "1,400.00" in column 4 on line 7, "-500.00" in column 4 on line 8, and "-100.00" in column 4 on line 10. Combine these amounts and enter "800.00" in column 4 on line 18.

Line 7	1,400.00
Line 8	-500.00
Line 10	-100.00
Line 18	800.00

19a. Claiming or Correcting the COBRA Premium Assistance Credit

Effective for tax periods beginning after December 31, 2013, the COBRA premium assistance credit cannot be claimed on Form 941 or 941-SS. Instead, use Form 941-X, lines 19a and 19b, to claim the credit.

Enter 65% of the total COBRA premium assistance payments for all assistance eligible individuals in column 1. Report the premium assistance payments on this line only after the assistance eligible individual's 35% share of the premium has been paid. For COBRA coverage provided under a self-insured plan, COBRA premium assistance is treated as having been made for each assistance eligible individual who paid 35% of the COBRA premium. Do not include the assistance eligible individual's 35% of the premium in the amount entered on this line.

For tax periods ending before January 1, 2014, enter any COBRA premium assistance payments previously claimed on Form 941 or 941-SS, line 12a, in column 2. For tax periods beginning after December 31, 2013, enter -0- in column 2, unless you are correcting a COBRA premium assistance payment previously reported on a Form 941-X. If you or the IRS previously corrected the amount reported, the amount entered in column 2 should take into account all previous corrections.

Enter the difference between column 1 and 2 in column 3. Copy the amount in column 3 to column 4. However, to properly show the amount as a credit or balance due item, enter a positive number in column 3 as a negative number in column 4 or a negative number in column 3 as a positive number in column 4.

 The COBRA premium assistance credit is treated as a credit on the first day of the return period (that is, January 1, April 1, July 1, or October 1). However, because the credit is now claimed on Form 941-X filed AFTER submission of the Form 941, an employer that reduces its required deposits in anticipation of the credit will receive a system-generated notice reflecting a balance due and associated penalties and interest, if applicable. The balance due, including any related penalties and interest, resulting from the reduction in deposits in anticipation of the credit will be abated when the credit is applied. Such abatement will generally occur without any further action from the employer. Alternatively, to prevent triggering a system-generated balance due notice, the employer can make its deposits without a reduction in anticipation of the COBRA premium assistance credit and follow these instructions for claiming the COBRA premium assistance credit.

For more information on the COBRA premium subsidy, visit IRS.gov and enter "COBRA" in the search box.

19b. Number of Individuals Provided COBRA Premium Assistance on line 19a

Enter the total number of assistance eligible individuals provided COBRA premium assistance in column 1. Count each assistance eligible individual who paid a reduced COBRA premium in the quarter as one individual, whether or not the reduced premium was for insurance that covered more than one assistance eligible individual. For example, if the reduced COBRA premium was for coverage for a former employee, spouse, and two children, you would include one individual in the number entered on line 19b for the premium assistance entered on line 19a. Further, each individual is reported only once per quarter. For example, an assistance eligible individual who made monthly premium payments during the quarter would only be reported as one individual on line 19b for that quarter.

For tax periods ending before January 1, 2014, enter the number of assistance eligible individuals provided COBRA premium assistance previously reported on Form 941 or 941-SS, line 12b, in column 2. For tax periods beginning after December 31, 2013, enter -0- in column 2, unless you are correcting a previously filed Form 941-X. If you or the IRS previously corrected the number of individuals reported, the number entered in column 2 should take into account all previous corrections.

20. Total

Combine the amounts on lines 18 and 19a of column 4 and enter the result on line 20.

Your credit. If the amount entered on line 20 is less than zero, for example, "-115.00," you have a credit because you overreported your federal employment taxes.
- If you checked the box on line 1, include this amount on Form 941, line 11 ("Total deposits" line), for the quarter during which you filed Form 941-X or Form 944, line 8 ("Total deposits" line), for the year during which you filed Form 941-X. Do not make any changes to your record of federal tax liability reported on Form 941, line 14, or Schedule B (Form 941), if your Form 941-X is filed timely. The amounts reported on the record should reflect your actual tax liability for the period.
- If you checked the box on line 2, you are filing a claim for refund or abatement of the amount shown.

If your credit is less than $1, we will send a refund or apply it only if you ask us in writing to do so.

Amount you owe. If the amount on line 20 is a positive number, you must pay the amount you owe by the time you file Form 941-X. You may not use any credit that you show on another Form 941-X to pay the amount you owe, even if you filed for the amount you owe and the credit at the same time.

If you owe tax and are filing a timely Form 941-X, do not file an amended Schedule B (Form 941) unless you were assessed an FTD penalty caused by an incorrect, incomplete, or missing Schedule B (Form 941). Do not include the tax increase reported on Form 941-X on any amended Schedule B (Form 941) you file.

If you owe tax and are filing a late Form 941-X, that is, after the due date for Form 941 for the quarter in which you discovered the error, you must file an amended Schedule B (Form 941) with the Form 941-X. Otherwise, the IRS may assess an "averaged" FTD penalty. The total tax reported on the "Total liability for the quarter" line of Schedule B (Form 941), must match the corrected tax (Form 941, line 10, combined with any correction reported on Form 941-X, line 18) for the quarter, less any previous abatements and interest-free tax assessments.

Payment methods. You may pay the amount you owe on line 20 electronically using the Electronic Federal Tax Payment System (EFTPS), by credit or debit card, or by a check or money order.
- The preferred method of payment is EFTPS. For more information, visit *www.eftps.gov*, call EFTPS Customer Service at 1-800-555-4477 or 1-800-733-4829 (TDD), or see Pub. 966, Electronic Federal Tax Payment System: A Guide To Getting Started.

- To pay by credit or debit card, visit the IRS website at *www.irs.gov/e-pay*.
- If you pay by check or money order, make it payable to "United States Treasury." On your check or money order, be sure to write your EIN, "Form 941-X," the calendar quarter you corrected (for example "Quarter 2"), and the calendar year of the quarter you corrected.

You do not have to pay if the amount you owe is less than $1.

Previously assessed FTD penalty. If line 20 reflects overreported tax and the IRS previously assessed a failure-to-deposit (FTD) penalty, you may be able to reduce the penalty. For more information, see the Instructions for Schedule B (Form 941).

Part 4: Explain Your Corrections for This Quarter

21. Correction of Both Underreported and Overreported Amounts

Check the box on line 21 if any corrections you entered on lines 7-19a, column 3, reflect both underreported and overreported amounts.

Example. If you had an increase to social security wages of $15,000 for employee A and a decrease to social security wages of $5,000 for employee B, you would enter $10,000 on line 8, column 3. That $10,000 represents the net change from corrections.

On line 23, you must explain the reason for both the $15,000 increase and the $5,000 decrease.

22. Did You Reclassify Any Workers?

Check the box on line 22 if you reclassified any workers to be independent contractors or nonemployees. Also check this box if the IRS (or you) determined that workers you treated as independent contractors or nonemployees should be classified as employees. On line 23, give us a detailed reason why any worker was reclassified and, if you used section 3509 rates on lines 14-17, for any worker reclassified as an employee, explain why section 3509 rates apply and what rates you used.

Return not filed because you did not treat any workers as employees. If you did not previously file Form 941 because you mistakenly treated all workers as independent contractors or as nonemployees, file a Form 941 for each delinquent quarter.

On each Form 941 for which you are entitled to use section 3509 rates, complete the following steps.
- Write **"Misclassified Employees"** in **bold** letters across the top margin of page 1.
- Enter a zero on line 10 ("Total taxes after adjustments").
- Complete the signature area.
- Attach a completed Form 941-X (see instructions next).

On each Form 941-X complete the following steps.
- Complete the top of Form 941-X, including the date you discovered the error.
- Enter the wage amounts on lines 14-17, column 1.
- Enter zeros on lines 14-17, column 2.
- Complete columns 3 and 4 as instructed in Part 3.
- Provide a detailed statement on line 23.
- Complete the signature area.

⚠️ **CAUTION** *If you cannot use section 3509 rates (for example, because the workers you treated as nonemployees were certain statutory employees), file a Form 941 for each delinquent quarter. Write "**Misclassified Employees**" in **bold** letters across the top margin of page 1 of each Form 941. Complete Form 941 using the Instructions for Form 941. Attach a Form 941-X to each Form 941. Complete the top of Form*

941-X, including the date you discovered the error, and provide a detailed explanation on line 23.

23. Explain Your Corrections

Treasury regulations require you to explain in detail the grounds and facts relied upon to support each correction. On line 23, describe in detail each correction you entered in column 4 on lines 7-17 and 19a. Also use line 23 to describe corrections made on line 19b. If you need more space, attach additional sheets, but be sure to write your name, EIN, "Form 941-X," the quarter you are correcting (for example, "Quarter 2"), and the calendar year of the quarter you are correcting on the top of each sheet.

You must describe the events that caused the underreported or overreported amounts. Explanations such as "social security and Medicare wages were overstated" or "administrative/payroll errors were discovered" are insufficient and may delay processing your Form 941-X because the IRS may need to ask for a more complete explanation.

Provide the following information in your explanation for each correction.
- Form 941-X line number(s) affected.
- Date you discovered the error.
- Difference (amount of the error).
- Cause of the error.

You may report the information in paragraph form. The following paragraph is an example.

"The $1,000 difference shown in column 3 on lines 6, 8, and 10 was discovered on May 15, 2015, during an internal payroll audit. We discovered that we included $1,000 of wages for one of our employees twice. This correction removes the reported wages that were never paid."

For corrections shown on lines 14-17, column 3, explain why the correction was necessary and attach any notice you received from the IRS.

Part 5. Sign Here

You must complete all three pages of Form 941-X and sign it on page 3. If you do not sign, processing of Form 941-X will be delayed.

Who must sign the Form 941-X? The following persons are authorized to sign the return for each type of business entity.
- **Sole proprietorship**—The individual who owns the business.
- **Corporation (including a limited liability company (LLC) treated as a corporation)**—The president, vice president, or other principal officer duly authorized to sign.
- **Partnership (including an LLC treated as a partnership) or unincorporated organization**—A responsible and duly authorized member, partner, or officer having knowledge of its affairs.
- **Single member LLC treated as a disregarded entity for federal income tax purposes**—The owner of the LLC or a principal officer duly authorized to sign.
- **Trust or estate**—The fiduciary.

Form 941-X may also be signed by a duly authorized agent of the taxpayer if a valid power of attorney has been filed.

Alternative signature method. Corporate officers or duly authorized agents may sign Form 941-X by rubber stamp, mechanical device, or computer software program. For details and required documentation, see Rev. Proc. 2005-39. You can find Rev. Proc. 2005-39, 2005-28 I.R.B. 82, at *www.irs.gov/irb/2005-28_IRB/ar16.html*.

Paid Preparer Use Only

A paid preparer must sign Form 941-X and provide the information in the *Paid Preparer Use Only* section of Part 5 if the preparer was paid to prepare Form 941-X and is not an employee of the filing entity. Paid preparers must sign paper returns with a manual signature. The preparer must give you a copy of the return in addition to the copy to be filed with the IRS.

If you are a paid preparer, enter your Preparer Tax Identification Number (PTIN) in the space provided. Include your complete address. If you work for a firm, enter the firm's name and the EIN of the firm. You can apply for a PTIN online or by filing Form W-12, IRS Paid Preparer Tax Identification Number (PTIN) Application and Renewal. For more information about applying for a PTIN online, visit the IRS website at *www.irs.gov/ptin*. You cannot use your PTIN in place of the EIN of the tax preparation firm.

Generally, you are not required to complete this section if you are filing the return as a reporting agent and have a valid Form 8655, Reporting Agent Authorization, on file with the IRS. However, a reporting agent must complete this section if the reporting agent offered legal advice, for example, advising the client on determining whether its workers are employees or independent contractors for federal tax purposes.

How Can You Order Forms, Instructions, and Publications from the IRS?

Visit the IRS website at *www.irs.gov/formspubs*.

Call 1-800-TAX-FORM (1-800-829-3676).

Additional Information

You may find the following products helpful when using Form 941-X.
* Form W-2, Wage and Tax Statement
* Form W-3, Transmittal of Wage and Tax Statements
* General Instructions for Forms W-2 and W-3
* Form W-2AS, American Samoa Wage and Tax Statement
* Form W-2CM, Wage and Tax Statement (Northern Mariana Islands)
* Form W-2GU, Guam Wage and Tax Statement
* Form W-2VI, U.S. Virgin Islands Wage and Tax Statement
* Form W-3SS, Transmittal of Wage and Tax Statements

* Form W-2c, Corrected Wage and Tax Statement
* Form W-3c, Transmittal of Corrected Wage and Tax Statements
* Instructions for Form 843
* Instructions for Form 941
* Instructions for Schedule B (Form 941)
* Instructions for Form 941-SS
* Pub. 1, Your Rights as a Taxpayer
* Pub. 15 (Circular E), Employer's Tax Guide
* Pub. 80 (Circular SS), Federal Tax Guide for Employers in the U.S. Virgin Islands, Guam, American Samoa, and the Commonwealth of the Northern Mariana Islands
* Pub. 966, Electronic Federal Tax Payment System: A Guide To Getting Started

Paperwork Reduction Act Notice We ask for the information on Form 941-X to carry out the Internal Revenue laws of the United States. We need it to figure and collect the right amount of tax. Subtitle C, Employment Taxes, of the Internal Revenue Code imposes employment taxes on wages, including income tax withholding. This form is used to determine the amount of taxes that you owe. Section 6011 requires you to provide the requested information if the tax is applicable to you.

You are not required to provide the information requested on a form that is subject to the Paperwork Reduction Act unless the form displays a valid OMB control number. Books and records relating to a form or instructions must be retained as long as their contents may become material in the administration of any Internal Revenue law.

The time needed to complete and file Form 941-X will vary depending on individual circumstances. The estimated average time is:

Recordkeeping	16 hr., 15 min.
Learning about the law or the form	30 min.
Preparing and sending the form to the IRS	47 min.

If you have comments concerning the accuracy of these time estimates or suggestions for making Form 941-X simpler, we would be happy to hear from you. You can send us comments from *www.irs.gov/formspubs*. Click on *More Information* and then click on *Give us feedback*. Or you can send your comments to: Tax Forms and Publications Division, 1111 Constitution Ave. NW, IR-6526, Washington, DC 20224. **Do not** send Form 941-X to this address. Instead, see *Where Should You File Form 941-X*, earlier.

Form **945**

Department of the Treasury
Internal Revenue Service

Annual Return of Withheld Federal Income Tax

▶ For withholding reported on Forms 1099 and W-2G.
▶ For more information on income tax withholding, see Pub. 15 and Pub. 15-A.
▶ Information about Form 945 and its separate instructions is at *www.irs.gov/form945*.

OMB No. 1545-1430

20**15**

Type or Print

Name (as distinguished from trade name)	Employer identification number (EIN)
Trade name, if any	
Address (number and street)	
City or town, state or province, country, and ZIP or foreign postal code	

If address is different from prior return, check here. ▶ ☐

A If you **do not have to file** returns in the future, check here ▶ ☐ and enter date final payments made. ▶ ----------------

1	Federal income tax withheld from pensions, annuities, IRAs, gambling winnings, etc.	**1**	
2	Backup withholding	**2**	
3	**Total taxes.** If $2,500 or more, this must equal line 7M below or Form 945-A, line M	**3**	
4	Total deposits for 2015, including overpayment applied from a prior year and overpayment applied from Form 945-X	**4**	
5	**Balance due.** If line 3 is more than line 4, enter the difference and see the separate instructions .	**5**	

6 **Overpayment.** If line 4 is more than line 3, enter the difference ▶ $ _____

Check one: ☐ Apply to next return. ☐ Send a refund.

- **All filers:** If line 3 is less than $2,500, **do not** complete line 7 or Form 945-A.
- **Semiweekly schedule depositors:** Complete **Form 945-A** and check here . . . . ▶ ☐
- **Monthly schedule depositors:** Complete **line 7, entries A through M,** and check here . . . . ▶ ☐

7 **Monthly Summary of Federal Tax Liability. (Do not** complete if you were a semiweekly schedule depositor.)

	Tax liability for month		Tax liability for month		Tax liability for month
A January . . .		**F** June		**K** November . .	
B February . .		**G** July		**L** December . .	
C March . . .		**H** August		**M** Total liability for year (add lines **A** through **L**) . .	
D April		**I** September . . .			
E May		**J** October			

Third-Party Designee

Do you want to allow another person to discuss this return with the IRS (see the instructions)? ☐ Yes. Complete the following. ☐ No.

Designee's name ▶ ___   Phone no. ▶ ___   Personal identification number (PIN) ▶ ☐☐☐☐☐

Sign Here

Under penalties of perjury, I declare that I have examined this return, including accompanying schedules and statements, and to the best of my knowledge and belief, it is true, correct, and complete. Declaration of preparer (other than taxpayer) is based on all information of which preparer has any knowledge.

Signature ▶ ___   Print Your Name and Title ▶ ___   Date ▶ ___

Paid Preparer Use Only

Print/Type preparer's name	Preparer's signature	Date	Check ☐ if self-employed	PTIN
Firm's name ▶			Firm's EIN ▶	
Firm's address ▶			Phone no.	

For Privacy Act and Paperwork Reduction Act Notice, see the separate instructions.   Cat. No. 14584B   Form **945** (2015)

Form 945-V,
Payment Voucher

Purpose of Form

Complete Form 945-V if you are making a payment with Form 945. We will use the completed voucher to credit your payment more promptly and accurately, and to improve our service to you.

Making Payments With Form 945

To avoid a penalty, make your payment with your 2015 Form 945 **only if**:

• Your total taxes for the year (Form 945, line 3) are less than $2,500 and you are paying in full with a timely filed return, or

• You are a monthly schedule depositor making a payment in accordance with the Accuracy of Deposits Rule. See section 11 of Pub. 15 for details. In this case, the amount of your payment may be $2,500 or more.

Otherwise, you must make deposits by electronic funds transfer. See section 11 of Pub. 15 for deposit instructions. Don't use Form 945-V to make federal tax deposits.

 Use Form 945-V when making any payment with Form 945. However, if you pay an amount with Form 945 that should have been deposited, you may be subject to a penalty. See Deposit Penalties *in section 11 of Pub. 15.*

Specific Instructions

Box 1—Employer identification number (EIN). If you don't have an EIN, you may apply for one online. Go to IRS.gov and type "EIN" in the search box. You may also apply for an EIN by faxing or mailing Form SS-4 to the IRS. If you haven't received your EIN by the due date of Form 945, write "Applied For" and the date you applied in this entry space.

Box 2—Amount paid. Enter the amount paid with Form 945.

Box 3—Name and address. Enter your name and address as shown on Form 945.

• Enclose your check or money order made payable to "United States Treasury." Be sure to enter your EIN, "Form 945," and "2015" on your check or money order. Don't send cash. Don't staple Form 945-V or your payment to the return (or to each other).

• Detach Form 945-V and send it with your payment and Form 945 to the address provided in the Instructions for Form 945.

Note: You must also complete the entity information above line A on Form 945.

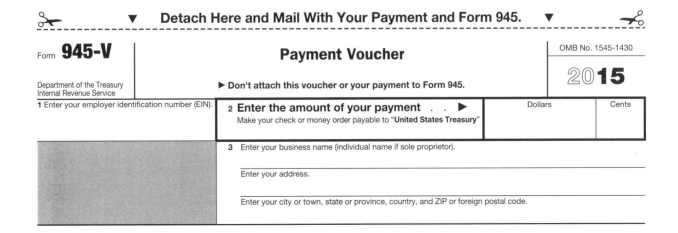

✂ ▼ **Detach Here and Mail With Your Payment and Form 945.** ▼ ✂

Form **945-V**	**Payment Voucher**	OMB No. 1545-1430
Department of the Treasury Internal Revenue Service	▶ **Don't attach this voucher or your payment to Form 945.**	20**15**

1 Enter your employer identification number (EIN).	2 **Enter the amount of your payment** . . ▶ Make your check or money order payable to "**United States Treasury**"	Dollars	Cents
	3 Enter your business name (individual name if sole proprietor).		
	Enter your address.		
	Enter your city or town, state or province, country, and ZIP or foreign postal code.		

20**15**

![Department of the Treasury Internal Revenue Service]

**Department of the Treasury
Internal Revenue Service**

Instructions for Form 945

Annual Return of Withheld Federal Income Tax

Section references are to the Internal Revenue Code unless otherwise noted.

Future Developments

For the latest information about developments related to Form 945 and its instructions, such as legislation enacted after they were published, go to *www.irs.gov/form945*.

Reminders

Correcting a previously filed Form 945. If you discover an error on a previously filed Form 945, make the correction using Form 945-X, Adjusted Annual Return of Withheld Federal Income Tax or Claim for Refund. Form 945-X is a stand-alone form, meaning taxpayers can file Form 945-X when an error is discovered. For more information, see the Instructions for Form 945-X or visit IRS.gov and enter "correcting employment taxes" in the search box.

Federal tax deposits must be made by electronic funds transfer (EFT). You must use EFT to make all federal tax deposits. Generally, an EFT is made using the Electronic Federal Tax Payment System (EFTPS). If you don't want to use EFTPS, you can arrange for your tax professional, financial institution, payroll service, or other trusted third party to make electronic deposits on your behalf. Also, you may arrange for your financial institution to initiate a same-day wire payment on your behalf. EFTPS is a free service provided by the Department of Treasury. Services provided by your tax professional, financial institution, payroll service, or other third party may have a fee.

For more information on making federal tax deposits, see section 11 of Pub. 15. To get more information about EFTPS or to enroll in EFTPS, visit the EFTPS website at *www.eftps.gov*, or call 1-800-555-4477 or 1-800-733-4829 (TDD). Additional information about EFTPS is also available in Pub. 966.

 For an EFTPS deposit to be on time, you must submit the deposit by 8 p.m. Eastern time the day before the date the deposit is due.

Same-day wire payment option. If you fail to submit a deposit transaction on EFTPS by 8 p.m. Eastern time the day before the date a deposit is due, you can still make your deposit on time by using the Federal Tax Collection Service (FTCS). To use the same-day wire payment method, you will need to make arrangements with your financial institution ahead of time. Please check with your financial institution regarding availability, deadlines, and costs. Your financial institution may charge you a fee for payments made this way. To learn more about the information you will need to provide your financial institution to make a same-day wire payment, visit the IRS

website at *www.irs.gov/payments* and click on *Same-day wire*.

Timeliness of federal tax deposits. If a deposit is required to be made on a day that isn't a business day, the deposit is considered timely if it is made by the close of the next business day. A business day is any day other than a Saturday, Sunday, or legal holiday. The term "legal holiday" for deposit purposes includes only those legal holidays in the District of Columbia. Legal holidays in the District of Columbia are provided in Pub. 15.

Electronic filing and payment. Now, more than ever before, businesses can enjoy the benefits of filing tax returns and paying their federal taxes electronically. Whether you rely on a tax professional or handle your own taxes, the IRS offers you convenient programs to make filing and paying easier. Spend less time worrying about taxes and more time running your business. Use e-file and EFTPS to your benefit.

- For e-file, visit the IRS website at *www.irs.gov/efile* for additional information.
- For EFTPS, visit *www.eftps.gov* or call EFTPS Customer Service at 1-800-555-4477 or 1-800-733-4829 (TDD) for additional information.

 If you are filing your tax return or paying your federal taxes electronically, a valid employer identification number (EIN) is required at the time the return is filed or the payment is made. If a valid EIN isn't provided, the return or payment won't be processed. This may result in penalties.

Electronic funds withdrawal (EFW). If you file Form 945 electronically, you can e-file and e-pay (electronic funds withdrawal) the balance due in a single step using tax preparation software or through a tax professional. However, don't use EFW to make federal tax deposits. For more information on paying your taxes using EFW, visit the IRS website at *www.irs.gov/payments*. A fee may be charged to file electronically.

Credit or debit card payments. Payors can pay the balance due shown on Form 945 by credit or debit card. Don't use a credit or debit card to make federal tax deposits. For more information on paying your taxes with a credit or debit card, visit the IRS website at *www.irs.gov/payments*.

Online payment agreement. You may be eligible to apply for an installment agreement online if you have a balance due when you file your return. For more information, see *What if you can't pay in full*, later.

Paid preparers must sign Form 945. Paid preparers must complete and sign the paid preparer's section of Form 945.

Outsourcing your tax duties. You are responsible to ensure that tax returns are filed and deposits and payments are made, even if you contract with a third party to perform these acts. You remain responsible if the third party fails to perform any required action. If you choose to outsource any of your tax duties (that is, withholding, reporting, and paying over federal income tax) to a third-party payer, such as a payroll service provider or reporting agent, visit IRS.gov and enter "outsourcing payroll duties" in the search box for helpful information on this topic.

How to get forms and publications. You can get most IRS forms and publications at *www.irs.gov/orderforms*.

Where can you get telephone help? For answers to your questions about completing Form 945 or tax deposit rules, you can call the IRS at 1-800-829-4933 (Business and Specialty Tax Line) or 1-800-829-4059 (TDD/TTY for persons who are deaf, hard of hearing, or have a speech disability) Monday–Friday from 7:00 a.m. to 7:00 p.m. local time (Alaska and Hawaii follow Pacific time).

Additional information. Pub. 15 explains the rules for withholding, depositing, and reporting federal income tax. Pub. 15-A includes information on federal income tax withholding from pensions, annuities, and Indian gaming profits. For information on withholding from gambling winnings, see the Instructions for Forms W-2G and 5754.

For a list of employment tax products, visit the IRS website at *www.irs.gov/businesses* and click on the *Employment Taxes* link under *Businesses Topics*.

Photographs of missing children. The IRS is a proud partner with the National Center for Missing and Exploited Children. Photographs of missing children selected by the Center may appear in instructions on pages that would otherwise be blank. You can help bring these children home by looking at the photographs and calling 1-800-THE-LOST (1-800-843-5678) if you recognize a child.

General Instructions

Purpose of Form 945

Use Form 945 to report withheld federal income tax from nonpayroll payments. Nonpayroll payments include:

- Pensions (including distributions from tax-favored retirement plans, for example, section 401(k), section 403(b), and governmental section 457(b) plans) and annuities;
- Military retirement;
- Gambling winnings;
- Indian gaming profits;
- Voluntary withholding on certain government payments;
- Voluntary withholding on dividends and other distributions by an Alaska Native Corporation (ANC); and
- Backup withholding.

Report all federal income tax withholding from nonpayroll payments or distributions annually on one Form 945. Don't file more than one Form 945 for any calendar year.

All federal income tax withholding reported on

Forms 1099 (for example, Form 1099-R, Distributions From Pensions, Annuities, Retirement or Profit-Sharing Plans, IRAs, Insurance Contracts, etc.; or 1099-MISC, Miscellaneous Income) or Form W-2G, Certain Gambling Winnings, must be reported on Form 945. Don't report federal income tax withholding from wages on Form 945.

All employment taxes and federal income tax withholding reported on Form W-2, Wage and Tax Statement, must be reported on Form 941, Employer's QUARTERLY Federal Tax Return, or Form 944, Employer's ANNUAL Federal Tax Return; Form 943, Employer's Annual Federal Tax Return for Agricultural Employees; Schedule H (Form 1040), Household Employment Taxes; or Form CT-1, Employer's Annual Railroad Retirement Tax Return.

Don't report on Form 945 federal income tax withheld on distributions to participants from nonqualified pension plans (including nongovernmental section 457(b) plans) and some other deferred compensation arrangements that are treated as wages and are reported on Form W-2. Report such withholding on Form 941 or Form 944. See Pub. 15 for more information.

Compensation paid to H-2A visa holders. Generally, report compensation of $600 or more paid to foreign agricultural workers who entered the country on H-2A visas on Form W-2 and Form 943. However, if an H-2A visa worker did not provide the employer with a taxpayer identification number, the employee is subject to backup withholding. The employer must report the wages and backup withholding on Form 1099-MISC. The employer must also report the backup withholding on Form 945, line 2.

Who Must File

If you withhold federal income tax (including backup withholding) from nonpayroll payments, you must file Form 945. See *Purpose of Form 945,* earlier. You don't have to file Form 945 for those years in which you don't have a nonpayroll tax liability. Don't report on Form 945 withholding that is required to be reported on Form 1042, Annual Withholding Tax Return for U.S. Source Income of Foreign Persons.

When To File

For 2015, file Form 945 by February 1, 2016. However, if you made deposits on time in full payment of the taxes for the year, you may file the return by February 10, 2016. Your return will be considered timely filed if it is properly addressed and mailed First-Class or sent by an IRS-designated private delivery service on or before the due date. See Pub. 15 for more information on IRS-designated private delivery services.

Where To File

In the following list, find the location of your legal residence, principal place of business, office, or agency. Send Form 945 to the address listed for your location.

 Where you file depends on whether or not you are including a payment with the return.

If you are in . . .		Without a payment . . .	With a payment . . .
Connecticut Delaware District of Columbia Florida Georgia Illinois Indiana Kentucky Maine Maryland Massachusetts Michigan New Hampshire	New Jersey New York North Carolina Ohio Pennsylvania Rhode Island South Carolina Tennessee Vermont Virginia West Virginia Wisconsin	Department of the Treasury Internal Revenue Service Cincinnati, OH 45999-0042	Internal Revenue Service P. O. Box 804524 Cincinnati, OH 45280-4524
Alabama Alaska Arizona Arkansas California Colorado Hawaii Idaho Iowa Kansas Louisiana Minnesota Mississippi	Missouri Montana Nebraska Nevada New Mexico North Dakota Oklahoma Oregon South Dakota Texas Utah Washington Wyoming	Department of the Treasury Internal Revenue Service Ogden, UT 84201-0042	Internal Revenue Service P. O. Box 37945 Hartford, CT 06176-7945
No legal residence or principal place of business in any state:		Internal Revenue Service P.O. Box 409101 Ogden, UT 84409	Internal Revenue Service P. O. Box 37945 Hartford, CT 06176-7945
If you are filing Form 945 for an exempt organization or government entity (federal, state, local, or Indian tribal government), use the following addresses, regardless of your location:		Department of the Treasury Internal Revenue Service Ogden, UT 84201-0042	Internal Revenue Service P. O. Box 37945 Hartford, CT 06176-7945

Employer Identification Number (EIN)

If you don't have an EIN, you may apply for one online. Go to IRS.gov and enter "EIN" in the search box.

You may also apply for an EIN by faxing or mailing Form SS-4 to the IRS. If you haven't received your EIN by the due date of Form 945, write "Applied For" and the date you applied in this entry space.

 If you are filing your tax return electronically, a valid EIN is required at the time the return is filed. If a valid EIN isn't provided, the return won't be accepted. This may result in penalties.

 Always be sure the EIN on the form you file exactly matches the EIN the IRS assigned to your business. Don't use your social security number (SSN) or individual taxpayer identification number (ITIN) on forms that ask for an EIN. Filing a Form 945 with an incorrect EIN or using another business's EIN may result in penalties and delays in processing your return.

Name or Address Change

Notify the IRS immediately if you change your business name or address.
• Write to the IRS office where you file your returns (using the *Without a payment* address under *Where To File,*

earlier) to notify the IRS of any name change. See Pub. 1635 to see if you need to apply for a new EIN.
• Complete and mail Form 8822-B to notify the IRS of an address change.

Penalties and Interest

There are penalties for filing Form 945 late and for paying or depositing taxes late, unless there is reasonable cause. See section 11 of Pub. 15 for more information on deposit penalties. There are also penalties for failure to furnish information returns (for example, Forms 1099-MISC, 1099-R, or W-2G) to payees and failure to file copies with the IRS. Interest is charged on taxes paid late at a rate set by law.

If you receive a notice about a penalty after you file this return, reply to the notice with an explanation and we will determine if you meet reasonable-cause criteria. Don't attach an explanation when you file your return.

Use Form 843 to request abatement of assessed penalties or interest. Don't request abatement of assessed penalties or interest on Form 945 or Form 945-X.

 If amounts that must be withheld aren't withheld or aren't deposited or paid to the United States Treasury, the trust fund recovery penalty may apply. The penalty is the full amount of the unpaid trust fund tax. This penalty may apply to you if these unpaid taxes can't be immediately collected from the employer or business.

The penalty may be imposed on all persons who are determined by the IRS to be responsible for collecting, accounting for, or paying over these taxes, and who acted willfully in not doing so. For more information, see section 11 of Pub. 15.

Voluntary Income Tax Withholding

States must allow unemployment compensation recipients to elect to have federal income tax withheld at a 10% rate. Recipients paid under the Railroad Unemployment Insurance Act may also elect withholding at a 10% rate.

Recipients of any of the following payments may request federal income tax withholding at a rate of 7%, 10%, 15%, or 25%.
• Social security and Tier 1 railroad retirement benefits.
• Certain crop disaster payments.
• Commodity Credit Corporation loans.
• Dividends and other distributions by an ANC.

The payee may request withholding on Form W-4V or you may develop your own substitute form. Any voluntary withholding on these payments must be reported on Form 945 (and on the required information return—Form 1099-G, Form SSA-1099, or Form RRB-1099) and is subject to the deposit rules.

Depositing Withheld Taxes

Deposit all nonpayroll (Form 945) withheld federal income tax, including backup withholding, by EFT. Combine all Form 945 taxes for deposit purposes. Don't combine deposits for Forms 941, 943, 944, or Form CT-1 with deposits for Form 945.

Generally, the deposit rules that apply to Form 941 also apply to Form 945. However, because Form 945 is an annual return, the rules for determining your deposit schedule (discussed below) are different from those for Form 941. See section 11 of Pub. 15 for a detailed discussion of the deposit rules.

 If the total amount of tax for 2015 is less than $2,500, you aren't required to make deposits during the year.

Determining Your Deposit Schedule

There are two deposit schedules—**monthly** or **semiweekly**— for determining when you must deposit withheld federal income tax. These schedules tell you when a deposit is due after a tax liability arises (that is, you make a payment subject to federal income tax withholding, including backup withholding). Before the beginning of each calendar year, you must determine which of the two deposit schedules you must use.

For 2016, you are a monthly schedule depositor for Form 945 if the total tax reported on your 2014 Form 945 (line 3) was $50,000 or less. If the total tax reported for 2014 was more than $50,000, you are a semiweekly schedule depositor.

 If you are a monthly schedule depositor and accumulate a $100,000 liability or more on any day during a calendar month, your deposit schedule changes on the next day to semiweekly for the remainder of the year and for the following year. For more information, see the $100,000 Next-Day Deposit Rule in section 11 of Pub. 15.

Specific Instructions

Line A. Final Return

If you go out of business or end operations and you will not have to file Form 945 in the future, file a final return. Be sure to check the box on line A and enter the date that final nonpayroll payments were made.

Line 1. Federal Income Tax Withheld

Enter the federal income tax that you withheld (or were required to withhold) from pensions (including distributions from tax-favored retirement plans, for example, section 401(k), section 403(b), and governmental section 457(b) plans), annuities, IRA distributions, military retirement, Indian gaming profits, and gambling winnings (regular gambling withholding only). Also enter any voluntary amount that you withheld on certain government payments. If you are required to report federal income tax withholding on Forms 1099 (for example, Form 1099-R or 1099-MISC) or Form W-2G, you must report the federal income tax withheld on Form 945.

 Federal income tax withholding reported on Form W-2 must be reported on Form 941, Form 943, Form 944, or Schedule H (Form 1040), as appropriate.

Line 2. Backup Withholding

Enter any backup withholding, including backup withholding on gambling winnings.

Regulated investment companies (RICs) and real estate investment trusts (REITs) must report any backup withholding on Form 945 in the year that the dividends are actually paid. This includes January payments of dividends declared during October, November, and December of the prior year. See the Instructions for Form 1099-DIV for special reporting requirements.

Line 3. Total Taxes

Add lines 1 and 2. If total taxes are $2,500 or more, the amount reported on line 3 must equal the total liability for the year reported on line 7M of the Monthly Summary of Federal Tax Liability, or line M of Form 945-A, Annual Record of Federal Tax Liability.

Line 4. Total Deposits

Enter your total Form 945 deposits for the year, including any overpayment that you applied from filing Form 945-X and any overpayment that you applied from your 2014 return.

Line 5. Balance Due

If line 3 is more than line 4, enter the difference on line 5. Otherwise, see *Overpayment*, later. You don't have to pay if line 5 is under $1. Generally, you should have a balance due only if your total taxes for the year (line 3) are less than $2,500. If you made payments under the accuracy of deposits rule, see section 11 of Pub. 15.

If you were required to make federal tax deposits, pay the amount shown on line 5 by EFT. If you weren't required to make federal tax deposits, you may pay the amount shown on line 5 by EFT, credit card, debit card, check, money order, or EFW. For more information on electronic payment options, visit the IRS website at *www.irs.gov/payments*.

If you pay by EFT, credit card, or debit card, file your return using the *Without a payment* address under *Where To File*, earlier. Don't file Form 945-V, Payment Voucher. If you pay by check or money order, make it payable to "United States Treasury." Enter your EIN, Form 945, and the tax period on your check or money order. Complete Form 945-V and enclose with Form 945.

If line 3 is $2,500 or more and you deposited all taxes when due, the amount on line 5 should be zero.

 If you didn't make deposits as required and instead pay the taxes with Form 945, you may be subject to a penalty.

What if you can't pay in full? If you can't pay the full amount of tax you owe, you can apply for an installment agreement online.

You can apply for an installment agreement online if:
- You can't pay the full amount shown on line 5,
- The total amount you owe is $25,000 or less, and
- You can pay the liability in full in 24 months.

To apply using the Online Payment Agreement Application, go to IRS.gov, click on *Tools*, then click on *Online Payment Agreement*.

Under an installment agreement, you can pay what you owe in monthly installments. There are certain conditions you must meet to enter into and maintain an installment agreement, such as paying the liability within 24 months, and making all required deposits and timely filing tax returns during the length of the agreement.

If your installment agreement is accepted, you will be charged a fee and you will be subject to penalties and interest on the amount of tax not paid by the due date of the return.

Line 6. Overpayment

If line 4 is more than line 3, enter the difference on line 6. **Never make an entry on both lines 5 and 6.**

If you deposited more than the correct amount for the year, you can have the overpayment refunded or applied to your next return by checking the appropriate box. Check only one box below line 6. If you don't check either box or if you check both boxes, generally we will apply the overpayment to your account. We may apply your overpayment to any past due tax account that is shown in our records under your EIN. If line 6 is under $1, we will send a refund or apply it to your next return only if you ask us in writing to do so.

Line 7. Monthly Summary of Federal Tax Liability

 This is a summary of your monthly tax liability, not a summary of deposits made. If line 3 is less than $2,500, don't complete line 7 or Form 945-A.

Complete line 7 only if you were a **monthly schedule depositor** for the entire year and line 3 is $2,500 or more. See *Determining Your Deposit Schedule,* earlier.

 The amount entered on line 7M must equal the amount reported on line 3.

Report your liabilities on Form 945-A instead of on line 7 if either of the following apply.
* You were a **semiweekly schedule depositor** during 2015. Don't complete entries A through M of line 7. Instead, complete and file Form 945-A with Form 945.
* You were a **monthly schedule depositor** for 2015 and during any month you accumulated nonpayroll taxes of $100,000 or more. Because this converted you to a semiweekly schedule depositor for the remainder of 2015 (and for 2016), you must report your liabilities on Form 945-A for the entire year. Don't complete entries A through M of line 7. For more information, see the *$100,000 Next-Day Deposit Rule* in section 11 of Pub. 15.

Third-Party Designee

If you want to allow an employee, a paid tax preparer, or another person to discuss your Form 945 with the IRS, check the "Yes" box in the "Third-Party Designee" section of Form 945. Enter the name, phone number, and five-digit personal identification number (PIN) of the specific person to speak with—not the name of the firm that prepared your return. The designee may choose any five numbers as his or her PIN.

By checking "Yes," you authorize the IRS to talk to the person you named (your designee) about any questions we may have while we process your return. You also authorize your designee to do all of the following.
* Give us any information that is missing from your return.
* Call us for information about the processing of your return.
* Respond to certain IRS notices that you have shared with your designee about math errors and return preparation. The IRS won't send notices to your designee.

You aren't authorizing your designee to bind you to anything (including additional tax liability) or to otherwise represent you before the IRS. If you want to expand the designee's authorization, see Pub. 947.

The authorization will automatically expire 1 year from the due date (without regard to extensions) for filing your Form 945. If you or your designee wants to terminate the authorization, write to the IRS office for your locality using *Without a payment* address under *Where To File,* earlier.

Who Must Sign (Approved Roles)

The following persons are authorized to sign the return for each type of business entity.
* **Sole proprietorship**—The individual who owns the business.
* **Corporation (including a limited liability company (LLC) treated as a corporation)**—The president, vice president, or other principal officer duly authorized to sign.
* **Partnership (including an LLC treated as a partnership) or unincorporated organization**— A responsible and duly authorized partner, member, or officer having knowledge of its affairs.
* **Single member LLC treated as a disregarded entity for federal tax purposes**—The owner of the LLC or a principal officer duly authorized to sign.
* **Trust or estate**—The fiduciary.

Form 945 may also be signed by a duly authorized agent of the taxpayer if a valid power of attorney has been filed.

Alternative signature method. Corporate officers or duly authorized agents may sign Form 945 by rubber stamp, mechanical device, or computer software program. For details and required documentation, see Rev. Proc. 2005-39, 2005-28 I.R.B. 82, available at *www.irs.gov/irb/2005-28_IRB/ar16.html.*

Paid Preparer Use Only

A paid preparer must sign Form 945 and provide the information in the *Paid Preparer Use Only* section if the preparer was paid to prepare Form 945 and isn't an employee of the filing entity. Paid preparers must sign paper returns with a manual signature. The preparer must give you a copy of the return in addition to the copy to be filed with the IRS.

If you are a paid preparer, enter your Preparer Tax Identification Number (PTIN) in the space provided. Include your complete address. If you work for a firm, enter the firm's name and the EIN of the firm. You can apply for a PTIN online or by filing Form W-12. For more information about applying for a PTIN online, visit the IRS website at _www.irs.gov/ptin_. You can't use your PTIN in place of the EIN of the tax preparation firm.

Generally, don't complete this section if you are filing the return as a reporting agent and have a valid Form 8655 on file with the IRS. However, a reporting agent must complete this section if the reporting agent offered legal advice, for example, advising the client on determining whether federal income tax withholding is required on certain payments.

Privacy Act and Paperwork Reduction Act Notice.
We ask for the information on Form 945 to carry out the Internal Revenue laws of the United States. We need it to figure and collect the right amount of tax. Sections 3402, 3405, and 3406 of the Internal Revenue Code require taxpayers to pay over to the IRS federal income tax withheld from certain nonpayroll payments and distributions, including backup withholding. Form 945 is used to report these withholdings. Section 6011 requires you to provide the requested information if the tax is applicable to you. Section 6109 requires you to provide your identification number. If you fail to provide this information in a timely manner, or provide false or fraudulent information, you may be subject to penalties.

You aren't required to provide the information requested on a form that is subject to the Paperwork Reduction Act unless the form displays a valid OMB control number. Books or records relating to a form or instructions must be retained as long as their contents may become material in the administration of any Internal Revenue law.

Generally, tax returns and return information are confidential, as required by section 6103. However, section 6103 allows or requires the IRS to disclose or give the information shown on your tax return to others described in the Code. For example, we may disclose your tax information to the Department of Justice for civil and criminal litigation, and to cities, states, the District of Columbia, and U.S. commonwealths and possessions for use in administering their tax laws. We may also disclose this information to other countries under a tax treaty, to federal and state agencies to enforce federal nontax criminal laws, or to federal law enforcement and intelligence agencies to combat terrorism.

The time needed to complete and file Form 945 will vary depending on individual circumstances. The estimated average time is: **Recordkeeping,** 5 hr., 58 min.; **Learning about the law or the form,** 24 min.; and **Preparing and sending the form to the IRS,** 30 min. If you have comments concerning the accuracy of these time estimates or suggestions for making Form 945 simpler, we would be happy to hear from you. You can send us comments from _www.irs.gov/formspubs_. Click on _More Information_ and then click on _Give us feedback_. Or you can send your comments to the Internal Revenue Service, Tax Forms and Publications Division, 1111 Constitution Ave. NW, IR-6526, Washington, DC 20224. Don't send Form 945 to this address. Instead, see _Where To File,_ earlier.

A-107

Form **945-A**	**Annual Record of Federal Tax Liability**	OMB No. 1545-1430

(Rev. February 2015)

Department of the Treasury
Internal Revenue Service

▶ Information about Form 945-A and its instructions is at *www.irs.gov/form945a*.

▶ File with Form 945, 945-X, CT-1, CT-1 X, 944, or 944-X.

_____ _____ _____ _____
Calendar Year

Name (as shown on Form 945, 945-X, CT-1, CT-1 X, 944, or 944-X)	Employer identification number (EIN)

You must complete this form if you are required to deposit on a semiweekly schedule or if your tax liability during any month was $100,000 or more. Show tax liability here, not deposits. (The IRS gets deposit data from electronic funds transfers.) **DO NOT change your tax liability by adjustments reported on any Form 945-X, 944-X, or CT-1 X.**

January Tax Liability				February Tax Liability				March Tax Liability			
1		17		1		17		1		17	
2		18		2		18		2		18	
3		19		3		19		3		19	
4		20		4		20		4		20	
5		21		5		21		5		21	
6		22		6		22		6		22	
7		23		7		23		7		23	
8		24		8		24		8		24	
9		25		9		25		9		25	
10		26		10		26		10		26	
11		27		11		27		11		27	
12		28		12		28		12		28	
13		29		13		29		13		29	
14		30		14				14		30	
15		31		15				15		31	
16				16				16			
A Total for month ▶				**B** Total for month ▶				**C** Total for month ▶			

April Tax Liability				May Tax Liability				June Tax Liability			
1		17		1		17		1		17	
2		18		2		18		2		18	
3		19		3		19		3		19	
4		20		4		20		4		20	
5		21		5		21		5		21	
6		22		6		22		6		22	
7		23		7		23		7		23	
8		24		8		24		8		24	
9		25		9		25		9		25	
10		26		10		26		10		26	
11		27		11		27		11		27	
12		28		12		28		12		28	
13		29		13		29		13		29	
14		30		14		30		14		30	
15				15		31		15			
16				16				16			
D Total for month ▶				**E** Total for month ▶				**F** Total for month ▶			

For Paperwork Reduction Act Notice, see page 4.   Cat. No. 14733M   Form **945-A** (Rev. 2-2015)

July Tax Liability

1		17	
2		18	
3		19	
4		20	
5		21	
6		22	
7		23	
8		24	
9		25	
10		26	
11		27	
12		28	
13		29	
14		30	
15		31	
16			

G Total for month ▶

August Tax Liability

1		17	
2		18	
3		19	
4		20	
5		21	
6		22	
7		23	
8		24	
9		25	
10		26	
11		27	
12		28	
13		29	
14		30	
15		31	
16			

H Total for month ▶

September Tax Liability

1		17	
2		18	
3		19	
4		20	
5		21	
6		22	
7		23	
8		24	
9		25	
10		26	
11		27	
12		28	
13		29	
14		30	
15			
16			

I Total for month ▶

October Tax Liability

1		17	
2		18	
3		19	
4		20	
5		21	
6		22	
7		23	
8		24	
9		25	
10		26	
11		27	
12		28	
13		29	
14		30	
15		31	
16			

J Total for month ▶

November Tax Liability

1		17	
2		18	
3		19	
4		20	
5		21	
6		22	
7		23	
8		24	
9		25	
10		26	
11		27	
12		28	
13		29	
14		30	
15			
16			

K Total for month ▶

December Tax Liability

1		17	
2		18	
3		19	
4		20	
5		21	
6		22	
7		23	
8		24	
9		25	
10		26	
11		27	
12		28	
13		29	
14		30	
15		31	
16			

L Total for month ▶

M Total tax liability for the year (add lines **A** through **L**). This should equal line 3 on Form 945 (line 15 on Form CT-1, line 7 on Form 944). . . . . ▶

Future Developments

For the latest information about developments related to Form 945-A and its instructions, such as legislation enacted after they were published, go to *www.irs.gov/form945a*.

Reminders

Reporting prior period adjustments. Prior period adjustments are reported on Form 945-X, Adjusted Annual Return of Withheld Federal Income Tax or Claim for Refund; Form CT-1 X, Adjusted Employer's Annual Railroad Retirement Tax Return or Claim for Refund; or Form 944-X, Adjusted Employer's ANNUAL Federal Tax Return or Claim for Refund; and are not taken into account when figuring the tax liability for the current year.

When you file Form 945-A with your Form 945, CT-1, or 944, **do not** change your tax liability by adjustments reported on any Form 945-X, CT-1 X, or 944-X.

Amended Form 945-A. If you have been assessed a failure-to-deposit (FTD) penalty, you may be able to file an amended Form 945-A. For more information, see *Correcting Previously Reported Tax Liability*, later.

General Instructions

Purpose of form. Use Form 945-A to report your federal tax liability (based on the dates payments were made or wages were paid) for the following tax returns.

• Forms 945 and 945-X for federal income tax withholding on nonpayroll payments. Nonpayroll withholding includes backup withholding and federal income tax withholding on pensions, annuities, IRAs, Indian gaming profits, gambling winnings, and military retirement.

• Forms CT-1 and CT-1 X for both employee and employer Tier 1 and Tier 2 taxes.

• Forms 944 and 944-X for federal income tax withheld plus both employee and employer social security and Medicare taxes.

Forms 944(SP), 944-X (SP), and 944-X (PR). If you are a semiweekly schedule depositor who files Formulario 944(SP), Declaración Federal ANUAL de Impuestos del Patrono o Empleador, you should use Formulario 943A-PR, Registro de la Obligación Contributiva Federal del Patrono Agrícola, to report your tax liability. You should also file Form 943A-PR if you file Form 944-X (SP) or Form 944-X (PR) and you need to amend a previously filed Form 943A-PR.

Who must file. Semiweekly schedule depositors must complete and file Form 945-A with their tax return. **Do not** file Form 945-A if your tax liability for the return period is less than $2,500. **Do not** file this form if you are a monthly schedule depositor unless you accumulated a tax liability of $100,000 during any month of the year. Monthly schedule depositors who accumulate $100,000 become semiweekly schedule depositors on the next day and for the remainder of the year (and the next year) and must complete Form 945-A for the entire year.

The deposit rules, including the $100,000 Next-Day Deposit Rule, are explained in section 11 of Pub. 15 (Circular E), Employer's Tax Guide, and in the instructions for your tax return.

Caution. IRS uses Form 945-A to match the tax liability you reported on the returns indicated above with your deposits. The IRS also uses Form 945-A to determine if you have deposited your tax liabilities on time. Unless Form 945-A is properly completed and filed (if applicable) with your tax return, the IRS may propose an "averaged" FTD penalty. See *Deposit Penalties* in section 11 of Pub. 15 (Circular E) for more information.

Specific Instructions

If you must report your tax liabilities on Form 945-A as discussed above, file it with your tax return. Each numbered space on Form 945-A corresponds to a date during the year. Report your tax liabilities in the spaces that correspond to the dates you made payments, not the date tax deposits were made. For example, if you became liable for a pension distribution on December 31, 2013, but did not make the distribution until January 3, 2014, the federal income tax withholding liability for the distribution must be reported on Form 945-A for 2014, on line 3 under January Tax Liability.

Enter your business information. Carefully enter your employer identification number (EIN) and name at the top of the form. Make sure that they exactly match the name of your business and the EIN that the IRS assigned to your business and also agree with the name and EIN shown on the attached Form 945, 945-X, CT-1, CT-1 X, 944, or 944-X.

Calendar year. Enter the calendar year of the Form 945, 945-X, CT-1, CT-1 X, 944, or 944-X to which Form 945-A is attached.

Form 945 filers. Do not complete entries A through M of the Monthly Summary of Federal Tax Liability (Form 945, line 7). Be sure to mark the semiweekly schedule depositor checkbox above line 7 on Form 945.

Form CT-1 filers. Do not complete the Monthly Summary of Railroad Retirement Tax Liability (Form CT-1).

Form 944 filers. On Form 944, check the box for "Line 7 is $2,500 or more" at line 13, and leave blank lines 13a–13m.

Enter your tax liability by month. Enter your tax liabilities in the spaces that correspond to the dates you **paid** wages to your employees or made nonpayroll payments, not the date deposits were made. The total tax liability for the year (line M) must equal net taxes on Form 945 (line 3), Form 944 (line 7), or Form CT-1 (line 15). Report your tax liabilities on this form corresponding to the dates of each wage payment or nonpayroll payment, **not** to when the liabilities are accrued. Enter the monthly totals on lines A, B, C, D, E, F, G, H, I, J, K, and L. Enter the total for the year on line M.

For example, if you are a Form 945 filer, your payroll period ended on December 31, 2013, and you **paid** the nonpayroll payments for that period on January 7, 2014, you would:

• Go to January (on Form 945-A filed with your 2014 return), and

• Enter your tax liability on line 7 (because line 7 represents the seventh day of the month).

 Make sure you have checked the appropriate box above line 7 of Form 945 to show that you are a semiweekly schedule depositor.

Example 1. Cedar Co., which has a semiweekly deposit schedule, makes periodic payments on gambling winnings on the 15th day of each month. On December 24, 2014, in addition to its periodic payments, it withheld from a payment on gambling winnings under the backup withholding rules. Since Cedar Co. is a semiweekly schedule depositor, it **must** record these nonpayroll withholding liabilities on Form 945-A. It must report tax liabilities on line 15 for each month and line 24 for December.

Cedar Co. enters the monthly totals on lines **A** through **L**. It adds these monthly subtotals and enters the total tax liability for the year on line **M**. The amount on line **M** should equal Form 945, line 3.

Example 2. Fir Co. is a semiweekly schedule depositor. During January, it withheld federal income tax on pension distributions as follows: $52,000 on January 10; $35,000 on January 24. Since Fir Co. is a semiweekly schedule depositor, it **must** record its federal income tax withholding liabilities on Form 945-A. It must record $52,000 on line 10 and $35,000 on line 24 for January.

Example 3. Because Elm Co. is a new business, it is a monthly schedule depositor at the beginning of 2014. During January, it withheld federal income tax on nonpayroll payments as follows: $2,000 on January 10; $99,000 on January 24. The deposit rules require that a monthly schedule depositor begin depositing on a semiweekly deposit schedule when a $100,000 or more tax liability is accumulated on any day within a month (see section 11 of Pub. 15 (Circular E) for details). Since Elm Co. accumulated $101,000 ($2,000 + $99,000) on January 24, 2014, it became a semiweekly schedule depositor on January 25, 2014. Elm Co. must complete Form 945-A and file it with Form 945. It must record $2,000 on line 10 and $99,000 on line 24 for January. **No entries** should be made on Form 945, line 7, although Elm Co. was a monthly schedule depositor until January 25.

Correcting Previously Reported Tax Liability

Semiweekly schedule depositors. If you have been assessed an FTD penalty and you made an error on Form 945-A and the correction will not change the total liability you reported on Form 945-A, you may be able to reduce your penalty by filing an amended Form 945-A.

Example. You reported a tax liability of $3,000 on January 1. However, the liability was actually for March. Prepare an amended Form 945-A showing the $3,000 liability on March 1. Also, you must enter the liabilities previously reported for the year that did not change. Write "Amended" at the top of Form 945-A. The IRS will refigure the penalty and notify you of any change in the penalty.

Monthly schedule depositors. You can file Form 945-A if you have been assessed an FTD penalty and you made an error on the monthly tax liability section of Form 945. When completing Form 945-A, only enter the monthly totals. The daily entries are not required.

Where to file. File your amended Form 945-A, or, for monthly schedule depositors, your original Form 945-A at the address provided in the penalty notice you received. If you are filing an amended Form 945-A, you do not have to submit your original Form 945-A.

Forms 945-X, CT-1 X, and 944-X

Tax decrease. If you are filing Form 945-X, CT-1 X, or 944-X, you can file an amended Form 945-A with the form if **both** of the following apply.

1. You have a tax decrease.

2. You were assessed an FTD penalty.

File your amended Form 945-A with Form 945-X, CT-1 X, or 944-X. The total liability reported on your amended Form 945-A must equal the corrected amount of tax reported on Form 945-X, CT-1 X, or 944-X. If your penalty is decreased, the IRS will include the penalty decrease with your tax decrease.

Tax increase—Form 945-X, CT-1 X, or 944-X filed timely. If you are filing a timely Form 945-X, CT-1 X, or 944-X showing a tax increase, do not file an amended Form 945-A, unless you were assessed an FTD penalty caused by an incorrect, incomplete, or missing Form 945-A. Do not include the tax increase reported on Form 945-X, CT-1 X, or 944-X on an amended Form 945-A you file.

Tax increase—Form 945-X, CT-1 X, or 944-X filed late. If you owe tax and are filing late, that is, after the due date of the return for the filing period in which you discovered the error, you must file the form with an amended Form 945-A. Otherwise, IRS may assess an "averaged" FTD penalty.

The total tax reported on line M of Form 945-A must match the corrected tax (Form 945, line 3; Form 944, line 7; Form CT-1, line 15 (line 13 for years before 2013); combined with any correction reported on Form 945-X, line 5 (Form 944-X, line 17; Form CT-1 X, line 19) for the year, less any previous abatements and interest-free tax assessments.

Paperwork Reduction Act Notice. We ask for the information on this form to carry out the Internal Revenue laws of the United States. You are required to give us the information. We need it to ensure that you are complying with these laws and to allow us to figure and collect the right amount of tax.

You are not required to provide the information requested on a form that is subject to the Paperwork Reduction Act unless the form displays a valid OMB control number. Books or records relating to a form or its instructions must be retained as long as their contents may become material in the administration of any Internal Revenue law. Generally, tax returns and return information are confidential, as required by Code section 6103.

The time needed to complete and file this form will vary depending on individual circumstances. The estimated average time is:

Recordkeeping . . . . 6 hr., 27 min.

Learning . . . . 6 min.

Preparing and sending the form to the IRS . . . . 12 min.

If you have comments concerning the accuracy of these time estimates or suggestions for making this form simpler, we would be happy to hear from you. You can write to the IRS at the address listed in the Privacy Act Notice for your tax return.

9595 ☐ VOID ☐ CORRECTED

PAYER'S name, street address, city or town, state or province, country, ZIP or foreign postal code, and telephone no.		1 Rents $	OMB No. 1545-0115 2016 Form 1099-MISC	Miscellaneous Income
		2 Royalties $		
		3 Other income $	4 Federal income tax withheld $	Copy A For
PAYER'S federal identification number	RECIPIENT'S identification number	5 Fishing boat proceeds $	6 Medical and health care payments $	Internal Revenue Service Center File with Form 1096.
RECIPIENT'S name		7 Nonemployee compensation $	8 Substitute payments in lieu of dividends or interest $	For Privacy Act and Paperwork Reduction Act Notice, see the
Street address (including apt. no.)		9 Payer made direct sales of $5,000 or more of consumer products to a buyer (recipient) for resale ▶ ☐	10 Crop insurance proceeds $	2016 General Instructions for Certain
City or town, state or province, country, and ZIP or foreign postal code		11	12	Information Returns.
Account number (see instructions)	FATCA filing requirement ☐	2nd TIN not. ☐	13 Excess golden parachute payments $	14 Gross proceeds paid to an attorney $
15a Section 409A deferrals $	15b Section 409A income $	16 State tax withheld $ $	17 State/Payer's state no.	18 State income $ $

Form **1099-MISC**   Cat. No. 14425J   www.irs.gov/form1099misc   Department of the Treasury - Internal Revenue Service

Do Not Cut or Separate Forms on This Page — Do Not Cut or Separate Forms on This Page

A-112

9898 ☐ VOID ☐ CORRECTED

PAYER'S name, street address, city or town, state or province, country, and ZIP or foreign postal code		1 Gross distribution $	OMB No. 1545-0119 2016 Form 1099-R	Distributions From Pensions, Annuities, Retirement or Profit-Sharing Plans, IRAs, Insurance Contracts, etc.
		2a Taxable amount $		
		2b Taxable amount not determined ☐	Total distribution ☐	Copy A For Internal Revenue Service Center
PAYER'S federal identification number	RECIPIENT'S identification number	3 Capital gain (included in box 2a) $	4 Federal income tax withheld $	File with Form 1096.
RECIPIENT'S name		5 Employee contributions /Designated Roth contributions or insurance premiums $	6 Net unrealized appreciation in employer's securities $	For Privacy Act and Paperwork Reduction Act Notice, see the 2016 General Instructions for Certain Information Returns.
Street address (including apt. no.)		7 Distribution code(s) ☐ IRA/ SEP/ SIMPLE	8 Other $ %	
City or town, state or province, country, and ZIP or foreign postal code		9a Your percentage of total distribution %	9b Total employee contributions $	
10 Amount allocable to IRR within 5 years $	11 1st year of desig. Roth contrib.	FATCA filing requirement ☐	12 State tax withheld $ $	13 State/Payer's state no.	14 State distribution $ $
Account number (see instructions)			15 Local tax withheld $ $	16 Name of locality	17 Local distribution $ $

Form **1099-R**   Cat. No. 14436Q   www.irs.gov/form1099r   Department of the Treasury - Internal Revenue Service

Do Not Cut or Separate Forms on This Page   —   Do Not Cut or Separate Forms on This Page

A-113

SOCIAL SECURITY ADMINISTRATION
Application for a Social Security Card

Applying for a Social Security Card is free!

USE THIS APPLICATION TO:

- Apply for an original Social Security card
- Apply for a replacement Social Security card
- Change or correct information on your Social Security number record

IMPORTANT: You MUST provide a properly completed application and the required evidence before we can process your application. We can only accept original documents or documents certified by the custodian of the original record. Notarized copies or photocopies which have not been certified by the custodian of the record are not acceptable. We will return any documents submitted with your application. For assistance call us at 1-800-772-1213 or visit our website at www.socialsecurity.gov.

Original Social Security Card

To apply for an original card, you must provide at least two documents to prove age, identity, and U.S. citizenship or current lawful, work-authorized immigration status. If you are not a U.S. citizen and do not have DHS work authorization, you must prove that you have a valid non-work reason for requesting a card. See page 2 for an explanation of acceptable documents.

NOTE: If you are age 12 or older and have never received a Social Security number, you must apply in person.

Replacement Social Security Card

To apply for a replacement card, you must provide one document to prove your identity. If you were born outside the U.S., you must also provide documents to prove your U.S. citizenship or current, lawful, work-authorized status. See page 2 for an explanation of acceptable documents.

Changing Information on Your Social Security Record

To change the information on your Social Security number record (i.e., a name or citizenship change, or corrected date of birth) you must provide documents to prove your identity, support the requested change, and establish the reason for the change. For example, you may provide a birth certificate to show your correct date of birth. A document supporting a name change must be recent and identify you by both your old and new names. If the name change event occurred over two years ago or if the name change document does not have enough information to prove your identity, you must also provide documents to prove your identity in your prior name and/or in some cases your new legal name. If you were born outside the U.S. you must provide a document to prove your U.S. citizenship or current lawful, work-authorized status. See page 2 for an explanation of acceptable documents.

LIMITS ON REPLACEMENT SOCIAL SECURITY CARDS

Public Law 108-458 limits the number of replacement Social Security cards you may receive to 3 per calendar year and 10 in a lifetime. Cards issued to reflect changes to your legal name or changes to a work authorization legend do not count toward these limits. We may also grant exceptions to these limits if you provide evidence from an official source to establish that a Social Security card is required.

IF YOU HAVE ANY QUESTIONS

If you have any questions about this form or about the evidence documents you must provide, please visit our website at www.socialsecurity.gov for additional information as well as locations of our offices and Social Security Card Centers. You may also call Social Security at 1-800-772-1213. You can also find your nearest office or Card Center in your local phone book.

EVIDENCE DOCUMENTS

The following lists are examples of the types of documents you must provide with your application and are not all inclusive. Call us at 1-800-772-1213 if you cannot provide these documents.

IMPORTANT : If you are completing this application on behalf of someone else, you must provide evidence that shows your authority to sign the application as well as documents to prove your identity and the identity of the person for whom you are filing the application. We can only accept original documents or documents certified by the custodian of the original record. Notarized copies or photocopies which have not been certified by the custodian of the record are not acceptable.

Evidence of Age

In general, you must provide your birth certificate. In some situations, we may accept another document that shows your age. Some of the other documents we may accept are:

- U.S. hospital record of your birth (created at the time of birth)
- Religious record established before age five showing your age or date of birth
- Passport
- Final Adoption Decree (the adoption decree must show that the birth information was taken from the original birth certificate)

Evidence of Identity

You must provide current, unexpired evidence of identity in your legal name. Your legal name will be shown on the Social Security card. Generally, we prefer to see documents issued in the U.S. Documents you submit to establish identity must show your legal name AND provide biographical information (your date of birth, age, or parents' names) **and/or** physical information (photograph, or physical description - height, eye and hair color, etc.). If you send a photo identity document but do not appear in person, the document must show your biographical information (e.g., your date of birth, age, or parents' names). Generally, documents without an expiration date should have been issued within the past two years for adults and within the past four years for children.

As proof of your identity, you must provide a:

- U.S. driver's license; or
- U.S. State-issued non-driver identity card; or
- U.S. passport

If you do not have one of the documents above or cannot get a replacement within 10 work days, we may accept other documents that show your legal name and biographical information, such as a U.S. military identity card, Certificate of Naturalization, employee identity card, certified copy of medical record (clinic, doctor or hospital), health insurance card, Medicaid card, or school identity card/record. For young children, we may accept medical records (clinic, doctor, or hospital) maintained by the medical provider. We may also accept a final adoption decree, or a school identity card, or other school record maintained by the school.

If you are not a U.S. citizen, we must see your current U.S. immigration document(s) and your foreign passport with biographical information or photograph.

WE CANNOT ACCEPT A BIRTH CERTIFICATE, HOSPITAL SOUVENIR BIRTH CERTIFICATE, SOCIAL SECURITY CARD STUB OR A SOCIAL SECURITY RECORD as evidence of identity.

Evidence of U.S. Citizenship

In general, you must provide your U.S. birth certificate or U.S. Passport. Other documents you may provide are a Consular Report of Birth, Certificate of Citizenship, or Certificate of Naturalization.

Evidence of Immigration Status

You must provide a current unexpired document issued to you by the Department of Homeland Security (DHS) showing your immigration status, such as Form I-551, I-94, or I-766. If you are an international student or exchange visitor, you may need to provide additional documents, such as Form I-20, DS-2019, or a letter authorizing employment from your school and employer (F-1) or sponsor (J-1). We CANNOT accept a receipt showing you applied for the document. If you are not authorized to work in the U.S., we can issue you a Social Security card only if you need the number for a valid non-work reason. Your card will be marked to show you cannot work and if you do work, we will notify DHS. See page 3, item 5 for more information.

HOW TO COMPLETE THIS APPLICATION

Complete and sign this application LEGIBLY using ONLY black or blue ink on the attached or downloaded form using only 8 ½" x 11" (or A4 8.25" x 11.7") paper.

GENERAL: Items on the form are self-explanatory or are discussed below. The numbers match the numbered items on the form. If you are completing this form for someone else, please complete the items as they apply to that person.

4. Show the month, day, and full (4 digit) year of birth; for example, "1998" for year of birth.

5. If you check "Legal Alien Not Allowed to Work" or "Other," you must provide a document from a U.S. Federal, State, or local government agency that explains why you need a Social Security number and that you meet all the requirements for the government benefit. NOTE: Most agencies do not require that you have a Social Security number. Contact us to see if your reason qualifies for a Social Security number.

6., 7. Providing race and ethnicity information is voluntary and is requested for informational and statistical purposes only. Your choice whether to answer or not does not affect decisions we make on your application. If you do provide this information, we will treat it very carefully.

9.B., 10.B. If you are applying for an original Social Security card for a child under age 18, you MUST show the parents' Social Security numbers unless the parent was never assigned a Social Security number. If the number is not known and you cannot obtain it, check the "unknown" box.

13. If the date of birth you show in item 4 is different from the date of birth currently shown on your Social Security record, show the date of birth currently shown on your record in item 13 and provide evidence to support the date of birth shown in item 4.

16. Show an address where you can receive your card 7 to 14 days from now.

17. WHO CAN SIGN THE APPLICATION? If you are age 18 or older and are physically and mentally capable of reading and completing the application, you must sign in item 17. If you are under age 18, you may either sign yourself, or a parent or legal guardian may sign for you. If you are over age 18 and cannot sign on your own behalf, a legal guardian, parent, or close relative may generally sign for you. If you cannot sign your name, you should sign with an "X" mark and have two people sign as witnesses in the space beside the mark. Please do not alter your signature by including additional information on the signature line as this may invalidate your application. Call us if you have questions about who may sign your application.

HOW TO SUBMIT THIS APPLICATION

In most cases, you can take or mail this signed application with your documents to any Social Security office. Any documents you mail to us will be returned to you. Go to https://secure.ssa.gov/apps6z/FOLO/fo001.jsp to find the Social Security office or Social Security Card Center that serves your area.

PROTECT YOUR SOCIAL SECURITY NUMBER AND CARD

Protect your SSN card and number from loss and identity theft. DO NOT carry your SSN card with you. Keep it in a secure location and only take it with you when you must show the card; e.g., to obtain a new job, open a new bank account, or to obtain benefits from certain U.S. agencies. Use caution in giving out your Social Security number to others, particularly during phone, mail, email and Internet requests you did not initiate.

PRIVACY ACT STATEMENT
Collection and Use of Personal Information

Sections 205(c) and 702 of the Social Security Act, as amended, authorize us to collect this information. The information you provide will be used to assign you a Social Security number and issue a Social Security card.

The information you furnish on this form is voluntary. However, failure to provide the requested information may prevent us from issuing you a Social Security number and card.

We rarely use the information you supply for any purpose other than for issuing a Social Security number and card. However, we may use it for the administration and integrity of Social Security programs. We may also disclose information to another person or to another agency in accordance with approved routine uses, which include but are not limited to the following:

1. To enable a third party or an agency to assist Social Security in establishing rights to Social Security benefits and/or coverage;

2. To comply with Federal laws requiring the release of information from Social Security records (e.g., to the Government Accountability Office and Department of Veterans' Affairs);

3. To make determinations for eligibility in similar health and income maintenance programs at the Federal, State, and local level; and

4. To facilitate statistical research, audit or investigative activities necessary to assure the integrity of Social Security programs.

We may also use the information you provide in computer matching programs. Matching programs compare our records with records kept by other Federal, State, or local government agencies. Information from these matching programs can be used to establish or verify a person's eligibility for Federally-funded or administered benefit programs and for repayment of payments or delinquent debts under these programs.

Complete lists of routine uses for this information are available in System of Records Notice 60-0058 (Master Files of Social Security Number (SSN) Holders and SSN Applications). The Notice, additional information regarding this form, and information regarding our systems and programs, are available on-line at www.socialsecurity.gov or at any local Social Security office.

This information collection meets the requirements of 44 U.S.C. §3507, as amended by Section 2 of the Paperwork Reduction Act of 1995 . You do not need to answer these questions unless we display a valid Office of Management and Budget control number. We estimate that it will take about 8.5 to 9.5 minutes to read the instructions, gather the facts, and answer the questions. You may send comments on our time estimate to: SSA, 6401 Security Blvd., Baltimore, MD 21235-6401. **Send only comments relating to our time estimate to this address, not the completed form.**

SOCIAL SECURITY ADMINISTRATION
Application for a Social Security Card

Form Approved
OMB No. 0960-0066

1

NAME TO BE SHOWN ON CARD	First	Full Middle Name	Last
FULL NAME AT BIRTH IF OTHER THAN ABOVE	First	Full Middle Name	Last
OTHER NAMES USED			

2 Social Security number previously assigned to the person listed in item 1

☐☐☐ – ☐☐ – ☐☐☐☐

3 PLACE OF BIRTH _____
(Do Not Abbreviate) City   State or Foreign Country

Office Use Only   FCI

4 DATE OF BIRTH _____ MM/DD/YYYY

5 CITIZENSHIP (Check One)
☐ U.S. Citizen
☐ Legal Alien Allowed To Work
☐ Legal Alien **Not** Allowed To Work(See Instructions On Page 3)
☐ Other (See Instructions On Page 3)

6 ETHNICITY
Are You Hispanic or Latino? (Your Response is Voluntary)
☐ Yes   ☐ No

7 RACE
Select One or More (Your Response is Voluntary)
☐ Native Hawaiian   ☐ American Indian   ☐ Other Pacific Islander
☐ Alaska Native   ☐ Black/African American   ☐ White
☐ Asian

8 SEX   ☐ Male   ☐ Female

9

A. PARENT/ MOTHER'S NAME AT HER BIRTH	First	Full Middle Name	Last

B. PARENT/ MOTHER'S SOCIAL SECURITY NUMBER (See instructions for 9 B on Page 3)
☐☐☐ – ☐☐ – ☐☐☐☐   ☐ Unknown

10

A. PARENT/ FATHER'S NAME	First	Full Middle Name	Last

B. PARENT/ FATHER'S SOCIAL SECURITY NUMBER (See instructions for 10B on Page 3)
☐☐☐ – ☐☐ – ☐☐☐☐   ☐ Unknown

11 Has the person listed in item 1 or anyone acting on his/her behalf ever filed for or received a Social Security number card before?
☐ Yes (If "yes" answer questions 12-13)   ☐ No   ☐ Don't Know (If "don't know," skip to question 14.)

12 Name shown on the most recent Social Security card issued for the person listed in item 1

First	Full Middle Name	Last

13 Enter any different date of birth if used on an earlier application for a card
_____ MM/DD/YYYY

14 TODAY'S DATE _____ MM/DD/YYYY

15 DAYTIME PHONE NUMBER _____ _____ Area Code   Number

16 MAILING ADDRESS (Do Not Abbreviate)
Street Address, Apt. No., PO Box, Rural Route No.
City   State/Foreign Country   ZIP Code

17 I declare under penalty of perjury that I have examined all the information on this form, and on any accompanying statements or forms, and it is true and correct to the best to my knowledge.
YOUR SIGNATURE

18 YOUR RELATIONSHIP TO THE PERSON IN ITEM 1 IS:
☐ Self   ☐ Natural Or Adoptive Parent   ☐ Legal Guardian   ☐ Other Specify _____

DO NOT WRITE BELOW THIS LINE (FOR SSA USE ONLY)

NPN			DOC	NTI	CAN		ITV
PBC	EVI	EVA	EVC	PRA	NWR	DNR	UNIT

EVIDENCE SUBMITTED

SIGNATURE AND TITLE OF EMPLOYEE(S) REVIEWING EVIDENCE AND/OR CONDUCTING INTERVIEW

_____ DATE

DCL _____ DATE

Form **SS-5** (08-2011) ef (08-2011)   Destroy Prior Editions   Page 5

A-118

Form **SS-8**

(Rev. May 2014)

Department of the Treasury
Internal Revenue Service

Determination of Worker Status for Purposes of Federal Employment Taxes and Income Tax Withholding

▶ Information about Form SS-8 and its separate instructions is at *www.irs.gov/formss8*.

OMB. No. 1545-0004

For IRS Use Only:
Case Number:

_____

Earliest Receipt Date:

Name of firm (or person) for whom the worker performed services	Worker's name

Firm's mailing address (include street address, apt. or suite no., city, state, and ZIP code)	Worker's mailing address (include street address, apt. or suite no., city, state, and ZIP code)

Trade name	Firm's email address	Worker's daytime telephone number	Worker's email address
Firm's fax number	Firm's website	Worker's alternate telephone number	Worker's fax number
Firm's telephone number (include area code)	Firm's employer identification number	Worker's social security number	Worker's employer identification number (if any)

Note. If the worker is paid for these services by a firm other than the one listed on this form, enter the name, address, and employer identification number of the payer. ▶ --

Disclosure of Information

The information provided on Form SS-8 may be disclosed to the firm, worker, or payer named above to assist the IRS in the determination process. For example, if you are a worker, we may disclose the information you provide on Form SS-8 to the firm or payer named above. The information can only be disclosed to assist with the determination process. If you provide incomplete information, we may not be able to process your request. See *Privacy Act and Paperwork Reduction Act Notice* in the separate instructions for more information. **If you do not want this information disclosed to other parties, do not file Form SS-8.**

Parts I–V. All filers of Form SS-8 must complete all questions in Parts I–IV. Part V must be completed if the worker provides a service directly to customers or is a salesperson. If you cannot answer a question, enter "Unknown" or "Does not apply." If you need more space for a question, attach another sheet with the part and question number clearly identified. Write your firm's name (or worker's name) and employer identification number (or social security number) at the top of each additional sheet attached to this form.

Part I   General Information

1   This form is being completed by: ☐ Firm ☐ Worker; for services performed _____ to _____ .
     (beginning date)   (ending date)

2   Explain your reason(s) for filing this form (for example, you received a bill from the IRS, you believe you erroneously received a Form 1099 or Form W-2, you are unable to get workers' compensation benefits, or you were audited or are being audited by the IRS). ------------------------
     ----
     ----

3   Total number of workers who performed or are performing the same or similar services: _____ .

4   How did the worker obtain the job? ☐ Application   ☐ Bid   ☐ Employment Agency   ☐ Other (specify) _____

5   **Attach copies of all supporting documentation (for example, contracts, invoices, memos, Forms W-2 or Forms 1099-MISC issued or received, IRS closing agreements or IRS rulings).** In addition, please inform us of any current or past litigation concerning the worker's status. If no income reporting forms (Form 1099-MISC or W-2) were furnished to the worker, enter the amount of income earned for the year(s) at issue $ _____ .

     If both Form W-2 and Form 1099-MISC were issued or received, explain why. --
     ----

6   Describe the firm's business. --

For Privacy Act and Paperwork Reduction Act Notice, see the separate instructions.   Cat. No. 16106T   Form **SS-8** (Rev. 5-2014)

Part I   General Information (continued)

7   If the worker received pay from more than one entity because of an event such as the sale, merger, acquisition, or reorganization of the firm for whom the services are performed, provide the following: Name of the firm's previous owner:
_____

Previous owner's taxpayer identification number: _____ Change was a: ☐ Sale ☐ Merger ☐ Acquisition ☐ Reorganization
☐ Other (specify) _____

Description of above change: _____
_____

Date of change (MM/DD/YY): _____

8   Describe the work done by the worker and provide the worker's job title. _____
_____
_____

9   Explain why you believe the worker is an employee or an independent contractor. _____
_____
_____

10 Did the worker perform services for the firm in any capacity before providing the services that are the subject of this determination request?
☐ Yes   ☐ No   ☐ N/A

If "Yes," what were the dates of the prior service? _____

If "Yes," explain the differences, if any, between the current and prior service. _____
_____
_____

11 If the work is done under a written agreement between the firm and the worker, attach a copy (preferably signed by both parties). Describe the terms and conditions of the work arrangement. _____
_____
_____

Part II   Behavioral Control (Provide names and titles of specific individuals, if applicable.)

1   What specific training and/or instruction is the worker given by the firm? _____

2   How does the worker receive work assignments? _____

3   Who determines the methods by which the assignments are performed? _____

4   Who is the worker required to contact if problems or complaints arise and who is responsible for their resolution? _____

5   What types of reports are required from the worker? Attach examples. _____

6   Describe the worker's daily routine such as his or her schedule or hours. _____
_____

7   At what location(s) does the worker perform services (for example, firm's premises, own shop or office, home, customer's location)? Indicate the appropriate percentage of time the worker spends in each location, if more than one. _____

8   Describe any meetings the worker is required to attend and any penalties for not attending (for example, sales meetings, monthly meetings, staff meetings). _____

9   Is the worker required to provide the services personally? .   .   .   .   ☐ Yes   ☐ No

10 If substitutes or helpers are needed, who hires them? _____

11 If the worker hires the substitutes or helpers, is approval required? .   .   .   .   ☐ Yes   ☐ No
If "Yes," by whom? _____

12 Who pays the substitutes or helpers? _____

13 Is the worker reimbursed if the worker pays the substitutes or helpers? .   .   .   .   ☐ Yes   ☐ No
If "Yes," by whom?

Part III **Financial Control** (Provide names and titles of specific individuals, if applicable.)

1 List the supplies, equipment, materials, and property provided by each party:
   The firm: _____
   The worker: _____
   Other party: _____

2 Does the worker lease equipment, space, or a facility? . . . . ☐ **Yes** ☐ **No**
   If "Yes," what are the terms of the lease? (Attach a copy or explanatory statement.) _____

3 What expenses are incurred by the worker in the performance of services for the firm? _____

4 Specify which, if any, expenses are reimbursed by:
   The firm: _____
   Other party: _____

5 Type of pay the worker receives: ☐ Salary   ☐ Commission   ☐ Hourly Wage   ☐ Piece Work
   ☐ Lump Sum   ☐ Other (specify) _____
   If type of pay is commission, and the firm guarantees a minimum amount of pay, specify amount. $ _____

6 Is the worker allowed a drawing account for advances? . . . . ☐ **Yes** ☐ **No**
   If "Yes," how often? _____
   Specify any restrictions. _____

7 Whom does the customer pay? . . . . ☐ Firm   ☐ Worker
   If worker, does the worker pay the total amount to the firm? ☐ **Yes**   ☐ **No**   If "No," explain. _____

8 Does the firm carry workers' compensation insurance on the worker? . . . . ☐ **Yes** ☐ **No**

9 What economic loss or financial risk, if any, can the worker incur beyond the normal loss of salary (for example, loss or damage of equipment, material)? _____

10 Does the worker establish the level of payment for the services provided or the products sold? . . . . ☐ **Yes** ☐ **No**
    If "No," who does? _____

Part IV **Relationship of the Worker and Firm**

1 Please check the benefits available to the worker: ☐ Paid vacations   ☐ Sick pay   ☐ Paid holidays
   ☐ Personal days   ☐ Pensions   ☐ Insurance benefits   ☐ Bonuses
   ☐ Other (specify) _____

2 Can the relationship be terminated by either party without incurring liability or penalty? . . . . ☐ **Yes** ☐ **No**
   If "No," explain your answer. _____

3 Did the worker perform similar services for others during the time period entered in Part I, line 1? . . . . ☐ **Yes** ☐ **No**
   If "Yes," is the worker required to get approval from the firm? . . . . ☐ **Yes** ☐ **No**

4 Describe any agreements prohibiting competition between the worker and the firm while the worker is performing services or during any later period. Attach any available documentation. _____

5 Is the worker a member of a union? . . . . ☐ **Yes** ☐ **No**

6 What type of advertising, if any, does the worker do (for example, a business listing in a directory or business cards)? Provide copies, if applicable. _____

7 If the worker assembles or processes a product at home, who provides the materials and instructions or pattern? _____

8 What does the worker do with the finished product (for example, return it to the firm, provide it to another party, or sell it)? _____

9 How does the firm represent the worker to its customers (for example, employee, partner, representative, or contractor), and under whose business name does the worker perform these services? _____

10 If the worker no longer performs services for the firm, how did the relationship end (for example, worker quit or was fired, job completed, contract ended, firm or worker went out of business)? _____

Part V	For Service Providers or Salespersons. Complete this part if the worker provided a service directly to customers or is a salesperson.

1   What are the worker's responsibilities in soliciting new customers? _____

2   Who provides the worker with leads to prospective customers? _____

3   Describe any reporting requirements pertaining to the leads. _____

4   What terms and conditions of sale, if any, are required by the firm? _____

5   Are orders submitted to and subject to approval by the firm? . . . . ☐ **Yes** ☐ **No**

6   Who determines the worker's territory? _____

7   Did the worker pay for the privilege of serving customers on the route or in the territory? . . . . ☐ **Yes** ☐ **No**
    If "Yes," whom did the worker pay? _____
    If "Yes," how much did the worker pay? . . . . $ _____

8   Where does the worker sell the product (for example, in a home, retail establishment)? _____

9   List the product and/or services distributed by the worker (for example, meat, vegetables, fruit, bakery products, beverages, or laundry or dry cleaning services). If more than one type of product and/or service is distributed, specify the principal one. _____

10 Does the worker sell life insurance full time? . . . . ☐ **Yes** ☐ **No**

11 Does the worker sell other types of insurance for the firm? . . . . ☐ **Yes** ☐ **No**
    If "Yes," enter the percentage of the worker's total working time spent in selling other types of insurance . . . . . _____ %

12 If the worker solicits orders from wholesalers, retailers, contractors, or operators of hotels, restaurants, or other similar establishments, enter the percentage of the worker's time spent in the solicitation . . . . _____ %

13 Is the merchandise purchased by the customers for resale or use in their business operations? . . . . ☐ **Yes** ☐ **No**
    Describe the merchandise and state whether it is equipment installed on the customers' premises. _____

Sign Here	►	Under penalties of perjury, I declare that I have examined this request, including accompanying documents, and to the best of my knowledge and belief, the facts presented are true, correct, and complete.

_____ Title ► _____ Date ► _____
Type or print name below signature.

Form **SS-8** (Rev. 5-2014)

A-122

Instructions for Form SS-8

Department of the Treasury
Internal Revenue Service

(Rev. May 2014)

Determination of Worker Status for Purposes of Federal Employment Taxes and Income Tax Withholding

Section references are to the Internal Revenue Code unless otherwise noted.

Future Developments

Information about any future developments affecting Form SS-8 (such as legislation enacted after we release it) will be posted at *www.irs.gov/formss8*.

General Instructions

Purpose of Form

Firms and workers file Form SS-8 to request a determination of the status of a worker under the common law rules for purposes of federal employment taxes and income tax withholding. Generally, under the common law rules a worker is an employee if the firm has the right to control what will be done and how it will be done. See Publication 15–A, Employer's Supplemental Tax Guide, for more information on how to determine whether a worker providing services is an employee or independent contractor.

A Form SS-8 determination may be requested only in order to resolve federal tax matters. If Form SS-8 is submitted for a tax year for which the statute of limitations on the tax return has expired, a determination letter will not be issued.

The IRS does not issue a determination letter for proposed transactions or on hypothetical situations or for other reasons not in the best interests of tax administration. We may, however, issue an information letter when it is considered appropriate.

Definition

Firm. For the purposes of this form, the term "firm" means any individual, business enterprise, organization, state, or other entity for which a worker has performed services. The firm may or may not have paid the worker directly for these services.

 If the firm was not responsible for payment for services, be sure to enter the name, address, and employer identification number of the payer on the first page of Form SS-8, below the identifying information for the firm and the worker.

Note. Workers for state and local governments and/or interstate instrumentalities may be covered by a Section 218 Agreement. A Section 218 Agreement is a written, voluntary agreement between the State Social Security Administrator and the Social Security Administration. All 50 states, Puerto Rico, the Virgin Islands and approximately 60 interstate instrumentalities have Section 218 Agreements extending social security coverage to specified employees. Workers covered under a Section 218 Agreement are subject to social security and Medicare tax regardless of any determinations made under the common law rules.

Whether a state or local government worker is subject to social security and Medicare tax depends on which of the following three categories the worker falls into:

1. Subject to social security under a Section 218 Agreement, or

2. Subject to social security under mandatory coverage provisions, or

3. Excluded from social security because there is no Section 218 Agreement **and** the employee is covered by a qualified retirement plan.

If the worker is uncertain whether a Section 218 Agreement covers the state or local government entity, he or she should contact the entity before submitting Form SS-8. If the entity is uncertain about whether a Section 218 Agreement covers the position in question, the entity should contact the State Social Security Administrator for the state in which it operates.

The Form SS-8 Determination Process

The IRS will acknowledge the receipt of your Form SS-8. Because there are usually two (or more) parties who could be affected by a determination of employment status, the IRS attempts to get information from all parties involved by sending those parties blank Forms SS-8 for completion. Some or all of the information provided on this Form SS-8 may be shared with the other parties listed on page 1. The case will be assigned to a technician who will review the facts, apply the law, and render a decision. The technician may ask for additional information from the requestor, from other involved parties, or from third parties that could help clarify the work relationship before rendering a decision. The IRS will generally issue a formal determination to the firm or payer (if that is a different entity), and will send a copy to the worker. A determination letter applies only to a worker (or a class of workers) requesting it, and the decision is binding on the IRS if there is no change in the facts or law that form the basis for the ruling. In certain cases, a formal determination will not be issued. Instead, an information letter may be issued. Although an information letter is advisory only and is not binding on the IRS, it may be used to assist the worker to fulfill his or her federal tax obligations. In other very limited circumstances the IRS may issue a courtesy letter that the worker may rely on to fulfill his or her federal tax obligations.

Neither the Form SS-8 determination process nor the review of any records in connection with the determination constitutes an examination (audit) of any federal tax return. If the periods under consideration have previously been examined, the Form SS-8 determination process will not constitute a reexamination under IRS reopening procedures. Because this is not an examination of any federal tax return, the appeal rights available in connection with an examination do not apply to a Form SS-8 determination. If you disagree with a determination, you can identify facts that were part of the original submission that you think were not fully considered. If you have additional information concerning the relationship that was not part of the original submission, you can submit the additional information and request that the office reconsider the determination.

Completing Form SS-8

Answer all questions as completely as possible. Attach additional sheets if you need more space. Provide information for all years the worker provided services for the firm. Determinations are based on the entire relationship between the firm and the worker. Also indicate if there were any significant changes in the work relationship over the service term.

May 16, 2014

Cat. No. 66200M

Form SS-8 will be returned to the requestor if all required information is not provided.

Additional copies of this form may be obtained on IRS.gov or by calling 1-800-TAX-FORM (1-800-829-3676).

Fee

There is no fee for requesting a Form SS-8 determination letter.

Signature

Form SS-8 must be signed and dated by the taxpayer. A stamped signature will not be accepted.

The person who signs for a corporation must be an officer of the corporation who has personal knowledge of the facts. If the corporation is a member of an affiliated group filing a consolidated return, it must be signed by an officer of the common parent of the group.

The person signing for a trust, partnership, or limited liability company must be, respectively, a trustee, general partner, or member-manager who has personal knowledge of the facts.

A Form SS-8 that is not properly signed and dated by the taxpayer cannot be processed and will be returned.

Where To File

Send the completed and signed Form SS-8 to:

Internal Revenue Service
Form SS-8 Determinations
P.O. Box 630
Stop 631
Holtsville, NY 11742-0630

Faxed, photocopied, or electronic versions of Form SS-8 are not acceptable for the initial request for the Form SS-8 determination. **Do not submit Form SS-8 with your tax return as that will delay processing time.**

Instructions for Workers

If you are requesting a determination for more than one firm, complete a separate Form SS-8 for each firm.

 Form SS-8 is not a claim for refund of social security and Medicare taxes or federal income tax withholding.

If the IRS determines that you are an employee, you are responsible for filing an amended return for any corrections related to this decision. A determination that a worker is an employee does not necessarily reduce any current or prior tax liability. For more information, call 1-800-829-1040.

Time for filing a claim for refund. Generally, you must file your claim for a credit or refund within 3 years from the date your original return was filed or within 2 years from the date the tax was paid, whichever is later.

Filing Form SS-8 does not prevent the expiration of the time in which a claim for a refund must be filed. If you are concerned about a refund, and the statute of limitations for filing a claim for refund for the year(s) at issue has not yet expired, you should file Form 1040X, Amended U.S. Individual Income Tax Return, to protect your statute of limitations. File a separate Form 1040X for each year.

On the Form 1040X you file, do not complete lines 1 through 23 on the form. Write "Protective Claim" at the top of the form, sign and date it. In addition, enter the following statement in Part III: "Filed Form SS-8 with the Internal Revenue Service Office in Holtsville, NY. By filing this protective claim, I reserve the right to file a claim for any refund that may be due after a determination of my employment tax status has been completed."

Filing Form SS-8 does not alter the requirement to timely file an income tax return. Do not delay filing your tax return in anticipation of an answer to your Form SS-8 request. In addition, if applicable, do not delay in responding to a request for payment while waiting for a determination of your worker status.

Instructions for Firms

If a **worker** has requested a determination of his or her status while working for you, you will receive a request from the IRS to complete a Form SS-8. In cases of this type, the IRS usually gives each party an opportunity to present a statement of the facts because any decision will affect the employment tax status of the parties. Failure to respond to this request will not prevent the IRS from issuing a determination letter based on the information available to it so that the worker may fulfill his or her federal tax obligations. However, the information that you provide is extremely valuable in determining the status of the worker.

If you are requesting a determination for a particular class of worker, complete the form for one individual who is representative of the class of workers whose status is in question. If you want a written determination for more than one class of workers, complete a separate Form SS-8 for one worker from each class whose status is typical of that class. A written determination for any worker will apply to other workers of the same class if the facts are not materially different for these workers. Please provide a list of names and addresses of all workers potentially affected by this determination so that the IRS can contact them for information.

If you have a reasonable basis for not treating a worker as an employee, you may be relieved from having to pay employment taxes for that worker under section 530 of the Revenue Act of 1978. However, this relief provision cannot be considered in conjunction with a Form SS-8 determination because the determination does not constitute an examination of any tax return. For more information regarding section 530 of the Revenue Act of 1978 and to determine if you qualify for relief under this section, visit IRS.gov.

How To Get Help

To get IRS forms and publications, go to IRS.gov or call 1-800-TAX-FORM (1-800-829-3676).

The Taxpayer Advocate Service Is Here To Help You

The Taxpayer Advocate Service (TAS) is your voice at the IRS. Our job is to ensure that every taxpayer is treated fairly and that you know and understand your rights.

What can TAS do for you? We can offer you free help with IRS problems that you can't resolve on your own. We know this process can be confusing, but the worst thing you can do is nothing at all! TAS can help if you can't resolve your problems with the IRS and:
• Your problem is causing financial difficulties for you, your family, or your business.
• You face (or your business is facing) an immediate threat of adverse action.
• You have tried repeatedly to contact the IRS but no one has responded, or the IRS has not responded to you by the date promised.

If you qualify for our help, you'll be assigned to one advocate who'll be with you at every turn and will do everything possible to resolve your problem. Here's why we can help:
- TAS is an independent organization within the IRS.
- Our advocates know how to work with the IRS.
- Our services are free and tailored to meet your needs.
- We have offices in every state, the District of Columbia, and Puerto Rico.

How can you reach us? If you think TAS can help you, call your local advocate, whose number is in your local directory and at *www.irs.gov/advocate*, or call us toll-free at 1-877-777-4778.

How else does TAS help taxpayers?

TAS also handles large-scale, systemic problems that affect many taxpayers. If you know of one of these broad issues, please report it through the Systemic Advocacy Management System at *www.irs.gov/sams*.

For additional information about TAS, visit *www.taxpayeradvocate.irs.gov* or see Pub. 1546, The Taxpayer Advocate Service of the IRS – How to Get Help With Unresolved Tax Problems.

Low Income Taxpayer Clinics

Low Income Taxpayer Clinics (LITCs) serve individuals whose income is below a certain level and need to resolve tax problems such as audits, appeals and tax collection disputes. Some clinics can provide information about taxpayer rights and responsibilities in different languages for individuals who speak English as a second language. Visit *www.irs.gov/litc* or see IRS Publication 4134, Low Income Taxpayer Clinic List.

Representation

You may either represent yourself or, with proper written authorization, have someone else represent you. Your representative must be someone who is allowed to practice before the IRS, such as an attorney, certified public accountant, or enrolled agent (a person enrolled to practice before the IRS). Use Form 2848, Power of Attorney and Declaration of Representative, to authorize someone else to represent you before the IRS.

Privacy Act and Paperwork Reduction Act Notice. We ask for the information on Form SS-8 to carry out the Internal Revenue laws of the United States. This information will be used to determine the employment status of the worker(s) described on the form. Subtitle C, Employment Taxes, of the Internal Revenue Code imposes employment taxes on wages, including income tax withholding. Sections 3121(d), 3306(a), and 3401(c) and (d) and the related regulations define employee and employer for purposes of employment taxes imposed under Subtitle C. Section 6001 authorizes the IRS to request information needed to determine if a worker(s) or firm is subject to these taxes. Section 6109 requires you to provide your identification number. Neither workers nor firms are required to request a status determination, but if you choose to do so, you must provide the information requested on this form. Failure to provide the requested information may prevent us from making a status determination. If any worker or the firm has requested a status determination and you are being asked to provide information for use in that determination, you are not required to provide the requested information. However, failure to provide such information will prevent the IRS from considering it in making the status determination. Providing false or fraudulent information may subject you to penalties. Generally, tax returns and return information are confidential, as required by section 6103. However, section 6103 allows or requires the IRS to disclose or give the information shown on this form to others as described in the Code. Routine uses of this information include providing it to the Department of Justice for use in civil and criminal litigation, to the Social Security Administration for the administration of social security programs, and to cities, states, the District of Columbia, and U.S. commonwealths and possessions for the administration of their tax laws. We also may disclose this information to other countries under a tax treaty, to federal and state agencies to enforce federal nontax criminal laws, or to federal law enforcement and intelligence agencies to combat terrorism. We may provide this information to the affected worker(s), the firm, or payer as part of the status determination process.

You are not required to provide the information requested on a form that is subject to the Paperwork Reduction Act unless the form displays a valid OMB control number. Books or records relating to a form or its instructions must be retained as long as their contents may become material in the administration of any Internal Revenue law.

The time needed to complete and file this Form SS-8 will vary depending on individual circumstances. The estimated average time is: **Recordkeeping,** 23 hrs., 55 min.; **Learning about the law or the form,** 1 hr., 48 min.; **Preparing the form,** 5 hrs., 03 min.; and **Sending the form to the IRS,** 48 min. If you have comments concerning the accuracy of these time estimates or suggestions for making this form simpler, we would be happy to hear from you. You can send your comments from *www.irs.gov/formspubs*. Click on "More Information" and then on "Give us feedback." Or you can send your comments to the Internal Revenue Service, Tax Forms and Publications, 1111 Constitution Ave. NW, IR-6526, Washington, DC 20224. **Do not** send the form to this address. Instead, see *Where To File*, earlier.

Instructions for Employment Eligibility Verification

Department of Homeland Security
U.S. Citizenship and Immigration Services

Read all instructions carefully before completing this form.

Anti-Discrimination Notice. It is illegal to discriminate against any work-authorized individual in hiring, discharge, recruitment or referral for a fee, or in the employment eligibility verification (Form I-9 and E-Verify) process based on that individual's citizenship status, immigration status or national origin. Employers **CANNOT** specify which document(s) they will accept from an employee. The refusal to hire an individual because the documentation presented has a future expiration date may also constitute illegal discrimination. For more information, call the Office of Special Counsel for Immigration-Related Unfair Employment Practices (OSC) at 1-800-255-7688 (employees), 1-800-255-8155 (employers), or 1 800 237-2515 (TDD), or visit **www.justice.gov/crt/about/osc**.

What Is the Purpose of This Form?

Employers must complete Form I-9 to document verification of the identity and employment authorization of each new employee (both citizen and noncitizen) hired after November 6, 1986, to work in the United States. In the Commonwealth of the Northern Mariana Islands (CNMI), employers must complete Form I-9 to document verification of the identity and employment authorization of each new employee (both citizen and noncitizen) hired after November 27, 2011. Employers should have used Form I-9 CNMI between November 28, 2009 and November 27, 2011.

General Instructions

Employers are responsible for completing and retaining Form I-9. For the purpose of completing this form, the term "employer" means all employers, including those recruiters and referrers for a fee who are agricultural associations, agricultural employers, or farm labor contractors.

Form I-9 is made up of three sections. Employers may be fined if the form is not complete. Employers are responsible for retaining completed forms. Do not mail completed forms to U.S. Citizenship and Immigration Services (USCIS) or Immigration and Customs Enforcement (ICE).

Section 1. Employee Information and Attestation

Newly hired employees must complete and sign Section 1 of Form I-9 **no later than the first day of employment**. Section 1 should never be completed before the employee has accepted a job offer.

Provide the following information to complete Section 1:

Name: Provide your full legal last name, first name, and middle initial. Your last name is your family name or surname. If you have two last names or a hyphenated last name, include both names in the last name field. Your first name is your given name. Your middle initial is the first letter of your second given name, or the first letter of your middle name, if any.

Other names used: Provide all other names used, if any (including maiden name). If you have had no other legal names, write "N/A."

Address: Provide the address where you currently live, including Street Number and Name, Apartment Number (if applicable), City, State, and Zip Code. Do not provide a post office box address (P.O. Box). Only border commuters from Canada or Mexico may use an international address in this field.

Date of Birth: Provide your date of birth in the mm/dd/yyyy format. For example, January 23, 1950, should be written as 01/23/1950.

U.S. Social Security Number: Provide your 9-digit Social Security number. Providing your Social Security number is voluntary. However, if your employer participates in E-Verify, you must provide your Social Security number.

E-mail Address and Telephone Number (Optional): You may provide your e-mail address and telephone number. Department of Homeland Security (DHS) may contact you if DHS learns of a potential mismatch between the information provided and the information in DHS or Social Security Administration (SSA) records. You may write "N/A" if you choose not to provide this information.

A-126

All employees must attest in Section 1, under penalty of perjury, to their citizenship or immigration status by checking one of the following four boxes provided on the form:

1. **A citizen of the United States**

2. **A noncitizen national of the United States:** Noncitizen nationals of the United States are persons born in American Samoa, certain former citizens of the former Trust Territory of the Pacific Islands, and certain children of noncitizen nationals born abroad.

3. **A lawful permanent resident:** A lawful permanent resident is any person who is not a U.S. citizen and who resides in the United States under legally recognized and lawfully recorded permanent residence as an immigrant. The term "lawful permanent resident" includes conditional residents. If you check this box, write either your Alien Registration Number (A-Number) or USCIS Number in the field next to your selection. At this time, the USCIS Number is the same as the A-Number without the "A" prefix.

4. **An alien authorized to work:** If you are not a citizen or national of the United States or a lawful permanent resident, but are authorized to work in the United States, check this box.

    If you check this box:

    a. Record the date that your employment authorization expires, if any. Aliens whose employment authorization does not expire, such as refugees, asylees, and certain citizens of the Federated States of Micronesia, the Republic of the Marshall Islands, or Palau, may write "N/A" on this line.

    b. Next, enter your Alien Registration Number (A-Number)/USCIS Number. At this time, the USCIS Number is the same as your A-Number without the "A" prefix. If you have not received an A-Number/USCIS Number, record your Admission Number. You can find your Admission Number on Form I-94, "Arrival-Departure Record," or as directed by USCIS or U.S. Customs and Border Protection (CBP).

        (1) If you obtained your admission number from CBP in connection with your arrival in the United States, then also record information about the foreign passport you used to enter the United States (number and country of issuance).

        (2) If you obtained your admission number from USCIS *within the United States*, or you entered the United States without a foreign passport, you must write "N/A" in the Foreign Passport Number and Country of Issuance fields.

Sign your name in the "Signature of Employee" block and record the date you completed and signed Section 1. By signing and dating this form, you attest that the citizenship or immigration status you selected is correct and that you are aware that you may be imprisoned and/or fined for making false statements or using false documentation when completing this form. To fully complete this form, you must present to your employer documentation that establishes your identity and employment authorization. Choose which documents to present from the Lists of Acceptable Documents, found on the last page of this form. You must present this documentation no later than the third day after beginning employment, although you may present the required documentation before this date.

Preparer and/or Translator Certification

The Preparer and/or Translator Certification must be completed if the employee requires assistance to complete Section 1 (e.g., the employee needs the instructions or responses translated, someone other than the employee fills out the information blocks, or someone with disabilities needs additional assistance). The employee must still sign Section 1.

Minors and Certain Employees with Disabilities (Special Placement)

Parents or legal guardians assisting minors (individuals under 18) and certain employees with disabilities should review the guidelines in the *Handbook for Employers: Instructions for Completing Form I-9 (M-274)* on **www.uscis.gov/ I-9Central** before completing Section 1. These individuals have special procedures for establishing identity if they cannot present an identity document for Form I-9. The special procedures include **(1)** the parent or legal guardian filling out Section 1 and writing "minor under age 18" or "special placement," whichever applies, in the employee signature block; and **(2)** the employer writing "minor under age 18" or "special placement" under List B in Section 2.

A-127

Section 2. Employer or Authorized Representative Review and Verification

Before completing Section 2, employers must ensure that Section 1 is completed properly and on time. Employers may not ask an individual to complete Section 1 before he or she has accepted a job offer.

Employers or their authorized representative must complete Section 2 by examining evidence of identity and employment authorization within 3 business days of the employee's first day of employment. For example, if an employee begins employment on Monday, the employer must complete Section 2 by Thursday of that week. However, if an employer hires an individual for less than 3 business days, Section 2 must be completed no later than the first day of employment. An employer may complete Form I-9 before the first day of employment if the employer has offered the individual a job and the individual has accepted.

Employers cannot specify which document(s) employees may present from the Lists of Acceptable Documents, found on the last page of Form I-9, to establish identity and employment authorization. Employees must present one selection from List A **OR** a combination of one selection from List B and one selection from List C. List A contains documents that show both identity and employment authorization. Some List A documents are combination documents. The employee must present combination documents together to be considered a List A document. For example, a foreign passport and a Form I-94 containing an endorsement of the alien's nonimmigrant status must be presented together to be considered a List A document. List B contains documents that show identity only, and List C contains documents that show employment authorization only. If an employee presents a List A document, he or she should **not** present a List B and List C document, and vice versa. If an employer participates in E-Verify, the List B document must include a photograph.

In the field below the Section 2 introduction, employers must enter the last name, first name and middle initial, if any, that the employee entered in Section 1. This will help to identify the pages of the form should they get separated.

Employers or their authorized representative must:

1. Physically examine each original document the employee presents to determine if it reasonably appears to be genuine and to relate to the person presenting it. The person who examines the documents must be the same person who signs Section 2. The examiner of the documents and the employee must both be physically present during the examination of the employee's documents.

2. Record the document title shown on the Lists of Acceptable Documents, issuing authority, document number and expiration date (if any) from the original document(s) the employee presents. You may write "N/A" in any unused fields.

   If the employee is a student or exchange visitor who presented a foreign passport with a Form I-94, the employer should also enter in Section 2:

   a. The student's Form I-20 or DS-2019 number (Student and Exchange Visitor Information System-SEVIS Number); **and** the program end date from Form I-20 or DS-2019.

3. Under Certification, enter the employee's first day of employment. Temporary staffing agencies may enter the first day the employee was placed in a job pool. Recruiters and recruiters for a fee do not enter the employee's first day of employment.

4. Provide the name and title of the person completing Section 2 in the Signature of Employer or Authorized Representative field.

5. Sign and date the attestation on the date Section 2 is completed.

6. Record the employer's business name and address.

7. Return the employee's documentation.

Employers may, but are not required to, photocopy the document(s) presented. If photocopies are made, they should be made for **ALL** new hires or reverifications. Photocopies must be retained and presented with Form I-9 in case of an inspection by DHS or other federal government agency. Employers must always complete Section 2 even if they photocopy an employee's document(s). Making photocopies of an employee's document(s) cannot take the place of completing Form I-9. Employers are still responsible for completing and retaining Form I-9.

Unexpired Documents

Generally, only unexpired, original documentation is acceptable. The only exception is that an employee may present a certified copy of a birth certificate. Additionally, in some instances, a document that appears to be expired may be acceptable if the expiration date shown on the face of the document has been extended, such as for individuals with temporary protected status. Refer to the *Handbook for Employers: Instructions for Completing Form I-9 (M-274)* or I-9 Central (www.uscis.gov/I-9Central) for examples.

Receipts

If an employee is unable to present a required document (or documents), the employee can present an acceptable receipt in lieu of a document from the Lists of Acceptable Documents on the last page of this form. Receipts showing that a person has applied for an initial grant of employment authorization, or for renewal of employment authorization, are not acceptable. Employers cannot accept receipts if employment will last less than 3 days. Receipts are acceptable when completing Form I-9 for a new hire or when reverification is required.

Employees must present receipts within 3 business days of their first day of employment, or in the case of reverification, by the date that reverification is required, and must present valid replacement documents within the time frames described below.

There are three types of acceptable receipts:

1. A receipt showing that the employee has applied to replace a document that was lost, stolen or damaged. The employee must present the actual document within 90 days from the date of hire.

2. The arrival portion of Form I-94/I-94A with a temporary I-551 stamp and a photograph of the individual. The employee must present the actual Permanent Resident Card (Form I-551) by the expiration date of the temporary I-551 stamp, or, if there is no expiration date, within 1 year from the date of issue.

3. The departure portion of Form I-94/I-94A with a refugee admission stamp. The employee must present an unexpired Employment Authorization Document (Form I-766) or a combination of a List B document and an unrestricted Social Security card within 90 days.

When the employee provides an acceptable receipt, the employer should:

1. Record the document title in Section 2 under the sections titled List A, List B, or List C, as applicable.

2. Write the word "receipt" and its document number in the "Document Number" field. Record the last day that the receipt is valid in the "Expiration Date" field.

By the end of the receipt validity period, the employer should:

1. Cross out the word "receipt" and any accompanying document number and expiration date.

2. Record the number and other required document information from the actual document presented.

3. Initial and date the change.

See the *Handbook for Employers: Instructions for Completing Form I-9 (M-274)* at **www.uscis.gov/I-9Central** for more information on receipts.

Section 3. Reverification and Rehires

Employers or their authorized representatives should complete Section 3 when reverifying that an employee is authorized to work. When rehiring an employee within 3 years of the date Form I-9 was originally completed, employers have the option to complete a new Form I-9 or complete Section 3. When completing Section 3 in either a reverification or rehire situation, if the employee's name has changed, record the name change in Block A.

For employees who provide an employment authorization expiration date in Section 1, employers must reverify employment authorization on or before the date provided.

Some employees may write "N/A" in the space provided for the expiration date in Section 1 if they are aliens whose employment authorization does not expire (e.g., asylees, refugees, certain citizens of the Federated States of Micronesia, the Republic of the Marshall Islands, or Palau). Reverification does not apply for such employees unless they chose to present evidence of employment authorization in Section 2 that contains an expiration date and requires reverification, such as Form I-766, Employment Authorization Document.

Reverification applies if evidence of employment authorization (List A or List C document) presented in Section 2 expires. However, employers should not reverify:

1. U.S. citizens and noncitizen nationals; or

2. Lawful permanent residents who presented a Permanent Resident Card (Form I-551) for Section 2.

Reverification does not apply to List B documents.

If both Section 1 and Section 2 indicate expiration dates triggering the reverification requirement, the employer should reverify by the earlier date.

For reverification, an employee must present unexpired documentation from either List A or List C showing he or she is still authorized to work. Employers CANNOT require the employee to present a particular document from List A or List C. The employee may choose which document to present.

To complete Section 3, employers should follow these instructions:

1. Complete Block A if an employee's name has changed at the time you complete Section 3.

2. Complete Block B with the date of rehire if you rehire an employee within 3 years of the date this form was originally completed, and the employee is still authorized to be employed on the same basis as previously indicated on this form. Also complete the "Signature of Employer or Authorized Representative" block.

3. Complete Block C if:

    a. The employment authorization or employment authorization document of a current employee is about to expire and requires reverification; or

    b. You rehire an employee within 3 years of the date this form was originally completed and his or her employment authorization or employment authorization document has expired. (Complete Block B for this employee as well.)

    To complete Block C:

    a. Examine either a List A or List C document the employee presents that shows that the employee is currently authorized to work in the United States; and

    b. Record the document title, document number, and expiration date (if any).

4. After completing block A, B or C, complete the "Signature of Employer or Authorized Representative" block, including the date.

    For reverification purposes, employers may either complete Section 3 of a new Form I-9 or Section 3 of the previously completed Form I-9. Any new pages of Form I-9 completed during reverification must be attached to the employee's original Form I-9. If you choose to complete Section 3 of a new Form I-9, you may attach just the page containing Section 3, with the employee's name entered at the top of the page, to the employee's original Form I-9. If there is a more current version of Form I-9 at the time of reverification, you must complete Section 3 of that version of the form.

What Is the Filing Fee?

There is no fee for completing Form I-9. This form is not filed with USCIS or any government agency. Form I-9 must be retained by the employer and made available for inspection by U.S. Government officials as specified in the **"USCIS Privacy Act Statement"** below.

USCIS Forms and Information

For more detailed information about completing Form I-9, employers and employees should refer to the *Handbook for Employers: Instructions for Completing Form I-9 (M-274)*.

You can also obtain information about Form I-9 from the USCIS Web site at www.uscis.gov/I-9Central, by e-mailing USCIS at **I-9Central@dhs.gov**, or by calling **1-888-464-4218**. For TDD (hearing impaired), call **1-877-875-6028**.

To obtain USCIS forms or the *Handbook for Employers*, you can download them from the USCIS Web site at www.uscis.gov/forms. You may order USCIS forms by calling our toll-free number at **1-800-870-3676**. You may also obtain forms and information by contacting the USCIS National Customer Service Center at **1-800-375-5283**. For TDD (hearing impaired), call **1-800-767-1833**.

Information about E-Verify, a free and voluntary program that allows participating employers to electronically verify the employment eligibility of their newly hired employees, can be obtained from the USCIS Web site at www.dhs.gov/E-Verify, by e-mailing USCIS at **E-Verify@dhs.gov** or by calling **1-888-464-4218**. For TDD (hearing impaired), call **1-877-875-6028**.

Employees with questions about Form I-9 and/or E-Verify can reach the USCIS employee hotline by calling **1-888-897-7781**. For TDD (hearing impaired), call **1-877-875-6028**.

Photocopying and Retaining Form I-9

A blank Form I-9 may be reproduced, provided all sides are copied. The instructions and Lists of Acceptable Documents must be available to all employees completing this form. Employers must retain each employee's completed Form I-9 for as long as the individual works for the employer. Employers are required to retain the pages of the form on which the employee and employer enter data. If copies of documentation presented by the employee are made, those copies must also be kept with the form. Once the individual's employment ends, the employer must retain this form for either 3 years after the date of hire or 1 year after the date employment ended, whichever is later.

Form I-9 may be signed and retained electronically, in compliance with Department of Homeland Security regulations at 8 CFR 274a.2.

USCIS Privacy Act Statement

AUTHORITIES: The authority for collecting this information is the Immigration Reform and Control Act of 1986, Public Law 99-603 (8 USC 1324a).

PURPOSE: This information is collected by employers to comply with the requirements of the Immigration Reform and Control Act of 1986. This law requires that employers verify the identity and employment authorization of individuals they hire for employment to preclude the unlawful hiring, or recruiting or referring for a fee, of aliens who are not authorized to work in the United States.

DISCLOSURE: Submission of the information required in this form is voluntary. However, failure of the employer to ensure proper completion of this form for each employee may result in the imposition of civil or criminal penalties. In addition, employing individuals knowing that they are unauthorized to work in the United States may subject the employer to civil and/or criminal penalties.

ROUTINE USES: This information will be used by employers as a record of their basis for determining eligibility of an employee to work in the United States. The employer will keep this form and make it available for inspection by authorized officials of the Department of Homeland Security, Department of Labor, and Office of Special Counsel for Immigration-Related Unfair Employment Practices.

Paperwork Reduction Act

An agency may not conduct or sponsor an information collection and a person is not required to respond to a collection of information unless it displays a currently valid OMB control number. The public reporting burden for this collection of information is estimated at 35 minutes per response, including the time for reviewing instructions and completing and retaining the form. Send comments regarding this burden estimate or any other aspect of this collection of information, including suggestions for reducing this burden, to: U.S. Citizenship and Immigration Services, Regulatory Coordination Division, Office of Policy and Strategy, 20 Massachusetts Avenue NW, Washington, DC 20529-2140; OMB No. 1615-0047. **Do not mail your completed Form I-9 to this address.**

Employment Eligibility Verification

Department of Homeland Security
U.S. Citizenship and Immigration Services

USCIS
Form I-9
OMB No. 1615-0047
Expires 03/31/2016

▶**START HERE.** Read instructions carefully before completing this form. **The instructions must be available during completion of this form.**
ANTI-DISCRIMINATION NOTICE: It is illegal to discriminate against work-authorized individuals. Employers **CANNOT** specify which document(s) they will accept from an employee. The refusal to hire an individual because the documentation presented has a future expiration date may also constitute illegal discrimination.

Section 1. Employee Information and Attestation (Employees must complete and sign Section 1 of Form I-9 no later than the **first day of employment**, but not before accepting a job offer.)

Last Name (Family Name)	First Name (Given Name)	Middle Initial	Other Names Used (if any)

Address (Street Number and Name)	Apt. Number	City or Town	State	Zip Code

Date of Birth (mm/dd/yyyy)	U.S. Social Security Number	E-mail Address	Telephone Number
	☐☐☐-☐☐-☐☐☐☐		

I am aware that federal law provides for imprisonment and/or fines for false statements or use of false documents in connection with the completion of this form.

I attest, under penalty of perjury, that I am (check one of the following):

☐ A citizen of the United States

☐ A noncitizen national of the United States (See instructions)

☐ A lawful permanent resident (Alien Registration Number/USCIS Number): _____

☐ An alien authorized to work until (expiration date, if applicable, mm/dd/yyyy) _____ . Some aliens may write "N/A" in this field.
    (See instructions)

   *For aliens authorized to work, provide your Alien Registration Number/USCIS Number **OR** Form I-94 Admission Number:*

   1. Alien Registration Number/USCIS Number: _____

   ### OR

   2. Form I-94 Admission Number: _____

   If you obtained your admission number from CBP in connection with your arrival in the United States, include the following:

   Foreign Passport Number: _____

   Country of Issuance: _____

   Some aliens may write "N/A" on the Foreign Passport Number and Country of Issuance fields. (See instructions)

3-D Barcode
Do Not Write in This Space

Signature of Employee:	Date (mm/dd/yyyy):

Preparer and/or Translator Certification (To be completed and signed if Section 1 is prepared by a person other than the employee.)

I attest, under penalty of perjury, that I have assisted in the completion of this form and that to the best of my knowledge the information is true and correct.

Signature of Preparer or Translator:	Date (mm/dd/yyyy):

Last Name (Family Name)	First Name (Given Name)

Address (Street Number and Name)	City or Town	State	Zip Code

🛑 *Employer Completes Next Page* 🛑

A-132

Section 2. Employer or Authorized Representative Review and Verification

(Employers or their authorized representative must complete and sign Section 2 within 3 business days of the employee's first day of employment. You must physically examine one document from List A OR examine a combination of one document from List B and one document from List C as listed on the "Lists of Acceptable Documents" on the next page of this form. For each document you review, record the following information: document title, issuing authority, document number, and expiration date, if any.)

Employee Last Name, First Name and Middle Initial from Section 1:

List A	OR	List B	AND	List C
Identity and Employment Authorization		**Identity**		**Employment Authorization**

List A	List B	List C
Document Title:	Document Title:	Document Title:
Issuing Authority:	Issuing Authority:	Issuing Authority:
Document Number:	Document Number:	Document Number:
Expiration Date *(if any)(mm/dd/yyyy)*:	Expiration Date *(if any)(mm/dd/yyyy)*:	Expiration Date *(if any)(mm/dd/yyyy)*:
Document Title:		
Issuing Authority:		
Document Number:		
Expiration Date *(if any)(mm/dd/yyyy)*:		
Document Title:		**3-D Barcode**
Issuing Authority:		**Do Not Write in This Space**
Document Number:		
Expiration Date *(if any)(mm/dd/yyyy)*:		

Certification

I attest, under penalty of perjury, that (1) I have examined the document(s) presented by the above-named employee, (2) the above-listed document(s) appear to be genuine and to relate to the employee named, and (3) to the best of my knowledge the employee is authorized to work in the United States.

The employee's first day of employment *(mm/dd/yyyy)*: _____ (*See instructions for exemptions.*)

Signature of Employer or Authorized Representative	Date *(mm/dd/yyyy)*	Title of Employer or Authorized Representative	
Last Name *(Family Name)*	First Name *(Given Name)*	Employer's Business or Organization Name	
Employer's Business or Organization Address *(Street Number and Name)*	City or Town	State	Zip Code

Section 3. Reverification and Rehires *(To be completed and signed by employer or authorized representative.)*

A. New Name *(if applicable)* Last Name *(Family Name)* First Name *(Given Name)*	Middle Initial	**B.** Date of Rehire *(if applicable)* *(mm/dd/yyyy)*:

C. If employee's previous grant of employment authorization has expired, provide the information for the document from List A or List C the employee presented that establishes current employment authorization in the space provided below.

Document Title:	Document Number:	Expiration Date *(if any)(mm/dd/yyyy)*:

I attest, under penalty of perjury, that to the best of my knowledge, this employee is authorized to work in the United States, and if the employee presented document(s), the document(s) I have examined appear to be genuine and to relate to the individual.

Signature of Employer or Authorized Representative:	Date *(mm/dd/yyyy)*:	Print Name of Employer or Authorized Representative:

LISTS OF ACCEPTABLE DOCUMENTS
All documents must be UNEXPIRED

Employees may present one selection from List A
or a combination of one selection from List B and one selection from List C.

LIST A **Documents that Establish Both Identity and Employment Authorization**	OR	LIST B **Documents that Establish Identity**	AND	LIST C **Documents that Establish Employment Authorization**
1. U.S. Passport or U.S. Passport Card 2. Permanent Resident Card or Alien Registration Receipt Card (Form I-551) 3. Foreign passport that contains a temporary I-551 stamp or temporary I-551 printed notation on a machine-readable immigrant visa 4. Employment Authorization Document that contains a photograph (Form I-766) 5. For a nonimmigrant alien authorized to work for a specific employer because of his or her status: 　a. Foreign passport; and 　b. Form I-94 or Form I-94A that has the following: 　　(1) The same name as the passport; and 　　(2) An endorsement of the alien's nonimmigrant status as long as that period of endorsement has not yet expired and the proposed employment is not in conflict with any restrictions or limitations identified on the form. 6. Passport from the Federated States of Micronesia (FSM) or the Republic of the Marshall Islands (RMI) with Form I-94 or Form I-94A indicating nonimmigrant admission under the Compact of Free Association Between the United States and the FSM or RMI		1. Driver's license or ID card issued by a State or outlying possession of the United States provided it contains a photograph or information such as name, date of birth, gender, height, eye color, and address 2. ID card issued by federal, state or local government agencies or entities, provided it contains a photograph or information such as name, date of birth, gender, height, eye color, and address 3. School ID card with a photograph 4. Voter's registration card 5. U.S. Military card or draft record 6. Military dependent's ID card 7. U.S. Coast Guard Merchant Mariner Card 8. Native American tribal document 9. Driver's license issued by a Canadian government authority **For persons under age 18 who are unable to present a document listed above:** 10. School record or report card 11. Clinic, doctor, or hospital record 12. Day-care or nursery school record		1. A Social Security Account Number card, unless the card includes one of the following restrictions: 　(1) NOT VALID FOR EMPLOYMENT 　(2) VALID FOR WORK ONLY WITH INS AUTHORIZATION 　(3) VALID FOR WORK ONLY WITH DHS AUTHORIZATION 2. Certification of Birth Abroad issued by the Department of State (Form FS-545) 3. Certification of Report of Birth issued by the Department of State (Form DS-1350) 4. Original or certified copy of birth certificate issued by a State, county, municipal authority, or territory of the United States bearing an official seal 5. Native American tribal document 6. U.S. Citizen ID Card (Form I-197) 7. Identification Card for Use of Resident Citizen in the United States (Form I-179) 8. Employment authorization document issued by the Department of Homeland Security

Illustrations of many of these documents appear in Part 8 of the Handbook for Employers (M-274).

Refer to Section 2 of the instructions, titled "Employer or Authorized Representative Review and Verification," for more information about acceptable receipts.

A-134

INCOME WITHHOLDING FOR SUPPORT

☐ **ORIGINAL INCOME WITHHOLDING ORDER/NOTICE FOR SUPPORT (IWO)**
☐ **AMENDED IWO**
☐ **ONE-TIME ORDER/NOTICE FOR LUMP SUM PAYMENT**
☐ **TERMINATION OF IWO**   **Date:** _____

☐ Child Support Enforcement (CSE) Agency ☐ Court ☐ Attorney ☐ Private Individual/Entity (Check One)

NOTE: This IWO must be regular on its face. Under certain circumstances you must reject this IWO and return it to the sender (see IWO instructions **www.acf.hhs.gov/programs/css/resource/income-withholding-for-support-instructions**). If you receive this document from someone other than a state or tribal CSE agency or a court, a copy of the underlying order must be attached.

State/Tribe/Territory _____   Remittance ID (include w/payment) _____
City/County/Dist./Tribe _____   Order ID _____
Private Individual/Entity _____   CSE Agency Case ID _____

_____   RE: _____
Employer/Income Withholder's Name   Employee/Obligor's Name (Last, First, Middle)

_____   _____
Employer/Income Withholder's Address   Employee/Obligor's Social Security Number

_____   _____
                                      Custodial Party/Obligee's Name (Last, First, Middle)
_____

Employer/Income Withholder's FEIN _____

Child(ren)'s Name(s) (Last, First, Middle)   Child(ren)'s Birth Date(s)

_____   _____
_____   _____
_____   _____
_____   _____
_____   _____
_____   _____

ORDER INFORMATION: This document is based on the support or withholding order from _____
(State/Tribe). You are required by law to deduct these amounts from the employee/obligor's income until further notice.
$ _____ Per _____ current child support
$ _____ Per _____ past-due child support - **Arrears greater than 12 weeks?** ☐ Yes ☐ No
$ _____ Per _____ current cash medical support
$ _____ Per _____ past-due cash medical support
$ _____ Per _____ current spousal support
$ _____ Per _____ past-due spousal support
$ _____ Per _____ other (must specify) _____ .
for a **Total Amount to Withhold of $** _____ per _____ .

AMOUNTS TO WITHHOLD: You do not have to vary your pay cycle to be in compliance with the *Order Information*. If your pay cycle does not match the ordered payment cycle, withhold one of the following amounts:
$ _____ per weekly pay period $ _____ per semimonthly pay period (twice a month)
$ _____ per biweekly pay period (every two weeks) $ _____ per monthly pay period
$ _____ **Lump Sum Payment:** Do not stop any existing IWO unless you receive a termination order.

Document Tracking ID _____   OMB 0970-0154

1

A-135

Employer's Name: _____ Employer FEIN: _____

Employee/Obligor's Name: _____ SSN: _____

CSE Agency Case Identifier: _____ Order Identifier: _____

REMITTANCE INFORMATION: If the employee/obligor's principal place of employment is_____
(State/Tribe), you must begin withholding no later than the first pay period that occurs ____days after the date
of _____ . Send payment within ____ working days of the pay date. If you cannot withhold the full amount of support
for any or all orders for this employee/obligor, withhold up to ____ % of disposable income. If the obligor is a nonemployee, obtain withholding limits from Supplemental Information on page 3. If the employee/obligor's principal place of
employment is not _____ (State/Tribe), obtain withholding limitations, time requirements,
and any allowable employer fees at www.acf.hhs.gov/programs/css/resource/state-income-withholding-contacts-and-
program-information for the employee/obligor's principal place of employment.

For electronic payment requirements and centralized payment collection and disbursement facility information (State
Disbursement Unit (SDU)), see www.acf.hhs.gov/programs/css/employers/electronic-payments.

Include the *Remittance ID* with the payment and if necessary this FIPS code: _____ .

Remit payment to _____ (SDU/Tribal Order Payee)
at _____ (SDU/Tribal Payee Address)

[ ] **Return to Sender [Completed by Employer/Income Withholder].** Payment must be directed to an SDU in
accordance with 42 USC §666(b)(5) and (b)(6) or Tribal Payee (see Payments to SDU below). If payment is not directed
to an SDU/Tribal Payee or this IWO is not regular on its face, you *must* check this box and return the IWO to the sender.

Signature of Judge/Issuing Official (if Required by State or Tribal Law): _____ Print Name of Judge/Issuing Official: _____ Title of Judge/Issuing Official: _____ Date of Signature: _____

If the employee/obligor works in a state or for a tribe that is different from the state or tribe that issued this order, a copy of
this IWO must be provided to the employee/obligor.
[ ] If checked, the employer/income withholder must provide a copy of this form to the employee/obligor.

ADDITIONAL INFORMATION FOR EMPLOYERS/INCOME WITHHOLDERS

State-specific contact and withholding information can be found on the Federal Employer Services website located at
www.acf.hhs.gov/programs/css/resource/state-income-withholding-contacts-and-program-information.

Priority: Withholding for support has priority over any other legal process under State law against the same income (42
USC §666(b)(7)). If a federal tax levy is in effect, please notify the sender.

Combining Payments: When remitting payments to an SDU or tribal CSE agency, you may combine withheld amounts
from more than one employee/obligor's income in a single payment. You must, however, separately identify each
employee/obligor's portion of the payment.

Payments To SDU: You must send child support payments payable by income withholding to the appropriate SDU or to a
tribal CSE agency. If this IWO instructs you to send a payment to an entity other than an SDU (e.g., payable to the
custodial party, court, or attorney), you must check the box above and return this notice to the sender. Exception: If this
IWO was sent by a court, attorney, or private individual/entity and the initial order was entered before January 1, 1994 or
the order was issued by a tribal CSE agency, you must follow the "Remit payment to" instructions on this form.

Reporting the Pay Date: You must report the pay date when sending the payment. The pay date is the date on which the
amount was withheld from the employee/obligor's wages. You must comply with the law of the state (or tribal law if
applicable) of the employee/obligor's principal place of employment regarding time periods within which you must
implement the withholding and forward the support payments.

Multiple IWOs: If there is more than one IWO against this employee/obligor and you are unable to fully honor all IWOs
due to federal, state, or tribal withholding limits, you must honor all IWOs to the greatest extent possible, giving priority to
current support before payment of any past-due support. Follow the state or tribal law/procedure of the employee/obligor's
principal place of employment to determine the appropriate allocation method.

OMB Expiration Date - 7/31/2017. The OMB Expiration Date has no bearing on the termination date of the IWO; it identifies the
version of the form currently in use.   2

A-136

Employer's Name: _____ Employer FEIN: _____

Employee/Obligor's Name: _____ SSN: _____

CSE Agency Case Identifier: _____ Order Identifier: _____

Lump Sum Payments: You may be required to notify a state or tribal CSE agency of upcoming lump sum payments to this employee/obligor such as bonuses, commissions, or severance pay. Contact the sender to determine if you are required to report and/or withhold lump sum payments.

Liability: If you have any doubts about the validity of this IWO, contact the sender. If you fail to withhold income from the employee/obligor's income as the IWO directs, you are liable for both the accumulated amount you should have withheld and any penalties set by state or tribal law/procedure.

_____
_____
_____
_____
_____

Anti-discrimination: You are subject to a fine determined under state or tribal law for discharging an employee/obligor from employment, refusing to employ, or taking disciplinary action against an employee/obligor because of this IWO.

_____
_____
_____
_____
_____

Withholding Limits: You may not withhold more than the lesser of: 1) the amounts allowed by the Federal Consumer Credit Protection Act (CCPA) (15 USC §1673(b)); or 2) the amounts allowed by the state of the employee/obligor's principal place of employment or tribal law if a tribal order (see *Remittance Information*). Disposable income is the net income after mandatory deductions such as: state, federal, local taxes; Social Security taxes; statutory pension contributions; and Medicare taxes. The federal limit is 50% of the disposable income if the obligor is supporting another family and 60% of the disposable income if the obligor is not supporting another family. However, those limits increase 5% --to 55% and 65% --if the arrears are greater than 12 weeks. If permitted by the state or tribe, you may deduct a fee for administrative costs. The combined support amount and fee may not exceed the limit indicated in this section.

For tribal orders, you may not withhold more than the amounts allowed under the law of the issuing tribe. For tribal employers/income withholders who receive a state IWO, you may not withhold more than the limit set by tribal law.

Depending upon applicable state or tribal law, you may need to consider amounts paid for health care premiums in determining disposable income and applying appropriate withholding limits.

Arrears greater than 12 weeks? If the *Order Information* does not indicate that the arrears are greater than 12 weeks, then the employer should calculate the CCPA limit using the lower percentage.

Supplemental Information:

_____
_____
_____
_____
_____
_____
_____
_____
_____
_____

IMPORTANT: The person completing this form is advised that the information may be shared with the employee/obligor.

A-137

Employer's Name: _____ Employer FEIN: _____

Employee/Obligor's Name: _____ SSN: _____

CSE Agency Case Identifier: _____ Order Identifier: _____

NOTIFICATION OF EMPLOYMENT TERMINATION OR INCOME STATUS: If this employee/obligor never worked for you or you are no longer withholding income for this employee/obligor, you must promptly notify the CSE agency and/or the sender by returning this form to the address listed in the contact information below:

☐ This person has never worked for this employer nor received periodic income.

☐ This person no longer works for this employer nor receives periodic income.

Please provide the following information for the employee/obligor:

Termination date: _____ Last known phone number: _____

Last known address: _____

_____

Final payment date to SDU/tribal payee: _____ Final payment amount:_____

New employer's name: _____

New employer's address: _____

_____

CONTACT INFORMATION:

To Employer/Income Withholder: If you have questions, contact _____ (issuer name)

by phone:_____ , by fax:_____ , by e-mail or website: _____ .

Send termination/income status notice and other correspondence to:

_____ (issuer address).

To Employee/Obligor: If the employee/obligor has questions, contact _____ (issuer name)

by phone: _____ , by fax:_____ , by e-mail or website: _____ .

A-138

1. Tables for Figuring Amount Exempt from Levy on Wages, Salary, and Other Income (Forms 668-W(ACS), 668-W(c)(DO) and 668-W(ICS))

The tables below show the amount of an individual's income that is exempt from a notice of levy used to collect delinquent tax in 2016

2016

Filing Status: Single

Pay Period	Number of Exemptions Claimed on Statement						
	1	2	3	4	5	6	More Than 6
Daily	39.81	55.38	70.96	86.54	102.12	117.69	24.23 plus 15.58 for each exemption
Weekly	199.04	276.92	354.81	432.69	510.58	588.46	121.15 plus 77.89 for each exemption
Biweekly	398.08	553.85	709.62	865.38	1021.15	1176.92	242.31 plus 155.77 for each exemption
Semimonthly	431.25	600.00	768.75	937.50	1106.25	1275.00	262.50 plus 168.75 for each exemption
Monthly	862.50	1200.00	1537.50	1875.00	2212.50	2550.00	525 plus 337.50 for each exemption

Filing Status: Married Filing Joint Return (and Qualifying Widow(er)s)

Pay Period	Number of Exemptions Claimed on Statement						
	1	2	3	4	5	6	More Than 6
Daily	64.04	79.62	95.19	110.77	126.35	141.92	48.47 plus 15.58 for each exemption
Weekly	320.19	398.08	475.96	553.85	631.73	709.62	242.30 plus 77.89 for each exemption
Biweekly	640.38	796.15	951.92	1107.69	1263.46	1419.23	484.62 plus 155.77 for each exemption
Semimonthly	693.75	862.50	1031.25	1200.00	1368.75	1537.50	525 plus 168.75 for each exemption
Monthly	1387.50	1725.00	2062.50	2400.00	2737.50	3075.00	1050 plus 337.50 for each exemption

Filing Status: Head of Household

Pay Period	Number of Exemptions Claimed on Statement						
	1	2	3	4	5	6	More Than 6
Daily	51.35	66.92	82.50	98.08	113.65	129.23	35.77 plus 15.58 for each exemption
Weekly	256.73	334.62	412.50	490.38	568.27	646.15	178.84 plus 77.89 for each exemption
Biweekly	513.46	669.23	825.00	980.77	1136.54	1292.31	357.69 plus 155.77 for each exemption
Semimonthly	556.25	725.00	893.75	1062.50	1231.25	1400.00	387.50 plus 168.75 for each exemption
Monthly	1112.50	1450.00	1787.50	2125.00	2462.50	2800.00	775.00 plus 337.50 for each exemption

Filing Status: Married Filing Separate Return

Pay Period	Number of Exemptions Claimed on Statement						
	1	2	3	4	5	6	More Than 6
Daily	39.81	55.38	70.96	86.54	102.12	117.69	24.23 plus 15.58 for each exemption
Weekly	199.04	276.92	354.81	432.69	510.58	588.46	121.15 plus 77.89 for each exemption
Biweekly	398.08	553.85	709.62	865.38	1021.15	1176.92	242.31 plus 155.77 for each exemption
Semimonthly	431.25	600.00	768.75	937.50	1106.25	1275.00	262.50 plus 168.75 for each exemption
Monthly	862.50	1200.00	1537.50	1875.00	2212.50	2550.00	525 plus 337.50 for each exemption

2. Table for Figuring Additional Exempt Amount for Taxpayers at Least 65 Years Old and/or Blind

Filing Status	*	Additional Exempt Amount				
		Daily	Weekly	Biweekly	Semi-monthly	Monthly
Single or Head of Household	1	5.96	29.81	59.62	64.58	129.17
	2	11.92	59.62	119.23	129.17	258.33
Any Other Filing Status	1	4.81	24.04	48.08	52.08	104.17
	2	9.62	48.08	96.15	104.17	208.33
	3	14.42	72.12	144.23	156.25	312.50
	4	19.23	96.15	192.31	208.33	416.67

* ADDITIONAL STANDARD DEDUCTION claimed on Parts 3,4, and 5 of levy.

Examples

These tables show the amount exempt each pay period from a levy on wages, salary, and other income.

1. A single taxpayer who is paid weekly and claims three exemptions (including one for the taxpayer) has $354.81 exempt from levy.

2. If the taxpayer in number 1 is over 65 and writes 1 in the ADDITIONAL STANDARD DEDUCTION space on Parts 3, 4, & 5 of the levy, $384.62 is exempt from this levy ($354.81 plus $29.81).

3. A taxpayer who is married, files jointly, is paid bi-weekly, and claims two exemptions (including one for the taxpayer) has $796.15 exempt from levy.

4. if the taxpayer in number 3 is over 65 and has a spouse who is blind, this taxpayer should write 2 in the ADDITIONAL STANDARD DEDUCTION space on Parts 3,4, and 5 of the levy. If so, $892.30 is exempt from this levy ($796.15 plus $96.15).

Publication 1494 (2016) www.irs.gov Catalog Number 11439T Department of Treasury -- Internal Revenue Service

Department of the Treasury
Internal Revenue Service

Publication 15
Cat. No. 10000W

(Circular E), Employer's Tax Guide

For use in **2016**

Get forms and other information faster and easier at:
- *IRS.gov* (English)   • *IRS.gov/Korean* (한국어)
- *IRS.gov/Spanish* (Español)   • *IRS.gov/Russian* (Русский)
- *IRS.gov/Chinese*···   • *IRS.gov/Vietnamese* (TiếngViệt)

Dec 23, 2015

Contents

Future Developments

For the latest information about developments related to Pub. 15, such as legislation enacted after it was published, go to *www.irs.gov/pub15*.

What's New

Social security and Medicare tax for 2016. The social security tax rate is 6.2% each for the employee and employer, unchanged from 2015. The social security wage base limit is $118,500, unchanged from 2015.

A-140

The Medicare tax rate is 1.45% each for the employee and employer, unchanged from 2015. There is no wage base limit for Medicare tax.

Social security and Medicare taxes apply to the wages of household workers you pay $2,000 or more in cash or an equivalent form of compensation. Social security and Medicare taxes apply to election workers who are paid $1,700 or more in cash or an equivalent form of compensation.

2016 withholdng tables. This publication includes the 2016 Percentage Method Tables and Wage Bracket Tables for Income Tax Withholding.

Withholding allowance. The 2016 amount for one withholding allowance on an annual basis is $4,050.

New filing due date for 2016 Forms W-2, W-3, and 1099-MISC. Both paper and electronically filed 2016 Forms W-2 and W-3 must be filed with the Social Security Administration (SSA) by January 31, 2017. Both paper and electronically filed 2016 Form 1099-MISC must be filed with the IRS by January 31, 2017.

Work opportunity tax credit for qualified tax-exempt organizations hiring qualified veterans extended. The work opportunity tax credit is now available for eligible unemployed veterans who begin work after December 31, 2014, and before January 1, 2020. Qualified tax-exempt organizations that hire eligible unemployed veterans can claim the work opportunity tax credit against their payroll tax liability using Form 5884-C. For more information, visit IRS.gov and enter "work opportunity tax credit" in the search box.

New Pub. 5146 explains employment tax examinations and appeal rights. Pub. 5146 provides employers with information on how the IRS selects employment tax returns to be examined, what happens during an exam, and what options an employer has in responding to the results of an exam, including how to appeal the results. Pub. 5146 also includes information on worker classification issues and tip exams.

Motion picture project employers. Beginning January 1, 2016, all wages paid by a motion picture project employer to a motion picture project worker during a calendar year are subject to a single social security tax wage base ($118,500 for 2016) and a single FUTA tax wage base ($7,000 for 2016) regardless of the worker's status as a common law employee of multiple clients of the motion picture project employer. For more information, including the definition of a motion picture project employer and motion picture project worker, see Internal Revenue Code section 3512.

Reminders

COBRA premium assistance credit. Effective for tax periods beginning after December 31, 2013, the credit for COBRA premium assistance payments can't be claimed on Form 941, Employer's QUARTERLY Federal Tax Return (or Form 944, Employer's ANNUAL Federal Tax Return). Instead, after filing your Form 941 (or Form 944), file Form 941-X, Adjusted Employer's QUARTERLY Federal Tax Return or Claim for Refund (or Form 944-X, Adjusted Employer's ANNUAL Federal Tax Return or Claim for Refund), respectively, to claim the COBRA premium assistance credit. Filing a Form 941-X (or Form 944-X) before filing a Form 941 (or Form 944) for the return period may result in errors or delays in processing your Form 941-X (or Form 944-X). For more information, see the Instructions for Form 941 (or the Instructions for Form 944), or visit IRS.gov and enter "COBRA" in the search box.

Medicaid waiver payments. Notice 2014-7 provides that certain Medicaid waiver payments are excludable from income for federal income tax purposes. See Notice 2014-7, 2014-4 I.R.B. 445, available at *www.irs.gov/irb/ 2014-4_IRB/ar06.html*. For more information, including questions and answers related to Notice 2014-7, visit IRS.gov and enter "Medicaid waiver payments" in the search box.

No federal income tax withholding on disability payments for injuries incurred as a direct result of a terrorist attack directed against the United States. Disability payments for injuries incurred as a direct result of a terrorist attack directed against the United States (or its allies) aren't included in income. Because federal income tax withholding is only required when a payment is includable in income, no federal income tax should be withheld from these payments.

Voluntary withholding on dividends and other distributions by an Alaska Native Corporation (ANC). A shareholder of an ANC may request voluntary income tax withholding on dividends and other distributions paid by an ANC. A shareholder may request voluntary withholding by giving the ANC a completed Form W-4V. For more information see Notice 2013-77, 2013-50 I.R.B. 632, available at *www.irs.gov/irb/2013-50_IRB/ar10.html*.

Same-sex marriage. For federal tax purposes, marriages of couples of the same sex are treated the same as marriages of couples of the opposite sex. The term "spouse" includes an individual married to a person of the same sex. However, individuals who have entered into a registered domestic partnership, civil union, or other similar relationship that isn't considered a marriage under state law aren't considered married for federal tax purposes. For more information, see Revenue Ruling 2013-17, 2013-38 I.R.B. 201, available at *www.irs.gov/irb/ 2013-38_IRB/ar07.html* .

Notice 2013-61 provides special administrative procedures for employers to make claims for refunds or adjustments of overpayments of social security and Medicare taxes with respect to certain same-sex spouse benefits before expiration of the period of limitations. Notice 2013-61, 2013-44 I.R.B. 432, is available at *www.irs.gov/ irb/2013-44_IRB/ar10.html*. You may correct errors to federal income tax withholding and Additional Medicare Tax withheld for prior years if the amount reported on your employment tax return doesn't agree with the amount you actually withheld. This type of error is an administrative error. You may also correct errors to federal income tax withholding and Additional Medicare Tax withheld for prior years if section 3509 rates apply.

Additional Medicare Tax withholding. In addition to withholding Medicare tax at 1.45%, you must withhold a 0.9% Additional Medicare Tax from wages you pay to an employee in excess of $200,000 in a calendar year. You are required to begin withholding Additional Medicare Tax in the pay period in which you pay wages in excess of $200,000 to an employee and continue to withhold it each pay period until the end of the calendar year. Additional Medicare Tax is only imposed on the employee. There is no employer share of Additional Medicare Tax. All wages that are subject to Medicare tax are subject to Additional Medicare Tax withholding if paid in excess of the $200,000 withholding threshold.

For more information on what wages are subject to Medicare tax, see the chart, *Special Rules for Various Types of Services and Payments*, in section 15. For more information on Additional Medicare Tax, visit IRS.gov and enter "Additional Medicare Tax" in the search box.

Outsourcing payroll duties. You are responsible to ensure that tax returns are filed and deposits and payments are made, even if you contract with a third party to perform these acts. You remain responsible if the third party fails to perform any required action. If you choose to outsource any of your payroll and related tax duties (that is, withholding, reporting, and paying over social security, Medicare, FUTA, and income taxes) to a third-party payer, such as a payroll service provider (PSP) or reporting agent, visit IRS.gov and enter "outsourcing payroll duties" in the search box for helpful information on this topic. For more information on the different types of third party payer arrangements, see section 16.

Severance payments are subject to social security and Medicare taxes, income tax withholding, and FUTA tax. Severance payments are wages subject to social security and Medicare taxes. As noted in section 15, *Special Rules for Various Types of Services and Payments*, severance payments are also subject to income tax withholding and FUTA tax.

You must receive written notice from the IRS to file Form 944. If you have been filing Forms 941 (or Forms 941-SS, Employer's QUARTERLY Federal Tax Return—American Samoa, Guam, the Commonwealth of the Northern Mariana Islands, and the U.S. Virgin Islands, or Formularios 941-PR, Planilla para la Declaración Federal TRIMESTRAL del Patrono), and believe your employment taxes for the calendar year will be $1,000 or less, and you would like to file Form 944 instead of Forms 941, you must contact the IRS to request to file Form 944. You must receive written notice from the IRS to file Form 944 instead of Forms 941 before you may file this form. For more information on requesting to file Form 944, see the Instructions for Form 944.

Employers can request to file Forms 941 instead of Form 944. If you received notice from the IRS to file Form 944 but would like to file Forms 941 instead, you must contact the IRS to request to file Forms 941. You must receive written notice from the IRS to file Forms 941 instead of Form 944 before you may file these forms. For more information on requesting to file Form 941, see the Instructions for Form 944.

Federal tax deposits must be made by electronic funds transfer (EFT). You must use EFT to make all federal tax deposits. Generally, an EFT is made using the Electronic Federal Tax Payment System (EFTPS). If you don't want to use EFTPS, you can arrange for your tax professional, financial institution, payroll service, or other trusted third party to make electronic deposits on your behalf. Also, you may arrange for your financial institution to initiate a same-day wire payment on your behalf. EFTPS is a free service provided by the Department of Treasury. Services provided by your tax professional, financial institution, payroll service, or other third party may have a fee.

For more information on making federal tax deposits, see *How To Deposit* in section 11. To get more information about EFTPS or to enroll in EFTPS, visit *www.eftps.gov*, or call 1-800-555-4477 or 1-800-733-4829 (TDD). Additional information about EFTPS is also available in Pub. 966.

Aggregate Form 941 filers. Agents must complete Schedule R (Form 941), Allocation Schedule for Aggregate Form 941 Filers, when filing an aggregate Form 941. Aggregate Forms 941 may only be filed by agents approved by the IRS under section 3504 of the Internal Revenue Code (IRC). To request approval to act as an agent for an employer, the agent files Form 2678 with the IRS.

Aggregate Form 940 filers. Agents must complete Schedule R (Form 940), Allocation Schedule for Aggregate Form 940 Filers, when filing an aggregate Form 940, Employer's Annual Federal Unemployment (FUTA) Tax Return. Aggregate Forms 940 can be filed by agents acting on behalf of home care service recipients who receive home care services through a program administered by a federal, state, or local government. To request approval to act as an agent on behalf of home care service recipients, the agent files Form 2678 with the IRS.

Electronic Filing and Payment

Now, more than ever before, businesses can enjoy the benefits of filing and paying their federal taxes electronically. Whether you rely on a tax professional or handle your own taxes, the IRS offers you convenient programs to make filing and payment easier.

Spend less time and worry on taxes and more time running your business. Use *e-file* and EFTPS to your benefit.

- For *e-file,* visit *www.irs.gov/efile* for additional information.

- For EFTPS, visit *www.eftps.gov* or call EFTPS Customer Service at 1-800-555-4477 or 1-800-733-4829 (TDD).

- For electronic filing of Forms W-2, Wage and Tax Statement, visit *www.socialsecurity.gov/employer*.

 If you are filing your tax return or paying your federal taxes electronically, a valid EIN is required. If a valid EIN isn't provided, the return or payment won't be processed. This may result in penalties and delays in processing your return or payment.

Electronic funds withdrawal (EFW). If you file Form 940, Form 941, Form 944, or Form 945 electronically, you can e-file and e-pay (electronic funds withdrawal) the balance due in a single step using tax preparation software or through a tax professional. However, don't use EFW to make federal tax deposits. For more information on paying your taxes using EFW, visit the IRS website at *www.irs.gov/payments*. A fee may be charged to file electronically.

Credit or debit card payments. For information on paying your taxes with a credit or debit card, visit the IRS website at *www.irs.gov/payments*. However, don't use credit or debit cards to make federal tax deposits.

Online payment agreement. You may be eligible to apply for an installment agreement online if you have a balance due when you file your employment tax return. For more information, see the instructions for your employment tax return or visit the IRS website at *www.irs.gov/payments*.

Forms in Spanish

You can provide Formulario W-4(SP), Certificado de Exención de Retenciones del Empleado, in place of Form W-4, Employee's Withholding Allowance Certificate, to your Spanish-speaking employees. For more information, see Pub. 17(SP), El Impuesto Federal sobre los Ingresos (Para Personas Físicas). For nonemployees, Formulario W-9(SP), Solicitud y Certificación del Número de Identificación del Contribuyente, may be used in place of Form W-9, Request for Taxpayer Identification Number and Certification.

Hiring New Employees

Eligibility for employment. You must verify that each new employee is legally eligible to work in the United States. This includes completing the U.S. Citizenship and Immigration Services (USCIS) Form I-9, Employment Eligibility Verification. You can get Form I-9 from USCIS offices or by calling 1-800-870-3676. For more information, visit the USCIS website at *www.uscis.gov*, or call 1-800-375-5283 or 1-800-767-1833 (TDD).

New hire reporting. You are required to report any new employee to a designated state new hire registry. A new employee is an employee who hasn't previously been employed by you or was previously employed by you but has been separated from such prior employment for at least 60 consecutive days.

Many states accept a copy of Form W-4 with employer information added. Visit the Office of Child Support Enforcement website at *www.acf.hhs.gov/programs/cse/newhire* for more information.

W-4 request. Ask each new employee to complete the 2016 Form W-4. See section 9.

Name and social security number (SSN). Record each new employee's name and SSN from his or her social security card. Any employee without a social security card should apply for one. See section 4.

Paying Wages, Pensions, or Annuities

Correcting Form 941 or Form 944. If you discover an error on a previously filed Form 941 or Form 944, make the correction using Form 941-X or Form 944-X. Forms 941-X and 944-X are stand-alone forms, meaning taxpayers can file them when an error is discovered. Forms 941-X and 944-X are used by employers to claim refunds or abatements of employment taxes, rather than Form 843. See section 13 for more information.

Income tax withholding. Withhold federal income tax from each wage payment or supplemental unemployment compensation plan benefit payment according to the employee's Form W-4 and the correct withholding table. If you have nonresident alien employees, see *Withholding income taxes on the wages of nonresident alien employees* in section 9.

Withhold from periodic **pension and annuity payments** as if the recipient is married claiming three withholding allowances, unless he or she has provided Form W-4P, Withholding Certificate for Pension or Annuity Payments, either electing no withholding or giving a different number of allowances, marital status, or an additional amount to be withheld. Don't withhold on direct rollovers from qualified plans or governmental section 457(b) plans. See section 9 and Pub. 15-A, Employer's Supplemental Tax Guide. Pub. 15-A includes information about withholding on pensions and annuities.

Zero wage return. If you haven't filed a "final" Form 941 or Form 944, or aren't a "seasonal" employer, you must continue to file a Form 941 or Form 944, even for periods during which you paid no wages. The IRS encourages you to file your "Zero Wage" Forms 941 or 944 electronically using IRS e-file at *www.irs.gov/efile*.

Information Returns

You may be required to file information returns to report certain types of payments made during the year. For example, you must file Form 1099-MISC, Miscellaneous Income, to report payments of $600 or more to persons not treated as employees (for example, independent contractors) for services performed for your trade or business. For details about filing Forms 1099 and for information about required electronic filing, see the General Instructions for Certain Information Returns for general information and the separate, specific instructions for each information return you file (for example, Instructions for Form 1099-MISC). Generally, don't use Forms 1099 to report wages and other compensation you paid to employees; report these on Form W-2. See the General Instructions for Forms W-2 and W-3 for details about filing Form W-2 and for information about required electronic filing. If you file 250 or more Forms 1099, you must file them electronically. If you file 250 or more Forms W-2, you must file them electronically. IRS and SSA won't accept information returns filed on magnetic media.

Information reporting customer service site. The IRS operates an information return customer service site to answer questions about reporting on Forms W-2, W-3, 1099, and other information returns. If you have questions related to reporting on information returns, call 1-866-455-7438 (toll free), 304-263-8700 (toll call), or 304-579-4827 (TDD/TTY for persons who are deaf, hard of hearing, or have a speech disability). The center can also be reached by email at *mccirp@irs.gov*. Don't include tax identification numbers (TINs) or attachments in email correspondence because electronic mail isn't secure.

Nonpayroll Income Tax Withholding

Nonpayroll federal income tax withholding (reported on Forms 1099 and Form W-2G, Certain Gambling Winnings) must be reported on Form 945, Annual Return of Withheld Federal Income Tax. Separate deposits are required for payroll (Form 941 or Form 944) and nonpayroll (Form 945) withholding. Nonpayroll items include:

- Pensions (including distributions from tax-favored retirement plans, for example, section 401(k), section 403(b), and governmental section 457(b) plans) and annuities.

- Military retirement.

- Gambling winnings.

- Indian gaming profits.

- Certain other payments, such as unemployment compensation, social security, and Tier 1 railroad retirement benefits, subject to voluntary withholding.

- Payments subject to backup withholding.

For details on depositing and reporting nonpayroll income tax withholding, see the Instructions for Form 945.

Distributions from nonqualified pension plans and deferred compensation plans. Because distributions to participants from some nonqualified pension plans and deferred compensation plans (including section 457(b) plans of tax-exempt organizations) are treated as wages and are reported on Form W-2, income tax withheld must be reported on Form 941 or Form 944, not on Form 945. However, distributions from such plans to a beneficiary or estate of a deceased employee aren't wages and are re-ported on Forms 1099-R, Distributions From Pensions,

Employer Responsibilities

Employer Responsibilities: The following list provides a brief summary of your basic responsibilities. Because the individual circumstances for each employer can vary greatly, responsibilities for withholding, depositing, and reporting employment taxes can differ. Each item in this list has a page reference to a more detailed discussion in this publication.

A-144

Annuities, Retirement or Profit-Sharing Plans, IRAs, Insurance Contracts, etc.; income tax withheld must be reported on Form 945.

Backup withholding. You generally must withhold 28% of certain taxable payments if the payee fails to furnish you with his or her correct taxpayer identification number (TIN). This withholding is referred to as "backup withholding."

Payments subject to backup withholding include interest, dividends, patronage dividends, rents, royalties, commissions, nonemployee compensation, payments made in settlement of payment card or third-party network transactions, and certain other payments you make in the course of your trade or business. In addition, transactions by brokers and barter exchanges and certain payments made by fishing boat operators are subject to backup withholding.

 Backup withholding doesn't apply to wages, pensions, annuities, IRAs (including simplified employee pension (SEP) and SIMPLE retirement plans), section 404(k) distributions from an employee stock ownership plan (ESOP), medical savings accounts (MSAs), health savings accounts (HSAs), long-term-care benefits, or real estate transactions.

You can use Form W-9 or Formulario W-9(SP) to request payees to furnish a TIN. Form W-9 or Formulario W-9 (SP) must be used when payees must certify that the number furnished is correct, or when payees must certify that they aren't subject to backup withholding or are exempt from backup withholding. The Instructions for the Requester of Form W-9 or Formulario W-9(SP) includes a list of types of payees who are exempt from backup withholding. For more information, see Pub. 1281, Backup Withholding for Missing and Incorrect Name/TIN(s).

Recordkeeping

Keep all records of employment taxes for at least 4 years. These should be available for IRS review. Your records should include the following information.

- Your EIN.
- Amounts and dates of all wage, annuity, and pension payments.
- Amounts of tips reported to you by your employees.
- Records of allocated tips.
- The fair market value of in-kind wages paid.
- Names, addresses, social security numbers, and occupations of employees and recipients.
- Any employee copies of Forms W-2 and W-2c returned to you as undeliverable.
- Dates of employment for each employee.
- Periods for which employees and recipients were paid while absent due to sickness or injury and the amount

and weekly rate of payments you or third party payors made to them.

- Copies of employees' and recipients' income tax withholding allowance certificates (Forms W-4, W-4P, W-4(SP), W-4S, and W-4V).
- Dates and amounts of tax deposits you made and acknowledgment numbers for deposits made by EFTPS.
- Copies of returns filed and confirmation numbers.
- Records of fringe benefits and expense reimbursements provided to your employees, including substantiation.

Change of Business Name

Notify the IRS immediately if you change your business name. Write to the IRS office where you file your returns, using the *Without a payment* address provided in the instructions for your employment tax return, to notify the IRS of any business name change. See Pub. 1635 to see if you need to apply for a new EIN.

Change of Business Address or Responsible Party

Notify the IRS immediately if you change your business address or responsible party. Complete and mail Form 8822-B to notify the IRS of a business address or responsible party change. For a definition of "responsible party," see the Form 8822-B instructions.

Private Delivery Services

You can use certain private delivery services designated by the IRS to mail tax returns and payments. The list includes only the following:

- Federal Express (FedEx): FedEx First Overnight, FedEx Priority Overnight, FedEx Standard Overnight, FedEx 2 Day, FedEx International Next Flight Out, FedEx International Priority, FedEx International First, and FedEx International Economy
- United Parcel Service (UPS): UPS Next Day Air Early AM, UPS Next Day Air, UPS Next Day Air Saver, UPS 2nd Day Air, UPS 2nd Day Air A.M., UPS Worldwide Express Plus, and UPS Worldwide Express

For the IRS mailing address to use if you are using a private delivery service, go to IRS.gov and enter "private delivery service" in the search box.

Your private delivery service can tell you how to get written proof of the mailing date.

Private delivery services can't deliver items to P.O. boxes. You must use the U.S. Postal Service to mail any item to an IRS P.O. box address.

Telephone Help

Tax questions. You can call the IRS Business and Specialty Tax Line with your employment tax questions at 1-800-829-4933.

Help for people with disabilities. You may call 1-800-829-4059 (TDD/TTY for persons who are deaf, hard of hearing, or have a speech disability) with any employment tax questions. You may also use this number for assistance with unresolved tax problems.

Additional employment tax information. Visit IRS.gov and enter "employment taxes" in the search box.

Ordering Employer Tax Forms and Publications

You can order employer tax forms and publications and information returns online at *www.irs.gov/orderforms*.

Instead of ordering paper Forms W-2 and W-3, consider filing them electronically using the SSA's free e-file service. Visit the SSA's Employer W-2 Filing Instructions & Information website at *www.socialsecurity.gov/employer* to register for Business Services Online. You will be able to create Forms W-2 online and submit them to the SSA by typing your wage information into easy-to-use fill-in fields. In addition, you can print out completed copies of Forms W-2 to file with state or local governments, distribute to your employees, and keep for your records. Form W-3 will be created for you based on your Forms W-2.

Filing Addresses

Generally, your filing address for Forms 940, 941, 943, 944, 945, and CT-1 depends on the location of your residence or principal place of business and whether or not you are including a payment with your return. There are separate filing addresses for these returns if you are a tax-exempt organization or government entity. See the separate instructions for Forms 940, 941, 943, 944, 945, or CT-1 for the filing addresses.

Dishonored Payments

Any form of payment that is dishonored and returned from a financial institution is subject to a penalty. The penalty is $25 or 2% of the payment, whichever is more. However, the penalty on dishonored payments of $24.99 or less is an amount equal to the payment. For example, a dishonored payment of $18 is charged a penalty of $18.

Photographs of Missing Children

The IRS is a proud partner with the National Center for Missing and Exploited Children. Photographs of missing children selected by the Center may appear in this publication on pages that would otherwise be blank. You can help bring these children home by looking at the photographs and calling 1-800-THE-LOST (1-800-843-5678) if you recognize a child.

Calendar

The following is a list of important dates. Also see Pub. 509, Tax Calendars.

 If any date shown next for filing a return, furnishing a form, or depositing taxes falls on a Saturday, Sunday, or legal holiday, use the next business day. A statewide legal holiday delays a filing due date only if the IRS office where you are required to file is located in that state. However, a statewide legal holiday doesn't delay the due date of federal tax deposits. See Deposits on Business Days Only *in section 11. For any filing due date, you will meet the "file" or "furnish" requirement if the envelope containing the return or form is properly addressed, contains sufficient postage, and is postmarked by the U.S. Postal Service on or before the due date, or sent by an IRS-designated private delivery service on or before the due date. See* Private Delivery Services *under Reminders for more information.*

By January 31

Furnish Forms 1099 and W-2. Furnish each employee a completed Form W-2. Furnish each other payee a completed Form 1099 (for example, Form 1099-MISC).

File Form 941 or Form 944. File Form 941 for the fourth quarter of the previous calendar year and deposit any undeposited income, social security, and Medicare taxes. You may pay these taxes with Form 941 if your total tax liability for the quarter is less than $2,500. File Form 944 for the previous calendar year instead of Form 941 if the IRS has notified you in writing to file Form 944 and pay any undeposited income, social security, and Medicare taxes. You may pay these taxes with Form 944 if your total tax liability for the year is less than $2,500. For additional rules on when you can pay your taxes with your return, see *Payment with return* in section 11. If you timely deposited all taxes when due, you may file by February 10.

File Form 940. File Form 940 to report any FUTA tax. However if you deposited all of the FUTA tax when due, you may file by February 10.

File Form 945. File Form 945 to report any nonpayroll federal income tax withheld. If you deposited all taxes when due, you may file by February 10. See *Nonpayroll Income Tax Withholding* under *Reminders* for more information.

By February 15

Request a new Form W-4 from exempt employees. Ask for a new Form W-4 from each employee who claimed exemption from income tax withholding last year.

On February 16

Forms W-4 claiming exemption from withholding expire. Any Form W-4 claiming exemption from withholding for the previous year has now expired. Begin withholding for any employee who previously claimed exemption from withholding but hasn't given you a new Form W-4 for the current year. If the employee doesn't give you a new Form W-4, withhold tax based on the last valid Form W-4 you have for the employee that doesn't claim exemption from withholding or, if one doesn't exist, as if he or she is single with zero withholding allowances. See section 9 for more information. If the employee furnishes a new Form W-4 claiming exemption from withholding after February 15, you may apply the exemption to future wages, but don't refund taxes withheld while the exempt status wasn't in place.

 Both paper and electronically filed 2016 Forms W-2 and W-3 must be filed with the SSA by January 31, 2017. Both paper and electronically filed 2016 Form 1099-MISC must be filed with the IRS by January 31, 2017.

By February 28

File paper 2015 Forms 1099 and 1096. File Copy A of all paper 2015 Forms 1099 with Form 1096, Annual Summary and Transmittal of U.S. Information Returns, with the IRS. For electronically filed returns, see *By March 31* below.

By February 29

File paper 2015 Forms W-2 and W-3. File Copy A of all paper 2015 Forms W-2 with Form W-3, Transmittal of Wage and Tax Statements, with the SSA. For electronically filed returns, see *By March 31* below.

File paper Form 8027. File paper Form 8027, Employer's Annual Information Return of Tip Income and Allocated Tips, with the IRS. See section 6. For electronically filed returns, see *By March 31* next.

By March 31

File electronic 2015 Forms 1099, 8027, and W-2. File electronic 2015 Forms 1099 and 8027 with the IRS. File electronic 2015 Forms W-2 with the SSA. For

information on reporting Form W-2 information to the SSA electronically, visit the Social Security Administration's Employer W-2 Filing Instructions & Information webpage at *www.socialsecurity.gov/employer*. For information on filing information returns electronically with the IRS, see Pub. 1220, Specifications for Electronic Filing of Forms 1097, 1098, 1099, 3921, 3922, 5498, 8935, and W-2G; and Pub. 1239, Specifications for Electronic Filing of Form 8027, Employer's Annual Information Return of Tip Income and Allocated Tips.

By April 30, July 31, October 31, and January 31

Deposit FUTA taxes. Deposit FUTA tax due if it is more than $500.

File Form 941. File Form 941 and deposit any undeposited income, social security, and Medicare taxes. You may pay these taxes with Form 941 if your total tax liability for the quarter is less than $2,500. If you timely deposited all taxes when due, you may file by May 10, August 10, November 10, or February 10, respectively.

Before December 1

New Forms W-4. Remind employees to submit a new Form W-4 if their marital status or withholding allowances have changed or will change for the next year.

Introduction

This publication explains your tax responsibilities as an employer. It explains the requirements for withholding, depositing, reporting, paying, and correcting employment taxes. It explains the forms you must give to your employees, those your employees must give to you, and those you must send to the IRS and SSA. This guide also has tax tables you need to figure the taxes to withhold from each employee for 2016. References to "income tax" in this guide apply only to "federal" income tax. Contact your state or local tax department to determine if their rules are different.

When you pay your employees, you don't pay them all the money they earned. As their employer, you have the added responsibility of withholding taxes from their paychecks. The federal income tax and employees' share of social security and Medicare taxes that you withhold from your employees' paychecks are part of their wages that you pay to the United States Treasury instead of to your employees. Your employees trust that you pay the withheld taxes to the United States Treasury by making federal tax deposits. This is the reason that these withheld taxes are called trust fund taxes. If federal income, social security, or Medicare taxes that must be withheld aren't withheld or aren't deposited or paid to the United States Treasury, the trust fund recovery penalty may apply. See section 11 for more information.

Additional employment tax information is available in Pub. 15-A. Pub. 15-A includes specialized information supplementing the basic employment tax information provided in this publication. Pub. 15-B, Employer's Tax Guide to Fringe Benefits, contains information about the employment tax treatment and valuation of various types of noncash compensation.

Most employers must withhold (except FUTA), deposit, report, and pay the following employment taxes.

- Income tax.

- Social security tax.

- Medicare tax.

- FUTA tax.

There are exceptions to these requirements. See section 15 for guidance. Railroad retirement taxes are explained in the Instructions for Form CT-1.

Comments and suggestions. We welcome your comments about this publication and your suggestions for future editions. You can send us comments from *www.irs.gov/formspubs*. Click on *More Information* and then click on *Give us feedback*.

Or you can write to:

Internal Revenue Service
Tax Forms and Publications
1111 Constitution Ave. NW, IR-6526
Washington, DC 20224

We respond to many letters by telephone. Therefore, it would be helpful if you would include your daytime phone number, including the area code, in your correspondence.

Although we can't respond individually to each comment received, we do appreciate your feedback and will consider your comments as we revise our tax forms, instructions, and publications.

Federal Government employers. The information in this publication, including the rules for making federal tax deposits, applies to federal agencies.

State and local government employers. Payments to employees for services in the employ of state and local government employers are generally subject to federal income tax withholding but not FUTA tax. Most elected and appointed public officials of state or local governments are employees under common law rules. See chapter 3 of Pub. 963, Federal-State Reference Guide. In addition, wages, with certain exceptions, are subject to social security and Medicare taxes. See section 15 for more information on the exceptions.

If an election worker is employed in another capacity with the same government entity, see Revenue Ruling 2000-6 on page 512 of Internal Revenue Bulletin 2000-6 at *www.irs.gov/pub/irs-irbs/irb00-06.pdf*.

You can get information on reporting and social security coverage from your local IRS office. If you have any questions about coverage under a section 218 (Social Security Act) agreement, contact the appropriate state official. To find your State Social Security Administrator, visit the National Conference of State Social Security Administrators website at *www.ncsssa.org*.

Disregarded entities and qualified subchapter S subsidiaries (QSubs). Eligible single-owner disregarded entities and QSubs are treated as separate entities for employment tax purposes. Eligible single-member entities that haven't elected to be taxed as corporations must report and pay employment taxes on wages paid to their employees using the entities' own names and EINs. See Regulations sections 1.1361-4(a)(7) and 301.7701-2(c)(2)(iv).

COBRA premium assistance credit. The Consolidated Omnibus Budget Reconciliation Act of 1985 (COBRA) provides certain former employees, retirees, spouses, former spouses, and dependent children the right to temporary continuation of health coverage at group rates. COBRA generally covers multiemployer health plans and health plans maintained by private-sector employers (other than churches) with 20 or more full and part-time employees. Parallel requirements apply to these plans under the Employee Retirement Income Security Act of 1974 (ERISA). Under the Public Health Service Act, COBRA requirements apply also to health plans covering state or local government employees. Similar requirements apply under the Federal Employees Health Benefits Program and under some state laws. For the premium assistance (or subsidy) discussed below, these requirements are all referred to as COBRA requirements.

Under the American Recovery and Reinvestment Act of 2009 (ARRA), employers are allowed a credit against "payroll taxes" (referred to in this publication as "employment taxes") for providing COBRA premium assistance to assistance eligible individuals. For periods of COBRA continuation coverage beginning after February 16, 2009, a group health plan must treat an assistance eligible individual as having paid the required COBRA continuation coverage premium if the individual elects COBRA coverage and pays 35% of the amount of the premium.

An assistance eligible individual is a qualified beneficiary of an employer's group health plan who is eligible for COBRA continuation coverage during the period beginning September 1, 2008, and ending May 31, 2010, due to the involuntarily termination from employment of a covered employee during the period and elects continuation COBRA coverage. The assistance for the coverage can last up to 15 months.

Employees terminated during the period beginning September 1, 2008, and ending May 31, 2010, who received a severance package that delayed the start of the COBRA continuation coverage, may still be eligible for premium assistance for COBRA continuation coverage. For more information see Notice 2009-27, 2009-16 I.R.B. 838, available at *www.irs.gov/irb/2009-16_irb/ar09.html*.

Administrators of the group health plans (or other entities) that provide or administer COBRA continuation coverage must provide notice to assistance eligible individuals of the COBRA premium assistance.

The 65% of the premium not paid by the assistance eligible individuals is reimbursed to the employer maintaining the group health plan. The reimbursement is made through a credit against the employer's employment tax liabilities. For information on how to claim the credit, see the Instructions for Form 941-X or the Instructions for Form 944-X. The credit is treated as a deposit made on the first day of the return period (quarter or year). In the case of a multiemployer plan, the credit is claimed by the plan, rather than the employer. In the case of an insured plan subject to state law continuation coverage requirements, the credit is claimed by the insurance company, rather than the employer.

Anyone claiming the credit for COBRA premium assistance payments must maintain the following information to support their claim, including the following.

- Information on the receipt of the assistance eligible individuals' 35% share of the premium, including dates and amounts.

- In the case of an insurance plan, a copy of invoice or other supporting statement from the insurance carrier and proof of timely payment of the full premium to the insurance carrier required under COBRA.

- In the case of a self-insured plan, proof of the premium amount and proof of the coverage provided to the assistance eligible individuals.

- Attestation of involuntary termination, including the date of the involuntary termination for each covered employee whose involuntary termination is the basis for eligibility for the subsidy.

- Proof of each assistance eligible individual's eligibility for COBRA coverage and the election of COBRA coverage.

- A record of the SSNs of all covered employees, the amount of the subsidy reimbursed with respect to each covered employee, and whether the subsidy was for one individual or two or more individuals.

For more information, visit IRS.gov and enter "COBRA" in the search box.

1. Employer Identification Number (EIN)

If you are required to report employment taxes or give tax statements to employees or annuitants, you need an EIN.

The EIN is a nine-digit number the IRS issues. The digits are arranged as follows: 00-0000000. It is used to identify the tax accounts of employers and certain others who have no employees. Use your EIN on all of the items you send to the IRS and SSA. For more information, see Pub. 1635.

If you don't have an EIN, you may apply for one online. Visit IRS.gov and enter "EIN" in the search box. You may also apply for an EIN by faxing or mailing Form SS-4 to the IRS. Employers outside of the United States may also apply for an EIN by calling 267-941-1099 (toll call). Don't use an SSN in place of an EIN.

You should have only one EIN. If you have more than one and aren't sure which one to use, call 1-800-829-4933 or 1-800-829-4059 (TDD/TTY for persons who are deaf, hard of hearing, or have a speech disability). Give the numbers you have, the name and address to which each was assigned, and the address of your main place of business. The IRS will tell you which number to use.

If you took over another employer's business (see *Successor employer* in section 9), don't use that employer's EIN. If you have applied for an EIN but don't have your EIN by the time a return is due, file a paper return and write "Applied For" and the date you applied for it in the space shown for the number.

2. Who Are Employees?

Generally, employees are defined either under common law or under statutes for certain situations. See Pub. 15-A for details on statutory employees and nonemployees.

Employee status under common law. Generally, a worker who performs services for you is your employee if you have the right to control what will be done and how it will be done. This is so even when you give the employee freedom of action. What matters is that you have the right to control the details of how the services are performed. See Pub. 15-A for more information on how to determine whether an individual providing services is an independent contractor or an employee.

Generally, people in business for themselves aren't employees. For example, doctors, lawyers, veterinarians, and others in an independent trade in which they offer their services to the public are usually not employees. However, if the business is incorporated, corporate officers who work in the business are employees of the corporation.

If an employer-employee relationship exists, it doesn't matter what it is called. The employee may be called an agent or independent contractor. It also doesn't matter how payments are measured or paid, what they are called, or if the employee works full or part time.

Statutory employees. If someone who works for you isn't an employee under the common law rules discussed above, don't withhold federal income tax from his or her pay, unless backup withholding applies. Although the following persons may not be common law employees, they are considered employees by statute for social security, Medicare, and FUTA tax purposes under certain conditions.

- An agent (or commission) driver who delivers food, beverages (other than milk), laundry, or dry cleaning for someone else.

- A full-time life insurance salesperson who sells primarily for one company.

- A homeworker who works by guidelines of the person for whom the work is done, with materials furnished by and returned to that person or to someone that person designates.

A-149

- A traveling or city salesperson (other than an agent-driver or commission-driver) who works full time (except for sideline sales activities) for one firm or person getting orders from customers. The orders must be for merchandise for resale or supplies for use in the customer's business. The customers must be retailers, wholesalers, contractors, or operators of hotels, restaurants, or other businesses dealing with food or lodging.

Statutory nonemployees. Direct sellers, qualified real estate agents, and certain companion sitters are, by law, considered nonemployees. They are generally treated as self-employed for all federal tax purposes, including income and employment taxes.

H-2A agricultural workers. On Form W-2, don't check box 13 (Statutory employee), as H-2A workers aren't statutory employees.

Treating employees as nonemployees. You will generally be liable for social security and Medicare taxes and withheld income tax if you don't deduct and withhold these taxes because you treated an employee as a nonemployee. You may be able to calculate your liability using special IRC section 3509 rates for the employee share of social security and Medicare taxes and the federal income tax withholding. The applicable rates depend on whether you filed required Forms 1099. You can't recover the employee share of social security tax, Medicare tax, or income tax withholding from the employee if the tax is paid under IRC section 3509. You are liable for the income tax withholding regardless of whether the employee paid income tax on the wages. You continue to owe the full employer share of social security and Medicare taxes. The employee remains liable for the employee share of social security and Medicare taxes. See IRC section 3509 for details. Also see the Instructions for Form 941-X.

IRC section 3509 rates aren't available if you intentionally disregard the requirement to withhold taxes from the employee or if you withheld income taxes but not social security or Medicare taxes. IRC section 3509 isn't available for reclassifying statutory employees. See *Statutory employees*, earlier.

If the employer issued required information returns, the IRC section 3509 rates are:

- For social security taxes; employer rate of 6.2% plus 20% of the employee rate (see the Instructions for Form 941-X).

- For Medicare taxes; employer rate of 1.45% plus 20% of the employee rate of 1.45%, for a total rate of 1.74% of wages.

- For Additional Medicare Tax; 0.18% (20% of the employee rate of 0.9%) of wages subject to Additional Medicare Tax.

- For income tax withholding, the rate is 1.5% of wages.

If the employer didn't issue required information returns, the IRC section 3509 rates are:

- For social security taxes; employer rate of 6.2% plus 40% of the employee rate (see the Instructions for Form 941-X).

- For Medicare taxes; employer rate of 1.45% plus 40% of the employee rate of 1.45%, for a total rate of 2.03% of wages.

- For Additional Medicare Tax; 0.36% (40% of the employee rate of 0.9%) of wages subject to Additional Medicare Tax.

- For income tax withholding, the rate is 3.0% of wages.

Relief provisions. If you have a reasonable basis for not treating a worker as an employee, you may be relieved from having to pay employment taxes for that worker. To get this relief, you must file all required federal tax returns, including information returns, on a basis consistent with your treatment of the worker. You (or your predecessor) must not have treated any worker holding a substantially similar position as an employee for any periods beginning after 1977. See Pub. 1976, Do You Qualify for Relief Under Section 530.

IRS help. If you want the IRS to determine whether a worker is an employee, file Form SS-8.

Voluntary Classification Settlement Program (VCSP). Employers who are currently treating their workers (or a class or group of workers) as independent contractors or other nonemployees and want to voluntarily reclassify their workers as employees for future tax periods may be eligible to participate in the VCSP if certain requirements are met. File Form 8952 to apply for the VCSP. For more information visit IRS.gov and enter "VCSP" in the search box.

Business Owned and Operated by Spouses

If you and your spouse jointly own and operate a business and share in the profits and losses, you are partners in a partnership, whether or not you have a formal partnership agreement. See Pub. 541 for more details. The partnership is considered the employer of any employees, and is liable for any employment taxes due on wages paid to its employees.

Exception—Qualified joint venture. For tax years beginning after December 31, 2006, the Small Business and Work Opportunity Tax Act of 2007 (Public Law 110-28) provides that a "qualified joint venture," whose only members are spouses filing a joint income tax return, can elect not to be treated as a partnership for federal tax purposes. A qualified joint venture conducts a trade or business where:

- The only members of the joint venture are spouses who file a joint income tax return,

- Both spouses materially participate (see *Material participation* in the Instructions for Schedule C (Form 1040), line G) in the trade or business (mere joint ownership of property isn't enough),

- Both spouses elect to not be treated as a partnership, and

- The business is co-owned by both spouses and isn't held in the name of a state law entity such as a partnership or limited liability company (LLC).

To make the election, all items of income, gain, loss, deduction, and credit must be divided between the spouses, in accordance with each spouse's interest in the venture, and reported on separate Schedules C or F as sole proprietors. Each spouse must also file a separate Schedule SE to pay self-employment taxes, as applicable.

Spouses using the qualified joint venture rules are treated as sole proprietors for federal tax purposes and generally don't need an EIN. If employment taxes are owed by the qualified joint venture, either spouse may report and pay the employment taxes due on the wages paid to the employees using the EIN of that spouse's sole proprietorship. Generally, filing as a qualified joint venture won't increase the spouses' total tax owed on the joint income tax return. However, it gives each spouse credit for social security earnings on which retirement benefits are based and for Medicare coverage without filing a partnership return.

Note. If your spouse is your employee, not your partner, see *One spouse employed by another* in section 3.

For more information on qualified joint ventures, visit IRS.gov and enter "qualified joint venture" in the search box.

Exception—Community income. If you and your spouse wholly own an unincorporated business as community property under the community property laws of a state, foreign country, or U.S. possession, you can treat the business either as a sole proprietorship (of the spouse who carried on the business) or a partnership. You may still make an election to be taxed as a qualified joint venture instead of a partnership. See *Exception—Qualified joint venture*, earlier.

3. Family Employees

Child employed by parents. Payments for the services of a child under age 18 who works for his or her parent in a trade or business aren't subject to social security and Medicare taxes if the trade or business is a sole proprietorship or a partnership in which each partner is a parent of the child. If these payments are for work other than in a trade or business, such as domestic work in the parent's private home, they aren't subject to social security and Medicare taxes until the child reaches age 21. However, see *Covered services of a child or spouse* below. Payments for the services of a child under age 21 who works for his or her parent, whether or not in a trade or business, aren't subject to FUTA tax. Payments for the services of a child of any age who works for his or her parent are gener-

ally subject to income tax withholding unless the payments are for domestic work in the parent's home, or unless the payments are for work other than in a trade or business and are less than $50 in the quarter or the child isn't regularly employed to do such work.

One spouse employed by another. The wages for the services of an individual who works for his or her spouse in a trade or business are subject to income tax withholding and social security and Medicare taxes, but not to FUTA tax. However, the payments for services of one spouse employed by another in other than a trade or business, such as domestic service in a private home, aren't subject to social security, Medicare, and FUTA taxes.

Covered services of a child or spouse. The wages for the services of a child or spouse are subject to income tax withholding as well as social security, Medicare, and FUTA taxes if he or she works for:

- A corporation, even if it is controlled by the child's parent or the individual's spouse;

- A partnership, even if the child's parent is a partner, unless each partner is a parent of the child;

- A partnership, even if the individual's spouse is a partner; or

- An estate, even if it is the estate of a deceased parent.

Parent employed by son or daughter. When the employer is a son or daughter employing his or her parent the following rules apply.

- Payments for the services of a parent in the son's or daughter's (the employer's) trade or business are subject to income tax withholding and social security and Medicare taxes.

- Payments for the services of a parent not in the son's or daughter's (the employer's) trade or business are generally not subject to social security and Medicare taxes.

 Social security and Medicare taxes do apply to payments made to a parent for domestic services if all of the following apply:

- *The parent is employed by his or her son or daughter;*

- *The son or daughter (the employer) has a child or stepchild living in the home;*

- *The son or daughter (the employer) is a widow or widower, divorced, or living with a spouse who, because of a mental or physical condition, can't care for the child or stepchild for at least 4 continuous weeks in a calendar quarter; and*

- *The child or stepchild is either under age 18 or requires the personal care of an adult for at least 4 continuous weeks in a calendar quarter due to a mental or physical condition.*

Payments made to a parent employed by his or her child aren't subject to FUTA tax, regardless of the type of services provided.

4. Employee's Social Security Number (SSN)

You are required to get each employee's name and SSN and to enter them on Form W-2. This requirement also applies to resident and nonresident alien employees. You should ask your employee to show you his or her social security card. The employee may show the card if it is available.

 Don't accept a social security card that says "Not valid for employment." A social security number issued with this legend doesn't permit employment.

You may, but aren't required to, photocopy the social security card if the employee provides it. If you don't provide the correct employee name and SSN on Form W-2, you may owe a penalty unless you have reasonable cause. See Pub. 1586, Reasonable Cause Regulations & Requirements for Missing and Incorrect Name/TINs, for information on the requirement to solicit the employee's SSN.

Applying for a social security card. Any employee who is legally eligible to work in the United States and doesn't have a social security card can get one by completing Form SS-5, Application for a Social Security Card, and submitting the necessary documentation. You can get Form SS-5 from the SSA website at *www.socialsecurity.gov/online/ss-5.html*, at SSA offices, or by calling 1-800-772-1213 or 1-800-325-0778 (TTY). The employee must complete and sign Form SS-5; it can't be filed by the employer. You may be asked to supply a letter to accompany Form SS-5 if the employee has exceeded his or her yearly or lifetime limit for the number of replacement cards allowed.

Applying for an SSN. If you file Form W-2 on paper and your employee applied for an SSN but doesn't have one when you must file Form W-2, enter "Applied For" on the form. If you are filing electronically, enter all zeros (000-00-000) in the SSN field. When the employee receives the SSN, file Copy A of Form W-2c, Corrected Wage and Tax Statement, with the SSA to show the employee's SSN. Furnish copies B, C, and 2 of Form W-2c to the employee. Up to 25 Forms W-2c for each Form W-3c, Transmittal of Corrected Wage and Tax Statements, may now be filed per session over the Internet, with no limit on the number of sessions. For more information, visit the SSA's Employer W-2 Filing Instructions & Information webpage at *www.socialsecurity.gov/employer*. Advise your employee to correct the SSN on his or her original Form W-2.

Correctly record the employee's name and SSN. Record the name and SSN of each employee as they are shown on the employee's social security card. If the employee's name isn't correct as shown on the card (for example, because of marriage or divorce), the employee should request an updated card from the SSA. Continue to report the employee's wages under the old name until the employee shows you the updated social security card with the corrected name.

If the SSA issues the employee an updated card after a name change, or a new card with a different SSN, file a Form W-2c to correct the name/SSN reported for the most recently filed Form W-2. It isn't necessary to correct other years if the previous name and number were used for years before the most recent Form W-2.

IRS individual taxpayer identification numbers (ITINs) for aliens. Don't accept an ITIN in place of an SSN for employee identification or for work. An ITIN is only available to resident and nonresident aliens who aren't eligible for U.S. employment and need identification for other tax purposes. You can identify an ITIN because it is a nine-digit number, formatted like an SSN, that starts with the number "9" and has a range of numbers from "70–88", "90–92", and "94–99" for the fourth and fifth digits (for example, 9NN-7N-NNNN).

 An individual with an ITIN who later becomes eligible to work in the United States must obtain an SSN. If the individual is currently eligible to work in the United States, instruct the individual to apply for an SSN and follow the instructions under Applying for an SSN above. Don't use an ITIN in place of an SSN on Form W-2.

Verification of SSNs. Employers and authorized reporting agents can use the Social Security Number Verification Service (SSNVS) to instantly verify up to 10 names and SSNs (per screen) at a time, or submit an electronic file of up to 250,000 names and SSNs and usually receive the results the next business day. Visit *www.socialsecurity.gov/employer/ssnv.htm* for more information.

Registering for SSNVS. You must register online and receive authorization from your employer to use SSNVS. To register, visit SSA's website at *www.socialsecurity.gov/bso* and click on the *Register* link under *Business Services Online*. Follow the registration instructions to obtain a user identification (ID) and password. You will need to provide the following information about yourself and your company.

- Name.

- SSN.

- Date of birth.

- Type of employer.

- EIN.

- Company name, address, and telephone number.

- Email address.

When you have completed the online registration process, SSA will mail a one-time activation code to your employer. You must enter the activation code online to use SSNVS.

5. Wages and Other Compensation

Wages subject to federal employment taxes generally include all pay you give to an employee for services performed. The pay may be in cash or in other forms. It includes salaries, vacation allowances, bonuses, commissions, and fringe benefits. It doesn't matter how you measure or make the payments. Amounts an employer pays as a bonus for signing or ratifying a contract in connection with the establishment of an employer-employee relationship and an amount paid to an employee for cancellation of an employment contract and relinquishment of contract rights are wages subject to social security, Medicare, and FUTA taxes and income tax withholding. Also, compensation paid to a former employee for services performed while still employed is wages subject to employment taxes.

More information. See section 6 for a discussion of tips and section 7 for a discussion of supplemental wages. Also, see section 15 for exceptions to the general rules for wages. Pub. 15-A provides additional information on wages, including nonqualified deferred compensation, and other compensation. Pub. 15-B provides information on other forms of compensation, including:

- Accident and health benefits,

- Achievement awards,

- Adoption assistance,

- Athletic facilities,

- De minimis (minimal) benefits,

- Dependent care assistance,

- Educational assistance,

- Employee discounts,

- Employee stock options,

- Employer-provided cell phones,

- Group-term life insurance coverage,

- Health Savings Accounts,

- Lodging on your business premises,

- Meals,

- Moving expense reimbursements,

- No-additional-cost services,

- Retirement planning services,

- Transportation (commuting) benefits,

- Tuition reduction, and

- Working condition benefits.

Employee business expense reimbursements. A reimbursement or allowance arrangement is a system by which you pay the advances, reimbursements, and charges for your employees' business expenses. How you report a reimbursement or allowance amount depends on whether you have an accountable or a nonaccountable plan. If a single payment includes both wages and an expense reimbursement, you must specify the amount of the reimbursement.

These rules apply to all ordinary and necessary employee business expenses that would otherwise qualify for a deduction by the employee.

Accountable plan. To be an accountable plan, your reimbursement or allowance arrangement must require your employees to meet all three of the following rules.

1. They must have paid or incurred deductible expenses while performing services as your employees. The reimbursement or advance must be payment for the expenses and must not be an amount that would have otherwise been paid to the employee as wages.

2. They must substantiate these expenses to you within a reasonable period of time.

3. They must return any amounts in excess of substantiated expenses within a reasonable period of time.

Amounts paid under an accountable plan aren't wages and aren't subject to income, social security, Medicare, and FUTA taxes.

If the expenses covered by this arrangement aren't substantiated (or amounts in excess of substantiated expenses aren't returned within a reasonable period of time), the amount paid under the arrangement in excess of the substantiated expenses is treated as paid under a nonaccountable plan. This amount is subject to income, social security, Medicare, and FUTA taxes for the first payroll period following the end of the reasonable period of time.

A reasonable period of time depends on the facts and circumstances. Generally, it is considered reasonable if your employees receive their advance within 30 days of the time they incur the expenses, adequately account for the expenses within 60 days after the expenses were paid or incurred, and return any amounts in excess of expenses within 120 days after the expenses were paid or incurred. Also, it is considered reasonable if you give your employees a periodic statement (at least quarterly) that asks them to either return or adequately account for outstanding amounts and they do so within 120 days.

Nonaccountable plan. Payments to your employee for travel and other necessary expenses of your business under a nonaccountable plan are wages and are treated as supplemental wages and subject to income, social security, Medicare, and FUTA taxes. Your payments are treated as paid under a nonaccountable plan if:

- Your employee isn't required to or doesn't substantiate timely those expenses to you with receipts or other documentation,

- You advance an amount to your employee for business expenses and your employee isn't required to or doesn't return timely any amount he or she doesn't use for business expenses,

- You advance or pay an amount to your employee regardless of whether you reasonably expect the employee to have business expenses related to your business, or

- You pay an amount as a reimbursement you would have otherwise paid as wages.

See section 7 for more information on supplemental wages.

Per diem or other fixed allowance. You may reimburse your employees by travel days, miles, or some other fixed allowance under the applicable revenue procedure. In these cases, your employee is considered to have accounted to you if your reimbursement doesn't exceed rates established by the Federal Government. The 2015 standard mileage rate for auto expenses was 57.5 cents per mile. The rate for 2016 is 54 cents per mile.

The government per diem rates for meals and lodging in the continental United States can be found by visiting the U.S. General Services Administration website at *www.GSA.gov* and entering "per diem rates" in the search box. Other than the amount of these expenses, your employees' business expenses must be substantiated (for example, the business purpose of the travel or the number of business miles driven). For information on substantiation methods, see Pub. 463.

If the per diem or allowance paid exceeds the amounts substantiated, you must report the excess amount as wages. This excess amount is subject to income tax withholding and payment of social security, Medicare, and FUTA taxes. Show the amount equal to the substantiated amount (for example, the nontaxable portion) in box 12 of Form W-2 using code "L."

Wages not paid in money. If in the course of your trade or business you pay your employees in a medium that is neither cash nor a readily negotiable instrument, such as a check, you are said to pay them "in kind." Payments in kind may be in the form of goods, lodging, food, clothing, or services. Generally, the fair market value of such payments at the time they are provided is subject to federal income tax withholding and social security, Medicare, and FUTA taxes.

However, noncash payments for household work, agricultural labor, and service not in the employer's trade or business are exempt from social security, Medicare, and FUTA taxes. Withhold income tax on these payments only

if you and the employee agree to do so. Nonetheless, noncash payments for agricultural labor, such as commodity wages, are treated as cash payments subject to employment taxes if the substance of the transaction is a cash payment.

Moving expenses. Reimbursed and employer-paid qualified moving expenses (those that would otherwise be deductible by the employee) paid under an accountable plan aren't includible in an employee's income unless you have knowledge the employee deducted the expenses in a prior year. Reimbursed and employer-paid nonqualified moving expenses are includible in income and are subject to employment taxes and income tax withholding. For more information on moving expenses, see Pub. 521.

Meals and lodging. The value of meals isn't taxable income and isn't subject to income tax withholding and social security, Medicare, and FUTA taxes if the meals are furnished for the employer's convenience and on the employer's premises. The value of lodging isn't subject to income tax withholding and social security, Medicare, and FUTA taxes if the lodging is furnished for the employer's convenience, on the employer's premises, and as a condition of employment.

"For the convenience of the employer" means you have a substantial business reason for providing the meals and lodging other than to provide additional compensation to the employee. For example, meals you provide at the place of work so that an employee is available for emergencies during his or her lunch period are generally considered to be for your convenience.

However, whether meals or lodging are provided for the convenience of the employer depends on all of the facts and circumstances. A written statement that the meals or lodging are for your convenience isn't sufficient.

50% test. If over 50% of the employees who are provided meals on an employer's business premises receive these meals for the convenience of the employer, all meals provided on the premises are treated as furnished for the convenience of the employer. If this 50% test is met, the value of the meals is excludable from income for all employees and isn't subject to federal income tax withholding or employment taxes. For more information, see Pub. 15-B.

Health insurance plans. If you pay the cost of an accident or health insurance plan for your employees, including an employee's spouse and dependents, your payments aren't wages and aren't subject to social security, Medicare, and FUTA taxes, or federal income tax withholding. Generally, this exclusion also applies to qualified long-term care insurance contracts. However, for income tax withholding, the value of health insurance benefits must be included in the wages of S corporation employees who own more than 2% of the S corporation (2% shareholders). For social security, Medicare, and FUTA taxes, the health insurance benefits are excluded from the wages only for employees and their dependents or for a class or classes of employees and their dependents. See Announcement 92-16 for more information. You can find

Announcement 92-16 on page 53 of Internal Revenue Bulletin 1992-5.

Health Savings Accounts and medical savings accounts. Your contributions to an employee's Health Savings Account (HSA) or Archer medical savings account (MSA) aren't subject to social security, Medicare, or FUTA taxes, or federal income tax withholding if it is reasonable to believe at the time of payment of the contributions they will be excludable from the income of the employee. To the extent it isn't reasonable to believe they will be excludable, your contributions are subject to these taxes. Employee contributions to their HSAs or MSAs through a payroll deduction plan must be included in wages and are subject to social security, Medicare, and FUTA taxes and income tax withholding. However, HSA contributions made under a salary reduction arrangement in a section 125 cafeteria plan aren't wages and aren't subject to employment taxes or withholding. For more information, see the Instructions for Form 8889.

Medical care reimbursements. Generally, medical care reimbursements paid for an employee under an employer's self-insured medical reimbursement plan aren't wages and aren't subject to social security, Medicare, and FUTA taxes, or income tax withholding. See Pub. 15-B for an exception for highly compensated employees.

Differential wage payments. Differential wage payments are any payments made by an employer to an individual for a period during which the individual is performing service in the uniformed services while on active duty for a period of more than 30 days and represent all or a portion of the wages the individual would have received from the employer if the individual were performing services for the employer.

Differential wage payments are wages for income tax withholding, but aren't subject to social security, Medicare, or FUTA taxes. Employers should report differential wage payments in box 1 of Form W-2. For more information about the tax treatment of differential wage payments, visit IRS.gov and enter "employees in a combat zone" in the search box.

Fringe benefits. You generally must include fringe benefits in an employee's gross income (but see *Nontaxable fringe benefits* next). The benefits are subject to income tax withholding and employment taxes. Fringe benefits include cars you provide, flights on aircraft you provide, free or discounted commercial flights, vacations, discounts on property or services, memberships in country clubs or other social clubs, and tickets to entertainment or sporting events. In general, the amount you must include is the amount by which the fair market value of the benefits is more than the sum of what the employee paid for it plus any amount the law excludes. There are other special rules you and your employees may use to value certain fringe benefits. See Pub. 15-B for more information.

Nontaxable fringe benefits. Some fringe benefits aren't taxable (or are minimally taxable) if certain conditions are met. See Pub. 15-B for details. The following are some examples of nontaxable fringe benefits.

1. Services provided to your employees at no additional cost to you.

2. Qualified employee discounts.

3. Working condition fringes that are property or services the employee could deduct as a business expense if he or she had paid for it. Examples include a company car for business use and subscriptions to business magazines.

4. Certain minimal value fringes (including an occasional cab ride when an employee must work overtime and meals you provide at eating places you run for your employees if the meals aren't furnished at below cost).

5. Qualified transportation fringes subject to specified conditions and dollar limitations (including transportation in a commuter highway vehicle, any transit pass, and qualified parking).

6. Qualified moving expense reimbursement. See *Moving expenses*, earlier in this section, for details.

7. The use of on-premises athletic facilities, if substantially all of the use is by employees, their spouses, and their dependent children.

8. Qualified tuition reduction an educational organization provides to its employees for education. For more information, see Pub. 970.

9. Employer-provided cell phones provided primarily for a noncompensatory business reason.

However, don't exclude the following fringe benefits from the income of highly compensated employees unless the benefit is available to other employees on a nondiscriminatory basis.

- No-additional-cost services.

- Qualified employee discounts.

- Meals provided at an employer operated eating facility.

- Reduced tuition for education.

For more information, including the definition of a highly compensated employee, see Pub. 15-B.

When fringe benefits are treated as paid. You may choose to treat certain noncash fringe benefits as paid by the pay period, by the quarter, or on any other basis you choose as long as you treat the benefits as paid at least once a year. You don't have to make a formal choice of payment dates or notify the IRS of the dates you choose. You don't have to make this choice for all employees. You may change methods as often as you like, as long as you treat all benefits provided in a calendar year as paid by December 31 of the calendar year. See Pub. 15-B for more information, including a discussion of the special accounting rule for fringe benefits provided during November and December.

Valuation of fringe benefits. Generally, you must determine the value of fringe benefits no later than January

A-155

31 of the next year. Before January 31, you may reasonably estimate the value of the fringe benefits for purposes of withholding and depositing on time.

Withholding on fringe benefits. You may add the value of fringe benefits to regular wages for a payroll period and figure withholding taxes on the total, or you may withhold federal income tax on the value of the fringe benefits at the optional flat 25% supplemental wage rate. However, see *Withholding on supplemental wages when an employee receives more than $1 million of supplemental wages during the calendar year* in section 7.

You may choose not to withhold income tax on the value of an employee's personal use of a vehicle you provide. You must, however, withhold social security and Medicare taxes on the use of the vehicle. See Pub. 15-B for more information on this election.

Depositing taxes on fringe benefits. Once you choose when fringe benefits are paid, you must deposit taxes in the same deposit period you treat the fringe benefits as paid. To avoid a penalty, deposit the taxes following the general deposit rules for that deposit period.

If you determine by January 31 you overestimated the value of a fringe benefit at the time you withheld and deposited for it, you may claim a refund for the overpayment or have it applied to your next employment tax return. See *Valuation of fringe benefits*, earlier. If you underestimated the value and deposited too little, you may be subject to a failure-to-deposit (FTD) penalty. See section 11 for information on deposit penalties.

If you deposited the required amount of taxes but withheld a lesser amount from the employee, you can recover from the employee the social security, Medicare, or income taxes you deposited on his or her behalf, and included in the employee's Form W-2. However, you must recover the income taxes before April 1 of the following year.

Sick pay. In general, sick pay is any amount you pay under a plan to an employee who is unable to work because of sickness or injury. These amounts are sometimes paid by a third party, such as an insurance company or an employees' trust. In either case, these payments are subject to social security, Medicare, and FUTA taxes. These taxes don't apply to sick pay paid more than 6 calendar months after the last calendar month in which the employee worked for the employer. The payments are always subject to federal income tax. See Pub. 15-A for more information.

6. Tips

Tips your employee receives from customers are generally subject to withholding. Your employee must report cash tips to you by the 10th of the month after the month the tips are received. The report should include tips you paid over to the employee for charge customers, tips the employee received directly from customers, and tips received from other employees under any tip-sharing arrangement. Both directly and indirectly tipped employees

must report tips to you. No report is required for months when tips are less than $20. Your employee reports the tips on Form 4070 or on a similar statement. The statement must be signed by the employee and must include:

- The employee's name, address, and SSN,

- Your name and address,

- The month and year (or the beginning and ending dates, if the statement is for a period of less than 1 calendar month) the report covers, and

- The total of tips received during the month or period.

Both Forms 4070 and 4070-A, Employee's Daily Record of Tips, are included in Pub. 1244, Employee's Daily Record of Tips and Report to Employer.

 You are permitted to establish a system for electronic tip reporting by employees. See Regulations section 31.6053-1(d).

Collecting taxes on tips. You must collect income tax, employee social security tax, and employee Medicare tax on the employee's tips. The withholding rules for withholding an employee's share of Medicare tax on tips also apply to withholding the Additional Medicare Tax once wages and tips exceed $200,000 in the calendar year.

You can collect these taxes from the employee's wages or from other funds he or she makes available. See *Tips treated as supplemental wages* in section 7 for more information. Stop collecting the employee social security tax when his or her wages and tips for tax year 2016 reach $118,500; collect the income and employee Medicare taxes for the whole year on all wages and tips. You are responsible for the employer social security tax on wages and tips until the wages (including tips) reach the limit. You are responsible for the employer Medicare tax for the whole year on all wages and tips. File Form 941 or Form 944 to report withholding and employment taxes on tips.

Ordering rule. If, by the 10th of the month after the month for which you received an employee's report on tips, you don't have enough employee funds available to deduct the employee tax, you no longer have to collect it. If there aren't enough funds available, withhold taxes in the following order.

1. Withhold on regular wages and other compensation.

2. Withhold social security and Medicare taxes on tips.

3. Withhold income tax on tips.

Reporting tips. Report tips and any collected and uncollected social security and Medicare taxes on Form W-2 and on Form 941, lines 5b, 5c, and 5d (Form 944, lines 4b, 4c, and 4d). Report an adjustment on Form 941, line 9 (Form 944, line 6), for the uncollected social security and Medicare taxes. Enter the amount of uncollected social security tax and Medicare tax on Form W-2, box 12, with codes "A" and "B." Don't include any uncollected Additional Medicare Tax in box 12 of Form W-2. For additional information on reporting tips, see section 13 and the General Instructions for Forms W-2 and W-3.

Revenue Ruling 2012-18 provides guidance for employers regarding social security and Medicare taxes imposed on tips, including information on the reporting of the employer share of social security and Medicare taxes under section 3121(q), the difference between tips and service charges, and the section 45B credit. See Revenue Ruling 2012-18, 2012-26 I.R.B. 1032, available at *www.irs.gov/irb/2012-26_IRB/ar07.html*.

FUTA tax on tips. If an employee reports to you in writing $20 or more of tips in a month, the tips are also subject to FUTA tax.

Allocated tips. If you operate a large food or beverage establishment, you must report allocated tips under certain circumstances. However, don't withhold income, social security, or Medicare taxes on allocated tips.

A large food or beverage establishment is one that provides food or beverages for consumption on the premises, where tipping is customary, and where there were normally more than 10 employees on a typical business day during the preceding year.

The tips may be allocated by one of three methods—hours worked, gross receipts, or good faith agreement. For information about these allocation methods, including the requirement to file Forms 8027 electronically if 250 or more forms are filed, see the Instructions for Form 8027. For information on filing Form 8027 electronically with the IRS, see Pub. 1239.

Tip Rate Determination and Education Program. Employers may participate in the Tip Rate Determination and Education Program. The program primarily consists of two voluntary agreements developed to improve tip income reporting by helping taxpayers to understand and meet their tip reporting responsibilities. The two agreements are the Tip Rate Determination Agreement (TRDA) and the Tip Reporting Alternative Commitment (TRAC). A tip agreement, the Gaming Industry Tip Compliance Agreement (GITCA), is available for the gaming (casino) industry. To get more information about TRDA and TRAC agreements, see Pub. 3144. Additionally, visit IRS.gov and enter "MSU tips" in the search box to get more information about GITCA, TRDA, or TRAC agreements.

7. Supplemental Wages

Supplemental wages are wage payments to an employee that aren't regular wages. They include, but aren't limited to, bonuses, commissions, overtime pay, payments for accumulated sick leave, severance pay, awards, prizes, back pay, retroactive pay increases, and payments for nondeductible moving expenses. Other payments subject to the supplemental wage rules include taxable fringe benefits and expense allowances paid under a nonaccountable plan. How you withhold on supplemental wages depends on whether the supplemental payment is identified as a separate payment from regular wages. See Regulations section 31.3402(g)-1 for additional guidance for wages paid after January 1, 2007. Also see Revenue

Ruling 2008-29, 2008-24 I.R.B. 1149, available at *www.irs.gov/irb/2008-24_IRB/ar08.html*.

Withholding on supplemental wages when an employee receives more than $1 million of supplemental wages from you during the calendar year. Special rules apply to the extent supplemental wages paid to any one employee during the calendar year exceed $1 million. If a supplemental wage payment, together with other supplemental wage payments made to the employee during the calendar year, exceeds $1 million, the excess is subject to withholding at 39.6% (or the highest rate of income tax for the year). Withhold using the 39.6% rate without regard to the employee's Form W-4. In determining supplemental wages paid to the employee during the year, include payments from all businesses under common control. For more information, see Treasury Decision 9276, 2006-37 I.R.B. 423, available at *www.irs.gov/irb/2006-37_IRB/ar09.html*.

Withholding on supplemental wage payments to an employee who doesn't receive $1 million of supplemental wages during the calendar year. If the supplemental wages paid to the employee during the calendar year are less than or equal to $1 million, the following rules apply in determining the amount of income tax to be withheld.

Supplemental wages combined with regular wages. If you pay supplemental wages with regular wages but don't specify the amount of each, withhold federal income tax as if the total were a single payment for a regular payroll period.

Supplemental wages identified separately from regular wages. If you pay supplemental wages separately (or combine them in a single payment and specify the amount of each), the federal income tax withholding method depends partly on whether you withhold income tax from your employee's regular wages.

1. If you withheld income tax from an employee's regular wages in the current or immediately preceding calendar year, you can use one of the following methods for the supplemental wages.

   a. Withhold a flat 25% (no other percentage allowed).

   b. If the supplemental wages are paid concurrently with regular wages, add the supplemental wages to the concurrently paid regular wages. If there are no concurrently paid regular wages, add the supplemental wages to alternatively, either the regular wages paid or to be paid for the current payroll period or the regular wages paid for the preceding payroll period. Figure the income tax withholding as if the total of the regular wages and supplemental wages is a single payment. Subtract the tax withheld from the regular wages. Withhold the remaining tax from the supplemental wages. If there were other payments of supplemental wages paid during the payroll period made before the current payment of supplemental wages, aggregate all the payments of supplemental wages paid during the payroll period with the regular wages paid during the payroll period, calculate the tax on the total, subtract the tax already withheld from the regular wages and the previous supplemental wage payments, and withhold the remaining tax.

2. If you didn't withhold income tax from the employee's regular wages in the current or immediately preceding calendar year, use method 1-b. This would occur, for example, when the value of the employee's withholding allowances claimed on Form W-4 is more than the wages.

Regardless of the method you use to withhold income tax on supplemental wages, they are subject to social security, Medicare, and FUTA taxes.

Example 1. You pay John Peters a base salary on the 1st of each month. He is single and claims one withholding allowance. In January he is paid $1,000. Using the wage bracket tables, you withhold $50 from this amount. In February, he receives salary of $1,000 plus a commission of $2,000, which you combine with regular wages and don't separately identify. You figure the withholding based on the total of $3,000. The correct withholding from the tables is $336.

Example 2. You pay Sharon Warren a base salary on the 1st of each month. She is single and claims one allowance. Her May 1 pay is $2,000. Using the wage bracket tables, you withhold $186. On May 14 she receives a bonus of $1,000. Electing to use supplemental wage withholding method 1-b, you:

1. Add the bonus amount to the amount of wages from the most recent base salary pay date (May 1) ($2,000 + $1,000 = $3,000).

2. Determine the amount of withholding on the combined $3,000 amount to be $336 using the wage bracket tables.

3. Subtract the amount withheld from wages on the most recent base salary pay date (May 1) from the combined withholding amount ($336 − $186 = $150).

4. Withhold $150 from the bonus payment.

Example 3. The facts are the same as in Example 2, except you elect to use the flat rate method of withholding on the bonus. You withhold 25% of $1,000, or $250, from Sharon's bonus payment.

Example 4. The facts are the same as in Example 2, except you elect to pay Sharon a second bonus of $2,000 on May 28. Using supplemental wage withholding method 1-b, you:

1. Add the first and second bonus amounts to the amount of wages from the most recent base salary pay date (May 1) ($2,000 + $1,000 + $2,000 = $5,000).

2. Determine the amount of withholding on the combined $5,000 amount to be $771 using the wage bracket tables.

3. Subtract the amounts withheld from wages on the most recent base salary pay date (May 1) and the amounts withheld from the first bonus payment from the combined withholding amount ($771 − $186 − $150 = $435).

4. Withhold $435 from the second bonus payment.

Tips treated as supplemental wages. Withhold income tax on tips from wages earned by the employee or from other funds the employee makes available. If an employee receives regular wages and reports tips, figure income tax withholding as if the tips were supplemental wages. If you haven't withheld income tax from the regular wages, add the tips to the regular wages. Then withhold income tax on the total. If you withheld income tax from the regular wages, you can withhold on the tips by method 1-a or 1-b discussed earlier in this section under *Supplemental wages identified separately from regular wages*.

Vacation pay. Vacation pay is subject to withholding as if it were a regular wage payment. When vacation pay is in addition to regular wages for the vacation period, treat it as a supplemental wage payment. If the vacation pay is for a time longer than your usual payroll period, spread it over the pay periods for which you pay it.

---

8. Payroll Period

Your payroll period is a period of service for which you usually pay wages. When you have a regular payroll period, withhold income tax for that time period even if your employee doesn't work the full period.

No regular payroll period. When you don't have a regular payroll period, withhold the tax as if you paid wages for a daily or miscellaneous payroll period. Figure the number of days (including Sundays and holidays) in the period covered by the wage payment. If the wages are unrelated to a specific length of time (for example, commissions paid on completion of a sale), count back the number of days from the payment period to the latest of:

• The last wage payment made during the same calendar year,

• The date employment began, if during the same calendar year, or

• January 1 of the same year.

Employee paid for period less than 1 week. When you pay an employee for a period of less than one week, and the employee signs a statement under penalties of perjury indicating he or she isn't working for any other employer during the same week for wages subject to withholding, figure withholding based on a weekly payroll period. If the employee later begins to work for another employer for wages subject to withholding, the employee must notify you within 10 days. You then figure withholding based on the daily or miscellaneous period.

9. Withholding From Employees' Wages

Income Tax Withholding

Using Form W-4 to figure withholding. To know how much federal income tax to withhold from employees' wages, you should have a Form W-4 on file for each employee. Encourage your employees to file an updated Form W-4 for 2016, especially if they owed taxes or received a large refund when filing their 2015 tax return. Advise your employees to use the IRS Withholding Calculator on the IRS website at _www.irs.gov/individuals_ for help in determining how many withholding allowances to claim on their Forms W-4.

Ask all new employees to give you a signed Form W-4 when they start work. Make the form effective with the first wage payment. If a new employee doesn't give you a completed Form W-4, withhold income tax as if he or she is single, with no withholding allowances.

**Form in Spanish.** You can provide Formulario W-4(SP) in place of Form W-4, to your Spanish-speaking employees. For more information, see Pub. 17(SP). The rules discussed in this section that apply to Form W-4 also apply to Formulario W-4(SP).

**Electronic system to receive Form W-4.** You may establish a system to electronically receive Forms W-4 from your employees. See Regulations section 31.3402(f) (5)-1(c) for more information.

**Effective date of Form W-4.** A Form W-4 remains in effect until the employee gives you a new one. When you receive a new Form W-4 from an employee, don't adjust withholding for pay periods before the effective date of the new form. If an employee gives you a Form W-4 that replaces an existing Form W-4, begin withholding no later than the start of the first payroll period ending on or after the 30th day from the date when you received the replacement Form W-4. For exceptions, see _Exemption from federal income tax withholding_, _IRS review of requested Forms W-4_, and _Invalid Forms W-4_, later in this section.

 A Form W-4 that makes a change for the next calendar year won't take effect in the current calendar year.

**Successor employer.** If you are a successor employer (see _Successor employer_, later in this section), secure new Forms W-4 from the transferred employees unless the "Alternative Procedure" in section 5 of Revenue Procedure 2004-53 applies. See Revenue Procedure 2004-53, 2004-34 I.R.B. 320, available at _www.irs.gov/irb/2004-34_IRB/ar13.html_.

**Completing Form W-4.** The amount of any federal income tax withholding must be based on marital status and withholding allowances. Your employees may not base their withholding amounts on a fixed dollar amount or percentage. However, an employee may specify a dollar amount to be withheld in addition to the amount of withholding based on filing status and withholding allowances claimed on Form W-4.

Employees may claim fewer withholding allowances than they are entitled to claim. They may wish to claim fewer allowances to ensure they have enough withholding or to offset the tax on other sources of taxable income not subject to withholding.

See Pub. 505 for more information about completing Form W-4. Along with Form W-4, you may wish to order Pub. 505 for use by your employees.

Don't accept any withholding or estimated tax payments from your employees in addition to withholding based on their Form W-4. If they require additional withholding, they should submit a new Form W-4 and, if necessary, pay estimated tax by filing Form 1040-ES or by using EFTPS to make estimated tax payments.

Exemption from federal income tax withholding. Generally, an employee may claim exemption from federal income tax withholding because he or she had no income tax liability last year and expects none this year. See the Form W-4 instructions for more information. However, the wages are still subject to social security and Medicare taxes. See also _Invalid Forms W-4_, later in this section.

A Form W-4 claiming exemption from withholding is effective when it is filed with the employer and only for that calendar year. To continue to be exempt from withholding in the next calendar year, an employee must give you a new Form W-4 by February 15. If the employee doesn't give you a new Form W-4 by February 15, begin withholding based on the last Form W-4 for the employee that didn't claim an exemption from withholding or, if one wasn't furnished, then withhold tax as if he or she is single with zero withholding allowances. If the employee provides a new Form W-4 claiming exemption from withholding on February 16 or later, you may apply it to future wages but don't refund any taxes already withheld.

Withholding income taxes on the wages of nonresident alien employees. In general, you must withhold federal income taxes on the wages of nonresident alien employees. However, see Pub. 515 for exceptions to this general rule. Also see section 3 of Pub. 51 for guidance on H-2A visa workers.

Withholding adjustment for nonresident alien employees. Apply the procedure discussed next to figure the amount of income tax to withhold from the wages of nonresident alien employees performing services within the United States.

 Nonresident alien students from India and business apprentices from India aren't subject to this procedure.

Instructions. To figure how much income tax to withhold from the wages paid to a nonresident alien employee performing services in the United States, use the following steps.

Step 1. Add to the wages paid to the nonresident alien employee for the payroll period the amount shown in the chart next for the applicable payroll period.

Amount to Add to Nonresident Alien Employee's Wages for Calculating Income Tax Withholding Only

Payroll Period	Add Additional
Weekly	$ 43.30
Biweekly	86.50
Semimonthly	93.80
Monthly	187.50
Quarterly	562.50
Semiannually	1,125.00
Annually	2,250.00
Daily or Miscellaneous (each day of the payroll period)	8.70

Step 2. Use the amount figured in *Step 1* and the number of withholding allowances claimed (generally limited to one allowance) to figure income tax withholding. Determine the value of withholding allowances by multiplying the number of withholding allowances claimed by the appropriate amount from *Table 5* shown on page 45. If you are using the Percentage Method Tables for Income Tax Withholding, provided on pages 44–45, reduce the amount figured in *Step 1* by the value of withholding allowances and use that reduced amount to figure the income tax withholding. If you are using the Wage Bracket Method Tables for Income Tax Withholding, provided on pages 46–65, use the amount figured in *Step 1* and the number of withholding allowances to figure income tax withholding.

The amounts from the chart, earlier, are added to wages solely for calculating income tax withholding on the wages of the nonresident alien employee. The amounts from the chart shouldn't be included in any box on the employee's Form W-2 and don't increase the income tax liability of the employee. Also, the amounts from the chart don't increase the social security tax or Medicare tax liability of the employer or the employee, or the FUTA tax liability of the employer.

This procedure only applies to nonresident alien employees who have wages subject to income tax withholding.

Example. An employer using the percentage method of withholding pays wages of $500 for a biweekly payroll period to a married nonresident alien employee. The nonresident alien has properly completed Form W-4, entering marital status as "single" with one withholding allowance and indicating status as a nonresident alien on Form W-4, line 6 (see *Nonresident alien employee's Form W-4* below in this section). The employer determines the wages to be used in the withholding tables by adding to the $500

amount of wages paid the amount of $86.50 from the chart under *Step 1* ($586.50 total). The employer then applies the applicable tables to determine the income tax withholding for nonresident aliens (see *Step 2*). **Reminder:** If you use the Percentage Method Tables for Income Tax Withholding, reduce the amount figured in Step 1 by the value of withholding allowances and use that reduced amount to figure income tax withholding.

The $86.50 added to wages for calculating income tax withholding isn't reported on Form W-2, and doesn't increase the income tax liability of the employee. Also, the $86.50 added to wages doesn't affect the social security tax or Medicare tax liability of the employer or the employee, or the FUTA tax liability of the employer.

Supplemental wage payment. This procedure for determining the amount of income tax withholding doesn't apply to a supplemental wage payment (see section 7) if the 39.6% mandatory flat rate withholding applies or if the 25% optional flat rate withholding is being used to calculate income tax withholding on the supplemental wage payment.

Nonresident alien employee's Form W-4. When completing Forms W-4, nonresident aliens are required to:

- Not claim exemption from income tax withholding,

- Request withholding as if they are single, regardless of their actual marital status,

- Claim only one allowance (if the nonresident alien is a resident of Canada, Mexico, or South Korea, or a student or business apprentice from India, he or she may claim more than one allowance), and

- Write "Nonresident Alien" or "NRA" above the dotted line on line 6 of Form W-4.

If you maintain an electronic Form W-4 system, you should provide a field for nonresident aliens to enter nonresident alien status instead of writing "Nonresident Alien" or "NRA" above the dotted line on line 6.

 A nonresident alien employee may request additional withholding at his or her option for other purposes, although such additions shouldn't be necessary for withholding to cover federal income tax liability related to employment.

Form 8233. If a nonresident alien employee claims a tax treaty exemption from withholding, the employee must submit Form 8233 with respect to the income exempt under the treaty, instead of Form W-4. See Pub. 515 for details.

IRS review of requested Forms W-4. When requested by the IRS, you must make original Forms W-4 available for inspection by an IRS employee. You may also be directed to send certain Forms W-4 to the IRS. You may receive a notice from the IRS requiring you to submit a copy of Form W-4 for one or more of your named employees. Send the requested copy or copies of Form W-4 to the IRS at the address provided and in the manner directed by the notice. The IRS may also require you to submit copies of Form W-4 to the IRS as directed by Treasury Decision 9337, 2007-35 I.R.B. 455, which is available at _www.irs.gov/irb/2007-35_IRB/ar10.html_. When we refer to Form W-4, the same rules apply to Formulario W-4(SP), its Spanish translation.

After submitting a copy of a requested Form W-4 to the IRS, continue to withhold federal income tax based on that Form W-4 if it is valid (see _Invalid Forms W-4_ below in this section). However, if the IRS later notifies you in writing the employee isn't entitled to claim exemption from withholding or a claimed number of withholding allowances, withhold federal income tax based on the effective date, marital status, and maximum number of withholding allowances specified in the IRS notice (commonly referred to as a "lock-in letter").

Initial lock-in letter. The IRS also uses information reported on Form W-2 to identify employees with withholding compliance problems. In some cases, if a serious under-withholding problem is found to exist for a particular employee, the IRS may issue a lock-in letter to the employer specifying the maximum number of withholding allowances and marital status permitted for a specific employee. You will also receive a copy for the employee that identifies the maximum number of withholding allowances permitted and the process by which the employee can provide additional information to the IRS for purposes of determining the appropriate number of withholding allowances. You must furnish the employee copy to the employee within 10 business days of receipt if the employee is employed by you as of the date of the notice. Begin withholding based on the notice on the date specified in the notice.

Employee not performing services. If you receive a notice for an employee who isn't performing services for you, you must still furnish the employee copy to the employee and withhold based on the notice if any of the following apply.

- You are paying wages for the employee's prior services and the wages are subject to income tax withholding on or after the date specified in the notice.

- You reasonably expect the employee to resume services within 12 months of the date of the notice.

- The employee is on a leave of absence that doesn't exceed 12 months or the employee has a right to re-employment after the leave of absence.

Termination and re-hire of employees. If you must furnish and withhold based on the notice and the employment relationship is terminated after the date of the notice, you must continue to withhold based on the notice if you continue to pay any wages subject to income tax withholding. You must also withhold based on the notice or modification notice (explained next) if the employee resumes the employment relationship with you within 12 months after the termination of the employment relationship.

Modification notice. After issuing the notice specifying the maximum number of withholding allowances and marital status permitted, the IRS may issue a subsequent notice (modification notice) that modifies the original notice. The modification notice may change the marital status and/or the number of withholding allowances permitted. You must withhold federal income tax based on the effective date specified in the modification notice.

New Form W-4 after notice. After the IRS issues a notice or modification notice, if the employee provides you with a new Form W-4 claiming complete exemption from withholding or claims a marital status, a number of withholding allowances, and any additional withholding that results in less withholding than would result under the IRS notice or modification notice, disregard the new Form W-4. You must withhold based on the notice or modification notice unless the IRS notifies you to withhold based on the new Form W-4. If the employee wants to put a new Form W-4 into effect that results in less withholding than required, the employee must contact the IRS.

If, after you receive an IRS notice or modification notice, your employee gives you a new Form W-4 that doesn't claim exemption from federal income tax withholding and claims a marital status, a number of withholding allowances, and any additional withholding that results in more withholding than would result under the notice or modification notice, you must withhold tax based on the new Form W-4. Otherwise, disregard any subsequent Forms W-4 provided by the employee and withhold based on the IRS notice or modification notice.

For additional information about these rules, see Treasury Decision 9337, 2007-35 I.R.B. 455, available at _www.irs.gov/irb/2007-35_IRB/ar10.html_.

Substitute Forms W-4. You are encouraged to have your employees use the official version of Form W-4 to claim withholding allowances or exemption from withholding.

You may use a substitute version of Form W-4 to meet your business needs. However, your substitute Form W-4 must contain language that is identical to the official Form W-4 and your form must meet all current IRS rules for substitute forms. At the time you provide your substitute form to the employee, you must provide him or her with all tables, instructions, and worksheets from the current Form W-4.

You can't accept substitute Forms W-4 developed by employees. An employee who submits an employee-developed substitute Form W-4 after October 10, 2007, will be treated as failing to furnish a Form W-4. However, continue to honor any valid employee-developed Forms W-4 you accepted before October 11, 2007.

Invalid Forms W-4. Any unauthorized change or addition to Form W-4 makes it invalid. This includes taking out any language by which the employee certifies the form is correct. A Form W-4 is also invalid if, by the date an employee gives it to you, he or she indicates in any way it is false. An employee who submits a false Form W-4 may be subject to a $500 penalty. You may treat a Form W-4 as invalid if the employee wrote "exempt" on line 7 and also entered a number on line 5 or an amount on line 6.

A-161

When you get an invalid Form W-4, don't use it to figure federal income tax withholding. Tell the employee it is invalid and ask for another one. If the employee doesn't give you a valid one, withhold tax as if the employee is single with zero withholding allowances. However, if you have an earlier Form W-4 for this worker that is valid, withhold as you did before.

Amounts exempt from levy on wages, salary, and other income. If you receive a Notice of Levy on Wages, Salary, and Other Income (Forms 668-W(ACS), 668-W(c) (DO), or 668-W(ICS)), you must withhold amounts as described in the instructions for these forms. Pub. 1494 has tables to figure the amount exempt from levy. If a levy issued in a prior year is still in effect and the taxpayer submits a new Statement of Exemptions and Filing Status, use the current year Pub. 1494 to compute the exempt amount.

Social Security and Medicare Taxes

The Federal Insurance Contributions Act (FICA) provides for a federal system of old-age, survivors, disability, and hospital insurance. The old-age, survivors, and disability insurance part is financed by the social security tax. The hospital insurance part is financed by the Medicare tax. Each of these taxes is reported separately.

Generally, you are required to withhold social security and Medicare taxes from your employees' wages and pay the employer's share of these taxes. Certain types of wages and compensation aren't subject to social security and Medicare taxes. See section 5 and section 15 for details. Generally, employee wages are subject to social security and Medicare taxes regardless of the employee's age or whether he or she is receiving social security benefits. If the employee reported tips, see section 6.

Tax rates and the social security wage base limit. Social security and Medicare taxes have different rates and only the social security tax has a wage base limit. The wage base limit is the maximum wage subject to the tax for the year. Determine the amount of withholding for social security and Medicare taxes by multiplying each payment by the employee tax rate. There are no withholding allowances for social security and Medicare taxes.

For 2016, the social security tax rate is 6.2% (amount withheld) each for the employer and employee (12.4% total). The social security wage base limit is $118,500. The tax rate for Medicare is 1.45% (amount withheld) each for the employee and employer (2.9% total). There is no wage base limit for Medicare tax; all covered wages are subject to Medicare tax.

Additional Medicare Tax withholding. In addition to withholding Medicare tax at 1.45%, you must withhold a 0.9% Additional Medicare Tax from wages you pay to an employee in excess of $200,000 in a calendar year. You are required to begin withholding Additional Medicare Tax in the pay period in which you pay wages in excess of $200,000 to an employee and continue to withhold it each pay period until the end of the calendar year. Additional Medicare Tax is only imposed on the employee. There is no employer share of Additional Medicare Tax. All wages that are subject to Medicare tax are subject to Additional Medicare Tax withholding if paid in excess of the $200,000 withholding threshold.

For more information on what wages are subject to Medicare tax, see the chart, *Special Rules for Various Types of Services and Payments*, in section 15. For more information on Additional Medicare Tax, visit IRS.gov and enter "Additional Medicare Tax" in the search box.

Successor employer. When corporate acquisitions meet certain requirements, wages paid by the predecessor are treated as if paid by the successor for purposes of applying the social security wage base and for applying the Additional Medicare Tax withholding threshold (that is, $200,000 in a calendar year). You should determine whether or not you should file Schedule D (Form 941), Report of Discrepancies Caused by Acquisitions, Statutory Mergers, or Consolidations, by reviewing the Instructions for Schedule D (Form 941). See Regulations section 31.3121(a)(1)-1(b) for more information. Also see Revenue Procedure 2004-53, 2004-34 I.R.B. 320, available at *www.irs.gov/irb/2004-34_IRB/ar13.html*.

Example. Early in 2016, you bought all of the assets of a plumbing business from Mr. Martin. Mr. Brown, who had been employed by Mr. Martin and received $2,000 in wages before the date of purchase, continued to work for you. The wages you paid to Mr. Brown are subject to social security taxes on the first $116,500 ($118,500 minus $2,000). Medicare tax is due on all of the wages you pay him during the calendar year. You should include the $2,000 Mr. Brown received while employed by Mr. Martin in determining whether Mr. Brown's wages exceed the $200,000 for Additional Medicare Tax withholding threshold.

Withholding of social security and Medicare taxes on nonresident aliens. In general, if you pay wages to nonresident alien employees, you must withhold federal social security and Medicare taxes as you would for a U.S. citizen. However, see Pub. 515 for exceptions to this general rule.

International social security agreements. The United States has social security agreements, also known as totalization agreements, with many countries that eliminate dual taxation and dual coverage. Compensation subject to social security and Medicare taxes may be exempt under one of these agreements. You can get more information and a list of agreement countries from the SSA at *www.socialsecurity.gov/international* or see section 7 of Pub. 15-A.

Religious exemption. An exemption from social security and Medicare taxes is available to members of a recognized religious sect opposed to insurance. This exemption is available only if both the employee and the employer are members of the sect. For more information, see Pub. 517.

Foreign persons treated as American employers. Under IRC section 3121(z), for services performed after July 31, 2008, a foreign person who meets both of the following conditions is generally treated as an American employer for purposes of paying FICA taxes on wages paid to an employee who is a United States citizen or resident.

1. The foreign person is a member of a domestically controlled group of entities.

2. The employee of the foreign person performs services in connection with a contract between the U.S. Government (or an instrumentality of the U.S. Government) and any member of the domestically controlled group of entities. Ownership of more than 50% constitutes control.

Part-Time Workers

Part-time workers and workers hired for short periods of time are treated the same as full-time employees, for federal income tax withholding and social security, Medicare, and FUTA tax purposes.

Generally, it doesn't matter whether the part-time worker or worker hired for a short period of time has another job or has the maximum amount of social security tax withheld by another employer. See *Successor employer*, earlier, for an exception to this rule.

Income tax withholding may be figured the same way as for full-time workers or it may be figured by the part-year employment method explained in section 9 of Pub. 15-A.

10. Required Notice to Employees About the Earned Income Credit (EIC)

You must notify employees who have no federal income tax withheld that they may be able to claim a tax refund because of the EIC. Although you don't have to notify employees who claim exemption from withholding on Form W-4 about the EIC, you are encouraged to notify any employees whose wages for 2015 were less than $47,747 ($53,267 if married filing jointly) that they may be eligible to claim the credit for 2015. This is because eligible employees may get a refund of the amount of EIC that is more than the tax they owe.

You will meet this notification requirement if you issue the employee Form W-2 with the EIC notice on the back of Copy B, or a substitute Form W-2 with the same statement. You will also meet the requirement by providing Notice 797, Possible Federal Tax Refund Due to the Earned Income Credit (EIC), or your own statement that contains the same wording.

If a substitute for Form W-2 is given to the employee on time but doesn't have the required statement, you must notify the employee within 1 week of the date the

substitute for Form W-2 is given. If Form W-2 is required but isn't given on time, you must give the employee Notice 797 or your written statement by the date Form W-2 is required to be given. If Form W-2 isn't required, you must notify the employee by February 8, 2016.

11. Depositing Taxes

In general, you must deposit federal income tax withheld and both the employer and employee social security and Medicare taxes. You must use EFT to make all federal tax deposits. See *How To Deposit*, later in this section, for information on electronic deposit requirements.

 The credit against employment taxes for COBRA assistance payments is treated as a deposit of taxes on the first day of your return period. See COBRA premium assistance credit *under* Introduction *for more information.*

Payment with return. You may make a payment with Form 941 or Form 944 instead of depositing, without incurring a penalty, if one of the following applies.

- Your Form 941 total tax liability for either the current quarter or the preceding quarter is less than $2,500, and you didn't incur a $100,000 next-day deposit obligation during the current quarter. If you aren't sure your total tax liability for the current quarter will be less than $2,500, (and your liability for the preceding quarter wasn't less than $2,500), make deposits using the semi-weekly or monthly rules so you won't be subject to an FTD penalty.

- You are a monthly schedule depositor (defined later) and make a payment in accordance with the *Accuracy of Deposits Rule*, discussed later in this section. This payment may be $2,500 or more.

Employers who have been notified to file Form 944 can pay their fourth quarter tax liability with Form 944 if the fourth quarter tax liability is less than $2,500. Employers must have deposited any tax liability due for the first, second, and third quarters according to the deposit rules to avoid an FTD penalty for deposits during those quarters.

Separate deposit requirements for nonpayroll (Form 945) tax liabilities. Separate deposits are required for nonpayroll and payroll income tax withholding. Don't combine deposits for Forms 941 (or Form 944) and Form 945 tax liabilities. Generally, the deposit rules for nonpayroll liabilities are the same as discussed next, except the rules apply on an annual rather than a quarterly return period. Thus, the $2,500 threshold for the deposit requirement discussed above applies to Form 945 on an annual basis. See the separate Instructions for Form 945 for more information.

When To Deposit

There are two deposit schedules—monthly and semi-weekly—for determining when you deposit social security,

Medicare, and withheld income taxes. These schedules tell you when a deposit is due after a tax liability arises (for example, when you have a payday). Before the beginning of each calendar year, you must determine which of the two deposit schedules you are required to use. The deposit schedule you must use is based on the total tax liability you reported on Form 941 during a lookback period, discussed next. Your deposit schedule isn't determined by how often you pay your employees or make deposits. See special rules for Forms 944 and 945, later. Also see *Application of Monthly and Semiweekly Schedules*, later in this section.

 These rules don't apply to FUTA tax. See section 14 for information on depositing FUTA tax.

Lookback period. If you are a Form 941 filer, your deposit schedule for a calendar year is determined from the total taxes reported on Forms 941, line 10, in a 4-quarter lookback period. The lookback period begins July 1 and ends June 30 as shown next in Table 1. If you reported $50,000 or less of taxes for the lookback period, you are a monthly schedule depositor; if you reported more than $50,000, you are a semiweekly schedule depositor.

Table 1. Lookback Period for Calendar Year 2016

July 1, 2014 through Sep. 30, 2014	Oct. 1, 2014 through Dec. 31, 2014	Jan. 1, 2015 through Mar. 31, 2015	Apr.1, 2015 through June 30, 2015

 The lookback period for a 2016 Form 941 filer who filed Form 944 in either 2014 or 2015 is calendar year 2014.

If you are a Form 944 filer for the current year or either of the preceding 2 years, your deposit schedule for a calendar year is determined from the total taxes reported during the second preceding calendar year (either on your Form 941 for all 4 quarters of that year or your Form 944 for that year). The lookback period for 2016 for a Form 944 filer is calendar year 2014. If you reported $50,000 or less of taxes for the lookback period, you are a monthly schedule depositor; if you reported more than $50,000, you are a semiweekly schedule depositor.

If you are a Form 945 filer, your deposit schedule for a calendar year is determined from the total taxes reported on line 3 of your Form 945 for the second preceding calendar year. The lookback period for 2016 for a Form 945 filer is calendar year 2014.

Adjustments and the lookback rule. Adjustments made on Form 941-X, Form 944-X, and Form 945-X don't affect the amount of tax liability for previous periods for purposes of the lookback rule.

Example. An employer originally reported a tax liability of $45,000 for the lookback period. The employer discovered, during January 2016, that the tax reported for one of the lookback period quarters was understated by $10,000 and corrected this error by filing Form 941-X. This

employer is a monthly schedule depositor for 2016 because the lookback period tax liabilities are based on the amounts originally reported, and they were $50,000 or less.

Deposit period. The term deposit period refers to the period during which tax liabilities are accumulated for each required deposit due date. For monthly schedule depositors, the deposit period is a calendar month. The deposit periods for semiweekly schedule depositors are Wednesday through Friday and Saturday through Tuesday.

Monthly Deposit Schedule

You are a monthly schedule depositor for a calendar year if the total taxes on Form 941, line 10, for the 4 quarters in your lookback period were $50,000 or less. Under the monthly deposit schedule, deposit employment taxes on payments made during a month by the 15th day of the following month. See also *Deposits on Business Days Only* and the *$100,000 Next-Day Deposit Rule*, later in this section. Monthly schedule depositors shouldn't file Form 941 or Form 944 on a monthly basis.

New employers. Your tax liability for any quarter in the lookback period before you started or acquired your business is considered to be zero. Therefore, you are a monthly schedule depositor for the first calendar year of your business. However, see the *$100,000 Next-Day Deposit Rule*, later in this section.

Semiweekly Deposit Schedule

You are a semiweekly schedule depositor for a calendar year if the total taxes on Form 941, line 10, during your lookback period were more than $50,000. Under the semiweekly deposit schedule, deposit employment taxes for payments made on Wednesday, Thursday, and/or Friday by the following Wednesday. Deposit taxes for payments made on Saturday, Sunday, Monday, and/or Tuesday by the following Friday. See also *Deposits on Business Days Only*, later.

Note. Semiweekly schedule depositors must complete Schedule B (Form 941), Report of Tax Liability for Semiweekly Schedule Depositors, and submit it with Form 941. If you file Form 944 and are a semiweekly schedule depositor, complete Form 945-A, Annual Record of Federal Tax Liability, and submit it with your return (instead of Schedule B).

Table 2. Semiweekly Deposit Schedule

IF the payday falls on a . . .	THEN deposit taxes by the following . . .
Wednesday, Thursday, and/or Friday	Wednesday
Saturday, Sunday, Monday, and/or Tuesday	Friday

Semiweekly deposit period spanning 2 quarters. If you have more than one pay date during a semiweekly period and the pay dates fall in different calendar quarters, you will need to make **separate deposits** for the separate liabilities.

Example. If you have a pay date on Thursday, March 31, 2016 (first quarter), and another pay date on Friday, April 1, 2016 (second quarter), two separate deposits would be required even though the pay dates fall within the same semiweekly period. Both deposits would be due Wednesday, April 6, 2016.

Summary of Steps to Determine Your Deposit Schedule

1. Identify your lookback period (see *Lookback period*, earlier in this section).
2. Add the total taxes you reported on Form 941, line 10, during the lookback period.
3. Determine if you are a monthly or semiweekly schedule depositor:

If the total taxes you reported in the lookback period were	Then you are a . . . .
$50,000 or less	Monthly Schedule Depositor
More than $50,000	Semiweekly Schedule Depositor

Example of Monthly and Semiweekly Schedules

Rose Co. reported Form 941 taxes as follows:

2015 Lookback Period		2016 Lookback Period	
3rd Quarter 2013	$12,000	3rd Quarter 2014	$12,000
4th Quarter 2013	12,000	4th Quarter 2014	12,000
1st Quarter 2014	12,000	1st Quarter 2015	12,000
2nd Quarter 2014	12,000	2nd Quarter 2015	15,000
	$48,000		$51,000

Rose Co. is a monthly schedule depositor for 2015 because its tax liability for the 4 quarters in its lookback period (third quarter 2013 through second quarter 2014) wasn't more than $50,000. However, for 2016, Rose Co. is a semiweekly schedule depositor because the total taxes exceeded $50,000 for the 4 quarters in its lookback period (third quarter 2014 through second quarter 2015).

Deposits on Business Days Only

If a deposit is required to be made on a day that isn't a business day, the deposit is considered timely if it is made by the close of the next business day. A business day is any day other than a Saturday, Sunday, or legal holiday. For example, if a deposit is required to be made on a Friday and Friday is a legal holiday, the deposit will be considered timely if it is made by the following Monday (if that Monday is a business day).

Semiweekly schedule depositors have at least 3 business days to make a deposit. If any of the 3 weekdays after the end of a semiweekly period is a legal holiday, you will have an additional day for each day that is a legal holiday to make the required deposit. For example, if a semiweekly schedule depositor accumulated taxes for payments made on Friday and the following Monday is a legal holiday, the deposit normally due on Wednesday may be made on Thursday (this allows 3 business days to make the deposit).

Legal holiday. The term "legal holiday" means any legal holiday in the District of Columbia. Legal holidays for 2016 are listed next.

- January 1— New Year's Day
- January 18— Birthday of Martin Luther King, Jr.
- February 15— Washington's Birthday
- April 15— District of Columbia Emancipation Day (observed)
- May 30— Memorial Day
- July 4— Independence Day
- September 5— Labor Day
- October 10— Columbus Day
- November 11— Veterans' Day
- November 24— Thanksgiving Day
- December 26— Christmas Day (observed)

Application of Monthly and Semiweekly Schedules

The terms "monthly schedule depositor" and "semiweekly schedule depositor" don't refer to how often your business pays its employees or even how often you are required to make deposits. The terms identify which set of deposit rules you must follow when an employment tax liability arises. The deposit rules are based on the dates when wages are paid (for example, cash basis); not on when tax liabilities are accrued for accounting purposes.

Monthly schedule example. Spruce Co. is a monthly schedule depositor with seasonal employees. It paid wages each Friday during May but didn't pay any wages during June. Under the monthly deposit schedule, Spruce Co. must deposit the combined tax liabilities for the May paydays by June 15. Spruce Co. doesn't have a deposit requirement for June (due by July 15) because no wages were paid and, therefore, it didn't have a tax liability for June.

Semiweekly schedule example. Green, Inc. is a semiweekly schedule depositor and pays wages once each month on the last Friday of the month. Although Green, Inc., has a semiweekly deposit schedule, it will deposit just once a month because it pays wages only once a month. The deposit, however, will be made under the semiweekly deposit schedule as follows: Green, Inc.'s tax liability for the April 29, 2016 (Friday), payday must be deposited by May 4, 2016 (Wednesday). Under the semiweekly deposit schedule, liabilities for wages paid on Wednesday through Friday must be deposited by the following Wednesday.

$100,000 Next-Day Deposit Rule

If you accumulate $100,000 or more in taxes on any day during a monthly or semiweekly deposit period (see *Deposit period*, earlier in this section), you must deposit the tax by the next business day, whether you are a monthly or semiweekly schedule depositor.

For purposes of the $100,000 rule, don't continue accumulating a tax liability after the end of a deposit period. For example, if a semiweekly schedule depositor has accumulated a liability of $95,000 on a Tuesday (of a Saturday-through-Tuesday deposit period) and accumulated a $10,000 liability on Wednesday, the $100,000 next-day deposit rule doesn't apply. Thus, $95,000 must be deposited by Friday and $10,000 must be deposited by the following Wednesday.

However, once you accumulate at least $100,000 in a deposit period, stop accumulating at the end of that day and begin to accumulate anew on the next day. For example, Fir Co. is a semiweekly schedule depositor. On Monday, Fir Co. accumulates taxes of $110,000 and must deposit this amount on Tuesday, the next business day. On Tuesday, Fir Co. accumulates additional taxes of $30,000. Because the $30,000 isn't added to the previous $110,000 and is less than $100,000, Fir Co. must deposit the $30,000 by Friday (following the semiweekly deposit schedule).

 If you are a monthly schedule depositor and accumulate a $100,000 tax liability on any day, you become a semiweekly schedule depositor on the next day and remain so for at least the rest of the calendar year and for the following calendar year.

Example. Elm, Inc., started its business on May 1, 2016. On Wednesday, May 4, it paid wages for the first time and accumulated a tax liability of $40,000. On Friday, May 6, Elm, Inc., paid wages and accumulated a liability of $60,000, bringing its total accumulated tax liability to $100,000. Because this was the first year of its business, the tax liability for its lookback period is considered to be zero, and it would be a monthly schedule depositor based on the lookback rules. However, since Elm, Inc., accumulated a $100,000 liability on May 6, it became a semiweekly schedule depositor on May 7. It will be a semiweekly schedule depositor for the remainder of 2016 and for 2017. Elm, Inc., is required to deposit the $100,000 by Monday, May 9, the next business day.

Accuracy of Deposits Rule

You are required to deposit 100% of your tax liability on or before the deposit due date. However, penalties won't be applied for depositing less than 100% if both of the following conditions are met.

- Any deposit shortfall doesn't exceed the greater of $100 or 2% of the amount of taxes otherwise required to be deposited.

- The deposit shortfall is paid or deposited by the shortfall makeup date as described next.

Makeup Date for Deposit Shortfall:

1. **Monthly schedule depositor.** Deposit the shortfall or pay it with your return by the due date of your return for the return period in which the shortfall occurred. You may pay the shortfall with your return even if the amount is $2,500 or more.

2. **Semiweekly schedule depositor.** Deposit by the earlier of:

   a. The first Wednesday or Friday (whichever comes first) that falls on or after the 15th of the month following the month in which the shortfall occurred, or

   b. The due date of your return (for the return period of the tax liability).

For example, if a semiweekly schedule depositor has a deposit shortfall during June 2016, the shortfall makeup date is July 15, 2016 (Friday). However, if the shortfall occurred on the required April 1, 2016 (Friday), deposit due date for a March 29, 2016 (Tuesday), pay date, the return due date for the March 29, 2016, pay date (May 2, 2016) would come before the May 18, 2016 (Wednesday), shortfall makeup date. In this case, the shortfall must be deposited by May 2, 2016.

How To Deposit

You must deposit employment taxes, including Form 945 taxes, by EFT. See *Payment with return*, earlier in this section, for exceptions explaining when taxes may be paid with the tax return instead of being deposited.

Electronic deposit requirement. You must use EFT to make all federal tax deposits (such as deposits of employment tax, excise tax, and corporate income tax). Generally, an EFT is made using EFTPS. If you don't want to use EFTPS, you can arrange for your tax professional, financial institution, payroll service, or other trusted third party to make electronic deposits on your behalf. EFTPS is a free service provided by the Department of Treasury. To get more information about EFTPS or to enroll in EFTPS, visit *www.eftps.gov*, or call 1-800-555-4477 or 1-800-733-4829 (TDD). Additional information about EFTPS is also available in Pub. 966.

When you receive your EIN. If you are a new employer that indicated a federal tax obligation when requesting an EIN, you will be pre-enrolled in EFTPS. You will receive information about Express Enrollment in your Employer Identification Number (EIN) Package and an additional mailing containing your EFTPS personal identification number (PIN) and instructions for activating

A-166

your PIN. Call the toll-free number located in your "How to Activate Your Enrollment" brochure to activate your enrollment and begin making your payroll tax deposits. If you outsource any of your payroll and related tax duties to a third party payer, such as a PSP or reporting agent, be sure to tell them about your EFTPS enrollment.

Deposit record. For your records, an EFT Trace Number will be provided with each successful payment. The number can be used as a receipt or to trace the payment.

Depositing on time. For deposits made by EFTPS to be on time, you must submit the deposit by 8 p.m. Eastern time the day before the date the deposit is due. If you use a third party to make a deposit on your behalf, they may have different cutoff times.

Same-day wire payment option. If you fail to submit a deposit transaction on EFTPS by 8 p.m. Eastern time the day before the date a deposit is due, you can still make your deposit on time by using the Federal Tax Collection Service (FTCS). To use the same-day wire payment method, you will need to make arrangements with your financial institution ahead of time. Please check with your financial institution regarding availability, deadlines, and costs. Your financial institution may charge you a fee for payments made this way. To learn more about the information you will need to provide to your financial institution to make a same-day wire payment, visit the IRS website at *www.irs.gov/payments* and click on *Same-day wire*.

How to claim credit for overpayments. If you deposited more than the right amount of taxes for a quarter, you can choose on Form 941 for that quarter (or on Form 944 for that year) to have the overpayment refunded or applied as a credit to your next return. Don't ask EFTPS to request a refund from the IRS for you.

Deposit Penalties

 Although the deposit penalties information provided next refers specifically to Form 941, these rules also apply to Form 945 and Form 944 (if the employer required to file Form 944 doesn't qualify for the exception to the deposit requirements discussed under Payment with return, *earlier in this section).*

Penalties may apply if you don't make required deposits on time or if you make deposits for less than the required amount. The penalties don't apply if any failure to make a proper and timely deposit was due to reasonable cause and not to willful neglect. If you receive a penalty notice, you can provide an explanation of why you believe reasonable cause exists. The IRS may also waive penalties if you inadvertently fail to deposit in the first quarter you were required to deposit any employment tax, or in the first quarter during which your frequency of deposits changed, if you timely filed your employment tax return.

For amounts not properly or timely deposited, the penalty rates are as follows.

2%	-	Deposits made 1 to 5 days late.
5%	-	Deposits made 6 to 15 days late.
10%	-	Deposits made 16 or more days late. Also applies to amounts paid within 10 days of the date of the first notice the IRS sent asking for the tax due.
10%	-	Amounts (that should have been deposited) paid directly to the IRS, or paid with your tax return. But see *Payment with return*, earlier in this section, for an exception.
15%	-	Amounts still unpaid more than 10 days after the date of the first notice the IRS sent asking for the tax due or the day on which you received notice and demand for immediate payment, whichever is earlier.

Late deposit penalty amounts are determined using calendar days, starting from the due date of the liability.

Special rule for former Form 944 filers. If you filed Form 944 for the prior year and file Forms 941 for the current year, the FTD penalty won't apply to a late deposit of employment taxes for January of the current year if the taxes are deposited in full by March 15 of the current year.

Order in which deposits are applied. Deposits generally are applied to the most recent tax liability within the quarter. If you receive an FTD penalty notice, you may designate how your deposits are to be applied in order to minimize the amount of the penalty if you do so within 90 days of the date of the notice. Follow the instructions on the penalty notice you received. For more information on designating deposits, see Revenue Procedure 2001-58. You can find Revenue Procedure 2001-58 on page 579 of Internal Revenue Bulletin 2001-50 at *www.irs.gov/pub/irs-irbs/irb01-50.pdf*.

Example. Cedar, Inc. is required to make a deposit of $1,000 on May 15 and $1,500 on June 15. It doesn't make the deposit on May 15. On June 15, Cedar, Inc. deposits $2,000. Under the deposits rule, which applies deposits to the most recent tax liability, $1,500 of the deposit is applied to the June 15 deposit and the remaining $500 is applied to the May deposit. Accordingly, $500 of the May 15 liability remains undeposited. The penalty on this underdeposit will apply as explained above.

Trust fund recovery penalty. If federal income, social security, or Medicare taxes that must be withheld aren't withheld or aren't deposited or paid to the United States Treasury, the trust fund recovery penalty may apply. The penalty is the full amount of the unpaid trust fund tax. This penalty may apply to you if these unpaid taxes can't be immediately collected from the employer or business.

The trust fund recovery penalty may be imposed on all persons who are determined by the IRS to be responsible for collecting, accounting for, or paying over these taxes, and who acted willfully in not doing so.

A **responsible person** can be an officer or employee of a corporation, a partner or employee of a partnership, an accountant, a volunteer director/trustee, or an employee of a sole proprietorship, or any other person or entity that is responsible for collecting, accounting for, or paying over trust fund taxes. A responsible person also may include one who signs checks for the business or otherwise has authority to cause the spending of business funds.

Willfully means voluntarily, consciously, and intentionally. A responsible person acts willfully if the person knows the required actions of collecting, accounting for, or paying over trust fund taxes aren't taking place, or recklessly disregards obvious and known risks to the government's right to receive trust fund taxes.

Separate accounting when deposits aren't made or withheld taxes aren't paid. Separate accounting may be required if you don't pay over withheld employee social security, Medicare, or income taxes; deposit required taxes; make required payments; or file tax returns. In this case, you would receive written notice from the IRS requiring you to deposit taxes into a special trust account for the U.S. Government.

 You may be charged with criminal penalties if you don't comply with the special bank deposit requirements for the special trust account for the U.S. Government.

"Averaged" FTD penalty. IRS may assess an "averaged" FTD penalty of 2% to 10% if you are a monthly schedule depositor and didn't properly complete Form 941, line 14, when your tax liability shown on Form 941, line 10, equaled or exceeded $2,500.

The IRS may also assess an "averaged" FTD penalty of 2% to 10% if you are a semiweekly schedule depositor and your tax liability shown on Form 941, line 10, equaled or exceeded $2,500 and you:

- Completed Form 941, line 14, instead of Schedule B (Form 941);

- Failed to attach a properly completed Schedule B (Form 941); or

- Improperly completed Schedule B (Form 941) by, for example, entering tax deposits instead of tax liabilities in the numbered spaces.

The FTD penalty is figured by distributing your total tax liability shown on Form 941, line 10, equally throughout the tax period. As a result, your deposits and payments may not be counted as timely because the actual dates of your tax liabilities can't be accurately determined.

You can avoid an "averaged" FTD penalty by reviewing your return before you file it. Follow these steps before submitting your Form 941.

- If you are a monthly schedule depositor, report your tax liabilities (not your deposits) in the monthly entry spaces on Form 941, line 14.

- If you are a semiweekly schedule depositor, report your tax liabilities (not your deposits) on Schedule B (Form 941) in the lines that represent the dates your employees were paid.

- Verify your total liability shown on Form 941, line 14, or the bottom of Schedule B (Form 941) equals your tax liability shown on Form 941, line 10.

- Don't show negative amounts on Form 941, line 14, or Schedule B (Form 941).

- For prior period errors don't adjust your tax liabilities reported on Form 941, line 14, or on Schedule B (Form 941). Instead, file an adjusted return (Form 941-X, 944-X, or 945-X) if you are also adjusting your tax liability. If you are only adjusting your deposits in response to an FTD penalty notice, see the Instructions for Schedule B (Form 941) or the Instructions for Form 945-X (for Forms 944 and 945).

12. Filing Form 941 or Form 944

Form 941. Each quarter, if you pay wages subject to income tax withholding (including withholding on sick pay and supplemental unemployment benefits) or social security and Medicare taxes you must file Form 941 unless you receive an IRS notification that you are required to file Form 944 or the following exceptions apply. Also, if you are required to file Form 941 but believe your employment taxes for the calendar year will be $1,000 or less, you may request to file Form 944 instead of Forms 941. See the Instructions for Form 941 for details. Form 941 must be filed by the last day of the month that follows the end of the quarter. See the *Calendar*, earlier.

Form 944. If you receive written notification you qualify for the Form 944 program, you must file Form 944 instead of Form 941. If you received this notification, but prefer to file Form 941, you can request to have your filing requirement changed to Form 941 if you satisfy certain requirements. See the Instructions for Form 944 for details. Employers who must file Form 944 have until the last day of the month that follows the end of the year to file Form 944.

Exceptions. The following exceptions apply to the filing requirements for Forms 941 and 944.

- **Seasonal employers who no longer file for quarters when they regularly have no tax liability because they have paid no wages.** To alert the IRS you won't have to file a return for one or more quarters during the year, check the "Seasonal employer" box on Form 941, line 16. When you fill out Form 941, be sure to check the box on the top of the form that corresponds to the quarter reported. Generally, the IRS won't inquire about unfiled returns if at least one taxable return is filed each year. However, you must check the "Seasonal employer" box on **every** Form 941 you file. Otherwise, the IRS will expect a return to be filed for each quarter.

- **Household employers reporting social security and Medicare taxes and/or withheld income tax.** If you are a sole proprietor and file Form 941 or Form 944 for business employees, you may include taxes for household employees on your Form 941 or Form 944. Otherwise, report social security and Medicare taxes and income tax withholding for household employees on Schedule H (Form 1040). See Pub. 926 for more information.

- **Employers reporting wages for employees in American Samoa, Guam, the Commonwealth of the Northern Mariana Islands, the U.S. Virgin Islands, or Puerto Rico.** If your employees aren't subject to U.S. income tax withholding, use Forms 941-SS, 944, or Formulario 944(SP). Employers in Puerto Rico use Formularios 941-PR, 944(SP), or Form 944. If you have both employees who are subject to U.S. income tax withholding and employees who aren't subject to U.S. income tax withholding, you must file only Form 941 (or Form 944 or Formulario 944(SP)) and include all of your employees' wages on that form. For more information, see Pub. 80, Federal Tax Guide for Employers in U.S. Virgin Islands, Guam, American Samoa, and the Commonwealth of the Northern Mariana Islands, or Pub. 179, Guía Contributiva Federal para Patronos Puertorriqueños.

- **Agricultural employers reporting social security, Medicare, and withheld income taxes.** Report these taxes on Form 943. For more information, see Pub. 51.

Form 941 e-file. The Form 941 e-file program allows a taxpayer to electronically file Form 941 or Form 944 using a computer with an internet connection and commercial tax preparation software. For more information, visit the IRS website at *www.irs.gov/efile*, or call 1-866-255-0654.

Electronic filing by reporting agents. Reporting agents filing Forms 941 or Form 944 for groups of taxpayers can file them electronically. See *Reporting Agents* in section 7 of Pub. 15-A.

Penalties. For each whole or part month a return isn't filed when required (disregarding any extensions of the filing deadline), there is a failure-to-file (FTF) penalty of 5% of the unpaid tax due with that return. The maximum penalty is generally 25% of the tax due. Also, for each whole or part month the tax is paid late (disregarding any extensions of the payment deadline), there is a failure-to-pay (FTP) penalty of 0.5% per month of the amount of tax. For individual filers only, the FTP penalty is reduced from 0.5% per month to 0.25% per month if an installment agreement is in effect. You must have filed your return on or before the due date of the return to qualify for the reduced penalty. The maximum amount of the FTP penalty is also 25% of the tax due. If both penalties apply in any month, the FTF penalty is reduced by the amount of the FTP penalty. The penalties won't be charged if you have a reasonable cause for failing to file or pay. If you receive a penalty notice, you can provide an explanation of why you believe reasonable cause exists.

Note. In addition to any penalties, interest accrues from the due date of the tax on any unpaid balance.

If income, social security, or Medicare taxes that must be withheld aren't withheld or aren't paid, you may be personally liable for the trust fund recovery penalty. See *Trust fund recovery penalty* in section 11.

Use of a third party payer, such as a PSP or reporting agent, doesn't relieve an employer of the responsibility to ensure tax returns are filed and all taxes are paid or deposited correctly and on time.

Don't file more than one Form 941 per quarter or more than one Form 944 per year. Employers with multiple locations or divisions must file only one Form 941 per quarter or one Form 944 per year. Filing more than one return may result in processing delays and may require correspondence between you and the IRS. For information on making adjustments to previously filed returns, see section 13.

Reminders about filing.

- Don't report more than 1 calendar quarter on a Form 941.

- If you need Form 941 or Form 944, get one from the IRS in time to file the return when due. See *Ordering Employer Tax Forms and Publications*, earlier.

- Enter your name and EIN on Form 941 or Form 944. Be sure they are exactly as they appeared on earlier returns.

- See the Instructions for Form 941 or the Instructions for Form 944 for information on preparing the form.

Final return. If you go out of business, you must file a final return for the last quarter (last year for Form 944) in which wages are paid. If you continue to pay wages or other compensation for periods following termination of your business, you must file returns for those periods. See the Instructions for Form 941 or the Instructions for Form 944 for details on how to file a final return.

If you are required to file a final return, you are also required to furnish Forms W-2 to your employees by the due date of your final return. File Forms W-2 and W-3 with the SSA by the last day of the month that follows the due date of your final return. Don't send an original or copy of your Form 941 or Form 944 to the SSA. See the General Instructions for Forms W-2 and W-3 for more information.

Filing late returns for previous years. If possible, get a copy of Form 941 or Form 944 (and separate instructions) with a revision date showing the year for which your delinquent return is being filed. See *Ordering Employer Tax Forms and Publications*, earlier. Contact the IRS at 1-800-829-4933 if you have any questions about filing late returns.

A-169

Table 3. **Social Security and Medicare Tax Rates** *(for 3 prior years)*

Calendar Year	Wage Base Limit (each employee)	Tax Rate on Taxable Wages and Tips
2015–Social Security	$118,500	12.4%
2015–Medicare	All Wages	2.9%
2014–Social Security	$117,000	12.4%
2014–Medicare	All Wages	2.9%
2013 Social Security	$113,700	12.4%
2013–Medicare	All Wages	2.9%

Reconciling Forms W-2, W-3, and 941 or 944. When there are discrepancies between Forms 941 or Form 944 filed with the IRS and Forms W-2 and W-3 filed with the SSA, the IRS must contact you to resolve the discrepancies.

Take the following steps to help reduce discrepancies.

1. Report bonuses as wages and as social security and Medicare wages on Forms W-2 and on Form 941 or Form 944.

2. Report both social security and Medicare wages and taxes separately on Forms W-2, W-3, 941, and 944.

3. Report employee share of social security taxes on Form W-2 in the box for social security tax withheld (box 4), not as social security wages.

4. Report employee share of Medicare taxes on Form W-2 in the box for Medicare tax withheld (box 6), not as Medicare wages.

5. Make sure the social security wage amount for each employee doesn't exceed the annual social security wage base limit (for example, $118,500 for 2016).

6. Don't report noncash wages that aren't subject to social security or Medicare taxes as social security or Medicare wages.

7. If you used an EIN on any Form 941 or Form 944 for the year that is different from the EIN reported on Form W-3, enter the other EIN on Form W-3 in the box for "Other EIN used this year" (box h).

8. Be sure the amounts on Form W-3 are the total of amounts from Forms W-2.

9. Reconcile Form W-3 with your four quarterly Forms 941 or annual Form 944 by comparing amounts reported for:

   a. Income tax withholding;

   b. Social security wages, social security tips, and Medicare wages and tips. Form W-3 should include Forms 941 or Form 944 adjustments only for the current year; and

   c. Social security and Medicare taxes.

Don't report backup withholding or withholding on nonpayroll payments, such as pensions, annuities, and gambling winnings, on Form 941 or Form 944. Withholding on nonpayroll payments is reported on Forms 1099 or W-2G and must be reported on Form 945. Only taxes and withholding reported on Form W-2 should be reported on Form 941 or Form 944.

Amounts reported on Forms W-2, W-3, and Forms 941 or Form 944 may not match for valid reasons. If they don't match, you should determine the reasons they are valid. Keep your reconciliation so you will have a record of why amounts didn't match in case there are inquiries from the IRS or the SSA. See the Instructions for Schedule D (Form 941) if you need to explain any discrepancies that were caused by an acquisition, statutory merger, or consolidation.

---

13. Reporting Adjustments to Form 941 or Form 944

Current Period Adjustments

In certain cases, amounts reported as social security and Medicare taxes on Form 941, lines 5a–5d, column 2 (Form 944, lines 4a–4d, column 2), must be adjusted to arrive at your correct tax liability (for example, excluding amounts withheld by a third party payor or amounts you weren't required to withhold). Current period adjustments are reported on Form 941, lines 7–9, or Form 944, line 6, and include the following types of adjustments.

Fractions-of-cents adjustment. If there is a small difference between total taxes after adjustments (Form 941, line 10; Form 944, line 7) and total deposits (Form 941, line 11; Form 944, line 10), it may have been caused, all or in part, by rounding to the nearest cent each time you computed payroll. This rounding occurs when you figure the amount of social security and Medicare tax to be withheld and deposited from each employee's wages. The IRS refers to rounding differences relating to employee withholding of social security and Medicare taxes as "fractions-of-cents" adjustments. If you pay your taxes with Form 941 (or Form 944) instead of making deposits because your total taxes for the quarter (year for Form 944) are less than $2,500, you also may report a fractions-of-cents adjustment.

To determine if you have a fractions-of-cents adjustment for 2016, multiply the total wages and tips for the quarter subject to:

- Social security tax reported on Form 941 or Form 944 by 6.2% (.062),

- Medicare tax reported on Form 941 or Form 944 by 1.45% (.0145), and

- Additional Medicare Tax reported on Form 941 or 944 by 0.9% (.009).

Compare these amounts (the employee share of social security and Medicare taxes) with the total social security

A-170

and Medicare taxes actually withheld from employees for the quarter (from your payroll records). The difference, positive or negative, is your fractions-of-cents adjustment to be reported on Form 941, line 7, or Form 944, line 6. If the actual amount withheld is less, report a negative adjustment using a minus sign (if possible, otherwise use parentheses) in the entry space. If the actual amount is more, report a positive adjustment.

 For the above adjustments, prepare and retain a brief supporting statement explaining the nature and amount of each. Don't attach the statement to Form 941 or Form 944.

Example. Cedar, Inc. was entitled to the following current period adjustments.

- **Fractions of cents.** Cedar, Inc. determined the amounts withheld and deposited for social security and Medicare taxes during the quarter were a net $1.44 more than the employee share of the amount figured on Form 941, lines 5a–5d, column 2 (social security and Medicare taxes). This difference was caused by adding or dropping fractions of cents when figuring social security and Medicare taxes for each wage payment. Cedar, Inc. must report a positive $1.44 fractions-of-cents adjustment on Form 941, line 7.

- **Third-party sick pay.** Cedar, Inc. included taxes of $2,000 for sick pay on Form 941, lines 5a and 5c, column 2, for social security and Medicare taxes. However, the third-party payor of the sick pay withheld and paid the employee share ($1,000) of these taxes. Cedar, Inc. is entitled to a $1,000 sick pay adjustment (negative) on Form 941, line 8.

- **Life insurance premiums.** Cedar, Inc. paid group-term life insurance premiums for policies in excess of $50,000 for former employees. The former employees must pay the employee share of the social security and Medicare taxes ($200) on the policies. However, Cedar, Inc. must include the employee share of these taxes with the social security and Medicare taxes reported on Form 941, lines 5a and 5c, column 2. Therefore, Cedar, Inc. is entitled to a negative $200 adjustment on Form 941, line 9.

Adjustment of tax on third-party sick pay. Report both the employer and employee shares of social security and Medicare taxes for sick pay on Form 941, lines 5a and 5c (Form 944, lines 4a and 4c). If the aggregate wages paid for an employee by the employer and third-party payor exceed $200,000 for the calendar year, report the Additional Medicare Tax on Form 941, line 5d (Form 944, line 4d). Show as a negative adjustment on Form 941, line 8 (Form 944, line 6), the social security and Medicare taxes withheld on sick pay by a third-party payor. See section 6 of Pub. 15-A for more information.

Adjustment of tax on tips. If, by the 10th of the month after the month you received an employee's report on tips, you don't have enough employee funds available to withhold the employee's share of social security and Medicare

taxes, you no longer have to collect it. However, report the entire amount of these tips on Form 941, lines 5b and 5c (Form 944, lines 4b and 4c). If the aggregate wages and tips paid for an employee exceed $200,000 for the calendar year, report the Additional Medicare Tax on Form 941, line 5d (Form 944, line 4d). Include as a negative adjustment on Form 941, line 9 (Form 944, line 6), the total uncollected employee share of the social security and Medicare taxes.

Adjustment of tax on group-term life insurance premiums paid for former employees. The employee share of social security and Medicare taxes for premiums on group-term life insurance over $50,000 for a former employee is paid by the former employee with his or her tax return and isn't collected by the employer. However, include all social security and Medicare taxes for such coverage on Form 941, lines 5a and 5c (Form 944, lines 4a and 4c). If the amount paid for an employee for premiums on group-term life insurance combined with other wages exceeds $200,000 for the calendar year, report the Additional Medicare Tax on Form 941, line 5d (Form 944, line 4d). Back out the amount of the employee share of these taxes as a negative adjustment on Form 941, line 9 (Form 944, line 6). See Pub. 15-B for more information on group-term life insurance.

No change to record of federal tax liability. Don't make any changes to your record of federal tax liability reported on Form 941, line 14, or Schedule B (Form 941) (Form 945-A for Form 944 filers) for current period adjustments. The amounts reported on the record reflect the actual amounts you withheld from employees' wages for social security and Medicare taxes. Because the current period adjustments make the amounts reported on Form 941, lines 5a–5d, column 2 (Form 944, lines 4a–4d, column 2), equal the actual amounts you withheld (the amounts reported on the record), no additional changes to the record of federal tax liability are necessary for these adjustments.

Prior Period Adjustments

Forms for prior period adjustments. Use Form 941-X or Form 944-X to make a correction after you discover an error on a previously filed Form 941 or Form 944. There are also Forms 943-X, 945-X, and CT-1 X to report corrections on the corresponding returns. Use Form 843 when requesting a refund or abatement of assessed interest or penalties.

 See Revenue Ruling 2009-39, 2009-52 I.R.B. 951, for examples of how the interest-free adjustment and claim for refund rules apply in 10 different situations. You can find Revenue Ruling 2009-39, at www.irs.gov/irb/2009-52_IRB/ar14.html.

Background. Treasury Decision 9405 changed the process for making interest-free adjustments to employment taxes reported on Form 941 and Form 944 and for filing a claim for refund of employment taxes. Treasury Decision 9405, 2008-32 I.R.B. 293, is available at www.irs.gov/irb/

2008-32_irb/ar13.html. You will use the adjustment process if you underreported employment taxes and are making a payment, or if you overreported employment taxes and will be applying the credit to the Form 941 or Form 944 period during which you file Form 941-X or Form 944-X. You will use the claim process if you overreported employment taxes and are requesting a refund or abatement of the overreported amount. We use the terms "correct" and "corrections" to include interest-free adjustments under sections 6205 and 6413, and claims for refund and abatement under sections 6402, 6414, and 6404 of the Internal Revenue Code.

Correcting employment taxes. When you discover an error on a previously filed Form 941 or Form 944, you must:

- Correct that error using Form 941-X or Form 944-X,

- File a separate Form 941-X or Form 944-X for each Form 941 or Form 944 you are correcting, and

- File Form 941-X or Form 944-X separately. Don't file with Form 941 or Form 944.

Continue to report current quarter adjustments for fractions of cents, third-party sick pay, tips, and group-term life insurance on Form 941 using lines 7–9, and on Form 944 using line 6.

Report the correction of underreported and overreported amounts for the same tax period on a single Form 941-X or Form 944-X unless you are requesting a refund. If you are requesting a refund and are correcting both underreported and overreported amounts, file one Form 941-X or Form 944-X correcting the underreported amounts only and a second Form 941-X or Form 944-X correcting the overreported amounts.

See the chart on the back of Form 941-X or Form 944-X for help in choosing whether to use the adjustment process or the claim process. See the Instructions for Form 941-X or the Instructions for Form 944-X for details on how to make the adjustment or claim for refund or abatement.

Income tax withholding adjustments. In a current calendar year, correct prior quarter income tax withholding errors by making the correction on Form 941-X when you discover the error.

You may make an adjustment only to correct income tax withholding errors discovered during the same calendar year in which you paid the wages. This is because the employee uses the amount shown on Form W-2 as a credit when filing his or her income tax return (Form 1040, etc.).

You can't adjust amounts reported as income tax withheld in a prior calendar year unless it is to correct an administrative error or IRC section 3509 applies. An administrative error occurs if the amount you entered on Form 941 or Form 944 isn't the amount you actually withheld. For example, if the total income tax actually withheld was incorrectly reported on Form 941 or Form 944 due to a mathematical or transposition error, this would be an administrative error. The administrative error adjustment corrects the amount reported on Form 941 or Form 944 to

agree with the amount actually withheld from employees and reported on their Forms W-2.

Additional Medicare Tax withholding adjustments. Generally, the rules discussed above under *Income tax withholding adjustments* apply to Additional Medicare Tax withholding adjustments. That is, you may make an adjustment to correct Additional Medicare Tax withholding errors discovered during the same calendar year in which you paid wages. You can't adjust amounts reported in a prior calendar year unless it is to correct an administrative error or IRC section 3509 applies. If you have overpaid Additional Medicare Tax, you can't file a claim for refund for the amount of the overpayment unless the amount wasn't actually withheld from the employee's wages (which would be an administrative error).

If a prior year error was a nonadministrative error, you may correct only the **wages and tips** subject to Additional Medicare Tax withholding.

Collecting underwithheld taxes from employees. If you withheld no income, social security, or Medicare taxes or less than the correct amount from an employee's wages, you can make it up from later pay to that employee. But you are the one who owes the underpayment. Reimbursement is a matter for settlement between you and the employee. Underwithheld income tax and Additional Medicare Tax must be recovered from the employee on or before the last day of the calendar year. There are special rules for tax on tips (see section 6) and fringe benefits (see section 5).

Refunding amounts incorrectly withheld from employees. If you withheld more than the correct amount of income, social security, or Medicare taxes from wages paid, repay or reimburse the employee the excess. Any excess income tax or Additional Medicare Tax withholding must be repaid or reimbursed to the employee before the end of the calendar year in which it was withheld. Keep in your records the employee's written receipt showing the date and amount of the repayment or record of reimbursement. If you didn't repay or reimburse the employee, you must report and pay each excess amount when you file Form 941 for the quarter (or Form 944 for the year) in which you withheld too much tax.

Correcting filed Forms W-2 and W-3. When adjustments are made to correct wages and social security and Medicare taxes because of a change in the wage totals reported for a previous year, you also need to file Form W-2c and Form W-3c with the SSA. Up to 25 Forms W-2c per Form W-3c may now be filed per session over the Internet, with no limit on the number of sessions. For more information, visit the Social Security Administration's Employer W-2 Filing Instructions & Information webpage at *www.socialsecurity.gov/employer*.

Exceptions to interest-free corrections of employment taxes. A correction won't be eligible for interest-free treatment if:

- The failure to report relates to an issue raised in an IRS examination of a prior return, or

- The employer knowingly underreported its employment tax liability.

A correction won't be eligible for interest-free treatment after the earlier of the following:

- Receipt of an IRS notice and demand for payment after assessment or

- Receipt of an IRS Notice of Determination of Worker Classification (Letter 3523).

Wage Repayments

If an employee repays you for wages received in error, don't offset the repayments against current-year wages unless the repayments are for amounts received in error in the current year.

Repayment of current year wages. If you receive repayments for wages paid during a prior quarter in the current year, report adjustments on Form 941-X to recover income tax withholding and social security and Medicare taxes for the repaid wages.

Repayment of prior year wages. If you receive repayments for wages paid during a prior year, report an adjustment on Form 941-X or Form 944-X to recover the social security and Medicare taxes. You can't make an adjustment for income tax withholding because the wages were income to the employee for the prior year. You can't make an adjustment for Additional Medicare Tax withholding because the employee determines liability for Additional Medicare Tax on the employee's income tax return for the prior year.

You also must file Forms W-2c and W-3c with the SSA to correct social security and Medicare wages and taxes. Don't correct wages (box 1) on Form W-2c for the amount paid in error. Give a copy of Form W-2c to the employee.

Employee reporting of repayment. The wages paid in error in the prior year remain taxable to the employee for that year. This is because the employee received and had use of those funds during that year. The employee isn't entitled to file an amended return (Form 1040X) to recover the income tax on these wages. Instead, the employee is entitled to a deduction (or credit in some cases) for the repaid wages on his or her income tax return for the year of repayment. However, the employee should file an amended return (Form 1040X) to recover any Additional Medicare Tax paid on the wages paid in error in the prior year.

14. Federal Unemployment (FUTA) Tax

The Federal Unemployment Tax Act, with state unemployment systems, provides for payments of unemployment compensation to workers who have lost their jobs. Most employers pay both a federal and a state unemployment tax. For a list of state unemployment agencies, visit the U.S. Department of Labor's website at

www.workforcesecurity.doleta.gov/unemploy/ agencies.asp. Only the employer pays FUTA tax; it isn't withheld from the employee's wages. For more information, see the Instructions for Form 940.

 Services rendered to a federally recognized Indian tribal government (or any subdivision, subsidiary, or business wholly owned by such an Indian tribe) are exempt from FUTA tax, subject to the tribe's compliance with state law. For more information, see Internal Revenue Code section 3309(d).

Who must pay? Use the following three tests to determine whether you must pay FUTA tax. Each test applies to a different category of employee, and each is independent of the others. If a test describes your situation, you are subject to FUTA tax on the wages you pay to employees in that category during the current calendar year.

1. **General test.**

    You are subject to FUTA tax in 2016 on the wages you pay employees who aren't farmworkers or household workers if:

    a. You paid wages of $1,500 or more in any calendar quarter in 2015 or 2016, or

    b. You had one or more employees for at least some part of a day in any 20 or more different weeks in 2015 or 20 or more different weeks in 2016.

2. **Household employees test.**

    You are subject to FUTA tax if you paid total cash wages of $1,000 or more to household employees in any calendar quarter in 2015 or 2016. A household employee is an employee who performs household work in a private home, local college club, or local fraternity or sorority chapter.

3. **Farmworkers test.**

    You are subject to FUTA tax on the wages you pay to farmworkers if:

    a. You paid cash wages of $20,000 or more to farmworkers during any calendar quarter in 2015 or 2016, or

    b. You employed 10 or more farmworkers during at least some part of a day (whether or not at the same time) during any 20 or more different weeks in 2015 or 20 or more different weeks in 2016.

Computing FUTA tax. For 2016, the FUTA tax rate is 6.0%. The tax applies to the first $7,000 you pay to each employee as wages during the year. The $7,000 is the federal wage base. Your state wage base may be different.

Generally, you can take a credit against your FUTA tax for amounts you paid into state unemployment funds. The credit may be as much as 5.4% of FUTA taxable wages. If you are entitled to the maximum 5.4% credit, the FUTA tax rate after credit is 0.6%. You are entitled to the maximum credit if you paid your state unemployment taxes in full, on time, and on all the same wages as are subject to FUTA tax, and as long as the state isn't determined to be a credit reduction state. See the Instructions for Form 940 to determine the credit.

In some states, the wages subject to state unemployment tax are the same as the wages subject to FUTA tax. However, certain states exclude some types of wages from state unemployment tax, even though they are subject to FUTA tax (for example, wages paid to corporate officers, certain payments of sick pay by unions, and certain fringe benefits). In such a case, you may be required to deposit more than 0.6% FUTA tax on those wages. See the Instructions for Form 940 for further guidance.

TIP *In years when there are credit reduction states, you must include liabilities owed for credit reduction with your fourth quarter deposit. You may deposit the anticipated extra liability throughout the year, but it isn't due until the due date for the deposit for the fourth quarter, and the associated liability should be recorded as being incurred in the fourth quarter. See the Instructions for Form 940 for more information.*

Successor employer. If you acquired a business from an employer who was liable for FUTA tax, you may be able to count the wages that employer paid to the employees who continue to work for you when you figure the $7,000 FUTA tax wage base. See the Instructions for Form 940.

Depositing FUTA tax. For deposit purposes, figure FUTA tax quarterly. Determine your FUTA tax liability by multiplying the amount of taxable wages paid during the quarter by 0.6%. Stop depositing FUTA tax on an employee's wages when he or she reaches $7,000 in taxable wages for the calendar year.

If your FUTA tax liability for any calendar quarter is $500 or less, you don't have to deposit the tax. Instead, you may carry it forward and add it to the liability figured in the next quarter to see if you must make a deposit. If your FUTA tax liability for any calendar quarter is over $500 (including any FUTA tax carried forward from an earlier quarter), you must deposit the tax by EFT. See section 11 for more information on EFT.

Household employees. You aren't required to deposit FUTA taxes for household employees unless you report their wages on Form 941, 943, or 944. See Pub. 926 for more information.

When to deposit. Deposit the FUTA tax by the last day of the first month that follows the end of the quarter. If the due date for making your deposit falls on a Saturday, Sunday, or legal holiday, you may make your deposit on the next business day. See *Legal holiday*, earlier, for a list of the legal holidays for 2016.

If your liability for the fourth quarter (plus any undeposited amount from any earlier quarter) is over $500, deposit the entire amount by the due date of Form 940 (January 31). If it is $500 or less, you can make a deposit, pay the tax with a credit or debit card, or pay the tax with your 2015 Form 940 by February 1, 2016. If you file Form 940 electronically, you can e-file and e-pay (EFW). For more information on paying your taxes with a credit or debit card or using EFW, visit the IRS website at *www.irs.gov/payments*.

Table 4. **When to Deposit FUTA Taxes**

Quarter	Ending	Due Date
Jan.–Feb.–Mar.	Mar. 31	Apr. 30
Apr.–May–June	June 30	July 31
July–Aug.–Sept.	Sept. 30	Oct. 31
Oct.–Nov.–Dec.	Dec. 31	Jan. 31

Reporting FUTA tax. Use Form 940 to report FUTA tax. File your 2015 Form 940 by February 1, 2016. However, if you deposited all FUTA tax when due, you may file on or before February 10, 2016.

Form 940 e-file. The Form 940 e-file program allows a taxpayer to electronically file From 940 using a computer with an internet connection and commercial tax preparation software. For more information, visit the IRS website at *www.irs.gov/efile*, or call 1-866-255-0654.

Household employees. If you didn't report employment taxes for household employees on Forms 941, 943, or 944, report FUTA tax for these employees on Schedule H (Form 1040). See Pub. 926 for more information. You must have an EIN to file Schedule H (Form 1040).

Electronic filing by reporting agents. Reporting agents filing Forms 940 for groups of taxpayers can file them electronically. See the *Reporting Agent* discussion in section 7 of Pub. 15-A.

15. Special Rules for Various Types of Services and Payments

Section references are to the Internal Revenue Code unless otherwise noted.

Special Classes of Employment and Special Types of Payments	Treatment Under Employment Taxes		
	Income Tax Withholding	Social Security and Medicare (including Additional Medicare Tax when wages are paid in excess of $200,000)	FUTA
Aliens, nonresident.	See Pub. 515 and Pub. 519.		
Aliens, resident:			
1. Service performed in the U.S.	Same as U.S. citizen.	Same as U.S. citizen. (Exempt if any part of service as crew member of foreign vessel or aircraft is performed outside U.S.)	Same as U.S. citizen.
2. Service performed outside U.S.	Withhold	Taxable if (1) working for an American employer or (2) an American employer by agreement covers U.S. citizens and residents employed by its foreign affiliates.	Exempt unless on or in connection with an American vessel or aircraft and either performed under contract made in U.S., or alien is employed on such vessel or aircraft when it touches U.S. port.
Cafeteria plan benefits under section 125.	If employee chooses cash, subject to all employment taxes. If employee chooses another benefit, the treatment is the same as if the benefit was provided outside the plan. See Pub. 15-B for more information.		
Deceased worker:			
1. Wages paid to beneficiary or estate in same calendar year as worker's death. See the Instructions for Forms W-2 and W-3 for details.	Exempt	Taxable	Taxable
2. Wages paid to beneficiary or estate after calendar year of worker's death.	Exempt	Exempt	Exempt
Dependent care assistance programs.	Exempt to the extent it is reasonable to believe amounts are excludable from gross income under section 129.		
Disabled worker's wages paid after year in which worker became entitled to disability insurance benefits under the Social Security Act.	Withhold	Exempt, if worker didn't perform any service for employer during period for which payment is made.	Taxable
Employee business expense reimbursement:			
1. Accountable plan.			
a. Amounts not exceeding specified government rate for per diem or standard mileage.	Exempt	Exempt	Exempt
b. Amounts in excess of specified government rate for per diem or standard mileage.	Withhold	Taxable	Taxable
2. Nonaccountable plan. See section 5 for details.	Withhold	Taxable	Taxable
Family employees:			
1. Child employed by parent (or partnership in which each partner is a parent of the child).	Withhold	Exempt until age 18; age 21 for domestic service.	Exempt until age 21
2. Parent employed by child.	Withhold	Taxable if in course of the son's or daughter's business. For domestic services, see section 3.	Exempt
3. Spouse employed by spouse.	Withhold	Taxable if in course of spouse's business.	Exempt
See section 3 for more information.			
Fishing and related activities.	See Pub. 334.		
Foreign governments and international organizations.	Exempt	Exempt	Exempt

Special Classes of Employment and Special Types of Payments	Treatment Under Employment Taxes		
	Income Tax Withholding	Social Security and Medicare (including Additional Medicare Tax when wages are paid in excess of $200,000)	FUTA
Foreign service by U.S. citizens:			
1. As U.S. government employees.	Withhold	Same as within U.S.	Exempt
2. For foreign affiliates of American employers and other private employers.	Exempt if at time of payment (1) it is reasonable to believe employee is entitled to exclusion from income under section 911 or (2) the employer is required by law of the foreign country to withhold income tax on such payment.	Exempt unless (1) an American employer by agreement covers U.S. citizens employed by its foreign affiliates or (2) U.S. citizen works for American employer.	Exempt unless (1) on American vessel or aircraft and work is performed under contract made in U.S. or worker is employed on vessel when it touches U.S. port or (2) U.S. citizen works for American employer (except in a contiguous country with which the U.S. has an agreement for unemployment compensation) or in the U.S. Virgin Islands.
Fringe benefits.	Taxable on excess of fair market value of the benefit over the sum of an amount paid for it by the employee and any amount excludable by law. However, special valuation rules may apply. Benefits provided under cafeteria plans may qualify for exclusion from wages for social security, Medicare, and FUTA taxes. See Pub. 15-B for details.		
Government employment:			
State/local governments and political subdivisions, employees of:			
1. Salaries and wages (includes payments to most elected and appointed officials.) See chapter 3 of Pub. 963.	Withhold	Generally, taxable for (1) services performed by employees who are either (a) covered under a section 218 agreement or (b) not covered under a section 218 agreement and not a member of a public retirement system (mandatory social security and Medicare coverage), and (2) (for Medicare tax only) for services performed by employees hired or rehired after 3/31/86 who aren't covered under a section 218 agreement or the mandatory social security provisions, unless specifically excluded by law. See Pub. 963.	Exempt
2. Election workers. Election individuals are workers who are employed to perform services for state or local governments at election booths in connection with national, state, or local elections.

Note: File Form W-2 for payments of $600 or more even if no social security, or Medicare taxes were withheld. | Exempt | Taxable if paid $1,700 or more in 2016 (lesser amount if specified by a section 218 social security agreement). See Revenue Ruling 2000-6. | Exempt |
| 3. Emergency workers. Emergency workers who were hired on a temporary basis in response to a specific unforeseen emergency and aren't intended to become permanent employees. | Withhold | Exempt if serving on a temporary basis in case of fire, storm, snow, earthquake, flood, or similar emergency. | Exempt |
| U.S. federal government employees. | Withhold | Taxable for Medicare. Taxable for social security unless hired before 1984. See section 3121(b)(5). | Exempt |

A-176

Special Classes of Employment and Special Types of Payments	Treatment Under Employment Taxes		
	Income Tax Withholding	Social Security and Medicare (including Additional Medicare Tax when wages are paid in excess of $200,000)	FUTA
Homeworkers (industrial, cottage industry):			
1. Common law employees.	Withhold	Taxable	Taxable
2. Statutory employees. See section 2 for details.	Exempt	Taxable if paid $100 or more in cash in a year.	Exempt
Hospital employees:			
1. Interns.	Withhold	Taxable	Exempt
2. Patients.	Withhold	Taxable (Exempt for state or local government hospitals.)	Exempt
Household employees:			
1. Domestic service in private homes. Farmers, see Pub. 51.	Exempt (withhold if both employer and employee agree).	Taxable if paid $2,000 or more in cash in 2016. Exempt if performed by an individual under age 18 during any portion of the calendar year and isn't the principal occupation of the employee.	Taxable if employer paid total cash wages of $1,000 or more in any quarter in the current or preceding calendar year.
2. Domestic service in college clubs, fraternities, and sororities.	Exempt (withhold if both employer and employee agree).	Exempt if paid to regular student; also exempt if employee is paid less than $100 in a year by an income-tax-exempt employer.	Taxable if employer paid total cash wages of $1,000 or more in any quarter in the current or preceding calendar year.
Insurance for employees:			
1. Accident and health insurance premiums under a plan or system for employees and their dependents generally or for a class or classes of employees and their dependents.	Exempt (except 2% shareholder-employees of S corporations).	Exempt	Exempt
2. Group-term life insurance costs. See Pub. 15-B for details	Exempt	Exempt, except for the cost of group-term life insurance includible in the employee's gross income. Special rules apply for former employees.	Exempt
Insurance agents or solicitors:			
1. Full-time life insurance salesperson.	Withhold only if employee under common law. See section 2.	Taxable	Taxable if (1) employee under common law and (2) not paid solely by commissions.
2. Other salesperson of life, casualty, etc., insurance.	Withhold only if employee under common law.	Taxable only if employee under common law.	Taxable if (1) employee under common law and (2) not paid solely by commissions.
Interest on loans with below-market interest rates (foregone interest and deemed original issue discount).	See Pub. 15-A.		
Leave-sharing plans: Amounts paid to an employee under a leave-sharing plan.	Withhold	Taxable	Taxable
Newspaper carriers and vendors: Newspaper carriers under age 18; newspaper and magazine vendors buying at fixed prices and retaining receipts from sales to customers. See Pub. 15-A for information on statutory nonemployee status.	Exempt (withhold if both employer and employee voluntarily agree).	Exempt	Exempt

A-177

Special Classes of Employment and Special Types of Payments	Treatment Under Employment Taxes		
	Income Tax Withholding	Social Security and Medicare (including Additional Medicare Tax when wages are paid in excess of $200,000)	FUTA
Noncash payments:			
1. For household work, agricultural labor, and service not in the course of the employer's trade or business.	Exempt (withhold if both employer and employee voluntarily agree).	Exempt	Exempt
2. To certain retail commission salespersons ordinarily paid solely on a cash commission basis.	Optional with employer, except to the extent employee's supplemental wages during the year exceed $1 million.	Taxable	Taxable
Nonprofit organizations.	See Pub. 15-A.		
Officers or shareholders of an S Corporation: Distributions and other payments by an S corporation to a corporate officer or shareholder must be treated as wages to the extent the amounts are reasonable compensation for services to the corporation by an employee. See the Instructions for Form 1120S.	Withhold	Taxable	Taxable
Partners: Payments to general or limited partners of a partnership. See Pub. 541 for partner reporting rules.	Exempt	Exempt	Exempt
Railroads: Payments subject to the Railroad Retirement Act. See Pub. 915 for more details.	Withhold	Exempt	Exempt
Religious exemptions.	See Pub. 15-A and Pub. 517.		
Retirement and pension plans:			
1. Employer contributions to a qualified plan.	Exempt	Exempt	Exempt
2. Elective employee contributions and deferrals to a plan containing a qualified cash or deferred compensation arrangement (for example, 401(k)).	Generally exempt, but see section 402(g) for limitation.	Taxable	Taxable
3. Employer contributions to individual retirement accounts under simplified employee pension plan (SEP).	Generally exempt, but see section 402(g) for salary reduction SEP limitation.	Exempt, except for amounts contributed under a salary reduction SEP agreement.	
4. Employer contributions to section 403(b) annuities.	Generally exempt, but see section 402(g) for limitation.	Taxable if paid through a salary reduction agreement (written or otherwise).	
5. Employee salary reduction contributions to a SIMPLE retirement account.	Exempt	Taxable	Taxable
6. Distributions from qualified retirement and pension plans and section 403(b) annuities. See Pub. 15-A for information on pensions, annuities, and employer contributions to nonqualified deferred compensation arrangements.	Withhold, but recipient may elect exemption on Form W-4P in certain cases; mandatory 20% withholding applies to an eligible rollover distribution that isn't a direct rollover; exempt for direct rollover. See Pub. 15-A.	Exempt	Exempt
7. Employer contributions to a section 457(b) plan.	Generally exempt but see section 402(g) limitation.	Taxable	Taxable
8. Employee salary reduction contributions to a section 457(b) plan.	Generally exempt but see section 402(g) salary reduction limitation.	Taxable	Taxable
Salespersons:			
1. Common law employees.	Withhold	Taxable	Taxable
2. Statutory employees.	Exempt	Taxable	Taxable, except for full-time life insurance sales agents.
3. Statutory nonemployees (qualified real estate agents, direct sellers, and certain companion sitters). See Pub. 15-A for details.	Exempt	Exempt	Exempt

A-178

Special Classes of Employment and Special Types of Payments	Treatment Under Employment Taxes		
	Income Tax Withholding	Social Security and Medicare (including Additional Medicare Tax when wages are paid in excess of $200,000)	FUTA
Scholarships and fellowship grants (includible in income under section 117(c)).	Withhold	Taxability depends on the nature of the employment and the status of the organization. See *Students, scholars, trainees, teachers, etc.* below.	
Severance or dismissal pay.	Withhold	Taxable	Taxable
Service not in the course of the employer's trade or business (other than on a farm operated for profit or for household employment in private homes).	Withhold only if employee earns $50 or more in cash in a quarter and works on 24 or more different days in that quarter or in the preceding quarter.	Taxable if employee receives $100 or more in cash in a calendar year.	Taxable only if employee earns $50 or more in cash in a quarter and works on 24 or more different days in that quarter or in the preceding quarter.
Sick pay. See Pub. 15-A for more information.	Withhold	Exempt after end of 6 calendar months after the calendar month employee last worked for employer.	
Students, scholars, trainees, teachers, etc.:			
1. Student enrolled and regularly attending classes, performing services for:			
a. Private school, college, or university.	Withhold	Exempt	Exempt
b. Auxiliary nonprofit organization operated for and controlled by school, college, or university.	Withhold	Exempt unless services are covered by a section 218 (Social Security Act) agreement.	Exempt
c. Public school, college, or university.	Withhold	Exempt unless services are covered by a section 218 (Social Security Act) agreement.	Exempt
2. Full-time student performing service for academic credit, combining instruction with work experience as an integral part of the program.	Withhold	Taxable	Exempt unless program was established for or on behalf of an employer or group of employers.
3. Student nurse performing part-time services for nominal earnings at hospital as incidental part of training.	Withhold	Exempt	Exempt
4. Student employed by organized camps.	Withhold	Taxable	Exempt
5. Student, scholar, trainee, teacher, etc., as nonimmigrant alien under section 101(a)(15)(F), (J), (M), or (Q) of Immigration and Nationality Act (that is, aliens holding F-1, J-1, M-1, or Q-1 visas).	Withhold unless excepted by regulations.	Exempt if service is performed for purpose specified in section 101(a)(15)(F), (J), (M), or (Q) of Immigration and Nationality Act. However, these taxes may apply if the employee becomes a resident alien. See the special residency tests for exempt individuals in chapter 1 of Pub. 519.	
Supplemental unemployment compensation plan benefits.	Withhold	Exempt under certain conditions. See Pub. 15-A.	
Tips:			
1. If $20 or more in a month.	Withhold	Taxable	Taxable for all tips reported in writing to employer.
2. If less than $20 in a month. See section 6 for more information.	Exempt	Exempt	Exempt
Worker's compensation.	Exempt	Exempt	Exempt

16. Third Party Payer Arrangements

An employer may outsource some or all of its federal employment tax withholding, reporting and payment obligations. An employer who outsources payroll and related tax duties (that is, withholding, reporting, and paying over social security, Medicare, FUTA, and income taxes) to a third party payer, generally will remain responsible for those duties, including liability for the taxes.

If an employer outsources some or all of its payroll responsibilities, the employer should consider the following information.

- The employer remains responsible for federal tax deposits and other federal tax payments even though the employer may forward the tax amounts to the third party payer to make the deposits and payments. If the third party fails to make the deposits and payments, the IRS may assess penalties and interest on the employer's account. As the employer, you may be liable for all taxes, penalties, and interest due. The employer may also be held personally liable for certain unpaid federal taxes.

- If the employer's account has any issues, the IRS will send correspondence to the employer at the address of record. We strongly recommend that the employer maintain its address as the address of record with the IRS. Having correspondence sent to the address of the third party payer may significantly limit the employer's ability to be informed about tax matters involving the employer's business.

The following are common third party payers who an employer may contract with to perform payroll and related tax duties.

- Payroll service provider (PSP).

- Reporting agent.

- Agent with approved Form 2678.

- Payer designated under section 3504.

Payroll service provider (PSP). A PSP helps administer payroll and payroll related tax duties on behalf of the employer. A PSP may prepare paychecks for employees, prepare and file employment tax returns, prepare Form W-2, and make federal tax deposits and other federal tax payments. A PSP performs these functions using the EIN of the employer. A PSP isn't liable as either an employer or an agent of the employer for the employer's employment taxes. If an employer is using a PSP to perform its tax duties, the employer remains liable for its employment tax obligations, including liability for employment taxes.

An employer who uses a PSP should ensure the PSP is using EFTPS to make federal tax deposits on behalf of the employer so the employer can confirm that the payments are being made on its behalf.

Reporting agent. A reporting agent is a type of PSP. A reporting agent helps administer payroll and payroll related tax duties on behalf of the employer, including authorization to electronically sign and file forms set forth on Form 8655. An employer uses Form 8655 to authorize a reporting agent to perform functions on behalf of the employer. A reporting agent performs these functions using the EIN of the employer. A reporting agent isn't liable as either an employer or an agent of the employer for the employer's employment taxes. If an employer is using a reporting agent to perform its tax duties, the employer remains liable for its employment obligations, including liability for employment taxes.

A reporting agent must use EFTPS to make federal tax deposits on behalf of an employer. The employer has access to EFTPS to confirm federal tax deposits were made on its behalf.

For more information on reporting agents, see Revenue Procedure 2012-32, 2012-34 I.R.B. 267, at *www.irs.gov/ irb/2012-34_IRB/ar08.html* and Pub. 1474, Technical Specifications Guide for Reporting Agent Authorization and Federal Tax Depositors.

Agent with an approved Form 2678. An agent with an approved Form 2678 helps administer payroll and related tax duties on behalf of the employer. An agent authorized under section 3504 may pay wages or compensation to some or all of the employees of an employer, prepare and file employment tax returns as set forth on Form 2678, prepare Form W-2, and make federal tax deposits and other federal tax payments. An employer uses Form 2678 to request authorization to appoint an agent to perform functions on behalf of the employer. An agent with an approved Form 2678 is authorized to perform these functions using its own EIN. The agent files a Schedule R (Form 941) to allocate wages and taxes to the employers it represents as an agent.

If an employer is using an agent with an approved Form 2678 to perform its tax duties, the agent and the employer are jointly liable for the employment taxes and related tax duties for which the agent is authorized to perform.

Form 2678 doesn't apply to FUTA taxes reportable on Form 940 unless the employer is a home care service recipient receiving home care services through a program administered by a federal, state, or local government agency.

For more information on an agent with an approved Form 2678, see Revenue Procedure 2013-39, 2013-52 I.R.B. 830, at *www.irs.gov/irb/2013-52_IRB/ar15.html*.

Payer designated under section 3504. In certain circumstances, the IRS may designate a third party payer to perform the acts of an employer. The IRS will designate a third party payer on behalf of an employer if the third party has a service agreement with the employer. A service agreement is an agreement between the third party payer and an employer in which the third party payer (1) asserts it is the employer of individuals performing services for the employer; (2) pays wages to the individuals that perform services for the employer; and (3) assumes responsibility to withhold, report, and pay federal employment taxes for the wages it pays to the individuals that perform services for the employer.

A payer designated under section 3504 performs tax duties under the service agreement using its own EIN. If the IRS designates a third party payer under section 3504, the designated payer and the employer are jointly liable for the employment taxes and related tax duties for which the third party payer is designated.

For more information on a payer designated under section 3504, see Regulations section 31.3504-2.

17. How To Use the Income Tax Withholding Tables

There are several ways to figure income tax withholding. The following methods of withholding are based on the information you get from your employees on Form W-4. See section 9 for more information on Form W-4.

 Adjustments aren't required when there will be more than the usual number of pay periods, for example, 27 biweekly pay dates instead of 26.

Wage Bracket Method

Under the wage bracket method, find the proper table (on pages 46–65) for your payroll period and the employee's marital status as shown on his or her Form W-4. Then, based on the number of withholding allowances claimed on the Form W-4 and the amount of wages, find the amount of income tax to withhold. If your employee is claiming more than 10 withholding allowances, see below.

If you can't use the wage bracket tables because wages exceed the amount shown in the last bracket of the table, use the percentage method of withholding described below. Be sure to reduce wages by the amount of total withholding allowances in *Table 5* before using the percentage method tables (pages 44–45).

Adjusting wage bracket withholding for employees claiming more than 10 withholding allowances. The wage bracket tables can be used if an employee claims up to 10 allowances. More than 10 allowances may be claimed because of the special withholding allowance, additional allowances for deductions and credits, and the system itself.

Adapt the tables to more than 10 allowances as follows:

1. Multiply the number of withholding allowances over 10 by the allowance value for the payroll period. The allowance values are in *Table 5* below.

2. Subtract the result from the employee's wages.

3. On this amount, find and withhold the tax in the column for 10 allowances.

This is a voluntary method. If you use the wage bracket tables, you may continue to withhold the amount in the "10" column when your employee has more than 10 allowances, using the method above. You can also use any other method described next.

Percentage Method

If you don't want to use the wage bracket tables on pages 46–65 to figure how much income tax to withhold, you can use a percentage computation based on *Table 5* below and the appropriate rate table. This method works for any number of withholding allowances the employee claims and any amount of wages.

Use these steps to figure the income tax to withhold under the percentage method.

1. Multiply one withholding allowance for your payroll period (see *Table 5* below) by the number of allowances the employee claims.

2. Subtract that amount from the employee's wages.

3. Determine the amount to withhold from the appropriate table on pages 44–45.

Table 5. **Percentage Method—2016 Amount for One Withholding Allowance**

Payroll Period	One Withholding Allowance
Weekly	$ 77.90
Biweekly	155.80
Semimonthly	168.80
Monthly	337.50
Quarterly	1,012.50
Semiannually	2,025.00
Annually	4,050.00
Daily or miscellaneous (each day of the payroll period)	15.60

Example. An unmarried employee is paid $800 weekly. This employee has in effect a Form W-4 claiming two withholding allowances. Using the percentage method, figure the income tax to withhold as follows:

1.	Total wage payment		$800.00
2.	One allowance	$77.90	
3.	Allowances claimed on Form W-4 . .	2	
4.	Multiply line 2 by line 3		$155.80
5	Amount subject to withholding (subtract line 4 from line 1)		$644.20
6.	Tax to be withheld on $644.20 from Table 1—single person, page 44 . . .		$81.23

To figure the income tax to withhold, you may reduce the last digit of the wages to zero, or figure the wages to the nearest dollar.

Annual income tax withholding. Figure the income tax to withhold on annual wages under the *Percentage Method* for an annual payroll period. Then prorate the tax back to the payroll period.

Example. A married person claims four withholding allowances. She is paid $1,000 a week. Multiply the weekly wages by 52 weeks to figure the annual wage of $52,000. Subtract $16,200 (the value of four withholding allowances for 2016) for a balance of $35,800. Using the table for the annual payroll period on page 45, $3,160.00 is withheld. Divide the annual tax by 52. The weekly income tax to withhold is $60.77.

Alternative Methods of Income Tax Withholding

Rather than the _Wage Bracket Method_ or _Percentage Method_ described in this section, you can use an alternative method to withhold income tax. Pub. 15-A describes these alternative methods and contains:

- Formula tables for percentage method withholding (for automated payroll systems),

- Wage bracket percentage method tables (for automated payroll systems), and

- Combined income, social security, and Medicare tax withholding tables.

Some of the alternative methods explained in Pub. 15-A are annualized wages, average estimated wages, cumulative wages, and part-year employment.

A-182

Percentage Method Tables for Income Tax Withholding

(For Wages Paid in 2016)

TABLE 1—WEEKLY Payroll Period

(a) SINGLE person (including head of household)—

If the amount of wages (after subtracting withholding allowances) is: Not over $43 . . . . The amount of income tax to withhold is: $0

Over—	But not over—		of excess over—
$43	—$222 . .	$0.00 plus 10%	—$43
$222	—$767 . .	$17.90 plus 15%	—$222
$767	—$1,796 . .	$99.65 plus 25%	—$767
$1,796	—$3,700 . .	$356.90 plus 28%	—$1,796
$3,700	—$7,992 . .	$890.02 plus 33%	—$3,700
$7,992	—$8,025 . .	$2,306.38 plus 35%	—$7,992
$8,025	. . . .	$2,317.93 plus 39.6%	—$8,025

(b) MARRIED person—

If the amount of wages (after subtracting withholding allowances) is: Not over $164 . . . . The amount of income tax to withhold is: $0

Over—	But not over—		of excess over—
$164	—$521 . .	$0.00 plus 10%	—$164
$521	—$1,613 . .	$35.70 plus 15%	—$521
$1,613	—$3,086 . .	$199.50 plus 25%	—$1,613
$3,086	—$4,615 . .	$567.75 plus 28%	—$3,086
$4,615	—$8,113 . .	$995.87 plus 33%	—$4,615
$8,113	—$9,144 . .	$2,150.21 plus 35%	—$8,113
$9,144	. . . .	$2,511.06 plus 39.6%	—$9,144

TABLE 2—BIWEEKLY Payroll Period

(a) SINGLE person (including head of household)—

If the amount of wages (after subtracting withholding allowances) is: Not over $87 . . . . The amount of income tax to withhold is: $0

Over—	But not over—		of excess over—
$87	—$443 . .	$0.00 plus 10%	—$87
$443	—$1,535 . .	$35.60 plus 15%	—$443
$1,535	—$3,592 . .	$199.40 plus 25%	—$1,535
$3,592	—$7,400 . .	$713.65 plus 28%	—$3,592
$7,400	—$15,985 . .	$1,779.89 plus 33%	—$7,400
$15,985	—$16,050 . .	$4,612.94 plus 35%	—$15,985
$16,050	. . . .	$4,635.69 plus 39.6%	—$16,050

(b) MARRIED person—

If the amount of wages (after subtracting withholding allowances) is: Not over $329 . . . . The amount of income tax to withhold is: $0

Over—	But not over—		of excess over—
$329	—$1,042 . .	$0.00 plus 10%	—$329
$1,042	—$3,225 . .	$71.30 plus 15%	—$1,042
$3,225	—$6,171 . .	$398.75 plus 25%	—$3,225
$6,171	—$9,231 . .	$1,135.25 plus 28%	—$6,171
$9,231	—$16,227 . .	$1,992.05 plus 33%	—$9,231
$16,227	—$18,288 . .	$4,300.73 plus 35%	—$16,227
$18,288	. . . .	$5,022.08 plus 39.6%	—$18,288

TABLE 3—SEMIMONTHLY Payroll Period

(a) SINGLE person (including head of household)—

If the amount of wages (after subtracting withholding allowances) is: Not over $94 . . . . The amount of income tax to withhold is: $0

Over—	But not over—		of excess over—
$94	—$480 . .	$0.00 plus 10%	—$94
$480	—$1,663 . .	$38.60 plus 15%	—$480
$1,663	—$3,892 . .	$216.05 plus 25%	—$1,663
$3,892	—$8,017 . .	$773.30 plus 28%	—$3,892
$8,017	—$17,317 . .	$1,928.30 plus 33%	—$8,017
$17,317	—$17,388 . .	$4,997.30 plus 35%	—$17,317
$17,388	. . . .	$5,022.15 plus 39.6%	—$17,388

(b) MARRIED person—

If the amount of wages (after subtracting withholding allowances) is: Not over $356 . . . . The amount of income tax to withhold is: $0

Over—	But not over—		of excess over—
$356	—$1,129 . .	$0.00 plus 10%	—$356
$1,129	—$3,494 . .	$77.30 plus 15%	—$1,129
$3,494	—$6,685 . .	$432.05 plus 25%	—$3,494
$6,685	—$10,000 . .	$1,229.80 plus 28%	—$6,685
$10,000	—$17,579 . .	$2,158.00 plus 33%	—$10,000
$17,579	—$19,813 . .	$4,659.07 plus 35%	—$17,579
$19,813	. . . .	$5,440.97 plus 39.6%	—$19,813

TABLE 4—MONTHLY Payroll Period

(a) SINGLE person (including head of household)—

If the amount of wages (after subtracting withholding allowances) is: Not over $188 . . . . The amount of income tax to withhold is: $0

Over—	But not over—		of excess over—
$188	—$960 . .	$0.00 plus 10%	—$188
$960	—$3,325 . .	$77.20 plus 15%	—$960
$3,325	—$7,783 . .	$431.95 plus 25%	—$3,325
$7,783	—$16,033 . .	$1,546.45 plus 28%	—$7,783
$16,033	—$34,633 . .	$3,856.45 plus 33%	—$16,033
$34,633	—$34,775 . .	$9,994.45 plus 35%	—$34,633
$34,775	. . . .	$10,044.15 plus 39.6%	—$34,775

(b) MARRIED person—

If the amount of wages (after subtracting withholding allowances) is: Not over $713 . . . . The amount of income tax to withhold is: $0

Over—	But not over—		of excess over—
$713	—$2,258 . .	$0.00 plus 10%	—$713
$2,258	—$6,988 . .	$154.50 plus 15%	—$2,258
$6,988	—$13,371 . .	$864.00 plus 25%	—$6,988
$13,371	—$20,000 . .	$2,459.75 plus 28%	—$13,371
$20,000	—$35,158 . .	$4,315.87 plus 33%	—$20,000
$35,158	—$39,625 . .	$9,318.01 plus 35%	—$35,158
$39,625	. . . .	$10,881.46 plus 39.6%	—$39,625

A-183

Percentage Method Tables for Income Tax Withholding (continued)

(For Wages Paid in 2016)

TABLE 5—QUARTERLY Payroll Period

(a) SINGLE person (including head of household)—				(b) MARRIED person—			
If the amount of wages (after subtracting withholding allowances) is:		The amount of income tax to withhold is:		If the amount of wages (after subtracting withholding allowances) is:		The amount of income tax to withhold is:	
Not over $563		$0		Not over $2,138		$0	
Over—	But not over—		of excess over—	Over—	But not over—		of excess over—
$563	—$2,881 . .	$0.00 plus 10%	—$563	$2,138	—$6,775 . .	$0.00 plus 10%	—$2,138
$2,881	—$9,975 . .	$231.80 plus 15%	—$2,881	$6,775	—$20,963 . .	$463.70 plus 15%	—$6,775
$9,975	—$23,350 . .	$1,295.90 plus 25%	—$9,975	$20,963	—$40,113 . .	$2,591.90 plus 25%	—$20,963
$23,350	—$48,100 . .	$4,639.65 plus 28%	—$23,350	$40,113	—$60,000 . .	$7,379.40 plus 28%	—$40,113
$48,100	—$103,900 . .	$11,569.65 plus 33%	—$48,100	$60,000	—$105,475 . .	$12,947.76 plus 33%	—$60,000
$103,900	—$104,325 . .	$29,983.65 plus 35%	—$103,900	$105,475	—$118,875 . .	$27,954.51 plus 35%	—$105,475
$104,325	. . . .	$30,132.40 plus 39.6%	—$104,325	$118,875	. . . .	$32,644.51 plus 39.6%	—$118,875

TABLE 6—SEMIANNUAL Payroll Period

(a) SINGLE person (including head of household)—				(b) MARRIED person—			
If the amount of wages (after subtracting withholding allowances) is:		The amount of income tax to withhold is:		If the amount of wages (after subtracting withholding allowances) is:		The amount of income tax to withhold is:	
Not over $1,125		$0		Not over $4,275		$0	
Over—	But not over—		of excess over—	Over—	But not over—		of excess over—
$1,125	—$5,763 . .	$0.00 plus 10%	—$1,125	$4,275	—$13,550 . .	$0.00 plus 10%	—$4,275
$5,763	—$19,950 . .	$463.80 plus 15%	—$5,763	$13,550	—$41,925 . .	$927.50 plus 15%	—$13,550
$19,950	—$46,700 . .	$2,591.85 plus 25%	—$19,950	$41,925	—$80,225 . .	$5,183.75 plus 25%	—$41,925
$46,700	—$96,200 . .	$9,279.35 plus 28%	—$46,700	$80,225	—$120,000 . .	$14,758.75 plus 28%	—$80,225
$96,200	—$207,800 . .	$23,139.35 plus 33%	—$96,200	$120,000	—$210,950 . .	$25,895.75 plus 33%	—$120,000
$207,800	—$208,650 . .	$59,967.35 plus 35%	—$207,800	$210,950	—$237,750 . .	$55,909.25 plus 35%	—$210,950
$208,650	. . . .	$60,264.85 plus 39.6%	—$208,650	$237,750	. . . .	$65,289.25 plus 39.6%	—$237,750

TABLE 7—ANNUAL Payroll Period

(a) SINGLE person (including head of household)—				(b) MARRIED person—			
If the amount of wages (after subtracting withholding allowances) is:		The amount of income tax to withhold is:		If the amount of wages (after subtracting withholding allowances) is:		The amount of income tax to withhold is:	
Not over $2,250		$0		Not over $8,550		$0	
Over—	But not over—		of excess over—	Over—	But not over—		of excess over—
$2,250	—$11,525 . .	$0.00 plus 10%	—$2,250	$8,550	—$27,100 . .	$0.00 plus 10%	—$8,550
$11,525	—$39,900 . .	$927.50 plus 15%	—$11,525	$27,100	—$83,850 . .	$1,855.00 plus 15%	—$27,100
$39,900	—$93,400 . .	$5,183.75 plus 25%	—$39,900	$83,850	—$160,450 . .	$10,367.50 plus 25%	—$83,850
$93,400	—$192,400 . .	$18,558.75 plus 28%	—$93,400	$160,450	—$240,000 . .	$29,517.50 plus 28%	—$160,450
$192,400	—$415,600 . .	$46,278.75 plus 33%	—$192,400	$240,000	—$421,900 . .	$51,791.50 plus 33%	—$240,000
$415,600	—$417,300 . .	$119,934.75 plus 35%	—$415,600	$421,900	—$475,500 . .	$111,818.50 plus 35%	—$421,900
$417,300	. . . .	$120,529.75 plus 39.6%	—$417,300	$475,500	. . . .	$130,578.50 plus 39.6%	—$475,500

TABLE 8—DAILY or MISCELLANEOUS Payroll Period

(a) SINGLE person (including head of household)—				(b) MARRIED person—			
If the amount of wages (after subtracting withholding allowances) divided by the number of days in the payroll period is:		The amount of income tax to withhold per day is:		If the amount of wages (after subtracting withholding allowances) divided by the number of days in the payroll period is:		The amount of income tax to withhold per day is:	
Not over $8.70		$0		Not over $32.90		$0	
Over—	But not over—		of excess over—	Over—	But not over—		of excess over—
$8.70	—$44.30 . .	$0.00 plus 10%	—$8.70	$32.90	—$104.20 . .	$0.00 plus 10%	—$32.90
$44.30	—$153.50 . .	$3.56 plus 15%	—$44.30	$104.20	—$322.50 . .	$7.13 plus 15%	—$104.20
$153.50	—$359.20 . .	$19.94 plus 25%	—$153.50	$322.50	—$617.10 . .	$39.88 plus 25%	—$322.50
$359.20	—$740.00 . .	$71.37 plus 28%	—$359.20	$617.10	—$923.10 . .	$113.53 plus 28%	—$617.10
$740.00	—$1,598.50 . .	$177.99 plus 33%	—$740.00	$923.10	—$1,622.70 . .	$199.21 plus 33%	—$923.10
$1,598.50	—$1,605.00 . .	$461.30 plus 35%	—$1,598.50	$1,622.70	—$1,828.80 . .	$430.08 plus 35%	—$1,622.70
$1,605.00	. . . .	$463.58 plus 39.6%	—$1,605.00	$1,828.80	. . . .	$502.22 plus 39.6%	—$1,828.80

A-184

Wage Bracket Method Tables for Income Tax Withholding

SINGLE Persons—WEEKLY Payroll Period

(For Wages Paid through December 31, 2016)

And the wages are—		And the number of withholding allowances claimed is—										
At least	But less than	0	1	2	3	4	5	6	7	8	9	10
		The amount of income tax to be withheld is—										
$0	$55	$0	$0	$0	$0	$0	$0	$0	$0	$0	$0	$0
55	60	1	0	0	0	0	0	0	0	0	0	0
60	65	2	0	0	0	0	0	0	0	0	0	0
65	70	2	0	0	0	0	0	0	0	0	0	0
70	75	3	0	0	0	0	0	0	0	0	0	0
75	80	3	0	0	0	0	0	0	0	0	0	0
80	85	4	0	0	0	0	0	0	0	0	0	0
85	90	4	0	0	0	0	0	0	0	0	0	0
90	95	5	0	0	0	0	0	0	0	0	0	0
95	100	5	0	0	0	0	0	0	0	0	0	0
100	105	6	0	0	0	0	0	0	0	0	0	0
105	110	6	0	0	0	0	0	0	0	0	0	0
110	115	7	0	0	0	0	0	0	0	0	0	0
115	120	7	0	0	0	0	0	0	0	0	0	0
120	125	8	0	0	0	0	0	0	0	0	0	0
125	130	8	1	0	0	0	0	0	0	0	0	0
130	135	9	1	0	0	0	0	0	0	0	0	0
135	140	9	2	0	0	0	0	0	0	0	0	0
140	145	10	2	0	0	0	0	0	0	0	0	0
145	150	10	3	0	0	0	0	0	0	0	0	0
150	155	11	3	0	0	0	0	0	0	0	0	0
155	160	11	4	0	0	0	0	0	0	0	0	0
160	165	12	4	0	0	0	0	0	0	0	0	0
165	170	12	5	0	0	0	0	0	0	0	0	0
170	175	13	5	0	0	0	0	0	0	0	0	0
175	180	13	6	0	0	0	0	0	0	0	0	0
180	185	14	6	0	0	0	0	0	0	0	0	0
185	190	14	7	0	0	0	0	0	0	0	0	0
190	195	15	7	0	0	0	0	0	0	0	0	0
195	200	15	8	0	0	0	0	0	0	0	0	0
200	210	16	8	1	0	0	0	0	0	0	0	0
210	220	17	9	2	0	0	0	0	0	0	0	0
220	230	18	10	3	0	0	0	0	0	0	0	0
230	240	20	11	4	0	0	0	0	0	0	0	0
240	250	21	12	5	0	0	0	0	0	0	0	0
250	260	23	13	6	0	0	0	0	0	0	0	0
260	270	24	14	7	0	0	0	0	0	0	0	0
270	280	26	15	8	0	0	0	0	0	0	0	0
280	290	27	16	9	1	0	0	0	0	0	0	0
290	300	29	17	10	2	0	0	0	0	0	0	0
300	310	30	19	11	3	0	0	0	0	0	0	0
310	320	32	20	12	4	0	0	0	0	0	0	0
320	330	33	22	13	5	0	0	0	0	0	0	0
330	340	35	23	14	6	0	0	0	0	0	0	0
340	350	36	25	15	7	0	0	0	0	0	0	0
350	360	38	26	16	8	0	0	0	0	0	0	0
360	370	39	28	17	9	1	0	0	0	0	0	0
370	380	41	29	18	10	2	0	0	0	0	0	0
380	390	42	31	19	11	3	0	0	0	0	0	0
390	400	44	32	20	12	4	0	0	0	0	0	0
400	410	45	34	22	13	5	0	0	0	0	0	0
410	420	47	35	23	14	6	0	0	0	0	0	0
420	430	48	37	25	15	7	0	0	0	0	0	0
430	440	50	38	26	16	8	0	0	0	0	0	0
440	450	51	40	28	17	9	1	0	0	0	0	0
450	460	53	41	29	18	10	2	0	0	0	0	0
460	470	54	43	31	19	11	3	0	0	0	0	0
470	480	56	44	32	21	12	4	0	0	0	0	0
480	490	57	46	34	22	13	5	0	0	0	0	0
490	500	59	47	35	24	14	6	0	0	0	0	0
500	510	60	49	37	25	15	7	0	0	0	0	0
510	520	62	50	38	27	16	8	0	0	0	0	0
520	530	63	52	40	28	17	9	1	0	0	0	0
530	540	65	53	41	30	18	10	2	0	0	0	0
540	550	66	55	43	31	20	11	3	0	0	0	0
550	560	68	56	44	33	21	12	4	0	0	0	0
560	570	69	58	46	34	23	13	5	0	0	0	0
570	580	71	59	47	36	24	14	6	0	0	0	0
580	590	72	61	49	37	26	15	7	0	0	0	0
590	600	74	62	50	39	27	16	8	1	0	0	0

Wage Bracket Method Tables for Income Tax Withholding

SINGLE Persons—WEEKLY Payroll Period

(For Wages Paid through December 31, 2016)

And the wages are—		And the number of withholding allowances claimed is—										
At least	But less than	0	1	2	3	4	5	6	7	8	9	10
		The amount of income tax to be withheld is—										
$600	$610	$75	$64	$52	$40	$29	$17	$9	$2	$0	$0	$0
610	620	77	65	53	42	30	18	10	3	0	0	0
620	630	78	67	55	43	32	20	11	4	0	0	0
630	640	80	68	56	45	33	21	12	5	0	0	0
640	650	81	70	58	46	35	23	13	6	0	0	0
650	660	83	71	59	48	36	24	14	7	0	0	0
660	670	84	73	61	49	38	26	15	8	0	0	0
670	680	86	74	62	51	39	27	16	9	1	0	0
680	690	87	76	64	52	41	29	17	10	2	0	0
690	700	89	77	65	54	42	30	19	11	3	0	0
700	710	90	79	67	55	44	32	20	12	4	0	0
710	720	92	80	68	57	45	33	22	13	5	0	0
720	730	93	82	70	58	47	35	23	14	6	0	0
730	740	95	83	71	60	48	36	25	15	7	0	0
740	750	96	85	73	61	50	38	26	16	8	0	0
750	760	98	86	74	63	51	39	28	17	9	1	0
760	770	99	88	76	64	53	41	29	18	10	2	0
770	780	102	89	77	66	54	42	31	19	11	3	0
780	790	104	91	79	67	56	44	32	21	12	4	0
790	800	107	92	80	69	57	45	34	22	13	5	0
800	810	109	94	82	70	59	47	35	24	14	6	0
810	820	112	95	83	72	60	48	37	25	15	7	0
820	830	114	97	85	73	62	50	38	27	16	8	0
830	840	117	98	86	75	63	51	40	28	17	9	1
840	850	119	100	88	76	65	53	41	30	18	10	2
850	860	122	102	89	78	66	54	43	31	19	11	3
860	870	124	105	91	79	68	56	44	33	21	12	4
870	880	127	107	92	81	69	57	46	34	22	13	5
880	890	129	110	94	82	71	59	47	36	24	14	6
890	900	132	112	95	84	72	60	49	37	25	15	7
900	910	134	115	97	85	74	62	50	39	27	16	8
910	920	137	117	98	87	75	63	52	40	28	17	9
920	930	139	120	100	88	77	65	53	42	30	18	10
930	940	142	122	103	90	78	66	55	43	31	20	11
940	950	144	125	105	91	80	68	56	45	33	21	12
950	960	147	127	108	93	81	69	58	46	34	23	13
960	970	149	130	110	94	83	71	59	48	36	24	14
970	980	152	132	113	96	84	72	61	49	37	26	15
980	990	154	135	115	97	86	74	62	51	39	27	16
990	1,000	157	137	118	99	87	75	64	52	40	29	17
1,000	1,010	159	140	120	101	89	77	65	54	42	30	19
1,010	1,020	162	142	123	103	90	78	67	55	43	32	20
1,020	1,030	164	145	125	106	92	80	68	57	45	33	22
1,030	1,040	167	147	128	108	93	81	70	58	46	35	23
1,040	1,050	169	150	130	111	95	83	71	60	48	36	25
1,050	1,060	172	152	133	113	96	84	73	61	49	38	26
1,060	1,070	174	155	135	116	98	86	74	63	51	39	28
1,070	1,080	177	157	138	118	99	87	76	64	52	41	29
1,080	1,090	179	160	140	121	101	89	77	66	54	42	31
1,090	1,100	182	162	143	123	104	90	79	67	55	44	32
1,100	1,110	184	165	145	126	106	92	80	69	57	45	34
1,110	1,120	187	167	148	128	109	93	82	70	58	47	35
1,120	1,130	189	170	150	131	111	95	83	72	60	48	37
1,130	1,140	192	172	153	133	114	96	85	73	61	50	38
1,140	1,150	194	175	155	136	116	98	86	75	63	51	40
1,150	1,160	197	177	158	138	119	99	88	76	64	53	41
1,160	1,170	199	180	160	141	121	102	89	78	66	54	43
1,170	1,180	202	182	163	143	124	104	91	79	67	56	44
1,180	1,190	204	185	165	146	126	107	92	81	69	57	46
1,190	1,200	207	187	168	148	129	109	94	82	70	59	47
1,200	1,210	209	190	170	151	131	112	95	84	72	60	49
1,210	1,220	212	192	173	153	134	114	97	85	73	62	50
1,220	1,230	214	195	175	156	136	117	98	87	75	63	52
1,230	1,240	217	197	178	158	139	119	100	88	76	65	53
1,240	1,250	219	200	180	161	141	122	102	90	78	66	55

$1,250 and over	Use Table 1(a) for a **SINGLE person** on page 44. Also see the instructions on page 42.

A-186

Wage Bracket Method Tables for Income Tax Withholding

MARRIED Persons—WEEKLY Payroll Period

(For Wages Paid through December 31, 2016)

And the wages are–		And the number of withholding allowances claimed is—										
At least	But less than	0	1	2	3	4	5	6	7	8	9	10
		The amount of income tax to be withheld is—										
$ 0	$170	$0	$0	$0	$0	$0	$0	$0	$0	$0	$0	$0
170	175	1	0	0	0	0	0	0	0	0	0	0
175	180	1	0	0	0	0	0	0	0	0	0	0
180	185	2	0	0	0	0	0	0	0	0	0	0
185	190	2	0	0	0	0	0	0	0	0	0	0
190	195	3	0	0	0	0	0	0	0	0	0	0
195	200	3	0	0	0	0	0	0	0	0	0	0
200	210	4	0	0	0	0	0	0	0	0	0	0
210	220	5	0	0	0	0	0	0	0	0	0	0
220	230	6	0	0	0	0	0	0	0	0	0	0
230	240	7	0	0	0	0	0	0	0	0	0	0
240	250	8	0	0	0	0	0	0	0	0	0	0
250	260	9	1	0	0	0	0	0	0	0	0	0
260	270	10	2	0	0	0	0	0	0	0	0	0
270	280	11	3	0	0	0	0	0	0	0	0	0
280	290	12	4	0	0	0	0	0	0	0	0	0
290	300	13	5	0	0	0	0	0	0	0	0	0
300	310	14	6	0	0	0	0	0	0	0	0	0
310	320	15	7	0	0	0	0	0	0	0	0	0
320	330	16	8	0	0	0	0	0	0	0	0	0
330	340	17	9	1	0	0	0	0	0	0	0	0
340	350	18	10	2	0	0	0	0	0	0	0	0
350	360	19	11	3	0	0	0	0	0	0	0	0
360	370	20	12	4	0	0	0	0	0	0	0	0
370	380	21	13	5	0	0	0	0	0	0	0	0
380	390	22	14	6	0	0	0	0	0	0	0	0
390	400	23	15	7	0	0	0	0	0	0	0	0
400	410	24	16	8	1	0	0	0	0	0	0	0
410	420	25	17	9	2	0	0	0	0	0	0	0
420	430	26	18	10	3	0	0	0	0	0	0	0
430	440	27	19	11	4	0	0	0	0	0	0	0
440	450	28	20	12	5	0	0	0	0	0	0	0
450	460	29	21	13	6	0	0	0	0	0	0	0
460	470	30	22	14	7	0	0	0	0	0	0	0
470	480	31	23	15	8	0	0	0	0	0	0	0
480	490	32	24	16	9	1	0	0	0	0	0	0
490	500	33	25	17	10	2	0	0	0	0	0	0
500	510	34	26	18	11	3	0	0	0	0	0	0
510	520	35	27	19	12	4	0	0	0	0	0	0
520	530	36	28	20	13	5	0	0	0	0	0	0
530	540	38	29	21	14	6	0	0	0	0	0	0
540	550	39	30	22	15	7	0	0	0	0	0	0
550	560	41	31	23	16	8	0	0	0	0	0	0
560	570	42	32	24	17	9	1	0	0	0	0	0
570	580	44	33	25	18	10	2	0	0	0	0	0
580	590	45	34	26	19	11	3	0	0	0	0	0
590	600	47	35	27	20	12	4	0	0	0	0	0
600	610	48	37	28	21	13	5	0	0	0	0	0
610	620	50	38	29	22	14	6	0	0	0	0	0
620	630	51	40	30	23	15	7	0	0	0	0	0
630	640	53	41	31	24	16	8	0	0	0	0	0
640	650	54	43	32	25	17	9	1	0	0	0	0
650	660	56	44	33	26	18	10	2	0	0	0	0
660	670	57	46	34	27	19	11	3	0	0	0	0
670	680	59	47	35	28	20	12	4	0	0	0	0
680	690	60	49	37	29	21	13	5	0	0	0	0
690	700	62	50	38	30	22	14	6	0	0	0	0
700	710	63	52	40	31	23	15	7	0	0	0	0
710	720	65	53	41	32	24	16	8	1	0	0	0
720	730	66	55	43	33	25	17	9	2	0	0	0
730	740	68	56	44	34	26	18	10	3	0	0	0
740	750	69	58	46	35	27	19	11	4	0	0	0
750	760	71	59	47	36	28	20	12	5	0	0	0
760	770	72	61	49	37	29	21	13	6	0	0	0
770	780	74	62	50	39	30	22	14	7	0	0	0
780	790	75	64	52	40	31	23	15	8	0	0	0
790	800	77	65	53	42	32	24	16	9	1	0	0

Wage Bracket Method Tables for Income Tax Withholding

MARRIED Persons—WEEKLY Payroll Period

(For Wages Paid through December 31, 2016)

And the wages are–		And the number of withholding allowances claimed is—										
At least	But less than	0	1	2	3	4	5	6	7	8	9	10
		The amount of income tax to be withheld is—										
$800	$810	$78	$67	$55	$43	$33	$25	$17	$10	$2	$0	$0
810	820	80	68	56	45	34	26	18	11	3	0	0
820	830	81	70	58	46	35	27	19	12	4	0	0
830	840	83	71	59	48	36	28	20	13	5	0	0
840	850	84	73	61	49	38	29	21	14	6	0	0
850	860	86	74	62	51	39	30	22	15	7	0	0
860	870	87	76	64	52	41	31	23	16	8	0	0
870	880	89	77	65	54	42	32	24	17	9	1	0
880	890	90	79	67	55	44	33	25	18	10	2	0
890	900	92	80	68	57	45	34	26	19	11	3	0
900	910	93	82	70	58	47	35	27	20	12	4	0
910	920	95	83	71	60	48	36	28	21	13	5	0
920	930	96	85	73	61	50	38	29	22	14	6	0
930	940	98	86	74	63	51	39	30	23	15	7	0
940	950	99	88	76	64	53	41	31	24	16	8	0
950	960	101	89	77	66	54	42	32	25	17	9	1
960	970	102	91	79	67	56	44	33	26	18	10	2
970	980	104	92	80	69	57	45	34	27	19	11	3
980	990	105	94	82	70	59	47	35	28	20	12	4
990	1,000	107	95	83	72	60	48	37	29	21	13	5
1,000	1,010	108	97	85	73	62	50	38	30	22	14	6
1,010	1,020	110	98	86	75	63	51	40	31	23	15	7
1,020	1,030	111	100	88	76	65	53	41	32	24	16	8
1,030	1,040	113	101	89	78	66	54	43	33	25	17	9
1,040	1,050	114	103	91	79	68	56	44	34	26	18	10
1,050	1,060	116	104	92	81	69	57	46	35	27	19	11
1,060	1,070	117	106	94	82	71	59	47	36	28	20	12
1,070	1,080	119	107	95	84	72	60	49	37	29	21	13
1,080	1,090	120	109	97	85	74	62	50	38	30	22	14
1,090	1,100	122	110	98	87	75	63	52	40	31	23	15
1,100	1,110	123	112	100	88	77	65	53	41	32	24	16
1,110	1,120	125	113	101	90	78	66	55	43	33	25	17
1,120	1,130	126	115	103	91	80	68	56	44	34	26	18
1,130	1,140	128	116	104	93	81	69	58	46	35	27	19
1,140	1,150	129	118	106	94	83	71	59	47	36	28	20
1,150	1,160	131	119	107	96	84	72	61	49	37	29	21
1,160	1,170	132	121	109	97	86	74	62	50	39	30	22
1,170	1,180	134	122	110	99	87	75	64	52	40	31	23
1,180	1,190	135	124	112	100	89	77	65	53	42	32	24
1,190	1,200	137	125	113	102	90	78	67	55	43	33	25
1,200	1,210	138	127	115	103	92	80	68	56	45	34	26
1,210	1,220	140	128	116	105	93	81	70	58	46	35	27
1,220	1,230	141	130	118	106	95	83	71	59	48	36	28
1,230	1,240	143	131	119	108	96	84	73	61	49	38	29
1,240	1,250	144	133	121	109	98	86	74	62	51	39	30
1,250	1,260	146	134	122	111	99	87	76	64	52	41	31
1,260	1,270	147	136	124	112	101	89	77	65	54	42	32
1,270	1,280	149	137	125	114	102	90	79	67	55	44	33
1,280	1,290	150	139	127	115	104	92	80	68	57	45	34
1,290	1,300	152	140	128	117	105	93	82	70	58	47	35
1,300	1,310	153	142	130	118	107	95	83	71	60	48	36
1,310	1,320	155	143	131	120	108	96	85	73	61	50	38
1,320	1,330	156	145	133	121	110	98	86	74	63	51	39
1,330	1,340	158	146	134	123	111	99	88	76	64	53	41
1,340	1,350	159	148	136	124	113	101	89	77	66	54	42
1,350	1,360	161	149	137	126	114	102	91	79	67	56	44
1,360	1,370	162	151	139	127	116	104	92	80	69	57	45
1,370	1,380	164	152	140	129	117	105	94	82	70	59	47
1,380	1,390	165	154	142	130	119	107	95	83	72	60	48
1,390	1,400	167	155	143	132	120	108	97	85	73	62	50
1,400	1,410	168	157	145	133	122	110	98	86	75	63	51
1,410	1,420	170	158	146	135	123	111	100	88	76	65	53
1,420	1,430	171	160	148	136	125	113	101	89	78	66	54
1,430	1,440	173	161	149	138	126	114	103	91	79	68	56
1,440	1,450	174	163	151	139	128	116	104	92	81	69	57
1,450	1,460	176	164	152	141	129	117	106	94	82	71	59
1,460	1,470	177	166	154	142	131	119	107	95	84	72	60
1,470	1,480	179	167	155	144	132	120	109	97	85	74	62
1,480	1,490	180	169	157	145	134	122	110	98	87	75	63

$1,490 and over — Use Table 1(b) for a **MARRIED person** on page 44. Also see the instructions on page 42.

Wage Bracket Method Tables for Income Tax Withholding

SINGLE Persons—BIWEEKLY Payroll Period

(For Wages Paid through December 31, 2016)

And the wages are—		And the number of withholding allowances claimed is—										
At least	But less than	0	1	2	3	4	5	6	7	8	9	10
		The amount of income tax to be withheld is—										
$ 0	$105	$0	$0	$0	$0	$0	$0	$0	$0	$0	$0	$0
105	110	2	0	0	0	0	0	0	0	0	0	0
110	115	3	0	0	0	0	0	0	0	0	0	0
115	120	3	0	0	0	0	0	0	0	0	0	0
120	125	4	0	0	0	0	0	0	0	0	0	0
125	130	4	0	0	0	0	0	0	0	0	0	0
130	135	5	0	0	0	0	0	0	0	0	0	0
135	140	5	0	0	0	0	0	0	0	0	0	0
140	145	6	0	0	0	0	0	0	0	0	0	0
145	150	6	0	0	0	0	0	0	0	0	0	0
150	155	7	0	0	0	0	0	0	0	0	0	0
155	160	7	0	0	0	0	0	0	0	0	0	0
160	165	8	0	0	0	0	0	0	0	0	0	0
165	170	8	0	0	0	0	0	0	0	0	0	0
170	175	9	0	0	0	0	0	0	0	0	0	0
175	180	9	0	0	0	0	0	0	0	0	0	0
180	185	10	0	0	0	0	0	0	0	0	0	0
185	190	10	0	0	0	0	0	0	0	0	0	0
190	195	11	0	0	0	0	0	0	0	0	0	0
195	200	11	0	0	0	0	0	0	0	0	0	0
200	205	12	0	0	0	0	0	0	0	0	0	0
205	210	12	0	0	0	0	0	0	0	0	0	0
210	215	13	0	0	0	0	0	0	0	0	0	0
215	220	13	0	0	0	0	0	0	0	0	0	0
220	225	14	0	0	0	0	0	0	0	0	0	0
225	230	14	0	0	0	0	0	0	0	0	0	0
230	235	15	0	0	0	0	0	0	0	0	0	0
235	240	15	0	0	0	0	0	0	0	0	0	0
240	245	16	0	0	0	0	0	0	0	0	0	0
245	250	16	1	0	0	0	0	0	0	0	0	0
250	260	17	1	0	0	0	0	0	0	0	0	0
260	270	18	2	0	0	0	0	0	0	0	0	0
270	280	19	3	0	0	0	0	0	0	0	0	0
280	290	20	4	0	0	0	0	0	0	0	0	0
290	300	21	5	0	0	0	0	0	0	0	0	0
300	310	22	6	0	0	0	0	0	0	0	0	0
310	320	23	7	0	0	0	0	0	0	0	0	0
320	330	24	8	0	0	0	0	0	0	0	0	0
330	340	25	9	0	0	0	0	0	0	0	0	0
340	350	26	10	0	0	0	0	0	0	0	0	0
350	360	27	11	0	0	0	0	0	0	0	0	0
360	370	28	12	0	0	0	0	0	0	0	0	0
370	380	29	13	0	0	0	0	0	0	0	0	0
380	390	30	14	0	0	0	0	0	0	0	0	0
390	400	31	15	0	0	0	0	0	0	0	0	0
400	410	32	16	1	0	0	0	0	0	0	0	0
410	420	33	17	2	0	0	0	0	0	0	0	0
420	430	34	18	3	0	0	0	0	0	0	0	0
430	440	35	19	4	0	0	0	0	0	0	0	0
440	450	36	20	5	0	0	0	0	0	0	0	0
450	460	37	21	6	0	0	0	0	0	0	0	0
460	470	39	22	7	0	0	0	0	0	0	0	0
470	480	40	23	8	0	0	0	0	0	0	0	0
480	490	42	24	9	0	0	0	0	0	0	0	0
490	500	43	25	10	0	0	0	0	0	0	0	0
500	520	46	27	11	0	0	0	0	0	0	0	0
520	540	49	29	13	0	0	0	0	0	0	0	0
540	560	52	31	15	0	0	0	0	0	0	0	0
560	580	55	33	17	2	0	0	0	0	0	0	0
580	600	58	35	19	4	0	0	0	0	0	0	0
600	620	61	37	21	6	0	0	0	0	0	0	0
620	640	64	40	23	8	0	0	0	0	0	0	0
640	660	67	43	25	10	0	0	0	0	0	0	0
660	680	70	46	27	12	0	0	0	0	0	0	0
680	700	73	49	29	14	0	0	0	0	0	0	0
700	720	76	52	31	16	0	0	0	0	0	0	0
720	740	79	55	33	18	2	0	0	0	0	0	0
740	760	82	58	35	20	4	0	0	0	0	0	0
760	780	85	61	38	22	6	0	0	0	0	0	0
780	800	88	64	41	24	8	0	0	0	0	0	0

Publication 15 (2016)

A-189

Wage Bracket Method Tables for Income Tax Withholding

SINGLE Persons—**BIWEEKLY** Payroll Period

(For Wages Paid through December 31, 2016)

And the wages are–		And the number of withholding allowances claimed is—										
At least	But less than	0	1	2	3	4	5	6	7	8	9	10
		The amount of income tax to be withheld is—										
$800	$820	$91	$67	$44	$26	$10	$0	$0	$0	$0	$0	$0
820	840	94	70	47	28	12	0	0	0	0	0	0
840	860	97	73	50	30	14	0	0	0	0	0	0
860	880	100	76	53	32	16	0	0	0	0	0	0
880	900	103	79	56	34	18	2	0	0	0	0	0
900	920	106	82	59	36	20	4	0	0	0	0	0
920	940	109	85	62	39	22	6	0	0	0	0	0
940	960	112	88	65	42	24	8	0	0	0	0	0
960	980	115	91	68	45	26	10	0	0	0	0	0
980	1,000	118	94	71	48	28	12	0	0	0	0	0
1,000	1,020	121	97	74	51	30	14	0	0	0	0	0
1,020	1,040	124	100	77	54	32	16	1	0	0	0	0
1,040	1,060	127	103	80	57	34	18	3	0	0	0	0
1,060	1,080	130	106	83	60	36	20	5	0	0	0	0
1,080	1,100	133	109	86	63	39	22	7	0	0	0	0
1,100	1,120	136	112	89	66	42	24	9	0	0	0	0
1,120	1,140	139	115	92	69	45	26	11	0	0	0	0
1,140	1,160	142	118	95	72	48	28	13	0	0	0	0
1,160	1,180	145	121	98	75	51	30	15	0	0	0	0
1,180	1,200	148	124	101	78	54	32	17	1	0	0	0
1,200	1,220	151	127	104	81	57	34	19	3	0	0	0
1,220	1,240	154	130	107	84	60	37	21	5	0	0	0
1,240	1,260	157	133	110	87	63	40	23	7	0	0	0
1,260	1,280	160	136	113	90	66	43	25	9	0	0	0
1,280	1,300	163	139	116	93	69	46	27	11	0	0	0
1,300	1,320	166	142	119	96	72	49	29	13	0	0	0
1,320	1,340	169	145	122	99	75	52	31	15	0	0	0
1,340	1,360	172	148	125	102	78	55	33	17	2	0	0
1,360	1,380	175	151	128	105	81	58	35	19	4	0	0
1,380	1,400	178	154	131	108	84	61	37	21	6	0	0
1,400	1,420	181	157	134	111	87	64	40	23	8	0	0
1,420	1,440	184	160	137	114	90	67	43	25	10	0	0
1,440	1,460	187	163	140	117	93	70	46	27	12	0	0
1,460	1,480	190	166	143	120	96	73	49	29	14	0	0
1,480	1,500	193	169	146	123	99	76	52	31	16	0	0
1,500	1,520	196	172	149	126	102	79	55	33	18	2	0
1,520	1,540	199	175	152	129	105	82	58	35	20	4	0
1,540	1,560	203	178	155	132	108	85	61	38	22	6	0
1,560	1,580	208	181	158	135	111	88	64	41	24	8	0
1,580	1,600	213	184	161	138	114	91	67	44	26	10	0
1,600	1,620	218	187	164	141	117	94	70	47	28	12	0
1,620	1,640	223	190	167	144	120	97	73	50	30	14	0
1,640	1,660	228	193	170	147	123	100	76	53	32	16	1
1,660	1,680	233	196	173	150	126	103	79	56	34	18	3
1,680	1,700	238	199	176	153	129	106	82	59	36	20	5
1,700	1,720	243	204	179	156	132	109	85	62	39	22	7
1,720	1,740	248	209	182	159	135	112	88	65	42	24	9
1,740	1,760	253	214	185	162	138	115	91	68	45	26	11
1,760	1,780	258	219	188	165	141	118	94	71	48	28	13
1,780	1,800	263	224	191	168	144	121	97	74	51	30	15
1,800	1,820	268	229	194	171	147	124	100	77	54	32	17
1,820	1,840	273	234	197	174	150	127	103	80	57	34	19
1,840	1,860	278	239	200	177	153	130	106	83	60	36	21
1,860	1,880	283	244	205	180	156	133	109	86	63	39	23
1,880	1,900	288	249	210	183	159	136	112	89	66	42	25
1,900	1,920	293	254	215	186	162	139	115	92	69	45	27
1,920	1,940	298	259	220	189	165	142	118	95	72	48	29
1,940	1,960	303	264	225	192	168	145	121	98	75	51	31
1,960	1,980	308	269	230	195	171	148	124	101	78	54	33
1,980	2,000	313	274	235	198	174	151	127	104	81	57	35
2,000	2,020	318	279	240	201	177	154	130	107	84	60	37
2,020	2,040	323	284	245	206	180	157	133	110	87	63	40
2,040	2,060	328	289	250	211	183	160	136	113	90	66	43
2,060	2,080	333	294	255	216	186	163	139	116	93	69	46
2,080	2,100	338	299	260	221	189	166	142	119	96	72	49

$2,100 and over	Use Table 2(a) for a **SINGLE person** on page 44. Also see the instructions on page 42.

A-190

Wage Bracket Method Tables for Income Tax Withholding

MARRIED Persons—BIWEEKLY Payroll Period

(For Wages Paid through December 31, 2016)

And the wages are–		And the number of withholding allowances claimed is—										
At least	But less than	0	1	2	3	4	5	6	7	8	9	10
		The amount of income tax to be withheld is—										
$ 0	$340	$0	$0	$0	$0	$0	$0	$0	$0	$0	$0	$0
340	350	2	0	0	0	0	0	0	0	0	0	0
350	360	3	0	0	0	0	0	0	0	0	0	0
360	370	4	0	0	0	0	0	0	0	0	0	0
370	380	5	0	0	0	0	0	0	0	0	0	0
380	390	6	0	0	0	0	0	0	0	0	0	0
390	400	7	0	0	0	0	0	0	0	0	0	0
400	410	8	0	0	0	0	0	0	0	0	0	0
410	420	9	0	0	0	0	0	0	0	0	0	0
420	430	10	0	0	0	0	0	0	0	0	0	0
430	440	11	0	0	0	0	0	0	0	0	0	0
440	450	12	0	0	0	0	0	0	0	0	0	0
450	460	13	0	0	0	0	0	0	0	0	0	0
460	470	14	0	0	0	0	0	0	0	0	0	0
470	480	15	0	0	0	0	0	0	0	0	0	0
480	490	16	0	0	0	0	0	0	0	0	0	0
490	500	17	1	0	0	0	0	0	0	0	0	0
500	520	18	3	0	0	0	0	0	0	0	0	0
520	540	20	5	0	0	0	0	0	0	0	0	0
540	560	22	7	0	0	0	0	0	0	0	0	0
560	580	24	9	0	0	0	0	0	0	0	0	0
580	600	26	11	0	0	0	0	0	0	0	0	0
600	620	28	13	0	0	0	0	0	0	0	0	0
620	640	30	15	0	0	0	0	0	0	0	0	0
640	660	32	17	1	0	0	0	0	0	0	0	0
660	680	34	19	3	0	0	0	0	0	0	0	0
680	700	36	21	5	0	0	0	0	0	0	0	0
700	720	38	23	7	0	0	0	0	0	0	0	0
720	740	40	25	9	0	0	0	0	0	0	0	0
740	760	42	27	11	0	0	0	0	0	0	0	0
760	780	44	29	13	0	0	0	0	0	0	0	0
780	800	46	31	15	0	0	0	0	0	0	0	0
800	820	48	33	17	1	0	0	0	0	0	0	0
820	840	50	35	19	3	0	0	0	0	0	0	0
840	860	52	37	21	5	0	0	0	0	0	0	0
860	880	54	39	23	7	0	0	0	0	0	0	0
880	900	56	41	25	9	0	0	0	0	0	0	0
900	920	58	43	27	11	0	0	0	0	0	0	0
920	940	60	45	29	13	0	0	0	0	0	0	0
940	960	62	47	31	15	0	0	0	0	0	0	0
960	980	64	49	33	17	2	0	0	0	0	0	0
980	1,000	66	51	35	19	4	0	0	0	0	0	0
1,000	1,020	68	53	37	21	6	0	0	0	0	0	0
1,020	1,040	70	55	39	23	8	0	0	0	0	0	0
1,040	1,060	73	57	41	25	10	0	0	0	0	0	0
1,060	1,080	76	59	43	27	12	0	0	0	0	0	0
1,080	1,100	79	61	45	29	14	0	0	0	0	0	0
1,100	1,120	82	63	47	31	16	0	0	0	0	0	0
1,120	1,140	85	65	49	33	18	2	0	0	0	0	0
1,140	1,160	88	67	51	35	20	4	0	0	0	0	0
1,160	1,180	91	69	53	37	22	6	0	0	0	0	0
1,180	1,200	94	71	55	39	24	8	0	0	0	0	0
1,200	1,220	97	73	57	41	26	10	0	0	0	0	0
1,220	1,240	100	76	59	43	28	12	0	0	0	0	0
1,240	1,260	103	79	61	45	30	14	0	0	0	0	0
1,260	1,280	106	82	63	47	32	16	1	0	0	0	0
1,280	1,300	109	85	65	49	34	18	3	0	0	0	0
1,300	1,320	112	88	67	51	36	20	5	0	0	0	0
1,320	1,340	115	91	69	53	38	22	7	0	0	0	0
1,340	1,360	118	94	71	55	40	24	9	0	0	0	0
1,360	1,380	121	97	74	57	42	26	11	0	0	0	0
1,380	1,400	124	100	77	59	44	28	13	0	0	0	0
1,400	1,420	127	103	80	61	46	30	15	0	0	0	0
1,420	1,440	130	106	83	63	48	32	17	1	0	0	0
1,440	1,460	133	109	86	65	50	34	19	3	0	0	0
1,460	1,480	136	112	89	67	52	36	21	5	0	0	0
1,480	1,500	139	115	92	69	54	38	23	7	0	0	0

Wage Bracket Method Tables for Income Tax Withholding

MARRIED Persons—**BIWEEKLY** Payroll Period

(For Wages Paid through December 31, 2016)

And the wages are–		And the number of withholding allowances claimed is—										
At least	But less than	0	1	2	3	4	5	6	7	8	9	10
		The amount of income tax to be withheld is—										
$1,500	$1,520	$142	$118	$95	$71	$56	$40	$25	$9	$0	$0	$0
1,520	1,540	145	121	98	74	58	42	27	11	0	0	0
1,540	1,560	148	124	101	77	60	44	29	13	0	0	0
1,560	1,580	151	127	104	80	62	46	31	15	0	0	0
1,580	1,600	154	130	107	83	64	48	33	17	2	0	0
1,600	1,620	157	133	110	86	66	50	35	19	4	0	0
1,620	1,640	160	136	113	89	68	52	37	21	6	0	0
1,640	1,660	163	139	116	92	70	54	39	23	8	0	0
1,660	1,680	166	142	119	95	72	56	41	25	10	0	0
1,680	1,700	169	145	122	98	75	58	43	27	12	0	0
1,700	1,720	172	148	125	101	78	60	45	29	14	0	0
1,720	1,740	175	151	128	104	81	62	47	31	16	0	0
1,740	1,760	178	154	131	107	84	64	49	33	18	2	0
1,760	1,780	181	157	134	110	87	66	51	35	20	4	0
1,780	1,800	184	160	137	113	90	68	53	37	22	6	0
1,800	1,820	187	163	140	116	93	70	55	39	24	8	0
1,820	1,840	190	166	143	119	96	73	57	41	26	10	0
1,840	1,860	193	169	146	122	99	76	59	43	28	12	0
1,860	1,880	196	172	149	125	102	79	61	45	30	14	0
1,880	1,900	199	175	152	128	105	82	63	47	32	16	0
1,900	1,920	202	178	155	131	108	85	65	49	34	18	2
1,920	1,940	205	181	158	134	111	88	67	51	36	20	4
1,940	1,960	208	184	161	137	114	91	69	53	38	22	6
1,960	1,980	211	187	164	140	117	94	71	55	40	24	8
1,980	2,000	214	190	167	143	120	97	73	57	42	26	10
2,000	2,020	217	193	170	146	123	100	76	59	44	28	12
2,020	2,040	220	196	173	149	126	103	79	61	46	30	14
2,040	2,060	223	199	176	152	129	106	82	63	48	32	16
2,060	2,080	226	202	179	155	132	109	85	65	50	34	18
2,080	2,100	229	205	182	158	135	112	88	67	52	36	20
2,100	2,120	232	208	185	161	138	115	91	69	54	38	22
2,120	2,140	235	211	188	164	141	118	94	71	56	40	24
2,140	2,160	238	214	191	167	144	121	97	74	58	42	26
2,160	2,180	241	217	194	170	147	124	100	77	60	44	28
2,180	2,200	244	220	197	173	150	127	103	80	62	46	30
2,200	2,220	247	223	200	176	153	130	106	83	64	48	32
2,220	2,240	250	226	203	179	156	133	109	86	66	50	34
2,240	2,260	253	229	206	182	159	136	112	89	68	52	36
2,260	2,280	256	232	209	185	162	139	115	92	70	54	38
2,280	2,300	259	235	212	188	165	142	118	95	72	56	40
2,300	2,320	262	238	215	191	168	145	121	98	75	58	42
2,320	2,340	265	241	218	194	171	148	124	101	78	60	44
2,340	2,360	268	244	221	197	174	151	127	104	81	62	46
2,360	2,380	271	247	224	200	177	154	130	107	84	64	48
2,380	2,400	274	250	227	203	180	157	133	110	87	66	50
2,400	2,420	277	253	230	206	183	160	136	113	90	68	52
2,420	2,440	280	256	233	209	186	163	139	116	93	70	54
2,440	2,460	283	259	236	212	189	166	142	119	96	72	56
2,460	2,480	286	262	239	215	192	169	145	122	99	75	58
2,480	2,500	289	265	242	218	195	172	148	125	102	78	60
2,500	2,520	292	268	245	221	198	175	151	128	105	81	62
2,520	2,540	295	271	248	224	201	178	154	131	108	84	64
2,540	2,560	298	274	251	227	204	181	157	134	111	87	66
2,560	2,580	301	277	254	230	207	184	160	137	114	90	68
2,580	2,600	304	280	257	233	210	187	163	140	117	93	70
2,600	2,620	307	283	260	236	213	190	166	143	120	96	73
2,620	2,640	310	286	263	239	216	193	169	146	123	99	76
2,640	2,660	313	289	266	242	219	196	172	149	126	102	79
2,660	2,680	316	292	269	245	222	199	175	152	129	105	82
2,680	2,700	319	295	272	248	225	202	178	155	132	108	85
2,700	2,720	322	298	275	251	228	205	181	158	135	111	88
2,720	2,740	325	301	278	254	231	208	184	161	138	114	91
2,740	2,760	328	304	281	257	234	211	187	164	141	117	94
2,760	2,780	331	307	284	260	237	214	190	167	144	120	97
2,780	2,800	334	310	287	263	240	217	193	170	147	123	100
2,800	2,820	337	313	290	266	243	220	196	173	150	126	103
2,820	2,840	340	316	293	269	246	223	199	176	153	129	106
2,840	2,860	343	319	296	272	249	226	202	179	156	132	109
2,860	2,880	346	322	299	275	252	229	205	182	159	135	112

| $2,880 and over | Use Table 2(b) for a **MARRIED person** on page 44. Also see the instructions on page 42. |

Wage Bracket Method Tables for Income Tax Withholding

SINGLE Persons—SEMIMONTHLY Payroll Period

(For Wages Paid through December 31, 2016)

And the wages are—		And the number of withholding allowances claimed is—										
At least	But less than	0	1	2	3	4	5	6	7	8	9	10
		The amount of income tax to be withheld is—										
$ 0	$115	$0	$0	$0	$0	$0	$0	$0	$0	$0	$0	$0
115	120	2	0	0	0	0	0	0	0	0	0	0
120	125	3	0	0	0	0	0	0	0	0	0	0
125	130	3	0	0	0	0	0	0	0	0	0	0
130	135	4	0	0	0	0	0	0	0	0	0	0
135	140	4	0	0	0	0	0	0	0	0	0	0
140	145	5	0	0	0	0	0	0	0	0	0	0
145	150	5	0	0	0	0	0	0	0	0	0	0
150	155	6	0	0	0	0	0	0	0	0	0	0
155	160	6	0	0	0	0	0	0	0	0	0	0
160	165	7	0	0	0	0	0	0	0	0	0	0
165	170	7	0	0	0	0	0	0	0	0	0	0
170	175	8	0	0	0	0	0	0	0	0	0	0
175	180	8	0	0	0	0	0	0	0	0	0	0
180	185	9	0	0	0	0	0	0	0	0	0	0
185	190	9	0	0	0	0	0	0	0	0	0	0
190	195	10	0	0	0	0	0	0	0	0	0	0
195	200	10	0	0	0	0	0	0	0	0	0	0
200	205	11	0	0	0	0	0	0	0	0	0	0
205	210	11	0	0	0	0	0	0	0	0	0	0
210	215	12	0	0	0	0	0	0	0	0	0	0
215	220	12	0	0	0	0	0	0	0	0	0	0
220	225	13	0	0	0	0	0	0	0	0	0	0
225	230	13	0	0	0	0	0	0	0	0	0	0
230	235	14	0	0	0	0	0	0	0	0	0	0
235	240	14	0	0	0	0	0	0	0	0	0	0
240	245	15	0	0	0	0	0	0	0	0	0	0
245	250	15	0	0	0	0	0	0	0	0	0	0
250	260	16	0	0	0	0	0	0	0	0	0	0
260	270	17	0	0	0	0	0	0	0	0	0	0
270	280	18	1	0	0	0	0	0	0	0	0	0
280	290	19	2	0	0	0	0	0	0	0	0	0
290	300	20	3	0	0	0	0	0	0	0	0	0
300	310	21	4	0	0	0	0	0	0	0	0	0
310	320	22	5	0	0	0	0	0	0	0	0	0
320	330	23	6	0	0	0	0	0	0	0	0	0
330	340	24	7	0	0	0	0	0	0	0	0	0
340	350	25	8	0	0	0	0	0	0	0	0	0
350	360	26	9	0	0	0	0	0	0	0	0	0
360	370	27	10	0	0	0	0	0	0	0	0	0
370	380	28	11	0	0	0	0	0	0	0	0	0
380	390	29	12	0	0	0	0	0	0	0	0	0
390	400	30	13	0	0	0	0	0	0	0	0	0
400	410	31	14	0	0	0	0	0	0	0	0	0
410	420	32	15	0	0	0	0	0	0	0	0	0
420	430	33	16	0	0	0	0	0	0	0	0	0
430	440	34	17	0	0	0	0	0	0	0	0	0
440	450	35	18	1	0	0	0	0	0	0	0	0
450	460	36	19	2	0	0	0	0	0	0	0	0
460	470	37	20	3	0	0	0	0	0	0	0	0
470	480	38	21	4	0	0	0	0	0	0	0	0
480	490	39	22	5	0	0	0	0	0	0	0	0
490	500	41	23	6	0	0	0	0	0	0	0	0
500	520	43	25	8	0	0	0	0	0	0	0	0
520	540	46	27	10	0	0	0	0	0	0	0	0
540	560	49	29	12	0	0	0	0	0	0	0	0
560	580	52	31	14	0	0	0	0	0	0	0	0
580	600	55	33	16	0	0	0	0	0	0	0	0
600	620	58	35	18	1	0	0	0	0	0	0	0
620	640	61	37	20	3	0	0	0	0	0	0	0
640	660	64	39	22	5	0	0	0	0	0	0	0
660	680	67	42	24	7	0	0	0	0	0	0	0
680	700	70	45	26	9	0	0	0	0	0	0	0
700	720	73	48	28	11	0	0	0	0	0	0	0
720	740	76	51	30	13	0	0	0	0	0	0	0
740	760	79	54	32	15	0	0	0	0	0	0	0
760	780	82	57	34	17	0	0	0	0	0	0	0
780	800	85	60	36	19	2	0	0	0	0	0	0

Publication 15 (2016)

Wage Bracket Method Tables for Income Tax Withholding

SINGLE Persons—SEMIMONTHLY Payroll Period

(For Wages Paid through December 31, 2016)

And the wages are—		And the number of withholding allowances claimed is—										
At least	But less than	0	1	2	3	4	5	6	7	8	9	10
		The amount of income tax to be withheld is—										
$800	$820	$88	$63	$38	$21	$4	$0	$0	$0	$0	$0	$0
820	840	91	66	40	23	6	0	0	0	0	0	0
840	860	94	69	43	25	8	0	0	0	0	0	0
860	880	97	72	46	27	10	0	0	0	0	0	0
880	900	100	75	49	29	12	0	0	0	0	0	0
900	920	103	78	52	31	14	0	0	0	0	0	0
920	940	106	81	55	33	16	0	0	0	0	0	0
940	960	109	84	58	35	18	1	0	0	0	0	0
960	980	112	87	61	37	20	3	0	0	0	0	0
980	1,000	115	90	64	39	22	5	0	0	0	0	0
1,000	1,020	118	93	67	42	24	7	0	0	0	0	0
1,020	1,040	121	96	70	45	26	9	0	0	0	0	0
1,040	1,060	124	99	73	48	28	11	0	0	0	0	0
1,060	1,080	127	102	76	51	30	13	0	0	0	0	0
1,080	1,100	130	105	79	54	32	15	0	0	0	0	0
1,100	1,120	133	108	82	57	34	17	0	0	0	0	0
1,120	1,140	136	111	85	60	36	19	2	0	0	0	0
1,140	1,160	139	114	88	63	38	21	4	0	0	0	0
1,160	1,180	142	117	91	66	41	23	6	0	0	0	0
1,180	1,200	145	120	94	69	44	25	8	0	0	0	0
1,200	1,220	148	123	97	72	47	27	10	0	0	0	0
1,220	1,240	151	126	100	75	50	29	12	0	0	0	0
1,240	1,260	154	129	103	78	53	31	14	0	0	0	0
1,260	1,280	157	132	106	81	56	33	16	0	0	0	0
1,280	1,300	160	135	109	84	59	35	18	2	0	0	0
1,300	1,320	163	138	112	87	62	37	20	4	0	0	0
1,320	1,340	166	141	115	90	65	40	22	6	0	0	0
1,340	1,360	169	144	118	93	68	43	24	8	0	0	0
1,360	1,380	172	147	121	96	71	46	26	10	0	0	0
1,380	1,400	175	150	124	99	74	49	28	12	0	0	0
1,400	1,420	178	153	127	102	77	52	30	14	0	0	0
1,420	1,440	181	156	130	105	80	55	32	16	0	0	0
1,440	1,460	184	159	133	108	83	58	34	18	1	0	0
1,460	1,480	187	162	136	111	86	61	36	20	3	0	0
1,480	1,500	190	165	139	114	89	64	38	22	5	0	0
1,500	1,520	193	168	142	117	92	67	41	24	7	0	0
1,520	1,540	196	171	145	120	95	70	44	26	9	0	0
1,540	1,560	199	174	148	123	98	73	47	28	11	0	0
1,560	1,580	202	177	151	126	101	76	50	30	13	0	0
1,580	1,600	205	180	154	129	104	79	53	32	15	0	0
1,600	1,620	208	183	157	132	107	82	56	34	17	0	0
1,620	1,640	211	186	160	135	110	85	59	36	19	2	0
1,640	1,660	214	189	163	138	113	88	62	38	21	4	0
1,660	1,680	218	192	166	141	116	91	65	40	23	6	0
1,680	1,700	223	195	169	144	119	94	68	43	25	8	0
1,700	1,720	228	198	172	147	122	97	71	46	27	10	0
1,720	1,740	233	201	175	150	125	100	74	49	29	12	0
1,740	1,760	238	204	178	153	128	103	77	52	31	14	0
1,760	1,780	243	207	181	156	131	106	80	55	33	16	0
1,780	1,800	248	210	184	159	134	109	83	58	35	18	1
1,800	1,820	253	213	187	162	137	112	86	61	37	20	3
1,820	1,840	258	216	190	165	140	115	89	64	39	22	5
1,840	1,860	263	221	193	168	143	118	92	67	42	24	7
1,860	1,880	268	226	196	171	146	121	95	70	45	26	9
1,880	1,900	273	231	199	174	149	124	98	73	48	28	11
1,900	1,920	278	236	202	177	152	127	101	76	51	30	13
1,920	1,940	283	241	205	180	155	130	104	79	54	32	15
1,940	1,960	288	246	208	183	158	133	107	82	57	34	17
1,960	1,980	293	251	211	186	161	136	110	85	60	36	19
1,980	2,000	298	256	214	189	164	139	113	88	63	38	21
2,000	2,020	303	261	218	192	167	142	116	91	66	40	23
2,020	2,040	308	266	223	195	170	145	119	94	69	43	25
2,040	2,060	313	271	228	198	173	148	122	97	72	46	27
2,060	2,080	318	276	233	201	176	151	125	100	75	49	29
2,080	2,100	323	281	238	204	179	154	128	103	78	52	31
2,100	2,120	328	286	243	207	182	157	131	106	81	55	33
2,120	2,140	333	291	248	210	185	160	134	109	84	58	35

$2,140 and over   Use Table 0(a) for a SINGLE person on page 44. Also see the instructions on page 42.

Wage Bracket Method Tables for Income Tax Withholding

MARRIED Persons—**SEMIMONTHLY** Payroll Period

(For Wages Paid through December 31, 2016)

And the wages are–		And the number of withholding allowances claimed is—										
At least	But less than	0	1	2	3	4	5	6	7	8	9	10
		The amount of income tax to be withheld is—										
$ 0	$360	$0	$0	$0	$0	$0	$0	$0	$0	$0	$0	$0
360	370	1	0	0	0	0	0	0	0	0	0	0
370	380	2	0	0	0	0	0	0	0	0	0	0
380	390	3	0	0	0	0	0	0	0	0	0	0
390	400	4	0	0	0	0	0	0	0	0	0	0
400	410	5	0	0	0	0	0	0	0	0	0	0
410	420	6	0	0	0	0	0	0	0	0	0	0
420	430	7	0	0	0	0	0	0	0	0	0	0
430	440	8	0	0	0	0	0	0	0	0	0	0
440	450	9	0	0	0	0	0	0	0	0	0	0
450	460	10	0	0	0	0	0	0	0	0	0	0
460	470	11	0	0	0	0	0	0	0	0	0	0
470	480	12	0	0	0	0	0	0	0	0	0	0
480	490	13	0	0	0	0	0	0	0	0	0	0
490	500	14	0	0	0	0	0	0	0	0	0	0
500	520	15	0	0	0	0	0	0	0	0	0	0
520	540	17	1	0	0	0	0	0	0	0	0	0
540	560	19	3	0	0	0	0	0	0	0	0	0
560	580	21	5	0	0	0	0	0	0	0	0	0
580	600	23	7	0	0	0	0	0	0	0	0	0
600	620	25	9	0	0	0	0	0	0	0	0	0
620	640	27	11	0	0	0	0	0	0	0	0	0
640	660	29	13	0	0	0	0	0	0	0	0	0
660	680	31	15	0	0	0	0	0	0	0	0	0
680	700	33	17	0	0	0	0	0	0	0	0	0
700	720	35	19	2	0	0	0	0	0	0	0	0
720	740	37	21	4	0	0	0	0	0	0	0	0
740	760	39	23	6	0	0	0	0	0	0	0	0
760	780	41	25	8	0	0	0	0	0	0	0	0
780	800	43	27	10	0	0	0	0	0	0	0	0
800	820	45	29	12	0	0	0	0	0	0	0	0
820	840	47	31	14	0	0	0	0	0	0	0	0
840	860	49	33	16	0	0	0	0	0	0	0	0
860	880	51	35	18	1	0	0	0	0	0	0	0
880	900	53	37	20	3	0	0	0	0	0	0	0
900	920	55	39	22	5	0	0	0	0	0	0	0
920	940	57	41	24	7	0	0	0	0	0	0	0
940	960	59	43	26	9	0	0	0	0	0	0	0
960	980	61	45	28	11	0	0	0	0	0	0	0
980	1,000	63	47	30	13	0	0	0	0	0	0	0
1,000	1,020	65	49	32	15	0	0	0	0	0	0	0
1,020	1,040	67	51	34	17	0	0	0	0	0	0	0
1,040	1,060	69	53	36	19	2	0	0	0	0	0	0
1,060	1,080	71	55	38	21	4	0	0	0	0	0	0
1,080	1,100	73	57	40	23	6	0	0	0	0	0	0
1,100	1,120	75	59	42	25	8	0	0	0	0	0	0
1,120	1,140	77	61	44	27	10	0	0	0	0	0	0
1,140	1,160	80	63	46	29	12	0	0	0	0	0	0
1,160	1,180	83	65	48	31	14	0	0	0	0	0	0
1,180	1,200	86	67	50	33	16	0	0	0	0	0	0
1,200	1,220	89	69	52	35	18	1	0	0	0	0	0
1,220	1,240	92	71	54	37	20	3	0	0	0	0	0
1,240	1,260	95	73	56	39	22	5	0	0	0	0	0
1,260	1,280	98	75	58	41	24	7	0	0	0	0	0
1,280	1,300	101	77	60	43	26	9	0	0	0	0	0
1,300	1,320	104	79	62	45	28	11	0	0	0	0	0
1,320	1,340	107	82	64	47	30	13	0	0	0	0	0
1,340	1,360	110	85	66	49	32	15	0	0	0	0	0
1,360	1,380	113	88	68	51	34	17	0	0	0	0	0
1,380	1,400	116	91	70	53	36	19	2	0	0	0	0
1,400	1,420	119	94	72	55	38	21	4	0	0	0	0
1,420	1,440	122	97	74	57	40	23	6	0	0	0	0
1,440	1,460	125	100	76	59	42	25	8	0	0	0	0
1,460	1,480	128	103	78	61	44	27	10	0	0	0	0
1,480	1,500	131	106	81	63	46	29	12	0	0	0	0
1,500	1,520	134	109	84	65	48	31	14	0	0	0	0
1,520	1,540	137	112	87	67	50	33	16	0	0	0	0
1,540	1,560	140	115	90	69	52	35	18	1	0	0	0
1,560	1,580	143	118	93	71	54	37	20	3	0	0	0
1,580	1,600	146	121	96	73	56	39	22	5	0	0	0

Wage Bracket Method Tables for Income Tax Withholding

MARRIED Persons—SEMIMONTHLY Payroll Period

(For Wages Paid through December 31, 2016)

And the wages are—		And the number of withholding allowances claimed is—										
At least	But less than	0	1	2	3	4	5	6	7	8	9	10
		The amount of income tax to be withheld is—										
$1,600	$1,620	$149	$124	$99	$75	$58	$41	$24	$7	$0	$0	$0
1,620	1,640	152	127	102	77	60	43	26	9	0	0	0
1,640	1,660	155	130	105	79	62	45	28	11	0	0	0
1,660	1,680	158	133	108	82	64	47	30	13	0	0	0
1,680	1,700	161	136	111	85	66	49	32	15	0	0	0
1,700	1,720	164	139	114	88	68	51	34	17	0	0	0
1,720	1,740	167	142	117	91	70	53	36	19	2	0	0
1,740	1,760	170	145	120	94	72	55	38	21	4	0	0
1,760	1,780	173	148	123	97	74	57	40	23	6	0	0
1,780	1,800	176	151	126	100	76	59	42	25	8	0	0
1,800	1,820	179	154	129	103	78	61	44	27	10	0	0
1,820	1,840	182	157	132	106	81	63	46	29	12	0	0
1,840	1,860	185	160	135	109	84	65	48	31	14	0	0
1,860	1,880	188	163	138	112	87	67	50	33	16	0	0
1,880	1,900	191	166	141	115	90	69	52	35	18	2	0
1,900	1,920	194	169	144	118	93	71	54	37	20	4	0
1,920	1,940	197	172	147	121	96	73	56	39	22	6	0
1,940	1,960	200	175	150	124	99	75	58	41	24	8	0
1,960	1,980	203	178	153	127	102	77	60	43	26	10	0
1,980	2,000	206	181	156	130	105	80	62	45	28	12	0
2,000	2,020	209	184	159	133	108	83	64	47	30	14	0
2,020	2,040	212	187	162	136	111	86	66	49	32	16	0
2,040	2,060	215	190	165	139	114	89	68	51	34	18	1
2,060	2,080	218	193	168	142	117	92	70	53	36	20	3
2,080	2,100	221	196	171	145	120	95	72	55	38	22	5
2,100	2,120	224	199	174	148	123	98	74	57	40	24	7
2,120	2,140	227	202	177	151	126	101	76	59	42	26	9
2,140	2,160	230	205	180	154	129	104	79	61	44	28	11
2,160	2,180	233	208	183	157	132	107	82	63	46	30	13
2,180	2,200	236	211	186	160	135	110	85	65	48	32	15
2,200	2,220	239	214	189	163	138	113	88	67	50	34	17
2,220	2,240	242	217	192	166	141	116	91	69	52	36	19
2,240	2,260	245	220	195	169	144	119	94	71	54	38	21
2,260	2,280	248	223	198	172	147	122	97	73	56	40	23
2,280	2,300	251	226	201	175	150	125	100	75	58	42	25
2,300	2,320	254	229	204	178	153	128	103	77	60	44	27
2,320	2,340	257	232	207	181	156	131	106	80	62	46	29
2,340	2,360	260	235	210	184	159	134	109	83	64	48	31
2,360	2,380	263	238	213	187	162	137	112	86	66	50	33
2,380	2,400	266	241	216	190	165	140	115	89	68	52	35
2,400	2,420	269	244	219	193	168	143	118	92	70	54	37
2,420	2,440	272	247	222	196	171	146	121	95	72	56	39
2,440	2,460	275	250	225	199	174	149	124	98	74	58	41
2,460	2,480	278	253	228	202	177	152	127	101	76	60	43
2,480	2,500	281	256	231	205	180	155	130	104	79	62	45
2,500	2,520	284	259	234	208	183	158	133	107	82	64	47
2,520	2,540	287	262	237	211	186	161	136	110	85	66	49
2,540	2,560	290	265	240	214	189	164	139	113	88	68	51
2,560	2,580	293	268	243	217	192	167	142	116	91	70	53
2,580	2,600	296	271	246	220	195	170	145	119	94	72	55
2,600	2,620	299	274	249	223	198	173	148	122	97	74	57
2,620	2,640	302	277	252	226	201	176	151	125	100	76	59
2,640	2,660	305	280	255	229	204	179	154	128	103	78	61
2,660	2,680	308	283	258	232	207	182	157	131	106	81	63
2,680	2,700	311	286	261	235	210	185	160	134	109	84	65
2,700	2,720	314	289	264	238	213	188	163	137	112	87	67
2,720	2,740	317	292	267	241	216	191	166	140	115	90	69
2,740	2,760	320	295	270	244	219	194	169	143	118	93	71
2,760	2,780	323	298	273	247	222	197	172	146	121	96	73
2,780	2,800	326	301	276	250	225	200	175	149	124	99	75
2,800	2,820	329	304	279	253	228	203	178	152	127	102	77
2,820	2,840	332	307	282	256	231	206	181	155	130	105	79
2,840	2,860	335	310	285	259	234	209	184	158	133	108	82
2,860	2,880	338	313	288	262	237	212	187	161	136	111	85
2,880	2,900	341	316	291	265	240	215	190	164	139	114	88
2,900	2,920	344	319	294	268	243	218	193	167	142	117	91

$2,920 and over	Use Table 3(b) for a **MARRIED person** on page 44. Also see the instructions on page 42.

Wage Bracket Method Tables for Income Tax Withholding

SINGLE Persons—MONTHLY Payroll Period

(For Wages Paid through December 31, 2016)

And the wages are–		And the number of withholding allowances claimed is—										
At least	But less than	0	1	2	3	4	5	6	7	8	9	10
		The amount of income tax to be withheld is—										
$ 0	$220	$0	$0	$0	$0	$0	$0	$0	$0	$0	$0	$0
220	230	4	0	0	0	0	0	0	0	0	0	0
230	240	5	0	0	0	0	0	0	0	0	0	0
240	250	6	0	0	0	0	0	0	0	0	0	0
250	260	7	0	0	0	0	0	0	0	0	0	0
260	270	8	0	0	0	0	0	0	0	0	0	0
270	280	9	0	0	0	0	0	0	0	0	0	0
280	290	10	0	0	0	0	0	0	0	0	0	0
290	300	11	0	0	0	0	0	0	0	0	0	0
300	320	12	0	0	0	0	0	0	0	0	0	0
320	340	14	0	0	0	0	0	0	0	0	0	0
340	360	16	0	0	0	0	0	0	0	0	0	0
360	380	18	0	0	0	0	0	0	0	0	0	0
380	400	20	0	0	0	0	0	0	0	0	0	0
400	420	22	0	0	0	0	0	0	0	0	0	0
420	440	24	0	0	0	0	0	0	0	0	0	0
440	460	26	0	0	0	0	0	0	0	0	0	0
460	480	28	0	0	0	0	0	0	0	0	0	0
480	500	30	0	0	0	0	0	0	0	0	0	0
500	520	32	0	0	0	0	0	0	0	0	0	0
520	540	34	1	0	0	0	0	0	0	0	0	0
540	560	36	3	0	0	0	0	0	0	0	0	0
560	580	38	5	0	0	0	0	0	0	0	0	0
580	600	40	7	0	0	0	0	0	0	0	0	0
600	640	43	10	0	0	0	0	0	0	0	0	0
640	680	47	14	0	0	0	0	0	0	0	0	0
680	720	51	18	0	0	0	0	0	0	0	0	0
720	760	55	22	0	0	0	0	0	0	0	0	0
760	800	59	26	0	0	0	0	0	0	0	0	0
800	840	63	30	0	0	0	0	0	0	0	0	0
840	880	67	34	0	0	0	0	0	0	0	0	0
880	920	71	38	4	0	0	0	0	0	0	0	0
920	960	75	42	8	0	0	0	0	0	0	0	0
960	1,000	80	46	12	0	0	0	0	0	0	0	0
1,000	1,040	86	50	16	0	0	0	0	0	0	0	0
1,040	1,080	92	54	20	0	0	0	0	0	0	0	0
1,080	1,120	98	58	24	0	0	0	0	0	0	0	0
1,120	1,160	104	62	28	0	0	0	0	0	0	0	0
1,160	1,200	110	66	32	0	0	0	0	0	0	0	0
1,200	1,240	116	70	36	2	0	0	0	0	0	0	0
1,240	1,280	122	74	40	6	0	0	0	0	0	0	0
1,280	1,320	128	78	44	10	0	0	0	0	0	0	0
1,320	1,360	134	84	48	14	0	0	0	0	0	0	0
1,360	1,400	140	90	52	18	0	0	0	0	0	0	0
1,400	1,440	146	96	56	22	0	0	0	0	0	0	0
1,440	1,480	152	102	60	26	0	0	0	0	0	0	0
1,480	1,520	158	108	64	30	0	0	0	0	0	0	0
1,520	1,560	164	114	68	34	0	0	0	0	0	0	0
1,560	1,600	170	120	72	38	4	0	0	0	0	0	0
1,600	1,640	176	126	76	42	8	0	0	0	0	0	0
1,640	1,680	182	132	81	46	12	0	0	0	0	0	0
1,680	1,720	188	138	87	50	16	0	0	0	0	0	0
1,720	1,760	194	144	93	54	20	0	0	0	0	0	0
1,760	1,800	200	150	99	58	24	0	0	0	0	0	0
1,800	1,840	206	156	105	62	28	0	0	0	0	0	0
1,840	1,880	212	162	111	66	32	0	0	0	0	0	0
1,880	1,920	218	168	117	70	36	3	0	0	0	0	0
1,920	1,960	224	174	123	74	40	7	0	0	0	0	0
1,960	2,000	230	180	129	78	44	11	0	0	0	0	0
2,000	2,040	236	186	135	84	48	15	0	0	0	0	0
2,040	2,080	242	192	141	90	52	19	0	0	0	0	0
2,080	2,120	248	198	147	96	56	23	0	0	0	0	0
2,120	2,160	254	204	153	102	60	27	0	0	0	0	0
2,160	2,200	260	210	159	108	64	31	0	0	0	0	0
2,200	2,240	266	216	165	114	68	35	1	0	0	0	0
2,240	2,280	272	222	171	120	72	39	5	0	0	0	0
2,280	2,320	278	228	177	126	76	43	9	0	0	0	0
2,320	2,360	284	234	183	132	82	47	13	0	0	0	0
2,360	2,400	290	240	189	138	88	51	17	0	0	0	0

Publication 15 (2016)

Wage Bracket Method Tables for Income Tax Withholding

SINGLE Persons—MONTHLY Payroll Period

(For Wages Paid through December 31, 2016)

And the wages are–		And the number of withholding allowances claimed is—										
At least	But less than	0	1	2	3	4	5	6	7	8	9	10
		The amount of income tax to be withheld is—										
$2,400	$2,440	$296	$246	$195	$144	$94	$55	$21	$0	$0	$0	$0
2,440	2,480	302	252	201	150	100	59	25	0	0	0	0
2,480	2,520	308	258	207	156	106	63	29	0	0	0	0
2,520	2,560	314	264	213	162	112	67	33	0	0	0	0
2,560	2,600	320	270	219	168	118	71	37	3	0	0	0
2,600	2,640	326	276	225	174	124	75	41	7	0	0	0
2,640	2,680	332	282	231	180	130	79	45	11	0	0	0
2,680	2,720	338	288	237	186	136	85	49	15	0	0	0
2,720	2,760	344	294	243	192	142	91	53	19	0	0	0
2,760	2,800	350	300	249	198	148	97	57	23	0	0	0
2,800	2,840	356	306	255	204	154	103	61	27	0	0	0
2,840	2,880	362	312	261	210	160	109	65	31	0	0	0
2,880	2,920	368	318	267	216	166	115	69	35	1	0	0
2,920	2,960	374	324	273	222	172	121	73	39	5	0	0
2,960	3,000	380	330	279	228	178	127	77	43	9	0	0
3,000	3,040	386	336	285	234	184	133	82	47	13	0	0
3,040	3,080	392	342	291	240	190	139	88	51	17	0	0
3,080	3,120	398	348	297	246	196	145	94	55	21	0	0
3,120	3,160	404	354	303	252	202	151	100	59	25	0	0
3,160	3,200	410	360	309	258	208	157	106	63	29	0	0
3,200	3,240	416	366	315	264	214	163	112	67	33	0	0
3,240	3,280	422	372	321	270	220	169	118	71	37	4	0
3,280	3,320	428	378	327	276	226	175	124	75	41	8	0
3,320	3,360	436	384	333	282	232	181	130	80	45	12	0
3,360	3,400	446	390	339	288	238	187	136	86	49	16	0
3,400	3,440	456	396	345	294	244	193	142	92	53	20	0
3,440	3,480	466	402	351	300	250	199	148	98	57	24	0
3,480	3,520	476	408	357	306	256	205	154	104	61	28	0
3,520	3,560	486	414	363	312	262	211	160	110	65	32	0
3,560	3,600	496	420	369	318	268	217	166	116	69	36	2
3,600	3,640	506	426	375	324	274	223	172	122	73	40	6
3,640	3,680	516	432	381	330	280	229	178	128	77	44	10
3,680	3,720	526	441	387	336	286	235	184	134	83	48	14
3,720	3,760	536	451	393	342	292	241	190	140	89	52	18
3,760	3,800	546	461	399	348	298	247	196	146	95	56	22
3,800	3,840	556	471	405	354	304	253	202	152	101	60	26
3,840	3,880	566	481	411	360	310	259	208	158	107	64	30
3,880	3,920	576	491	417	366	316	265	214	164	113	68	34
3,920	3,960	586	501	423	372	322	271	220	170	119	72	38
3,960	4,000	596	511	429	378	328	277	226	176	125	76	42
4,000	4,040	606	521	437	384	334	283	232	182	131	81	46
4,040	4,080	616	531	447	390	340	289	238	188	137	87	50
4,080	4,120	626	541	457	396	346	295	244	194	143	93	54
4,120	4,160	636	551	467	402	352	301	250	200	149	99	58
4,160	4,200	646	561	477	408	358	307	256	206	155	105	62
4,200	4,240	656	571	487	414	364	313	262	212	161	111	66
4,240	4,280	666	581	497	420	370	319	268	218	167	117	70
4,280	4,320	676	591	507	426	376	325	274	224	173	123	74
4,320	4,360	686	601	517	433	382	331	280	230	179	129	78
4,360	4,400	696	611	527	443	388	337	286	236	185	135	84
4,400	4,440	706	621	537	453	394	343	292	242	191	141	90
4,440	4,480	716	631	547	463	400	349	298	248	197	147	96
4,480	4,520	726	641	557	473	406	355	304	254	203	153	102
4,520	4,560	736	651	567	483	412	361	310	260	209	159	108
4,560	4,600	746	661	577	493	418	367	316	266	215	165	114
4,600	4,640	756	671	587	503	424	373	322	272	221	171	120
4,640	4,680	766	681	597	513	430	379	328	278	227	177	126
4,680	4,720	776	691	607	523	438	385	334	284	233	183	132
4,720	4,760	786	701	617	533	448	391	340	290	239	189	138
4,760	4,800	796	711	627	543	458	397	346	296	245	195	144
4,800	4,840	806	721	637	553	468	403	352	302	251	201	150
4,840	4,880	816	731	647	563	478	409	358	308	257	207	156
4,880	4,920	826	741	657	573	488	415	364	314	263	213	162
4,920	4,960	836	751	667	583	498	421	370	320	269	219	168
4,960	5,000	846	761	677	593	508	427	376	326	275	225	174
5,000	5,040	856	771	687	603	518	434	382	332	281	231	180
5,040	5,080	866	781	697	613	528	444	388	338	287	237	186

$5,080 and over   Use Table 4(a) for a **SINGLE person** on page 44. Also see the Instructions on page 42.

Wage Bracket Method Tables for Income Tax Withholding

MARRIED Persons—MONTHLY Payroll Period

(For Wages Paid through December 31, 2016)

And the wages are—		And the number of withholding allowances claimed is—										
At least	But less than	0	1	2	3	4	5	6	7	8	9	10
		The amount of income tax to be withheld is—										
$ 0	$720	$0	$0	$0	$0	$0	$0	$0	$0	$0	$0	$0
720	760	3	0	0	0	0	0	0	0	0	0	0
760	800	7	0	0	0	0	0	0	0	0	0	0
800	840	11	0	0	0	0	0	0	0	0	0	0
840	880	15	0	0	0	0	0	0	0	0	0	0
880	920	19	0	0	0	0	0	0	0	0	0	0
920	960	23	0	0	0	0	0	0	0	0	0	0
960	1,000	27	0	0	0	0	0	0	0	0	0	0
1,000	1,040	31	0	0	0	0	0	0	0	0	0	0
1,040	1,080	35	1	0	0	0	0	0	0	0	0	0
1,080	1,120	39	5	0	0	0	0	0	0	0	0	0
1,120	1,160	43	9	0	0	0	0	0	0	0	0	0
1,160	1,200	47	13	0	0	0	0	0	0	0	0	0
1,200	1,240	51	17	0	0	0	0	0	0	0	0	0
1,240	1,280	55	21	0	0	0	0	0	0	0	0	0
1,280	1,320	59	25	0	0	0	0	0	0	0	0	0
1,320	1,360	63	29	0	0	0	0	0	0	0	0	0
1,360	1,400	67	33	0	0	0	0	0	0	0	0	0
1,400	1,440	71	37	3	0	0	0	0	0	0	0	0
1,440	1,480	75	41	7	0	0	0	0	0	0	0	0
1,480	1,520	79	45	11	0	0	0	0	0	0	0	0
1,520	1,560	83	49	15	0	0	0	0	0	0	0	0
1,560	1,600	87	53	19	0	0	0	0	0	0	0	0
1,600	1,640	91	57	23	0	0	0	0	0	0	0	0
1,640	1,680	95	61	27	0	0	0	0	0	0	0	0
1,680	1,720	99	65	31	0	0	0	0	0	0	0	0
1,720	1,760	103	69	35	2	0	0	0	0	0	0	0
1,760	1,800	107	73	39	6	0	0	0	0	0	0	0
1,800	1,840	111	77	43	10	0	0	0	0	0	0	0
1,840	1,880	115	81	47	14	0	0	0	0	0	0	0
1,880	1,920	119	85	51	18	0	0	0	0	0	0	0
1,920	1,960	123	89	55	22	0	0	0	0	0	0	0
1,960	2,000	127	93	59	26	0	0	0	0	0	0	0
2,000	2,040	131	97	63	30	0	0	0	0	0	0	0
2,040	2,080	135	101	67	34	0	0	0	0	0	0	0
2,080	2,120	139	105	71	38	4	0	0	0	0	0	0
2,120	2,160	143	109	75	42	8	0	0	0	0	0	0
2,160	2,200	147	113	79	46	12	0	0	0	0	0	0
2,200	2,240	151	117	83	50	16	0	0	0	0	0	0
2,240	2,280	155	121	87	54	20	0	0	0	0	0	0
2,280	2,320	161	125	91	58	24	0	0	0	0	0	0
2,320	2,360	167	129	95	62	28	0	0	0	0	0	0
2,360	2,400	173	133	99	66	32	0	0	0	0	0	0
2,400	2,440	179	137	103	70	36	2	0	0	0	0	0
2,440	2,480	185	141	107	74	40	6	0	0	0	0	0
2,480	2,520	191	145	111	78	44	10	0	0	0	0	0
2,520	2,560	197	149	115	82	48	14	0	0	0	0	0
2,560	2,600	203	153	119	86	52	18	0	0	0	0	0
2,600	2,640	209	158	123	90	56	22	0	0	0	0	0
2,640	2,680	215	164	127	94	60	26	0	0	0	0	0
2,680	2,720	221	170	131	98	64	30	0	0	0	0	0
2,720	2,760	227	176	135	102	68	34	0	0	0	0	0
2,760	2,800	233	182	139	106	72	38	4	0	0	0	0
2,800	2,840	239	188	143	110	76	42	8	0	0	0	0
2,840	2,880	245	194	147	114	80	46	12	0	0	0	0
2,880	2,920	251	200	151	118	84	50	16	0	0	0	0
2,920	2,960	257	206	156	122	88	54	20	0	0	0	0
2,960	3,000	263	212	162	126	92	58	24	0	0	0	0
3,000	3,040	269	218	168	130	96	62	28	0	0	0	0
3,040	3,080	275	224	174	134	100	66	32	0	0	0	0
3,080	3,120	281	230	180	138	104	70	36	3	0	0	0
3,120	3,160	287	236	186	142	108	74	40	7	0	0	0
3,160	3,200	293	242	192	146	112	78	44	11	0	0	0
3,200	3,240	299	248	198	150	116	82	48	15	0	0	0
3,240	3,280	305	254	204	154	120	86	52	19	0	0	0
3,280	3,320	311	260	210	159	124	90	56	23	0	0	0
3,320	3,360	317	266	216	165	128	94	60	27	0	0	0
3,360	3,400	323	272	222	171	132	98	64	31	0	0	0

Publication 15 (2016)

Wage Bracket Method Tables for Income Tax Withholding

MARRIED Persons—MONTHLY Payroll Period

(For Wages Paid through December 31, 2016)

And the wages are—		And the number of withholding allowances claimed is—										
At least	But less than	0	1	2	3	4	5	6	7	8	9	10
		The amount of income tax to be withheld is—										
$3,400	$3,440	$329	$278	$228	$177	$136	$102	$68	$35	$1	$0	$0
3,440	3,480	335	284	234	183	140	106	72	39	5	0	0
3,480	3,520	341	290	240	189	144	110	76	43	9	0	0
3,520	3,560	347	296	246	195	148	114	80	47	13	0	0
3,560	3,600	353	302	252	201	152	118	84	51	17	0	0
3,600	3,640	359	308	258	207	166	122	88	55	21	0	0
3,640	3,680	365	314	264	213	162	126	92	59	25	0	0
3,680	3,720	371	320	270	219	168	130	96	63	29	0	0
3,720	3,760	377	326	276	225	174	134	100	67	33	0	0
3,760	3,800	383	332	282	231	180	138	104	71	37	3	0
3,800	3,840	389	338	288	237	186	142	108	75	41	7	0
3,840	3,880	395	344	294	243	192	146	112	79	45	11	0
3,880	3,920	401	350	300	249	198	150	116	83	49	15	0
3,920	3,960	407	356	306	255	204	154	120	87	53	19	0
3,960	4,000	413	362	312	261	210	160	124	91	57	23	0
4,000	4,040	419	368	318	267	216	166	128	95	61	27	0
4,040	4,080	425	374	324	273	222	172	132	99	65	31	0
4,080	4,120	431	380	330	279	228	178	136	103	69	35	1
4,120	4,160	437	386	336	285	234	184	140	107	73	39	5
4,160	4,200	443	392	342	291	240	190	144	111	77	43	9
4,200	4,240	449	398	348	297	246	196	148	115	81	47	13
4,240	4,280	455	404	354	303	252	202	152	119	85	51	17
4,280	4,320	461	410	360	309	258	208	157	123	89	55	21
4,320	4,360	467	416	366	315	264	214	163	127	93	59	25
4,360	4,400	473	422	372	321	270	220	169	131	97	63	29
4,400	4,440	479	428	378	327	276	226	175	135	101	67	33
4,440	4,480	485	434	384	333	282	232	181	139	105	71	37
4,480	4,520	491	440	390	339	288	238	187	143	109	75	41
4,520	4,560	497	446	396	345	294	244	193	147	113	79	45
4,560	4,600	503	452	402	351	300	250	199	151	117	83	49
4,600	4,640	509	458	408	357	306	256	205	155	121	87	53
4,640	4,680	515	464	414	363	312	262	211	160	125	91	57
4,680	4,720	521	470	420	369	318	268	217	166	129	95	61
4,720	4,760	527	476	426	375	324	274	223	172	133	99	65
4,760	4,800	533	482	432	381	330	280	229	178	137	103	69
4,800	4,840	539	488	438	387	336	286	235	184	141	107	73
4,840	4,880	545	494	444	393	342	292	241	190	145	111	77
4,880	4,920	551	500	450	399	348	298	247	196	149	115	81
4,920	4,960	557	506	456	405	354	304	253	202	153	119	85
4,960	5,000	563	512	462	411	360	310	259	208	158	123	89
5,000	5,040	569	518	468	417	366	316	265	214	164	127	93
5,040	5,080	575	524	474	423	372	322	271	220	170	131	97
5,080	5,120	581	530	480	429	378	328	277	226	176	135	101
5,120	5,160	587	536	486	435	384	334	283	232	182	139	105
5,160	5,200	593	542	492	441	390	340	289	238	188	143	109
5,200	5,240	599	548	498	447	396	346	295	244	194	147	113
5,240	5,280	605	554	504	453	402	352	301	250	200	151	117
5,280	5,320	611	560	510	459	408	358	307	256	206	155	121
5,320	5,360	617	566	516	465	414	364	313	262	212	161	125
5,360	5,400	623	572	522	471	420	370	319	268	218	167	129
5,400	5,440	629	578	528	477	426	376	325	274	224	173	133
5,440	5,480	635	584	534	483	432	382	331	280	230	179	137
5,480	5,520	641	590	540	489	438	388	337	286	236	185	141
5,520	5,560	647	596	546	495	444	394	343	292	242	191	145
5,560	5,600	653	602	552	501	450	400	349	298	248	197	149
5,600	5,640	659	608	558	507	456	406	355	304	254	203	153
5,640	5,680	665	614	564	513	462	412	361	310	260	209	159
5,680	5,720	671	620	570	519	468	418	367	316	266	215	165
5,720	5,760	677	626	576	525	474	424	373	322	272	221	171
5,760	5,800	683	632	582	531	480	430	379	328	278	227	177
5,800	5,840	689	638	588	537	486	436	385	334	284	233	183
5,840	5,880	695	644	594	543	492	442	391	340	290	239	189
5,880	5,920	701	650	600	549	498	448	397	346	296	245	195
5,920	5,960	707	656	606	555	504	454	403	352	302	251	201
5,960	6,000	713	662	612	561	510	460	409	358	308	257	207
6,000	6,040	719	668	618	567	516	466	415	364	314	263	213
6,040	6,080	725	674	624	573	522	472	421	370	320	269	219
6,080	6,120	731	680	630	579	528	478	427	376	326	275	225

$6,120 and over — Use Table 4(b) for a **MARRIED** person on page 44. Also see the instructions on page 12.

Wage Bracket Method Tables for Income Tax Withholding

SINGLE Persons—DAILY Payroll Period

(For Wages Paid through December 31, 2016)

And the wages are—		And the number of withholding allowances claimed is—										
At least	But less than	0	1	2	3	4	5	6	7	8	9	10
		The amount of income tax to be withheld is—										
$0	$15	$0	$0	$0	$0	$0	$0	$0	$0	$0	$0	$0
15	18	1	0	0	0	0	0	0	0	0	0	0
18	21	1	0	0	0	0	0	0	0	0	0	0
21	24	1	0	0	0	0	0	0	0	0	0	0
24	27	2	0	0	0	0	0	0	0	0	0	0
27	30	2	0	0	0	0	0	0	0	0	0	0
30	33	2	1	0	0	0	0	0	0	0	0	0
33	36	3	1	0	0	0	0	0	0	0	0	0
36	39	3	1	0	0	0	0	0	0	0	0	0
39	42	3	2	0	0	0	0	0	0	0	0	0
42	45	3	2	0	0	0	0	0	0	0	0	0
45	48	4	2	1	0	0	0	0	0	0	0	0
48	51	4	3	1	0	0	0	0	0	0	0	0
51	54	5	3	1	0	0	0	0	0	0	0	0
54	57	5	3	2	0	0	0	0	0	0	0	0
57	60	6	3	2	0	0	0	0	0	0	0	0
60	63	6	4	2	1	0	0	0	0	0	0	0
63	66	7	4	2	1	0	0	0	0	0	0	0
66	69	7	5	3	1	0	0	0	0	0	0	0
69	72	7	5	3	2	0	0	0	0	0	0	0
72	75	8	6	3	2	0	0	0	0	0	0	0
75	78	8	6	4	2	1	0	0	0	0	0	0
78	81	9	7	4	2	1	0	0	0	0	0	0
81	84	9	7	5	3	1	0	0	0	0	0	0
84	87	10	7	5	3	1	0	0	0	0	0	0
87	90	10	8	6	3	2	0	0	0	0	0	0
90	93	11	8	6	4	2	0	0	0	0	0	0
93	96	11	9	6	4	2	0	0	0	0	0	0
96	99	12	9	7	5	3	1	0	0	0	0	0
99	102	12	10	7	5	3	1	0	0	0	0	0
102	105	12	10	8	5	3	2	0	0	0	0	0
105	108	13	11	8	6	4	2	0	0	0	0	0
108	111	13	11	9	6	4	2	1	0	0	0	0
111	114	14	11	9	7	4	3	1	0	0	0	0
114	117	14	12	10	7	5	3	1	0	0	0	0
117	120	15	12	10	8	5	3	2	0	0	0	0
120	123	15	13	10	8	6	3	2	0	0	0	0
123	126	16	13	11	9	6	4	2	1	0	0	0
126	129	16	14	11	9	7	4	3	1	0	0	0
129	132	16	14	12	9	7	5	3	1	0	0	0
132	135	17	15	12	10	8	5	3	2	0	0	0
135	138	17	15	13	10	8	6	3	2	0	0	0
138	141	18	16	13	11	8	6	4	2	1	0	0
141	144	18	16	14	11	9	7	4	2	1	0	0
144	147	19	16	14	12	9	7	5	3	1	0	0
147	150	19	17	15	12	10	8	5	3	2	0	0
150	153	20	17	15	13	10	8	6	3	2	0	0
153	156	20	18	15	13	11	8	6	4	2	1	0
156	159	21	18	16	14	11	9	7	4	2	1	0
159	162	22	19	16	14	12	9	7	5	3	1	0
162	165	22	19	17	14	12	10	7	5	3	1	0
165	168	23	20	17	15	13	10	8	6	3	2	0
168	171	24	20	18	15	13	11	8	6	4	2	1
171	174	25	21	18	16	13	11	9	6	4	2	1
174	177	25	22	19	16	14	12	9	7	5	3	1
177	180	26	22	19	17	14	12	10	7	5	3	1
180	183	27	23	19	17	15	12	10	8	5	3	2
183	186	28	24	20	18	15	13	11	8	6	4	2
186	189	28	25	21	18	16	13	11	9	6	4	2
189	192	29	25	21	18	16	14	11	9	7	4	3
192	195	30	26	22	19	17	14	12	10	7	5	3
195	198	31	27	23	19	17	15	12	10	8	5	3
198	201	31	28	24	20	17	15	13	10	8	6	4
201	204	32	28	24	21	18	16	13	11	9	6	4
204	207	33	29	25	21	18	16	14	11	9	7	4
207	210	34	30	26	22	19	17	14	12	10	7	5
210	213	34	31	27	23	19	17	15	12	10	8	5
213	216	35	31	27	24	20	17	15	13	10	8	6
216	219	36	32	28	24	20	18	16	13	11	9	6
219	222	37	33	29	25	21	18	16	14	11	9	7
222	225	37	34	30	26	22	19	16	14	12	9	7

A-201

Wage Bracket Method Tables for Income Tax Withholding

SINGLE Persons—DAILY Payroll Period

(For Wages Paid through December 31, 2016)

And the wages are—		And the number of withholding allowances claimed is—										
At least	But less than	0	1	2	3	4	5	6	7	8	9	10
		The amount of income tax to be withheld is—										
$225	$228	$38	$34	$30	$27	$23	$19	$17	$15	$12	$10	$8
228	231	39	35	31	27	23	20	17	15	13	10	8
231	234	40	36	32	28	24	20	18	15	13	11	8
234	237	40	37	33	29	25	21	18	16	14	11	9
237	240	41	37	33	30	26	22	19	16	14	12	9
240	243	42	38	34	30	26	22	19	17	14	12	10
243	246	43	39	35	31	27	23	20	17	15	13	10
246	249	43	40	36	32	28	24	20	18	15	13	11
249	252	44	40	36	33	29	25	21	18	16	13	11
252	255	45	41	37	33	29	25	22	19	16	14	12
255	258	46	42	38	34	30	26	22	19	17	14	12
258	261	46	43	39	35	31	27	23	19	17	15	12
261	264	47	43	39	36	32	28	24	20	18	15	13
264	267	48	44	40	36	32	28	25	21	18	16	13
267	270	49	45	41	37	33	29	25	21	19	16	14
270	273	49	46	42	38	34	30	26	22	19	17	14
273	276	50	46	42	39	35	31	27	23	19	17	15
276	279	51	47	43	39	35	31	28	24	20	18	15
279	282	52	48	44	40	36	32	28	24	21	18	16
282	285	52	49	45	41	37	33	29	25	21	18	16
285	288	53	49	45	42	38	34	30	26	22	19	17
288	291	54	50	46	42	38	34	31	27	23	19	17
291	294	55	51	47	43	39	35	31	27	24	20	17
294	297	55	52	48	44	40	36	32	28	24	20	18
297	300	56	52	48	45	41	37	33	29	25	21	18
300	303	57	53	49	45	41	37	34	30	26	22	19
303	306	58	54	50	46	42	38	34	30	27	23	19
306	309	58	55	51	47	43	39	35	31	27	23	20
309	312	59	55	51	48	44	40	36	32	28	24	20
312	315	60	56	52	48	44	40	37	33	29	25	21
315	318	61	57	53	49	45	41	37	33	30	26	22
318	321	61	58	54	50	46	42	38	34	30	26	23
321	324	62	58	54	51	47	43	39	35	31	27	23
324	327	63	59	55	51	47	43	40	36	32	28	24
327	330	64	60	56	52	48	44	40	36	33	29	25
330	333	64	61	57	53	49	45	41	37	33	29	26
333	336	65	61	57	54	50	46	42	38	34	30	26
336	339	66	62	58	54	50	46	43	39	35	31	27
339	341	67	63	59	55	51	47	43	39	35	32	28
341	343	67	63	59	55	51	48	44	40	36	32	28
343	345	68	64	60	56	52	48	44	40	36	33	29
345	347	68	64	60	56	52	49	45	41	37	33	29
347	349	69	65	61	57	53	49	45	41	37	34	30
349	351	69	65	61	57	53	50	46	42	38	34	30
351	353	70	66	62	58	54	50	46	42	38	35	31
353	355	70	66	62	58	54	51	47	43	39	35	31
355	357	71	67	63	59	55	51	47	43	39	36	32
357	359	71	67	63	59	55	52	48	44	40	36	32
359	361	72	68	64	60	56	52	48	44	40	37	33
361	363	72	68	64	60	56	53	49	45	41	37	33
363	365	73	69	65	61	57	53	49	45	41	38	34
365	367	73	69	65	61	57	54	50	46	42	38	34
367	369	74	70	66	62	58	54	50	46	42	39	35
369	371	74	70	66	62	58	55	51	47	43	39	35
371	373	75	71	67	63	59	55	51	47	43	40	36
373	375	76	71	67	63	59	56	52	48	44	40	36
375	377	76	72	68	64	60	56	52	48	44	41	37
377	379	77	72	68	64	60	57	53	49	45	41	37
379	381	77	73	69	65	61	57	53	49	45	42	38
381	383	78	73	69	65	61	58	54	50	46	42	38
383	385	78	74	70	66	62	58	54	50	46	43	39
385	387	79	75	70	66	62	59	55	51	47	43	39
387	389	79	75	71	67	63	59	55	51	47	44	40
389	391	80	76	71	67	63	60	56	52	48	44	40
391	393	81	76	72	68	64	60	56	52	48	45	41

$393 and over Use Table 8(a) for a **SINGLE person** on page 45. Also see the instructions on page 42.

A-202

Wage Bracket Method Tables for Income Tax Withholding

MARRIED Persons—**DAILY** Payroll Period

(For Wages Paid through December 31, 2016)

At least	But less than	0	1	2	3	4	5	6	7	8	9	10
		\$0	\$0	\$0	\$0	\$0	\$0	\$0	\$0	\$0	\$0	\$0
\$0	\$39	\$0	\$0	\$0	\$0	\$0	\$0	\$0	\$0	\$0	\$0	\$0
39	42	1	0	0	0	0	0	0	0	0	0	0
42	45	1	0	0	0	0	0	0	0	0	0	0
45	48	1	0	0	0	0	0	0	0	0	0	0
48	51	2	0	0	0	0	0	0	0	0	0	0
51	54	2	0	0	0	0	0	0	0	0	0	0
54	57	2	1	0	0	0	0	0	0	0	0	0
57	60	3	1	0	0	0	0	0	0	0	0	0
60	63	3	1	0	0	0	0	0	0	0	0	0
63	66	3	2	0	0	0	0	0	0	0	0	0
66	69	3	2	0	0	0	0	0	0	0	0	0
69	72	4	2	1	0	0	0	0	0	0	0	0
72	75	4	3	1	0	0	0	0	0	0	0	0
75	78	4	3	1	0	0	0	0	0	0	0	0
78	81	5	3	2	0	0	0	0	0	0	0	0
81	84	5	3	2	0	0	0	0	0	0	0	0
84	87	5	4	2	1	0	0	0	0	0	0	0
87	90	6	4	2	1	0	0	0	0	0	0	0
90	93	6	4	3	1	0	0	0	0	0	0	0
93	96	6	5	3	1	0	0	0	0	0	0	0
96	99	6	5	3	2	0	0	0	0	0	0	0
99	102	7	5	4	2	1	0	0	0	0	0	0
102	105	7	6	4	2	1	0	0	0	0	0	0
105	108	7	6	4	3	1	0	0	0	0	0	0
108	111	8	6	5	3	1	0	0	0	0	0	0
111	114	8	6	5	3	2	0	0	0	0	0	0
114	117	9	7	5	4	2	0	0	0	0	0	0
117	120	9	7	5	4	2	1	0	0	0	0	0
120	123	10	7	6	4	3	1	0	0	0	0	0
123	126	10	8	6	4	3	1	0	0	0	0	0
126	129	11	8	6	5	3	2	0	0	0	0	0
129	132	11	9	7	5	4	2	0	0	0	0	0
132	135	12	9	7	5	4	2	1	0	0	0	0
135	138	12	10	7	6	4	3	1	0	0	0	0
138	141	12	10	8	6	4	3	1	0	0	0	0
141	144	13	11	8	6	5	3	2	0	0	0	0
144	147	13	11	9	7	5	3	2	0	0	0	0
147	150	14	11	9	7	5	4	2	1	0	0	0
150	153	14	12	10	7	6	4	3	1	0	0	0
153	156	15	12	10	8	6	4	3	1	0	0	0
156	159	15	13	10	8	6	5	3	2	0	0	0
159	162	16	13	11	9	7	5	3	2	0	0	0
162	165	16	14	11	9	7	5	4	2	1	0	0
165	168	16	14	12	9	7	6	4	2	1	0	0
168	171	17	15	12	10	8	6	4	3	1	0	0
171	174	17	15	13	10	8	6	5	3	2	0	0
174	177	18	15	13	11	8	6	5	3	2	0	0
177	180	18	16	14	11	9	7	5	4	2	1	0
180	183	19	16	14	12	9	7	6	4	2	1	0
183	186	19	17	15	12	10	7	6	4	3	1	0
186	189	20	17	15	13	10	8	6	5	3	1	0
189	192	20	18	15	13	11	8	6	5	3	2	0
192	195	21	18	16	14	11	9	7	5	4	2	0
195	198	21	19	16	14	12	9	7	5	4	2	1
198	201	21	19	17	14	12	10	7	6	4	3	1
201	204	22	20	17	15	13	10	8	6	5	3	1
204	207	22	20	18	15	13	11	8	6	5	3	2
207	210	23	20	18	16	13	11	9	7	5	4	2
210	213	23	21	19	16	14	12	9	7	5	4	2
213	216	24	21	19	17	14	12	10	7	6	4	3
216	219	24	22	19	17	15	12	10	8	6	4	3
219	222	25	22	20	18	15	13	11	8	6	5	3
222	225	25	23	20	18	16	13	11	9	7	5	3
225	228	25	23	21	18	16	14	11	9	7	5	4
228	231	26	24	21	19	17	14	12	10	7	6	4
231	234	26	24	22	19	17	15	12	10	8	6	4
234	237	27	24	22	20	17	15	13	10	8	6	5
237	240	27	25	23	20	18	16	13	11	9	7	5
240	243	28	25	23	21	18	16	14	11	9	7	5
243	246	28	26	24	21	19	16	14	12	9	7	6
246	249	29	26	24	22	19	17	15	12	10	8	6

Publication 15 (2016)

A-203

Wage Bracket Method Tables for Income Tax Withholding

MARRIED Persons—DAILY Payroll Period

(For Wages Paid through December 31, 2016)

And the wages are—		And the number of withholding allowances claimed is—										
At least	But less than	0	1	2	3	4	5	6	7	8	9	10
		The amount of income tax to be withheld is—										
$249	$252	$29	$27	$24	$22	$20	$17	$15	$13	$10	$8	$6
252	255	30	27	25	23	20	18	16	13	11	8	6
255	258	30	28	25	23	21	18	16	14	11	9	7
258	261	30	28	26	23	21	19	16	14	12	9	7
261	264	31	29	26	24	22	19	17	15	12	10	8
264	267	31	29	27	24	22	20	17	15	13	10	8
267	270	32	29	27	25	22	20	18	15	13	11	8
270	273	32	30	28	25	23	21	18	16	14	11	9
273	276	33	30	28	26	23	21	19	16	14	12	9
276	279	33	31	28	26	24	21	19	17	14	12	10
279	282	34	31	29	27	24	22	20	17	15	13	10
282	285	34	32	29	27	25	22	20	18	15	13	11
285	288	34	32	30	27	25	23	20	18	16	13	11
288	291	35	33	30	28	26	23	21	19	16	14	12
291	294	35	33	31	28	26	24	21	19	17	14	12
294	297	36	33	31	29	26	24	22	19	17	15	12
297	300	36	34	32	29	27	25	22	20	18	15	13
300	303	37	34	32	30	27	25	23	20	18	16	13
303	306	37	35	33	30	28	25	23	21	18	16	14
306	309	38	35	33	31	28	26	24	21	19	17	14
309	312	38	36	33	31	29	26	24	22	19	17	15
312	315	39	36	34	32	29	27	25	22	20	17	15
315	318	39	37	34	32	30	27	25	23	20	18	16
318	321	39	37	35	32	30	28	25	23	21	18	16
321	324	40	38	35	33	31	28	26	24	21	19	17
324	327	41	38	36	33	31	29	26	24	22	19	17
327	330	41	38	36	34	31	29	27	24	22	20	17
330	333	42	39	37	34	32	30	27	25	23	20	18
333	336	43	39	37	35	32	30	28	25	23	21	18
336	339	44	40	37	35	33	30	28	26	23	21	19
339	341	44	40	38	35	33	31	28	26	24	21	19
341	343	45	41	38	36	33	31	29	26	24	22	19
343	345	45	41	38	36	34	31	29	27	24	22	20
345	347	46	42	39	36	34	32	29	27	25	22	20
347	349	46	42	39	37	34	32	30	27	25	23	20
349	351	47	43	39	37	35	32	30	28	25	23	21
351	353	47	43	40	37	35	33	30	28	26	23	21
353	355	48	44	40	38	35	33	31	28	26	24	21
355	357	48	44	40	38	36	33	31	29	26	24	22
357	359	49	45	41	38	36	34	31	29	27	24	22
359	361	49	45	41	38	36	34	31	29	27	24	22
361	363	50	46	42	39	36	34	32	29	27	25	22
363	365	50	46	42	39	37	34	32	30	27	25	23
365	367	51	47	43	39	37	35	32	30	28	25	23
367	369	51	47	43	40	37	35	33	30	28	26	23
369	371	52	48	44	40	38	35	33	31	28	26	24
371	373	52	48	44	41	38	36	33	31	29	26	24
373	375	53	49	45	41	38	36	34	31	29	27	24
375	377	53	49	45	42	39	36	34	32	29	27	25
377	379	54	50	46	42	39	37	34	32	30	27	25
379	381	54	50	46	43	39	37	34	32	30	27	25
381	383	55	51	47	43	39	37	35	32	30	28	25
383	385	55	51	47	44	40	37	35	33	30	28	26
385	387	56	52	48	44	40	38	35	33	31	28	26
387	389	56	52	48	45	41	38	36	33	31	29	26
389	391	57	53	49	45	41	38	36	34	31	29	27
391	393	57	53	49	46	42	39	36	34	32	29	27
393	395	58	54	50	46	42	39	37	34	32	30	27
395	397	58	54	50	47	43	39	37	35	32	30	28
397	399	59	55	51	47	43	40	37	35	33	30	28
399	401	59	55	51	48	44	40	37	35	33	30	28
401	403	60	56	52	48	44	40	38	35	33	31	28
403	405	60	56	52	49	45	41	38	36	33	31	29
405	407	61	57	53	49	45	41	38	36	34	31	29
407	409	61	57	53	50	46	42	39	36	34	32	29

$409 and over	Use Table 8(b) for a **MARRIED person** on page 45. Also see the instructions on page 42.

A-204

How To Get Tax Help

If you have questions about a tax issue, need help preparing your tax return, or want to download free publications, forms, or instructions, go to IRS.gov and find resources that can help you right away.

Preparing and filing your tax return. Go to IRS.gov and click on the Filing tab to see your options.

 Getting answers to your tax law questions. On IRS.gov, get answers to your tax questions anytime, anywhere.

- Go to *www.irs.gov/Help-&-Resources* for a variety of tools that will help you with your taxes.

- Additionally, you may be able to access tax law information in your electronic filing software.

Tax forms and publications. You can download or print some of the forms and publications you may need on *www.irs.gov/formspubs*. Otherwise, you can go to *www.irs.gov/orderforms* to place an order and have forms mailed to you. You should receive your order within 10 business days.

Getting a transcript or copy of a return.

- Go to IRS.gov and click on "Get Transcript of Your Tax Records" under "Tools."

- Call the transcript toll-free line at 1-800-908-9946.

- Mail Form 4506-T (transcript request) or Form 4506 (copy of return) to the IRS.

Understanding identity theft issues.

- Go to *www.irs.gov/uac/Identity-Protection* for information and videos.

- If you suspect you are a victim of tax-related identity theft, visit *www.irs.gov/identitytheft* to learn what steps you should take.

Making a tax payment. The IRS uses the latest encryption technology so electronic payments are safe and secure. You can make electronic payments online, by phone, or from a mobile device. Paying electronically is quick, easy, and faster than mailing in a check or money order. Go to *www.irs.gov/payments* to make a payment using any of the following options.

- **Debit or credit card** (approved payment processors online or by phone).

- **Electronic Funds Withdrawal** (available during *e-file*).

- **Electronic Federal Tax Payment System** (best option for businesses; enrollment required).

- **Check or money order**.

IRS2Go provides access to mobile-friendly payment options. Simply download IRS2Go from Google Play, the Apple App Store, or the Amazon Appstore, and make your payments anytime, anywhere.

What if I can't pay now? Click on the "Pay Your Tax Bill" icon on IRS.gov for more information about these additional options.

- Apply for an *online payment agreement* to meet your tax obligation in monthly installments if you cannot pay your taxes in full today. Once you complete the online process, you will receive immediate notification of whether your agreement has been approved.

- An offer in compromise allows you to settle your tax debt for less than the full amount you owe. Use the *Offer in Compromise Pre-Qualifier* to confirm your eligibility.

Understanding an IRS notice or letter. Enter "Understanding your notice" in the search box on IRS.gov to find additional information about your IRS notice or letter.

Visiting the IRS. Locate the nearest Taxpayer Assistance Center using the Office Locator tool on IRS.gov. Enter "office locator" in the search box. Or choose the "Contact Us" option on the IRS2Go app and search Local Offices. Before you visit, use the Locator tool to check hours and services available.

Watching IRS videos. The IRS Video portal *www.irsvideos.gov* contains video and audio presentations for individuals, small businesses, and tax professionals. You'll find video clips of tax topics, archived versions of panel discussions and Webinars, and audio archives of tax practitioner phone forums.

Getting tax information in other languages. For taxpayers whose native language is not English, we have the following resources available.

1. Taxpayers can find information on IRS.gov in the following languages.

    a. *Spanish*.

    b. *Chinese*.

    c. *Vietnamese*.

    d. *Korean*.

    e. *Russian*.

2. The IRS Taxpayer Assistance Centers provide over-the-phone interpreter service in over 170 languages, and the service is available free to taxpayers.

The Taxpayer Advocate Service Is Here To Help You

What is the Taxpayer Advocate Service?

The Taxpayer Advocate Service (TAS) is an ***independent*** organization within the Internal Revenue Service that helps taxpayers and protects taxpayer rights. Our job is to ensure that every taxpayer is treated fairly and that you know and understand your rights under the _Taxpayer Bill of Rights_.

What Can the Taxpayer Advocate Service Do For You?

We can help you resolve problems that you can't resolve with the IRS. And our service is free. If you qualify for our assistance, you will be assigned to one advocate who will work with you throughout the process and will do everything possible to resolve your issue. TAS can help you if:

- Your problem is causing financial difficulty for you, your family, or your business,

- You face (or your business is facing) an immediate threat of adverse action, or

- You've tried repeatedly to contact the IRS but no one has responded, or the IRS hasn't responded by the date promised.

How Can You Reach Us?

We have offices _in every state, the District of Columbia, and Puerto Rico_. Your local advocate's number is in your local directory and at _www.taxpayeradvocate.irs.gov_. You can also call us at 1-877-777-4778.

How Can You Learn About Your Taxpayer Rights?

The Taxpayer Bill of Rights describes ten basic rights that all taxpayers have when dealing with the IRS. Our Tax Toolkit at _www.taxpayeradvocate.irs.gov_ can help you understand _what these rights mean to you_ and how they apply. These are **your** rights. Know them. Use them.

How Else Does the Taxpayer Advocate Service Help Taxpayers?

TAS works to resolve large-scale problems that affect many taxpayers. If you know of one of these broad issues, please report it to us at _www.irs.gov/sams_.

A-206

Index

To help us develop a more useful index, please let us know if you have ideas for index entries. See "Comments and Suggestions" in the "Introduction" for the ways you can reach us.

A-207

Index

I

Immigration Reform and Control Act (IRCA)
records retention requirements, 1-49
Imputed income, 4-3
Independent contractors
common law test, 1-3
worker status of, 1-2
Income statement, 6-10
Increased penalties for record retention requirements, 1-49
Integrated databases, computerized payroll systems, 2-5
Interfaces, computerized payroll systems, 2-3
Internal Revenue Code (IRC)
Section 125, 4-30
Section 401, 4-23. See also: 401(k) plans, 4-23
Section 403(b), 4-25
Section 457(b), 4-25
Internal Revenue Service (IRS)
Circular E, A-140
Involuntary deductions
guidelines for, 3-19

J

Journal accounting procedures, 6-4

L

Law enforcement workers
FLSA exemptions, 1-25
Legal advice, nonqualified deferred compensation plans, 4-27
Levies, guidelines for, 3-19
Liability
accounts, 6-5
federal tax deposit requirements, 5-3
Loan payments, 3-18
Lock-in letter, 1-57

Lookback period, federal tax deposit requirements, 5-3

M

Manager Self-Service, 2-3
Master files, maintenance guidelines, 1-47
Media imaging, record keeping and retention, 1-47
Medicare tax
depositing guidelines, 5-3
401(k) plan contributions, 4-24
nonqualified deferred compensation plans, 4-27
Section 125 flexible plans, 4-31
tips, 3-4
withholding requirements, 3-11
Meetings, 1-44
Minimum wages and salaries
federal requirements, 1-18
state regulations regarding, 1-18
Monthly deposits, federal tax, 5-4
Moving expenses, 4-9
Multiple child support orders, 3-24

N

New hire reporting, 1-11
No-additional-cost services, 4-6
Noncash fringe benefits, 4-4
Noncash payments FLSA, 1-33
Nonexempt employees, FLSA regulations, 1-15
Nonqualified deferred compensation plans, 4-26
Nonqualified Plan, Awards, 4-12
Nonreportable fringe benefits, 4-5
Nontaxable compensation, vs. taxable compensation, 4-1

Nontaxable fringe benefits, 4-5

O

$100,000 one-day rule, tax deposit requirements, 5-5
$1,000 annual deposit rule, 5-4
Off-cycle checks, posting procedures, 6-13
Optional flat 25% withholding method
calculation techniques, 3-8
guidelines for using, 3-8
OSHA documents, retention requirements, 1-48
Outside salespeople, FLSA category of, 1-17
Overpayments/repayments, 3-3
Overtime pay, 1-22, 1-33
in excess of requirements, 1-32
commission calculations, 1-37
exempt employees, 1-15
hospital employees, 1-25
hourly pay calculations, 1-33
hours included in, 1-41
piecework calculations, 1-35
regular pay rates, establishment of, 1-30
salaried employees calculations, 1-37
state regulations regarding, 1-23
time of payment, 1-23
weighted average calculations, 1-34
workweek calculations, 1-24

P

Parking, 4-8
Pay rates
hourly employees, 1-18
noncash payments, 1-33
nondiscretionary and discretionary bonuses, 1-31